W9-BZL-654

DISCARDED
JENKS LRC
GORDON COLLEGE

THE CAMBRIDGE COMPANION TO GALILEO

Each volume of this series of companions to major philosophers contains specially commissioned essays by an international team of scholars, together with a substantial bibliography, and will serve as a reference work for students and nonspecialists. One aim of the series is to dispel the intimidation such readers often feel when faced with the work of a difficult and challenging thinker.

Not only a hero of the scientific revolution, but after his conflict with the church, a hero of science, Galileo is today rivaled in the popular imagination only by Newton and Einstein. But what did Galileo actually do, and what are the sources of the popular image we have of him? This collection of essays is unparalleled in the depth of its coverage of all facets of Galileo's work. A particular feature of the volume is the treatment of Galileo's relationship with the church. It will be of particular interest to philosophers, historians of science, cultural historians, and those in religious studies.

New readers and nonspecialists will find this the most convenient, accessible guide to Galileo available. Advanced students and specialists will find a conspectus of recent developments in the interpretation of Galileo.

CAMBRIDGE COMPANIONS TO PHILOSOPHY

AQUINAS *Edited by* NORMAN KRETZMANN *and*
ELEANORE STUMP *(published)*
BACON *Edited by* MARKKU PELTONEN *(published)*
BERKELEY *Edited by* KENNETH WINKLER
DESCARTES *Edited by* JOHN COTTINGHAM *(published)*
EARLY GREEK PHILOSOPHY *Edited by* A. A. LONG
FICHTE *Edited by* GUENTER ZOELLER
FOUCAULT *Edited by* GARY GUTTING *(published)*
FREGE *Edited by* TOM RICKETTS
FREUD *Edited by* JEROME NEU *(published)*
HABERMAS *Edited by* STEPHEN K. WHITE *(published)*
HEGEL *Edited by* FREDERICK BEISER *(published)*
HEIDEGGER *Edited by* CHARLES GUIGNON
(published)
HOBBES *Edited by* TOM SORELL *(published)*
HUME *Edited by* DAVID FATE NORTON *(published)*
HUSSERL *Edited by* BARRY SMITH *and*
DAVID WOODRUFF SMITH *(published)*
WILLIAM JAMES *Edited by* RUTH ANNA PUTNAM
(published)
KANT *Edited by* PAUL GUYER *(published)*
KIERKEGAARD *Edited by* ALASTAIR HANNAY *and*
GORDON MARINO *(published)*
LEIBNIZ *Edited by* NICHOLAS JOLLEY *(published)*
LOCKE *Edited by* VERE CHAPPELL *(published)*
MALEBRANCHE *Edited by* STEPHEN NADLER
MARX *Edited by* TERRELL CARVER *(published)*
MILL *Edited by* JOHN SKORUPSKI *(published)*
NIETZSCHE *Edited by* BERND MAGNUS *and*
KATHLEEN M. HIGGINS *(published)*
OCKHAM *Edited by* PAUL VINCENT SPADE
PEIRCE *Edited by* CHRISTOPHER HOOKWAY
PLATO *Edited by* RICHARD KRAUT *(published)*
PLOTINUS *Edited by* LLOYD P. GERSON *(published)*
QUINE *Edited by* ROGER GIBSON
ROUSSEAU *Edited by* PATRICK RILEY
RUSSELL *Edited by* NICHOLAS GRIFFIN
SARTRE *Edited by* CHRISTINA HOWELLS *(published)*
SPINOZA *Edited by* DON GARRETT *(published)*
WITTGENSTEIN *Edited by* HANS SLUGA *and*
DAVID G. STERN *(published)*

The Cambridge Companion to

GALILEO

Edited by

Peter Machamer
University of Pittsburgh

CAMBRIDGE
UNIVERSITY PRESS

JENKS LIBRARY
GORDON COLLEGE
255 GRAPEVINE RD.
WENHAM, MA 01984

PUBLISHED BY THE PRESS SYNDICATE OF THE UNIVERSITY OF CAMBRIDGE
The Pitt Building, Trumpington Street, Cambridge, United Kingdom

CAMBRIDGE UNIVERSITY PRESS
The Edinburgh Building, Cambridge CB2 2RU, UK   www.cup.cam.ac.uk
40 West 20th Street, New York, NY 10011-4211, USA   www.cup.org
10 Stamford Road, Oakleigh, Melbourne 3166, Australia
Ruiz de Alarcón 13, 28014 Madrid, Spain

© Cambridge University Press 1998

This book is in copyright. Subject to statutory exception
and to the provisions of relevant collective licensing agreements,
no reproduction of any part may take place without
the written permission of Cambridge University Press.

First published 1998
Reprinted 1999

Printed in the United States of America

Typeset in Trump Medieval 10/13 pt. in LaTeX 2_ε [TB]

A catalog record for this book is available from the British Library

Library of Congress Cataloging in Publication Data is available

ISBN 0 521 58178 8 hardback
ISBN 0 521 58841 3 paperback

CONTENTS

vii

CONTRIBUTORS

RICHARD J. BLACKWELL is professor of philosophy at Saint Louis University.

RIVKA FELDHAY is the director and professor of the Cohen Institute for the History and Philosophy of Science and Ideas, Tel-Aviv University, Israel.

PAULO GALLUZZI is Director of the Institute and Museum of the History of Science in Florence, and professor of philosophy at the University of Florence, Italy.

WALLACE E. HOOPER, currently part of the American Indian Studies Research Institute at Indiana University, was the Galileo Postdoctoral fellow at the Museum of the History of Science in Florence, Italy in 1993–4, and Maria Luisa Righini Postdoctoral fellow in 1995–6.

PETER MACHAMER is professor of history and philosophy of science at the University of Pittsburgh.

ERNAN MCMULLIN is Director Emeritus of the Program in History and Philosophy of Science and O'Hara Professor Emeritus of philosophy at the University of Notre Dame.

MARCELLO PERA is professor of philosophy, on leave, at the University of Pisa, Italy. He is currently a Senator of the Italian Republic.

PIETRO REDONDI is associate professor of history of science at Universita di Bologna, Italy. He is the author of *Sadi Carnot et la technologie francaise* and *Galileo Heretic*.

MICHAEL SEGRE teaches history of science at the University of Munich. He is author of *In the Wake of Galileo*.

WILLIAM SHEA is Director of the Institute for Philosophy at Universite Louis Pasteur, Strasbourg, France.

N. M. SWERDLOW is professor in the Department of Astronomy and Astrophysics at The University of Chicago. His research is concerned with the history of the exact sciences, particularly astronomy from antiquity through the seventeenth century.

WILLIAM A. WALLACE is professor of philosophy at the University of Maryland and professor emeritus of philosophy and history at The Catholic University of America.

As in all such work this volume could not have come about without help and encouragement from many people. Those who have fostered my interest in Galileo go back many, many years. I am pleased to call many of the Galileo group my friends. Names leap to mind: From early days Bill Shea, Gerd Buchdahl, Tom Settle, Maria Louisa Bonelli Righini, Silvio Bedini, David Lindberg, Dudley Shapere, Noel Swerdlow, and Ed Collins all were important. Later Ernan McMullin, Bill Wallace, Bob Butts, Joe Pitt, Winifrid Wisan, Noretta Koertge, Sam Westfall, Raymond Fredette, Bob Westman, Larry Laudan, Maurice Finocchiaro, and Stillman Drake aided my inquires and corresponded with me on various topics. Still more recently, Rivka Feldhay, Maurizio Mamiani, Marcello Pera, Lorenz Kruger, Wallace Hooper, Michael Segre, Paolo Galluzzi, and Mario Biagioli have shared insights. Of course, Ted McGuire, my good old friend, is as always a source of encouragement and joy and a pain. Oh, the stories one could tell.

This project was conceived when Michael Ruse introduced me to Terry Moore at Cambridge University Press. The real work began while I was on sabbatical and living in Tuscany, in the country house of my friend and vineyard companion, Marcello Pera, who has now forsaken philosophy to become a senator in the Italian government. The Luccese hills, and the wines and foods of Toscano were a great support as I attempted to gather together people to contribute to the volume. Maurizio Mamiani and my students at Udine also propelled this endeavor forward. The proofing on this book was started in Athens, when I was teaching there. Samantha Statidaki was a great help in getting these original papers organized and edited. The early editing was done by my dear friend, Patty Tascarella, a reporter for the Pittsburgh Business Times, who unselfishly gave of her time and energy. It is in most part due to her that these papers have some consistency and structure. Debora Richards, in her careful and conscientious way, was a great help on the bibliography and the index.

It is with regret that I have to say that some papers originally intended for the volume will not appear. Francesco Barone became too ill to revise his work on Galileo's logic. Mario Biagioli, and then Biagioli and Al van Helden, originally had agreed to contribute, but their lives became so hectic that they had to drop out of the project. Alfonso Perez de Laborda did not finish his piece, having taken on the job as the first founder and rector of the newly established Universidada di Catholica di Avila, in Spain. Some others whom I asked to contribute were unable to for various reasons, so I am sorry not to have papers by Tom Settle, Gideon Freudenthal, and some others. The volume is the poorer for the lack of these contributions.

But to all who aided and abetted, in direct and indirect ways, many thanks.

Peter Machamer
Pittsburgh
September 1997

Introduction

Galileo is one of the larger than life heroes of history. This status was conferred during his lifetime and grew with each succeeding century. Not only was he the hero of the Scientific Revolution, but after his troubles with the Catholic Church he became the hero of science. Today, only the names of Newton and Einstein rival that of Galileo in popularity and imagination. But yet we must ask, to what is his popularity due? What did Galileo actually do that made his image so great and so long-standing?

Certainly, he was impressive with his telescope. The discoveries, in 1609–1610, of the mountains on the Moon, the numerous stars in the Milky Way, and, of course, the four satellites of Jupiter (which he called the Medician stars) caught the imagination of the time. His book was much remarked about, but its first edition was limited to 550 copies, and the later Frankfurt edition printing probably included not more than 1,000 or so. Mario Biagioli has commented that Galileo's control of the distribution of his book was impressive, making sure it got to the right important people.[1] Clearly, too, the invocation of the name of the Medici caused it to be looked at in court circles. Surely, too, books were even more shared and passed around then than in our own time, and, even more, the oral tradition of fame and status was still alive and accounted for a good bit of his popularity. Still, it is hard to fathom through the distance of centuries what caused such a ready reception of Galileo and his work.

Richard Westfall has noted that, at the time, Galileo had to build an audience for scientific work, while less than eighty years later, Newton could assume that such an audience was already in place.[2] So Galileo created the place of science in our intellectual life. He, of course, did not do so single-handedly; Francis Bacon had already published his *The Advancement of Learning* in 1605. However, Bacon's fame as a spokesperson for science would have to wait until the Royal Society was founded in 1662, though the Society's secretary, Henry Oldenburg, comments on the importance of Bacon's philosophy in his letter in 1656.[3] But even if Galileo was aided in promoting science and its importance by others, certainly his was the first main effort that fired the vision of science and the world that went well beyond limited intellectual circles.

Galileo's fame grew as he published more. The *Letters on the Sunspots* (1613) were widely read and circulated and increased the fervor for learning more about the realms of the heavens, as did his later *Il Saggiatore* (*The Assayer*) (1623). But there is no doubt that it is was the 1632 publication of *Dialogue on the Two Chief World Systems* (*Dialogo*), its subsequent condemnation by the Church, and then the trial of Galileo before the office of the Inquisition that projected Galileo's name into household status. This episode in the history of thought and science has been amply and elucidatingly commented upon by many people.[4]

But my question remains: Why was this event treated as being so important? Why did not the attention and public outcry that greeted Galileo emerge earlier, say with the burning of Giordano Bruno in 1600. One can argue that Bruno was not a scientist and was large ways toward being a crank, and so his situation compelled less interest. But this just begs the question: Why had science become so important to the people (at least to a large class of people, not even just the franchised, aristocratic class)?

The earlier discoveries and innovations in science and natural knowledge had helped to prepare the ground. Nicholas Copernicus's publication of *De Revolutionibus* in 1543, and Andrea Vesalius's *De Humani Corporis Fabrica...* in the same year, certainly showed to those who cared that science could change and was advancing new conceptions of theory and knowledge. Certainly, too, the rediscovery of the Greek texts of scientists and mathematicians and the new growth in practical mathematics helped make the ground fertile so Galileo could sow his seeds.

But somehow this background is insufficient to explain the phenomenon. There had been new discoveries and new innovations, in a very real way since the fourteenth century. But what, in general, had changed since that time? There was no scientific revolution, no enfranchisement of science as a publicly worthy and most important occupation, at that time.

I am well aware that some historians and some philosophers would challenge the claim that there really was a scientific revolution. Whatever might hang on the interpretation of the word "revolution" is unimportant to my theme. What cannot be in doubt is that between, say somewhat arbitrarily, the dates of 1543 and 1687, many things had radically changed and the world was, and was further becoming, a wildly different kind of place. Science, as any other human endeavor, does not exist in a vacuum. It is not an isolated, independent system of thought and practice. What happens in other realms of human life affects how science is practiced, perceived, and received.

At this point it might be good to quote the insightful words of the famous art historian Heinrich Wolfflin:

Even the most original talent cannot proceed beyond certain limits which are fixed for it by the date of its birth. Not everything is possible at all times, and certain thoughts can only be thought at certain stages of the development.[5]

What is true of thinking thoughts is also true of the reception of thoughts. People are not ready to receive and act upon just any thought at any time. The way must be prepared; the need must be felt. In an evolutionary metaphor, the environment must have changed, and the resulting pressure must lead to the selection of a new trait by allowing it to reproduce more successfully than its rivals. What was the change in environment that led to Galileo's fame? Why was the world ready to select for him?

SOCIAL AND CULTURAL CONDITIONS OF
LATE SIXTEENTH AND EARLY SEVENTEENTH
CENTURY: THE BACKGROUND TO GALILEO
AND HIS FAME

The end of the Renaissance brought in to being a new kind of person across the lands of Europe. Empowered by commerce and money, a person's goals, though often still very religious and, now, nationalistic, lay within his (and occasionally in her) own self-fulfillment, as seen to be in the accumulation of money and commodities for private use. Subjective individuality was the basis for privacy, and privacy came to mean private property and the ability to resist interference from other people. Out of this individualistic isolationism grew the doctrine of individual human rights.

The entrepreneurial capitalist, as a fairly widespread new type of power and cultural force, debuted in the late sixteenth and early seventeenth centuries. The type probably first appeared in Italy and southern Germany, and then later in the newly burgeoning cities of the North Atlantic, as centers of commerce shifted as the result of various national endeavors toward the silver and gold of the New World and trade with the Far East. This "class" (for class is an eighteenth century term) can be characterized by its commitment to the ideal of entrepreneurial individualism, wherein the individual person was taken as, and so enabled to become, a source of social and economic power and epistemic and moral value. In northern Europe, then, status, glory, and political power became highly attached to money and professional success rather than only to land and birthright as doled out and sanctioned by the courts and crowns of Europe. This shift contrasted with parts of central and southern Europe which retained, or rather reinstituted, an almost feudal structure based on nobles and court. Of course, these were not the parts of Europe where science, philosophy, and capitalism flourished and became important.

Obviously, this change in the locus of European power was connected with the breaking down of the previously existing sovereign based social and political power structure and the rupture of heretofore extant patterns of mutual support between church and state. One consequence was that the newly enfranchised people had to become educated in ways to use their power and develop their values, but such education was not necessarily to be gained in traditional or formal institutions or to be directed toward older educational goals.

The events that contributed to and were partial and overdetermined causes and effects of these changes extend over many seemingly different aspects of life and society. They cross cultural and national boundaries, and they shatter traditional, disciplinary lines of research. But one must begin to tell the story somehow.

One theme with which to begin to unwind this age is the relatively new phenomenon of printing. By the end of the sixteenth century, the new printing culture provided readily accessible books, pamphlets, and broadsides through which both formal and informal education and communication occurred. These were read and used in old institutions (schools and universities), new ones (ateliers, academies, and private tutorials), and, not the least, by individual readers alone in their homes. It is not just the greater accessibility, and consequent greater and more widespread literacy, among various people and classes that is worth noting. The spread of printed material across Europe, of course, meant that more people and different types of people were reading than ever had before, but much less noticed is the far-reaching consequence that education became more standardized, with many people reading the same books (and so getting the same information). This also meant that the information was presented in new forms confined to two-dimensional page layouts, in part, because this is what could be printed well and clearly (illustrations, tables, diagrams, etc.).

This new situation needs to be contrasted with what existed previously with learners hearing individual lectures or sermons, or workers and artisans being individually tutored in the idiosyncratic style of the master by whom they were taught. For the first time, someone learning anatomy in Padua would learn from the same text and diagrams that were used by another student in Pisa or even one in Paris. Even the Bible became more standardized so that many people could read the same text in their separate homes, and, though there were different editions, it was now possible for each individual to learn on his or her own and discuss what the Bible actually said, rather than rely on aural memory and the ultimate textual authority of the local priest or pastor.[6]

Printed texts were not only strings of sentences but contained representations in the form of spatial layouts, displays, tables, and pictures. These became the preferred forms of demonstration. Tables allowed a reader to follow a procedure, whether it was instruction for writing a letter, holding a civil conversation, determining the volume of a wine barrel, or performing an inductive discovery. Pictures, first reproduced as woodcuts and then as copperplates, provided visual awareness of fascinating new discoveries and forms of life from faraway lands, as well as serving as a source of knowledge and pleasure about events and practices closer to home. Diagrams and illustrations served as mechanical drawings and detailed models (as "blueprints") for those who would learn to construct and perform. This is one strong reason why geometry took on new life and excitement (while concurrently it was being revived by the reintroduction of classical geometrical texts by the humanists and mechanics). This should not be surprising since geometry, too, depended essentially on the construction of diagrams, which now could be clearly and easily reproduced on the printed page.

It cannot be overemphasized how much this way of learning by reading something held in one's hand was a new form of knowledge acquisition. Again, it is not just that printing provided the opportunity for more people to read, and that more people because of this opportunity did learn to read, and so literacy increased. Nor is it just that more books were printed in the vernacular so that they would appeal and sell to these newly literate audiences. These were important features of the new phenomenon, but even more importantly, something fundamentally different happens when a person sits down with a book in hand, and, concentrating on a page at a time, reads in an isolated act, rather than hearing the spoken words of another person. The very cognitive form of learning and memory was essentially changed.

Much has been written recently about the impact of television and the intellectual and cultural changes that have been wrought by the demise of the printed culture and the rise of the pictorial image. And it may be that today children primarily learn by watching moving images on the television screen, supplemented only by occasional spoken words, but this change is minimal compared to that brought by the "Gutenberg revolution." The individuality of the learning act and the publicly presented standardized content of what is learned are still preserved in today's new genre. But in the sixteenth century, individual private acts were new and had to be newly mastered, and we, having grown up with books abounding, can only imagine what new interior worlds were opened up for these new readers. It is small wonder that the imagination became a topic of much speculation, discussion, and publication.

It is most important to realize that the change to the printed page cannot be understood as an isolated phenomenon. The post-Reformation and anti-Aristotelian context in which these changes were occurring also emphasized an antiestablishment, proindividual, and humanistic ideology. Yet this need to devise a new, systematic way of codifying knowledge must be seen as part of an attempt to establish intellectual and social stability. For a moment, consider that the very things that comprised knowledge, that made up the inventory of stuff in the world – the very things that comprised the subjects to be known – had grown and changed. The voyages of exploration, east and west, introduced the Europeans to multitudinous new kinds of things, plants, animals, and peoples. These novelties caused a sense of wonder and awe and awakened a desire to collect them. Every king and every court, and, soon, every rich man would have to build his collection of the rare and wondrous. But these novelties needed to be understood.

Such new kinds of things did not fit well into the old systems of knowledge, and they raised many painful and difficult questions. There were questions about the nature of God (Did He give divine grace to the Indians, even though they were not Christians?), about the nature of human beings (Were the Indians really men at all, and what of the manlike apes from the East?), and about the natures of the flora and fauna in the world. In the late sixteenth century, botanical and zoological gardens began to be established because they provided places where the newly awakened curiosity could be appeased, and as well places to study the new natures. Such gardens were established at Padua and Parma in 1544 and in Bologna in 1568. Printed books and posters proliferated the images of the unusual for those who could not travel to see the live specimens.

The Reformation, too, played a large part in forming the intellectual and social climate of the seventeenth century. After the Reformation, many people, emotionally upset and intellectually confused, responded by pledging allegiances to a huge variety of evangelical dogmas or by retreating to a skeptical agnosticism. It was difficult for many to tell which God was the right one, or, more mundanely, to decide upon a righteous form of confessional, given the many factions that the Protestant movement took or the forms by which the Counter-Reformation responded. As in all things, though, such skeptical questions were countered by dogmatic fervor among those who had become convinced by one or another sect or retrenching movement.

There was one aspect of the new post-Reformation age that was growing among Catholics and dissenters alike: the idea of a personalized God who dwelt in the hearts of individuals. This, in varying degrees, extended individual sovereignty over Biblical interpretation and, perhaps, salvation. It also lessened the degree of obedience to whatever church hierarchy one accepted. Moreover, among all religious factions, these changes did make legitimate, and so increase, the amount of individual and family Bible reading, which helped to shift the educational burden away from the churches and schools and into the homes.

The need for new systematization was forced not only by the many novelties and religious foment but had been spurred on intellectually by strong feelings for a need for change. This was a time in which many people felt they were at the dawning of a new age, an age unlike any other that the world had seen. This led to much intellectual debate, theory construction, and experimentation, bringing new ways of thinking about God, the cosmos, human beings, and the stuff of the world. Proposals for many new systems, new philosophies, and new religions abounded. These promulgations of anti-Aristotelians, revisionist Scholastics, alternative cosmologists, natural and magical theories, and humanistic eclectic philosophers augmented the perceived need for change and were designed to establish or show the way toward a new systematization. They all raised questions about the existing patterns of thought and opened up the space of possibilities wherein people could contemplate alternatives.

However, not just intellectual forces were at work. The social changes in law, government, and, especially, forms of commerce that came along with the greater reliance upon and recognition of individuals ironically forced people from the land and bundled them together into the cities. These, in turn, required new forms of governments and institutions and their constituent individual-indifferent bureaucracies. This increasing urbanization, as Marx well pointed out, was due, in part, to the disenfranchisement of the peasant farmers and the newly initiated poor laws that forced them into the hands of the growing capitalist class.[7] This new population density greatly increased the number of poor. And with the numerous unemployed poor and their conditions of poverty came disease, famine, and death. The tenuous character of life was obvious to all.

Add to these devastating factors the piracy on the seas, the highwaymen on the land, and the increasing crime that went with this bursting growth of the cities, and it should be easy to feel the wretched insecurity and fear of the populace across Europe. Rape, pillage, and plunder was augmented by land grabbing that forced many peasants to flee the country for the cities, where they found new urban forms of starvation and death.

The combined new bureaucratic institutions and very pressing competing colonial and capitalistic interests brought along with them many great (and small) wars: Religion fought against religion, prince against prince, and national power against rival nations. Alliances and allegiances were shifting like windblown sands, and it was never clear for long who was on what side. In this regard it is of strange significance to note that Descartes, who would later seek to become the savior and new Aquinas of the Catholic Church, fought in his earlier years for the Protestant army of Prince Maurice, Duke of Orange. Such ongoing and changing battles meant that princes had to raise money for armies, would commandeer men and property, and were always looking for more wealth to support their ambitions. The main fodder, as always, were the common people.

Death was all around. People's sense of their future and their security was at a low point. The old forms and existing structures of government and social organization began to fracture even further, and new ideas and practices began to move in to replace them.

Economic changes, too, were driven in large part by the sea vessels that plied their trade and searched for new lands to make new wealth. The galley of the Mediterranean gave way to the sailing ships of the North Atlantic. Economic competition among the seafarers and the companies that funded them was reflected increasingly in a sense of nationalism at the home ports. The desire to protect one's possessions and property (the colonies) brought new nationalistic wars and new forms of warfare. On sea and on land, cannons grew more manageable and effective, and hand guns, for the first time accurate, replaced pikes and long bows as everyone's weapon of choice.

Great amounts of money were required for gun- and cannon-based warfare and for the manufacture of such weapons. Mining for lead, iron, and copper was required for the ordnance, as well as for ships and other constructions, and, of course, gained real importance as a way to gather (hopefully) great amounts of silver and gold to restock rapidly depleting treasuries. To outfit, man, and embark a set of ships required large amounts of money, as well as skill in navigation. This required new ways of raising and deploying capital.

One new way is nicely stated by C. R. Boxer:

A characteristic feature of seaborne trade – and other forms of business, for that matter – in the northern Netherlands was known as the *rederij*. This

was a highly flexible type of co-operative enterprise by which a group of people would join together to buy, own, build, charter, or freight a ship and its
cargo ... this practice facilitated wide spread investment in shipping and a
wide diffusion of ownership, integrating mercantile and maritime commu-
nities to a great extent."[8]

This form of market endeavor was the model employed not only
for the production of wealth but also for knowledge. Given the rapid-
ity of increase and the geographical extent of these money exchanges,
accounting and systematized trade practices became a new big business. People had to be trained in such practices. Even Galileo made
much of his money while in Padua by teaching practical mathematics to the young aspiring business types of many nations. And in
Amsterdam, the Bourse was founded, and from 1585 onward it published commodity price lists for potential investors. So it was that
new practices and occupations arose, driven by the new social, economic, and technical necessities. Many of these new practices did
not fit well with the old educational, cultural, or political patterns.

The state of society was one of many amazing novelties – no secure
governments or security from governments, increasing fear of death,
and the proselytizing in the marketplace of ideas of many incongru-
ous, if not contradictory, schemes of order that purported to be able
to put things right. Not surprisingly, this state of affairs led to real,
not only philosophical, widespread skepticism about any possibility
the future might hold.

It also made people chary of other people. The emphasis on the
individual and the recognition that no one could depend upon social
institutions, let alone other people, was reinforced and augmented
by a growing sense of privacy during this period. The idea of privacy really did not exist before. Before this time, there were very
few single-family houses, no private bedrooms, and even no privies.
In the older scheme of things, the extended family, often including
quite distant relatives, was the basis for social life in the houses,
while at court there was nothing that did not literally belong to the
king.

Large houses had public rooms into which tables were carried for
eating and then removed so that the work of the household could go
on; then at night, the beds would be brought in for sleeping. (This,

by the by, is why "furniture" in French is called *meubles* and in Italian, *mobilia*.) Even where there were separate rooms, they were directly connected so that passage to one would require transversing through another. In such settings, children learned about sex from direct observation, and illicit lovers needed to steal away into forests and dark garden recesses in order to practice the standing and sitting positions of intercourse they had learned from the newly popular pornographic books. In this new age of privacy, the Dutch, and concurrently the Italian and French Protestants, first developed smaller houses with corridors and private bedrooms. The new home separated public from private space in a real way and so became the haven and private refuge of the "nuclear family."

This new cultural phenomenon of individual personal identity spawned a number of philosophical problems. How can an individual person locked in the subjectivity of a particular soul and body lay claim to objective knowledge for all people? How does a person who claims control only over himself and his immediate extensions derive the right to control other people?

It is little wonder that many people sought to construct and implement some new system (world view, new philosophy) that would bring both social and intellectual order and security. However, any new system that could provide epistemic, methodological, conceptual, and social order had to have some sort of philosophical basis on which it could be built. But the conditions of the times, as outlined above, proscribed what kind of system would be adequate and acceptable.

Any new order had to have the individual human at its foundation. There was no other power that could be relied upon. Yet any claim of a system for one individual had to be generalizable to other individuals, and so it had to lay claim to universality. Practically, it had to be teachable. This meant it had to be something that would work within the new printed culture and its new way of learning. It had to somehow rely on printed, spatial forms of knowledge representation.

An acceptable system had to be thought to be new (at least, in the sense that it had to appear anti-Aristotelian and antiestablishment), which meant it had to appear anticourtly or antiaristocratic so as to be open to the new class of powerful entrepreneurial gentlemen, who would become its supporters and mainstay. This entailed that, somewhere in its set of implications, it had to be able to show not only how political power was within each individual, but also how governments could be justified without appealing to divine rights of aristocratic birth.

Theoretically, it had to provide a conceptual scheme, laying out new natures for things of the world, including those newly discovered. Replacing the old essences with new natures meant coming up with new ways of understanding. Concomitantly and constituatively, this required the construction and adoption of new metaphysical foundations. Species, final causes, intelligible matter, and the actualities and potentialities of the old Aristotelian system of science and knowledge would have to be replaced. Moliere later mocked of these explanations, when he parodied the Aristotelian doctor who explained a potion's power to induce sleep in terms of its *virtus dormitiva* (power to cause sleep) (*Le Malade Imaginaire*, 1673). Any new foundations would have to be easily intelligible to those not trained in the "old" ways and would, as we have seen, have to be amenable to the new forms of learning. A new system that showed how things were to be understood would have to provide a new model of intelligibility.

Yet the rampant skepticism and distrust brought its own conservative restrictions. To be acceptable, any new system could not be something totally unproved, something that introduced totally new concepts. It had to be, in form and content, something that was tried and true and that was accessible to nonadepts, whether initiated by a university or alchemical or magical training.

Moreover, an important test of accessibility and acceptability, for these pragmatically driven people, would have to be its usefulness. Any new system, to be accepted, would have to bring with it both some fruit or a promise of future harvest that could be measured in understandable gains (and goods). It would have to show people what to do with their time, money, and energy in order to lead the good life, now defined in terms of the new capitalistic commodities and private property.

Finally, for a new system to become part of the cultural fabric, it would have to have a set of practitioners. It would have to command the allegiance of a set of people, who, like the priests and theologians of old, dedicated their lives to professing and practicing that which was prescribed by the system. These people would be the professionals, who by their coordinated actions would institutionalize this noble work and its theoretical basis.

Thus in response to skepticism, and in line with the forces that recognized novelties and demanded a new system for certainty (intellectual security) and social stability, a democratic, individualistic, epistemology, and mechanical view of the world came to dominate Western thought. This new system of thought and practice was to be a new form of science (*scientia*), a new form of knowledge, and it was natural knowledge and dealt with the natures of things, including humans, in the world.

The truly fascinating historical fact was that, given these conditions, there was only one acceptable candidate among all the possible theoretical contenders. The system that took over did not, of course, spring full blown and fully developed from the head of Zeus. It would be many years in the making and articulation. But its structural and methodological parameters were laid down quite early in the seventeenth century and would not be substantially changed *in physics* until well after Newton. In the rest of the areas of human endeavor and aspiration, this new "modern" way of thinking, which began in this time long ago, is still with us. It is the way we think today about most things. It is still our model of what is intelligible to us.

We might, as some seventeenth-century people did, call this new model for making the world intelligible, the Mechanical Philosophy. This general world view and way of thinking had a number of aspects that were common to all who came to believe it, despite numerous individual differences. The new system, in its conceptual and representational fundamentals, would be what has held in common among Galileo, Bacon, Descartes, Gassendi, Hobbes, Huygens, Stevin, Hooke, Boyle, Wren, Wallis, and even to Leibniz and Newton. Of course, this is not to claim that there were not great and important differences among these thinkers. There were. And for some purposes, the differences are what is important and what needs to be accounted for historically and conceptually. Yet, there was a common basis that provided the basic model of what was intelligible, for all these people and to those who learned from them.

All forms of the mechanical philosophy were based on an individualistic epistemology and methodology. This required that one dealt with the book of nature by oneself, so experiments, experiences, constructions dealing with machines, found objects, and geometrical proofs all were individual epistemic practices. This meant it was *an individual* who had to have the experience, construct the proof, build the model, or use the machine. Essentially everything was based in and ultimately dependent upon first-person activities, both cognitive and practical. It was the age of the Epistemic I, the first-person knower.

Not surprisingly, the various inventors of "the method" for acquiring knowledge, for promulgating the new philosophy, and for discovering the new system of the world thought themselves, individually, to be quite unique. In this way each of them was an entrepreneur in the knowledge- or system-building business. Examples are provided in the persons of Rene Descartes, who wanted his new system, the new principles of philosophy, to become the next official text at the Sorbonne, and Francis Bacon, too, who wished to establish an institute that was structured and run along the principles of science as he outlined in his new logic. The same entrepreneurial spirit motivated Hobbes, Boyle, Gassendi, and even Mersenne and Hooke. This is to say, each version of the mechanical philosophy was comprised in part by a set of methodological pronouncements and rules that had to be followed if scientific knowledge was to be acquired in the correct way.

Because each proposer of the new philosophy thought his way was better than alternatives, not only the old systems but also contemporary competitors, each thought he was clearly brighter and better and ought to be followed more than any other. Each was convinced that his system and methodology was the right one, and so each tried hard to sell his system to other people, especially those who were in power. Each wanted to be a leader of men, *the* director of the new knowledge enterprise. In fact, it is probably fair to say that each and every one of the new philosophical scientists thought he was a unique genius, despite many seemingly humble protestations to the contrary.

However, these men of genius had to be able to train people to use their method. Each one of them held that virtually every person was trainable. There was some dispute amongst them as to who counted as a person. Some held that women and slaves could not be trained, others, like Robert Boyle, that personhood was restricted to Christians. Some, like Hobbes, even went so far as to say that even the savage Indians of the new world were in principle trainable in new philosophy, and so they could have come, if they had been properly trained, to enjoy the benefits of the civilized world and its commodities. It is this aspect of trainability and its potential for all, some, or many people that gave rise to the democratic vision of the equality of men. Thus, in its original form, before the contractarians got hold of it and used it for arguing for new foundations for governments, the democratic principle was one of educability and of the ability to come to know the truth.

As a more detailed example, let us look more closely at the seventeenth-century thinkers' concept of demonstration. The common model for rational representation is described in terms of what is easily visible or what can be clearly and distinctly seen. As Hobbes put it, "Demonstration was understood by them for that sort of ratiocination that placed the thing they were to prove, as it were before mens eyes."[9] The representations of knowledge are always spatial displays. Very often the preferred form is taken to be proportional geometry. But tables laying out agreements and exclusions, definitions in terms of subjects being included in predicates, and even pictorial diagrams also fall into the spatial modes of representations. Causal, and thus explanatory relations, are conceived in terms of spatial, often mechanical, models and metaphors.

Necessity attends to these representations because they can be seen to be true by anyone who properly looks and pays attention to them. Spatial relations as primary mode of understanding lends itself well to an ontology of body and motion, for these are easily picturable. This, despite subtle differences, was the ontology of the all new methodologists (even Kepler). The seventeenth-century thinker thought in spatial terms; this mode of understanding and representation they took to be the prototype of the intelligible.

The "things" represented in these demonstrations formed the basis for the new metaphysics. For natural, nonhuman things, the realm was the concrete, external world: the realm of extension, of shape, size, and bulk. The substances of old gave way to bodies in the form of corpuscles. These bodies also had the power to move, though theorists differed on the ultimate source of this power.

For human beings, the internal world was the realm of ideas – sensible images of bodies, connections among these images, and abstractions from both. This was the realm of understanding. In addition an intensity dimension was needed and was conceived of as power, or, sometimes, desire. This was the new mode of conception of the will. The practices associated with all these ideas and intensities were described in terms of control that led both to understanding (comprehension) and utility. To know is to be able to control things in accord with plans and desires. Emphasis on this dimension can be seen in the new wave of voluntaristic theology that became prevalent throughout the low countries, France, and England. One problem that would persist throughout subsequent ages was how to comprehend the nature of the human being and how to bring humans under control (for purposes of health or betterment of life) by utilizing models and devices taken from the nonhuman, mechanical realm.

The systematization of the material world, natural philosophy, was seen as a mechanical model. This provided a concrete, constructible representation as the basis for knowledge in this new world view. Thus, knowledge of any thing could be modeled by real machines or real bodies, for the world was constructed as a machine was. The world was merely a set of Archimedian simple machines hooked together or a set of colliding corpuscles that obeyed the laws of mechanical collision (i.e., laws of the balance).

What did it take to understand a machine? There were two paradigmatic mechanical devices at the start: The balance or the pendulum and the mechanical clock. The clock had more power as an image because it had visibly regular motions and was as trustworthy as it was well made. But it did not take long for those building the new system to show that a mechanical clock was just a form of pendulum, and the pendulum was just a bent and hinged balance, and that all the other simple machines could be treated as if they were balances. This was Galileo's vision, and from him it swept around Europe and even across the seas into China.

It was a short but interestingly different move from Galileo's representations of two forces seeking equilibrium along a balance beam into Descartes' separation of the forces, thus turning a balance problem into an equilibrium collision problem. This collision form is the geometrical model of the mechanical universe that persisted until algebra brought new, nongeometrical representations and new ways of thinking – a new model of intelligibility for the universe (which started about the time of Euler but came to full fruition only in the nineteenth century).

This mechanical model of thought also pushed its way into the political realm, in the form of contract theory. Institutions were now to be legitimized by establishing equilibria among individual human bodies, as they all, singly and equally, entered into contracts – one with each other. Contracts were designed, in Hobbes' or Locke's system, to ensure the solidity of the nation, the peace of the world, and the political stability of a government that could not be undermined by the assassination or decapitation of a king.

The world was indeed a new place. Such individualism in science and philosophy, as it was found now in England, Holland, France, and northern Germany, was not the only possible reaction to these social and cultural conditions. As always, people did not have to move along with the new forces shaping the world; it was possible to react and regress. Rather than change to the new ways, they could try to reinvent and reestablish an older form of life. This is what happened in southern Germany, Austria, and throughout the Hapsburg empire. This reactionary move also accounts for the increasing marginalization of Spain and Portugal.

I try, in my essay in this volume, to show how it was that Galileo fit into this new world picture or, better, how he helped to create it. I demonstrate there that Galileo forged a new model of intelligibility for human understanding. He established new criteria for coherent explanations of natural phenomena. But these criteria – that is, the form of adequate explanations or demonstrations – were those that came fit with the mechanical philosophy or the mechanical world picture.

BRIEF BIOGRAPHICAL CHRONOLOGY

What follows is but a very brief sketch of some of the important dates and activities that made up Galileo's life. It is meant to be useful to those who wish to have some sense of Galileo's chronological progress aside from that provided in the essays in this book. However, I would urge interested readers to consult the very readable, and mostly correct, biography, *Galileo: A Life*, by James Reston,

Jr.[10] For those seriously interested in Galileo's ideas as well as his life, the classic intellectual biography is that of Stillman Drake: *Galileo at Work: His Scientific Biography*.[11] For an overview of Galilean scholarship that discusses the many different interpretations and conceptions of Galileo's work, one should look at Ernan McMullin's masterful introduction to *Galileo: Man of Science*.[12] There have been a good number of important works on Galileo published since McMullin's essay was written. Most of these have to do with the social and cultural climate in which Galileo learned and worked, which was a neglected area of Galilean research until recently. On these issues the reader is referred to the general list of references at the end of this volume, especially those works by Biagioli, Feldhay, Moss, Redondi, and Wallace.

Galileo Galilei was born on February 15, 1564 in Pisa. He was the first son of Vincenzo Galilei and Giula Ammananti. Vincenzo was a well-known court musician who struggled against authority and tradition in music and theory and who experimented with finding the chords that were written by nature. In 1574, the family moved to Florence. Galileo's early training came from the monks at the Monastery of Santa Maria of Vallombrosa, until his father pulled him out of school. In 1581, he began studies at the University of Pisa, pursuing a course in medicine. But by 1583, he had dropped out and was studying mathematics with Ostilio Ricci.

During the period from 1583 to 1589, he seems to have discovered Archimedes, met Christopher Clavius, the Jesuit mathematician and "scientific" leader of the Collegio Romano in Rome, and made his living by tutoring and giving public lectures on numerous topics in Florence and Siena. In 1586, he wrote a small book, *La Balancitta* (*The Little Balance*), using Archimedes' method of deterring specific gravities using a balance.

In 1589, Galileo was appointed to teach mathematics at the University of Pisa. He had earlier applied and been turned down for a similar job at the University of Bologna. In 1590, he completed a book, *De Motu* (*On Motion*), in which he criticized the Aristotelian doctrines of motion based on lightness and heaviness. He used Archimedes and the techniques of reasoning based on floating bodies and the balance to develop his own position. It seems that during this Pisan period, Galileo was also attending lectures, or getting notes from lectures, given by the professors at the Collegio Romano in Rome. Presumably, in this way, he was preparing himself in philosophy.[13]

In 1592, he accepted the chair of mathematics at the University of Padua, having obtained permission of the Grand Duke of Florence to do so. He gave his inaugural lecture in December of 1592. While in Padua, he not only taught mathematics but, to supplement his income, continued to tutor students, many of whom were interested in learning practical mathematics for business. In 1600, Maria Gamba, Galileo's companion, gave birth to their daughter, Virginia, who was to become a major source of Galileo's solace and comfort. In 1601, another daughter, Livia, was born. Then, in 1606 there was born a son, Vincenzo.

From 1602 through 1604, Galileo again turned to his study of motion and worked with inclined planes and pendula. It was at this time that he formulated the law of falling bodies and determined that projectiles moved in parabolic paths. These results would not be published until 1638. In 1606, he devised a mechanical sector and published *A Geometrico-military Compass*, which he sold along with the instrument.

Galileo first became involved with astronomy when he decided to lecture on the new star (supernova) of 1604. In 1609, while on a trip to Venice, he heard of a Dutch invention, the telescope. He hurriedly went back to Padua and began to theorize and construct his own instrument. By the end of that year, he had a telescope that allowed him to see the mountains on the Moon and the many stars that comprised the Milky Way, and by assiduous and painstaking observation he discovered four "stars" that revolved around Jupiter.

In 1610, he published these discoveries in *The Starry Messenger* (*Sidereus Nuncius*). This book, despite some small controversy that surrounded it, became the basis for Galileo's scientific reputation. In 1611, The Jesuit Collegio Romano, which was the scientific authority of the Church, issued a opinion that supported all of Galileo's telescopic discoveries.

In 1609, Galileo had cast a horoscope for the Grand Duke Ferdinand I, foretelling a long and happy life. The Duke died a few months later, and Prince Cosimo, to whom Galileo had been a tutor, became the new Grand Duke. Galileo used his book, and the fact that he had named Jupiter's moons "the Medician stars," to successfully argue for a job back home in the Florentine court of the Medici. He was appointed chief philosopher and mathematician to the Grand Duke of Tuscany. He insisted that "philosopher" be added to his title, for philosophers had more respect and importance than mere mathematicians. This may be the last time in history that this was true.

In 1612, he became embroiled in a controversy at court regarding the nature of floating bodies, and he published his *Discourse on Floating Bodies*, which was soon followed by the publication of his further telescopic observations, *Letters on the Sunspots*, which was the result of another controversy with the Jesuit father Christopher Scheiner.

In this work, Galileo explicitly came out as a Copernican in favor of the heliocentric system, announced the phases of Venus, and argued rightly that the sunspots were on the surface of the Sun and not "stars" that revolved around it. It was published in 1613 by the Academia de Lincei (Academy of the Lynxes), which arguably was the first scientific society. The society was named after the catlike lynx, because it was thought the lynx could see in the dark and so could see what others could not – just like the true scientist.

In 1614, Galileo's daughters entered the Franciscan convent of Saint Matthew, located in Arcetri in the hills outside Florence. Virginia became Sister Maria Celeste, while Livia chose the name Sister Arcangela.

In 1615, Galileo argued, in his "Letter to the Grand Duchess Christina," that Biblical scripture had to be interpreted in the light of what was known by science about the world. He claimed that the language of the Bible was the language of men who were historically context-bound to their time and who had as their purpose the persuasion of others to accept the "true" faith.

In early 1616, the Holy Office in Rome condemned the teachings of Copernicus and put his book in the prohibited index, pending correction. Earlier, Galileo had gone before Cardinal Robert Bellarmine and defended Copernicus's work, but yet he left this interview by being warned about defending or teaching the Copernican theory. But this time, he had also written a draft of a manuscript dealing with the ebb and flow of the tides, which he thought could be used as a mechanical proof of Copernicanism. This formed the basis of the later Day Four of his *Dialogue Concerning Two Chief World Systems* (*Dialogo*).

In the fall of 1618, three comets were visible – one for quite a long time. In 1619, Horatio Grassi, who then held the chair of mathematics at The Jesuit Collegio Romano, published anonymously his observations on these comets. Galileo, as one of the most famous astronomers of Europe, was asked his opinion, and his reply was published in 1619, though the form it took was two published lectures by his disciple, Mario Guiducci. In that book, Galileo attacked Tycho Brahe.

In response later in 1619, under the name Lothario Sarsi, Grassi published a stinging, harsh reply targeting Galileo himself. This was *The Astronomical and Philosophical Balance, on which the opinions of Galileo Galilei regarding Comets are weighed, as well as those presented in the Florentine Academy by Mario Guiduccio.* Galileo's friends urged him to reply and not to let this challenge to his authority go unremarked. The reply, *The Assayer, In which With a precise and delicate scale will be weighed the things contained in the Astronomical and Philosophical Balance of Lothario Sarsi...* [*Il Saggiatore*], was published by the Academia Lincei in 1623.

This was a truly masterful piece of sarcastic invective and criticism. It is still read today in Italian language classes in Italy as a fine example of the use of the rhetoric devices in the Italian language. Three things need to be remarked about this inflamed controversy:

First, through this exchange, Galileo managed to really rile the Jesuits, who were quite powerful at this time in the Papal Court. Yet, second, Galileo used some of his best, most insightful prose to defend the patently false theory that the comets were really sublunary phenomena caused by some vagaries of optical refraction. Finally, and importantly, it should be noted that in 1623, Cardinal Maffeo Barberini became Pope Urban VIII. Barberini had sided with Galileo in the Florentine court controversy over floating bodies, back in 1611. He, in fact, had written a poem in praise of Galileo.

The final salvo in the battle was published, still under the name Sarsi, in 1626 in Paris: *A Reckoning of the Weights for the Balance and the Small Scale.* There, Grassi pretended that *saggiatore* meant *assagiatore* (a wine taster) and accused Galileo of drinking too much new wine. Ironically, we do know that Galileo was quite partial to his food and wine (a fact that was well brought out much later in Bertolt Brecht's play, *Galileo*).

In 1624, Galileo went to Rome to see his friend, the new Pope. He was warmly greeted and feted all around. He was encouraged in his scholarship and shortly thereafter began work on the *Dialogo*. What Galileo seemed not to grasp, on this trip nor subsequently, was that the new Pope was in a politically precarious position. The Thirty Years War was raging on, and charges of heresy were being bandied about all over. Urban VIII himself was accused by his enemies of being too lenient toward those who deviated from the true faith. The Counter-Reformation was trying to solidify its power and recapture lands and peoples that had been lost.

Throughout this period of his life, Galileo was recurrently threatened by serious illnesses. These bouts considerably delayed his work. In January 1630, Galileo had finished *Dialogo*. He brought it to Rome some months later, seeking an *imprimatur* for the book. Without this official permission from the Church censors, the book could not be published. Finally, in 1632, after much controversy and trouble, the permission was granted in Florence, rather than in Rome. In February of 1632, the *Dialogue on the Two Chief World Systems (Dialogo)* was published. It was dedicated to the Grand Duke of Tuscany. By August of that year, sales of the book had been suspended, and by October Galileo had been ordered to stand trial for heresy.

Now to understand all this, a brief description of the book is necessary. *Dialogo* consists of a discussion among three men over the period of four days. The chief protagonist is Salviati, named after a dead Florentine friend of Galileo's. This character is the spokesman for Galileo himself, and he will defend the Copernican side in the discourse. Next, there is Sagredo, named after a late Venetian friend. Finally, there is the Aristotelian, called Simplicio, after the famous Aristotelian commentator, Simplicius. Of course, Simplicio also means simple-minded or simpleton.

As Galileo himself describes the book, Day One consists of a discussion of the principles of natural motion and natural philosophy and defends the circular version of natural or "inertial" motion. The second part of this day illustrates some of the methods of natural philosophy through a discussion of optics and the lunar properties. This harks back to Galileo's earlier book, *Sidereus Nuncius*.

Day Two treats the daily, or diurnal, rotation of the Earth, and therein Salviati convincingly introduces the principle of the relativity of observed motion. The first two days, Galileo says in his preface, show that any experiments that are practiced on the Earth are indifferent between the Earth's being in motion or at rest. In other words, it's a draw to this point.

Day Three treats the annual or yearly motion of the Sun about the Earth. Here, Galileo gives a few celestial arguments that seem to strengthen the Copernican hypothesis "until it might seem that this must triumph absolutely," but, he says, these reflections will only simplify astronomy and will not show "any necessity imposed by nature."

In Day Four, he proposes his ingenious speculation that the ebb and flow of the tides is due to the three-fold Copernican motions of the Earth. This argument gains force, in part, because the alternative explanations all invoke mysterious or occult causes. At the end of the four days, the injunction, given by Urban VII himself to Galileo, is voiced. It holds that God in His infinite power and wisdom could have caused the tides to move using whatever means He chose, and our human minds cannot pretend to a knowledge and certainty about nature that would limit and restrict the Divine power and wisdom.

Yet, Galileo puts this speech in the mouth of Simplicio! Even worse, in Day One, Galileo had already argued that if one proceeds in natural philosophy using mathematics, then a human mind can be like the Divine mind, intensively if not extensively. It is small wonder that Urban felt his trust was betrayed and his injunction flaunted. And even the fact that the three promise to keep talking about the nature of motion before heading for the gondolas was not enough to assuage Urban's ire.

In 1633, Galileo finally arrived in Rome. The Grand Duke and his doctors had sent messages that Galileo was too ill to travel but to no avail. Two months later, he was examined twice by the Inquisitors. Then two months more passed before Galileo, under the Pope's explicit orders, was rigorously examined. On June 22, 1633, Galileo was pronounced "vehemently suspected of heresy" and condemned to formal imprisonment. *Dialogo* was prohibited. Galileo made his abjuration on the same, according to the prescribed formula:

I, Galileo, son of the late Vincenzo Galilei of Florence, seventy years of age ... abandon completely the false opinion that the sun is at the center of the world and does not move and that the earth is not the center of the world and moves...[14]

He was allowed to serve his sentence under house arrest, and he first went to the archbishop of Siena. Later he was allowed to live in his house in Arcetri, near Florence. As if this were not enough pain, the following year, in 1634, his daughter, Sister Maria Celeste, died. It was she who had seen him through his numerous illnesses and upon whom he depended heavily. He was crushed and could not work for months afterwards.

In 1635, Marin Mersenne translated Galileo's *Mechanics* into French, and a Latin translation of *Dialogo* was made and published in Strasbourg. Galileo had already begun work on his next (and last) book, *Discourses and Mathematical Demonstrations Concerning the Two New Sciences* (*Discorsi*). It was finally published in July 1638, in Leyden in Holland, after the manuscript was smuggled out of Italy.

Discorsi is Galileo's most rigorous work. Again, it was written in dialogue form. The first two days treat the problems of matter. It is often said that these deal with the strength of materials, but claiming this is the topic makes it difficult to see why Galileo would have considered this to be an important new science. More clearly, they are Galileo's attempt to show the mathematics necessary for and the problems inherent in treating the nature of matter. Days Three and Four are a sustained treatment of the problem of local motion, and they contain the results of his research during his earlier time in Padua.

The historian of science and Galileo scholar, Tom Settle, wrote about Galileo's death in a way that illustrates nicely the problems of doing history, of even getting the dates right:

Conventionally we say that Galileo died on 8 January, 1642. Unfortunately, there is more to be said than that because there were and are more than one convention. If we are talking about the conventions we use today, 1642 was the correct year. If we were to talk about the convention normal in Florence in the period, Galileo died in 1641. The Florentines before and after the 17th Century began the year on the 25th of March, so that January was still 1641 by the rules and norms of Galileo's locale.

Then there is the problem of the day of Galileo's death. We change days at midnight, but of course that is just a convention. In Florence and many other places in Italy the day began at sunset or conventionally one half hour after sunset. Now by convention we say that Galileo died in the evening of 8 January. For the moment I am not sure whether that is the modern author's translation or the actual reading of the death certificate. If the death

certificate read evening of 8 January, then by our reckoning it would have
been evening of 7 January. If the 8 January is a translated one the death
certificate would have read evening of 9 January.

The story of Galileo does not end with his death. Immediately
after he died a fight began as his friends and disciples attempted to
build him a monument.[15] Of course, his fame lived on, and the legend
of Galileo the hero began to take on epic proportions.[16]

NOTES

1 Mario Biagioli commented on this in correspondence with me, but see
  also his *Galileo Courtier*, Chicago: The University of Chicago Press,
  1993, Chapters 1 and 2.
2 Richard Westfall, "Galileo and Newton: Two Different Rhetorical Strategies," in Marcello Pera and William Shea, eds., *Persuading Science: The
  Art of Scientific Rhetoric*, Canton, MA: Science History Publications,
  1991, pp. 107–122.
3 Oldenburg to Honywood, April 1656, in Rupert Hall and Marie Boas
  Hall, *The Correspondence of Henry Oldenburg*, Vol. I, Madison, WI:
  The University of Wisconsin Press, 1965.
4 See, for example, the papers in this volume by McMullin, Blackwell,
  Pera, Redondi, and Swerdlow, all of whom draw distinct and somewhat
  diverse ways of looking at this event. These authors also provide the
  reader with the important historical, bibliographical references.
5 Heinrich Wolfflin, *Principles of Art History: The Problem of the Development of Style in Later Art*, translated by M. D. Hottinger, New York:
  Dover, 1950 (originally 1915). This quotation comes from the preface to
  the sixth edition of 1922.
6 Cf. Elizabeth L. Eisenstein, *The Printing Revolution in Early Modern
  Europe*, Cambridge University Press, 1983.
7 Karl Marx, *Capital*, Vol. 1, Part Eight, Chapters 27–30, translated by Ben
  Fowkes, London: Penguin Books, 1976, pp. 877–913.
8 C. R. Boxer, *The Dutch Seaborne Empire 1600–1800*, Penguin, 1993,
  originally 1965, pp. 6–7.
9 Thomas Hobbes, *De Corpore*, 1655, Molesworth Edition, p. 86.
10 James Reston, Jr., *Galileo: A Life*, New York: Harper Collins, 1994.
11 Stillman Drake, *Galileo at Work: His Scientific Biography*, Chicago:
   The University of Chicago Press, 1978.
12 Ernan McMullin, "Introduction: Galileo, Man of Science," in E. Mc-
   Mullin, ed., *Galileo: Man of Science*, New York: Basic Books, 1967,
   pp. 3–51.

13 See the essay by William Wallace in this volume.
14 Reprinted in Maurice A. Finocchiaro, ed., *The Galileo Affair: A Documentary History*, Berkeley, CA: University of California Press, 1989, pp. 292–3.
15 See Paolo Galluzzi's essay in this volume for the details of the fascinating aftermath.
16 See Michael Segre's essay in this volume.

1   Galileo's Pisan studies in science and philosophy

The aura surrounding Galileo as founder of modern science disposes many of those writing about him to start *in medias res* with an account of his discoveries with the telescope, or with his dialogues on the world systems and the two new sciences, or with the trial and the tragic events surrounding it. Frequently implicit in such beginnings is the attitude that Galileo had no forebears and stands apart from history, this despite the fact that he was forty-six years of age when he wrote his *Sidereus Nuncius* and then in his late sixties and early seventies when he composed his two other masterpieces.

Attempts have recently been made by scholars to dispel this myth by giving closer scrutiny to the historical record – closer, that is, than one gets from perusing the National Edition of Galileo's works.[1] This was a masterful collection, but begun as it was in the last decade of the nineteenth century and completed in the first decade of the twentieth, it perforce could not benefit from the historiographical techniques developed in our century. During the past twenty years, in particular, much research has been done on Galileo's manuscripts, and it sheds unexpected light on what has come to be known as Galileo's "early period" – that covering the first forty-five years of his life.[2] This period has been singularly neglected by historians, and to their disadvantage, if the adage *parvus error in initio magnus in fine* may be applied to the history of ideas.

PERSONS AND PLACES IN TUSCANY

Galileo's father, Vincenzio Galilei, was born in Florence in 1520 and flourished there as a teacher of music and a lutanist of ability (Drake 1970). Having studied music theory for a while with

Gioseffo Zarlini in Venice, he married Guilia Ammannati of Pescia in 1563 and settled in the countryside near Pisa. There their first child, Galileo Galilei, was born on February 15, 1564. The family returned to Florence in 1572, but the young Galileo was left in Pisa with a relative of Guilia by marriage, Muzio Tedaldi, a businessman and customs official.

Two years later, Galileo rejoined his family in Florence and was tutored there by Jacopo Borghini until he could be sent to the Camaldolese Monastery at nearby Vallombrosa to begin his classical education. While at that monastery, Galileo was attracted to the life of the monks and actually joined the order as a novice. Vincenzio was displeased with the development, so he brought his son back to Florence where he resumed his studies at a school run by the Camaldolese monks but no longer as a candidate for their order.

Vincenzio's plan for Galileo was to become a physician, following in the footsteps of a fifteenth-century member of the family, also named Galileo, who had achieved great distinction as a physician and also in public affairs. Accordingly, he arranged for his son to live again with Tedaldi in Pisa and had him enrolled at the university there as a medical student in the fall of 1581 (Drake 1978).

The next four years of his life Galileo spent at the University of Pisa, studying mainly philosophy, where his professors were Francesco Buonamici and Girolamo Borro, and mathematics (including astronomy) under a Camaldolese monk, Filippo Fantoni. He probably went back to Florence for the summers, however, and this provides a key to the way Galileo supplemented the instructions he received in mathematics from Father Fantoni.

It was the custom of the Tuscan court to move from Florence to Pisa from Christmas to Easter of each year, and the court mathematician at the time was Ostilio Ricci, a competent geometer who is said to have studied under Niccolò Tartaglia (Settle 1971, Masotti 1975). During the 1582–1583 academic year, Galileo met Ricci while the latter was at Pisa and sat in on lectures Ricci was giving on Euclid to the court pages.

The following summer, when Galileo was back home, supposedly reading Galen, he invited Ricci to meet his father. Vincenzio was impressed with Ricci and the two became friends. Ricci told Vincenzio that his son was little interested in medicine, that he wanted to become a mathematician, and sought permission to instruct him in that discipline. Despite Vincenzio's unhappiness with this request, Galileo was able to avail himself of Ricci's help and devote himself more and more to the study of Euclid and Archimedes, probably with the aid of Italian translations prepared by Tartaglia.

By 1585, Galileo dropped out of the University of Pisa and began to teach mathematics privately at Florence and at Siena, where he had a public appointment in 1585–1586, and then at Vallombrosa in the summer of 1585. In 1587, Galileo traveled to Rome to visit Christopher Clavius, the famous Jesuit mathematician at the Collegio Romano. And in 1588, he was invited to the Florentine Academy to give lectures on the location and dimensions of hell in Dante's *Inferno*.

In 1589, Fantoni relinquished the chair in mathematics at Pisa and Galileo was selected to replace him, partly because of the favorable impression he had made on the Tuscan court with his lectures on Dante and partly on the recommendation of Clavius and other mathematicians who had become acquainted with his work. Galileo began lecturing at Pisa in November 1589, along with Jacopo Mazzoni, a philosopher who taught both Plato and Aristotle and was also an expert on Dante, and the two quickly became friends (Purnell 1972, DePace 1993).

Mazzoni is of special interest because of his knowledge of the works of another mathematician, Giovan Battista Benedetti, and because he is given special mention by Galileo in a letter from Pisa addressed to his father in Florence and dated November 15, 1590. In it, Galileo requests that his seven-volume Galen and his *Sfera* be sent to him at Pisa and informs his father that he is applying himself "to study and learning from Signor Mazzoni," who sends his regards (EN10:44–5).

Galileo then taught at the University of Pisa until 1592, when financial burdens put on him as the eldest son at the death of his father in 1591 required him to obtain a better salary than the 60 florins he was being paid. He sought and received an appointment at the University of Padua at a salary of 180 florins, where he delivered his inaugural lecture on December 7, 1592.

He spent the next eighteen years in the Republic of Venice, which he later avowed were the happiest years of his life. Then he returned to the Florentine court in 1610 as mathematician and philosopher to Cosimo II de' Medici, the Grand Duke of Tuscany.

MANUSCRIPTS AND THE EXPANDED DATA BASE

We have touched on places and persons in Tuscany that played a significant role in Galileo's intellectual development. The principal locations are Pisa and Florence, with Vallombrosa and Siena of secondary importance, along with the outside trip to Rome, which fortunately gave rise to materials that greatly enlarge the data base on which we can work. Galileo left a number of manuscripts dating from about 1580 to 1592, most in his own hand and in Latin, much of it on watermarked paper. Antonio Favaro transcribed some of the manuscripts for the National Edition and made a few notations regarding Galileo's peculiar spelling of Latin terms.

He also was able to identify two sources Galileo used for note taking, both translations of Plutarch's *Opuscoli Morali*, one published at Venice in 1559 and the other at Lucca in 1560 (EN9:277–8). Apart from this, Favaro could only conjecture about Galileo's sources and the periods during which he composed the various manuscripts that make up his Tuscan heritage, most of which are still conserved in Florence's Biblioteca Nazionale Centrale.

Serious work on these materials began around 1970, when Stillman Drake worked out a technique for dating Galileo's manuscripts through a study of the watermarks on the paper on which they were written and when other scholars, myself included, began to uncover the source materials on which the natural philosophy contained in one of the manuscripts was based.[3] Over the past twenty-five years, this research has expanded to include full studies of watermarks (Camerota 1993), detailed paleographical studies of Galileo's handwriting and word choice (Hooper 1993), and analyses of the ink he used when writing the manuscripts (Hooper 1994).[4]

Research on the sources of Galileo's philosophy proved particularly fruitful, since it turned out that a large part of that philosophy was appropriated from notes of lectures given in Rome by Jesuit professors of the Collegio Romano – the prestigious university established in that city by the founder of the Jesuits, Ignatius Loyola. Although Galileo did not attend those lectures, he somehow obtained copies of them and then appropriated selected materials for his own use. Since the Jesuit notes can be dated, the discovery in them of passages with correspondences in Galileo's writings offers an additional way to determine the time and place of Galileo's compositions.

The manuscripts most important for this enterprise are all in Galileo's hand and are four in number. One is a special collection, *Filza Rinuccini* 2, and contains Galileo's lectures on Dante's *Inferno*; this was given in Florence and is written on paper bearing a Florentine watermark. The other three are in the group of manuscripts at the Biblioteca Nazionale entitled *Manoscritti Galileiani* and bear the numbers 27, 46, and 71.

Manuscript 27 is labeled *Dialettica*, the term used for the whole of logic in Galileo's day, and contains two treatises on logic. Antonio Favaro regarded this as a "scholastic exercise" of Galileo and only transcribed its titles and a sample question in the National Edition (EN9:275–82). It gives many indications of having been copied or appropriated from one or more sources, and many of its folios bear watermarks, all of Pisan origin.

Manuscript 46 bears the notation that it contains "an examination of Aristotle's *De caelo* made by Galileo around the year 1590" (EN1:9). This manuscript is essentially a notebook and it contains five treatises on different subjects, which Favaro transcribed and published in their entirety under the title *Juvenilia*, regarding it as a youthful composition (EN1:15–177). It, too, shows signs of copying, and its folios bear a variety of watermarks, most of either Pisan or Florentine origin.

Manuscript 71 differs from the other two in that there are crossouts and emendations in the manuscript but no signs of copying. It apparently contains original drafts of essays by Galileo on the subject of motion; on this account, is referred to as the *De Motu Antiquiora*, the "older" science of motion, to distinguish it from the "new" science of motion published by Galileo in 1638. The folios of this manuscript, like the others, bear watermarks, a majority from Pisa but a significant number from Florence. Favaro also transcribed and published this manuscript (EN1:251–408), but in so doing he changed the ordering of the essays as they occur at present in the manuscript.

There are errors of Latinity in some of the noted manuscripts and also peculiarities of spelling. There are also internal references that serve to show temporal connections between them. And, finally, there is now a substantial collection of possible source materials, some in print, others still in manuscript, on which Galileo could have drawn when writing them. Evaluating all of this material is the task one must face when trying to assess Galileo's intellectual formation. This took place mainly at the University of Pisa, but it was an ongoing process during the entire Tuscan period, prior to Galileo's move to the Veneto in 1592.

GALILEO'S APPROPRIATION OF JESUIT LEARNING

Of the material surveyed thus far, the most surprising is that associated with the Jesuits of the Collegio Romano, a source completely unsuspected for over four centuries.

I started my research on that subject at about the same time Drake was beginning his work on watermarks and have reported my findings in publications since then, principally 1981, 1984a, 1990, and 1992a, b. The path was tortuous and need not be reviewed here. The main conclusions were that the two manuscripts with the closest connections to the Jesuits, 27 and 46, were both composed at Pisa, the first in early 1589 and the second in late 1589 or early 1590 (Wallace, 1992b:39, 57).

The logic notes of manuscript 27 consist of two treatises relating to Aristotle's *Posterior Analytics*, one dealing with foreknowledge required for demonstration and the other with demonstration itself. Both treatises clearly derive from a course taught by Paulus Vallius in Rome, which did not conclude until August of 1588, and from which Galileo could not have appropriated his version until early 1589. Nothing in the watermark evidence and that derived from peculiarities in spelling alters this conclusion.

The situation is more complex with regard to Manuscript 46, labeled *Physical Questions* (Wallace 1977) to differentiate them from the *Logical Questions* of Manuscript 27. This is composed of three parts, the first containing portions of a questionary on Aristotle's *De caelo*, the second portions of a questionary on Aristotle's *De generatione*, and the third of series of memoranda on motion that are related to the composition of Manuscript 71, to be considered later. There are three treatises in the part pertaining to *De caelo*, the first concerning the subject of that work, the second on the universe as a whole, and the third on the heavens.

All three of these are written on paper with Pisan watermarks and show few peculiarities of spelling. Since they presume knowledge of the logic contained in Manuscript 27 and show signs of improved Latinity, their writing is best located at Pisa around 1590, within a year after the questions on logic. The particular Jesuit set of notes Galileo used for his appropriation is not known with certainty, but a good possibility is that taught by Antonius Menu on *De caelo* in 1580. This source clears up a problem in the dating of Manuscript 46 based on the chronology given in it by Galileo (Wallace 1977:42, 258–9) and otherwise fits in with considerations presented in Wallace (1981:217–28) and Wallace (1984a:89–96).[5]

The second part of Manuscript 46 contains three treatises pertaining to *De generatione*, the first on alteration, the second on the elements, and the third on primary qualities. These are written on paper different from the first part, with Florentine watermarks, and they contain irregularities in spelling. The irregularities relate to word forms that are written differently in Italian and Latin, as, for example, *santo* and *sancto*, and occur in words with letter grouping like -*nt*- and -*st*-. Thus for *elementum* Galileo will sometimes write *elemenctum*; for *contra*, *conctra*; for *momentum*, *momenctum*; for *distantia*, *dixtantia*; and so on. These variants have been studied by Wallace Hooper (1993) who sees them as evidence of Galileo's learning when, and when not, to insert a *c* or an *x* when changing from an Italian to a Latin spelling.

Apparently, Galileo overcompensated at first and inserted too many *c*'s or changed an *s* to an *x* too often, for these forms quickly disappear in his later compositions. Their presence, therefore, is a good indication that their author, who had been accustomed to writing in Italian, was beginning to write in Latin as he prepared himself for an academic career. On the basis of this evidence it seems likely that these treatises were written in Florence and at a date even earlier than Manuscript 27, probably 1588.

Which of the Jesuit courses Galileo used for his appropriation is difficult to decide, but the best candidate is that on *De generatione*, offered in Rome by Paulus Vallius, the same Jesuit whose logical questions were used by Galileo when writing his Manuscript 27.

Unfortunately, the exemplar of Vallius's work on the elements that shows close correspondences with Galileo's Manuscript 46 is found in a codex that is undated. We do know, however, that Vallius taught *De generatione* there in 1585, 1586, and 1589, and, of these, the 1586 version would fit best with the new evidence.

As I have argued in Wallace (1984a:91–2, 223–5), Galileo first gained access to all these lecture notes through his visit to Christopher Clavius in 1587. At that time, he left with Clavius some theorems he had composed on the center of gravity of solids. In correspondence between the two in 1588, which involved Guidobaldo del Monte also, Clavius questioned Galileo's proof of the first theorem on the grounds that it contained a *petitio principii* (EN10:24–5, 29–30).

Since this type of question pertains to the foreknowledge required for demonstration, and at that time Vallius was teaching the part of the logic sequence dealing with foreknowledge and demonstration, it seems reasonable to suppose that Clavius would have put Galileo in touch with Vallius and that the latter would have made his lecture notes available to the young mathematician. Also, Galileo could well have had queries for Clavius on *gravitas* and *levitas* as these pertain to the elements, and Vallius would again be the best resource to whom Galileo could turn for information on these topics. This would explain how Galileo obtained not only the materials on which Manuscript 27 were based but also how the earlier version of Vallius's *De Elementis* (say, that of 1586) came to be incorporated in his Manuscript 46.

From the point of view of philosophy, Galileo's Manuscript 27 contains some very sophisticated information on scientific methodology, especially on the use of suppositions in scientific reasoning and on the role of resolution and composition as employed in the demonstrative *regressus*. Scholars have tended to overlook the regress, a powerful method of discovery and proof developed at the University of Padua, which reached its perfection in Galileo's lifetime (Wallace 1995). These areas of logic have been described in detail in my study of Galileo's sources (Wallace 1984a: Chapters 3, 5, and 6), which documents the recurrence of expressions found in Manuscript 27 in all Galileo's later writings. The implications of these logical teachings are more fully delineated in my examination of Galileo's logic of discovery and proof (Wallace 1992a), the first part of which (*logica docens*, Chapters 1–4) systematically analyzes the logic contained in his logical treatises and the second part (*logica utens*, Chapters 5–6) how he used it in his works on astronomy and mechanics.

Manuscript 46 is almost four times longer than Manuscript 27, being composed of 110 folios as opposed to the latter's 31. Its material content covers the universe, the celestial spheres, and the elemental components of the terrestrial region, topics that engaged Galileo's attention throughout his life.

Two of its questions on the celestial spheres are clearly extracted from Clavius's commentary on the *Sphere* of Sacrobosco, either the 1581 or the 1585 edition. They show that Galileo was acquainted with Copernicus's teaching on the number and ordering of the spheres, even though he there defended the Ptolemaic teaching. He continued to teach Ptolemaic astronomy until the early 1600s, as is seen in his *Trattato della Sfera*, student copies of which were prepared from an original in Galileo's own hand between 1602 and 1606. The autograph has been lost, but Drake speculates that it was begun as early as 1586–1587, in conjunction with Galileo's private teaching of astronomy (Drake 1978:12). More likely, it was composed toward the end of 1590, when he wrote to his father requesting that his copy of the *Sfera* be sent to him at Pisa (*Sfera* here meaning the text with Clavius's commentary), and when he was writing the *De caelo* portion of Manuscript 46 containing the extract from Clavius (Wallace 1983, 1984a:255–61).

A striking but often unnoticed feature of Galileo's thought is his extraordinary grasp of Aristotelian teaching and his ability to engage the Peripatetics of his day on fine points of their interpretations. Such knowledge was not simply intuited by Galileo; he had to work to acquire it. He himself wrote to Belisario Vinta on May 7, 1610, when seeking the title of philosopher be added to that of mathematician to the Grand Duke of Tuscany, that he had "studied more years in philosophy than months in pure mathematics" (EN10:353). Surely the study and laborious appropriation of these lecture notes from Collegio Romano, a major portion of which is found in Manuscript 46, is to be counted among the "years in philosophy," to which Galileo there refers. As far as his use of the Jesuit questionaries on *De caelo* and *De generatione* is concerned, these have been partially investigated in my translation of Manuscript 46 (Wallace 1977:253–314) and more fully in later works (Wallace 1981, 1984a, 1991, and 1992a).

THE PHILOSOPHICAL AMBIENCE AT PISA

Galileo's formal study of philosophy, of course, took place at the University of Pisa from 1581 to 1585, and he had further contacts with the philosophers there when teaching mathematics at the university between 1589 and 1592. Possibly because Galileo later voiced his disagreement with the views of his teachers at Pisa, scholars have tended to undervalue his philosophical training there.

This may prove to be a mistake, since a number of studies are now available that connect his studies at the university with the manuscripts we have already discussed, as well as with Manuscript 71, which will occupy our attention in the following section. To lay the groundwork for that exposition, we now sketch the philosophical ambience at Pisa, with particular reference to Francesco Buonamici, Girolamo Borro and his influence on Filippo Fantoni, and Jacopo Mazzoni and the way in which he may have put Galileo in contact with the thought of Giovanni Batista Benedetti.[6]

Correspondences between the contents of Manuscripts 46 and 71 and the teachings of Buonamici have long been recognized and have been analyzed in some detail by Alexandre Koyré (1978). More helpful for our purposes is Mario Helbing's (1989) study of Buonamici's philosophy. This provides the complete background of Galileo's studies at Pisa, a full analysis of the contents of Buonamici's *De Motu*, and valuable reflections on his relations with Galileo. Helbing calls attention to the fact that the *De Motu* was already completed by 1587, though it was not published until 1591. Its importance derives from the fact that it records the fruits of Buonamici's teaching at the University of Pisa, where he taught natural philosophy from 1565 to 1587. His occasion for putting out the volume was, in Buonamici's own words, "a controversy that had arisen at the university among our students and certain of our colleagues on the motion of the elements" (Helbing 1989:54).

To appreciate the import of this statement one must be aware, Helbing points out, that professorial lectures were not the only means of transmitting knowledge to students at the time. Disputations were an additional component, and many of these seem to have centered on precisely the problems that interested Galileo. It could well be, therefore, that Galileo was one of the students to whom Buonamici refers. The colleagues mentioned most certainly include Borro, who published a treatise on the motion of heavy and light bodies in 1575, to which Galileo refers in Manuscript 71, and probably Fantoni, who left a manuscript on the same subject that shows Borro's influence.

Helbing's thesis is that Buonamici's teaching exerted a substantial influence on the young Galileo, so much so that his own writings reflect a polemic dialogue with his teacher that continued through the years. The subjects and problems that preoccupied him were all contained in Buonamici's massive treatise, whose technical terminology Galileo took over as his own, even though his investigations led him to markedly different results.

Buonamici's project was to write a definitive treatise on motion in general that would explain its many manifestations in the world of nature on the basis of philological and scholarly research. Galileo's project, by way of opposition (EN1:367), was to concentrate on only one motion, essentially that of heavy bodies, and to make a detailed study of that using mathematical techniques to reveal its true nature. In his lectures, Helbing argues, Buonamici probably introduced Galileo to the atomism of Democritus, to Philoponus's critiques of Aristotle's teachings, to Copernicus's innovations in astronomy, to Archimedes and his use of the buoyancy principle to explain upward motion, to Hipparchus's theory of impetus, and to the writings of many others, including those of Clavius and Benedetto Pereira at the Collegio Romano – references to all of which can be found in his *De Motu*.

Galileo, without doubt, explicitly rejected many of Buonamici's teachings. Helbing notes that this rejection is particularly evident in Galileo's early writings, where Buonamici's arguments against Archimedes are definitely his target. Galileo also makes references to his former teacher in terms that are far from complimentary, in both the *Two Chief World Systems* (EN7:200, 231–2) and the *Two New Sciences* (EN8:190).

But despite these negative reactions, Helbing also records several areas of substantial agreement between Buonamici and Galileo, two of which are relevant to our study. The first is the general methodology they employ in their study of motion. Both wish to use a *methodus* to put their science on an axiomatic base, imitating in this the reasoning processes of mathematicians (*De Motu* 3A–B). Both regard sense experience as the foundation of natural science, taking this in a sense broad enough to include experiment in the rudimentary form it was then assuming at Pisa. And both see causal reasoning and demonstration, with its twofold process of resolution and composition, as the normal road to scientific conclusions.

The second and more important area of agreement is the status each accords to mathematics both as a science in its own right and as an aid in investigating the secrets of nature. Buonamici lists the three speculative sciences as physics, mathematics, and metaphysics, and he insists that students should begin their study with mathematics, then proceed to physics, and ultimately to metaphysics.

Again, mathematics for him is the discipline that can raise one to divine science. It is also a true science that satisfies the requirements of the *Posterior Analytics*, against the teachings of Pereira, whom he cites explicitly. Its demonstrations are not limited to reductions to the impossible but include ostensive demonstrations of all three types: of the fact, of the reasoned fact, and, most powerful, making it the most exact of the human sciences. Buonamici further accords validity to the middle sciences (*scientiae mediae*) which he lists as optics, catoptrics, harmonics, astronomy, navigation, and mechanics, and he sees them as valuable adjuncts for the study of nature. This part of Buonamici's instruction seems to have deeply influenced Galileo and set him on the course that would bring him ultimately to Clavius and the Collegio Romano.

Two additional professors at Pisa, Borro the philosopher and Fantoni the mathematician, seem to have had less positive influence on Galileo. Borro was the type of philosopher against whom Galileo reacted most violently. Very different from Buonamici, he took most of his knowledge of Aristotle from medieval authors, especially Averroes in Latin translation. His writings show him much opposed to Platonism and the attempts being made in his day to reconcile Aristotle's ideas with those of his teacher.

Borro's anti-Platonism, coupled with his attraction to Averroes, are further revealed in his vehement rejection of mathematics and of the use of mathematical methods in the study of nature. He focused instead on the empirical side of Aristotelian philosophy, stressing the importance of observation and experience in uncovering the secrets of nature, and in this respect he undoubtedly exerted an influence on Galileo. This influence is seen in Manuscript 71, where Galileo shows his acquaintance with an experiment performed by Borro and described by him in *De Motu Gravium et Levium* (1575).

Fantoni is important for two *quaestiones* he left in manuscript form, one on the motion of heavy and light bodies, the other on the certitude of the mathematical sciences. His *De Motu* is of some significance for the fact that he wrote it not as a philosopher, as did Borro and Buonamici, but while teaching mathematics, and in so doing set a precedent for Galileo to prepare a similar treatise when he took over Fantoni's post. Actually, it presents little more than the kind of Averroist analysis found in Borro's book. The treatise on mathematics is also unoriginal, taking up positions similar to those defended by Buonamici in his massive text. What is noteworthy about it is that it is explicitly directed against Pereira. Fantoni argues that mathematics is a true science, that it fills all the requirements of the *Posterior Analytics* for certain knowledge, that it demonstrates through true causes, and that it can even achieve demonstrations that are most powerful – conclusions consonant with those of Clavius and the mathematicians at the Collegio Romano.

Possibly the strongest influence on Galileo from his years in Pisa, however, came not from his professors there, but from the colleague he encountered when he started teaching there, Jacopo Mazzoni. In 1590, when Galileo told his father that he was studying with Mazzoni, he was probably composing the notes on *De caelo* and *De generatione*, a course Mazzoni had taught the previous year.

Unlike his Pisan colleagues in philosophy, Mazzoni was not a monolithic Aristotelian. He also had Platonic sympathies, and in the summer of 1589 he had introduced a course in Plato's thought at the university. One of his major interests was comparing Aristotle with Plato, for he had made a concordance of their views in an early treatise published at Cesena in 1576. His major work on that subject, the *Praeludia*, did not appear until 1597, but there are indications Mazzoni was working on it over the intervening years. After its publication at Venice, in fact, Galileo wrote to him and remarked how their discussions at the beginning of their friendship were detectable in its composition (EN2:197).

Like Buonamici, Mazzoni takes a favorable view of the "mixed sciences," the *scientiae mediae*, and is explicit that Ptolemy's work pertains to that genre and also the work of Archimedes. It was Aristotle's shunning the use of mathematical demonstrations in physics, Mazzoni states, that caused him to err in his philosophizing about nature.

As an example, he cites Aristotle's teaching on the velocity of falling bodies. In detailing its particular errors and how they can be corrected, he turns to the work of Benedetti and particularly the way the latter used Archimedian principles to rectify Aristotle's teachings. Mazzoni's own treatment of the velocity problem, it turns out, more resembles that given by Galileo in Manuscript 71 than it does Benedetti's. This gives reason to believe that it was precisely these matters that Galileo and Mazzoni were studying late in 1590, the period during which it is commonly agreed Galileo was working on his *De Motu Antiquiora*.

Another comparison made by Mazzoni comes from his interest in pedagogy and concerns the relative merits of Plato and Aristotle for removing impediments encountered in the study of nature. Galileo discusses such impediments in his early writings and the various suppositions one may use to circumvent them. It is not unlikely that his studies with Mazzoni were seminal also in this respect.

With regard finally to Benedetti's work on falling motion, Koyré suspected a connection between it and the positions taken in Manuscript 71 but had little textual evidence for it, since Galileo nowhere makes any mention of Benedetti. In particular, the anti-Aristotelian tone Galileo adopts in his Manuscript 71 resonates strongly with the tone of Benedetti's major work on falling motion, *Diversarum Speculationum Mathematicarum et Physicarum Liber*, printed at Turin in 1585.

Since this was available before 1590 and figures prominently in Mazzoni's *Praeludia*, it seems reasonable to suppose that Benedetti's text was itself the object of Galileo's study with Mazzoni referred to in the letter to his father. As I have pointed out elsewhere (Wallace 1987), Benedetti's basic disagreement with Aristotle was over the latter's not using mathematical principles and methods in the study of nature, a theme recurring in both Mazzoni and Galileo. Benedetti's work likewise abounds in suppositions and thought experiments, many of which are similar to Galileo's, and he, like Galileo, is particularly intent on discovering the causes of various properties of local motion – what they both call the *verae causae*, the true causes, as opposed to those proposed by Aristotle.

Information gleaned from the philosophical ambience at Pisa thus complements the materials contained in Manuscripts 27 and 46 and provides a fuller understanding of Galileo's intellectual development during his years at Pisa. His interest in Archimedes undoubtedly dates from his studies with Buonamici and Ricci, the latter particularly because he helped Galileo hone his argumentative skills against his former teacher. His respect for Plato and his privileging Plato over Aristotle in some of his writings are at least partially explicable in terms of his contacts with Mazzoni (DePace 1992; Dollo 1989, 1990).

Nor does this type of influence from Mazzoni work at cross purposes with the materials Galileo appropriated from the Collegio Romano. In some matters, the Jesuits actually preferred Platonic teachings to those of Aristotle. For, as Crombie (1977) has amply demonstrated, they saw Platonism as fostering interest in the study of mathematics – which Calvius by 1589 had succeeded, over the objections of Pereira, in making a part of the *Ratio studiorum* at the Collegio Romano.

THE ARCHIMEDEAN – ARISTOTELIAN STUDY OF MOTION

This brings us back to Galileo's Manuscript 71 and his first sustained attack on the problem of falling motion, where, like Benedetti, he hoped to correct Aristotle with the aid of Archimedes. This manuscript has a number of components and the problem of ordering and dating these, partially explored by Favaro (EN1:245–9), has been the subject of renewed research on the basis of the new clues they present (Fredette 1972, 1975; Drake, 1986; Wallace, 1990; Camerota, 1993; Hooper 1993). We first review this development and then assess its import for the subsequent development of Galileo's science. The memoranda or jottings that Galileo made in preparation for his *De Motu* are found at the end of Manuscript 46, after the treatise on the elements, and this serves to tie the contents of Manuscript 71 to the physical questions.

These aside, the components of Manuscript 71 pertaining to the early *De Motu* are five in number and in the following order: a plan for the treatise, a dialogue on motion, a ten-chapter treatise on motion, a twenty-three-chapter treatise on motion, and variants of the first two chapters. In transcribing and publishing these, Favaro rearranged them, and the memoranda, in an order different from their appearance in the manuscripts, as can be seen from the following listing, which shows the foliation of the manuscripts on the left and the pagination of the National Edition on the right:

MS 46 102r–110v	Memoranda	EN1:408–17
MS 71 3v	Plan for *De Motu*	EN1:418–9
MS 71 4r–35v	Dialogue on motion	EN1:367–408
MS 71 43r–60v	10-chapter treatise	EN1:344–66
MS 71 61r–124v	23-chapter treatise	EN1:251–340
Ms 71 133r–134v	Variants of first two chapters	EN1:341–3

Inserted into this material and occupying folios not listed above, are two items which Favaro decided to publish in volumes two and nine of the National Edition:

MS 71 39r	*De Motu Accelerato*	EN2:259–66
MS 71 132v–125r	Latin transl. of Greek Isocrates	EN9:283–4

The last item here is bound in backwards, which explains its folio ordering.

Favaro's arrangement in EN1 suggests that, of the three main items, the twenty-three-chapter treatise on motion was written first, followed by the ten-chapter treatise, and the dialogue on motion last. To these, he inserted the variants between the first two items and appended the memoranda on motion and the plan at the end.

This ordering has been contested in all recent scholarship, starting with Drabkin and Drake (1960) and Fredette (1972). Both proposed the order of dialogue, twenty-three-chapter version, and then ten-chapter version, though they offered different reasons in its support.

To these, Drake (1986) added the evidence he was able to glean from watermarks and on that basis made further decisions regarding the time and place of their composition. In his view, the dialogue was written first, at Siena, between 1586 and 1587; then came the ten-chapter treatise, composed at Florence in 1588, and finally the twenty-three-chapter treatise, also at Pisa, between 1590 and 1591. His dating of the last item was based on my dating of the logical questions (Manuscript 27), whose influence he could also detect in the longer *De Motu*.

In my response to Drake's proposal, I agreed that the dialogue was written first, but at Pisa and in 1590, and I maintained that the other versions were composed there also, but in 1591 or 1592, before Galileo left for Padua (Wallace 1990:42–7).

This is the way things stood before Camerota began his detailed study of watermarks in Manuscript 71 and Hooper examined its various components for peculiar spellings of Latin terms. Their most important finding was that the ten-chapter *De Motu* was written on paper with the same Florentine watermarks as that of Galileo's lectures on Dante's *Inferno* (and Manuscript 46's treatise on the elements) and had many irregularities in spelling, suggesting that it was the first item of those preserved in Manuscript 71, written in 1588 or shortly thereafter. Of the remaining pieces, all but the last four chapters of the twenty-three-chapter treatise bear Pisan watermarks. These chapters, surprisingly, are written on sheets with Florentine watermarks. The ensemble shows very few peculiar spellings, with the exception of the variants of the first two chapters, which have more than half the percentage of irregular spellings in the ten-chapter treatise and are probably of early composition also.

Data such as these have led Hooper (using Camerota's data) to propose the following as the preferred order of the materials in Manuscript 71: the ten-chapter treatise, composed at Florence as early as 1588, the variants on the first two chapters, written at Pisa in 1590, the *Dialogus*, written at Pisa also in 1590, the first nineteen chapters of the twenty-three-chapter *De Motu*, likewise written at Pisa but in 1591–1592, and the last four chapters of that work, written at Florence in 1591–1592 (Hooper 1993, Camerota 1993).

As supporting evidence for their Pisa 1590 dating of the dialogue, Hooper-Camerota detect the influence of Mazzoni in that work. These results are in substantial agreement with my own datings (Wallace 1990, 1992b). The most important consideration is that the latest research confirms my line of reasoning to establish that the major part of the *De Motu Antiquiora*, and particularly the twenty-three-chapter version, was written after the composition of Manuscripts 27 and 46 (Wallace 1984a). This allows for an influence of the materials Galileo appropriated from the Jesuits on that work, with consequences I shall now explain.

The key teaching of Manuscript 27, already noted, is that on the demonstrative *regressus*, a type of reasoning that employs two demonstrations, one "of the fact" and the other "of the reasoned fact" (Galilei 1988, Berti 1991, Wallace 1992b:180–184). Galileo refers to these demonstrations as "progressions" and notes that they are separated by an intermediate stage.

The first progression argues from effect to cause and the second goes in the reverse direction, thus "regressing" from cause to effect. For the process to work, the demonstration of the fact must come first, and the effect must initially be more known than the cause, though in the end the two must be seen as convertible. The intermediate stage effects the transition to the second demonstration.

As explained in Galileo's time, this stage involved "a mental examination of the cause proposed," *mentale ipsius causae examen*, the wording used by Jacopo Zabarella.[7] The Latin *examen* is significant because it corresponds to the Greek *peira*, a term that is the root for the Latin *periculum*, meaning test, the equivalent of *experimentum* or experiment (Olivieri 1978:164–6, Wallace 1993). Thus the main task of the intermediate stage is one of testing, of investigating and eliminating other possibilities, and so seeing the cause as required wherever the effect is present.

Note here Galileo's major innovation in the *regressus*: It was his use of the *periculum* in the intermediate stage to determine the "true cause" of the phenomenon under study. In the case of the *De Motu Antiquiora* that phenomenon was the speed of a body's fall in various media. Here Galileo's major use of Archimedes was his replacement of Aristotle's concept of absolute weight by that of specific weight, that is, the weight of the body as affected by the medium in which it is immersed, and so corrected for the buoyancy effect of the medium.

This was Benedetti's contribution, of course, and is not original with Galileo. What was original was Galileo's use of the inclined plane to slow the descent of bodies under the influence of gravity. The basic insight behind this experiment is found in Chapter 14 of the twenty-three-chapter version of *De Motu* (EN1:296–302, Drabkin and Drake 1960:63–9) and may be stated as follows: If the effective weight of a body can be decreased by positioning it on an incline (analogous in some way to the decrease of effective weight by buoyancy), then its velocity down the incline will be slowed proportionately.

The demonstration Galileo offers is geometrical and consists in showing that the forces involved with weights on an inclined plane actually obey the law of the balance. It also invokes several suppositions and on this account may be seen as a demonstration *ex suppositione.* If these suppositions are granted, the conclusion follows directly: The ratio of speeds down the incline will be as the length of the incline to its vertical height, because the weight of the body varies precisely in that proportion.

Galileo uses the term *periculum* for test or experiment five times in the *De Motu* treatises (Schmitt 1981:VIII, 114–23). One occurrence is in connection with the basic supposition behind his reasoning, the Aristotelian principle that speed of fall is directly proportional to the falling body's weight, amended now to be its weight in the medium as opposed to its absolute weight. Galileo says that if one performs the *periculum* the proposed proportionality will not actually be observed, and he attributes the discrepancy to "accidental causes" (EN1:273).

Moreover, for the inclined plane reasoning to apply, one must suppose that there is no accidental resistance occasioned by the roughness of the moving body or of the plane or by the shape of the body; that the plane is, so to speak, incorporeal, or at least that it is very carefully smoothed and perfectly hard; and that the moving body is perfectly smooth and of a perfectly spherical shape (EN1:298–9). Under such conditions, one may suppose that any given body can be moved on a plane parallel to the horizon by a force smaller than any given force (EN1:299–300). Here Galileo states that one should not be surprised if a *periculum* does not verify this for two reasons: External impediments prevent it (which elicits the previous supposition) and a plane surface cannot be parallel to the horizon because the Earth's surface is spherical (EN1:301).

A more interesting *periculum* to which Galileo makes reference occurs in Chapter 22 of the *De Motu*, where he speaks of dropping objects from a high tower (EN1:333–7, Drabkin and Drake 1960:106–10). Here, he contests the results of Borro's *experimentum* which purported to show that when two equal bodies of lead and wood are thrown simultaneously from a window, the lighter body invariably reaches the ground before the heavier one.

Galileo's tests, which he says were often repeated, show the opposite. Although the lighter body moves more swiftly at the beginning of its motion, the heavier one quickly overtakes it and reaches the ground far ahead. The reasons Galileo offers is that the lighter body cannot conserve its upward impetus as well as the heavier body. Thus it falls quickly at first, but the heavier body then overcomes its upward impetus and so catches up with, and then passes, the lighter body.

This solution actually depends on Galileo's argument in Chapter 19 of *De Motu*, directed against Aristotle, to explain why bodies increase their speed, or accelerate, during fall (EN1:315–23, Drabkin and Drake 1960:85–94). There, Galileo bases his explanation on an upwardly directed impetus or levity impressed on the body that is self-expending with time. As opposed to Aristotle's cause, Galileo sees the *vera causa* of the velocity increase to lie in the decrease of effective weight throughout the body's fall.

All of these suppositional demonstrations, we now know, pertain to Galileo's Pisan period. They all can be put in the form of the demonstrative *regressus* as this is set out in Manuscript 27, samples of which are given in Wallace (1992a:241–7). Galileo wanted to publish the treatise on motion, but he clearly had doubts about the "true causes" he had proposed in it because of his failure to obtain experimental confirmation of his results. He kept the manuscript in his possession, nonetheless, and when he finally did discover the correct law of falling bodies, he inserted a draft of his discovery among the folios of Manuscript 71, thus signaling its role in the discovery process (Fredette 1972, Camerota 1992). This is the *De Motu Accelerato* fragment we have listed above, which Favaro correctly judged was composed in 1609, at the end of Galileo's early period, and so he published it in the second volume of the National Edition.

CONTINUATION AT PADUA, AND BEYOND

We move now to the next period of experimental and observational activity, this time at Padua and extending to 1610, at the end of which Galileo made his important discoveries with the telescope. In his teaching at Padua, he continued to use his treatise on the sphere, the *Trattato della Sfera*, also called the *Cosmografia*, which is significant for its showing how the demonstrative regress works in astronomy.

The simplest context is Galileo's explanation of the aspects and phases of the Moon and the ways these vary with the Moon's synoptic and sidereal periods (EN2:251–3). These phenomena depend only on relative positions within the Earth–Moon and Earth–Sun systems and do not require commitment to either geocentrism or heliocentrism, being equally well explained in either. Basic to the explanation is the conviction that these aspects and phases are effects (*effetti*) for which it is possible to assign the cause (*la causa*, EN2:250). Among the causes Galileo enumerates are that the Moon is spherical in shape, that it is not luminous by nature but receives its light from the Sun, and that the orientation of the two with respect to Earth is what causes the various aspects and the places and times of their appearances.

The argument is typically that of a *scientia media* and follows closely the paradigm provided by Aristotle in *Posterior Analytics* (Bk. 1, Ch. 13) to show that the Moon is a sphere. It involves only one supposition, that light travels in straight lines, and this is what governs the intermediate stage of the regress. It allows one to use projective geometry to establish the convertibility condition, namely that only external illumination falling on a shape that is spherical will cause the Moon to exhibit the phases it does at precise positions and times observable from the Earth. The reasoning is summarized in regress form in Wallace (1992a:194–7).

Galileo's first attempt at a science of mechanics followed soon after his *De Motu Antiquiora* and built on the progress he had made at Pisa in the study of the inclined plane. The earliest version of his mechanics, based on what was thought at the time to be Aristotle's *Quaestiones mechanicae*, survives in two early versions, one probably dating from 1593 and the other certainly from 1594.

The main point is to show how all the primary machines – the lever, the capstan, the pulley, the screw, and the wedge – can be reduced to the simplest of them – the lever – and this itself can be reduced to the balance. In it, Galileo uses a concept he had already mentioned in the *De Motu*, namely, that of a minimum force, or a force smaller than any given force, to prove that a force of 200 will move a weight of 2,000 if applied with a leverage of 10 times the distance of application. If one considers, he says, that any minimal moment added to the counterbalancing force will produce a displacement, by not taking account of this "insensible moment," one can say that motion will be produced by the same force as sustains the weight at rest.

The use here of what is clearly a supposition, one permitting the mathematical physicist to neglect insensible forces in his calculations, opened the door for him to treat both dynamic and static cases by the same mathematical principles. Thus, by this early date, he had begun to bridge the gap between Archimedean statics and the Aristotelian dynamical tradition of *De ponderibus* recently revived by Tartaglia, and he was moving in the direction of a unified science of statics and dynamics.

Galileo's more fully developed treatise on mechanics, written in Italian and titled *Le meccaniche* in some manuscripts, was completed by 1600 or 1602 and was modeled on Tartaglia's works. In it, Galileo attacked the difficult problem of the force required to move an object up an inclined plane. By invoking his principle that the force required to move a weight need only *insensibilmente* exceed the force require to sustain it, he was able to solve not only the problem of the inclined plane but that of the wedge and the screw also (EN2:183–4, Drabkin and Drake 1960:175–7). Again, this line of reasoning made use of the demonstrative regress, invoking in the intermediate stage suppositions of the type described above (Wallace 1992a:262–3).

Shortly after this, Galileo engaged in an extensive period of experimentation that is recorded in the folios uncovered by Drake and that enabled him finally to obtain empirical confirmation of his calculations for motion down an incline and in free fall. This required him to relinquish the Archimedean–Aristotelian ratios for velocity versus specific weight he had been employing at Pisa and, ultimately, by 1609, to arrive at the conclusion that in motions that are naturally accelerated the velocity increases uniformly with time of fall. The major steps in this program, which involved the so-called table top experiments (completely unknown before Drake's discoveries) employed demonstrations that can be arranged in the format of the *regressus*, as will be documented below.

Momentous as these investigations were, they were quickly surpassed by Galileo's discoveries with the telescope in late 1609 and 1610. Fortunately, the paradigm he had used for demonstrating the aspects and phases of the Moon was at hand for explaining the novelties he had revealed. Others before him had constructed telescopes, and some had even looked at the heavens with them, but none would formulate the "necessary demonstrations" Galileo would propose on the basis of his observations.

Within months, he established that there were mountains on the Moon, that Jupiter was carrying along four satellites in its twelve-year passage across the heavens, and, later, that Venus exhibited phases – a sure indication it was orbiting the Sun and not the Earth. So spectacular were these results, all of which could be shown to be demonstrations through the use of the *regressus*, that they changed

Galileo's life in a most profound way. His "early period" was completed and he set out on the fateful course of convincing his fellow scientists (and the Church) that the Copernican system actually portrayed the true construction of the world. This would not only occupy his "middle period," but it would determine the tragic course of his "later period" as well.

When we add these Paduan accomplishments to their Pisan beginnings, however, we can see how fruitful these times leading to Galileo's forty-fifth year had been. His spectacular results in astronomy, no more important than his laying the foundations of modern mechanics, as yet unknown to the world, had behind them the strong logical base contained in Manuscript 27, one of his first Pisan manuscripts. Precisely how he accomplished this is documented in Wallace (1984a, 1992a), the first providing textual selections that connect Manuscript 27 with the various discoveries, and the second showing how all employ a search for causes using a method of resolution and composition that fits into the general schema for the demonstrative regress. The results are tabulated below, with the subjects of proof indicated in the center, the page numbers in 1984a on the left, and those in 1992a on the right:

Text (1984a)	Subject of proof	Manuscript 27 (1992a)
230	1 Fall in Various Media (EN1)	242
233	2 Fall and Specific Weight (EN1)	248
236	3 Speed in Different Media (EN1)	250
239	4 Motion on Inclined Planes (EN1)	253
235	5 Speed Increase in Fall (EN1)	256
248	7 Aspects and Phases of the Moon (EN2)	195
—	8 Mountains on the Moon (EN3.1)	199
—	9 Satellites of Jupiter (EN3.1)	202
—	10 Phases of Venus (EN10)	202

Of these, the first five, all from the *De Motu Antiquiora*, were not strictly demonstrations, although Galileo originally proposed them as such. It surely is to his credit that he ultimately recognized this and withheld them from publication, undoubtedly for empirical reasons, because of their failure to meet the limited *pericula* he used to test them at Pisa. Of the remainder, and particularly the last four, he never doubted their apodictic character.

There remains now a final consideration, namely, whether Galileo's use of demonstrative techniques terminated in 1610 at the end of his early period or whether it extended into the other periods as well. There are excellent reasons to prefer the second alternative, especially when one sees Galileo as amending the Manuscript 27 doctrine to make of it a logic of discovery that can employ probable arguments as well as demonstrative proofs.

The first indication we see of this is his tentative proof for the Earth's motion based on the ebb and flow of the tides, which he presented to his friend Cardinal Alessandro Orsini on January 8, 1616 (EN5:377–95). There, Galileo speculates that "the cause of the tides could reside in some motion of the basins containing the seawater," thus focusing on the motion of the terrestrial globe as "more probable" than any other cause previously assigned (EN5:381). In concluding his proof, Galileo notes that he is able to harmonize the Earth's motion with the tides, "taking the former as the cause of the latter, and the latter as a sign of and an argument for the former" (EN5:393). This is an elegant way of reformulating the first and last stages of the demonstrative regress, while leaving the intermediate stage open for probable arguments as well as for those that would establish conclusive proof.

Using this enlarged understanding of the *regressus*, it is possible to analyze the key proofs Galileo worked out in his middle and later periods. These are presented below in a format similar to that used above for the early period:

Text (1984a)	Subject of proof	Manuscript 27 (1992a)
284	1 True Cause of Flotations (EN4)	277
288	2 Nature of Sunspots (EN5)	209
294	3 Early Tidal Argument (EN5)	212
300	4 Unity of the Universe (EN7)	220
303	5 Earth's Daily Rotation (EN7)	223
306	6 Earth's Annual Revolution (EN7)	225
308	7 Later Tidal Argument (EN7)	229
315	8 True Cause of Cohesion (EN8)	281
320	9 Breaking Strength of a Beam (EN8)	283
322	10 Naturally Accelerated Motion (EN8)	287
330	11 Motion of Projectiles (EN8)	292

The first of these, as well as the eighth to eleventh, Galileo seems to have proposed as demonstrative. The rest he proposed only as probable arguments, surely because of the Church's prohibition against Copernican teaching, but also because he may have recognized some of their logical limitations. By the time he came to the last two, however, there can be no doubt that he made the transition from *scientia media* to *nuova scienza* (Olivieri 1995) and it is for this we celebrate him as the Father of Modern Science.

Only sixteen months before his death, on September 14, 1640, Galileo wrote a letter to Fortunio Leceti, explaining what it meant to be a true follower of Aristotle and stating that, in matters of logic, he had been an Aristotelian all his life (EN18:248). In light of his many invectives against the Peripatetics of his day, this statement by Galileo is puzzling and has given rise to many interpretations, some calling into question his honesty and sincerity.

When the letter is read in light of the materials just presented, however, it is a simple matter to absolve Galileo of charges of this type. In effect, he does not commit himself to any of Aristotle's conclusions in the physical sciences but states instead that he has consistently followed Aristotle's logical methodology in his own scientific work.

This is what enabled him, he says, to reason well and to deduce necessary conclusions from his premises; coupled with what he has learned from pure mathematicians, it has given him skill in demonstration and the ability to avoid mistakes in argumentation. He concludes on the note that, if one takes reliance on Aristotle's logical canons to be the sign of a Peripatetic, he can rightfully be called a Peripatetic himself.

When the letter to Liceti is read in light of what is available in the National Edition alone, of course, the background required for its understanding is missing. But then the true problem posed by the letter becomes quite clear: It is not Galileo's identifying himself as an Aristotelian but rather how he could possess sufficient knowledge of Aristotelian logic to be able to employ it in the way he claims. The problem is insoluble when the manuscripts of his early period, and particularly his Manuscript 27, are overlooked or are not taken into account. Such omission is the *parvus error in initio* to which I referred at the outset of this essay. Only when it is rectified do we gain an understanding of the man within his full historical context.

NOTES

1 *Le Opere di Galileo Galilei*, ed. Antonio Favaro, 20 vols. in 21, Florence: G. Barbèra Editrice, 1890–1909, henceforth cited as EN: Vol. No., page no(s).

2 Following the lead of W. R. Shea (1972), the chronology of Galileo's life is now commonly divided into three periods – the early period, from his birth in 1564 to 1610; the middle period, from 1610 to 1632; and the later period, from 1632 to his death in 1642.

3 The pioneering study of the sources of Galileo's natural philosophy was that of Alistair Crombie (1975), who first discerned its connection with teachings of the Jesuits. He followed that essay with a study of the place of mathematics and Platonism in Jesuit educational policy (1977) and then with a fuller examination of Jesuit ideas of science and of nature that are reflected in Galileo's writings, which he coauthored with his student Adriano Carugo (1983). For a detailed account of my early investigations and their relationships to the work of Crombie and Carugo, see Wallace (1984b:xii–xiii, 1986b, 1986c, and 1992b:xi–xv).

4 Here, Hooper reported early results of a project at the Instituto Nazionale di Fisica Nucleare in Florence, in which accurate physical analyses are being made of the chemical composition of Galileo's inks and papers using nondestructive proton induced x-ray emissions (acronym PIXE).

5 Favaro dated the compositions of Manuscript 46 at 1584, on the basis of the internal evidence he gathered from that chronology (EN1:27), where he added the number of years Galileo gives "from the birth of Christ to the destruction of Jerusalem, 74; from then up to the present time, 1510," to get the result 1584. Apparently, Favaro was unaware that exegetes in Galileo's time had already established that Christ was born in the year 4 B.C., and thus he should have obtained the result 1580. What he also could have done was add A.D. 70 (a well-established date among historians for the destruction of Jerusalem) to 1510, and this would have given him 1580 directly. If Galileo used Menu's notes for the chronology, this would serve to explain the sum of 1580 in his appropriation. Part of Favaro's reason for defending his erroneous 1584 dating of Manuscript 46 seems to have been his opposition to Pierre Duhem, who used Galileo's mention of the *Doctores Parisienses* in that manuscript to connect him with medieval authors who were his so-called Parisian precursors. For details of the dispute between Favaro and Duhem, see Wallace (1978) which is enlarged and reprinted in Wallace (1981).

6 Works on the authors and subjects mentioned and on which I have drawn in what follows include Camerota (1989), DePace (1990, 1992), Lennox (1986), Machamer (1978), Manno (1987), Masotti (1976), and Schmitt (1981).

7 The expression occurs in Zabarella's *Opera logica*, Cologne: Zetzner, 1597, 486. For details of the connection between Galileo and Zabarella, see Wallace (1988), reprinted in Wallace (1991).

2 Galileo's machines, his mathematics, and his experiments[1]

Galileo's life and works, like Gaul, has generally been divided into three parts. There is his work on mechanics and local motion (with the science of the strength of bodies grudgingly admitted), his work on astronomy and Copernicanism, and, finally, his relations and tribulations with the Catholic Church. Occasionally, some scholars under the anachronistic rubric of methodology have attempted to tie the two scientific parts together to obtain a more coherent picture.

In the space of this essay, I cannot overcome this tripartite division that the centuries have sanctioned. I can, however, sketch a picture of Galileo that will be a step toward this goal. It seems to me that Galileo had only a few basic conceptions that directed his life and work in all these three areas. His first belief concerned the role of the properly thinking and working individual scientist as being able to obtain knowledge and certainty. This belief showed up in his writings about the role of the scientific elite individual, who saw and understood things that were not seen by the masses, or, especially, by groups dedicated to the authority of Aristotle. It also seems to lie at the heart of his thoughts about Biblical exegesis. This individualism is apparent in Galileo's texts by his ubiquitous and consistent use of the first person singular "I" ("io") and the use of proper names or descriptions to talk about insights, discoveries, and all the accomplishments of good science. I call this the entrepreneurial-I. In *Il Saggiatore*, Galileo wrote eloquently on this individualistic theme:

Sarsi perhaps believes that all hosts of good philosophers may be enclosed within walls of some sort. I believe, Sarsi, that they fly, and that they fly alone like eagles, and not like starlings [storni]. It is true that because eagles

53

are scarce they are a little seen and less heard, whereas birds that fly in flocks fill the sky with shrieks and cries wherever they settle, and befoul the earth beneath them. But if true philosophers are like eagles, and not like the phoenix instead, Sig. Sarsi, the crowd of fools who know nothing is infinite; many are those who know very little of philosophy, few, indeed, they who truly know some part of it, and only one knows all, for that is God.[2]

Tempering this vision of the entrepreneurial scientist, a moderate egalitarian character also emerges. Galileo sometimes seems to believe that anyone receiving proper tutelage and paying proper attention can learn what is true. This is his homage to the Platonic doctrine of recollection (anemnesis). The emphasis on individualism also is used to make the typical Renaissance points. Galileo was much in the "modern" tradition of being extremely anti-Scholastic, anti-Aristotelian, dogmatically antiauthoritarian, and, somewhat uniquely for an Italian philosopher, antioccult. However, I will not go further into how Galileo fits in with the seventeenth-century rise of epistemic, economic, and political individualism.[3]

I will concentrate on some aspects of what Galileo took to be intelligible and the model of intelligibility that he developed (or constructed, if you prefer.) This second theme is related to the structures of nature and how truth comes to be known and displayed in natural philosophy. I will argue that Galileo's model of what was intelligible comes from Archimedes and the simple machines. This model was, and was seen to be, a new philosophy of nature, and it provided a new model for subsequent generations of how to do natural philosophy. This is not to say that Galileo had no predecessors. Of course there were many.[4] But no one, until Galileo, made the mechanical way, the way of doing science, the way of knowledge.

The story has yet to be told of how Galileo, who was probably not the brightest nor the best of the mechanicians nor of the mathematicians nor of the philosophers, was the one who made the mathematical, mechanical way the future of science. One can speculate that his successes and international acclaim with the telescope made him Europe's popular and intellectual hero, and so people were more likely to take seriously what he said on other topics. Maybe it was because he was extremely smart about the topic of motion, and his work predated his telescopic period, and because studying the motion of things was in accord with the tenor of the times in claiming novelty and some historical precedent. Maybe it was because this mechanical way presented, even more than Galileo saw, an alternative, systematic approach to dealing with the world.[5]

His way of stating and solving problems in natural philosophy in mechanical ways became the model of natural philosophy for the seventeenth century. After Newton's work (solidified by Euler) things would change. No longer would statics, rational mechanics, and dynamics be taken to be the same discipline. Further, proportional geometry would be supplanted by algebra. This made the "new" science even newer.

From the 1930s through the 1960s much of the debate about the nature of early modern science revolved around attributing the labels of Platonism and Aristotelianism to various practitioners.[6] By and large these Plato–Aristotle debates were centered on the concept of the proper scientific method. The general lines were that Aristotelians went back to the *Posterior Analytics* and experience and, therefore, experiment, whereas the Platonists made use of mathematics. So Alexandre Koyré characterized the Renaissance debate between Aristotle and Plato by claiming that if a thinker believed in the descriptive power of mathematics, he was a Platonist.[7]

But obviously the lines dividing different practitioners were not so clear. Though we know that Albertus Magnos unmasked the *liber de causis* as not being the work of Aristotle, about two and a half centuries later, Francesco Patrizzi issued a Latin edition of the *Elements of Theology* under the name of Aristotle. Similarly, even before Koyré had characterized Platonism as mathematics, Ernst Cassirer had found over sixteen distinguishable types of Platonism in the sixteenth century.[8]

There were debates in the late sixteenth century over whether certitude was better attributed to mathematical or syllogistic reasoning, but these were not held under the guise of Plato and Aristotle, and Petrus Catena, in the mid sixteenth century, was busy in Venice publishing works that showed Aristotle's important use of mathematics.

Mathematics itself came in many guises both institutionally and extrainstitutionally. Certainly, geometry was taught at the universities, but also there were the mathematical sciences of astronomy, geography, and sometimes mechanics. Outside the sanctioned institutions mathematics reigned quite lively in the realms of natural magic, astrology, hermetic practices, and the cabala, as well as in the more mundane, pragmatic spheres such as the principles of painting, construction of fortifications, and the design of machines.

What is to be learned from the historical complexity concerning the earlier historiographic Plato–Aristotle debate? Basically this: The categories of the historian's debate were not actor's categories. They were anachronistically imposed structural categories used by historians in an attempt to bring some order to the complexity. Most often, the order imposed was related to the historian's vision of the correct nature of modern science.

It is arguable, and reasonably so, that virtually any historical study is anachronistic in some degree. Every historian must be selective, choosing his characters, texts, and institutions with an eye to what is deemed important. In chronological histories, the issue of precursorship looms large, and so everyone exhibits some degree of Whiggish prejudice.

Yet, as has been argued from Burkhardt onward, categorization is both useful and necessary in history. Similarly it is useful and necessary in psychology to ascribe categories for understanding how peoples, at any time, think and make sense of their world, what they use to make intelligible sense out of their experiences.

But the categories depicted by the names "Plato" and "Aristotle" by themselves as historical personages do not seem today to be of much help in understanding the precursorship of modern science. Certainly at the end of the sixteenth century there was a long-lasting and multicomplex Aristotelian tradition and a renewed and resurgent, somewhat oppositional, Platonic tradition (for example, Bologna had established a chair in Plato by the mid-sixteenth century), and certainly many forms of systematization were floating about in various degrees of completion that could be called neo-Platonic. But even these were mostly Christian hierarchical bastards designed for a variety of religious, educational, and political purposes.

Despite these categorical caveats, I think at least one other name needs to be added to the list of categorical types for understanding the development of modern science: Archimedes. Recently Olaf Pedersen made a similar suggestion, when he suggested seeing the development of scientific method in terms of three great traditions: Plato, Aristotle, and Pythagoras or Archimedes.[9] But I want to go somewhat further. Of these three, I would claim that in the early seventeenth century, only the name of Archimedes invoked the original vision of the person denominated.

Surely, those who followed Archimedes were also often Christians and held a wide variety of beliefs in addition to their Archimedian vision. But I will claim that the scientific revolution of the seventeenth century owes much to an almost pure form of the Archimedian mathematics. It is this pure form that gave rise to the mathematical and experimental structure of the mechanical world picture (though not to all aspects of its widespread power of intelligibility). There were other helpful models that captured the imagination of the seventeenth century and aided the acceptance and spread of this mechanical view, most notably the image of the mechanical clock. But the "guts" of the picture comes from Archimedes, and almost solely originally through one long sung "hero of science": Galileo. So today let me sketch for you what I take to be a new view of Galileo and his Archimedianism.[10]

MACHINES: GALILEO AND THE BALANCE

Much has been written about Galileo's artisan–engineering training. Leonard Olschki, Erwin Panofsky, Lynn White, and Tom Settle all have drawn attention to this aspect of Galileo's background.[11] Wallace Hooper most insightfully developed another aspect.[12] I think that this artisan story is right, but I want to treat it differently and make more of it than they do. I argued many years ago that Galileo belongs in the tradition of the mixed sciences (scientia media).[13] In effect, this means that his use of the traditional Aristotelian causes is specialized to cases where the phenomena can be seen as both physical and mathematical. So, for example, formal causes and efficient cause often collapse. In this essay I want to draw further implications from one type of mixed science, mechanics. I will argue that the Archimedian simple machines and the experiences related to them become Galileo's model both for theory and for experiment. William Wallace agrees with his mixed science perspective, and yet, he emphasizes Galileo's debt to the philosophy professors in the Collegio Romano.[14] But then the question is how do these two types of training and influence relate to one another.

The short summary is that Galileo is an Archimedian mechanic by training and temperament, working in the mixed science tradition, and desperately trying to advance himself intellectually, socially, and financially by seeking legitimacy as a philosopher. For this, he must use acceptable scholastic terminology and deal with the problems of traditional natural philosophy. So he tries to apply his mechanical interests and insights to Aristotelian and peripatetic questions of natural philosophy, and he makes every effort to use their accepted mode of philosophical speech.

This attempt first becomes clear in his *De Motu* (Galileo 1590). Galileo wrote *De Motu* (*On Motion*) in the early part of his career; the traditional date is 1590 (by Favaro and Drabkin, but see Hooper.[15]) Whatever the exact date of composition, the manuscript was written while Galileo was teaching at Pisa. It was never published. However, it stands as an early example of Galileo's model of good science, despite the basic mistake of treating the motive power of bodies as being the relative difference between their specific gravity and that of the media in which they are immersed. His discomfort, perhaps based on this mistake, may be the reason *De Motu* was never published. By 1604 in his letter to Paolo Sarpi he seems to have abandoned this mistaken conception.[16]

In *De Motu* Galileo attempted to show the inadequacies of the Aristotelian theory of natural motions (where it was held that the heavy and the light were two different causes of motion). He argued in favor of a unified causal theory of natural motion, where what needs to be known is the proportional relation of the weight per volume of a body (conceived as the force caused by the weight) to the weight per volume of its surrounding medium. This is Galileo's way of describing the forces that act upon the body to make it go up, down, or remain at rest. Put another way, he first transformed problems about falling bodies (freefall) into a problem of hydrostatics (floating bodies) in which the body is seen to be rising, falling, or floating in a medium.

He then argued that all these phenomena (falling, floating, etc.) should be seen as balance problems, so he titles his ninth section: "In which all that was demonstrated above is considered in physical terms, and bodies moving naturally are reduced to weights of a balance."[17] This balance model for solving motion problems he credited to Archimedes.

Galileo argued at greater length in Chapter 6 that "what moves, as it were by force"[18] and showed how "the motion of bodies moving naturally can be reduced to the motion of weights on a balance."[19]

The section title reads: "In which is explained the analogy [convenientia] between naturally moving things and the weights on a balance."[20] Interestingly, he says this is a physical, as opposed to a mathematical, argument:

We shall first examine what happens in the case of the balance, so that we may then show [ostendamus] that all these things happen in the case of bodies moving naturally.

Let line *ab*, then represent a balance, whose center, over which motion may take place, is the point *c* bisecting line *ab*. And let two weights, *e* and *o*, be suspended from points *a* and *b*.

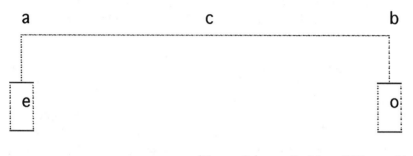

(Fig. 2, Balance, *De Motu*, [NE 1 257].)

Now in the case of weight *e* there are three possibilities: It may either be at rest, or move upward, or move downward. If therefore weight *e* is heavier than weight *o*, then *e* will move downward. But if *e* is less heavy, it will, of course, move upward, and not because it does not have weight, but because the weight of *o* is greater. From this it is clear that, in the case of the balance, motion upward as well as motion downward takes place because of weight but in a different way: For motion upward will occur for *e* on account of the weight of *o*, but motion downward will occur for *e* on account of its own weight. But if the weight of *e* is equal to that of *o*, then *e* will move neither upward nor downward.[21]

Next Galileo returns to the case of naturally moving bodies and tells us that a volume of water equal to a volume of wood will be heavier, which is why the wood cannot be submerged beneath the water. In general, he claims, all things can be explained in the same way, which of course disagrees with Aristotle:

In the case of bodies moving naturally, as in the case of the balance, the cause of all motions up or down can be referred to weight alone ... what is moved is moved, as it were by force, and by the extruding action of the medium.[22]

This anti-Aristotelian conclusion about the nature of motion, all being caused by weight, is most important because all natural motion (sublunary) is reduced to this one cause.

He repeats this same claim with further explication of the identity between floating bodies and the balance in Chapter 9:

Let us consider how and why bodies moving upward move with a force measured by the amount by which the weight of a volume of the medium (through which motion takes place) equal to the volume of the moving body exceeds the weight of the body itself ... [And later] For if the weights [on a scale] are in balance, and an additional weight is added to one side, then that side moves down, not in consequence of its whole weight, but only by reason of the weight by which it exceeds the weight on the other side.[23]

The principle to be noted is that for Galileo the whole schema of intelligibility becomes putting a question in the form of an equilibrium problem: What is the cause of (or force that causes) something becoming unbalanced? And what force will cause it to come back into balance? Where is the balance point? The geometrical diagrams Galileo used to represent these problems were always lines and angles inscribed in, circumscribed about, or tangent to circles. These literally described a real balance but also allowed him to use rules of geometry for constructions that went well beyond the balance. Ultimately it would allow him to construct the parabola as the curve describing projectiles.

A more general, and familiar, form of the model is stated later in Chapter 14, which has the title: "... a discussion of the ratios of the [speeds of] motions of the same body moving over various inclined planes."[24] Here Galileo wrote "... a heavy body tends to move downward with as much force as necessary to lift it up, i.e. it tends to move downward with the same force with which it resists rising."[25] This was his prelude to considering the force necessary to draw a given weight up an inclined plane, which, again, he immediately turns into a balance problem about the forces exerted by the weights of bodies depending upon the distances they are from a balance point. Galileo was causally tying together the concepts of weight, distance, force, and balance points (or equilibrium points) to solve his problems about the motions of bodies. He applied this model to bodies on inclined planes and pendulums.

Thus did Galileo, in *De Motu*, first lay out a model for solving all problems of motion. He argued that the problems of floating bodies (with which he started his text) could all be reduced to problems of the Archimedian balance. He went on to show that all simple machines (the lever, the inclined plane and the pendulum) could be also reduced to balance problems. Free fall of bodies came to be an instance of floating bodies or a balance that had no weight on one side.

In a later work, *Le Meccaniche* (*On Mechanics*)[26] (composed in 1600), he identifies the properties of all mechanical instruments with the motions of heavy bodies.[27] Galileo explicitly uses the concepts of the center of gravity (or center of proportional heaviness or weight) and moment to talk about the simple machines. "Thus, *moment* [momento] is that impetus to go downward composed of heaviness, position and of anything else by which this tendency may be caused."[28] The model by which such concepts were instantiated and illustrated again was the equilibrium balance model, balancing of the arms or weights on a steelyard – a single-arm balance or lever. Note also that *moment* (momento) is essentially a generalized force concept. Using this model, Galileo went on to explain the lever, the windlass, the capstan, the pulley, and the screw, and finally he made a first attempt at handling the force of percussion (or impact). These discussions are clearly within the Archimedian tradition and the tradition of the pseudo-Aristotelian mechanics. But it is the reduction of all the Archimedian simple machines and the problems of natural and unnatural motion to the problem of the balance to which I draw your attention.

Galileo used this equilibrium model all of his life. Prior to *De Motu* he had written *The Little Balance* (*La Balancitta*) in 1586.[29] In 1612 he wrote a *Discourse on Floating Bodies* (*Discorso Intorno alle Cose che Stanno in su' l'Acqua o che in Quella si Muovono*), which considered hydrostatic phenomena using a causal, equilibrium model.[30] The concern with water and its equilibrium came up again in his theory of the tides (*Discorso del Flusso e Reflusso del Mare*) first in 1616[31] and then in his *Dialogue on the Two Chief World Systems* (*Dialogo sopra i Due Massimi Sistemi del Mondo Tolemaico e Copernico*) in 1632.[32]

This balance model takes on larger epistemological force when, in 1623, it becomes the whole of the image in which he sets Lothario

Sarsi's (Orazio Grassi) claims about the comets in *The Assayer* (*Il Saggiatore*),[33] which he names in contrast to Grassi's 1619 tract, *The Astronomical and Philosophical Balance* (*Libra Astronomica ac Philosophica*).[34] There Galileo is contrasting ironically many meanings of "balance," from the balance scale (lances) to the alchemist's fire, to the true tester (*saggiatore*), to wisdom, to the very notion of justice herself, Libra.

In *Dialogo* (of 1632)[35] it was the model of the balance that provided Galileo the means by which to think about motion and the relativity of perceived motion. So in Day 2 we read:

Salviati: Do you not believe that the tendency of heavy bodies to move downward, for example, is equal to their resistance to being driven upward?
    Sagredo: I believe it is exactly so, and its for this reason that two equal weights in a balance are seen to remain steady and in equilibrium.[36]

In the next passage he goes on to introduce the steelyard, as a way of understanding.

Earlier in *Dialogo* the balance was again his metaphor for clear thought.

So let us hear the rest of the arguments favorable to his [Aristotle's] opinion so that we may proceed with their testing, refining them in the crucible and weighing them in the assayer's balance [ponderandole con bilancia del saggiatore].[37]

But balance and equilibrium also mean proper proportionality or right ratio (reason). Human understanding or reason (ragione) is having the correct measure (ratio) for things.

Sagredo: Please, Salviati let us waste no more time invoking these ratios against people who are ready to accept the most disproportionate things. . . [38]

Finally in his last work, the 1638 *Discourses and Mathematical Demonstrations Concerning Two New Sciences* (*Discorsi e Dimonstrazioni Mathematiche Intorno a Due Nuove Scienze*)[39] Galileo used the same concepts of impetus, moment, and center of gravity to solve motion problems about inclined planes, pendulua, free fall, and projectiles (and their parabolic curves.) In *Discorsi* his model for thinking about the world was the same. He dealt directly with natural motion mostly using the model of the inclined plane, "I assume that the degrees of speed acquired by the same movable over different inclinations of planes are equal whenever the heights of those planes are equal,"[40] and then immediately devised an experiment that used a pendulum to prove his point about inclined planes. From there he moved directly to Proposition I, Theorem I about falling bodies (free fall): The time in which a certain space is traversed by a movable in uniformly accelerated movement from rest is equal to the time in which the same space would be traversed by the same movable carried in uniform motion whose degree of speed is one half the maximum and final degree of speed of the previous, uniformly accelerated motion.[41] And from there, he proceeds to his famous result (Prop. II, Theorem II): If a movable descends from rest in uniformly accelerated motion, the spaces run through in any times whatever are to each other as the duplicate ratio of their times; that is, they are as the squares of those times.[42] All these solutions to problems were called "mechanical conclusions".[43] The inclined plane was again explained by using the balance and talking about equilibrium of weights.

It is of historical interest that this equilibrium model based on the balance and extended to the other simple machines, and using proportional geometry, remained the model for understanding motion problems through the seventeenth century. Descartes's collision models, Huygens' collision models and his general laws of motion, the work on the laws of motion by Wren and Wallis, and Hooke's work on the spring all used equilibrium as their fundamental problem-solving concept. Even Newton in *Principia Mathematica*, though he laid the ground for a change away from this relational, geometrical way of doing physics, relied on the Galilean form of proportional balance.

The treatment of all motion by means of Archimedian simple machines gives new insight as to why in this age nature was thought of as machinelike and why some seventeenth-century natural philosophers came to call themselves the mechanical philosophers. Mechanics was the theory of simple machines and so the term "mechanics" came to stand for a part of what now we call physics. But the practitioners of mechanics were artisan craftsmen, who, in contrast to the philosophers and mathematicians, were called "mechanics." So Simplicio in *Dialogo* contrasted Aristotle's approach:

... for the accelerated motions he [Aristotle] was content to supply the causes of accelerations, leaving to mechanics and other low artisans the investigation of the ratios of such accelerations and the other more detailed features."[44]

The balance as the model for what is intelligible during this period in history had a great and convoluted history. The balance was physically and metaphorically the model of intelligibility of the age. It was obviously observable when the balance was in equilibrium, when the weights and arms were equalized. Any individual could judge when a problem had been solved, when "things were right." And it was a concept of correctness or proof that could be easily taught. It was a way of interpreting phenomena that anybody could learn, and the standard for success was patent. There was no question of whether you had a proof or not; it was easily seen. Those who would not accept this model of intelligibility would not open their eyes. Personal ambition (such as claiming priority over Galileo) or dogmatism or authority blinded them.

In the late sixteenth century, with rising capitalism and the introduction of the concept of the nation state, the balance become the popular model for bourgeoisie bookkeeping with its "balanced accounts," for international commerce and its "balance of trade,"[45] and for the relation between nations with "balance of payments." Truly the model of Archimedes had permeated the whole of the fabric of society and social relations.[46] Later, with the idea of the contract as an equilibrium among individuals established by mutual agreement, social relations will come to have a new footing, and government itself will have a new legitimation. The legitimation is taken from the mathematics of mechanics, but this science itself took it from the mathematics and the ideas of commerce and trade for which that math was first used.

GALILEO'S MATHEMATICS

Galileo and other seventeenth-century practitioners of mathematics have been done ill by their anachronistic commentators. Never is it acceptable to put Galileo's proofs and theorems into algebraic form. To do so destroys the mind set, the schema, the very model of intelligibility with which they were working.

For Galileo, mathematics meant geometry. This is the way in which his famous claim in *Il Saggiatore* must be read:

Philosophy is written in this grand book – I mean the universe – which stands continuously open to our gaze, but it cannot be understood unless one first learns to comprehend the language and interpret the characters in which it is written. It is written in the language of mathematics, and its characters are triangles, circles, and other geometrical figures, without which it is humanly impossible to understand a single word of it; without these one is wandering about in a dark labyrinth.[47]

Galileo used a comparative, relativized geometry of ratios as the language of proof and mechanics, which was the language in which the book of nature was written. This is very different from what will follow in the eighteenth century and from the way we think of science today. In very few places in his work, and then mostly in talking about astronomical distances, does Galileo attempt to ascertain real values for any physical constant. Nowhere does Galileo attempt to find out, for example, what the real speed or weight of anything is. This proportional geometry is inherently comparative and relational, a matter of ratios. It measures one thing by showing its relation to another, which then may be quantitatively compared by supplying some arbitrarily or conveniently intelligible standard.[48] In this sort of geometry there are no absolute values, numbers that describe the true properties of things and so might serve as the touchstone for certainty or objectivity. Using this geometry one does not look for physical constants or solutions to problems in terms of absolute numerical values.[49]

Galileo was not interested in determination of specific numerical properties. Yet Baliani seems to agree and to understand part of Galileo when he writes to Galileo, commenting on his *Discorsi* to him:

I also think of reasoning about it thoroughly in a treatise I intend to publish on logic, and [there] show that science does nothing but to seek the causes [which] belong to a different habit called wisdom and just as the principles of the sciences are customarily definitions, axioms, and postulates, in physical things these are for the most part experiences, on which are founded astronomy, music, mechanics, optics, and all the rest. (July 20, 1639)[50]

The point is that experiences are the experiences, literally, of seeing mechanical, optical, and astronomical objects as the idealized objects of geometry. All experiences involve seeing things as they are accordingly to your model of intelligibility.

Galileo's geometry is the geometry of inscribed and proscribed circles. It is the geometry of mean proportionals (*media proportionales*). These are the ways Galileo brought the mixed science tradition to describe the balance. They are also the ways in which Galileo finds his chords theorem of descent (all bodies fall through the chord of a vertical circle in the same time-equal weight or not), and this gave him the times squared law for distances (in his 1602 letter to del Monte).[51] The relation between this ratio-geometry and the balance comes out clearly in *Discorsi*, Theorem IX, where he proves the chords theorem using the model of the balance.[52] Here is just a little part of the proof, to give a flavor of what Galileo's method is like:

Proposition IX. Theorem IX
    If any two planes are inclined from a point in a horizontal line, and are cut by a line that makes with them angles alternately equal to their angles with the horizontal, the movements in the parts cut off by the said line are made in equal times.
    From point C of horizontal line X let there be any two inclined planes CD and CE. At any point in line CD construct angle CDF equal to angle XCE; line DF cuts plane CE at F so that angles CDF and CFD equal angles XCE and LCD, taken alternately. I say that the times of descent through CD and CF are equal. Thus, the ratio of the heights of equal planes CD and CE is the same as the ratio of lengths DC and CF. Therefore, the times of descents in these will be equal; which was to be proved.[53]

This is just the geometry of co-alternate angles and similar triangles, and similar triangles are the balance.[54] But there is an important addition: These lines can move, just as the balance beam can move. There is a dynamic aspect to this mathematical mechanics. Galileo's commitment to ratios and proportionality as the true method is shown again by the text of the work he was dictating when he died: "On Euclid's Definitions of Ratios."[55]

    This proportional geometry also made it easy to think in terms of relative motion. It is only when one weight is heavier than another that the balance moves. When forces are equal there is no observable motion, though there is force acting. In Galilean relative motion the observer judges what is moving from his point of view, from his reference frame, neglecting all the motions that the observer and the objects have in common. So it is that since a person and all other earthly things, for instance, a boat, a cannon, or a bird, share the same circular motion, that person can only perceive motions that are added to the common motion.

    Yet in this person-relative way of looking at the world and judging when proofs had been successful, Galileo recognized a problem. The balance model of intelligibility and the equilibrium model of proof demanded subjectivity. Any one person could look at the balance, or even with many together, each could look, and judge. But this was insufficient and objectivity was needed.

In Day 1 of *Dialogo*, Galileo contrasted God's extensive knowledge with the human being's intensive knowledge.[56] When a person posed a puzzle in the language of proportional geometry where solutions were recognized by seeing that equilibrium was achieved, then the person was Godlike in insight and understanding of the case at hand. The universal can be seen in the particular. By contrast, God sees all of the infinite cases. God's extensive knowledge of all cases only contrasted with human certainty in its intensive, particular mode of operation. The individual could be assured of his certainty intensively by using a proper method of proof, a mechanical, mathematical method.

It was in this way that the *more geometrico* provided the model of intelligibility and proof for science. The geometry involved was not a pure geometry but the physical geometry of the mixed sciences. It was the geometry of Archimedes, the geometry of proportions and of the properties of machines considered relative (or in relation to) one another. The visual paradigm of equilibrium proof for the balance brought together the Galilean tenets of experiment, long observation, and rigorous demonstration.

Indeed, this proportional geometry and its attendant equilibrium balance was the model for all natural science until Newton changed the ground rules with algebra replacing proportional geometry, absolute space replacing relational place, true motion replacing relative motion, and God becoming an active intervener in the world in demonstrable ways and equilibrium. The balance as a model of intelligibility in physics gave way to algebraic equality; understanding the world by relating one thing to another in human terms became a problem of solving the equation in order to find a real number value for a given force. These changes gave science a new model of intelligibility and success.

GALILEO'S EXPERIMENTS AND EXPERIENCES

Experiments for Galileo were ways of providing for himself and others first-person experiences in order to discover or verify relationships holding in nature. They were ways of demonstrating that the phenomenon that had been geometrically described actually could produce the results claimed. These experiences made the terms of the natural mechanical explanations meaningful and real to the person constructing or discovering.

Mechanical models, comparable production of effects, and commonplace experiences all played the same set of roles in Galileo's thought. They were not merely rhetorical devices invoked to convince others about the certainty of conclusions, they were also epistemic requirements necessary to give the proper experience to the individual scientist putting forward the explanation. Thus in *Discorsi* Galileo has Salviati reply to Simplicio's query about falling bodies as to whether "this is the acceleration employed by nature in the motion of her falling heavy bodies."

Like a true scientist, you make a very reasonable demand, for this is usual and necessary in those sciences which apply mathematical demonstrations to physical conclusions, as may be seen among writers on optics, astronomers, mechanics, musicians and others who confirm their principles with sensory experiences that are the foundations of all the resulting structures. Therefore as to experiments, the Author [Galileo] has not failed to make them, and in order to be assured that the acceleration of heavy bodies falling naturally does follow the ratio expounded above, I have often made the following test [la prova] in the following manner.[57]

"Prova" here does mean test, but it is used similarly to "proof" in the phrase, "the proof (or test) of the pudding is in the eating." The proof lies literally in showing what happens. Even in his letter to Castelli in 1613, Galileo speaks of "those natural conclusions of which the manifest meaning or the necessary demonstration have made certain and sure."[58]

From the time of *De Motu* onwards (1590), Galileo held that the way to understand anything was to show how it worked in a mechanical way. As noted, this probably derived from his practical training in the mechanical arts, his so-called artisan–engineering background. This was also a reasonably new Renaissance enterprise and was quite individualistic in that training was given outside of traditional guilds and schools in an apprenticelike or tutorial fashion.

It was a practical do-it-yourself procedure. It was practical in that the practitioners designed instruments, built fortifications, and constructed machines. These were useful devices. But it was practical

in that it involved practices. One could understand how these machines worked by constructing them and seeing what they did. For
big projects one built models. But whether they worked or not was
tested by the very practice of constructing them and seeing if they
worked.

Intelligibility or having a true explanation for Galileo had to include
having a mechanical model or representation of the phenomenon.
In this sense, Galileo added something to the traditional criteria of
mathematical description (from the mixed sciences) and observation
(from astronomy) for constructing scientific objects (as some would
say) or for having adequate explanations of the phenomena observed
(as I would say). He puts it nicely in the negative, when criticizing alternative theories of the tide. But the moral is clear: To get at the true
cause, you must replicate or reproduce the effects by constructing an
artificial device, so that the effects can be seen.

I believe you do not have any stronger indication that the true cause of the
tides is one of those incomprehensibles than the mere fact that among all
the things so far adduced as *vera causa* there is not one that we can duplicate
for ourselves by means of appropriate artificial devices.[59]

Galileo did draw a diagram and construct a mechanical device to
prove that the Earth's motion was the true mechanical cause of the
flux and re-flux of the tides. Diagrams are useful but insufficient. In
talking again about the tides and Copernicus's third motion of the
Earth Salviati explains to Sagredo:

... Nevertheless, we shall see whether drawing the drawing of a little diagram will not shed some light on it. [However] It would be better to represent
this effect by means of solid bodies than a mere picture.[60]

For Galileo to have an explanation he had to have suitable experiences demonstrating that the explanatory cause is the true one and
that it works necessarily. These experiences are had by constructing
machines that duplicate the phenomenon in question and so demonstrate or make plain their workings. Where one cannot construct
a machine, one may use examples already constructed or found in
nature that exhibit or display how the phenomenon works. These
devices or analogic phenomena literally demonstrate how the phenomena occurs. One sees the machine or phenomenon as an instance

of mathematics in the world. In this way one can know that they are real and not imaginary.

This idea of mechanical models or real or constructed experiences being needed for demonstration fits well with the constructive geometrical tradition. To have a demonstration in geometry one must construct a proof, actually draw the diagram. This idea of active construction is also the force behind the persuasiveness of the passage in *Dialogo* where Salviati has Simplicio construct the diagram, using agreed upon experiences as constraints, that shows the relations among the planets.[61] In this way, Salviati says he will come to understand even though he does not believe. Of course, Simplicio ends up with a Copernican diagram. To have a demonstration in mechanics one must construct a geometrical proof and coordinate it with experiences.

For motion problems this meant the model of intelligibility was one of the Archimedian simple machines, first the balance and then later the inclined plane and pendulua. In the theory of the tides it was a constructed wheel with an embedded tube of water that could be rotated. In the *Letters on the Sunspots* it was throwing bitumen on a hot pan thereby creating clouds of smoke that were like the spots on the sun.[62] These are all models. These mechanical models were a necessary part of the "proof" or criteria of adequacy for determining if you had an explanation. What is mechanical in this sense can be drawn or reproduced in a picture or recipe book. Such things can be seen or made by everyone and anyone.

I would remind you of the extent to which little machines, constructions, and natural phenomena are used by Galileo as demonstrations or parts of arguments. I will provide a few interesting examples, but literally a hundred or so more fill the pages of this book. Just in *Dialogo* we have: pouring water on the pavement to demonstrate reflective properties of the Moon "to show this to your own senses,"[63] using a pendulum to represent motions,[64] observing flying animals while you are on a moving ship,[65] using steelyards and balances,[66] using a "material instrument" – an astronomical sphere – for representing facts about the Sun's rotation,[67] solving a ratio problem about the size of stars with a real piece of rope that blocks out the adventitious rays of the stars,[68] and arguing about the time of rotation of a body (the Earth) by showing how to regulate the time in wheel clocks.[69] Finally, Galileo feels the need to tackle the toughest problem for all of the mechanical philosophy and for any form of corpuscularianism, even atomism, when in *Dialogo*, he attempts to provide a mechanical explanation of Gilbert's magnetism in terms of smooth and touching particles that fill the holes of a sponge.[70]

PHILOSOPHICAL CONCLUSION: THE NATURE OF MODELS OF INTELLIGIBILITY[71]

I want to call Galileo's use of the balance, conceptual and real, a model of intelligibility. It is the model by which he actually does his science, and it directs what he looks for and how he thinks about the world. It also includes criteria for making it clear when he has succeeded in explaining something.

Talking about a model of intelligibility is not intended as a new way of speaking. It is similar in some aspects to many other concepts that have been used before. But the emphasis on its being a model (or representation) that directs thought, and the concomitant understanding, is stressed more by this locution. For example, Stephen Toulmin's ideals of natural order,[72] Stephen Peppers' world hypotheses,[73] and Gerald Holton's thematics[74] all were similar attempts to talk about ways of making sense of the world. But these seem too abstract, too diffuse, and too *weltanschaung*-like to capture the precision with which Galileo's model of intelligibility directs his work.

The mechanical world view, which is a favorite example of these writers, would not have been either possible or plausible without the intelligibility and form of understanding provided by Archimedian simple machines, especially the balance. Its physical concreteness, mathematical describability, and physical manipulability leading to experimental possibilities gave intelligibility and structure to the abstract concepts of the mechanical world picture.

Closer to my concept of a model of intelligibility is Thomas Kuhn's concept of an exemplar.[75] For Kuhn, an exemplar is a problem-solving schema that is learned through using it on problems. It is based on shared examples. Certainly this is a model of intelligibility. However, Kuhn sometimes seems to think of exemplars as rules of thumb used to solve algebraic story problems or, sometimes, abstract algorithms or mathematical schemas that are learned by use and then applied in similar kinds of cases. These lack an intuitive picturable intelligibility. Often they are too ad hoc, and seldom do they have a broad enough domain of application. In other cases, he seems to think they are generalized examples, and in some sense the balance and solving problems by reducing them to balance problems are examples, but these now are too general to fit the concrete idea of an exemplar that Kuhn seems to have in mind.

The picturable, perceptual character of our model of intelligibility is caught in some ways like some of Eleanor Rosch's perceptual prototypes.[76] A model of intelligibility does provide a meaning schema by directing attention to what is important in a problem and by exhibiting what relations exist among those important elements. The model directs attention to the elements or parts of the problem that need to be identified and selected, making the subject match one element on the model with one element in the problem.

However, there is no algorithm for adequate or correct mapping. Misidentification of the elements can occur. Also, parts of the problem may not have correlates in the model either because they have been suppressed (in which case they need to be supplied) or because the problem is not really of the type that can be solved by the model. In this latter case again, there is no certain way to tell when a problem solution by the model is possible. Further, prototypes of a type of phenomenon may all exhibit certain "accidental" features which must be ignored in order to find them intelligible. This is why Galileo insists always that science is based on perception *and* reason. Rosch's prototypes are too exclusively perceptual for my purposes.

Further, all models of intelligibility need not have a picturable, perceptual character. In fact, a model of intelligibility can be very abstract and highly conceptual. Maxwell's electromagnetic equations or the U.S. Constitution are examples.

In its cognitive aspects, a model of intelligibility resembles some theorists' descriptions of the workings of schemas,[77] plans,[78] theories or hypotheses,[79] mental models,[80] problem-solving processes,[81] or idealized cognitive models.[82] Models of intelligibility are rules for drawing inferences. The models also specify patterns of expectation, group certain phenomena or situations into classes, and constitute the structures or categories into which the world must fit for us to find it comprehensible and intelligible.

However, models of intelligibility depart from this psychological class of concepts by existing, in some sense, apart from the person.

They are not just abstractions but can be instantiated in concrete objects and are part of social or cultural conditions. Their use in thinking is as idealized objects; otherwise they could have no normative force. But their intelligibility and utilization derives much from the fact that often they are spatially representable and thus picturable. Further, their physical presence or representation allows actions to be performed on them, and relations among their parts can be literally discovered and seen. Thus, they lend themselves to experimental and observational possibilities. This also explains why they can be used to train students.

Part of this physical sense of the model and its independence of human beings was seen by J. J. Gibson[83] when he developed his realistic theory of perceptual invariants. These were physical, higher order relational properties of the environment that determined what people perceive.[84] However, Gibson made a firm distinction between perception and cognition, which is untenable at the level at which models of intelligibility function. They are perceptual *and* cognitive.

There are interesting parallels, too, between a model of intelligibility and stages of Piaget's developmental psychology, wherein a child moves from sensori-motor structures to concrete operations and then to the more abstract sphere of formal operations.[85] Even though a model is representable in the real world, it is not merely a concrete, real-world token. It also is an ideal psychological type that can be taught through its concrete exemplifications and through physical representations (drawings, diagrams, etc.). Because it is ideal, its structure can function to regulate and constrain applications or instantiations of itself. That is, its ideal character allows one to correct representations or applications of it by comparisons back to the ideal model. The model can thus function normatively as well as descriptively.

A model of intelligibility's structure can be accepted as understood or intelligible. A model of intelligibility can be extended and used to understand other types of cases, bringing unity to different domains and fields.

Finally, the intelligibility of a model of intelligibility allows it to help bring about agreement among people. Because a model exhibits all and only those properties that are important, people can check over the list of properties. This intelligibility and the normative character of the idealized model are what allows for objectivity. If a problem cannot be reduced to these elements, or if a participant in the investigation insists on attending to other aspects, then either the problem falls outside the scope of the model or the participant needs (re)training about what is important in the problem or what are the allowable procedures.[86] Because these are the factors that most often lead to disagreements and disputes, such disagreements can be used to test the scope and adequacy of models, and sometimes they give rise to "revolutions" in intelligibility when people become convinced that something important is being left out. This latter may cause them to abandon the model as inadequate for solving all problems or merely to establish it as limited in application to certain kinds of cases or problems.

This is what happened to the Galilean mechanical model of intelligibility after Newton changed the terms and the methods and began to change the mathematics of science.

NOTES

1 I offer great thanks to all those who have helped me with Galileo over the years. There are too many to name, but to all of you, I owe a great deal. I am sorry that most of you will not agree with this essay.

   Many of the Galileo references are to Antonio Favaro's *Le Opere di Galileo Galilei*, Edizione Nazionale, Firenze; reprinted in 1968. References to works in this edition will simply be listed by author, then EN, followed by volume number, and page number.

2 Galileo (Rome 1623), *The Assayer*, in S. Drake and C. D. O'Malley, *The Controversy of the Comets of 1618*, Philadelphia: University of Pennsylvania Press, 1960, p. 189; *Il Saggiatore*, Milano: Feltrinelli, 1992, p. 48.

3 For some more detail see Peter Machamer, "The Person Centered Rhetoric of Seventeenth Century Science," in Marcello Pera and William R. Shea, eds., *Persuading Science: The Art of Scientific Rhetoric*, Canton, MA: Science History Publications, 1991.

4 There were very many practitioners of the mechanical arts before Galileo, and they were becoming popular and intellectually recognized. Some immediate predecessors are collected in Stillman Drake and I. E. Drabkin, *Mechanics in Sixteenth Century Italy*, Madison, WI: The University of Wisconsin Press, 1969. But such arts predate the sixteenth century and even printing, see, e.g., Pamela Long, "Power, Patronage, and the Authorship of *Ars*: From Mechanical Know-How to Mechanical Knowledge in the Last Scribal Age," *Isis*, 88, 1997, pp. 1–41. There is much work to be done on this history of early machine theory and mechanics and its dissemination, and especially in its relation to printed, widely available

texts. Printing allowed mechanical diagrams for teaching, which was a radical new representation of knowledge.

5 See, for example, Otto Mayr, *Authority, Liberty and Automatic Machinery in Early Modern Europe*, Baltimore, MD: The Johns Hopkins University Press, 1986.

6 There were many participants in these method debates of Galileo, but the interested reader might look at Alexandre Koyré, *From the Closed World to the Infinite Universe*, Baltimore, MD: The Johns Hopkins University Press, 1957; Ludovico Geymonat, *Galileo Galilei: A Biography and Inquiry into His Philosophy of Science*, translated by Stillman Drake, New York: McGraw-Hill 1965; Ernan McMullin, "Introduction: Galileo, Man of Science," in Ernan McMullin, ed., *Galileo: Man of Science*, New York: Basic Books, 1967, pp. 3–51; Dudley Shapere, Galileo: A Philosophical Study, Chicago, IL: The University of Chicago Press, 1974; Thomas P. McTighe, "Galileo's Platonism: A Reconsideration," in Ernan McMullin, ed., *Galileo: Man of Science*, op. cit., pp. 365–87; William R. Shea, *Galileo's Intellectual Revolution*, New York: Science History Publications, 1972.

7 See Footnote 4.

8 Ernst Cassirer, *The Individual and the Cosmos in Renaissance Philosophy*, translated by Mario Domandi, Philadelphia, PA: University of Pennsylvania Press, 1972 (original 1927).

9 Olaf Pedersen, *The Book of Nature*, Vatican City: Vatican Observatory Publications, 1992.

10 Interestingly E. J. Dijksterhuis, though author of books of the mechanical world view and on Archimedes, misses the depth of this connection; see *The Mechanization of the World Picture*, translated by C. Dikshoorn, London: Oxford University Press, 1961 (original 1950).

11 See, for example, Leonardo Olschki, *Galileo und seine Zeit*, Halle, 1927 and "Galileo's Philosophy of Science," *Philosophical Review* 1943, pp. 349–65; Erwin Panofsky, *Galileo as a Critic of the Arts*, Nijhoff, 1954; Tom Settle, "Galileo's Use of Experiment as a Tool of Investigation," in E. McMullin, ed., *Galileo: Man of Science*, New York: Basic Books, 1967.

12 Wallace Hooper, *Galileo and the Problems of Motion*, Dissertation, Indiana University, 1992. Hooper's thesis is one of the best works on Galileo and motion that exists.

13 Peter Machamer "Galileo and the Causes," in Robert Butts and Joseph Pitt, eds., *New Perspectives on Galileo*, Dordrecht: D. Reidel, 1978, pp. 161–80. Cf. also James G. Lennox, "Aristotle, Galileo and the 'Mixed Sciences'," in William Wallace, ed., *Reinterpreting Galileo*, Washington, DC: The Catholic University of America Press, 1986.

14 William Wallace, *Galileo's Logic and Discovery and Proof*, Dordrecht: Kluwer 1992.

15 Galileo, *De Motu*, 1590, EN vol. 1, pp. 251–419; translation by I. E. Drabkin, *On Motion*, Madison WI: The University of Wisconsin Press, 1960. Hereafter, this translation is referred to as "Drabkin" followed by page number. As to the dating, see review of attempts by Wallace Hooper, *op. cit.*

16 See Wallace Hooper, *op. cit.*, p. 255 f.

17 Galileo, EN 1, 174; Drabkin 38.

18 Galileo, EN 1, 259; Drabkin 22.

19 Galileo EN 1, 259; Drabkin 23.

20 Galileo, EN 1, 257; Drabkin 20.

21 Galileo, EN 1, 257–8; Drabkin 20–21.

22 Galileo, EN 1, 259; Drabkin 22–23.

23 Galileo, EN 1, 274, 275; Drabkin 38, 39.

24 Galileo, EN 1, 296; Drabkin 63.

25 Galileo, EN 1, 297; Drabkin 64.

26 Galileo, EN 1; translated by Stillman Drake, *On Mechanics*, Madison, WI: The University of Wisconsin Press, 1960.

27 Galileo, EN 1; Drake 151.

28 Galileo, EN 1; Drake 151, my translation.

29 Galileo, EN 1, 215–16; translation in Laura Fermi and Gilberto Bernardini, *Galileo and the Scientific Revolution*, Greenwich, CT: Fawcett, 1961.

30 Galileo, EN 4; Stillman Drake translated this work and made it into a dialogue by adding his own thoughts, *Cause, Experiment and Science*, Chicago: The University of Chicago Press, 1981.

31 Galileo, EN 5, 378 ff.

32 Galileo, EN 7; translation by Stillman Drake, *Dialogue on the Two Chief World Systems*, Berkeley and Los Angeles: The University of California Press, 1962. Hereafter this work will be referred to as *Dialogo*.

33 Galileo EN 6; translation by Stillman Drake, *The Assayer in Galileo, et al.; Controversy of the Comets of* 1618, Philadelphia: The University of Pennsylvania Press, 1960.

34 Grassi, EN 6; translation by C. D. O'Malley, in *Galileo et al. Controversy of the Comets of* 1618, *op. cit.*

35 See Footnote 24.

36 Galileo, EN 7, 240; Drake 213–14.

37 Galileo, EN 7, 157; Drake 131.

38 Galileo, EN 7, 393–4; Drake 366.

39 Galileo, EN 8; translation by Stillman Drake, *Two New Sciences*, Madison, WI: The University of Wisconsin Press, 1974. Hereafter, this work is referred to as *Discorsi*.

40 Galileo, EN 7, 205; Drake 131.

41 Galileo, EN 8, 208; Drake 366.

42 Galileo, EN 8, 209; Drake 166.

43 Galileo, EN 8, 214; Drake 171.

44 Galileo, EN 7, 190; Drake 164.

45 W. H. Price, "Origins of the Phrase 'Balance of Trade'," *Quarterly Journal of Economics*, 1905, pp. 157–67.

46 For a review of some of this, see Philip Mirowski, *More Heat than Light: Economics as Social Physics, Physics as Nature's Economics*, Cambridge: Cambridge University Press, 1989.

47 Galileo Galilei, *Il Saggiatore*, 1623, Milano: Feltrinelli, 1965, p. 38; Drake translation in *Controversies of the Comets of 1618, op cit.* pp. 183–4.

48 I have struggled to find a way of describing Galileo's form of mathematico-physical reasoning. The ideas of ratio, proportionality, congruence, and dynamic motion are all part of it, but I still have no felicitous way of describing its character succinctly or precisely.

49 Stillman Drake understates this proportional character of Galileo's geometry when he writes:

> Unlike Galileo who concerned himself only with ratios, not only Baliani, but other scientists of his time and after (Mersenne, Cabeo, G. B. Ricioli, and the young Newton) sought number of feet or other arbitrary units traversed in fall from rest during a given number of astronomical seconds. Some figures given in the *Dialogo* as an example for purposes of calculation (EN 7, 50, Dialogue p. 223) were accordingly misunderstood as assertions of an experimental determination.

> Stillman Drake, *Galileo at Work*, Chicago: The University of Chicago Press, Footnote 7, p. 498.

50 Quoted in Drake, *Galileo at Work*, p. 398. Drake, of course, assumes Baliani is disagreeing with Galileo.

51 This development is brilliantly laid out in Wallace Hooper's *Galileo and the Problems of Motion, op. cit.*, p. 344 ff.

52 Galileo, EN 8, 227–8; Drake 184–5.

53 Galileo, EN 8, 227–8; Drake 184.

54 Wallace Hooper, *Galileo and the Problems of Motion, op. cit.*, p. 348.

55 Translated in Stillman Drake, *Galileo at Work, op. cit.*, pp. 422–36.

56 Galileo, EN 7, 128–9; Drake 103.

57 Galileo, EN 8, 212; Drake 169.

58 Galileo, EN V, 279–88.

59 Galileo, EN 7, 447; Drake 421.

60 Galileo, EN 7, 482; Drake 457. Unfortunately, even Galileo's artificial machine did not prevent him from accepting a wrong theory of the tides. But to his credit, lunar gravitation is a "miraculous force" and cannot be fit into the mechanical philosophy.

61 Galileo, EN 7, 350; Drake 322.

> But for your greater satisfaction and your astonishment, too, I want you to draw it yourself. You will see that however firmly you may believe yourself not to understand it, you do so perfectly and just by answering my questions you will describe it exactly.

62 For discussion of this technique and all the relevant quotations, see Rivka Feldhay, "Producing Sunspots on an Iron Pan: Galileo's Scientific Discourse" and my reply, both in Henry Krips, J. E. McGuire, and Trevor Melia, eds., *Science, Reason and Rhetoric*, University of Pittsburgh Press/Unveritatsverlag Konstanz, 1995, pp. 119–43, 145–52.

63 Galileo, EN 7, 123; Drake 97–9.

64 Galileo, EN 7, 177–8; Drake 152–3: "The pendulums have just shown us that the less a moving body partakes of weight, the less apt it is to conserve motion..." and EN 7, 454; Drake 428, for a swinging stone or pendulum representing the reciprocal motion of the tides.

65 Galileo, EN 7, 212–3; Drake 186–7.

> For a final indication of the nullity of the experiments brought forth, this seems to me the place to show you as a way to test [il modo di sperimentarle] them all very easily. Shut yourself up with some friend in the main cabin below decks on some large ship, and have with you there some flies, butterflies, and other small flying animals...

66 Galileo, EN 7, 240–1; Drake 213–4.

> Sagredo: But tell me what is this second force.
> Salviati: It is that which did not exist in the equal armed balance. Consider what there is that is new in the steelyard, and therein lies necessarily the cause of the new effect.

67 Galileo, EN 7, 375–6; Drake 348–9.

68 Galileo, EN 7, 388–9; Drake 361–2.

69 Galileo, EN 7, 474–5; Drake 449–50.

70 Galileo, EN 7, 435–6; Drake 409–10.

71 A version of this section appeared in Peter Machamer and Andrea Woody, "A Model of Intelligibility in Science: Using Galileo's Balance as a Model for Understanding the Motion of Bodies," *Science and Education* 3, 1994, pp. 215–44.

72 Stephen Toulmin, *Foresight and Understanding*, New York: Harper, 1961.

73 Stephen Pepper, *World Hypotheses*, Berkeley, CA: The University of California Press, 1948.

74 Gerald Holton, *Thematic Origins of Scientific Thought: Kepler to Einstein*, Cambridge, MA: Harvard University Press, 1972.

75 Thomas Kuhn, *The Structure of Scientific Revolutions*, second edition, Chicago, IL: The University of Chicago Press, 1970, "Postscript."

76 For example, Eleanor Rosch, "Cognitive Reference Points," *Cognitive Psychology*, 1975 7:532–47.

77 Ulrich Neisser, *Cognition and Reality*, San Francisco, CA: W. H. Freeman, 1976; Julian Hochberg, *Perception*, second edition, Englewood Cliffs, NJ: Prentice-Hall, 1978.

78 George A. Miller, E. Galanter, and K. Pribram, *Plans and the Structure of Behavior*, New York: Holt, Rinehart, and Winston, 1960.

79 Richard L. Gregory, "Choosing a Paradigm for Perception," in Edward C. Carterette and Morton P. Friedman, eds., *Handbook of Perception*, Vol. 1, New York: Academic Press, 1974.

80 Philip Johnson-Laird, *Mental Models*, Cambridge, MA: Harvard University Press, 1983.

81 For example, Herbert A. Simon, "Thinking by Computers" and "Scientific Discovery and the Psychology of Problem Solving," both in Robert G. Colodny, ed., *Mind and Cosmos*, Pittsburgh, PA: University of Pittsburgh Press, 1966, pp. 3–21, 22–40. Another, nonpsychological approach using problem solving as a model for how research traditions are structured is found in Larry Laudan, *Progress and Its Problems*, Berkeley, CA: University of California Press, 1977.

82 George Lakoff, *Women, Fire and Dangerous Things*, Chicago, IL: The University of Chicago Press, 1987.

83 James J. Gibson, *The Senses Considered as Perceptual Systems*, Boston, MA: Houghton Mifflin, 1966, and *The Ecological Approach to Visual Perception*, Boston, MA: Houghton Mifflin, 1979.

84 A theory, not unlike Gibson's, in some respects, is developed for the case of motion (and so for event perception) in James E. Cutting, *Perception with an Eye for Motion*, Cambridge, MA: MIT Press, 1986.

85 Piaget has developed this theory in numerous publications. For a summary, see Jean Piaget and Barbel Inhelder, *The Psychology of the Child*, translated by H. Weaver, New York: Basic Books, 1969 (originally 1966).

86 This theme is developed, albeit in a dated Wittgensteinian language of criteria, in William G. Lycan and Peter Machamer's, "A Theory of Critical Reasons," in B. R. Tilghman, ed., *Language and Aesthetics*, Witchita, KS: Kansas State University Press, 1971.

3 The use and abuse of mathematical entities: Galileo and the Jesuits revisited

INTRODUCTION

On the second day of the *Two New Sciences*[1] the three interlocutors Sagredo, Simplicio, and Salviati suspend their learned conversation on forces of fracture and resistance to indulge in yet another digression among many that have become well known as characteristic marks of Galileo's texts. Sagredo, the aristocratic amateur of natural philosophy and mathematics addresses Simplicio, the Aristotelian philosopher, with the following remark:

What shall we say, Simplicio? Must we not confess that the power of geometry is the most potent instrument of all to sharpen the mind and dispose it to reason perfectly, and to speculate? Didn't Plato have good reason to want his pupils to be first well grounded in mathematics? (133)

Simplicio, portrayed in this not very polemical text as an open-minded scholar, graciously responds:

Truly I begin to understand that although logic is a very excellent instrument to govern our reasoning, it does not compare with the sharpness of geometry in awakening the mind to discovery.

This unexpected agreement encourages Sagredo to further elaborate his position by saying:

It seems to me that logic teaches how to know whether or not reasonings and demonstrations already discovered are conclusive, but I do not believe that it teaches how to find conclusive reasonings and demonstrations.

The edge of Galileo's ambitious project is enfolded in this brief exchange. Suggesting that geometry is a tool of discovery, whereas logic serves for assessing and criticizing arguments already known, Sagredo hints at the need to restructure the body of natural knowledge, substituting mathematics for logic as the organon of philosophy.

Ever since the nineteenth century, the historiography of science has fruitfully oscillated between different interpretations of what really constituted the core of Galileo's project. Experimental practices,[2] mathematical Platonism,[3] Aristotelian method,[4] or some kind of a combination between experiment and mathematical deductivism[5] are just a few among many alternative clues suggested by scholars along the years, by means of which the "essence" of Galileo's enterprise was thought to be captured. Whatever may be the angle through which Galileo's theory and practice are to be examined, it is beyond doubt, however, that the transition from traditional natural philosophy to the new science was much effected by the role assigned to mathematics in Galilean discourse, though not necessarily by its actual mathematical techniques.

Many questions have been asked about the new status of mathematics in Galileo's scientific program. Some historians were most interested in the *origins* of Galileo's mathematical orientation, which could be found in classical mathematical texts, or perhaps among the medieval calculators, or the Parisian School, or among the mathematical practitioners of fifteenth- and sixteenth-century Italian courts.[6] Other historians were more interested in the *contents of the justifications*, devised by Galileo for using mathematics in the investigation of nature, and in their *philosophical validity*.[7] Yet others preferred to emphasize the *compatibility or incompatibility of mathematical arguments* with the established *method* of the official science of sixteenth-century universities.[8]

To this variety of points of view I would like to add yet another aspect. Assuming a breach within Galileo's scientific project (which has already been pointed out by other historians), but also taking into consideration the context of Galileo's project in the field of practicing mathematicians, Galileo's justification of the status of mathematics may be better understood if we realize and analyze the complexity of its various functions: on the one hand to create a bridge between the different and sometimes incompatible directions of his own inquiries, conferring upon them the coherence of a research program; on the other hand to construct for himself a differentiated position among other mathematicians working in the same cultural field.

My essay, then, is a preliminary attempt to provide a framework of some less discussed aspects of Galileo's politics of knowledge. The justification of the status of mathematics is not examined here as the source from which a coherent research project necessarily emerged but as a necessary strategy of creating coherence for a project whose inner connections were not yet clear. Furthermore, the cultural context within which such strategy was mainly practiced consisted in a newly reconstructed community of mathematicians whose field of research was in the process of being defined.

My point of departure is the debate over the mathematical sciences that broke out in Italy in the middle of the sixteenth century and has been known in historical literature as the controversy on the certainty of mathematics (*De certitudine mathematicarum disciplinarum*).[9] The cultural significance of this debate emerged as it began to play a role in the actual practices of mathematicians attempting to gain for their project a central educational role. Jesuit mathematicians made the first institutionally organized effort to place the mathematical disciplines at the heart of a broad cultural program.[10] Therefore, my focus in the first part of this essay is on the appropriation and development of the main themes of the debate as strategies of legitimizing their field of knowledge.

Galileo's science sprang from the same roots as the Jesuits' program, and it shared much of its spirit with Jesuit mathematicians. The dynamics of Galileo's own development, however, pushed him into formulating a different agenda. At the same time, Galileo never detached himself completely from his roots, which assumed the form of a counter-discourse, insisting in his texts but split from his later agenda. The second part of this paper comprises an analysis of various passages from Galileo's *Dialogue* that exemplify the structural split within his own scientific program.

The third part follows the traces left in Galileo's *Dialogue* by the debate on the certainty of mathematics. Galileo's final annihilation of the discourse on mathematical entities – used by the Jesuits as their main legitimation – was a way of covering up the split in his own program, as well as strategy of differentiating his position from that of the Jesuit mathematicians.

I. THE CONSTRUCTION OF A FIELD
FOR MATHEMATICIANS

In 1547 Alessandro Piccolomini, a member of the Accademia degli Infiammati, which was active in transmitting humanistic and Renaissance learning to the University of Padua, published a paraphrase of Aristotle's *Mechanical Questions*, appendiced by a commentary on the certitude of mathematics (*Commenatrium de certitudine mathematicarum disciplinarum*).[11] Piccolomini's treatise challenged the accepted interpretation of Averroes and the Latin commentators, according to which in the hierarchy of the speculative sciences (scientiae) the mathematical disciplines were the first in the order of *certainty*, because their demonstrations were the model for demonstrations *potissimae*, perceived as the strongest and most certain of all other forms of demonstration.[12] Following his reading of Proclus's *Commentary on the First Book of Euclid's Elements*, and of the Greek Commentators, whose recently translated work started to transform the reading of Aristotle in those same years,[13] Piccolomini changed his adolescent opinion on that matter and claimed that geometrical demonstrations had nothing to do with scientific demonstrations *potissimae*.[14]

Piccolomini's treatise is a natural point of departure for understanding the appropriation and rejection of the ancient discourse on mathematical entities in the cultural context of early modern science. Its arguments, recently represented and analyzed in detail by Anna De Pace amount to a strategy that attempted to establish a clear boundary between mathematics and natural philosophy, while still legitimizing mathematics as an autonomous but inferior science.

The ontology of mathematical entities delineated by Piccolomini consisted in a combination of his Averroistic interpretation of "quantity" as the most general accident of primary matter, his Aristotelian theory of abstraction, and his Aristotelian reading of Proclus's thesis about the middle position (*medietas*) of mathematics. The quantity that inheres in primary matter before it is embodied in any substantial form was, in Piccolomini's words, "quantum phantasiatum,"[15] the most common and basic of all sensible accidents[16] and undetermined by any specified form. Piccolomini calls it "indeterminate quantity" and describes it thus:

... since matter is by its own nature devoid of any substantial form, and nevertheless has in it the possibility and readiness for all forms: thus the quantity which is proper for it is likewise bare and devoid of any determination or figure; and is nevertheless able and disposed to receive all terms or figure...[17]

Quantity is the most immediate and manifest property of matter and hence the easiest to abstract. Mathematical entities are easily liberated from matter by simple abstraction. The certainty with which they may be known is connected to their simple being. Devoid of complexity and depth, they are the most accessible for human cognition.[18]

Piccolomini, however, denied that the certainty achieved by mathematical demonstrations, whose subject matter is quantity, can be identified with scientific demonstrations. Using Proclus's analysis of Euclid I, 32 [In any triangle, if one of the sides be produced, the exterior angle is equal to the two interior and opposite angles, and the three interior angles are equal to two right angles] as an example for a noncausal demonstration he claimed it could not be identified with demonstration *potissima*, and he generalized this critique to all Euclidean proofs. Thus, his conclusion was that mathematical demonstrations were not really scientific in the Aristotelian sense.[19]

The separation of mathematical objects from substance, which explains, according to Piccolomini, their capacity to be known with a high degree of certainty, but which differentiates them from the objects of natural philosophy entangled in the reality of matter and form, also accounts for the difference between geometrical and philosophical demonstrations. Together these differences justify the distinction between mathematics as a science of abstract being – "quantum phantasiatum" – and natural philosophy, the science of reality. Even the mixed sciences, which apply mathematics to the investigation of nature, are devoid of real scientificity, and though they are extremely useful for humanity they still represent an inferior form of knowledge compared to natural philosophy. One example used by Piccolomini to substantiate this difference concerned the sphericity of the Earth and heaven. Whereas the natural philosopher attempts to discover the *essential causes inherent in natural things*, the astronomer *considers their mathematical properties* without asking about their true nature:[20]

...the astronomer...even while considering that the heaven is spherical, or that the earth round, does not need, for this [purpose] to know the true nature and their substance, but solely from the positions, figures and aspects seen in the heaven argues that they are of such form...for this [reason] it can be concluded, that though the science of natural things often overlaps with other sciences in treating a certain subject, or in demonstrating a certain conclusion, nevertheless the natural philosopher differs from all the others in that never separating the concepts of the forms from those of their proper matter, he treats both natures as related to each other, namely the matter and the form: which are the two principles, and the intrinsic causes of natural things.

In the flourishing community of Paduan mathematicians and Averroist philosophers which sustained a rich technical and scientific tradition at the time,[21] including among its members people such as J. Contarini, D. Barbaro, G. Moleto, and N. Tartaglia, Piccolomini's treatise was received with much surprise and irritation. This was the natural audience for Francesco Barozzi, a young Venetian patrician. He had been lecturer of mathematics since 1559 and immersed in the study of Proclus's *Commentary* for some years, publishing (in 1560) his *Opusculum* – consisting in an oration and two questions on the certainty and the middle position of mathematics – in response to Piccolomini's startling innovation.[22] The work was dedicated to D. Barbaro, seeking his protection for daring to challenge Piccolomini's recent publication. Barbaro responded with a letter – thus leaving some testimony for the hostility toward Piccolomini in his circle – in which he expressed his long-term expectation for a refutation of Piccolomini's opinion as "new and unfounded" ("nova et non fondata").[23] In 1559 (the first year of his lectureship) Barozzi read Proclus's *Commentary* in his course and left his interpretation in manuscript form.[24] As a Venetian patron he corresponded extensively with prominent Italian mathematicians, among them Clavius, Guidobaldo del Monte, Giuseppe Moleto, and other eminent personalities.

Barozzi's work is of interest as a main source of interpretation and transmission of Proclus's *Commentary*, which he edited and published in the same year as he published his *Opusculum*.[25] Accepting Piccolomini's thesis about the *medietas* of mathematics (between philosophy and the "divine science" metaphysics) as the basis for reconciling Aristotle and Plato, Barozzi neglected Piccolomini's interpretation of this middle position in terms of abstraction and attempted to ground the certainty and scientificity of mathematical demonstrations in Proclus's claim to the innateness and priority of mathematical entities.

Thus Barozzi was the first to legitimize a reading of Aristotle in terms of a Neo-Platonic ontology of the objects of mathematical discourse. Barozzi, following Proclus, claimed that Plato arranged the sciences according to the perfection of their entities. Therefore, according to him: "Divine philosophy holds the first place, mathematics the second, natural philosophy the third."[26] At first glance it seems that Aristotle refused this order, since he gave priority to natural philosophy. This opposition is superficial, however, according to Barozzi. In truth, Aristotle accepted the middle nature of mathematical entities, since they mediate between matter and the purely abstract entities of metaphysics. "And indeed, this middle essence cannot be anything else but mathematical."[27] But the middle position of mathematics means that the certainty of knowledge of its objects is superior to that of the knowledge of the objects of natural philosophy. And because there must always be a correspondence between the objects of a science and its demonstrations, it follows that mathematical demonstrations are more certain than any other kind of demonstration.[28]

Two historical facts may echo something about the diffusion and transmission of Barozzi's ideas. That Galileo owned the *Opusculum* is known from the description of his library by Antonio Favaro.[29] Also, in the "Prolegomena" to his commentary on Euclid's *Elements* discussed below, Christopher Clavius admitted to the inspiration of Barozzi and his work on Proclus. Thus, Barozzi's reluctance to take issue with Piccolomini's Aristotelian theory of abstraction – in spite of his rejection of other parts of Piccolomini's reading – and his preference for blurring Proclus's harsh critique of this theory allowed mathematicians of different convictions to draw upon his ideas without giving full account of the profound differences between the Platonic and the Aristotelian position on the mathematical entities.

A more radical opposition to Piccolomini, entangled with a more radical reading of Aristotle in Proclean terms, characterizes the work of Pietro Catena, who held the chair of mathematics in Padua for almost thirty years (1547–1576) and developed his ideas in three works, all touching upon the relation between mathematics and philosophy, their objects, their demonstrations, and their status in the hierarchy of the speculative sciences.[30]

The main thesis common to Piccolomini and Barozzi, but rejected by Catena, was that of the middle position of mathematical entities, for which Catena substituted a view of mathematical universals as predicates of the rational soul that he derived from his Platonic reading of the *Posterior Analytics*. Unlike physical phenomena, which are perceived primarily through sense experience, mathematical entities are pure intelligibles, constituted only through a rational process of thought and in no need of the senses to be recognized.[31] Catena believed in their innateness and invoked the theory of reminiscence to justify the pure intellectual nature of their recognition.[32] But more generally, Catena subscribed to the view that all knowledge was first anchored in universals preexisting in the intellect, rather than in abstraction from particulars. Above all, the objects of geometricians – lines, points, and planes – originate in the soul, not in sense images.[33]

The clue to Catena's position may be his presupposition that any particular participates in a universal mathematical nature, although particulars cannot be reduced to such entities, because they also contain other elements in which they are distinguished as particulars. Science, according to Catena consisted essentially in the application of universal intelligibles to particulars, thus transforming recognition into actual knowledge.

To illustrate this process Catena used Aristotle's example of a bronze triangle recognized as participating in a universal (in this case a mathematical triangle) through an examination of the equality of the sum of its angles to two straight ones. The mind presupposes a bronze triangle and gradually excludes some of its properties (its bronzeness, for example) until it realizes that with the elimination of the three sides the property of the sum of the angles disappears.[34] Aristotle and Euclid agreed on this idea of science, but they used different logical procedures – syllogism and mathematical demonstration respectively – as their practice. Therefore, Aristotle, in his *Posterior Analytics*, referred to two kinds of inductions,[35] although he did not clarify the differences between them. Catena took upon himself to do just that, and this was probably the most original part of his contribution. Definition played an essential role in a syllogistic procedure, but a mere classificatory role in a geometrical one. To show this Catena picked up again Proclus's and Piccolomini's example of Euclid 1, 32,[36] only to claim the opposite of their conclusion, namely that in spite of its difference from a demonstration *potissima*, it still led to true, certain, and actual knowledge of the particular.[37] Thus, Catena agreed with Piccolomini about the difference between mathematical and syllogistic demonstrations, but insinuated – without actually articulating this conclusion clearly – that only mathematical demonstrations could serve in the discovery of new truths, whereas syllogisms were effective in the orderly presentation of old ones.

Catena's interpretation of the concept of universal science, which he deemed common to Aristotle and Euclid, enabled him to include the mixed mathematical disciplines within this framework, without any need to distinguish their status from the rest of the sciences. The basic difference was that in the constitution of corporeal entities (such as rays of light, for example, compared to geometrical lines) as objects of science not only pure rational thought but also experience played a major role. Still, the principles of the science as well as its basic concepts were universal intelligibles and the causes discovered were the product of rational discourse, not of the senses.[38]

The positions of Piccolomini, Barozzi, and Catena – who were the first to construct some archetypal strategies in early modern politics of knowledge – may be summed up as follows: Piccolomini recognized the superior certainty of mathematics but was most interested in bounding it within a separate, autonomous domain. The high degree of certainty attributed to mathematics was related by Piccolomini to the inferiority of its objects, which were, in his perception, the most simplistic in the ontological sense and therefore the easiest to acquire knowledge about. In this sense they were radically differentiated from the objects of natural philosophy, representing a higher degree of complexity and allowing for intrinsic knowledge of their essence through a much more complex rational process culminating in the demonstration *potissima*. The boundary between mathematics and philosophy was clearly at the center of Piccolomini's interest. Barozzi, using a Proclean reading of mathematical entities, focused his interest on proving the scientificity – and not just certainty – of mathematics by stressing its middle position (*medietas*) between philosophy and metaphysics, both in the order of nature (ontology) and in the order of knowing (epistemology). This doctrine he deemed common to Aristotle and Plato and was the source of recognizing mathematical demonstrations as equivalent to demonstrations *potissimae*. The compatibility between the objects of a science and the kind of demonstrations it used led, according to Barozzi, to the inescapable recognition of the higher status of mathematics relative to philosophy. However, the question of the use of mathematics in natural philosophy was not really predominant in his writing. In fact, De Pace's interpretation emphasizes that it played a minor role in his mind.[39] But this was the main focus of Catena's arguments. Attributing a common ideal of science to Aristotle and Euclid – in spite of a deep divergence of methods – Catena thought that mathematical demonstrations were superior to demonstrations *potissimae* as instruments of acquiring new knowledge. Hence, he claimed that knowledge of the world was only possible through the use of mathematical methods.

All three writers presupposed some kind of agreement between Aristotle, Plato, and sometimes Proclus on the certainty of mathematics, in spite of their different and sometimes oppository readings of their sources: Piccolomini stressed the agreement of Aristotle and Proclus on the middle position of mathematics – wrongly attributing to Aristotle a theory of abstraction – and used Proclus's occasional critique of some Euclidean proofs to claim the incompatibility of mathematical demonstration and demonstration *potissima*. Barozzi attempted to reconcile the Aristotelian and Platonic position on the *medietas* of mathematics but ignored the Aristotelian theory of abstraction. Catena attempted a Platonic reading of the *Posterior Analytics* in order to prove an idea of science common to Aristotle and Plato. It is thus clear that all three writers attributed a major role to the ancient authorities in their attempts to gain legitimation for their respective positions.

The debate over the status of mathematics in the sixteenth century signaled the beginning of a structural shift on the medieval map of knowledge toward a different understanding of the place of mathematics. The change was initiated by a variety of separate developments such as the activities of mathematical practitioners in Italian courts, the renaissance of Greek mathematical texts, the spread of Archimedean discourse, the emergence of Copernican astronomy, and the rise of the new algebra. But it was among the Jesuits that the first efforts were made to assimilate all these changes into an institutionalized research program with a special cultural and educational vocation. It is also in the context of the Jesuit program that the debate over the certainty of mathematics was appropriated and developed as a source for a variety of practices in the politics of knowledge. The history of the efforts of Jesuit mathematicians to create for themselves a separate identity within a humanistic–scholastic educational project and to secure their status vis-à-vis the theologians and philosophers of the society has not yet been written. Recent historical scholarship, however, points to tensions between philosophers and mathematicians – concerning the scope and place of mathematics in the Jesuit curriculum, the interpretation of cosmological phenomena such as the nova of 1604, the motion of the Earth, the critique of Archimedes, etc.[40] – all of which touched upon the problematic boundary between mathematical and philosophical discourse. In some of my previous work I have argued that the Jesuit policy of constructing boundaries between fields of knowledge functioned as a cultural mechanism of control enabling the reproduction of a Thomistic framework, in spite of the transgression of its boundaries which became common practice among Jesuit mathematicians.[41] The traditional mathematical disciplines were the science of numbers, the science of continuous magnitudes, and pure and mixed mathematics. Two examples may illustrate the kind of dynamics created by the Jesuit appropriation of new areas of mathematical research that tended to undermine these traditional boundaries within the mathematical disciplines (or between mathematics and natural philosophy) and the practice of keeping the boundaries, which was also exercised by Jesuit mathematicians.

The Jesuits' involvement is particularly interesting in two areas. The first concerns their role in the reception, assimilation, and transition of Vietà's algebra. Whereas Clavius himself praised algebra, publishing his textbook on the subject in 1608, his work did not really assimilate the "new art" and the innovations of recent Italian algebraists.[42] His student Staserio, however, who dedicated much of his life to building up the mathematical program of studies in the Jesuit college in Naples, succeeded in integrating the new algebra into the Jesuit curriculum.[43] Baldini's historical researches have taught us that around 1600 the Collegio Romano became a center of debate over the innovations springing from the use of algebra in solving geometrical problems.[44] The intense preoccupation with algebra could not take place, however, without challenging the boundary between discrete numbers and continuous magnitudes, as has been shown by

Jacob Klein, and more recently by Lachterman.[45] Nevertheless, the famous controversy between Paulus Guldin and Cavallieri over the method of indivisibles[46] echoes the tendency of many Jesuit mathematicians to defend the traditional disciplinary divisions, in spite of their interest and even promotion of research topics that clearly endangered them.

No less significant was the involvement of Jesuit mathematicians in the Archimedean revival that took place exactly in the same years. The origins of this involvement go back both to Torres – the first professor of mathematics at the Collegio Romano – who was a student of Maurolico, and to Clavius who was in close contact with Maurolico and planned to publish his manuscripts.[47] It is Baldini, again, who has pointed out the impact of these connections with Maurolico and through him also with Commandino's work, which was felt both through the emphasis on geometry and on Archimedean problems of measuring as well as through an interest in the Archimedean statical tradition of mechanics, thoroughly brought into contact with the medieval dynamical tradition in the context of the Jesuit "mixed mathematical science."[48] A most compelling piece of evidence for the new horizons opened up by the integration of the Archimedean tradition may be found in the plurality of works on centers of gravity, written by Jesuit mathematicians at the turn of the seventeenth century and later on.

It is well known that Clavius wrote on centers of gravity, but his work was not preserved. Staserio, Villalpando, Luca Valerio, and later on Guldin and Saint Vincent (all of them trained by Clavius in Rome) wrote on centers of gravity, testifying to the continuation of that tradition in Jesuit circles. Work on centers of gravity, however, was situated exactly on the borderline between mathematical and physical discourse. In fact, the concept of "weight" itself was conceptualized in qualitative terms in the context of Aristotelian physics and in terms of "quantity" in the Archimedean mathematical one. This exemplifies a clear point of interference and of potential tensions between mathematicians and philosophers.

The institutionalization and success of a mathematical program of studies and research was the context in which the debate on the certainty of mathematics was replicated, intensified, and developed in Jesuit circles. Benedictus Perera was the first to elaborate and deepen Alessandro Piccolomini's arguments with clear implications for the status of the mathematicians of the society. This strategy was countered by a rather intense campaign of Christopher Clavius, the architect of the program and the founder of a Jesuit mathematical tradition, who replicated some of Barozzi's arguments in his effort to buttress the position of the mathematicians. A certain climax was achieved, though, in the work of Josephus Blancanus who developed an ontology of mathematical entities in an attempt to ground the mathematical disciplines in a firm philosophical basis. In briefly reconstructing these three positions as strategies in the Jesuit politics of knowledge, my aim is to clarify the background against which Galileo's later rejection of the discourse on mathematical entities should be understood.

Perera developed his position in long passages of the widely circulated *De Communibus Omnium Rerum Naturalium Principiis*, first published in 1576, and reprinted nine times until the end of the century.[49] Departing from Piccolomini's suggestion that "quantity" inheres in prime matter as indeterminate extension independently of any substantial form, Perera securely anchored this contention in the Greek commentators and in Averroes.[50] He thus deepened the ontological dimension of Piccolomini's thesis and inferred the fully consistent conclusions from it. Stressing the radical separation of quantity not only from sensible substances – as did Albertus Magnus, Thomas Aquinas, and other Latin commentators[51] – but from any substance, he then attempted to prove their complete disjunction from real physical or metaphysical essences. Quantity thus became fully extrinsic to form. Hence it was the most superficial dimension of things, easy to separate and abstract, although instrumental for understanding certain aspects of them. Perera illustrated his contention through the example of the mathematical property of the sphere touching the plane in one point only. Whereas this is true for the sphere as a mathematical – or abstract – extension, he argued, it is not true for the sphere as physical extension.[52]

Perera's rejection of the theory of mathematical "medietas" – adopted by Piccolomini from Proclus but interpreted in an Aristotelian sense as abstraction from sensible matter – was effectively carried out through an attack on the Platonic doctrine of reminiscence, essential for the idea that mathematical entities are innate in the human soul. God has given us a human soul that is "tabula nuda," not inscribed with any contents and capable of learning all sciences, Perera argued.[53] For if knowledge is truly acquired through reminiscence, how would one explain the necessity of the senses – which even the Platonists cannot deny? And if the senses are necessary for acquiring knowledge, then it is not possible to maintain the theory of reminiscence.[54]

Perera's radical rejection of the middle position of mathematical entities and his elaboration of the ontology of *indeterminate extension* as inhering in prime matter – independently of any substance – constitute his main contributions to the development of Piccolomini's position. If quantity was disconected from substance, then it had nothing to do with the explanation of causes, not even formal causes. Furthermore, Perera followed in the footsteps of Piccolomini denying mathematical demonstrations the status of a model for demonstration *potissima* and criticizing Euclid I, 32 as a noncausal and nonessential proof. Who cannot see, he argued, that the geometer proves the sum of the angles of a triangle equaling two right ones through a construction of the external angle, which cannot be considered a cause since it is completely accidental to the essential nature of the triangle.[55]

Perera's negation of the innate nature of mathematical entities together with his peculiar understanding of geometrical demonstrations led him to a clearer and more radical distinction between the *certainty* of mathematics, which he explains by its rigorous structure, accepting and even strengthening the arguments to substantiate it, and the *scientificity* of demonstrations *potissimae*, which are the only ones capable of treating real, material, physical substances and heading to true conclusions. Thus, in the order of the nobility of the sciences, mathematics was the most inferior, according to him, both because of the simplicity of its subject matter, and because of the kind of demonstrations it used. Moreover, the rigorous structure of mathematics secures its status as a discipline, but its objects and demonstrations excluded it from the realm of the sciences:

For the mathematician neither considers the essence of quantity, nor treats of its affections as they flow from such essence, nor declares them by the proper causes on account of which they are in quantity, nor makes his demonstrations from proper and per se but from common and accidental predicates. It is my opinion, that the mathematical disciplines are not proper sciences.[56]

No wonder that Perera's conception of the mixed sciences was completely instrumental. When the astronomer thinks of the magnitude, shape, form, and motion of the heavens, he is not preoccupied with true causes that explain the nature of things, Perera claimed, but with some reasonings that can save the appearances. This, according to him, was the nature of eccentrics, epicycles, some irregular motions of celestial bodies, trepidation, etc.[57]

The first chapter of Clavius's "Prolegomena" to his *Commentary on Euclid's Elements*[58] reads as a direct and concise answer to Perera's arguments. First, he argued, the meaning of the word Mathesis in Greek was discipline, or doctrine, for only the arts of quantity used causal and *potissimae* proofs. The Pythagoreans and the Platonists believed that rational souls in some sense contained determined number, and therefore they could acquire these disciplines. Countering Perera's rejection of the theory of reminiscence, Clavius, quoting from the *Meno*, suggested that the process of remembering, was, in fact, a process of disciplining. This was understood by Plato in terms of a Socratic interrogation – which he exemplified in the story of *Meno* – and led to the ascent of the soul toward eternal truths. Clavius expressed a certain ambivalence toward Plato's theory, which presupposed, according to him, the migration of souls from one body to another – a possibility condemned as erroneous and false by Christian doctrine. Nevertheless, he massively relied upon quotations from Plato and from Proclus with which he became acquainted through the edition and interpretation of Barozzi. Following Barozzi too, however, he did not exclude Aristotle from his list of authorities, emphasizing the compatibility of mathematical disciplines with the canons of the *Posterior Analytics* and their rigorous structure – using only preknown principles and proved propositions – which justified their status as doctrine or discipline.[59]

Praising the nobility of the mathematical sciences in the third chapter, Clavius emphasized the certainty of their demonstration, which he contrasted with demonstrations practiced in the other sciences. Whereas those were incapable of actually demonstrating their claims (a fact resulting in endless unresolved disputations and in the plurality of philosophical sects) Euclid's propositions were unambiguous, and the certainty of mathematical demonstrations led to the pure truth.[60] Clavius supported this contention with a quotation from Plato's *Philebus*, where the truth of geometry is connected to supreme goodness.[61]

Moving, in the fourth chapter of the "Prolegomena," to the utility of mathematics, Clavius departed from their utility in administrating and governing the public sphere to their necessity for the study of all other disciplines. First he quoted Proclus showing how mathematics facilitated the passage from physical, sensible, and thus murky reality to the clear, enlightened reality of metaphysics.[62] In Platonic terms, the passage from the sensible to the intelligible world was called ascent to the contemplation of divine things, and for this ascent the mathematical disciplines prepared the soul.[63] Last, Clavius turned to the educational context, quoting both from *Philebus* and from the seventh book of the *Republic*, to stress again the necessity of mathematics as a basis for all other studies, as well as for leadership of political life in a city state.[64]

It is Clavius's strategy, throughout the "Prolegomena," to indicate the basic agreement between Plato and Aristotle on the nobility, utility, and necessity of the mathematical sciences, even though their respective justifications may sometimes be formulated by different vocabularies or anchored in different philosophical world views. This means that the simple dichotomization between Platonists as lovers of mathematics and Aristotelians as ignorant in this realm did not hold true for Jesuits mathematicians,[65] who refused to choose between Platonic and Aristotelian legitimation of their sciences, preferring to recruit both in the process of constructing their professional identity.

The controversy between Perera and Clavius represented in the hidden (but obvious) counterarguments of Clavius's "Prolegomena" testifies to the need of both philosophers and mathematicians to recruit ancient authorities for strengthening their positions. Plato and Aristotle were read and interpreted in accordance with contemporary needs, and their works functioned as imaginary constructions. Rather than a source of inspiration for mathematical innovation, they were used as topics for the symbolic capital contained in their figures.

In response to Piccolomini's and Perera's attempts to introduce a breach between mathematical entities and real, substantial forms, Clavius, relying upon Proclus's judgment, contended that the objects of mathematics, although considered in abstraction from matter, treated things immersed in matter. Adopting Barozzi's thesis of the *medietas* of mathematics he conceptualized mathematical entities as ontologically bridging between the complete abstractness of metaphysical objects and the full sensibility and materiality of physical ones:

> Since the mathematical diciplines deal with things which are considered apart from any sensible matter, although they are immersed in material things, it is clear that they hold a place intermediate between metaphysics and natural science, if we consider their subject matter. For as has been rightly shown by Proclus, the subject of metaphysics is seperated from any matter, both from the point of view of the thing itself, and from the point of view of reason. The subject of physics is truly connected to sensible matter, from the point of view of the thing itself as well as from the point of view of reason. And since the mathematical disciplines consider their subject separately from any matter, even though it [matter] is found in the thing itself, it is established that they are intermediate between two.[66]

The chapter on the division of the mathematical sciences in Clavius's "Prolegomena" aimed at redrawing and broadening the traditional map of knowledge, to fit better the project of Jesuit mathematicians. In restructuring the field Clavius drew upon the argument about mathematical entities, being immersed in material things, although considered in abstraction from it. The Pythagoreans and quite a number of philosophers believed that the mathematical disciplines essentially consisted of four branches, each having a specific subject: arithmetics with discrete numbers, geometry with continous magnitudes, music with numbers in relation to voices, and astronomy with continous magnitudes in relation to the motion of celestial bodies. However, there was another division, anchored in the writings of other ancient authors – especially Geminus and Proclus, according to Barozzi's interpretation. The first considered mathematical entities as purely intellectual and absolutely seperated from matter. But in truth, mathematical entities belonged to things connected with matter.[67] Without explicitly stating this, Clavius's juxtaposition of "intellectibles"versus mathematical entities immersed in material things seems to provide the justification for augmenting the number of mathematical diciplines concerned with physical phenomena to six, namely astrology, perspective, geodesy, canonics (music), suppotatrics (practical arithmetics), and mechanics, each being further divided into more specific branches.

There is a sense in which Clavius's practice of restructuring the map of knowledge can be derived from his (quasi)theoretical conception of mathematical entities as inherent in things immersed in matter. His theoretical arguement, however, was not anchored in any wide philosophical framework. Rather, it was an isolated insight, a reworking and reinterpretation of one passage from Proclus. His real justification came from the practice of mathematics itself. His elaborate descriptions of the various branches of knowledge pertaining to the physical world that have been successfully treated by mathematicians with mathematical methods was his proof. His insistence on the necessity and utility of mathematics for studying all other diciplines, which he supported with quotations from many ancient writers, Christians (St. Peter and St. Augustine) as well as non-Christians (Plato, Aristotle, Proclus, and others), was rheotrical by nature, based on repetition and accumulation of historical evidence, not on scholastic subtleties.[68]

More than anything else it is Clavius's style of arguing in many contexts, measured against what is known about his scientific career, that justifies the interpretation of the "Prolegomena" in terms of a cultural practice more than in terms of a philosophical justifications of the status of mathematics. His text comprised an attempt to restructure the map of knowledge so that more space be allowed for the discourse of mathematicians and thus deepening and stabilizing their authority compared to that of the philosophers. Departing from the Aristotelian premise that a science is defined by its specific subject matter, and by the kind of demonstrations it uses, he interpreted the nature of mathematical entities as a bridge between physical and metaphysical ones, being immersed in sensible matter and considered in abstraction from it. But although a boundary was thus created between natural philosophy and the mathematical sciences on the one hand, and between mathematics and metaphysics on the other hand (a boundary necessary for securing the autonomy of mathematics), Clavius's main strategy was to narrate the successes of mathematics in dealing with problems of the concrete physical world throughout history and in the present and to label anew as many mathematical subdisciplines as he could. Furthermore, although Clavius identified arithmetic and geometry as the two main mathematical fields of knowledge, he abstained from drawing too clear a boundary between *pure* and *applied* mathematics, suppressing the term "mixed sciences," which he had used in his preface to Sacrobosco's *Sphere*.

Compared with Clavius's "Prolegomena," Josephus Blancanus's "Treatise on the Nature of Mathematics"[69] was a much more comprehensive attempt to rebut the attacks of opponents in an articulated, well-informed way, relying upon philosophical and metaphysical thinking of the period. Blancanus's text signals the crystallization of a meta-discourse among Jesuit mathematicians concerning the status of their field of knowledge and its justification.

Blancanus's point of departure, like that of Clavius's, was the subject matter of the mathematical disciplines, which he attempted to distinguish both from that of natural philosophers as well as from that of the metaphysicians. However, the content of his arguments differed substantially from that of his mentor. Recognizing Perera's contention that the subject matter of metaphysical discourse is quantity but rejecting Perera's judgement about the nonessential nature of that quantity and hence his denial of the status of mathematics as science, Blancanus defined a special kind of quantity called "delimited" or "finite" quantity (*quantitas terminata*), which he distinguished from Perera's "indeterminate quantity" (*quantitas indeterminata*). The entities considered by the mathematicians, according to him,

are entirely different from those that the natural scientist and the metaphysician consider in quantity absolutely. . .from this delimitation there result the various figures and numbers which the mathematician defines and of which he demonstrates various theorems.[70]

Drawing upon Clavius's insight that mathematical entities inhere in things immersed in matter, even though they are considered separately from it, but following much more closely Aristotle's own argumentation about the problem, Blancanus used the Aristotelian terminology concerning the abstract matter of mathematical entities which Aristotle had called "intelligible matter":

But this [delimited quantity] is the quantity that is usually called intelligible matter, in contradistinction to sensible matter, which concerns the natural scientist, for the former is seperated by the intellect from the latter and it is perceived by the intellect alone.[71]

However, it was precisely because of the abstract nature of intelligible matter that mathematicians had been attacked for the nonexistence of mathematical entities. Blancanus answered to such a projection in the following terms:

...many [people] object to mathematicians that mathematical entities do not exist, except only by the intellect. However, we should know that even if these mathematical entities do not exist in that perfection, this is merely accidental... Therefore, even though these [perfect mathematical figures] do not exist in the nature of things, since in the mind of the Author of Nature, as well as in the human mind, their ideas do exist as the exact archetypes of all things, indeed, as exact mathematical entities, the mathematician investigates their ideas, which are primarily intended per se, and which are [the] true entities.[72]

To the contention of some philosophers that mathematicians use suppositions and argue in a mere accidental way, Blancanus responded that mathematical definitions were essential – not just nominal – and that only in mathematics is it possible to give definitions in which

the entire nature of the subject is primarily given to us: So it follows that the mathematical sciences proceed from what is better known to us as well as from what is better known by nature...And this is the reason why geometrical demonstrations are always so efficient and possess the highest degree of certitude.[73]

Arguing for the reality of mathematical entities and the essentiality of mathematical definitions constitutes the core of Blancanus's "apologia." The certainty and scientificity of mathematical demonstrations stem naturally from the nature of the objects, which, he emphasized, no writer had ever doubted before Piccolomini, who had very few followers, nobody other, in fact, than Perera, Fonesca, and the Coimbran commentators. The rest of the tradition – Aristotelians and Platonists alike (and here Blancanus was following Clavius's narratological techniques) – all admitted that mathematical proofs were the strongest given in any science.

The implications of Blancanus's insistence on elaborating a sound "metaphysical" foundation for justifying the mathematical disciplines were uncertain from the point of view of the mathematicians' politics of knowledge. No doubt Blancanus's "apologia" was a much stronger response to the philosophers' critique than Clavius's pragmatic arguments. In Jesuit culture it could have meant a real resource for legitimation. However, Blancanus also tied up the fortunes of the mathematicians' project to a philosophical discourse and to an ontology that would soon become obtrusive to major trends developing within the mathematics of his time, especially to the use of indivisbles and infinitesimals in the practice of mathematicians. One immediate effect of his vision was already apparent in his own text: The boundaries imposed in his treatise between mathematics and philosophy and between pure and applied mathematics were much more effectively constructed.

First we are going to discuss pure mathematics, i.e., geometry and arithmetic, which differs in kind from applied mathematics, namely, astronomy, optics, [perspectiva], mechanics and music. Quantity abstracted from sensible matter is usually considered in two ways. For it is considered by the natural scientist and the metaphysicians in itself...but the geometer and the arithmeticians consider [quantity] not absolutely, but insofar as it is delimited...[74]

This may have expressed the need to conform to the general policy of the Jesuit order, already implemented in the *Ratio studiorum*, which used the construction of boundaries as a strategy of control. In any case, the policy endorsed in Blancanus's text differed in nuance from Clavius's philosophically less committed solutions, which enabled both conformity with the policy of the order and maneuvering of the boundaries according to the needs of the mathematicians.

II. GALILEO'S MATHEMATICAL STRATEGIES:
BETWEEN ''MIXED MATHEMATICS'' AND
MATHEMATICAL PHYSICS

Galileo's early work should be read against the background of the debate on the certitude of mathematics and its appropriation by Jesuit mathematicians in the attempt to legitimize their ever broadening interests. The work on centers of gravity (*Theoremata Circa Centrum Gravitatis Solidorum*, 1585–7), the *Bilancetta* (1585–6), and even the project of *De Motu* (1590), which intended to combine Aristotelian dynamics with Archimedian statics, perfectly suited the spirit of the field of knowledge delineated by Jesuit mathematicians.

As mentioned above, writing on centers of gravity was rather popular among mathematicians of the Jesuit Society, and at this stage Galileo was not exceptional in choosing this topic. Neither did Galileo's range of problems and applications exceed the realm of pure geometry. No attempt was made to cope with gravity in a physical sense or even with the effect of weight at different distances from the fulcrum. Rather, Galileo restricted himself to treatment of pure geometrical entities.

Slightly different was the case of *Bilancetta*, which used the theory of the lever and was concerned with its application to various practical problems. Here the objects of discourse were real and material, having weight and varying in volume and even in the medium in which they were immersed. In their different styles of arguing Galileo's first two texts corresponded to the two main directions in which Archimedes's work was received in sixteenth-century Italy: one axiomatic and purely geomatrical, springing from Archimedes's *On the Equilibrium of Planes*, and the other more physical, local, ad-hoc, and stemming from the discussion of *On Floating Bodies*.[75]

Galileo's project of studying motion as it emerged in the premature text of the *De Motu*, however, already transgressed, or even broke through, the boundaries between mathematics and natural philosophy which had only started to become a sensitive issue in the Jesuit politics of knowledge during the same years. Natural motions of terrestrial bodies were certainly not typical subjects of mathematical discourse in the last decade of the sixteenth century. At the same time, expanding the field of application of Archimedean models was not as unknown strategy.

Galileo's project consisted in an attempt to offer a unified explanation of all motions – natural up and down motions, as well as violent projectile ones – in mathematical terms, by using Archimedean models to cope with problems in the sphere of Aristotelian dynamics. Eventually this attempt failed to explain one basic feature of the motions, namely acceleration. Galileo tended to use one Archimedean model – the hydrostatic – to explain the difference in the velocities of bodies moving up and down as a difference between their specific weights in relation to the mediums in which they moved. At the same time he used the balance model to visualize the analogy between rest (equilibrium) and up and down motions and to experiment with the same body along differently inclined planes.

The two models were not compatible, as the one considered specific weights, whereas the other dealt with absolute weights. Moreover, the full effect of weight on motion was not taken into consideration, as Galileo did not include in his balance model the distance of the weight from the center of the system. The velocity, in any case, came out of the theory as directly proportional to the body's (specific) weight. Hence, it could only be uniform. But that was incompatible with the facts known from experience.

Galileo proposed two ways of coping with this difficulty, which in retrospect read more as excuses for a failure rather than as real solutions to his problems. First, he suggested that acceleration was an accidental feature of motion, caused by the levity impressed in the body externally (either by the hand throwing a projectile or a property thought to be kept in the body from previous elevation) and intensifying its motion in its first stages.[76] This explanation pushed him back to treating levity as a substance, not as a state relative to gravity, thus undermining his radical critique against the Aristotelian physics that was one of the main targets of the his text. But the second way of treating the supposed "accident" of acceleration was even worse, because it put in doubt the rationale of his whole enterprise. The direct proportion between the velocity of a body and its weight could not be observed by the one doing the experiment, Galileo claimed.[77]

In admitting his failure to identify the mathematical results expected from his theory in experience, Galileo, in fact, invoked the main objection to the scientificity of mathematics which had first been used by Piccolomini and entered the circles of Jesuit philosophers mainly through Perera. In the context of the complicated field of positions concerning the status of mathematics, and the arguments adopted by the different participants, Galileo's admittance of the difficulty of mathematical reasoning to capture processes pertaining to material objects could be read as a declaration of defeat.

Against this background, the project of his *Mecaniche*,[78] seems as a return to the boundaries of mathematics accepted within the original discourse of the "mixed sciences," neglecting the problem of natural motion and free fall and concentrating on a problem in the traditional realm of mechanics, namely, the force necessary to elevate a weight along planes of different inclinations. This force was now differentiated into two components: the weight of the body and the distance from the center of the system, expressed the body's inclination to fall. The inclination to fall – conceptually differentiated from *gravitas* by the term moment (*momento*) – was measured by setting two limits: maximum momento on the perpendicular plane and minimum on the horizontal plane. Thus, the law of the moment stated that moments on the inclined plane and the perpendicular plane related to each other as the perpendicular line is to the inclined line. Moment, then, was constructed as a purely geometrical entity.[79]

Following Galluzzi, I would like to emphasize that the *Mecaniche* embodies a different type of project than the *De Motu*: Unlike *De Motu*, Galileo's *Mecaniche* did not present a quest for a unified explanation of all motions. Rather, it was an attempt to ground the study of motion and build it upon mechanical foundations, rooted in the traditions of the "mixed sciences," which acquired their renewed legitimacy in the environment of Jesuit mathematicians.[80] This means that the question of velocity remained on the margins of the discussion, coming up either as an addition of *momento* to weight or as an effect of a force that was constant. Velocity, then, if discussed at all, could only be conceived as uniform velocity. Galileo's use of the term *momento*, however, points to the possibility of translating it into dynamical terms. Thus translated, the law of the moment would entail that in determinate periods of time the body would pass distances on the inclined plane that relate to the distances on the perpendicular like the inclined line is to the perpendicular. Still, because the velocity was conceived as a product of a constant force, the prominent fact of acceleration could not be integrated into this framework. That, probably, was the origin of the dead end that forced Galileo to go beyond his original association of velocity with constant forces and beyond mechanical motions toward a different type of mathematical analysis of natural motion.[81]

Galileo's split from the "mixed sciences" and his conscious attempt to create an alternative science of mechanics – which brought about his growing estrangement from the discourse of Jesuit mathematicians – will be illustrated, in this paper, by a detailed analysis of his treatment of local motion in some passages of the *Dialogue* (1632).[82] Traditionally these passages have been read as an expression of the miraculous birth of modern science in Galileo's text, a reading that used to emphasize the break between Galileo's early and mature science, and obviously between the old and the new science. Recent readings, however, criticizing, developing, and documenting suggestions already made in the late nineteenth century have tended to stress Galileo's embeddedment in Aristotelian science.[83] Whereas nineteenth-century historians such as P. Duhem discovered the continuity between Galileo's work and that of the fourteenth-century calculators, for example, contemporary historians have stressed his anchorage in the work of Jesuit philosophers and mathematicians.[84] Continuing this last line of argument, my reading of selected passages of Galileo's *Dialogue* aims to represent, and interpret in a more contextual way, suggestions first made by Galluzzi in his *Momento* and then developed by Renn and others.[85]

In this reading, the attempt to broaden the discourse on mechanical motion by applying some of its concepts and techniques to the study of natural motion eventually led Galileo to a theory of acceleration in which weight was neglected as a cause and velocity moved into the center of discussion. But velocity was now thought of as the sum total of degrees of velocity, and it was represented geometrically by the infinity of parallel lines making up the surface of a geometrical figure. Thus, Galileo's project may be seen as an Aristotelian–Archimedean synthesis that violated the basic rules of both discourses. A reading of passages from the *Dialogue* in terms of this "problematique" is the focus of the second part of the paper.

As is well known, the first day of the *Dialogue* opens with a discussion of Aristotle's "general discourse upon universal first principles" (18), which leads, rather quickly, to a critical examination of his fundamental distinctions between two kinds of natural motions – along straight and circular lines – and also between two kinds of motions along straight lines: natural up and down motions on the one hand and violent motion on the other. Salviati raises many objections against this discourse, complaining that it seemed as if "he [Aristotle] was pulling cards of his sleeve, and trying to accommodate the architecture to the building instead of modeling the building after the precepts of architecture" (16) and that "whenever defects are seen in the foundations, it is reasonable to doubt everything else that is built upon them"(18). Suggesting that "basic principles and fundamentals must be secure, firm, and well established, so that one may build confidently upon them" (ibid.), he raises the reader's expectations for a foundational discourse built upon alternative "basic principles with sounder architectural precepts" (ibid.). What follows, however, does not really meet such expectations.

Every body constituted in a state of rest but *naturally* capable of motion will move when set at liberty only if it has a *natural* tendency towards some particular place; for if it were indifferent to all places it would remain at rest, having no more *cause* to move one way than another. Having such a tendency, it *naturally* follows that in its motion it will be continually accelerating. (20, my emphasis).

This passage opens a long digression from the critique of Aristotle that constitutes the major part of the first day to a modified, but still Aristotelian, discussion of accelerated motion, a digression in which Galileo's alternative is condensely presented for the first time. The passage consists of two statements: 1) The cause of motion is a natural inclination toward a place. 2) Natural motion is accelerated. In another famous passage in the *Dialogue*, Galileo reveals to the attentive reader that invocation of "nature" in scientific practice is always an indication for lack of explanation:

...*we do not really understand what principle* or what force it is that *moves* stones downward, any more than we understand what moves them upward after they leave the thrower's hand, or what moves the moon around. We have merely...assigned to the first the more specific and definite *name* "gravity"...and as the *cause* of infinite other *motions* we give *"Nature."* (235)

In the light of this confession it looks as if the creation of an alternative mathematical science of motion involves resignation of the effort to suggest *causal explanation* either to motion or to acceleration. Instead, already at this early stage Salviati offers a conceptual analysis of the continuum that he applies to accelerated motion:

Beginning with the slowest motion, it [a moving body] will never acquire any degree of speed without first having passed through all the gradations of lesser speed – or should I say of greater slowness? For, leaving a state of rest, which is the infinite degree of slowness, there is no way whatever for it to enter a definite degree of speed before having entered into a lesser, and another still less before that. It seems much more reasonable for it to pass first through those degrees nearest to that from which it set out, and from this to those farther on. But the degree from which the movable body began to move was that of most extreme slowness, that it to say from rest. (21)

Salviati suggests that acceleration involves a continuous increase or decrease of degrees of speed (or slowness). Sagredo, however, demands an explanation to the obvious paradox (finally formulated by Salviati) such a description entails: How can a body pass infinite degrees of slowness (or speed) in finite time? Salviati tries to "solve" this difficulty by saying that "the movable body does pass through the said gradations, but without pausing in any of them" (20). This "solution" conceals a lifetime of reflection on problems of infinity, the continuum and indivisibles that Galileo could not settle. Used here as a strategy of excluding further discussion, Salviati, however, takes up the opportunity to make a very condense presentation of the core of Galilean innovations in the field of the new science of motion, stemming from his new conceptualization of impetus and from the choice to focus on acceleration as the central phenomenon of the analysis of motion.

This choice leads to the privileging of a few limited areas of research of local motion, especially the falling of a stone, namely, free fall, and the motion of a cannon ball, namely, projectile motion. Through a short discussion touching upon these subjects Salviati attempts to engage his hearers' and interlocutors' interest and consent by claiming the following:

(1) That free fall and projectile motion are accelerated or deccelerated. He acquires quick consent for this claim by translating his concepts of "acceleration" and "degrees of speed" (and slowness) into the well-known but poorly defined traditional terms of impetus and velocity: "Tell me," he asks Sagredo, "if you have any trouble granting that the ball, in descending is always gaining greater impetus and velocity." The obvious answer to which is: "I am quite confident of that" (22).

(2) That the impetus acquired in fall is enough to lift the falling body up to the same height from which it started falling. This is a much more problematic assumption, for which Galileo acquired a real proof only after publication of the *Two New Sciences*, but which he used as a postulate there. Here the claim is justified by pointing out experiments that could confirm it.

From these two statements Salviati concludes that two equal bodies falling from the same height, one in free fall and another on an inclined plane, will arrive with the same "impetus" – which we have

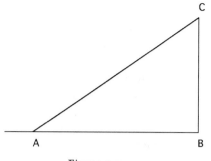

Figure 3.1.

seen him treating as synonymous with "velocity":

So will you not put an end to your difficulty by conceding that two *equal* movable bodies, descending by different lines and without any impediment, will have acquired *equal impetus* whenever their approaches to the center are *equal*? (23, my emphasis)

Sagredo's difficulty in understanding the claim leads to Salviati's explication and to the use of a geometrical figure (see Figure 3.1) to represent free fall by the perpendicular and descent along the inclined plane by the oblique. The geometrical representation, serving here as a tool for clarifying the meaning of concepts,[86] allows Salviati to try and disperse the ambiguity with which the term "impetus" has traditionally been stricken, and which still pervades Galileo's texts:

I ask you to concede that the impetus of that which descends by the plane CA, upon arriving at point A, would be equal to the impetus acquired by the other at point B after falling along the perpendicular CB. (23)

If before impetus and velocity were interchangeable, here equal impetuses seem to unambiguously mean that the two equal bodies acquire the same degree of speed upon arrival. Sagredo, however, responds by first conceding the conclusion, and then, bringing back the ambiguity: "In fact," he says, "they have both advanced *equally* toward the center" (Ibid.). *Equally* in what sense?

At first it seems obvious that the claim about the equal impetus acquired at the point of arrival by the free-falling body and the body on the inclined plane entails that they both move with the *same velocity*. Salviati, however, takes this opportunity to point out a fundamental incompatibility between the two concepts of velocity – one deriving from Aristotle's *Physics* and the other from Archimedes,[87] applied, however, to *accelerated motions*. According to the first definition of equal velocity – reiterated by Simplicio as equal spaces passed in equal times (24) – the body on the perpendicular moves *faster* than that on the inclined plane. According to the second definition – the equal proportion between spaces traversed and times elapsed – their velocities are *equal*. Salviati's explanation of this situation tends to calm down Sagredo's initially strong doubts. Still, he demands a real proof of the last conclusion, that the times of fall of both bodies relate to each other as the distances they traverse, which Salviati promises to supply from the mouth of his academic friend. Indeed, this had been Galileo's key theorem in his work on inclined planes. It is to be found in *De Motu*[88] and has been labeled by some scholars as the length–time theorem.

Four statements concerning acceleration have been established by Salviati up to this point:

1) That free-fall motion and motion on the inclined plane are accelerated.
2) That the impetus acquired in accelerated motion starting from the same point suffices to lift the bodies to the same height.
3) That the impetus or degree of speed acquired at the point of arrival is equal for both bodies.
4) That the velocity of both bodies is equal according to an Archimedean concept of velocity.

Nevertheless, the claim for the continuity of acceleration made immediately afterwards goes back again to the Aristotelian concept of velocity, relying on the growing slowness of motion as the body moves on lesser and lesser inclined planes, until it comes to rest on the horizon. Yet, this is combined with an Archimedean argument according to which: the degree of velocity acquired at a given point of the inclined plane is equal to the velocity of the body falling along the perpendicular to its point of intersection with a parallel to the horizon through the given point of the inclined plane. (28)

The strong tensions characteristic of Galileo's discourse emerge even in this cryptic presentation of some of his major discoveries. The recognition (pointed out above[89]) of a gap in our knowledge concerning the cause of local motion and its acceleration seems to lead to the attempt to understand acceleration first on a phenomenological level: by a conceptual analysis of the continuum and the geometrical representation of continuous acceleration and by comparing different accelerated motions. This presentation, however, raises two fundamental problems. First, while Saliviati's argument is unfolding, its origins in the old mechanics understood as a "mixed science" crop up with greater clarity. They finally become evident in the following passage:

Let us remember that we agreed that bodies descending along the perpendicular CB and the incline CA were found to have acquired equal degrees of velocity at the point B and A. Now, proceeding from there, I believe you will have no difficulty in granting that upon another plane less steep than AC – for example, AD – the motion of the descending body would be still *slower* than along the plane AC. Hence one cannot doubt the possibility of planes so little elevated above the horizontal AB that the ball may take any amount of time to reach the point A. If it moved along the plane BA, an infinite time would not suffice, and the motion is retarded according as the slope is diminished. (27)

In Galileo's *Mecaniche*, the speed of motion depends upon the body's weight and on the distance from the center of the system, called the *moment* of weight. The same bodies, therefore, moving on lesser and lesser inclined planes, acquire lesser and lesser *momenti*. The way to measure this motion is by assigning maximum *moment* to the perpendicular and minimum to the horizontal. Therefore, the speed on the less inclined planes is considered smaller.

Salviati's analysis in the *Dialogue* suppresses the traditional mechanical considerations in terms of weight and *moments* of weight. It leaves the notion of *velocity* connected with this discourse, in spite of its basic incompatibility with the definition of *velocity* as the proportion of times elapsed and traversed distances, which is used in the attempt to convince us that the *velocity* of a falling body and that of a body moving on the inclined plane are equal. This example clearly shows that the decomposition of velocity into infinitesimal degrees presented at the beginning of the text and the substitution of the traditional Aristotelian definition of velocity with the Archimedean definition cannot in fact be conceptually truncated from the traditional discourse of mechanics, in which weight played a major role.

The same uncertainty is evident in Salviati's *formulation* of the comparison between two *equal* bodies, one free falling and the other moving on an inclined plane. Speaking about two *equal* bodies means that *weight* is considered relevant to the discussion. At the same time the main thrust of the argument points to the horizon of the constancy of "impetus" – that is, the increase or decrease of the *degree* of velocity – and the equal velocity of the two bodies according to the Archimedean definition. If the *degrees of velocity* acquired by two bodies in free fall and on the incline are always the same, and if their *velocities* are also the same, what is the relevance of their *equal* weight?

The second fundamental problem raised by Salviati's presentation concerns the decomposition of velocity into infinite degrees of velocity and its relation to the Archimedean definition of velocity as a proportion between times elapsed and distances traversed. In fact, decomposition of velocity means that the proportion is not between lines, but rather between infinite sets of points. Galileo, however, lacked the philosophical justification to deal with such proportions. Furthermore, the switch between velocity decomposed into infinitesimal degrees for conceptual analysis and the application of the Archimedean proportion has the effect of blurring the distinction between *degrees of velocity* and *velocity* altogether. Salviati's conclusion from the following two statements – that the motion downwards is accelerated and that the impetus gained suffices to lift the bodies to the same height – reads as follows:

Two equal movable bodies, descending by different lines and without any impediment, will have acquired *equal impetus* whenever their approaches to the center are *equal*.

However, the next two references to the same issue – "In fact, they [the free falling body and the one moving on the inclined plane] have both advanced *equally* toward the center" (23) and "the speeds of the bodies falling by the perpendicular and by the incline are *equal*" (24) – remain ambiguous. Such ambiguity bordering on the obscure, culminates in Salviati's summary, which reiterates both that the motion is *slower* as the inclination above the horizon gets smaller and simultaneously that:

We may likewise suppose that the degree of velocity acquired at a given point of the inclined plane is *equal* to the velocity of the body falling along the perpendicular to its point of intersection with a parallel to the horizon through the given point of the inclined plane. (28)

Simplicio's failure to understand this opaque formulation brings about Sagredo's last attempt at clarification:

Whence no doubt can remain that the ball [namely, a cannon ball projected upwards which starts to lose its velocity and continues with slower and slower motion until it stops] before reaching the point of rest, passes through all the greater and greater gradations of slowness, and consequently through that one at which it would not traverse the distance of one inch in a thousand years. Such being the case, as it certainly is, it should not seem improbable to you, Simplicio, that the same ball, in returning downward, *recovers the velocity* of its motion by returning through those same degrees of slowness through which it passed going up. (31)

At first glance it seems that Sagredo's explanation is based upon a complete nonsequitur. How is the continuous nature of acceleration connected to the need of the body to "recover" its velocity? In fact, however, this passage, coming from the mouth of Sagredo, testifies to the model of accelerated motion lurking in Galileo's mind, in spite of its being erased from the text. In this model acceleration is still considered as the effect of an external force that the body loses while going up (in the *De Motu* hydrostatic model it is called levity, in analogy to the loss of weight in a medium of smaller specific gravity) and that it regains while going down. In contradistinction to Salviati's arguments, in Sagredo's explanation the abstract mathematical considerations are substituted with a picture easy to imagine and clearly present to the senses, which appeals to Simplicio's discursive habits and squeezes his long-awaited consent: "This argument convinces me much more than the previous mathematical subtleties" (ibid.).

The second and last discussion of free fall in the *Dialogue* taking place on the second day exhibits a very similar structure. This time the digression is made in response to Simplicio's quotation from a recent book written by a Jesuit mathematician,[90] who tried to calculate the velocity of a cannon ball falling from the orbit of the Moon to the center of the Earth. Salviati's quest to understand the rules underlying this calculation is met with the answer that the falling ball continues to move at uniform velocity equal to the motion along the Moon's orbit. Salviati's and Sagredo's sarcastic dismissal of this answer is followed by the presentation of alternative principles for analyzing the fall, and by an alternative calculation, including an explanation of the method by which it could be arrived at.

"The movement of descending bodies is not uniform," claims Salviati, "but…starting from rest they are continually accelerated" (221). There follows a straightforward statement – missing in the previous presentation – of the law of fall, that is the *exact mathematical ratio* of acceleration: "The acceleration of straight motion in heavy bodies proceeds according to the old numbers beginning from one" (222). This acceleration is then *explicitly* said to be equal to all falling bodies, without any connection to their weight: "for a ball of one, ten, a hundred, or a thousand pounds will all cover the same hundred yards in the same time" (223).

To understand the principles of the cannon ball's fall from the orbit of the Moon, Salviati quotes one more theorem and some "conjectures." The theorem he refers to is the "double distance rule,"[91] which establishes the relationship between accelerated and uniform motions. In accordance with this rule the falling cannon ball would acquire a degree of speed equal to the velocity of a body uniformly traversing double the space at the same time (255). This means that the cannon ball whose motion was calculated by the Jesuit in fact moves much faster than he had claimed in his book.

The "conjectures" to which Salviati then refers consist of observations of pendulums, conclusions from the work on inclined planes, a geometrical demonstration of the double distance rule based on medieval techniques of proving the mean speed theorem, and the representation of velocities by the infinity of lines making up the surfaces of a triangle and a parallelogram. All these provide the broad framework in which Salviati wishes to anchor his mathematical conclusions concerning the cannon ball and its velocity.

The example of a pendulum leads Sagredo to report of an impression he formulated to himself as a result of observation: "I have sometimes thought that the ascending arc [of a ball of lead suspended by a thread and removed from the perpendicular] would be equal to the descending one" (226). From this observation Salviati concludes that the impetus in both cases – descent and ascent – is the same:

"...The impetus acquired in the descending arc, in which the motion is natural, is able by itself to drive the same ball upward by a forced motion through as much space in the ascending arc" (ibid.). But whereas impetus, in this case, is expressed in terms of the equal space traversed by the body going down and up, immediately afterwards impetus is expressed in terms of velocity: "...Just as in the descending arc the velocity goes on increasing to the lowest point of the perpendicular, so in the ascending arc it keeps diminishing all the way to the highest point" (ibid.). Moreover, the increase and decrease of velocity is also said to be in the same ratio, and thus: "...The degrees of speed at points equally distant from the lowest point are equal to each other" (227).

The pendulum serves Salviati as a model for another kind of accelerated motion: that of a cannon ball imagined to be descending down to the center of the Earth and ascending to the other side through a hole perforated at the center. The model of the pendulum applied to the cannon ball yields the further conclusion that because the velocity upon ascent diminishes in the same ratio as it increased along descent, and because the spaces passed by the ball on its motion down and on its motion up are in the same ratio, so is the time of descent.

This also leads to the understanding of accelerated motion in terms of an equivalent uniform motion: "it certainly seems reasonable that if it were always to move with this *highest degree of speed*, it would pass through both these distances in an equal amount of time." Salviati thus formulates the "double distance rule," stating that a falling body passing from accelerated motion to uniform motion would traverse double the space while continuing with the highest degree of speed for an equal time. The purpose of all these steps becomes clear as Salviati at last moves to his final conclusion: "Therefore all the space passed through with all the degrees of speed, increasing and decreasing...must be equal to the space passed in as many of the maximum speeds as number one half the total of the increasing and decreasing ones" (ibid.).

But Salviati does not stop here. Rather, he declares the degrees of speeds to be "indeterminate" infinitesimals: "the increases in the accelerated motion being continuous, one cannot divide the ever-increasing degrees of speed into any determinate number; changing from moment to moment, they are always infinite" (228) and

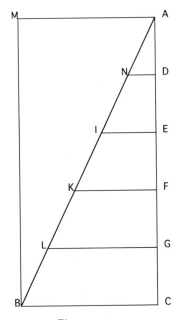

Figure 3.2.

suggests a powerful geometrical analogy through which they can be imagined. Representing the time continuum of the fall by the perpendicular of a rectangle triangle, he imagines the degrees of speed as all the lines parallel to the base (see Figure 3.2):

Therefore, to represent the infinite degrees of speed...there must be understood to be infinite lines, always shorter and shorter...this infinity of lines is ultimately represented here by the *surface* of the triangle... (229).

However, the representation serves as more than just illustration. By completing the triangle into a parallelogram the surface of which represents uniform degrees of velocities equal to the maximum degree achieved by the falling body, he proceeds to drawing the comparison between accelerated and uniform motion through a kind of geometrical demonstration, although he avoids assigning to it the status of a proof:

...While the whole surface of the triangle was the sum total of all the speeds with which such a distance was traversed in the time AC, so the parallelogram becomes the total and aggregate of just as many degrees of speed but with each one of them equal to the maximum BC. This total of speeds is *double* that of the total of the increasing speeds in the triangle, just as the parallelogram is *double* the triangle. And therefore if the falling body makes use of the accelerated degrees of speed conforming to the triangle ABC and has passed over a certain space in a certain time, it is indeed reasonable and probable that by making use of the uniform velocities corresponding to the parallelogram it would pass with uniform motion during the same time through double the space which it passed with the accelerated motion. (229)

A careful reading of the two digressions on local motion in the first and second day of the *Dialogue* reveals some of the conceptual difficulties symptomatic of Galileo's project, which were, at the same time, also problems in the politics of knowledge. As usual, it is Sagredo who dares – in the first digression – to pose a challenge which signals these difficulties: "A great part of your difficulty consists in accepting this very rapid passage of the movable body through the *infinite* gradations of slowness antecedent to the velocity acquired during the *given* time..." (22) Salviati's "solution" to this problem is then given in terms of the "infinite instants" contained in every "single instant of time": "The movable body does pass through the said gradations, but without pausing in any of them. So that even if the passage requires but a *single instant of time*, still, since a very *small time* contains *infinite* instants, we shall not lack a sufficiency of them to assign to each its own part of the infinite degrees of slowness, *though the time be as short as you please.*" (Ibid., my emphasis, R.F.) Another aspect of the same difficulty is raised by Salviati himself on the second day, and is immediately silenced by recognizing the impossibility of dividing continuous motion into discrete units: "For the increases in the accelerated motion being *continuous*, one cannot divide the ever-increasing degrees of speed into any *determinate number*, changing from moment to moment, they are always infinite." (228) This, however, does not deter him from imagining velocity – in the very next passage – in terms of the sum total of *all the lines* making up a *geometrical figure*: "And just as BC was the maximum of all the infinitude in the triangle, representing the highest degree of speed acquired by the moving body in its accelerated motion, while the whole surface of the triangle was the sum total of all the speeds with which such a distance was traversed in the time AC, so the parallelogram becomes the total and aggregate of just as many degrees of speed but with each one of them equal to the maximum BC." (229)

Two features characterize, then, Galileo's analysis of the continuous nature of acceleration in both digressions: first, decomposition of continuous magnitudes in terms of discrete units is attempted, in spite of the serious critique of such attempts by a long tradition, streching back to the Greeks. Galileo offered no philosophical justification for this daring analysis. Second, in both digressions Galileo made no distinction between physical and mathematical arguments. In fact, he conflated both spheres of knowledge in a seemingly nonproblematic way. Salviati's cryptic "excuses" for the conceptual difficulties: that the body passes all the gradations of velocity and slowness without pausing in any of them, and that the "infinitesimals" of time, velocity, and mathematical magnitudes are not "determinate" numbers could not – in fact – rid the text from the anxiety of paradoxes, and remained enormously problematical for his science. At the same time Galileo exposed himself to the blame of transgressions of two kinds of boundaries: between the sciences of continuous magnitudes and discrete number within mathematical discourse on the one hand, and between physical and mathematical science on the other. These boundaries, however, were invested with disciplinary interests, and became a sensitive area of dispute among philosophers and mathematicians after the debate on mathematical certitude. Thus, the conceptual analysis of the continuum, and its application to a mathematical science of motion were heavily involved in the contemporary politics of knowledge.

But it was precisely the analysis of the continuum which served as a necessary assumption for comparing two accelerated motions of two bodies, one free falling along the perpendicular, the other rolling along an inclined plane, and thus for realizing the *constant ratio* of acceleration in all naturally accelerated motions. Granted that their grades of velocity increase and decrease continuously and that their distances relate to each other as the times of fall (the "lengh-time rule"), Salviati demands consent for his conclusion that their velocities are *equal*. Again it is Sagredo who points out the difficulty such an inference purports. And again it is Salviati who offers a solution by pointing out a contradiction. "The speeds of the bodies falling by the perpendicular and by the incline are equal. Yet this proposition is quite true, just as it is also true that the body moves more swiftly

along the perpendicular than along the incline." (24) Salviati expla
this gap by the difference between two definitions of velocitie:
narrow, Aristotelian definition stipulating that bodies moving with
equal velocities traverse equal spaces in equal times; and its broad-
ened and Archimedean version, according to which equal velocities
of two moving bodies entails *equal proportion* of distances to times
in accelerated motion. Modern scholarship, however, has shown that
these two definitions are in fact incompatible in the case of accelerated motions, and that Galileo was not unaware of the difficulty involved in applying the Archimedean definition to the phenomenon of
acceleration. Thus, Galileo's identification in nature of two accelerated motions with different distances and different times – which he
interpreted mathematically in terms of the "double distance rule" –
actually involved an uneasy co-existence and unbearable tensions between the *Archimedean* and the *Aristotelian* approaches that guided
his investigations, and had to be transgressed in order to give birth
to his mathematical–physical discourse.

All the tensions involved in the analysis of the continuum on the
one hand, and in the Aristotelian–Archimedean synthesis when applied to the investigation of naturally accelerated motions reappear
in any attempt to understand the status and function of "degree of
velocity" in its relation to "impetus" and "speed." As we have seen,
these terms are often used by Galileo interchangeably. Thus, Salviati
asks his interlocutors to grant that "the *impetus* of that which descends by the plane CA upon arriving at the point A would be *equal*
to the *impetus* acquired by the other at point B after falling along
the perpendicular" (23); at the same time both bodies "have as much
impetus (that is, the same *degree of velocity*)" (24); and also, the "*impetus* of each should be equally sufficient to carry it back to the same
height," (23) and the "*speeds* of the bodies falling by the perpendicular and by the incline are equal." (24)

The terminological confusion between "degrees of velocity," "impetus" and "speed" has been subject to endless debates among historians culminating in "historiographical traditions" around this
problem. The Duhem–Clagett tradition stresses Galileo's anchorage
in fourteenth-century development of "impetus physics" by Buridan, and the development of tools for the mathematical representation of degrees of intensity of qualities (among them velocity) by
Oresme; Koyré and his followers tend to emphasize the "deductive"

character of Galileo's discourse stemming from a new mathematical metaphysics which guided the minds of the great scientists of the seventeenth century, and especially that of Galileo; and the Drake–Wisan–Naylor tradition built a lot upon the results of experimental work used by Galileo to corroborate his mathematical deductions, thus characterizing his method as hypothetico-deductive in different senses. More convincing to me, however, is Galluzzi's account in *Momento*. Galluzzi anchors Galileo's inconsistencies in the inner development of his science from its earliest beginnings in the theorems on centers of gravity, through *On Motion*, the *Mechanics*, the *Discourse on Floating Bodies*, the unpublished manuscripts of 1600–1609, and up to the *Dialogue* and the *Two New Sciences*. In very broad terms (and therefore unfaithful to the subtlety of his discussion), Galluzzi's thesis is that around 1610 a break occurred in the very heart of Galileo's project, which had aimed at a causal and mathematical explanation of all motions in terms of weight, force, and velocity and at a synthesis of statics and dynamics into a new science of mechanics. The concept of *moment*, according to Galluzzi, in fact allowed for a mediation between a geometrical science of weight (statics) stemming from Archimedean sources, and the more dynamical approach of the Aristotelian *Mechanical Questions*, allowing for the interchageability and compensation of weight by motion. Galileo's ambition was to apply a combination of these approaches to the study of natural motion by modeling his dynamical concept of "moments of velocity" upon the static concept of "moments of weight," and by an attempt to understand acceleration in free fall and projectile motion in terms of a series of increasing and decreasing "moments of velocity" reduced to a series of moments of uniform velocity. Within this broad framework "moments of velocity" were never divorced from "moments of weight," since weight and motion always compensate for each other. On the other hand, the justification for the constancy of acceleration expressed in the proportion between distances and the square of times was only to be found in the Merton rule, and thus in the Buridan–Oresme tradition of impetus theory, which did not aspire for causal explanation of natural motions, and was unrelated to considerations of weight or gravity of bodies. The strongest proof for Galluzzi's thesis can be found in one fragment of the famous Ms. 72, where Galileo identifies between "moment" and "grade of velocity" (speaking about "momentum seu gradus velocitatis"). After 1609, however, Galileo apparently gave up upon his broadest and most ambitious project, and developed his analysis of accelerated motion around the decomposition of "velocity" into "degrees of velocity" independently of weight, and around a concept of velocity as the sum total of "infinitesimal" (instantaneous) velocities. Thus, the concept of "moment" was more or less suppressed in his published texts. Instead, he developed his "length-time" theorem already proved for uniform velocity in the *De Motu*, and applied it to accelerated motion combined with the decomposition of velocity into its degrees.

In the light of Galluzzi's thesis it is now possible to read Galileo's confusion of "degrees of velocity," "impetus," and "speed" as a result of the split characterizing his discourse after he had to give up his ambition to find new foundations for a science of all motions based on the combination between the Archimedean statical approach, the Aristotelian tradition of the *Mechanical Questions* and the Oxfordian–Parisian development of impetus physics. Thus, "degrees of velocity" were never wholly divorced from "moments of velocity," closely connected to "moments of weight." Velocity, or speed remained undifferentiated from its degrees in any explicit way, although such differentiation is implied in many of the texts. Likewise, "impetus" remained immersed in ambiguities, sometimes conflated with *momento* and thus expressing some kind of "energy" accumulated along the fall and sufficient to elevate the body to the same height from which it started the fall, other times expressing velocity translated from dynamic to kinematic terms.

The *Dialogue Concerning the Two Chief World Systems* was written when Galileo's investigations of motion began to look like a science without foundations, a project whose coherence was torn by an inner split between proper physical considerations of weight in relation to velocity which survived only in the form of a subtext and were mainly confined to the application of results achieved in the framework of his old *Mechanics*, (especially the length-time rule), and a conceptual-mathematical analysis of accelerated motion and its geometrical representation on the other hand. Excluding either a philosophical justification of the analysis of the continuum, as well as causal explanations of motion in terms of weight or force, it also conflated different types of discourses, and transgressed the boundaries between mathematical and physical science. Thus, when the

Dialogue was finally being written, Galileo badly needed some kind of justification both for the inner coherence of his project as well as for his peculiar position within the cultural field of mathematical and philosophical discourse.

III. MATHEMATICAL ENTITES AND THE POLITICS OF KNOWLEDGE

A clue to Galileo's reflective perspective on his own project may be found in a short exchange among Simplicio, Salviati, and Sagredo, which takes place on the second day of the *Dialogue*: "I have frequently studied your manner of arguing," says Simplicio, "which gives me the impression that you lean toward Plato's opinion that *nostrum scire sit quoddam reminisci.*" Salviati's response to this challenge is complex. Neither explicitly affirming, nor else denying Simplicio's observation, he chooses to remain indirect about his debt to Plato, stressing instead his commitment to deeds, which do not, however, exclude words:

> How I feel about Plato's opinion I can indicate to you by means of words and also by deeds. In my previous arguments I have more than once explained myself with deeds. I shall pursue the same method in the matter at hand, which may then serve as an example, making it easier for you to comprehend my ideas about the acquisition of knowledge if there is time for them some other day, and if Sagredo will not be annoyed by our making such a digression.

Sagredo, of course, graciously expresses his intense interest in probing into any discourse that may provide an alternative to the one practiced in the schools:

> Rather, I shall be much obliged. For I remember that when I was studying logic, I never was able to convince myself that Aristotle's method of demonstration, so much preached, was very powerful. (190–1)

Traditionally, such passages as the one quoted above have been interpreted in terms of the epistemological revolution that necessarily accompanied the new "scientific" – mainly mathematical – contents suggested by Galileo. Some philosophers and historians of sceince have cherished the idea that it was Platonic (mathematical) epistemology, or even ontology, which actually enabled – not just accompanied – the emergence of mathematical physics. The old–new Platonic epistemology, they have claimed, substituted for the Aristotelian – logical, but nonmathematical – epistemology, accepted, for many centuries as the adequate framework for practicing Aristotelian physics.

A close reading of some more passages in the *Dialogue*, however, may suggest a different view. In conformity with the spirit of Salviati's words, such a view will accentuate practice, in speechacts rather than epistemology, as the basic clue to understanding the process by which Galileo's dispersed insights crystallized into a project that seemed coherent at the time. Such reading will also point out the futility of any attempt to reduce Galileo's options into the dichotomy of a Platonic or Aristotelian discourse. Again, Salviati's reluctance to commit himself to any given epistemology may provide a hint in this direction. This does not mean that Platonism and Aristotelianism had no ideological role in Galileo's politics of knowledge. It means, however, that the labels must be deconstructed, in order to understand their function as one cultural practice among others used by many sixteenth- and seventeenth-century intellectuals, among them Galileo.

The *Dialogue Concerning the Two Chief World Systems* offers relatively easy access to the map of options that constituted the cultural field in which Galileo operated and where he attempted to create for himself a recognized, legitimate, and well-specified position as a mathematical philosopher. In the remainder of this paper an attempt is made to interpret Galileo's position and the way he differentiated it from others' by reconstructing the network of debates among mathematicians and philosophers lurking behind the text or on its surface. Galileo's position, so the argument goes, can only be understood in the context of the positions he is aligning himself with or differentiating himself from. It was determined at the same time by considerations stemming from the inner problematics of his science (analyzed in the previous section) as well as by the dynamics of the field of positions in which he was trying to play.

Galileo needed to justify a discourse that conceptualized velocity as the sum total of an infinity of degrees of speeds and stated the irrelevance of weight for their mathematical determination. Nevertheless, it still left open queries about the role of weight in relation to natural motion and acceleration, which were suppressed but not totally excluded from the text. The preliminary exchange among Simplicio, Salviati, and Sagredo prepares the stage for the differentiation of an intersubjective field out of which Galileo's position emerges, and whose initial conditions are: a vague association with a Socratic mode of inquiry, an understanding of discourse as a set of practices, including speech ("deeds" and "words," in Galileo's terminology), and a vision of some alternative to the Aristotelian method of logical demonstration in natural philosophy.

Two kinds of arguments immediately followed Salviati's general comments on the "acquisition of knowledge" (191). The first argument was a purely geometrical refutation of objections to the motion of the Earth, making use of the geometrical notion of the "angle of contact" (the angle between the tangent and the curve). Indirectly and nonexplicitly, it implied a position on the two major conceptual problems discussed in the previous section: the translation of a (noncommonsensical) mathematical construct (angle of contact parallel to degrees of velocity) into a claim on the conditions of possibility of physical motion on the one hand and a very problematic assumption about the relation between two incommensurables, finite and "infinite" quantity, on the other. The second reflection on the acquisition of knowledge concerned the "point of contact between two spheres" and suggested a direct, explicit, and radical position on the nature of mathematical entities, their relation to physical objects, and the consequences for the justification of a mathematical knowledge of nature.

The "angle of contact" was used by Galileo in the context of a counterargument to the objection of Ptolematic astronomers to the diurnal motion of the Earth, whose whirling was claimed to cause stones, animals, and other heavy bodies on its surface to be ejected as a result of the impetus created by this kind of movement. Salviati contends that such projection is a physical nonpossibility, and he offers a subtle geometrical reasoning to support this claim. First he proves that the proportion between the tangent and the secant grows infinitely toward the point of contact. Then he argues that if a physical body were to be separated from the surface of the Earth it would be subject to two opposing motions: a projection along the tangent outside the circumference of the Earth's orbit and the tendency of the body to fall toward the center of the Earth along the secant. The velocity along the tangent, he concludes, would necessarily be

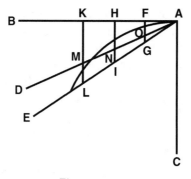

Figure 3.3.

smaller than the velocity along the secant. This conclusion is based upon the analysis of velocity in terms of moments of velocity, represented by the parallel lines lying between the two sides of an angle: "the degrees of speed infinitely diminished... correspond to the parallels included between the two straight lines meeting in an angle" (200–201). Since the angle of contact is always smaller than the angle between the tangent and the secant (see Figure 3.3), it is clear that the parallel lines between its two sides (corresponding to the degrees of velocity) are smaller than those between the tangent and the secant. Therefore, the motion along the tangent will never prevail over the motion along the secant, for, according to Salviati: "To have projection occur, it is required that the impetus along the tangent prevail over the tendency along the secant" (196).

In fact, Salviati's argument is far more obscure that the summary presented here. I believe, however, that this summary is not distorting and will prove useful for the initiation of my discussion. It is Galileo's use of a geometrical notion – the angle of contact as smaller than any other angle – and its translation into physical reality – the condition of possibility of motion – rather than the details of an argument that captures my attention right now, and it is the emergence of a position relative to other positions on the same question that constitutes the core of this story, parallel, and in connection, with the internal story about the problematic structure of Galileo's mathematical–philosophical discourse.

Between 1579 and 1589, the rich knot of controversies associated with a Euclidean proposition concerning the angle of contact began to take place among mathematicians all over Europe and became a "topos" around which logical, philological, methodological, and mathematical issues of fundamental importance to the organization of the map of knowledge were articulated.[92] A long list of participants in these debates, which spread widely up to the end of the seventeenth century and beyond, is quoted by L. Maieru. Among them are some of the greatest early modern mathematicians, such as Galilei, Borelli, Wallis, and Jacob Bernoulli.

The core of the polemics sprang from the work of J. Peletier, one of the earliest critics of Euclid in the modern era. Peletier was the first to point out the conceptual incompatibility between Euclid III.16, which implied that a geometrical magnitude – the angle of contact – should be considered "minimal quantity" – a discrete – and the two major rules that had been guiding the Euclidean project almost uninterruptedly since antiquity: namely, the principle of the continuous nature of geometrical magnitudes, implied by X, 1, and the principle of homogeneity invoked by the definition of ratio and proportion in the fifth book (V.3).[93] If indeed, Peletier argued, the angle of contact is smaller than any acute rectilinear angle, it cannot be multiplied and exceed an acute rectilinear one. In other words, there cannot be a ratio between the angle of contact and a rectilinear angle. In response to such difficulty, Peletier suggested – in two early texts from 1557 and 1563 – excluding the angle of contact from the realm of mathematical discourse. He then elaborated his critique in a public response – labeled an *Apology* (1579) – to Clavius's defenses of Euclid, which he first included in the first edition of his *Commentary* (1574) and repeated in the next two editions of 1586 and 1589. In the same spirit Peletier also argued that Euclid's proofs by superposition (I.4, for example) should be discarded, since there was something "mechanical" about moving triangles that did not fit the "nobility" of geometry.

Peletier's strategies testify to the crystallization of one position among sixteenth-century mathematicians that tended to privilege the norms behind the traditional boundaries implied by the Euclidean project: between discrete and continuous entities as exclusive objects of arithmetic and geometry, respectively, as well as between the objects of mathematical discourse as separate from matter and motion on the one hand and those of natural philosophy on the other hand. The application of the theory of proportion and the Eudoxian method of exhaustion enabled relations between the different kinds of mathematical entities to be established, and allowed for the application of mathematical methods to physical phenomena under specific conditions, but created many constraints against blurring the boundaries. Peletier's insistence that the angle of contact not be considered a quantity was a strategy of exclusion considered by him as an act of defense of necessary boundaries, even against Euclid himself, in a place where his own writings seemed to violate the norm of his own discourse. It was easier to argue for exclusion, however, than to actually practice it while still doing Euclidean geometry. This becomes very obvious when one looks into Peletier's attempt to provide a universal proof of the problem of constructing a curvilinear angle equal to a rectilinear one and is forced to add the angle of contact to another angle, treating it, then, as a quantity.[94]

The conflict between declared norms of the Euclidean discourse on the one hand and the need to solve geometrical problems on the other, which arose in the context of Peletier's critique of Euclid, should be remembered when Clavius's position in the polemic is being reconstructed and interpreted. As in most of his other polemics,[95] here too Clavius took a middle position, trying to defend both Euclid's proposition (III, 16) as well as the accepted boundary between continuous and discrete quantities, while still preserving the status of mathematical entities as separate from matter and motion. Thus, against Peletier he argued that the angle of contact was a quantity. However, he also contended that it was not a "minimal quantity," since it could be divided endlessly by a curve of the same type, so that there were, in fact, infinite angles of contact greater than a fixed one, and they could be compared to each other by superposition.[96] Still, even while defending Euclid's technique of superposition, Clavius was careful not to mix motion with geometrical entities. While speaking about superposition, he claimed, Euclid was referring to an operation of the mind, not to any mechanical moving of triangles or angles.[97]

No doubt Clavius was motivated by pragmatic reasons in his defense of Euclid. He rightly pointed out that because in geometry propositions depended on each other, exclusion of any Euclidean proposition meant that many others had to be excluded too. Peletier's own difficulties in discarding the angle of contact was a living demonstration to the legitimacy of Clavius's concerns, remembering that in his prominent position as the leading mathematician of the age he had far greater stake in practicing geometry than did Peletier. Nonetheless, Clavius's enormous caution in defending the boundaries of the mathematical sciences, and between its various disciplines, should not be interpreted solely from the mathematical point of view, for it also reflected the politics of knowledge peculiar to the Society of Jesus.

The complexity of the Jesuit attitude toward the boundaries of the mathematical sciences has already been pointed out in the first section of this paper. In their attempts to gain a higher status than had traditionally been assigned to mathematicians within the context of medieval and renaissance universities, Jesuit mathematicians were concerned with securing the autonomy of their field of knowledge. The quest for autonomy, however, often involved destabilization of the old boundaries.

New developments within the body of knowledge, such as the integration of algebra and of Archimedean materials, seemed to be leading toward the reconceptualization of the boundaries between pure and mixed mathematics and between mathematics and natural philosophy. It also began to destabilize the boundary, within pure mathematics, between the fields treating discrete and continuous quantities. The analysis of the continuum, however, had a long and controversial history connected to deep philosophical and theological issues.[98] No wonder that some of the philosophers were suspicious of those innovations and insisted on the subordination of the "mixed sciences" to the higher parts of speculative philosophy and on the inadequacy of mathematics to solve problems in physics. Clavius's position, which had a deep impact on the official policy of the order was marked by the conviction that the traditional boundaries should be reproduced and by the acceptance of a kind of compromise between philosophers and mathematicians about their division of labor, in spite of many transgressions on both sides.[99]

It should be stressed, however, that the implementation of the boundaries of mathematical discourse was just one aspect of the Jesuits' broader attempt to structure post-Tridentine culture in accordance with their theological and educational orientation. Clavius's tendency to reproduce the traditional boundaries – even though they were not always maintained in practice – conformed with the order's policy, applied in other spheres of knowledge, which combined an openness toward innovation with sophisticated means of control.[100]

Galileo's refutation of the argument about projection of bodies from the surface of the Earth and his interpretation of the "angle of contact" as minimal quantity thus pushed him to take a position against Clavius and many of the mathematicians who followed him, not only against philosophers or theologians. Simplicio's comment, however, that the argument may be very subtle, but that "these mathematical subtleties do very well in the abstract, but they do not work out when applied to sensible and physical matters," develops into a far more explicit discussion of the application of mathematical truths to material reality, provoked by the contention that: "mathematicians may prove well enough in theory that *sphaera tangit planum in puncto*, a preoposition similar to the one at hand; but when it comes to matter things happen otherwise"(203).

What follows is a surprisingly poor discussion of the relationship between mathematical abstractions and the concrete reality of physical, material bodies, which contrasts enormously with the rich philosophical, methodological, mathematical, and even theological and philological debates around the same topic in the sixteenth and seventeenth century, relying upon a long tradition since Greek antiquity.[101] Salviati's arguments proceed in three steps: First of all, he claimed, doubting that a *material sphere* is a *sphere* amounts to stating a contradiction, similar in kind to the saying that a sphere is not a sphere. This first step relies on the most basic agreement among human beings about the use of terms, necessary to maintain a community of speakers. Reverting, then, to the definition of the sphere as that form upon whose surface all points are equally distant from the center, Salviati provides the geometrical proof of this proposition – two spheres touch each other in one point – showing that to assume that two spheres touch each other at more than one point means assuming points on the surface that are not equally distant from the center, which is absurd. Simplicio easily accepts the proof, but rightly clings to his original problematics, which concerns the *application* of abstract concepts, not a proof in the abstract. Salviati, then, on the edge of impatience, argues last by analogy:

It would be novel indeed if computations and ratios made in abstract numbers should not thereafter correspond to concrete gold and silver coins and merchandise. Do you know what does happen, Simplicio? Just as the computer who wants his calculations to deal with sugar, silk, and wool must discount the boxes, bales, and other packings, so the mathematical scientist (filosofo geometra), when he wants to recognize in the concrete the effects which he has proved in the abstract, must deduct the material hindrances, and if he is able to do so, I assure you that things are in no less agreement than arithmetical computations. The errors, then, lie not in the abstractness or concreteness, not in geometry or physics, but in a calculator who does not know how to make a true accounting. (207–8)

The task of the philosopher–geometrician is analogous to that of the merchant in the market, Salviati argues. Both are calculators, the first of physical effects in nature and the last of goods in the market.

At first reading it is indeed hard to accept that Salviati's discussion of the most fundamental feature of Galileo's project is so dull, simplistic, and unconvincing, especially in comparison with the polemical background against which it was originally written. A second reading is therefore required. This second reading will focus on two aspects: Following the allusions dispersed along the text, which were certainly clear to contemporaries, but much less so to historians, I shall point out the political implications of Galileo's choice to structure his self-justification in this particular form. I shall then point out how his self-justification functioned to fill a void (unresolved conceptual problems and inner split) within his own scientific discourse.

A closer look at the text reveals that it begins by delineating two positions regarding the role of mathematics in the investigation of nature. The first is represented by Sagredo, who concludes from Salviati's argument on the angle of contact that: "It must be admitted that trying to deal with physical problems without geometry is attempting the impossible" (203). Simplicio, then, is presented as a philosopher who chooses a middle way: He is not "one of those Peripatetics who discourage their disciples from the study of mathematics," but somebody who still agrees with Aristotle "that he [Plato] plunged into geometry too deeply and became too fascinated by it" (ibid.).

Contrary to common belief Simplicio is far from being represented as a simpleton. In fact, he expresses a well-differentiated position that casts doubt upon the role of mathematics in the investigation of nature, without, however, being too blunt about it. Simplicio is said to differ from those philosophers who "discourage their disciples from the study of mathematics as a thing that disturbs the reason and renders it less fit for contemplation" (ibid.). The accusation cannot but echo Clavius's words in his *De Mathematicis* (one of three treatises written in the 1580s as part of the preparatory work for the *Ratio Studiorum*), where he commented that: "It will also contribute much...if the teachers of philosophy abstained from those questions which do not help in the understanding of natural things and very much detract from the authority of the mathematical disciplines in the eyes of the students."[102] One Jesuit notorious for becoming the target of Clavius's complaints was Benedictus Perera, from whom Simplicio seems to be distinguished at first. However, two of Simplicio's arguments inevitably bring Perera to the mind of the reader. First, he sounds skeptical about Salviati's Platonic orientation invoked by his understanding knowledge in terms of Plato's theory of reminiscence (190–1). Second, he quotes a great Peripatetic philosopher who accused Archimedes of assuming something instead of proving it (204). Both complaints resonate with Perera's interpretation of a passage from Plato's *Republic* VII, where he had written that "mathematicians dream about quantity, and in treating their demonstrations proceed not scientifically, but from certain suppositions."[103]

The dense web of allusions lingering over Simplicio's positioning, as it is crafted by Galileo, suggests the need to probe further into the cultural field in which the text was embedded. Simplicio's attitude toward the role of mathematics, which is affirmative in a sense, but insists on the clear boundaries of the mathematical disciplines and their limitations in dealing with sensible matter clearly alludes to Perera. Galileo's choice to focus the discussion on *"sphaera tangit planum in puncto"* also follows Perera, who had selected the most commonplace topos in a long and continuous tradition of writing – originating from the Platonic texts – on the objects of mathematical discourse.[104] Are mathematical spheres real? What is the difference between a mathematical sphere and a bronze sphere? What is the significance of the ontological status of mathematical objects for the kind of principles, arguments, and proofs produced by mathematicians? These were recurring questions raised and answered in different ways by the ongoing debate within a tradition, which nevertheless shared one basic assumption: Platonists, Aristotelians, and even Archimedeans believed in the uniqueness of mathematical objects and their difference from physical ones. This assumption was also reproduced in the Jesuit *Ratio Studiorum* of 1599, which explicitly mentioned the difference between a physical and a mathematical point as a subject of studies to be inculcated during the second year of the philosophical cycle in Jesuit universities.[105]

The rich intertextuality of Galileo's *Dialogue* enables him to differentiate various positions among Jesuit mathematicians and philosophers on that question and allowed for their (tacit) representation. Thus, Perera was represented by Simplicio. Clavius's middle position on the angle of contact – considering it a quantity, but not infinitesimal – may also be said to exist through Galileo's presentation of a debate in which Clavius was one of the most outstanding participators. Scheiner was represented by the *Disquisitiones Mathematicae*, quoted by Simplicio in the second day. What is missing from Galileo's text, however, is Blancanus's justification of the role of mathematics which he attempted to ground philosophically in his *Treatise on the Nature of Mathematics*.[106]

To understand this omission one should look at the exact configuration of problems in the midst of which Galileo chooses to locate his argument on mathematics and physics.

Salviati has just presented his refutation of the anti-Copernican claim concerning the projection of objects from the Earth's surface as a result of its speedy whirling. Galileo modeled the situation of a body on the surface of a moving Earth upon his analysis of a stone attached to a stick moving in a circle around a center. According to this model the impetus of the circular motion is impressed on the body which leaves the notch and starts moving along the tangent from the point of separation. The weight of the body is then the cause of a downward motion in the direction of the center. However, the tendency downwards – along the secant – always prevails over the motion along the tangent, because the velocity at the beginning of the latter motion is extremely slow: "For the distance traveled being so extremely small at the beginning of its seperation (because of the infinite acuteness of the angle of contact), any tendency that would draw it back toward the center of the wheel, however small, would suffice to hold it on the circumference." As mentioned before, the geometrical argument consists of showing that the angle of contact is always smaller than any acute rectilinear angle, and therefore the motion along the tangent will never prevail over the motion downwards.

Many of the characteristics of Galileo's discourse, pointed out above, crop up in this analysis. At first, both motions are described in terms of their causes: The tangential one is perceived as caused by the impetus of the whirling; the downward motion by the weight of the body. Immediately afterwards, however, the discussion shifts into another conceptual framework, and the motion is analyzed in terms of velocity and moments of velocity, which have nothing to do with weight and cannot offer a *causal* explanation of fall and acceleration. Within such a framework there is no way to contend that the velocity of the motion along the tangent might in some circumstances prevail: "Saying this is false; not from any deficiency in logic or physics or metaphysics, but merely in geometry." But the framework chosen by Galileo for this discussion does open the door to an objection coming from the mouth of Sagredo, which points out a major difficulty. The objection relates to the weight of the body, which has been presented as the cause of the downward motion at the beginning of the argument. Just as speed diminishes infinitely, so may weight be susceptible to the same analysis, in the case of very light bodies on the surface of the Earth.

Sagredo's objection sets the stage for Salviati's final clarification of the situation of a stone on the surface of the Earth, in terms of the diminishing *degrees of velocity* toward the point of rest and the diminution of speed as the weight of the body is diminished infinitely. As against this "twofold diminution ad infinitum" (200) he analyzes the diminishing degrees of speed of the body moving along the tangent, which are represented as those parts of the parallels lying between the rectilinear and the curve of the circle (i.e., between the sides of the angle of contact):

They grow always less than these parallels of which they are parts, and diminish in an increasing ratio as they approach the point of contact...Thus the shortness of such lines is reduced until it far surpasses what is needed to make the projectile, however, light, return to (or rather be kept on) the circumference. (201)

Sagredo, however, remains unhappy with this final clarification. Targeting his last objection at the weakest link in Salviati's argument – his complete ignorance of the mathematical relation between weight and velocity – he raises his last question. It is possible to imagine, he contends, that the weight of the body diminishes in a greater proportion that the speeds. Wouldn't the speed along the tangent suffice then to carry the body away? Salviati's response to this last challenge is threefold. First, he denies, but in a rather ambivalent way, that weight is really relevant for his discussion: "I have been taking it as true that the speeds of naturally falling bodies follow the proportions of their weights out of regard to Simplicio and Aristotle, who declares this in many places as an evident proposition." This ambivalence is rather incompatible with his very clear position regarding irrelevance of weight for analyzing free fall, which we have seen him stating in another passage of the dialogue. Yet, he claims, even if weight is relevant, it certainly is the case that the proportion of the speed is much less than that of the weights, which he can easily show by experiment. The third reaction, however, is the most interesting. For, he contends, even if the speed would decrease in a much greater ratio, even the lightest materials would not be projected:

Now weight never does diminish clear to its last term, for then the moving body would be weightless; but the space of return for the projectile to the circumference does reduce to its ultimate smallness, which happens when the moving body rests upon the circumference at that very point of contact, so that no space whatever is required for its return. Therefore let the tendency to downward motion be as small as you please, yet it will always be more than enough to get the moving body back to the circumference from which it is distant by the minimum distance, which is none at all. (203)

Salviati's arguments, I claim, exhibit in an exemplary form the split between two incompatible discourses that is visible all along the *Dialogue*: one rooted in mechanics as a "mixed science" but unable to provide the mathematical conceptualization of accelerated motion and the other phenomenological and mathematical but unable to integrate the physical cause of acceleration into its framework. As has been pointed out before, Salviati's preliminary analysis is performed within the conceptual framework of the old mechanics, in which the motion along the tangent is caused by some force impressed upon the body – the impetus. Downward motion is caused by the weight of the body, and the speed of the motion is measured in relation to the distance traversed by the body at equal times.

Posed in these terms, however, the solution is not clear, for Salviati cannot make any mathematical claim about the relationship between the impetus and the weight. Salviati, then, switches to his analysis of accelerated motion in terms of degrees of velocity, and he succeeds in offering a brilliant solution, unable, however, to incorporate weight into this explanation although it had been the point of departure of the whole argument.

It is exactly at this point that the discussion is interrupted by Sagredo's remark, claiming that "it must be admitted that trying to deal with physical problems without geometry is attempting the impossible" (203). Exactly at the moment when the failure to incorporate weight into the physical–mathematical construction of quantity is most transparent, Salviati's radical position about the complete reducibility of physical entities to mathematical ones is inserted, and Blancanus's intricate deliberations about mathematical objects and physical objects are erased from the text.

Now, in a way, Blancanus's arguments about mathematical entities, although cast in a different language and drawing upon the tradition, carried much of the same message as Galileo's. By arguing that "if there were given a material sphere and plane which were perfect and remained so, they would touch one another in a single point" he expressed his belief in the ideal nature of mathematical entities and in the exact correspondence between these ideal forms and material conditions in the physical world. Clavius, when arguing that mathematical entities are separated from matter although they are immersed in it, and Blancanus, in stressing the materiality of mathematical entities and the essentiality of mathematical definition, were likewise expressing the same vision. However, this vision functioned very differently in Galileo's discourse and in the Jesuits'. To cover up the gap between his physical causal discourse and his mathematical analysis, Galileo attempted to deny any boundary between mathematics and physics in the *Dialogue* and to erase the traditional discourse on mathematical entities. Comparing the mathematical philosopher to the calculator, he posed the ideal of a man of deeds who opted for practical solutions and who knew how to construct ideal realities that would also be true in the world of matter. In contradistinction Clavius and Blancanus attempted to use the discourse of mathematical entities for legitimating their discipline within a cultural project whose boundaries they were forced to accept and reproduce, even while sometimes committing their own transgressions.

NOTES

1 G. Galilei, *Two New Sciences*, translated with introduction by S. Drake, Madison, Wisconsin: University of Wisconsin Press, 1974 . Page numbers of original texts will be inserted within parentheses.
2 See, for example: T. Settle, "An Experiment in the History of Science," *Science*, 1961, 133:19–23; S. Drake, *Galileo at Work: His Scientific Biography*, Chicago & London: Dover Publications, 1978; D. K. Hill, "Galileo's Work on 116v: A New Analysis," *Isis*, 1986, 77:283–91; idem, "Dissecting Trajectories: Galileo's Early Experiments on Projectile Motion and the Law of Fall," *Isis*, 1988, 79:646–68.
3 A. E. Burtt, *Metaphysical Foundations of Modern Physical Science*, revised ed. London: Humanities Press, 1949; A. Koyré, *Etudes Galiléennes*, Paris: Hermann, 1939; idem, "Galileo and Plato," reprinted in P. P. Wiener and A. Noland, eds., *Roots of Scientific Thought*, New York: Basic Books, 1957, 147–75; P. Galluzzi, "Il Platonismo del tardo cinquecento e la filosofia di Galileo," in P. Zambelli, ed., *Ricerche sulla Cultura dell'Italia Moderna*, Bari: Laterza, 1973, 39–79; M. De Caro, "Galileo's Mathematical Platonism," in J. Czermak, ed., *Philosophie der Mathematik*, Wien: Hölder-Pichler-Tempsky, 1993.
4 The major writer in this tradition is: W. A. Wallace, *Galileo and His Sources: The Heritage of the Collegio Romano in Galileo's Science*, Princeton, NJ: Princeton University Press, 1984.
5 See, for example: W. L. Wisan, "The New Science of Motion: A Study of Galileo's De Motu Locali," *Archive for the History of Exact Sciences*, 1974, 13:103–306; idem, "Galileo's Scientific Method: A Reexamination," in R. E. Butts and J. C. Pitt, eds., *New Perspectives on Galileo*, Boston: Kluwer, 1978; idem, "Galileo and the Process of Scientific Creation," *Isis*, 1984, 75:269–86; R. H. Naylor, "Galileo and the Problem of Free Fall," *British Journal for the History of Science*, 1974, 7:105–34; idem, "Galileo's Theory of Motion: Processes of Conceptual Change in the Period 1604–1610," *Annals of Science*, 1977, 34:365–92; idem, "Galileo's Theory of Projectile Motion," *Isis*, 1980, 71:550–70 and others by the same author.
6 See, for example: Koyré's *Etudes* for classical texts; P. Galluzzi, *Momento. Studi Galileiani*, Rome: Allneo and Bizzarri, 1979; W. A. Wallace, *Prelude to Galileo: Essays on Medieval and Sixteenth-Century Sources of Galileo's Thought*, Boston: Kluwer, 1981; E. Sylla, "Galileo and the Oxford *Calculatores*: Analytical Languages and the Mean-Speed Theorem for Accelerated Motion," in W. A. Wallace, ed., *Reinterpreting Galileo*, Washington: Catholic University of America Press, 1986; E. W. Strong, *Procedures and Metaphysics. A study in the Philosophy and*

Mathematical-Physical Science in the Sixteenth and Seventeenth Centuries, Hildesheim, Germany: Georgolms, 1966 (1st ed., Berkeley, 1936); S. Drake and I. E. Drabkin, *Mechanics in Sixteenth-Century Italy*, Madison, Milwaukee, & London: University of Wisconsin Press, 1969; P. L. Rose, *The Italian Renaissance of Mathematics. Studies on Humanists and Mathematicians from Petrarch to Galileo*, Geneve: Droz, 1975; M. Biagioli, "The Social Status of Italian Mathematicians 1450–1600," *History of Science*, 1989, 27:41–95.

7 J. Pitt, *Galileo, Human Knowledge, and the Book of Nature: Method Replaces Metaphysics*, Dordrecht: Kluwer, 1992.

8 J. H. Randall, *The School of Padua and the Emergence of Modern Science*, Padua: Antenore, 1961; D. W. Edwards, "Randall on the Development of Scientific Method in the School of Padua – a Continuing Reappraisal," in J. P. Anton, ed., *Naturalism and Historical Understanding. Essays on the Philosophy of J. H. Randall, Jr.*, Albany: State University of New York Press, 1967, 42–5; C. B. Schmitt, "Experience and Experiment: A Comparison of Zabarella's View with Galileo's in De Motu," *Studies in the Renaissance*, 1969, XVI:80–138; W. A. Wallace, *Galileo and His Sources . . .* (1984a).

9 The first historian who drew attention to the reflections of sixteenth-century humanists, mathematicians, and philosophers on the status of mathematics was N. Gilbert in his *Concepts of Method in the Renaissance*, New York: State University of New York Press, 1960, 86–91. Other historians who followed Gilbert's original suggestions were: G. C. Giacobbe, "Il commentarium de certitudine mathematicarum disciplinarum di Alessandro Piccolomini," *Physis*, 1972, XIV, 2:162–93; idem, "Francesco Barozzi e la Quaestio de certitudine mathematicarum," *Physis*, 1972, XIV, 4:357–74; idem, "La riflessione metamatematica di Pietro Catena, *Physis*, 1973, XV, 2:178–96; idem, "Epigoni nel seicento della 'Quaestio de certitudine mathematicarum': Giuseppe Biancani," *Physis*, 1976, XVIII, 1:5–40; idem, "Un gesuita progressista nella 'Quaestio de certitudine mathematicarum' rinascimentale: Benito Pereyra," *Physis*, 1977, XIX, 51–86; idem, *Alle Radici della Rivoluzione Scientifica Rinascimentale: Le Opere di Pietro Catena Sui Rapporti tra Matematica e Logica*, Pisa: Domus Galileana, 1981; A. Carugo, "Giuseppe Moleto: Mathematics and the Aristotelian Theory of Science at Padua in the Second Half of the 16th-Century," in L. Olivieri, ed., *Aristotelismo Veneto e Scienza Moderna*, Padua, 1983, 509–17; idem, "L'insegnamento della matematica all'universita di Padova prima e dopo Galileo," in *Storia della Cultura Veneta: Nen Pozza*, 1984, 151–99. The most comprehensive treatment, however, upon which I have heavily drawn in A. De Pace, *Le Matematiche e il Mondo: Ricerche su*

un *Dibattito in Italia nella Seconda Metà del Cinquecento*, Milano: Francoangeli, 1993.

10 Some slected references relevant for studying the institutionalization of the Jesuit mathematical program are: F. de Dainville, *L'Education des Jésuites XVIe–XVIIIe Siecles*, Paris: Editions de Minuit, 1978; G. Cosentino, "L'insegnamento delle matematiche nei collegi Gesuitici nell'Italia settentrionale: Nota introduttiva," *Physis*, 1971, 13:205–17; idem, "Le matematiche nella 'Ratio studiorum' della Compagnia di Gesu," *Miscellanea Storica Ligure*, 1970, 2/2:171–213; W. A. Wallace, *Galileo and His Sources*... (1984a); P. Dear, *Mersenne and the Learning of the Schools*, Ithaca, NY: Cornell University Press, 1988; idem, *Discipline & Experience: The Mathematical Way in the Scientific Revolution*, Chicago, IL: University of Chicago Press, 1995; U. Baldini, *Legem Impone Subactis: Studi su Filosofia e Scienza dei Gesuiti in Italia 1540–1632*, Rome: Bulzoni, 1992; R. Gatto, *Tra Scienza e Immaginazione: Le Matematiche Presso il Collegio Gesuitico Napoletano (1552–1670 ca.)*, Firenze: Olschki, 1994; S. J. Harris, "Les chaires de mathematiques," in L. Giard, ed., *Les Jesuites a la Renaissance*, Paris: Presses Universitaires de France, 1995, 239–161; R. Feldhay, *Galileo and the Church: Political Inquisition or Critical Dialogue?*, Cambridge, NY: Cambridge University Press, 1995.

11 A. Piccolomini, In *Mechanicas Quaestiones Aristotelis... Eiusdem Commentarium de Certitudine Mathematicarum Disciplinarum*, Rome, 1547. On Piccolomini, see R. Suter, "The Scientific Work of Allesandro [sic] Piccolomini," *Isis*, 1969, 60:210–22.

12 *De certitudine...*, c. 69r, quoted by De Pace, 22, n. 3:

Mathematicas demonstrationes, in primo esse ordine certitudinis... testatur Averroes 2. Metaph. com. 16. super illis verbis Aristotelis, videlicet: "Certitudo mathematica non in omnibus expetenda." Quam quidem Averrois authoritatem, omnes fere latini, quos ego viderim, veluti ex antiquioribus, Divus Albertus, Divus Thomas, Marsilius, et Egidius; ex recentioribus vero, Zimarra, Suessanus, Acciaiolus, et plerique alii; si quando in eam inciderunt, uno ore, quasi alius alium sequens, ita interpretati sunt, ut propterea Averroes illud asserat, quia Mathematicus ex notioribus et nobis et naturae demonstrat, quippe qui vel solus, vel maxime, demonstratione illa, quam potissimam appellant, utatur, qua scilicet simul, et quod effectus sit, et cur sit liquido innotescit.

13 R. Sorabji, *Aristotle Transformed. The Ancient Commentators and Their Influence*, Ithaca, NY: Cornell University Press, 1990.

14 *De certitudine...*, cc. 69r–69v, quoted by De Pace, 26, n. 14:

Ego vero, quamvis in adolescentia mea, tantorum virorum authoritate ductus, in eorum opinionem ... descenderim, deinceps tamen,

dum mathematicas disciplinas assidue versans, intimius pertrac-
tavi, tantum abest, ut in scientia diutius permanserim, ut non solum
demonstrationes Geometrarum, reliquorumque mathematicorum,
non esse illas potissimas, sed ne vix ad illas accedere, existimaverim.
Verum enimvero, hanc meam sententiam, quamvis mihi constan-
tissime probaretur, ac quampluribus rationibus fulciretur,in me ipso
tamen, ne quid, quasi παρ'αδοξον a me dictum videretur, eousque
comprimendam duxi, donec Proclum ipsum, hoc idem sentire
cognoscens, maxima animi laetitia affectus, testem tam locupletem
nactus, id ipsum dehinc clara voce frequenter asserui.

15 Ibid, c. 95r, De Pace, 39, n. 42:

res ipsae mathematicae, de quibus fiunt demonstrationes, nec omnino in subiecto, sensibiles sunt, nec penitus ab ipso liberatae, sed in
ipsa phantasia reperiuntur figurae illae mathematicae, habita tamen
occasione a quantitatibus in materia sensibili repertis... Materia
ergo harum scientiarum, erit quantum ipsum, hoc modo, ut ita
dicam, phantasiatum, et id a plerisque, quamvis non satis proprie,
materia intelligibilis nuncupatur.

16 Ibid., c. 106v, De Pace, 43: "...quantitas vero est omnium sensatissi-
morum sensatissimum."

17 A. Piccolomini, *Parte Prima della Filosofia Naturale...*, Venice, 1576,
cc. 17v–18r, De Pace, 42.

18 *De certitudine...*, c. 107r, De Pace, 43:

...res illae... abstrahibiles erunt maxime, et iccirco faciles cognitu,
certae, ac manifestae. Quantitas igitur, quia... nulli materiae lima-
tatae adducitur, iccirco nihil habet arcani, seque totam nobis expli-
cat et manifestat.

19 Ibid., 102r, De Pace, 30, nn. 24, 25:

Quod autem [demonstrationes Mathematicae] non invenianturm
etiam in hac causa formali, arguo primum. Omnis demonstrationis
potissimae, est medium diffinitio, vel passionis, vel subiecti. Demonstrationum mathematicarum, non est tale medium ... Praeterea,
omnis demonstratio potissima, medium habet, quod est causa
immediata, ipsius effectus, idest passionis. Sed nulla mathematica reperitur talis... si Theorema...32. primi Elem. perpendatur, cogn-
oscetur quod angulus extrinsecus, qui ponitur ibi medium, ad decla-
randam passionem, quae est habere tres, de triangulo, non est diffinitio, neque trianguli (ut patet) nec passionis. Tam enim triangulus,
quam habere tres, non indiget in sui diffinitione angulo extrinseco.
Quo non existente, etiam est triangulus, et habet tres. Idem patebit
in omnibus fere aliis Euclidis Theorematibus et Problematibus.

20 *Parte Prima della Filosofia Naturale*, cc. 24v–25r, De Pace, 56:

... l'astrologo...quantonque consideri il Cielo essere sferico, o la
terra rotonda; non per questo ha egli dibisogno di conoscere la vera
natura, et sostanza loro, anzi solamente da' siti, figure, et aspetti

che si veggano in Cielo, argomenta esser di tal figura...Per la qual
cosa si puo concludere, che se ben la scientia delle cose naturali,
convien molto volte con altra scientia, in trattar d'alcun soggetto, o
in dimostrare alcuna conclusione, nondimeno in questo da tutti gli
altri è differente il filosofo naturale, che non separando mai i con-
cetti delle forme da quei delle proprie materie loro, ambedue queste
nature abbraccia come rispettiva l'una dell'altra; ciè la materia, et
la forme: le quali sono i due principji, et le cause intrinseche delle
cose naturali.

21 M.Tafuri, *Venezia e il Rinascimento*, Torino: Einaudi, 1985.

22 F. Barozzi, *Opusculum, in quo una Oratio, et duae Quaestiones: altera
de certitudine, et altera de medietate Mathematicarum continentur*,
Padua, 1560. On Barozzi see: P. L. Rose, "A Venetian Patron and Mathematician of the Sixteenth Century: Francesco Barozzi (1537–1604)," in
Studi Veneziani, New Series, 1977, I:119–77.

23 Quoted by De Pace, p. 126, n. 18.

24 Transcribed with an introduction by De Pace, *Le Matematiche...*, 339–
430.

25 *Procli Diadochi Lycii Philosophi Platonic iac Mathematici probatis-
simi in Primum Euclidis Elementorum librum Commentariorum...
Libri IIII. A Francisco Barocio Patritio Veneto summa opera, cura, ac
diligentia cunctis mendis expurgati*, Padua: 1560.

26 *Opusculum*, c. 38v, De Pace, 129.

27 Ibid., 38r, De Pace, 131.

28 Ibid., c. 20v, De Pace, 139, n. 52:

in unaquaque scientia tum iuxta subiectam materiam, tum etiam
iuxta scientiae illius methodum certitudinem requirendam esse,
ut doctrinae methodus subiectae materiae correspondeat. Si igitur
subiectam Mathematicarum materiam maximum in se se habere
certitudinem fatemur, cur demonstrationes etiam mathematicas cer-
tissimas esse non dicemus?

29 A. Favaro, "La libreria di Galileo Galilei descritta ed illustrata," in *Bul-
letino di Bibliografia e di Storia delle Scienze Matematiche e Fisiche*,
1886, XIX:219–93.

30 P. Catena, *Universa loca in logicam Aristotelis in mathematicas disciplinas*, Venice, 1556; idem, *Super loca mathematica contenta in Topicis
et Elenchis Aristotelis*, Venice, 1561; idem, *Oratio pro Idea Methodi*,
Padua, 1563. On Catena see: P. L. Rose, "Professors of Mathematics at
Padua University 1521–1588," *Physis*, 1975, XVII:302–33.

31 *Universa loca*, 70–71, De Pace, 191:

natura enim et per sensum notum est quoniam calidum est, ideo
non est opus praecipere mente et suppositione aliqua intellectuali,
et quadam scrupolosa indagine suum quia de calido, quando calidum

est subiectum, seu datum vel genus; hoc casu, quando est notum quia est dati, despicitur praecognoscere mentis indagatione de dato, an sit. Quod non contingit similiter de numero, quando numerus est datum: de eo est necesse mente et intellectuali actu praeaccipere quia numeri, videlicet quod numerus actu est mente conceptus, ac si existeret, vel aptitudinem ad existendum habeat, et hoc quidem propter hoc, quod numerus neque natura neque sensu actualiter percipitur quod sit, sed tantum intellectu dignoscitur.

32 Ibid., 25, De Pace, 200.
33 Ibid., 72, De Pace, 197:

si illa linea, quae altramento pingitur, vel penna aut stilo protrahitur recta non sit, non ob id tamen dicendum est Geometram errare, quia non ad id intentionem dirigit Geometra quod oculis subijcitur, sed ad id potius, quod intus animo concipit, dirigit intentionem.

34 Ibid., 44, De Pace, 210–11, n. 52.
35 Ibid., 26, De Pace, 212, n. 54: "Verbum hoc *inducens*, duas inductiones significat: Alteram Geometricam, reliquam syllogisticam."
36 Ibid., 25–6, De Pace, 213. One should note, however, that Catena changes a few of Euclid's terms – speaking about a triangle inscribed in a semicircle – in order to make this proposition comparable with Aristotle's discussion of the sum of angles of the triangle in the *Posterior Analytics*, 71, 19–27.
37 Ibid., 28:

et simpliciter scitur per Geometricam inductionem, quae semper ex veris, primis, causis illativis conclusionis, et ex magis notis procedit, non autem ex immediatis semper, neque ex causis quae dant esse, sed ex his tantum, quae dant propter quid illationis, tale instrumentum quod inductionem Geometricam voco,non est una consequentia, sed plures, ut plurimum, neque per immediata semper procedit, sed alternatim per immediata, et per ea qua probata sunt procedit, immediata autem, voco propositiones per se notas, et etiam illas propositiones demonstratas, quae immediate probant sequentes.

Quoted from Giacobbe, *Le opere di Pietro Catena...*, 130.
38 Ibid., 97–8, De Pace, 240–1, n. 120.
39 See De Pace, especially 170–85.
40 Baldini, "La nova del 1604 e i matematici e filosofi del Collegio Romano," *Annali dell'Istituto e Museo di Storia della Scienza*, 1981, VI: 63–98; idem, *Legem Impone Subactis....*
41 See Feldhay, *Galileo and the Church...* Chapter 8.
42 Baldini, *Legem Impone Subactis...*, 56.
43 Gatto, *Tra Scienza e Immaginazione...*, 153–8.
44 Baldini, *Legem Impone Subactis...*, 54–5.
45 J. Klein, *Greek Mathematical Thought and the Origin of Algebra*, transl.

by E. Brann, New York: Dover, 1992 (second ed.); D. R. Lachterman, *The Ethics of Geometry: A Genealogy of Modernity*, New York: Routledge, 1989, Part 2.

46 See E. Giusti, *Bonaventura Cavallieri and the Theory of Indivisibles*, Rome, 1982; P. Mancosu, *Philosophy of Mathematics and Mathematical Practice in the Seventeenth Century*, New York: Oxford University Press, 1996.

47 Baldini, *Legem Impone Subactis...*, 54; Gatto, *Tra Scienza e Immaginazione...*, 83.

48 Ibid., 44, 54. It should be noted, however, that Baldini has been very cautious in drawing conclusions from these facts. His tendency is to see them as promising beginnings that never developed into real fruitful research. My aim, however, is to show that exactly in the years of Galileo's formation an institutional structured space existed where the type of problems he was interested in were discussed. Further research on Jesuit mathematics currently under quite vigorous pursuit will show whether Jesuit science was seriously constrained and for which reasons. Alternatively an excavation of the sources will point out the results of all these beginnings, which are still obscure in modern historical research.

49 The edition quoted by De Pace is that of Rome, 1585.

50 Ibid., 209 col. b, quoted by De pace, "Interpretazione di Aristotele e comprensione matematica della natura," in G. Canziani and Y. C. Zarka, *L'Interpretazione nei Secoli XVI e XVII*, Milano: Franco angeli, 1993, p. 284–5, n. 45: "Vocatur autem quantitas hae proxime inhaerens materiae primae ab Averre indeterminata."

51 Ibid., 373 col. b–374 col. a, in De Pace, *Le Matematiche...*, 88, n. 148: "Albertus, D. Thomas, Aegidius et alii, existimant quantitatem Mathematicam non posse abstrahi ad omni substantia, sed tantum a sensibili."

52 Ibid., 375 col. b, De Pace, 88.

53 Ibid., 86 col. a, De Pace, 92–3, n. 164:

A principio... donatur a Deo animus, immortalis ille quidem et capax omnium disciplinarum, sed rudis expersque scientiarum, et ut pulchre inquit Aristoteles ceu tabula quaedam nuda, in qua nihil omnino pictum est.

54 Ibid., 86 col. b, De Pace, 94, n. 166:

Si animus noster olim habuit scientiam omnium rerum, quam postea dum est in corpore per disciplinam institutionem exercitationemque reminiscitur, cur ad reminiscendum adeo egemus sensibus, ut his subaltis nulla quoat scientia comparari? Nos enim experimur, cum

quidpiam reminisci volumus quod antea cognovimus, non valde in-
digere aut uti opera sensuum exteriorum; et sine his non solum
posse sed interdum etiam fieri solere multarum rerum reminiscen-
tiam sola vi et ope imaginatricis vel cogitatricis facultatis.

55 Ibid., 26 cols. a–b, De Pace, 90, n. 154.
56 This passage has been frequently quoted by historians of science in-
    terested in Jesuit mathematics. See A. Crombie, "Mathematics and
    Platonism in the Sixteenth-Century Italian Universities and in Jesuit
    Educational Policy," in Y. Maeyama and W. G. Saltzer, eds., *Prismata,
    Naturwissenschaftsgeschichtliche Studien*, Wiesbaden, 1977, 67. See
    also Mancosu, *Philosophy of Mathematics...*, 13, from which I am
    quoting.
57 Ibid., 51 col. a, in De Pace, "Interpretazioni di Aristotele...," 287.
58 C. Clavius, *Commentaria in Euclidis Elementorum Libri XV...*, 3d ed.,
    Rome, 1591.
59 Ibid., 4: "Cur sic ditae sint."
60 Ibid., 5: 'Nobilitas atque praestantia scientiarum mathematicarum':

Si vero nobilitas, atque praestantia scientiae ex certitudine demonstrationum, quibus utitur, sit udicanda: haud dubie Mathematicae
disciplinae inter caeteras omnes principem habebunt locum. Demo-
nstrant enim omnia, de quibus suscipiunt disputationem, firmiss-
mis rationibius, confirmantque, ita ut vere scientiam in auditoris animo gignant, omnemque prorsus dubitationem tollant... Theoremata enim Euclidis, caeterorumque Mathematicorum, eandem hodie,
quam ante tot annos, in Scholis retinent veritatis puritatem, rerum
certitudinem, demonstrationum robur, ac firmitatem.

61 Ibid.: "Huc accedit id, quod Plato ait in Philebo, seu Dialogo, qui de
    summo bono inscribitur. Eam scientiam esse digniorem, praestantio-
    remque, quae magis synceritatis, veritatisque est amans."
62 Ibid., p. 5:

Nam si a rebus sensibilibus, quas Physicus considerat, ad res ab
omni materia sensibili secretas, seiunctasque, quas contemplatur.
Metaphysicus, vires, aciemque nostri intellectus attollere absque
ullo medio tentemus: nos metipsos excaecabimus; non secus ac ei
contingit, qui e carcere aliquo tenebricoso, in quo dix latuit in lucem
Soliis clarissimam emittitur. Quam ob rem, antequam a rebus physi-
cis, quae materiae sensibus obnoxiae sunt coniununctae, ad res meta-
physicas, quae sunt ab eadem maxime anulsae, intellectus ascendat;
necesse est, ne harum claritate offundatur, prius eum assuefieri rebus minus abstractis, quales a Mathematicis considerantur, ut facil-
ius illas possit comprehendere.

63 Ibid.: "Quocirca recte Divinus Plato Mathematicas disciplinas erigere
    animum, & ad divinarum rerum contemplationem exdocere mentis

aciem affirmat."

64 Ibid.:

Immo vero idem Plato in Philebo, omnes disciplinas sine Mathematicis viles esse non dubitavit asserere, Qua de causa in 7. de
Republ. praecipit: Mathematicas disciplinas primo omnium esse
addiscendas, propter varias, ac multiplices earum utilitates (ut co-
piose scribit) non solum ad reliquas artes rectius percipiendas, verum
etaim ad Rem publicam bene administrandam.

65 This, of course, has already been noticed by most readers of Jesuit mathematical texts. See Crombie, Galluzzi, Wallace, or Dear.

66 Clavius, "Prolegomena," 5:

Quoniam disciplinae Mathematicae de rebus agunt, quae absque ulla
materia sensibili considerantur, quamvis re ipsa materiae sint im-
mersae; perspicuum est eas medium inter Metaphysicam, et naturalem scientiam obtinere locum, si subjectum earum considere-
menus, ut recte a Proclo probatur, Metaphysices etenim subiectum
ab omni est materia seiunctum, & re, & ratione; Physices vero sube-
ictum & re & ratione materiae sensibili est coniunctum: Unde cum
subiectum Mathematicarum disciplinarum extra omnem materiam
consideretur, quamvis re ipsa in ea reperiatur, liquido constat, hoc
medium esse inter alia duo.

67 Ibid., 4: "Volunt itaque praedicti auctores, scientiarum Mathematicarum quasdam in intellectibilibus duntaxat ab omni materia sepa-
ratis, quasdam vero in sensibilibus, ita ut attingant materiam sensibus
obnoxiam, versai."

68 Ibid., 6:

Non parum etiam conducunt hae artes ad Philosophiam naturalem,
moralem, Dialecticam, & ad reliquaas id genus doctrinas, artesque
perfecte acquirendas, ut perspicue docet Proclus. His adde, quod
omnia volumina antiquorum Philosophorum, maxime Aristotelis,
& Platonis quosmerite duces nobis sequendos, ad bene recteque
philosophandum proponimus, eorumque fere omnium interpretum
cum Graecorum, tum Latinorum, exemplis Mathematicis sunt refe-
rta, ea potissimum de causa, ut ea quae alioquin multis obstructa
difficultatibus videbantur esse, per exempla huiusmodi clariora, mag-
isque perspicua fierent: ...Quantum vero emolumenti hae disciplinae ad sacras literas recte percipiendas, interpretandasque confer-
ant, multis pulcherrime nobis exponit B. Augustinus lib. 2 cap. 16
de Doctrina Christiana demonstrans...Quo item loco, Geometriam
magnam asserre Theologis utilitatem perhibet.

69 J. Blancanus, "De Mathematicarum Natura Dissertatio," Bologona,
1615. The text was published as an appendix to Blancanus's *Aristotelis
Loca Mathematica*. Five years later Blancanus published another treatise on the mathematical sciences, his "Preparation for Learning and
Advancing the Mathematical Disciplines" ("Apparatus ad mathematicas addiscendas et promovendas"). The "Treatise on the Nature of

Mathematics" was lately translated into English; it is published as an appendix to Mancosu, *Philosophy of Mathematics*.... I've used this translation in all my quotations from the "Treatise...".

70 Blancanus, "Treatise..." in Mancosu, 179.

71 Ibid., 179–80.

72 Ibid., 180.

73 Ibid., 184.

74 Ibid., 179.

75 On the development of these two directions see U. Baldini, "Archimede nel Seicento Italiano," in C. Dollo, ed., *Archimede: Mito Tradizione Scienza*, Florence: Olschki, 1992, 248 ff.

76 A. Favaro, ed., *Le Opere di Galileo Galilei*, 20 Vols. in 21, Florence, 1968 (1st edition 1890), I, 318:

> Quia igitur grave mobile...descendens, tardius movetur in principio, ergo necessarium est, illud minus esse grave in principio sui motus quam in medio vel in fine; cum certo sciamus, ex demonstratis in primo libro, velocitatem et tarditatem, gravitatem et levitatem sequi...Verum naturalis et intrinseca mobilis gravitas certe non est diminuta, quia nec diminuta est moles nec densitas illius: restat ergo, imminutionem illam gravitatis esse praeternaturalem et accidentariam... Videamus ergo et diligenter perscrutemur, an forte virtus ista sit causa diminuendae gravitatis mobilis in principio sui motus.

77 Ibid, 273: "Sed animadvertentum est, quod magna hic oritur difficultas: quod proportiones istae, ab eo qui periculum fecerit, non observari comperientur."

78 Traditionally dated to 1593, but see also A. Carugo and A. C. Crombie, "The Jesuits and Galileo's Ideas of Science and of Nature," *Annali del Museo di Storia della Scienza di Firenze*, 1983, VIII:1–68.

79 See Galluzzi's discussion in *Momento*, 199–227.

80 See also Harris, "Les chaires des mathématiques," See note 10.

81 It should be noted, however, that Galluzzi thinks Galileo's project in the *Mecaniche* is much more ambiguous than I stated here. For him, Galileo's choice of the term "momento" to indicate a concept he could not differentiate before demonstrates the dynamical considerations underlying the *Mecaniche* in its very foundations.

82 All citations from Galileo's *Dialogue* are taken from: *Dialogue Concerning the Two Chief World System – Ptolemaic and Copernican*, transl. with revised notes by S. Drake, Berkeley: University of California Press, 1992.

83 See, for example, P. Damerow, G. Freudenthal, P. MacLaughlin, and J. Renn, *Exploring the Limits of Preclassical Mechanics*, New York: Springer, 1962.

84 See Wallace, *Galileo and His Sources*....

85 Galluzi, *Momento...*; Renn, *Exploring....*
86 See *Exploring...*; 18–19.
87 See the discussion of the definition of velocity and of "Mirandum Paradox" in *Exploring ...*, pp. 13–5, 194–9.
88 *Opere*, "De Motu," ch. 14, 296–302.
89 See above, p. 105.
90 The book referred to is probably a thesis defended by a student of Christopher Scheiner, *Disquisitiones mathematicae, de controversiis et novitatibus astronomicis...*sub praesidio Christophori Scheiner... Nobilis et Doctissimis iuvenis, Ioannes Georgius Locher, Boius Monacensis, Artium et Philosophiae Baccalaureus, Magisterij Candidatus, Ingolstadt, 1614.
91 See the fascinating discussion of the rule in *Explorations ...* (note 83), pp. 171–4; 178–85.
92 L. Maierù, "... in Christophorum Clavium de Contactu Linearum Apologia": Considerazioni attorno all a Polemica tra Peletier e Clavio circa l'angolo di contatto (1579–1589)," *Archive for the History of Exact Sciences*, 1990, 41/1:115–37.
93 Heath, *Euclid's Elements*, III, 16: "The straight line drawn at right angles to the diameter of a circle from its extremity will fall outside the circle, and into the space between the straight line and the circumference another straight line cannot be interposed; further the angle of the semicircle is greater, and the remaining angle less than any acute rectilinear angle."
X, 1: "Two unequal magnitudes set out, if from the greater there be substracted a magnitude greater than its half, and from that which is left a magnitude greater than its half, and if this process be repeated continually, there will be left some magnitude which will be less than the lesser magnitude set out."
V, 3: "a ratio is a sort of relation in respect of size between two magnitudes of the *same kind*" (My emphasis, R.F.).
94 Maierù, "... in Christophorum Clavium," 129.
95 A good example is his middle position in the debate between homocentrists and Copernicans on epicycles and eccentrics; see J. M. Lattis, *Between Copernicus and Galileo*, Chicago, IL: University of Chicago Press, 1995, Chapter 5.
96 Maierú, In Christophorum clavium ... op. cit.
97 Ibid. p. 133.
98 For this history, see N. Kretzmann, ed., *Infinity and Continuity in Ancient and Medieval Thought*, Ithaca: NY Cornell University Press, 1982.

99 About such compromise common among sixteenth-century astronomers, see N. Jardine, *The Birth of History and Philosophy of Science: Kepler's* A Defence of Tycho against Ursus *with Essays of its
Provenance and Significance*, Cambridge: Cambridge University Press,
1984, II, 7.

100 See Feldhay, *Galileo and the Church*, Chapters 7, 8, 11.

101 For the Greek background see R. Feldhay and S. Unguru, "Greek
Mathematical Discourse: Some Examples of Tensions and Gaps," in
T. Berggnen, ed. *Proceedings of the Third International Conference on
Ancient Mathematics, Delphi*. Vancouver, British Columbia: Simon
Fraser University Press, 1997, 45–7.

102 Quoted from Crombie, "Mathematics and Platonism...," 66.

103 Perera, *De communibus...*, 1576, 24, in Mancosu, *Philosophy of Mathematics...*, 214, n. 12, translation by Crombie, ibid., 67:

Confirmatio Minoris ducitur ex his, quae scribit Plato in 7, lib.
de Republ. dicens Mathematicos *somniare* circa quantitatem, & in
tractandis suis demonstrationibus non scientificè sed ex quibusdam
suppositionibus procedere, quamobrem non vult doctrinam eorum
appellare intellegetiam aut scientiam, sed tantum cogitationem.

104 See discussion of Perera's position in the *De Certitudine... above*, 92

105 See the discussion of *Ratio* in Feldhay, *Galileo and the Church*, 223–32.

106 See discussion of Blanianus' treatise, in this essay, pp. 98–100.

4   Inertial problems in Galileo's preinertial framework

Galileo made essential contributions to the development of inertial mechanics. His two most basic contributions were to collect the set of problems that held the keys to inertial mechanics and then address them all with an effective, consistent mechanics.

Classical mechanics is still taught by referring new students to the core set of problems that had to be solved by the original investigators like Descartes, Gassendi, Huygens, Wallis, Wren, Hooke, and Newton, all following Galileo's original line of attack. These problems include the analysis of motion on an inclined plane, the motion of a pendulum, the action of a lever, the force of a spring or pull in a rope, the result of collisions between impacting and moving bodies, and so on.

Inertial mechanics was extended to a far wider range of problems, but no writer before Galileo had put so many of the basic problems together in a single, articulate discussion. For that reason alone we may describe Galileo's work as modern in character and properly within the bounds and spirit of classical mechanics, even though the elements of the latter system were not successfully elaborated for almost fifty years after his passing and in spite of the fact that he sometimes proposed mistaken ideas to solve the basic problems.

Galileo's two major works (1632 and 1638) first defined space, time, and speed, and then moved on to uniform acceleration.[1] Galileo analyzed projectile motion into two component motions, the first horizontal and uniform, the other vertical and accelerated. Galileo discussed the motions of bodies upon the moving Earth and of planets around the Sun. He asked questions that led his fellows and successors directly toward inertial mechanics and gave them some of the essential tools to build it.

146

Yet his own terrestrial and celestial mechanics were not fully inertial. He did, for example, think in terms of impressed forces and the impetus acquired in descent, and he continued to speak of intrinsic motions, both of which were banished from inertial mechanics.

Galileo is best known in mechanics for contributions to kinetics, the analysis of motion in terms of distance, time, speed, and acceleration. About 1602 or, at the latest, 1604, he discovered the times squared law for distance fallen, $s \alpha t^2$. This rule says, for example, that during the first five units of time, that is, 1, 2, 3, 4, and 5, the distances fallen are as the squares of the times, 1, 4, 9, 16, and 25. The differences between those distances are the distances fallen in equal successive times, and they are as the odd numbers, 1, 3, 5, 7, and 9. In the *Discourses on the Two New Sciences of Motion and Mechanics* (1638), he stated the definition for uniformly accelerated motion from which he derived the times squared law and the odd number rule as deductive results:

...we shall not depart from the correct rule if we assume that intensification of speed is made according to the extension of time; from which the definition of the motion of which we are going to treat may be put thus:

We shall call that motion equably or uniformly accelerated which, abandoning rest, adds on to itself equal moments of swiftness in equal times.[2]

The amount of speed acquired in the first second is added again in the second second, and in the third, and so on. Thus, for example, after a descent of two seconds, the body has acquired twice the speed as it had at one second (2:1). By the times square law, it has also fallen four times as far ($2^2:1^2$). The speeds acquired in vertical descent are in direct proportion to the times of descent, $v_{acquired} \alpha t$.

If the descending body were deflected onto the horizontal plane, it would stop accelerating and continue moving uniformly with the final velocity it acquired. The accelerated motion of the first two seconds is transformed into a uniform horizontal motion that, in the next two seconds, travels twice the distance just fallen.

In other words, half of the final uniform speed would cover the distance fallen in the same time as the fall itself. This relation is called the mean speed theorem, and the expression of it given in the previous sentence is called the double distance rule. The mean speed theorem is Theorem One of *On Accelerated Motions*, and is the first result derived from Galileo's definition and postulate in the

Latin treatise *De Motu Locali*, in the Third Day of the *Two New Sciences*. There is evidence that Galileo performed experiments to work with these ideas, especially folio 116 verso in Volume 72 of the *Manoscritti Galileiani*.[3]

Galileo's double distance rule and mean speed theorem allow him to compare uniform and accelerated motions by the measures of time and distance. Working without the calculus, he reduces all accelerated motions to their uniform equivalents by this theorem.

Their uniform equivalents can then be compared with other accelerated motions or directly with uniform motions by the simple rules of uniform motion. Galileo uses his rules for uniform motion to resolve important problems of accelerating motion, and in this he is rather Aristotelian in his understanding of velocity.[4]

Galileo also postulated the equality of the speeds of all motions falling through equal vertical descents:

Salviati: This definition established, the Author requires and takes as true one single assumption, that is: [Postulate]

I assume that the degrees of speed acquired by the same movable over different inclinations of planes are equal whenever the heights of those planes are equal.[5]

If several inclined planes have the same height, bodies descending them would all acquire the same velocity when they reached the bottom – they simply take different amounts of time to reach bottom and acquire the velocity.

Galileo drew the new science of motion out of these beginnings as Euclid had drawn the *Elements* out of its opening propositions. Galileo's Theorem One, the mean speed theorem, and Theorem Two, the times squared law, follow immediately from the definition of uniform acceleration. Historically, Galileo knew the times squared law (1602–4) before he learned to define uniform acceleration (about 1608–9), but the postulate of equal velocities for equal descents appeared very early in Galileo's work, in the Paduan *De meccaniche* 1597.

THE ADVENT OF INERTIAL MECHANICS

Galileo put his new mechanics and physics before the educated world in 1612–1613, in *On Bodies That Float Atop Water* and *Letters on the*

Sunspots. He undoubtedly discussed them again during the various stages of his public defense of Copernicus at Rome from 1612 to 1616. He wrote about them again, at length, in his two major works published in the 1630s.

His new mechanics did inspire further enquiry. Some of his readers investigated the laws of motion and mechanical action along lines he had suggested, including Marin Mersenne, Pierre Fermat, and Pierre Gassendi in the late 1630s and 1640s and Christian Huygens in the 1640s and 1650s.

These investigators did find some discrepancies between Galileo's descriptions of events and the results of their own experimental trials, but many of his offerings held up under scrutiny. René Descartes also read the *Two New Sciences* in Mersenne's translation in the late 1630s and remarked that though Galileo philosophized rather better than most, he had failed to begin from first principles and thus could not arrive at a full understanding of matters.[6]

In 1613, the same year as the *Letters on Sunspots,* Isaac Beeckman had quietly rejected the ideas of impressed forces in notes in his journal. He proposed that a body continued to move as it had been moving as long as there was no cause acting to slow it down or to stop it.

Beeckman was the rector of the Latin School at Dordrecht, a steady investigator of natural phenomena and a keeper of scientific journals. Prior to 1620, Beeckman had befriended Simon Stevin, court mathematician to Prince Maurice of Orange and notable natural philosopher, who had argued in 1586 that all bodies fall at the same rate.

Beeckman developed the elements of his new approach in discussions in 1619 and after with his younger colleague, Rene Descartes. Descartes was, in those years, a soldier in the army of Prince Maurice and already a well-regarded mathematician. After those initial discussions, Descartes quietly worked with Beeckman's principle of indifferent conservation and improved it in his successive mechanical systems.

Pierre Gassendi had taken up Galileo's research almost as soon as it had been published in the *Two New Sciences* in 1638. He made experiments with inclined planes and dropped stones from the mast of a moving ship and confirmed Galileo's results and predictions. On paper, he studied Galileo's unaccelerated and unretarded uniform horizontal motion in an imaginary space outside the world and succeeded in abstracting the first statement of the principle of inertia from both the intrinsic gravity and circular motion that had enthralled Galileo. Horizontal motion in such a space would be rectilinear in the absence of intrinsic accelerating tendencies. Gassendi published this work in *De Motu Impresso a Motore Translato* (1642).[7]

Descartes published his laws of motion, including the principle of inertia, in *Principles of Philosophy* (1644) in two laws that Newton subsumes under his own first law.[8] Descartes's first rule said that a body will persevere in its state of rest or motion in the absense of resisting or impelling forces. The second rule said that a body is conserved in rectilinear motion. Descartes's *Principles* set out an extensive system of philosophy and nature and included his theories of impact and planetary vortices. His solution for impact was not correct and led to further enquiry.

Problems of collision engaged European mathematicians in the 1650s and 1660s. Huygens merged the mechanical approach of Galileo with the algebraic methods and inertial directions indicated by Gassendi, Descartes, and Beeckman in his analysis of shared and exchanged motions. Wren, Wallis, and Huygens independently worked out the solution and presented it to the Royal Society as Newton related.[9] Newton embraced all their problems and undertook many more original ones in the 1680s in his completed inertial mechanics.

NEWTON'S INERTIA

Newton built his universal mechanics on a small, rigorous logical structure. The eight definitions (and scholium) and the three laws of motion – the principle of inertia, the proportionality of force and mass and acceleration, and the equality of actions and reactions – and their corollaries are all stated in the first forty pages of the *Mathematical Principles of Natural Philosophy* (1687). The definitions are followed by a scholium on the measurement of time and space, while the third law is augmented by six corollaries outlining the composition of forces. His laws are:

Law I. Every body perseveres in its state of rest, or of uniform motion in a right line, unless it is compelled to change that state by forces impress'd thereon.

Law II. The alteration of motion is ever proportional to the motive force impress'd; and is made in the direction of the right line in which that force is impress'd.

Law III. To every Action there is always opposed an equal Reaction: or the mutual actions of two bodies upon each other are always equal, and directed to contrary parts.[10]

The first law, the principle of inertia, connotes several sets of problems. There is a recognition that motion persists in its current uniform state, and that it tends in a right direction as it persists, and that it incurs forces that accelerate or otherwise change it. The principle even includes a notice of the fundamental equivalence of rest and motion.

The first two corollaries to the third law demonstrate the parallelogram of forces and the composition of forces from two others. Galileo's *Two New Sciences* had demonstrated a parallelogram of motions and had shown how to compose motions when more than one motion was applied to a body at the same time. Important successors also used the same principle.

The three laws are followed by a second scholium resolving the problems of simple machines. This scholium is said to have concluded the enquiries of the science of mechanics as it had been known for the previous two millennia.

Kepler (1609) and Leibniz (1710) had previously published the term *inertia* as a principle of inactivity, but mentions of it also appeared in Descartes's *Correspondence*, where Newton probably learned it.[11] Newton did, however, change its meaning when he employed the term himself.

For Kepler, the *vis inertiae* was a force that kept a body at rest or brought it to rest if in motion. The classical *vis inertiae* stood for an accelerating or decelerating force in the equations of action and reaction, and it was regarded as the principle by which uniform motion continued.

Definition III. The *Vis Insita*, or Innate Force of Matter, is a power of resisting, by which every body, as much as in it lies, endeavors to persevere in its present state, whether it be of rest, or of moving uniformly forward in a right line.

This force is ever proportional to the body whose force it is; and differs nothing from the inactivity of the Mass, but in our manner of conceiving it

... This Vis Insita may, by a most significant name, be called *Vis Inertiae*, or force of inactivity ... a body exerts this force only, when another force impress'd upon it, endeavors to change its condition; ... it is resistance in so far as the body, for maintaining its present state withstands the force impressed; ... it is impulse in so far as it endeavors to change the state of that other.[12]

In the *Opticks* (1717), Newton remarked that the vis inertiae by itself does not add to motion but rather acts to conserve motion or rest:

The *Vis inertiae* is a passive Principle by which Bodies persist in their Motion or Rest, receive Motion in proportion to the Force impressing it, and resist as much as they are resisted. By this principle alone there never could have been any Motion in the World.[13]

Although it explains why bodies persist in their motions, the *vis inertiae* is nothing like a moving force that would push the body along, as in the medieval theories of *virtus impressa* or *impetus*.

Newton's view of the impressed force was distinguished explicitly from the medieval theories of *virtus impressa* or *impetus*. Those arguments had been advanced against Aristotle's theory of projectile motion, first by John Philoponus, a Greek neo-Platonist of sixth century AD, then in another version by Fransiscus de Marchia in the eleventh, and then restated by John Buridan and Nicole Oresme in fourteenth-century Paris.

The medieval *virtus impressa* was imparted to a projectile by its projector and continued to be present in the projectile; it served to move it after contact with the projector was broken. Newton's persisted only during the contact, doing all its work then. Their *virtus impressa* could keep a body moving at a given speed but Newton's changed the speed as long as it was applied.

Definition IV. An impress'd force is an action exerted upon a body, in order to change its state, either of rest, or of moving uniformly forward in a right line.

This force consists in the action only; and remains no longer in the body, when the action is over. For a body maintains every new state it acquires, by its Vis Inertiae only.[14]

The fourth definition gave a historic new meaning to an old term, impressed force, by assigning its traditional role in projectile motion – sustaining the flight of the body – to the force of inertia or inactivity. Under the fourth definition, impressed force, which "consists in the action only," did not remain in the body when the action was over. The definition rescued the traditional term by giving it an exact meaning that includes its intuitive, useful, and traditional sense as "a cause of action" in mechanics.

Recent works of interest on the history of the idea of inertia argue that the three laws have a strong experimental base in Newton's thought and work. It had become useful and common to think of the laws as a set of definitions and axioms in a rational mechanics, yet Newton went to great pains to produce the phenomena of inertia experimentally for observers.[15]

INERTIA-LIKE IDEAS IN GALILEO'S MECHANICS

Newton gave us his own exegis of the laws and corollaries in the scholium immediately following Corollary VI of the third law. There he gave Galileo credit for some important contributions to mechanics – credit that was largely owed to himself:

Hitherto, I have laid down such principles as have been received by mathematicians, and are confirmed by the abundance of experiments. By the first two laws and the first two corollaries, Galileo discovered that the descent of bodies observed the duplicate ratio of the time, and that the motion of projectiles was in the curve of a parabola; experience agreeing with both, unless so far as these motions are a little retarded by the resistance of the air.[16]

Galileo did not, however, work with Newton's notion of an accelerating force. Indeed, Galileo's concept of force was closely tied to ideas of static force. And in the broader realm of physics, Galileo did not regard gravity as an external force but always regarded it as an intrinsic property of a body, and that had many consequences for the development of his views.[17]

Alexandre Koyré often said that there were two strong indications that Newton had not read Galileo, this attribution of the first two laws and corollaries being one of them.[18]

I. B. Cohen said that only a Newton could have seen his laws in Galileo's work.[19]

Galileo did say that a body would persist perpetually in its current motion on a horizontal plane if there were no cause for deceleration or acceleration. The idea that gives Galileo's system its inertialike properties is derived from his work with inclined planes. A body set in motion on a horizontal plane would suffer no acceleration and no deceleration and could have the same uniform motion indefinitely. From *Letters on Sunspots*:

I have observed that physical bodies have an inclination toward some motion, as heavy bodies downward, which motion is exercised by them through an intrinsic property and without need of a special external mover, whenever they are not impeded by some obstacle. And to some other motion, they have a repugnance, as the same heavy bodies to motion upward, wherefore they never move in that manner unless thrown violently upward by an external mover.

Finally, to some movements they are indifferent, as are heavy bodies to horizontal movements they are indifferent as are heavy bodies to horizontal motion, to which they have neither inclination ... nor repugnance. And, therefore, all external impediments being removed, a heavy body on a spherical surface concentric with the earth will be indifferent to rest or to movement toward any part of the horizon. And it will remain in that state in which it has once been placed, that is, if placed in a state of rest, it will conserve that, and if placed in a movement toward the west, for example, it will maintain itself in that movement.

Thus a ship, for instance, having once received some impetus through the tranquil sea, would move continually around our globe without ever stopping; and placed at rest it would perpetually remain at rest, if in the first case all extrinsic impediments could be removed, and in the second case no external cause of motion were added.[20]

For Galileo, uniform horizontal motions imperceptibly become circular motions. The global circular dimension is much larger than the local scope of the laws for free fall, where the horizontal plane merely appears flat and rectilinear, as it does in his f.116v trajectory experiments.

Galileo's analysis of motion on the terrestrial horizontal plane is actually a composition of two component motions. The first component of a terrestrial motion is the downward, center-seeking, and accelerated motion of vertical descent. This component is governed by the times square law for distances fallen. The second component is a horizontal motion, usually uniform, and tending in the direction that its impetus or impressed form impels. That composition of motions is at the heart of Galileo's inertialike thinking.[21] Galileo first produced a limited version of this construction about 1590 in his Pisan mechanics, the *De Motu Antiquiora*, which he abandoned by 1602. It appears there in the absence of any discussion of the Earth's motion. While he was working with balance analogies circa 1590, he had used the arrangement to demonstrate that a body can be moved by the least possible force on a horizontal plane:

A body subject to no external resistance on a plane sloping no matter how little ... will move down in natural motion ... And the same body on a plane sloping upward, no matter how little, above the horizon, does not move up except by force. And so the conclusion remains that on the horizontal plane itself the motion of the body is neither natural nor forced. But if its motion is not forced motion, then it can be made to move by the smallest of all possible forces.[22]

Notice that this reflection on inclined planes leads to a challenge of the distinction between natural and forced motions for the horizontal plane. Galileo added an interesting marginal note on mixed motions:

From this it follows that mixed motion ["except circular" is canceled] does not exist. For since the forced motion of heavy bodies is away from the center, and their natural motion toward the center, a motion which is partly upward and partly downward cannot be compounded from these two; unless perhaps we should say that such a mixed motion is that which takes place on the circumference of a circle around the center of the universe. But such a motion will be better described as "neutral" than as "mixed." For "mixed" partakes of both, "neutral" of neither.[23]

This was an idea that Galileo would return to throughout his working life. Galileo presented very similar views prominently in the ill-fated *Dialogue on the Two Chief World Systems* (1632), and a version of it appears in the *Two New Sciences* (1638).

In Galileo's view, the impetus imparts a uniform speed to the body, and the speed is proportional to the amount of impressed force or impetus acquired and present in the body. Its presence is properly measured from the body's speed and weight. Accelerations add impetus and decelerations consume it, but in the absence of them, the impetus and the state of motion it entails are ineradicable.

Within a year of the trajectory experiments, Galileo launched his telescopic discoveries and began to think of Copernicus in great seriousness. When Galileo put the Earth into uniform rotation in his mind's eye, he used the circular horizontal construction we just saw in *Letters on the Sunspots*. The version in *Sunspots* is a case that does not incorporate the motion of the Earth – the horizontal impetus imparted to the ship has come from something else. Once the Earth is assumed to be rotating, as in the *Two Chief World Systems*, the horizontal impetus can be seen as due to the Earth's motion.[24]

The motion of a body at rest on the surface would be circular on the global scale. Among terrestrial bodies that share the Earth's motion, the only motions we can perceive or participate in are those made in addition to the Earth's rotation. A body in motion over the surface or one falling to the center adds any horizontal motions to its intrinsic vertical tendencies and the general rotational motion of the Earth to produce a circular path.

Galileo compares the motions of a body falling uniformly along a circular path from a tower to the center of the Earth with the motion of another ball that remains at rest at the top of the tower while it turns with the Earth.[25] From the geometry, the path of the body on the tower is the same length as the path of the body falling to the center of gravity. Finally, after one rotation of the Earth, the two paths are completed uniformly and in the same time. An accelerated vertical motion, freefall to the center, becomes a uniform circular motion when the rotation is taken into account. Galileo is led to declare that nature prefers to use uniform circular motions and that neither rectilinear nor accelerated motions ever occur in nature.

The *Two Chief World Systems* worked to show that when bodies share the same motion, the shared motion is "as if it did not exist" in relations between them. As Galileo explains, motion is made and perceived relative to other objects that stayed fixed or do not share the motion:

Motion, in so far as it is and acts as motion, to that extent exists relatively to things that lack it; and among things which all share equally in any motion, it does not act, and is as if it did not exist.[26]

Galileo uses the example of the cargo at rest on a ship bound from Venice to Aleppo. All the boxes and bundles were transported equally and yet the boxes were less affected by the ship's motion than by the small changes of position among themselves. All the bodies in our common experience share the rotational motion of the Earth, but the massive effect of that rotation is insensible to us optically and mechanically.

Galileo believed that his formula had important advantages for the defense of Copernicus. It does admit noninertial results chiefly because it views the circle as the path of conservation of impetus or motion on the surface of the Earth and in the heavens. A circular orbit is not a continually accelerated motion in Galileo's mind; rather it is a uniform motion capable of enduring eternally. Galileo contrasted circular motion with the rectilinear natural motion proposed by Aristotle. Aristotle's rectilinear natural motion was generally vertical and accelerated.

There are other, usually less successful analogies and formal homologies between elements of classical inertia and the structure of Galileo's definitions, theorems, and mechanical ideas. When systems of bodies are Galilean-invariant according to classical mechanics, for example, they preserve the properties of space and time and relative speed defined by Galileo's definitions of uniform motion and acceleration.

Galileo's own version of invariance, as stated in the *Dialogue on the Two Chief World Systems*, is not Galilean-invariant in the classical sense, as Alan Chalmers (1992) has recently shown, yet Galileo's analysis at least shows in broad strokes what a good invariance conclusion would have to look like.[27]

WHETHER GALILEO HAD INERTIAL IDEAS

Alexandre Koyré's *Études Galiléennes* (1939) was probably the most influential treatment of Galileo's mechanics written in the twentieth century.[28] Koyré pointed out that Beeckman and Descartes had written statements that were, word for word, very similar to Newton's first law, while there were no such statements, *expressis verbis*, in Galileo's works. Koyré said that Descartes's clear expression of the idea of rectilinear inertia marked a real advance over the suggestive and incomplete work of immediate predecessors including Beeckman, Gassendi, and Galileo. The view that Galileo did not grasp the idea of inertia has generally been accepted by the learned world for several reasons.

Nevertheless, Koyré argued that Galileo did succeed in working his way out of the old medieval and Parisian theories of impressed

force and impetus and out of the old division of motions into natural
and violent. Koyré described how Galileo broke down the distinction
between natural and violent.

The discussion of Aristotle's arguments picks up at the point where it had
been left by Copernicus: namely, with a *qualitative* distinction between
natural and violent motion as the explanation for the difference between
their effects. Now there is subtle modification, and the earth's natural motion (which, logically, is explained by its 'nature' or 'form') comes to be
attributed to bodies which are on earth, no longer as a result of a common-
ness of nature but solely because of the fact that they participate in this
motion. Another subtle change and now the earth's motion is no longer
seen as having any special status over and above the fact that it is circular, and this property, by yet another shift, is attributed by extension to
the motion of a ship moving across the sea. The special status of natural motion has now completely vanished. Henceforth, motion is conserved
not because it is natural but simply because it is motion. It is motion as
such which is conserved and which is ineradicably impressed on the moving body.[29]

Similarly, Koyré sees reflected in Galileo's description and analysis of accelerated motions implicit classical and inertial views even
though Galileo continued to use the language of impetus and impressed forces and of the natural and the violent in *Two Chief World
Systems.*

The same tactics are applied to the transformation of the idea of impetus.
Galileo opens his attack on Aristotelian physics with the help of objections
and ideas accumulated and developed by 'Parisian' physics. The time comes,
however, when being convinced of its hybrid and muddled character, Galileo
abandons the concept of *impetus*, seen as the origin and cause of motion. So
as the *Dialogue* progresses *impetus* can be found identified with moment,
with motion, with speed – these successive subtle modifications which imperceptibly guide the reader toward the conception of the paradox of motion
which is conserved by itself in the moving body, and of speed, which is
'ineradicably impressed' on bodies in motion.
   In theory the special status of circular motion is now ready for destruction.
It is motion as such which is conserved and not circular motion. But this
is in theory. In practice, the *Dialogue* does not take this step. Regardless of
what others have claimed, this move is not in fact taken, and not [neither]
is the move to the principle of inertia.[30]

Koyré maintained that Galileo did not reach the principle of inertia but defended him against Duhem's conclusion that his system was an impetus physics throughout. Koyré believed that a great "mutation of thought" occurred in the works of Copernicus, Kepler, Galileo, Descartes, and Newton that swept away much of what had stood as astronomy, physics, and natural philosophy. Something was at work in Galileo's mechanics besides a repetition of the scholastic's *virtus impressa* and *impetus*.

Koyré believed that when Galileo used the term impetus he had in mind not an impressed mover like Buridan's but the product of a body's weight and speed. Everywhere a reader looks in the *Two Chief World Systems*, one encounters discussion of impetus and impressed forces. Koyré writes:

Thus the proof of Galileo's postulate, the relation between distance and duration, depends on dynamical concepts; the speed of the descending body is explicitly related to the magnitude of the initial *impetus*.

Have we, then, reverted to *impetus* physics? Or have we, as Duhem thinks, never left it at all? This is a serious problem, and it requires very close examination. What, in fact, is this Galilean *impetus*?

'Let us consider first of all,' says Galileo, 'the well known fact that the moments or speeds of a given moving body are different on planes at different inclinations. The speed reaches a maximum along a vertical direction, and for other directions diminishes as the plane diverges from the vertical. Therefore, the *impetus*, ability, energy [*l'impeto, il talento, l'energia*] or, one might say, the momentum of descent of the moving body is diminished by the place upon which it is supported and along which it rolls ...'

So the *impetus* of the moving body is nothing other than the dynamic impulse given to it by its gravity. It is no longer in any way the internal cause producing the motion, as it was in Parisian physics. It is the same thing as its 'moment,' i.e., the product of its weight and speed. In the moving body at the end of its descent it is the total energy, or total *impetus*; in the body at the beginning of its motion it is the product of its weight and its initial speed ... Finally, for the body at rest the *impetus* is none other than the virtual speed.[31]

For example, a reader of either major work will readily find examples of *impetum seu gradum velocitatis*, or *momentum seu gradum velocitatis*, which express a practical equivalence or homology between the three terms *impetus, momentum*, and *gradum velocitatis*.

Galileo's proof of the postulate in *Two New Sciences* is his bridge between the science of weight and the rules of accelerated motion. In motion on inclined planes, the *momenta gravitatis*, which are due to the angle of descent, are shown to be congruent to the *momenta velocitatis* given by the rules of speed, and are taken as the explanation and cause of the latter. *Momentum gravitatis* appears to have more in common with the classical acceleration vector than it does with Galileo's *momentum velocitatis* or with Descartes's momentum, or Newton's. Galileo had first discussed the relations of planes and forces on which the idea of *momentum gravitatis* was framed in *On Motion* (ca. 1590). Paolo Galluzzi has written an important study of the semantics of Galileo's use of *momentum* and shown that there are stages in the development of meaning of the term.[32]

There is some justice in what Koyré intends here, but there are also some important problems. First, in an important paper in 1951, Ernest Moody pointed out that Koyré had not fully explored or understood the two versions of impetus and impressed force theory of the middle ages and, thus, had misread Galileo's change to his definition of *virtus impressa*, between 1590 and 1604.[33]

Galileo discussed the *virtus impressa* at some length in *On Motion*. There it appeared as a "praeternatural" lightness, sufficient to overcome the body's intrinsic gravity and carry it away. This view was in tune with his idea that motions could be understood as operations on a balance.

A body's intrinsic motion of descent balanced against the media in which it moved and progressed with an arithmetically reduced speed. All bodies have gravity. A force of projection clearly overcomes the tendency of the gravity and the projectile moves.

Galileo had a stronger view of natural and violent in *On Motion* than he possessed later. The projecting force was not a natural one and so would cease of its own accord. It tended to decay while the motion continued, and when it was exhausted, its influence stopped, even without deceleration. Galileo's later uses of *virtus impressa*, as found in his scientific papers, especially after 1604, and in publications in 1612–1613, all reflect the usage in the *Letters on the Sunspots*. The later version of *virtus impressa* does not decay unless it is forced into motion away from the center of gravity of the Earth.

Koyré identified Galileo's first version of impressed force with the medieval Parisian impetus theory. He identified Galileo's second version with a new, emerging terminology that was freeing itself from the ambiguities of the other, presumably Parisian impetus.

As Moody showed and Clagett's work sustains, however, Galileo's second version is similar to the Parisian version (ca. 1360) (fourteenth century) of impetus theory, whereas his first, decaying, version is similar to the views of Franciscus de Marchia (ca. 1320) and others who spoke of a *vis derelicta* decaying over time in projectiles.[34] In other words, Galileo was working within the bounds of impressed force theories before and after his important change of position on "impetus" and "impressed force." This has important consequences for our view of and intuitions for his dynamics.

Earlier in the *Études*, Koyré argued that Galileo had modified the meaning of *impetus*, to identify it with motion itself, stripping its sense of 'cause of motion'. Koyré say this about certain passages in the Second Day of the *Two Chief World Systems*:

The Aristotelians' strongest objection against the *impetus* theory was an ontological objection: An accident does not pass from one body to another. Therefore *impetus* cannot do this. This is true, replies Galileo, if *impetus* means a force which causes a motion; but the motion itself can be transmitted.[35]

This is, perhaps, too strong a reading of Galileo, whose actual reply to the ontological question in the passage just discussed took a much more traditional turn. He began with this indicative exchange:

Salv.: Patience all in good time. Tell me: Seeing that your objection is based entirely upon the nonexistence of impressed force, then if I were to show you that the medium plays no part in the continuation of motion in projectiles after they are separated from their throwers, would you allow impressed force to exist? Or would you merely move on to some other attack directed towards its destruction?

Simp.: If the action of the medium were removed, I do not see how recourse could be had to anything else than the property impressed by the motive force.[36]

Galileo actively took the same side of the traditional antiperistasis argument that Buridan and others had, and he would retain his commitment to it. The property impressed here was now, as Koyré says, functionally the quantity of motion imparted. Galileo makes this clear immediately in his treatment of a rider dropping a ball. The terms were being defined anew here but little of the traditional language had been discarded yet.

Historians of medieval philosophy have repeatedly argued against Duhem's claims that Galileo plagiarized the Parisians.[37] Koyré was right to look instead to Benedetti, Bruno, and Tartaglia as reflections of the contemporary usages of impressed force and impetus.[38] This group was recasting the scholastic language in a fundamentally new, geometry-based discourse about terrestrial and celestial motions. The results were, as we know, revolutionary.

For all its medieval connotations, Galileo's later impetus is consistent enough to be precisely the product of the body's weight and its speed of motion, wv, compared with momentum, mv, in the classical sense. Of course, the existence of the agency of motion in a projectile was a distraction from the real issue, but in Galileo's time, there persisted a perfunctory debate over the adequacy of Aristotle's account of projectile motion. The reader can hear Galileo's reluctance to rehearse the antiperistasis argument in the *Two Chief World Systems*, yet he was consistently anti-Aristotelian enough to pick up the cudgels on each occasion.[39]

Koyré said Galileo tried to mathematize impetus and found it impossible. Galileo clearly did attempt to mathematize his impetus theories. From his point of view, however, his mathematization continued to succeed within his expectations as far as he tried to push it. His results for impetus and speed are usually closely homologous to classical momentum and speed and are familiar enough to a modern reader to seem identical.

BEECKMAN, GALILEO, AND THE CONSERVATION OF MOTION

Beeckman made the crucial step to a properly inertial perspective by denying the existence of any *virtus impressa* in a moving body and citing indifference to change as the cause of continued uniform motion. A comparison of Beeckman's and Galileo's views will highlight some of the differences between impetus and inertial views.

Beeckman followed the argument initiated by William of Ockham almost four centuries earlier to deny the existence of the *virtus impressa*. Beeckman explained the cause of persevering uniform motion by saying there was insufficient reason for any change of motion (note that, like Newton, he does use the verb *perseverare*):

The stone which has been thrown form a hand persists (perjit) in moving not because of some force (vim) which comes upon it, nor because of abhorrence of the vacuum, but because it cannot not persevere (perseverare) in that motion, arising in that hand by which it was moved.[40]

In 1613, six years before he met Descartes, Beeckman wrote out the following principle, which differs from the impetus-based principles of perseverance offered by Jean Buridan, Nicole Oresme, and Galileo insofar as it denies a motor cause or force of continued motion, the *virtus impressa*, with a lack of cause of change of motion. Beeckman wrote:

Once moved things never come to rest, unless impeded. Once any thing is set in motion it never comes to rest, except because of an external impediment. Furthermore, as the impediment is weaker, by that is the moved thing moved of greater duration; truly, if it is projected on high and moved circularly at the same time, it is evident to the senses that it does not come to rest before its return to earth; and if it were to come to rest at length, that would not come about because of an equable impediment, but because of an inequable impediment since one and another parts of the air touch the moved thing in succession.[41]

Koyré says that both the usual trajectory motion and the circular motion are conserved according to Beeckman.[42] In other words, Beeckman's principle admits the persistence not just of uniform, straight line motion, but of motion in general, regardless of the immediate direction and curvature of their path (i.e., their determinations). Many forms of motion could persist under this principle. Beeckman argued for example that if a candelabra once received "the form of swinging motion," it would persist therein until brought to rest by an overwhelming, inequable resistance set up by the air.

Beeckman's principle does concern itself with the conservation of motion and the formal causes of the indifferent persistence of motion. "Once a thing is set in motion, it never comes to rest, except because of external impediment." The parsimonious nature of Beeckman's version of perseverance emerges clearly in the passage, which he composed in 1614, where he denies the existence of the *virtus impressa*.

...Truly what philosophers say about a force which is impressed in the stone, is seen to be without reason; who truly can conceive, that if it should be thus, or how does the stone continue to move, then in what part of the stone does it make its seat? However, by an easier mind one conceives that in a vacuum, a moving object never comes to rest since no cause mutating (changing) the motion occurs; truly nothing is changed without some cause of mutation.[43]

Beeckman's views offer an instructive contrast for Galileo's answers to the same question, "in what part of the stone does the impressed force sit?" as he gave it explicitly in his Paduan *On Mechanics*, circa 1600, or as he answered implicitly in the *Two Chief World Systems*. The seat of the impetus is the body's center of gravity in this definition from the *Mechanics*:

Center of Gravity is defined to be that point in every heavy body around which parts of equal moments are arranged ... And this is that point which would go to unite itself with the general center of all heavy things – that is, with the center of the earth – if it could descend in some free medium.
    Whence let us draw this supposition: Any heavy body will move downward in such a way that its center of gravity will never depart from the straight line produced from this center (placed at the first point of the motion) to the general center of heavy things...
    And in the second place we may suppose: Every heavy body gravitates principally upon its center of gravity and receives therein as its proper seat, every impetus, every heaviness, and in sum every *moment*.[44]

Much later, in the *Two Chief World Systems*, Galileo discussed the center of gravity of the earth again in very similar terms:

Salv.: "And I shall say that I believe that heavy things exist prior to the common center of gravity; hence it is not a center (which is nothing but an indivisible point and therefore incapable of acting) that attracts heavy materials to itself, but simply that these materials, cooperating naturally toward a juncture, would give rise to a common center, this being that around which parts of equal moments are arranged."[45]

Then we come to the question of what the impressed force or impetus actually was in Galileo's view. In 1590, the young Galileo had also tried to describe what precisely passed from hand to stone and was called impressed force, saying,

Do you wonder what it is that passes from the hand of a projector and is impressed upon the projectile? Yet you do not wonder what passes from the hammer and is transferred to the bell of the clock, and how it happens that so loud a sound is carried over from the silent hammer to the silent bell, and is preserved in the bell when the hammer which struck it is no longer in contact ... A sonorous quality is imparted to the bell contrary to its natural silence; a motive quality is imparted to the stone contrary to its state of rest. The sound is preserved in the bell, when the striking object is no longer in contact; motion is preserved in the stone when the mover is no longer in contact. The sonorous quality gradually diminishes in the bell; the motive quality gradually diminishes in the stone.[46]

Beeckman and young Galileo were kindred spirits, but Galileo still supposed that impressed force and impetus were physical entities – similar to the vibrations of the bell – that converge on a body's center of gravity and sum together to cause the resultant motion. Even in 1590, the quality that was passed to a projectile was a simple extension of a familiar mechanical property (i.e., weight). A sufficient projecting force overcomes the intrinsic gravity of a body and literally impresses a praeternatural lightness on it, and so moves it. In 1632, the quality was usually speed, but Galileo was less interested in what precisely the impetus was – it was in fact a mystery, like the true nature of gravity.

Salv.: "Simplicio ... what you ought to say that every one knows that it is called gravity. But we do not really understand what principle or what force it is that moves stones downward, any more that we understand what moves them upward after they leave the thrower's hand, or what moves the moon around."[47]

What mattered was that we could know how they operated. We may not know what these principles or forces are, but we do understand their consequences and can derive the laws of descent toward the center and the continuation of acquired motions.

There is no evidence that Galileo had abandoned his realist interpretation of impetus and impressed forces by 1609, when he did the trajectory experiments. Whether he had abandoned it in 1638 is unclear, even if his usage of "impetus," "impressed force," and "velocity" paralleled classical usage for simple "inertia," "momentum," and "velocity." The traditional words and ideas appear everywhere there. Yet, in spite of this extra baggage of "exchanged accidents," his formulations and analysis of the facts of motion are wide ranging and deeply perceptive – he often points directly at the large features of the classical solutions without being in a position to properly solve them himself.

RESISTANCE AND THE VIS INERTIAE

One of the themes that is basic to inertia is the idea of resistance. There is a clue that the use of *perseverare* to mean "persist indifferently," which Beeckman, Descartes, and Newton all adopted for the first law, may have had its origins in scholastic discussions of resistance, especially in regard to the intension and remission of forms.

Among Galileo's papers there is an interesting collection of notebooks on questions in Aristotelian natural philosophy that he probably composed at Pisa in the late 1580s and early 1590s. Galileo is working his way through discussions of resistance found in lectures of Jesuit professors on physics, and perhaps choosing his positions in his notes for his *De Elementis*, in a specific collection we now call the *Notebooks on the Physical Questions*.[48] At the end of the discussion, there appears this summary conclusion:

[7] It follows, third that three factors can be found in any resistance. The first is what it formally connotes, and this is permanence in a proper state; the second is what it implies connotatively and this is the impeded action of the contrary; the third is the cause of such permanence, i.e., the cause that makes the thing persevere in its state easily and resist the contrary action. And this cause can be manifold, e.g., the act of resisting, as when an animal by its own powers guards itself through appropriate action; or weight and hardness, as in a stone; or the binding of matter by which the action of a contrary is slowed down, etc.[49]

Here we actually find, in Galileo's own hand, what are tantamount to the words of the first law, *expressive verbis*, or at least Descartes's first law. But with what effect? Galileo did not see the full blinding importance of this idea, even as he wrote it out.

Yet Galileo was very interested in resistance then, especially the resistance of media in local motion. His chief aim was to refute Aristotle's rules of motion, and these passages may be considered as a source of reflection when reading his analysis of Aristotle's rules in *On Motion*.

He sought to show that the main phenomena of motions, their direction upward or downward, and their speeds, were readily resolved by applications of Archimedean mechanics. Here, in the *De Elementis*, however, Galileo is working with Aristotelian forms in a larger discussion about intension and remission of forms – another order of discourse entirely. This is the problem and replies that led to the summary statement just quoted:

[1] The first problem is what is resistance? Vallesius, in the first Controversies, chapter 5, and others say that resistance is action and that to resist is somehow to act...

[2] I say, first: Resistance is not action formally, because a stone resists a hand pressing on it and yet there is no action; because the least heat resists the greatest coldness – for otherwise alteration would take place in an instant – and nonetheless heat does not react on cold; because the medium resists in local motion and yet it does not react per se; and finally, because bodies here below resist the action of the heavens and nonetheless do not react on them.

[3] I say, a second; resistance is not reception. For, when iron is pressed it does not receive, though it resists ...

[4] I say, third, resistance is permanence in a proper state against a contrary action. I say "against a contrary action," for resistance, while not an action, nonetheless connotes the action of the contrary that it impedes. I say "is permanence in a proper state," because I do not differentiate resistance from the things' very existence whereby it endures; indeed resistance formally bespeaks this permanence of a thing in its state and connotes the impeding of a contrary action ...[50]

Some of the most important properties we associate with inertia are linked in these passages with resistance – the permanence in a state and the opposition to contrary actions. And resistance was firmly linked in Galileo's work then with the problem of motion in a medium. There is no overt suggestion here that a body's resistance to change could be its cause of motion, except for that tantalizing hint that a body could "persevere in its state easily." Either the seed had fallen too soon, or perhaps, his idea of indifferent horizontal motion in *On Motion* may be an incomplete echo of this passage.

William Wallace has determined the various origins from which Galileo drew this material, including many Jesuit writers. There is a consensus that the *Notebooks on the Physical Questions* were either reading notes or preparations for lecture notes. Did he ever believe them or defend them? Historians have not decided fully what to make of the Physical Questions. Yet here are the indicative phrases of the later statement of the principle of inertia.

This discussion of resistance came from a literature already in place in the Jesuit system of colleges across Europe. With all of its own foretaste of the context in which inertia was found, this passage indicates that all of the basic elements of the inertial view were coming into hand all over Europe. It only needed the spark of geometry to bring it to life.

In *Two Chief World Systems*, Galileo provided a more developed discussion of resistance in motion:

> Now fix it well in mind as a true and well-known principle that the resistance coming from the speed of motion compensates that which depends on the weight of another moving body, and consequently that a body weighing one pound and moving with a speed of 100 units resists restraint as much as another of 100 pounds whose speed is but a single unit.[51]

Here are the inklings of the idea of conservation of momentum, but based on and measured in terms of resistance.

CIRCULAR OR RIGHT? THE IMPOSSIBLE MOTION

Koyré regarded Galileo's fascination with uniform circular motion as a basic stumbling block that kept him from grasping the principle of inertia. Specifying the rectilinear direction is an important feature of the principle.

One may recall Gassendi's correction of Galileo's views, or Descartes's amendment, or Newton's insistence on it. Stillman Drake once argued that if one wished to say that Galileo's concepts were inertial, it would be sufficient to show that his motions persisted indifferently, and the direction did not matter, but it appears to be important. Galileo did say in *Two Chief World Systems* that all motions were circular and denied that rectilinear motions ever occurred in nature. He also said nature really never uses accelerated vertical motion but achieves everything by uniform circular motion.

Yet his circular motions were always composed from two components, and one of those was a rectilinear tangential tendency to persist in the line of the impetus or impressed force – the same tangent that figures in the classical analysis of slings and orbits.

Galileo admits the tangent and works with it in all of the important examples in the Second Day of the *Two Chief World Systems*. Rectilinear motions are never manifest for noticeable distances in nature, either for Galileo or for Newton. Koyré explains:

Contrary to what has often been said the law of inertia does not have its origin in common sense experience, and is neither a generalization nor an idealization of it. What we find in experience is circular motions, or more generally curved motion. We never see rectilinear motion, except in the untypical case of free fall, and this is precisely not a case of inertial motion. Yet it was curved motion that classical physics would struggle to explain on the basis of the latter, rectilinear motion. This is a very strange approach ... what it involves, strictly speaking, is the explanation of that which *exists* by reference to that which *does not exist*, which never exists, by reference even to that which *never could exist*.[52]

In fact, the situation is less paradoxical than it seems. The inertial tangential motions defined in Newton's first law are, of course, found all around us, subsumed as components in all normal motions. Therefore, in one sense, the best example we have of inertial motion is a properly accelerated trajectory, rather than yards of pure inertial motion found only far from the Earth or in our imaginations.

Galileo was, however, well aware of the rectilinear tangential initial tendency of motions, of a body in a sling for example. In *Two Chief World Systems*, he says:

Salv.: "Up to this point you knew all by yourself that the circular motion of the projector impresses an impetus upon the projectile to move, when they separate, along the straight line tangent to the circle of motion at the point of separation, and that continuing with this motion, it travels farther from the thrower. And you have said that the projectile would continue to move along that line if it were not inclined downward by its own weight, from which fact the line of motion derives its curvature. It seems to me that you also know by yourself that this bending always bends toward the center of the earth, for all heavenly bodies tend that way."[53]

Galileo recognizes the existence and meaning of the rectilinear tangential tendency. He does understand this feature of basic classical motion. Yet he argues strenuously for circular motion, consciously refuting Aristotle's rectilinear natural motions, and unwittingly clouding his own appreciation of rectilinear motion.

The most astonishing thing about the world of Copernicus is that all naturally occurring motions are curved motions because they share the Earth's rotational motion. That draws Galileo's focus, especially because of the rhetorical contrast it offered to Aristotle's rectilinear natural motions of the elements.

The rectilinear tendencies in the line of the impressed force at the point of departure of the stone from its sling, which Galileo identified, are deemphasized and neglected. They are not, however, rejected by Galileo either.

It is Galileo's misfortune that his campaign against Aristotle's rectilinear natural motions was carried to the extreme point that he says that straight motions never occur in nature. This leads us to question whether he could have been an inertial thinker at all. But his large-scale circular motions are always composite motions and the inertial tangent is always present, of course.

Galileo didn't see the importance of stating the inertial tangential tendency as a basic principle of motion or analysis. His neglect is borne of the exuberance of a discoverer of new worlds. There was much that was new to see at every turn, and much that was more provocative than this tangent that he admitted, even if it were never produced in nature because of intrinsic and extrinsic forces, much like Newton's right inertial motion. Yet Galileo's analysis always noticed that there was potential straight motion "in the line of the impressed force," even if he did not write it out.

THE HISTORICAL PRINCIPLE OF INERTIA

The principle of inertia, as stated here in the first law, consists of four historically separable elements. At the base is Galileo's contention that moving bodies will continue in their unchanging motion when there is no cause to decelerate or accelerate them. Over that lies Beeckman's insistence that the body perseveres – not because of an impetus or impressed force, but because of a lack of sufficient cause to change its motion.

Galileo had thought the conservation of unchanging motion or rest was due to the action of the impressed force or impetus persisting in the absence of accelerations and decelerations. That impetus actually connected the body to the vast shared motion of the Earth.

Beeckman saw, however, that the world rested or moved uniformly – persevered was Beeckman's word – precisely in the absence of such impressed forces, as would Descartes and Newton who followed him. But, like Galileo, Beeckman thought a body could persevere in a circular orbit.

With Beeckman's principle of perseverance as its basis, Descartes's principle of right perseverance declares that perseverance only occurs in uniform and unvarying straight line motions – the crucial amendment made by Descartes. He argued that because God sustains Creation from instant to instant, He uses the simplest and most direct means of recreating motions, which is to have bodies continue in right motion to the next point in the next time frame or instant. In Descartes's view, any circular planetary orbit was sustained by outward pressing centrifugal force that balanced pressures from outside the planet's orbit.

Finally, there is Newton's clear recognition that the actions and reactions of the *vis inertiae* occur as accelerations, that is, as forces. In the works of Descartes and Galileo, the action of an impressed force sustained the speed of a body and did not change it. Newton's forces cause accelerations, and inertial forces change the speeds and directions of motion of colliding bodies. Newton is clear on all the points in Definition III, stated as a preamble to the three laws of motion.

In conclusion, the evidence indicates that Galileo did understand the conservation of motion, but he did not reject the idea of impetus and impressed forces. Impetus had many of the functions of classical inertia, including sustaining motion. He had understood the composition of motions, and his fascination with circular motion was a fascination with composite motions.

In essence then, in the end, he almost had all of the principles of inertia: conservation, rectilinear tangential tendency, and the equivalence of rest and motion. But he still thought in terms of impetus and for that reason failed in understanding the operation of dynamic forces. That, in turn, hindered his analysis of the forces and agencies of nature like gravitation.

NOTES

1 Galileo Galilei, *Two Chief World Systems*, 1632, and *Two New Sciences*, 1638.
2 *Two New Sciences*, pp. 161–2.

3 The document was first published by Stillman Drake, *Galileo's Experimental Confirmation of Horizontal Inertia: Unpublished Manuscripts*. A considerable literature had developed around this document and others in Volume 72 of the *Manoscritti Galileiani*, preserved at the Biblioteca Nazionale Centrale, Firenze. Other authors to consult concerning the experiment include Ronald Naylor, Winifred Wisan, James Maclachlan, and Kenneth Hill. Other treatments are cited elsewhere in this article. From the early years of the twentieth century until the 1960s, scholars believed that Galileo had not performed any experiments; Thomas Settle was the first historian to challenge this conclusion, cf. "Galileo's Use of Experiment," in *Galileo. Man of Science*. Edited by Ernan McMullin. (New York: Basic Books, 1967), pp. 315–337. Volume 72 contains undated and unordered notes on motion and mechanics that are currently the subject of much scholarly interest.

4 P. Damerow, G. Freudenthal, P. McLaughlin, and J. Renn, *Exploring the Limits of Preclassical Mechanics* (New York; Springer–Verlag, 1992), pp. 243–7.

5 Galileo, *Two New Sciences*, pp. 161–2.

6 Rene Descartes, letter to Mersenne, Oct. 11, 1638. Cf., S. Drake, *Galileo at Work* (1978), p. 387.

7 Alexandre Koyré, "*Gassendi and the Science of His Time*," in *Metaphysics and Measurement*. (London: Chapman and Hall, 1968), pp. 126–7.

8 Descartes, *Principes de Philosophie*, II, 37, in *Oeuvres de Descartes*. C. Adam and P. Tannery, eds. (Paris: L. Cerf, 1897–1913). Cf., Koyré, *Galileo Studies* translated by J. Mepham (Atlantic City, N.J.; Humanities Press, 1978), pp. 262–3.

9 Isaac Newton, *Mathematical Principles*, pp. 31–2.

10 Newton, *Mathematical Principles*, pp. 19–21.

11 I. B. Cohen, *Newtonian Revolution* (Cambridge; University Press, 1980), pp. 182–93.

12 Newton, *Mathematical Principles*, pp. 2–3.

13 Newton, *Opticks*, cf. Cohen, *Newtonian Revolution*, p. 397.

14 Newton, *Mathematical Principles*, p. 3.

15 Cohen, *Newtonian Revolution*. Bernd Ludwig, "*What is Newton's Law About?*" *Science in Context* 5 (1992), 139–62. Another scholar writing about inertia in Newton's work is Zev Bechler, "*Newton's Ontology of the Force of Inertia*," in *The Investigation of Difficult Things*. P. Harmon and A. Shapiro, eds. (New York; Cambridge University Press, 1992) urging that the natural verus enforced motion distinction not be applied to Newton.

16 Newton, *Mathematical Principles*, p. 31.

17 Cf. R. S. Westfall, *Force and Newton's Physics* (New York; American Elsevier, 1971). Chapter 1.

18 Koyré, *Newtonian Studies*, pp. 207ff.

19 I. B. Cohen, *Birth of a New Physics* (Garden City, N.Y.; Anchor Books, 1960), pp. 158–61.

20 *Letters on the Sunspots*, pp. 113–14.

21 *Two Chief World Systems*, p. 149.

22 *On Motion and On Mechanics*, pp. 66–8.

23 Ibid., p. 67.

24 *Two Chief World Systems*, pp. 164–5.

25 *Two Chief World Systems*, pp. 163–7.

26 *Two Chief World Systems*, p. 116.

27 Alan Chalmers, "*Galilean Relativity and Galileo's Relativity*" in S. French and H. Kamminga (eds.), *Correspondence, Invariance, and Heuristics* (Amsterdam; Kluwer, 1993), pp. 189–205.

28 Koyré, *Etudes Galileennes* 3 vols., (Paris; Hermann and Cie, 1939).

29 Koyré, *Galileo Studies*, p. 174.

30 Koyré, *Galileo Studies*, p. 174.

31 Koyré, *Galileo Studies*, pp. 184–5.

32 Paolo Galluzzi, *Momento: Studi Galileiani*. Cf. Galileo, *On Motion, and On Mechanics*. Translated by I. Drabkin and S. Drake (Madison; University of Wisconsin Press, 1960). Especially Chapter 14 of *On Motion*, and the discussion of the screw in *On Mechanics*.

33 Ernest Moody, *Galileo and Avempace*.

34 Moody, "*Galileo and Avempace*," Journal of the History of Ideas 12 (1951): 163–93, 375–422, pp. 392–6. Clagett, *Science of Mechanics in the Middle Ages* (Madison; University of Wisconsin Press, 1959), pp. 505–32.

35 Koyré, *Galileo Studies*, p. 169.

36 Galileo, *Two Chief World Systems*, p. 150.

37 Cf. James A. Weisheipel, "Galileo and his precursors," in *Galileo. Man of Science*. Ernan McMullin, ed. (New York: Basic Books, 1967). Especially pp. 87–9. Also, Murdoch, John E. and Edith D. Scylla. "The Science of Motion," Chapter 7 in *Science in the Middle Ages*. David C. Lindberg, ed. (Chicago: Chicago University Press, 1978), especially pp. 246–51.

38 Cf. S. Drake, *Mechanics in Sixteenth Century Italy* (Madison; University of Wisconsin Press, 1969).

39 Galileo, *Two Chief World Systems* (translated by S. Drake. Berkeley; University of California Press, 1953, 1962, and 1967), pp. 150–1.

40 Isaac Beeckman, *Journal*, I, wan der Wald edition (LeHayre; Nijhoff), p. 24. The translation from the Latin is my own.

41 Ibid. The translation from the Latin is my own.

42 Koyré, *Galileo Studies*, pp. 117–18, n. 61.
43 Beeckman, *Journal*, I, wan der Wald edition (LeHaye: Nijhoff), p. 24. The translation from the Latin is my own.
44 Galileo, *On Motion and On Mechanics*, pp. 151–2.
45 Galileo, *Two Chief World Systems*, pp. 245–6.
46 Galileo, *On Motion and On Mechanics*, pp. 79–80.
47 Galileo, *Two Chief World Systems*, p. 234.
48 Galileo, *De Elementis*, SY2 in Wallace, *Galileo's Early Notebooks* (Notre Dame; University Press, 1977), pp. 243–4.
49 Ibid.
50 Ibid.
51 Galileo, *Two Chief World Systems*, p. 215.
52 Koyré, *Galileo Studies*, p. 155.
53 Galileo, *Two Chief World Systems*, pp. 189–94.

5 From Galileo to Augustine

Posuit Deus omnia in numero, pondere et mensura

Galileo, EN, vol. 4, 52

In this essay, I will examine the relationship between Galileo's physics and his theology, focusing primarily on the latter. It is not my intention to minimize his commitment to physics – quite the contrary. But Galileo's interest in theology might seem remote given the secular status held by science today and, as a result, it would be tempting to dismiss theology as a textual relic corresponding to a fideistic atavism that is no longer present. However, it is precisely this secular perception of history that forces us to consider cultural relics of this sort.

Several recent studies of Galileo have tended to present his religious beliefs in one of two ways: as reflecting "genuine piety and devotion to the Church"[1] or else as grounded in Baroque-court rhetoric and compliance with the Church's position.[2] Otherwise, because of his Copernican campaign and trial, Galileo has also been included in the group of other theologically minded scientists such as Descartes, Boyle, and Newton – not to mention Pascal or Leibniz. Compared to these figures, Galileo's theological concerns appear as self-defense in the struggle between Copernican astronomy and biblical exegesis and completely separate from his physics.

My question is quite different. I would like to explore the role religious formulas played in the genesis of Galileo's mechanics vis-à-vis atomism and cosmology. To do this, I will trace the transformation of his law of fall from its initial framework to its final published version which merged terrestrial and celestial motion. Finally, I will argue

175

that Galileo's theological commitment was essential to his scientific journey. That is to say, Galileo's physics required God.

MACROPHYSICS

Let me begin by briefly summarizing Galilean physics. At the end of the Renaissance, physics consisted of the study of things as they really were. Given that all things were endowed with movement (excluding, of course, the Earth) – from the divine heavenly spheres in perpetual revolution to the irregular paths of the sublunar bodies – physics dealt with the study of motion. Galileo agreed with the theory held by Democritus and Archimedes that all things are heavy and naturally move downward:

If it is true, as ancient philosophers believed, that there is a single kind of matter in all bodies, and those bodies are heavier which enclose more particles of that matter in a narrower space ... and also occupy narrower places, such are those that are nearer the center.[3]

Trained as he was in Jacopo Mazzoni's Christian natural philosophy, Galileo was referring to the *prisca physica* of the "most ancient philosophers" rather than to Aristotle. A Christian physicist had to justify the cosmos as a world created *ex novo* to comply with the providential meaning of nature – a creation defined as a separation of chaos.[4] Indeed, this notion of creation can also be found in Plato's *Timaeus*:

Just as when things are shaken and winnowed by means of winnowing-basket and other instruments for cleaning corn, the dense and heavier things go one way, while the rare and light are carried to another place and settle there.[5]

Lucretius also believed that creation consisted of moving downward those bodies that contained smaller particles closer to the center of the universe.[6] Among his early writings on mechanics, and specifically in *De Motu Antiquiora*, Galileo subscribed to this cosmogonic, geocentric view in which specific weight was wedded to the biblical genesis:

After the marvelous construction of the vast celestial sphere, the divine Creator pushed the refuse that remained into the center of that very sphere and hid it there ... and in order that this great region might not be unused and unoccupied he tore apart that heavy, confused mass ... and the earth was left in the center. And, similarly, the denser bodies were placed near the earth.[7]

The weight of all terrestrial bodies was a function of the medium surrounding them, including air, and this was an Archimedean idea which could also be found in the Book of Job: "He has weighed out the wind."[8] Weight, or gravity, was the universal source of motion – equally for a speck of dust as for a drop of water. This idea could be further reinforced by a passage in the Book of Wisdom: "You have disposed all things by measure, and number and weight ... before you the whole universe is as a grain from a balance, or a drop of morning dew come down upon the earth."[9]

Just as a grain of sand can tip the scales, so Galileo, when teaching his course on mechanics at Padua, adopted the general postulate that if all impediments were removed, heavy bodies could be moved along a horizontal plane by any minimal force whatsoever.[10] This axiom furnished the basis by which the force acting on an object along an inclined plane could be reduced to the static equilibrium established by a lever, in particular, momentum, the product of weight and speed.

But natural fall raised a phenomenological problem. If motion is a function of an object's gravity, or its density, then it should remain constant; however, free-falling bodies naturally accelerate. With respect to dynamics, the influential mathematician Benedetti had understood that acceleration represented as much a terrestrial accident as a questionable (and discriminating) factor between linear and circular motion.[11]

In principle, the essence of perfect motion in nature was circularity. Ever since Plato and Aristotle, but especially after Copernicus, the natural order of the cosmos was thought to be guaranteed by the uniformity of celestial revolutions. Galileo never doubted that circular motion was uniform and inertial, at least at slow speeds.

In contrast, downward acceleration remained a temporary and accidental attribute of linear motion in the sublunar realm. Aristotelian philosophers were inclined to believe that acceleration occurred at the end of the fall where the stratum of the resistant medium was less thick. Yet for someone like Benedetti, who followed medieval theories of dynamics, acceleration depended on the distance from the starting point – as impetus accumulated – produced by its weight.

Initially following in Benedetti's footsteps, Galileo had described acceleration as a continuously increasing speed in the case of an object projected upwards that then begins to fall. In other words, gravity gradually prevails on the object's lightness, which has been artificially created by the projector.[12] Time, as a variable, was dismissed in such a qualitative explanation of acceleration in terms of difference of heaviness and lightness.

But at the beginning of the seventeenth century, Galileo attempted to develop a geometrical framework of natural motion worthy of Hipparchus and Archimedes and sought mathematical regularities in both rectilinear and circular constrained fall. In measuring pendular oscillations along the arcs of circles as well as falling motions along inclined planes, Galileo made two discoveries, the implications of which were beyond the scope of his genius.

First, he realized that pendulums of equal length produce isochronous oscillations. As a result, they could measure time on Earth in much the same way as the stars did in the heavens.

According to Aristotle,

Neither qualitative modification nor growth nor genesis has the kind of uniformity that rotation has; and so time is regarded as the rotation of the sphere, inasmuch as all other orders of motion are measured by it, and time itself is standardized by reference to it ... time itself is conceived as coming round.[13]

In both the heavenly and terrestrial realms, physical time was nothing more than a quantity derived from periodic circular motions. To convince his master, Guidobaldo del Monte, of this "marvelous" discovery, Galileo intuitively arrived at the following comparison. He confronted the pendular isochronism along different arcs of circumference to the very disproportionate distances covered by a falling body in an equal amount of time, assuming its descent is vertical or along a very slowly moving river. Mistakenly believing that the pendulum moved in equal time along any arc of a circle, Galileo did not realize that these periodic oscillations were equivalent to the accelerated motions of linear descent.[14]

Perhaps the cosmological hiatus between rectilinear and circular movement as well as the fact that the latter defined time played a part in Galileo's understanding of his second discovery of a new mathematical regularity. In his famous letter to Paolo Sarpi in 1604, Galileo announced that he had formulated a rule according to which falling bodies accelerated uniformly in proportion to the squares of the time elapsed from rest.

However, he was unable to recognize the essential implications of such a law. In fact, he dismissed the possibility that rectilinear acceleration could be connected to time. Instead, he preferred to adopt another "completely indubitable principle to put as an axiom"[15] as the cornerstone of his geometrical framework on natural motion. This principle reflected the more traditional and intuitive proportion between the uniformity of acceleration and the distance from the starting point.

The traditional assumptions – that gravity acted as a motive force and acceleration as a spatial effect – were rooted as they were in scholastic physics. They represented two lines of research that Galileo continued to explore, proof after proof, in his unpublished papers on motion.[16] And yet almost thirty years would pass before he published radical revisions in this subject, first in the *Dialogue Concerning the Two Chief World Systems* (1632) and later in the *Two New Sciences* (1638).

By then he preferred to discard the conventional explanations of acceleration as "fancies" (*fantasie*), claiming that the true law of acceleration depended on a different ontological cause. Nature is perfect and simple and creates nothing in vain:

After continual agitation of mind ... it is as though we have been led by the hand to the investigation of naturally accelerated motion by consideration of the custom and procedure of nature itself in all her other works, in the performance of which she habitually employs the first, simplest and easiest means. And indeed, no one of judgment believes that swimming or flying can be accomplished in simpler or easier way than that which fish and birds employ by natural instinct.[17]

Assuming this teleological stance, Galileo now resurrected the axiomatic primacy of the proportion of uniform acceleration with respect to time; in short, "... that the intensification of speed is made according to the (*extensionem*) of time."[18]

How did this shift come about? Why had Galileo found it so difficult to acknowledge in 1604 "the closest affinity between time and motion"[19] whereas thirty years later he argued that it was an evident and necessary correspondence?

We need not enter here into the vexed question of how Galileo originally arrived at the law of fall. We are only interested in what might have prevented him from considering acceleration in temporal, rather than spatial, terms. Indeed, for Galileo and his contemporaries, the concept of uniform generation of speed as a function of elapsed time from rest was counterintuitive.

TIME

We can discuss this problem by recalling how time was conceptualized during the seventeenth century. True, natural time depended on Creation. This religious time focused on the mystery of the Incarnation and all orthodox mathematicians and annalists based their calculations on this chronology.

"The world was created by God in time" went the formula of the late Renaissance[20] and, as a professor of mathematics at Pisa, Galileo subscribed to these pious computations. Moreover, in his notes we find him agreeing with the Platonic doxography of the created world exemplified in Basilius and Ambrose's *Exameron* and Augustine's *The City of God*: "According to many authors, Plato thought that the world had been created in time from matter animated by a disordered motion."[21]

We can now understand why, in 1607, Galileo's pupil and closest collaborator, Father Castelli, wrote to his teacher expressing concern over the problem of Creation:

Because of the fact that we point out the production of everything, nothing can be found before, *ex nihilo nihil* must be necessarily understood and limited to nothing but the particular productions, not at all to the production of everything.[22]

A few years later, Galileo revealed that at the time he had envisioned an "immense theory full of philosophy, astronomy and geometry," which he tentatively entitled *De Systemate Mundi seu Constitutione Universi*.[23] According to Castelli, Galileo had also advanced an impressive conception of inertia: "That motion was anything but the mutation of something with regard to another one."

In this same letter, Castelli went on to argue about the danger of holding that the world had been created "by motion"; this was tantamount to claiming that motion was as eternal as God. Those Aristotelians who deduced the eternity of the world from the perpetual revolutions of the heavens ("if they are created, then it is by motion") were impious. However, enthusiasts who took God to be the initial source of an inertial rectilinear motion were also wrong:

Then, from the doctrine of Your Lordship that a motive cause is necessary to start the motion, but the lack of obstacles is sufficient to continue it, makes me want to laugh when they magnify such a doctrine as though it made the existence of God known to me.[24]

To be sure, mechanics involved a theological drift. This problematic link between motion and creation was indeed very close to the problem of time as discussed by Augustine against the Manichees. The Manichees had also believed in the eternal, cyclical return of things and dismissed the idea that the universe had not been built in a day. In Plato's *Timaeus*, a work recommended by Augustine for Christian philosophers, God's will established the regular planetary motions as "a mobile likeness of eternity."[25] In his biblical cosmogony, *De Opificio Mundi*, Philo of Alexandria, had maintained as well that eternity meant God's existence outside of time. Therefore, everything – including time – was instantaneously created *ex nihilo*: "The Maker made all things simultaneously, order was none the less an attribute of all that came into existence."[26] Thus the continuity of time was brought about by the ordered succession of things as they came into existence.

In *The City of God*, Augustine had integrated time with God's will, and the creation of the universe was explained as a uniform generative action through timeless or instantaneous degrees: "with one and the same will, eternal and unchanging, he created things which didn't exist until they existed and then existed as soon as they began to be."[27] Continuing in this same vein, he held that time consisted of a coming-into-being into the present. Furthermore, in his *Confessions*, Augustine disconnected time itself from the Aristotelian eternity of circular orbits:

Let no man therefore say unto me hereafter, that the motions of the celestial bodies be the times; because that when at the prayer of a certain man [Joshua], the sun had stood still, till he could achieve his victorious battle.[28]

This biblical miracle of the Sun stopping at the Battle of Gabaon proved that "... the sun stood indeed but time went on: for in a certain space of time of his own, (enough to serve his turn) was that battle strucken and gotten. I perceive time therefore to be a certain stretching (distensio)."[29]

And so Augustine asked, "What time should be by which we measure the circuit of the sun ... I desire to understand the force and nature of time by which we measure the motion of bodies and this motion is twice longer than that."[30]

Time was no longer measured by motion; rather, motion was measured by time. Augustine had portrayed the generative act of cosmic time together with the physical laws of the universe as an infinite succession of moments lacking extension. In other words, it was a temporal continuum of instants without dimensions, identical to geometrical points – in puncto[31] – as "if any instant of time could be conceived, which can not be divided either into more, or at most into the smallest particles of moments (In minutissimas momentorum partes)."[32]

Such an instantaneous view of Creation could hold for the ontology of time, but how does one correlate it with motion? In fact, motion marked discreet physical time measured on Earth by intervals. Thus time was kept by lunar periods, weight-driven clocks, one's pulse, or the length of an Ave Maria. How could one discuss motion in terms of instantaneous time if all natural timekeepers lasted no longer than one second?[33]

Augustine's metaphysics of time remained an untapped source for natural philosophers. Crede ut intelligas. But until then no one had applied it to dynamics. Not even the medieval, Augustinian natural philosopher Nicolas Oresme had conceived of instantaneous speed; nor in 1607 was Castelli as ingenious a theologian as Descartes to postulate inertia on the immovability of God. Castelli had only his faith to rely on when he reminded Galileo at the end of his letter that, "if it is true that motion is eternal, I could begin to be atheistic (ateista) and say that we don't need God. What a wicked blasphemy!"[34]

As we have already mentioned, at that time Galileo's physics was a physics of gravity or, as Koyré labeled it in his *Etudes Galiléennes,* a *"physique de le chute."* But Koyré himself later recognized that he had underestimated another kind of physics:

> ... by a mathematical approach to nature, atomism – in the works of Galileo, Boyle, Newton, etc. – became a scientifically valid conception and Lucretius and Epicurus appeared as forerunners of modern science. Obviously it is possible and even probable that in linking mathematics with atomism, modern science revived the deepest intuitions and intentions of Democritus.[35]

It is true that since 1610, Galileo was dealing more and more with extremely tenuous entities called corpuscles, particles, "aculeous of fire," *minima*, and atoms – all of which were weightless or nearly so. He was also investigating magnetic and cohesive forces, motions of penetration, and condensation and rarefaction of substances rather than a mechanics of gravity. So it would be more exact to say that Galileo had developed two different ideas of physics: a macrophysics of fall and a microphysics of weightlessness.

MICROPHYSICS

Until *The Assayer* appeared in 1623, Galileo continued with this corpuscular agenda which actually dated to his *Discourse on Floating Bodies* (1612). Here he and Castelli dealt with the paradox of imponderable objects, that is, those objects that seemed to be in perpetual suspension: "... impalpable and imperceptible atoms of earth which by their very tiny force take six days to down half a hands breadth."[36]

Surpassing Archimedes in hydromechanics, Galileo was able to take into account both the dimensions of the container and the level of the floating body. According to Galileo, the weight of the liquid volume generated by the surface of the container counterbalanced a sinking body until it floated, the rate of which was determined by the container's dimensions. The vertical component of buoyancy acted like a lever, and in such a physics of rigid reactions, water was an ideal fluid lacking resistance and viscous force.

That even those tiny particles suspended in cloudy water eventually settled was proof that water had no internal resistance. Therefore Galileo could "imagine" water as a structure of contact between "...

innumerable little spheres, smaller than any you can imagine, round and very clean or shaped according to the figure that Plato assigned to them."[37]

As luck would have it, his Aristotelian adversaries provided persuasive evidence that real, physical water was not an ideal fluid. This was because even bodies more dense than water could float as long as they were thinly shaped. Thus the viscosity of water became the "main point" under discussion.[38]

For his part, Galileo observed little liquid banks (arginetti) surrounding the thin bodies when they were half-submerged. He could then suppose that the air enclosed by the arginetti offered a plausible Archimedean explanation for the anomalous buoyancy. However, he was still puzzled by the force that sustained the arginetti. Was it not perhaps the same force that made heavy raindrops cling to a rain spout after a storm?[39]

Galileo discarded the idea that such a cohesive force could be explained by Gilbert and Kepler's magnetic attraction because he believed that magnetic force – like cohesion – must be attributed to more geometrical "exquisite contacts" of matter.[40]

Nevertheless, an answer to the puzzle of liquid cohesion continued to elude him, forcing him to admit in the Two New Sciences that, "... inability on my part should not detract from the clarity of truth (candidezza della verità). In the first place, I confess that I don't know how that business of sustaining large and elevated globules of water is accomplished."[41] He was blinded by such clarity, or "whiteness" (candidezza), because such an elementary phenomenon prevented him from generalizing a mechanics of gravity.

The puzzle lay in the cosmological value of spherical cohesion of the single drop of water. In fact, Copernicus opened his De Revolutionibus by saying that things move downward not because of their weight but rather the natural tendency (appetentia) of matter to aggregate as a sphere: "... as is apparent in drops of water and other fluid bodies when they seek to be spontaneously self-contained (per se terminari cupiunt). Hence no one will question the attribution of this form to the divine bodies."[42]

Gutta cavat lapidem. Cohesion, surface tension, and attraction were as mysterious as gravity. Given the well-known physical anomalies of atomism, such as condensation and rarefaction, in the Discourse, Galileo appealed in vain to Democritus, who was "...

not happy with mere names wanted to determine more particularly what weight and lightness were."[43]

One of his opponents, Vincenzio de Grazia, had argued – in the medieval tradition – that to admit the existence of indivisible atoms was to claim that lines were composed of a finite number of indivisible points; meaning that the diagonal and the side of a square would have the same ratio as the whole number of points of their lengths.[44]

Another critic of Galileo's Archimedean physics, Giorgio Coresio, had also objected that those particles suspended in cloudy water simply proved that the resistance of the medium was the essence of motion: No instantaneous motion existed since neither vacuums nor instants existed. According to Plato's concept of time as a moving image of eternity, motion meant duration. In particular, as Coresio pointed out, Aristotle defined motion as temporal, "... because it is measured by time and not because motion is produced in time, in the manner of an action like an intellection or an illumination which are in fact instantaneous."[45]

Until then, nature had seemed to Galileo a transparent realm of mechanical knowledge, one that was capable of proving "the true, intrinsic and total cause"[46] of all things. But now "the vain presumption of understanding everything"[47] was replaced with the *docta ignorantia* of the Socratic aphorisms scattered throughout *The Assayer* and *Dialogue*: "... there is not a single effect in nature, even the least that exists such that the most ingenious theorist can arrive at a complete understanding of it."[48]

Not only distant comets but even the most elementary phenomena of the world were locked in mystery – a flash of light, a persistent smell, those large dewdrops on the cabbage leaves, the chirp of a cicada. Meanwhile, gravity itself was becoming more and more mysterious: "... it is called gravity. What I am asking you for is not the name, but its essence, of which essence you know not a bit more than you know about the essence of whatever moves the stars around."[49]

Thus, in his physics Galileo abandoned universals and causes for another epistemological space. I am not talking about a flight into the Pythagorean mysticism of numbers, but of another optics, another logic, and other methods of knowledge. Here, the cause of natural effects was neither a name nor a mathematical essence but nature itself, created according to "number, weight and measure" as Galileo wrote in a fragment of the *Discourse on Floating Bodies*.

This is why, before arriving at Galileo's theology, I had to make such a long detour to reach the point in which his mechanics of weight was eclipsed by the sunspots.

ASTROPHYSICS

Is it possible, or even correct, to extrapolate from Galileo's celestial discoveries a transcendent image of nature? Four centuries later, we still find it difficult to understand the religious investiture of knowledge associated with the novelties presented in the *Sidereus Nuncius* in 1610. In this work, Galileo introduced himself as a prophet who had perfected the telescope "illuminated before by divine grace" and had discovered, "led by what fate, I don't know," the planets of Jupiter, which "... indeed the Maker of the stars itself has seemed by clear indications" to have suggested that he dedicate them to the Medici.[50]

Were both Protestant and Catholic readers, like Kepler and the Jesuit astronomers of the Roman College, wrong in welcoming the author of the *Sidereus* as a real "celestial messenger"?[51] To say nothing of Thomas Seggett's glorification of Galileo as an angel or of the religious praise of his discoveries by theologians like Campanella and Libert Froidmont.[52]

With Galileo's new astronomical commitment to the Copernican system, he made repeated appeals to divine inspiration and insisted to the Vatican prelate, Piero Dini, that "...One should not lose confidence that the divine Goodness sometimes decides to instill a beam of its immense wisdom in humble minds, especially when they are adorned with sincerity and holy zeal."[53] However, in this missionary zeal, the Holy Office had prevented him from publishing these precise words in his *Letters on Sunspots* (1613).

During this period, Galileo had adopted the pro-Copernican biblical conciliation that several Carmelite theologians were popularizing within the Catholic Church as well. He was displaying an intensive reading of patristic sources and theology. Augustine was his most frequently quoted author but Galileo was also inspired by the negative theology of Dionysius the Areopagite (and revived by Nicholas Cusanus).

To paraphrase Augustine, God is defined by what He is not.[54] So Galileo's *Letters on Sunspots* began as follows: "These considerations

... still make me hesitate to do more than advance a rather negative cause by appearing to know rather what sunspots are *not* than what they really are ...."[55] Like shadows on the bottom of a cavern, those dark spots moved through the image of the solar disk, projected by the telescope onto a sheet of paper. The identification of such a remote and indirect phenomenon implied a doubt: Reason would probably never attain the status of absolute truth, or discover the very essence of things, "... for that knowledge is withheld from us, and is not to be understood until we reach the state of blessedness [*stato di beatitudine*]."[56]

Nevertheless, when the senses fail, cognition is still possible. Mathematical demonstrations provide "the means" of entering a terrain of uncertain, conjectural knowledge founded on similitudes, analogies, and metaphors. Until then, Galileo had followed a strictly apodictic and Euclidian method. But how could such a weak and conjectural form of knowledge offer a legitimate alternative to the "true" science?

Faith provided such legitimation. In fact, the *Third Letter on Sunspots* opened with an epistemological prayer on the Augustinian theme of the divine intellectual light "... for which we now search almost like blind men in the impure and material sun shall come to us from the grace of the true, pure, and immaculate Sun, together with all other truths in Him."[57]

Why did solar physics require God? Castelli's diagrams had already offered geometrical proof that the sunspots lay on the solar surface or in its near vicinity, increasing in speed at the edges of the solar equator. Thus solar rotation could be proved without necessarily appealing to a fideistic position. Certainly, in Galileo's eyes, mathematical demonstrations as such proved that "... the human mind is a work of God and one of the most excellent." Of course, they were infinitely fewer than the mathematical properties of nature which were "... infinite and perhaps but one in their essence and in the Divine mind ... and run through the Divine mind like light in an instant."[58]

"God is always doing geometry," Plato is said to have remarked.[59] And this was exactly what Galileo was doing. But in this case, what he was really after was a superior contemplation through "divine grace" in order

... to be able to philosophize better about other and more controversial qualities of natural substances. And finally by elevating us to the ultimate end of our labors, which is the love of the divine Artificer, this will keep us steadfast in the hope that we shall learn every other truth in Him, the source of light and verity.[60]

At the very end of the *Third Letter*, Galileo made two conjectures. The first, given as a dubious hypothesis, was that, owing to their similarity to terrestrial clouds of smoke or to marks of burned tar on a plate, sunspots must be marks of luminous, solar combustion. The second, which he developed elsewhere to Castelli and presented as "quite probable and reasonable," was that "... the sun, as the instrument and highest minister of nature, as if it were the heart of the world, gives not only light, as it clearly does, but also motion to all the planets which revolve around it."[61]

This last point carried a theological implication. For the critics of Copernicanism, the biblical battle scene at Gabaon described the Sun's rotation around the Earth. Galileo, however, emphasized something quite different in this text: namely, that the miracle lay in stopping the Sun's axial rotation. In other words, interrupting the Sun's rotation was all that was necessary for the entire planetary system to come to a halt. And in this way God had lengthened the Earth's day.

This planetary dynamics was in fact supported by the famous neo-platonic and Copernican metaphor of the Sun reigning over and administering the planets with its light at the center of the celestial orbits like a "... lantern of the universe, its mind, its ruler ... the sun governs the family of planets revolving around it." But Copernicus had also employed an Aristotelian, physiological metaphor concerning the close kinship between the Sun and Earth, almost as if the latter was the Sun's own flesh and blood: "... the earth has intercourse with the sun, and is impregnated for its yearly parturition."[62]

Instead, Galileo not only discarded any neoplatonic identification of the Sun with God but also Kepler's ideas of a magnetic Sun moving the planets by irradiating immaterial light. Even though it was "... a most spiritual, tenuous and fast moving substance, which penetrates everything without resistance, and which warms, vivifies and fecundates all living creatures,"[63] solar light belonged to the realm of physics, or better still, physiology.

Likewise, in Cesalpino's theory of cardiac circulation to and from the lungs, the vital heat spread and regenerated itself by "circulating" hot blood from the heart. The heart was like a heat-propelling center of motion and nutrition for the entire human body. Galileo extended this model to solar activity: The Sun was like a hot, beating heart which emanated toward the stars and, in return, received a tenuous thermo-luminous fluid. It was this spherical propagation of light that could perhaps allow the planets to continue revolving around the Sun.[64]

In his letter of March 1615 to Monsignor Dini, Galileo explained in further detail this cardiac model, with the intention of providing a physical interpretation of the verses of Psalm 18, *The heavens declare the glory of God*:

... He has pitched a tent there for the sun which comes forth like the groom from his bridal chamber and like a giant, joyfully runs its course. At one end of the heavens it comes forth, and its course is to their other end; nothing escapes from its heat.

Galileo explained that "... the emanations of the sun's rays ..., which in a way occur by fits and starts" because solar light runs in an undulatory motion to and from the stars and is "reflected and emitted about very vigorously ... just as the heart of an animal continually regenerates the vital spirits."[65] Here, Galileo was arguing that the circular planetary orbits were maintained from the center, according to a pulsating, spherical propagation.

Indeed, with the biblical miracle of the Sun stopping "in medio caeli," it was almost as if God had come to Galileo's aid. In his famous *Letter to the Grand Duchess Christina*, Galileo had written that this phrase literally meant "in the midst of the heavens" and not at all "at midday" as it had been traditionally understood:

... in the "midst" – that is in the center – of the celestial orbs and planetary motions, as it is necessary to do ... that is in the center where it resides ... for the true and only "midst" of a spherical body such as the sky is its center.[66]

This meant that the Book of Revelations and the Book of Nature legitimated one another: Their propositions had to coincide because their author was one and the same. From this Augustinian postulate, Galileo formulated not only a criterion of a scientifically based scriptural exegesis, but also the theological status of physics insofar as the latter had something to say on the mysteries of creation, providence, and omnipotence:

... nor is God any less excellently revealed in Nature's actions than in sacred statements of the Bible. Perhaps this is what Tertullian meant by these words: We conclude that God is known first through Nature, and then again more particularly by doctrine.[67]

So Galileo invited "... the holy Church to say that God has placed the sun in the center of the heaven, and that by rotating it like a wheel gave to the moon and the other wandering stars their appointed courses" in accordance with Scripture and concluded by repeating with Augustine Ambrose's hymn, *Deus creator omnium*, "Who creating on the fourth day/the flaming disk of the sun/gave order to the moon/and wandering courses of the stars."[68]

Galileo was referring to the idea expressed in *Genesis* that God had imparted something like a rotatory push, or angular momentum, to the planetary orbits, or wheels.

It would seem that the Christian metaphor of "the Book of the World" adopted by Galileo since his *Letters on Sunspots* was an emblem of his religious voluntarism.[69] Galileo's mysticism was certainly inspired by Augustine's epistemological creed concerning the divine Word as an intellectual substitute for the weakness (*infirmitas*) of the human mind:

... first, the human mind perceives created things through the senses and understands them according to the limits of human weakness. Then it looks for their causes ... which primarily and constantly lie in the Word of God and in this way, the mind intellectually recognizes God's invisible perfections in His Work.[70]

But the *Letter to the Grand Duchess Christina* also contained the following declaration:

... within its pages are couched mysteries so profound and concepts so sublime that the vigils, labors and studies of hundreds upon hundreds of the most acute minds have still not pierced them even after continual investigations for thousands of years.[71]

One might ask whether the ecclesiastic condemnation in 1616 of a Copernican interpretation of the Bible might not have incited

Galileo to a more effective theodicy. As a matter of fact, at the end of the *Dialogue* he acknowledged that he meant "... to discover the work of His hands ... to recognize and thereby so much the more admire His greatness, however much less fit we may find ourselves to penetrate the profound depths of His infinite wisdom." And in this conclusion, Galileo was paraphrasing *Ecclesiastes*.[72]

COSMOGONY

As we know, in 1616 Galileo was expressly forbidden to use the Bible in order to defend Copernicus. Miracles, however, were not mentioned. At a certain point in the *Dialogue,* Sagredo remarks that "... all works of nature and of God appear miraculous" and Salviati agrees, replying "...that is the way I feel about it, and saying that the natural cause of tides is the motion of the earth does not exclude this operation from being miraculous."[73] In fact, tides are miraculous precisely because they obey "... Nature and in this alone may be recognized an infinite wisdom; hence one may conclude that Divine wisdom is infinitely infinite."[74]

Need I rehearse what has often been said about the metaphysical tones of the Galilean *mathesis universalis* and the geometrical language of both the divine knowledge and the universe itself ? In doing so, would I not arrive at a very general philosophical interpretation of the natural mysteries that so fascinated our author?

A cosmogonical theory framed the physics of the *Dialogue* and was reiterated in the *Two New Sciences*. The world was generated from chaos and reached its symmetry through primogenital, rectilinear motions that drove bodies to their most consonant places. Nevertheless, Galileo wanted to avoid the eventuality that the world would slip back into chaos through such continuous motions in undetermined directions.

This meant that he needed something like Lucretius's *clinamen* of atoms in order to redirect the linear motions to circular orbits in which "... the bodies have ever since been preserved and maintained."[75] However, Lucretius's *clinamen* was fortuitous whereas Galileo needed divine, intelligent agency to bring the world to a *universe* around a center.

Finis est prima causa. For such an intentional *clinamen,* Galileo required God. However because the Holy Office had forbidden him to advocate the hypothesis that God moved celestial orbits like wheels on the basis of Scripture, he shifted gears and told us the "true story" of Creation.

This was a mechanical proof, fully consonant with Christian faith, that was based on a Platonic myth of God who lets the planets fall and then redirects them to uniform circular motions once they reach a proper speed. This was mathematically demonstrable for, given the orbital distances and speeds, one could calculate the unique point from which God really made the planets fall.

While in Padua, we know that Galileo had drafted similar astronomical computations in his notes for *De Systemate Mundi*. Indeed, he confessed on the Fourth Day of the *Two New Sciences* that he had successfully calculated such a "sublimity" from which planets fell. Yet he preferred to remain silent in light of the fact that he ". . . had discovered too many novelties that have provoked the anger of many, and others might kindle still more sparks."[76]

In ascending the scale of cosmic time to the miraculous singularity of Creation, Galileo was not performing a mere mathematical simulation. On the contrary, these words revealed that he understood the theological effect of his alleged discovery of the divine law of accelerated fall.

But to Castelli's mind, wouldn't a divine, first mechanical action of the universe imply the impious idea of an eternity of motion? In the *Dialogue*, Salviati actually reveals that such a creationist physics came from ". . . a sublime concept, and worthy indeed of Plato, which I remember having heard discussed by our friend, the Lyncean Academician [Galileo]."[77] Galileo's reasoning about "Plato's concept" on the simultaneous birth of time and planetary motions dealt with the actual continuity of an accelerated motion in nature:

... a moving body, departing from rest and entering into the motion for which it has a natural inclination, passes through all the antecedent gradations of slowness that exist between a state of rest and any assigned degree of velocity, these gradations being infinite."[78]

Specifically, how had the Platonic (and Christian) concept of the creation of time inspired Galileo to conclude that an accelerated speed meant continuous degrees of slowness? In fact, common sense would suggest that such an instantaneous view of speed was misleading because our senses would recognize this as simply motionlessness. As

Coresio reminded us, Aristotle had stressed that neither an instantaneous motion, nor for that matter, an instant, could exist in nature. But, according to Augustine:

... Who indeed are we petty men to presume to set limits to God's knowledge by saying that, unless the same temporal things are repeated in the same periodic cycles, He cannot either foreknow all that he does in order to do it or know it when He has done it. For God's wisdom, which is simple in its multiformity comprehends all incomprehensible things.[79]

Similarly, Sagredo repeated in the *Dialogue*,

... To me, a great ineptitude exists on the part of those who would have it that God made the universe more in proportion to the small capacity of their reason than to His immense, His infinite power.[80]

Indeed, God could have decided otherwise. He might immediately have conferred a high speed to the falling bodies or else created circular motion but, "... *de facto* nature does not do so that the doing of this would be something outside the course of nature, and therefore miraculous."[81] As Aquinas and especially Nicholas Cusanus had recommended in their theology, Galileo's physics dealt with what God had actually done through divinely ordered power. Galileo's God was omnipotent yet parsimonious.

Around 1631, Galileo revealed that the new physics of motion that he was about to publish in the *Dialogue* was founded on the Augustinian representation of the divine wisdom of nature as expressed in the allegory of the perfect creation of birds and fish in order to fly in the air and swim underwater.[82]

In fact, Galileo wrote that God could have made birds fly with solid gold feathers and fish swim with veins full of quicksilver as further proof of His own omnipotence. Instead, their composition followed a teleological necessity: Birds have light bones and fish weigh as much as water. Moreover, Galileo's teleological foundation of natural philosophy was consistent with Aquinas's metaphysical principle of least action that nature doesn't make anything at random, for no purpose. Nature's providential order implied the shortest and most economical way of acting:

... in searching for hidden propositions of how God works, one finds that with respect to what is known, He always complies with the easiest and simplest rules, so that His power could be all the more revealed through his most difficult ways [*modo*].[83]

As for the complicated issue of accelerated motion, Nature continued to work as God had during Creation. A generative increase of speed *ex nihilo* had to be construed as truly instantaneous velocity; this goes against common sense and in accordance with the Augustinian instantaneous view of Creation. In fact, Galileo would specify in the Third Day of the *Two New Sciences*[84] that, "... in any finite time, however small, there are infinitely many instants."

This general definition would allow Galileo to derive his times-squared law of free fall, imbued as it was with the scholastic terminology and medieval, geometrical visualization of the mean-speed rule. On this point, d'Oresme agreed with Augustine and, in his *Traité du Ciel et du Monde*, attempted to refute Aristotelian physics in the name of God's creation with his famous analogy that God had released the heavens "... like a man lets go a clock." In turn, Augustine's framework was infused with the Platonic concept of the creationistic affinity between time and the universal laws of motion. And so Galileo was right to say that he had correctly revealed in physical–mathematical terms the creation "hidden under a mask or a poetic feature"[85] in Plato's cosmic myth.

Let us look at how Galileo had corrected this famous myth. In the *Timaeus*, we find that God chose uniform circular motion for the regular, or direct planetary motion. Plato also referred to this motion as "the Same" and it took precedence over "the Different." By the latter, as Proclus confirmed, Plato intended the variable, opposite, or retrograde motion along the inclined plane of the ecliptic. According to this geocentric theory, planets appear to move from west to east – sometimes faster, sometimes slower – and pass from the Sun through angles of divergence:

... And he gave the supremacy to the revolution of the Same and uniform ... In order that Time might be brought into being, Sun and Moon and five other stars ... were made to define and preserve the numbers of Time. Having made a body for each of them, the god set them in the circuits in which the revolution of the Different was moving, in seven circuits seven bodies .... Then they began to revolve by way of the motion of the Different, which was aslant, crossing the movement of the Same and subject to it: some moving in greater circles, some in lesser; those in the lesser circles moving faster, those in the greater more slowly.[86]

Of course, the Platonic myth of the creation of time through plane-tary motion was incorrect for the Copernican Galileo. In reality, such initial retrograde motion existed only in Plato's geocentric view. For Galileo, it was simply an apparent phenomenon caused by the Earth's revolution. His correction lay in transforming this astronomical mis-understanding of the initial variable and oblique motion of planets and claiming instead that it represented accelerated motion along an inclined line.

This mechanical adjustment to the Platonic–Augustinian cosmo-gony was also consistent with Galileo's earlier discussion of the bibli-cal craftsmanship of the planetary "wheels" introduced in the *Letter to the Grand Duchess Christina*. The kinematics of fall could now be generalized as the universal foundation of natural motion. In fact, true natural motion was the accelerated one of free fall.

The hiatus between terrestrial and celestial motions had now been bridged. The latter had been miraculously derived from the primo-genital and rectilinear falling motion. The establishment of the nat-ural symmetry of the cosmos lay in one miraculous act of the di-vine Wisdom of Creation. Natural motion could now comply with the divine law according to which God created the planets from rest in order to generate and mark time.

These ideas of identity between planetary dynamics and two terres-trial timekeepers were developed in the fourth part of the *Dialogue* and exemplified by the tides and the clock. Galileo had appropriated clockwork mechanics in his explanation of the monthly tidal cycle. Thus, the systemic relationship of the Sun, Moon, and Earth was similar to the static bond created by the weights attached to a *foliot* (the oscillating rod that also acts as the clock's regulator). By exten-sion, the positions of the Moon with respect to the Sun influenced the speed of the Earth's revolution. Monthly tides were the result of such a variation.[87]

So if the Earth's revolution around the Sun was not really a proper uniform motion, what could maintain it in a circular motion? As we know, in 1615 Galileo had conjectured that all planets orbited by the periodical motion of thermo-luminous fluid propagated spherically by the Sun. By the Third Day of the *Two New Sciences*, a geometrical theorem of the symmetrical rules of the universe now confirmed this natural mystery.

In introducing this theorem, Sagredo minimized its meaning as a *visio intellectualis*: "... I have resolved a certain idea that is now turning over in my mind. If it is not a fallacy, then it borders on a sprightly prank as are all pranks of nature or necessity."[88]

Just as a stone thrown into a pond – Sagredo said – makes uniform waves forming greater circles, so bodies falling from the same point along differently inclined lines are situated on larger and larger circumferences according to time. In other words, both periodic propagation and accelerated motion produce bigger and bigger circles.

As minimalist as Galileo's God was, nature could continue maintaining planetary motions from the center in perfect harmony with the cosmogonical falling motions from the primordial sublimity. So Simplicio, the third, naive character of the Galilean dialogues, was not wrong in observing that

...some great mystery of the universe may perhaps be contained in this true and admirable demonstration. I mean a mystery that relates the creation of the universe which I suppose to be spherical in shape, and perhaps relates to the residence of the first cause.[89]

The understatement with which Salviati restated the case emerges in his confesses that

...I feel no repugnance to that same belief. But such profound contemplations belong to doctrines much higher than ours, and we must be content to remain the less worthy artificers who discover and extract from quarries that marble in which industrious sculptors later made marvelous figures to appear that were lying hidden under those rough and formless exteriors.[90]

Galileo's metaphor of the relationship between physics and theology echoed Michelangelo's sonnet quoted in the *Dialogue*:

> The best of artists hath no thought to show
> Which the rough stone in its superfluous shell
> Does not include; to break the marble shell
> Is all the hand that serves the brain can do.[91]

Michelangelo's *David* was already present within the block of marble. The sculptor (that is, theology) had only to set the figure free from the raw block which the quarryman (that is, physics) had brought to light.

Apparently, objections to such a clear theological commitment were circulating even before the *Dialogue* was published, for Galileo remarked that, "... these unwelcome opinions are not mine at all. My opinions are those of Augustine, Aquinas and all the holy authors."[92]

In dedicating the *Dialogue* to the Grand Duke of Florence, Galileo had claimed the religious supremacy of his creationistic physics by reaffirming metaphors such as the divine Book of Nature and craftsmanship of the heavens:

... And though whatever we read in that book is the creation of the omnipotent Craftsman, and is accordingly excellently proportioned, nevertheless that part most suitable and most worthy which makes His works and His craftsmanship most evident to our view.[93]

It was this theological intention that became the target of the *Esercitationi Filosofiche* (Venice 1633), written by the Aristotelian philosopher and priest, Antonio Rocco, and appearing in the wake of the Church's condemnation of the Copernican opinions contained in the *Dialogue*. In the dedication of his book to Pope Urban VIII, Rocco explained that Galileo's cosmo-theology was impious because

... God can be known without mistake and adored without impiety only by the senses ... the only means through which we enter into the *penetralia* of Paradise: He who wants an alternate access is a thief and will be justly exterminated for such rashly held blessedness.[94]

According to Rocco, God was manifest "in the essence of both true God and true man" and detected through the human senses. However, Christian faith was founded on the Incarnation rather than the Creation. Indeed, Galileo's Old Testament view of the natural theology of the Glory of God was far from an orthodox theology of the Cross.

In any case, Rocco's accusation dealt precisely with the epistemological sacrilege of subverting the proper path to knowledge in accordance with the mystery of Redemption: "...the very pure intelligence being God, it can't be separated from Him, he who hopes to find it completely in creatures pretends to limit actual infinity in one point."[95] In his foresight, Father Antonio Rocco proved to be not only an orthodox theologian, but also a good prophet.

In 1634, after revising Galileo's new physical speculations in the manuscript of the *Two New Sciences*, Father Micanzio, Sarpi's Servite pupil, wrote, "I felt myself transported to meditate on the greatness

of God the Creator."[96] In fact, Galileo had introduced these preliminary reflections as "... a kind of fantasy full of undigested things
that I subject to your higher contemplations."[97]

Father Micanzio had discovered a dynamical, infinite theory of
matter in this manuscript that was very different from Sarpi's and
Galileo's corpuscularism. To tell the truth, in *The Assayer*, Galileo
had already announced a shift toward a physics of the continuum to
explain the generation and expansion of light from atomic matter as
instantaneous as an intellectual act:

> ... when the ultimate and highest resolution of the bodies in atoms into truly
> indivisible atoms is arrived at, light is created. This may have an instanta-
> neous motion, or rather an instantaneous expansion and diffusion, rendering
> it capable of occupying immense spaces but its – I know not whether to say
> its subtlety, its rarity, its immateriality, or some other property which differs
> from all this and is nameless.[98]

The proper name that would define the properties of the diffusion
of light sought by Galileo was really "infinity."

INFINITISM

Compared to his earlier works, the leap into an infinitesimal conception of the continuum of time, speed, and matter was the most
significant and unpredictable result of Galileo's final two books. Supporting evidence of this commitment to the concept of infinity dates
to 1619 when he wrote, "... the infinite lies in the proportion between anything and something."[99]

Nevertheless, there is evidence to suggest that such a decisive shift
occurred even earlier and, as a result, would have affected Galileo's
final formulation of the mathematical laws of matter and motion.
In replying to Micanzio's ecstatic letter of 1634, Galileo hinted that
he had held these views as far back as 1616. In fact, to Micanzio he
emphasized the novelty of a theory of the continuum of matter with
respect to his earlier atomism and that of Sarpi:

> ... At that time [in Padua] I had nothing but problems with the condensation
> and rarefaction [of substances]; but 18 years ago [1616], when I was staying
> at Salviati's villa, during Mass one morning, an idea flashed into my mind,
> and after I had more deeply immersed myself in it, I went to confirm for

myself and since then I have been considering it as worthy of admiration as a marvelous example [*modo*] of how Nature works.[100]

Galileo considered the solid state as the effect on a corpuscular scale of "matter's abhorrence of a vacuum" or, in anachronistic terms, negative pressure. This acted as an elementary force on material particles which were simultaneously separated and attracted by microscopic vacuities.

How many were contained in a body? And what was their dimension?

Here, Galileo had jumped into an actual infinite view of matter analogous to the medieval conception of a physico–geometrical continuum that had emerged from the controversies over the Eucharist.

Galileo was probably aware of this for he cautiously appealed to "those theological doctrines that are the only true and sure judges of our controversies" before introducing the idea that all physical bodies could contain an infinite number of vacuities on condition that they lacked dimensions (i.e., a line containing infinite points which are nondimensional or an interval of time containing infinite instants).[101] Instead of Plato's geometrically shaped atoms, one might claim that in any given body there were also infinite, indivisible, and nondimensional atoms – like points of a line.

This was the solution to the problem of condensation and rarefaction of matter Galileo mentioned to Micanzio. He reduced such phenomena to the property of being infinitely divisible and infinitely increasing along the geometrical continuum. In arriving at this position, Galileo employed two sorts of paradoxes. The first involved speculative geometry and was based on Cusanus's identification of an arc with its chord in order to establish the equivalence between the circumference of a circle and a regular polygon.[102] The second concerned the physical continuum and this was Ockham's famous paradox that the whole universe could be contained in a bean. Galileo also subscribed to the idea that as the entire Earth could be condensed in a walnut, so, too, a grain of gunpowder could rarefy through immense spaces, symmetrically, by its "dissolution with very swift motion."[103]

Nevertheless, in exploring the properties of the infinite by mathematical reasoning Galileo reached the limits of human cognition. When he realized that the square and cubic numbers were as infinite as their roots, he preferred to follow Augustine in maintaining the Euclidian axiom that the whole is greater than its parts. So he admitted that the mathematical properties, valid in the finite, could not be applied to the infinite. Infinity does not admit comparison. There is nothing greater, but by the same token, nothing smaller than the infinite: "... not only may one infinite not be said to be greater than another infinite, but it may not even be said that an infinite is greater than a finite."[104] In other words, both infinity and the indivisibles could not be understood in a rational way, but only contemplated, or imagined, through a *visio intellectualis*. "That numbers are infinite is indeed beyond all doubt," Augustine wrote in *The City of God*. Yet the epistemological status of the infinite was as nameless and as far from the bounds of human knowledge as God was. In fact, both Augustine and Aquinas emphasized that the infinite was as inscrutable as God: "... the infinity of number, although there is no set number of infinite numbers, nevertheless is not incomprehensible to God."[105]

Actually, among so many paradoxes Father Micanzio could recognize at least one true, positive demonstration. From the point of view of Cusanus's logic of *coincidentia oppositorum*, Galileo had in fact proven a proposition that was as mathematically problematic as it was theologically attractive. Galileo observed that if we want to seek a number capable of including all numbers and their powers, this number would be "one," or the unity: "... we conclude that there is no infinite number other than unity. These are among the marvels that surpass the bounds of our imagination."[106]

Maximum and minimum coincide. Concerning "the infinite unity which includes all numbers," Cusanus had also remarked that "... if one could understand or name such a unity which is everything and both the least and the most, he would properly call it God."[107] But Galileo would disappoint those who questioned the scope of such crude speculations on the actual infinite, or "higher contemplations." He suggested that the answer lay in Scripture. In 1639, Galileo wrote to the philosopher Fortunio Liceti:

... The infinite belongs to those questions which are, by chance, inexplicable through human discourse, like perhaps predestination, free will, and others about which only the holy pages and the divine statements can definitively persuade us.[108]

And in fact, we read in the Bible that "the sand of the seashore, the drops of rain, the days of the eternity: who can number these?"[109] I confess that at this point it would be tempting for me to conclude, like Koyré, that it is possible, and even probable, that Democritus's deepest intuitions and intentions lived on in such a mathematical atomism. But were they indeed identical to Galileo's? In the case of the latter, we find, in fact, a heroism of truth which until now has been treated as a trivial question but one we can no longer ignore.

CONCLUSION

The creationist and theological framework of Galileo's physics expressed in the *Dialogue* and the *Two New Sciences* attest to his efforts to make natural and supernatural truth coincide. Such a fideism was aimed at a Christian knowledge of the world. It was through Scripture and Plato that Galileo was able to modify significantly his mechanics from the Aristotelian logical framework in which accelerated motion, matter, and time were conceived.

By subordinating mechanical laws of nature to divine guidance, mathematical physics provided the key to knowledge of God. In the scientific culture of early–modern Europe, Galileo becomes the forerunner of Descartes, Malebranche, and Newton rather than the follower of Lucretius, Epicurus, and Democritus.

However, what seems probable to us is that Galileo's insight of an inner compatibility between physical and religious conceptions was the result of a spiritual experience stemming from the genius of his discoveries and the infinite slowness of his interlocutors. The conclusion of my reconstruction is that Galileo's faith was not restricted to his religion: For Galileo, theology and science were inseparable and not simply independent concerns much like Michelangelo's *David* was inseparable from its marble.

What I have tried to demonstrate here is the existence of a manifest program in Galileo's last works that aimed at establishing science in a Christian culture. Of course, with hindsight it would be easy to claim that Galileo was going to transfer the absolute attributes of God's craftsmanship to matter itself and to the secular skill of mathematicians, virtuosi, clock makers, and engineers (like those of the Arsenal in Venice). Yet since we have no clear evidence of Galileo's "deepest intentions" concerning such an eventual secularization, my reconstruction cannot prove that Galileo was a libertine or a saint. And because I myself feel as ignorant about Galileo's "deepest beliefs" as Simplicio when confronted with the intricacies of mathematics, I would like him to supply the closing argument.

When vacuums and atoms are discussed in the *Two New Sciences*, the author's spokesman, Salviati, reminds the reader of the old accusation, made by an eminent professor at the *Collegio Romano*, that "... our Academician [Galileo] followed a certain ancient philosopher who denied divine providence." Simplicio responds:

... yet I shall not touch on that, not only on reason of the bonds of good taste, but because I know how far such ideas are from the temperate and orderly mind of such a man as you, who are not only religious and pious, but Catholic and saintly.[110]

NOTES

I wish to thank Rachel Bindman for the English version of this paper.

1 Winifred L. Wisan, "Galileo and God's Creation," *Isis*, 77, 1986, 473–86. On Galileo's "religious sincerity" see also Giorgio Spini, "The Rationale of Galileo's Religiousness," in Carlo L. Golino, ed., *Galileo Reappraised*, Berkeley, University of California Press, 1966, 44–66; Olaf Pedersen, "Galileo's Religion," in George V. Coyne, ed., *The Galileo Affair: A Meeting of Faith and Science*, Città del Vaticano, Specola Vaticana, 1985, 75–102.

2 Mario Biagioli, *Galileo Courtier*, Chicago, University of Chicago Press, 1993, 303. On Galileo's religious rhetoric see Maurice A. Finocchiaro, *Galileo and the Art of Reasoning*, Dordrecht, Reidel, 1980, 6–18; Jean D. Moss, *Novelties in the Heavens*, Chicago, University of Chicago Press, 1993.

3 Antonio Favaro, ed., *Le Opere di Galileo Galilei*, 20 vols., Firenze, G. Barbera, 1890–1909, repr. 1968 (hereafter EN), vol. 1, 252; transl. Israel Edward Drabkin and Stillman Drake, eds., *Galileo Galilei on Motion and Mechanics*, Madison, University of Wisconsin Press, 1960, 14.

4 See Jacopo Mazzoni, *In Universam Platonis et Arisitotelis Philosophiam Praeludia*, Venetiis, I. Guerilium, 1597, 52, 189, and especially 202–4, 213–14. On the relationship between Galileo's and Mazzoni's atomism, see also William R. Shea, *Galileo's Intellectual Revolution*, New York, Science History Publ., 2nd ed., 1977, 108, n. 58; Frederick

Purnell, "Jacopo Mazzoni and Galileo," *Physis*, 14, 1972, 273–94. For Mazzoni's defense of corpuscularism as expresssed in Proclus's *Commentaria*, and against Aristotle's *De caelo*, see especially 285–6.

5   See *Timaeus*, 52E–53A; transl. Francis M. Cornford, ed., *Plato's Cosmology*, London, Routledge and Kegan Paul, 1977 (repr.), 198;202–3.

6   *De rerum natura*, V:450–5.

7   EN, 1, 344, transl. Drabkin and Drake, *Galileo on Motion*, 116.

8   *Job*, 28:25; transl. *The Holy Bible*, Good Counsel Publ. Co, Chicago, 1961, 425.

9   *Wis.* 11:20; 22; transl. ibid., 547.

10 Cf. Galileo's unpublished *Mechanics* completed in Padua by 1602 in EN, 2, 180; 189. For Galileo's theory of momentum see Paolo Galluzzi, *Momento*, Roma, Ateneo e Bizzarri, 1979, especially 70–9.

11 See Giovanbattista Benedetti, *Diversarum Speculationum Mathematicarum et Physicarum Liber*, Taurini, Haeres Bevilaquae, 1585, 195; transl. Drake, Drabkin, eds., *Mechanics in Sixteenth-Century Italy*, Madison, University of Wisconsin Press, 1969, 220–1. On the bifurcation of natural motion in Galileo's *De Motu*, see also EN, 1, 302–4.

12 EN, I, 315; 318–19. See Dudley Shapere, *Galileo, a Philosophical Study*, Chicago and London, University of Chicago Press, 1974, 69–70.

13 *Physica*, IV:14, 223b; transl. Philip H. Wicksteed, ed., *Aristotle, The Physics*, London, Loeb, Heinemann, 1929, vol. 2, 425.

14 See EN, vol. 10, 97–100:99. In his final work, *Two New Sciences*, ibid., vol. 8, 95, Galileo considered motion along the arcs as equivalent to ones along chords by imagining a regular polygon of an infinite number of sides which would eventually approximate the dimensions of a circle. For the path to the proof of pendular isochronism see W. L. Wisan, "The New Science of Motion," *Archive for History of Exact Sciences*, 13, 1974, 103–306; 176–7.

15 EN, 10, 114. Cf. Jurgen Renn, "Proofs and Paradoxes: Free Fall and Projectile Motion in Galileo's Physics," in Peter Damerow and others, *Exploring the Limits of Preclassical Mechanics*, New York, Berlin, Springer-Verlag, 1992, 127–268; 161.

16 Cf. Renn, "Proofs and Paradoxes," 227–40.

17 EN, 8, 197; transl. Drake, Galileo, *Two New Sciences*, 2nd ed., Toronto, Wall and Thompson, 1974, 153.

18 Ibid., 198; transl. ibid., 154.

19 Ibid., 202; transl. ibid., 159.

20 EN, 1, 27. On Galileo's chronology see William Wallace, *Prelude to Galileo*, Dordrecht, Reidel, 1981, 219–25.

21 EN, 1, 23. For the doxography of *Timaeus* see Jean Pépin, *Théologie cosmique et théologie chrétienne*, Paris, PUF, 1964.

22 Castelli to Galileo, April 1, 1607, EN 10, 169–70. On this document see Drabkin and Drake, *On Motion*, 171, n. 26; Libero Sosio, "Galileo e la cosmologia," in Galileo, *Dialogo sopra i due massimi sistemi*, Torino, Einaudi, 1970, xl, 28, n. 1; Bernard Vinaty, "La formation du système solaire d'après Galilée," *Angelicum*, 60, 1983, 333–85; 379. For an alternative interpretation, see Massimo Bucciantini, "Atomi, geometria e teologia nella filosofia galileiana di Benedetto Castelli," in Maurizio Torrini, ed., *Geometria e atomismo nella scuola galileiana*, Firenze, L. Olschki, 1992, 171–91; 174.

23 Galileo to Vinta, May 7, 1610, EN, 10, 348–56; 351. See S. Drake, "Galileo's Platonic Cosmogony and Kepler's *Prodromus*," *Journal for the History of Astronomy*, 4, 1973, 174–91; W. L. Wisan, "Galileo's *De Systemate Mundi* and the New Mechanics," in P. Galluzzi, ed., *Novità celesti e crisi del sapere, Supplemento agli Annali dell'Istituto et Museo di Storia della scienza*, 2, 1983, 41–9.

24 EN, 10, 170.

25 *Timaeus*, 37D, transl. Cornford, 98. Cf. *Gen.*, 1:14.

26 *De Opificio Mundi*, 1:27, transl. Francis M. Colson, *Philo in Then Volumes*, London and Cambridge, MA, Loeb, Heinemann, 1929, vol. 1, 23.

27 *De Civitate Dei*, 12:18; transl. Philip Levine, *The City of God*, London, Loeb, Heinemann, 1966, vol. 4, 88.

28 *Confessions*, 11:23 (29); transl. William Watts, *St. Augustine, Confessions* (1631), Cambridge and London, Harvard University Press, Loeb, Heinemann, 1912 (repr. 1988), vol. 2, 263.

29 Ibid.

30 Ibid., 11:23 (29–30); transl. ibid., 259.

31 Ibid., 11:28 (37); transl. ibid., 277.

32 Ibid., 11:15 (19); transl. ibid., 243. See James J. O'Donnell, ed., *Augustine, Confessions*, Oxford, Clarendon Press, 1992, 155.

33 See David S. Landes, *Revolution in Time*, Cambridge, MA, Harvard University Press, 1983, 114–21; Krzysztof Pomian, *L'Ordre du Temps*, Paris, Gallimard, ch. V. On the best definition of time allowed by sundials cf. Anthony Turner, *Early Scientific Instruments*, London, Sotheby's Publ., 1987, 173–80.

34 EN, 10, 170. For Castelli's pious science cf. *Alcuni Opuscoli Scientifici*, Bologna, Dozza, 1669, 8–9; 34; 37; 78. See also A. Favaro, "Intorno ad un Discorso sopra la calamita del p. B. Castelli," *Bullettino di bibliografia e di storia delle scienze matematiche e fisiche*, 16, 1883, 545–64; 549; 559–60 and M. Bucciantini, "Gli scritti di Benedetto Castelli sui numeri negativi," *Giornale critico della filosofia italiana*, 64; 1985, 215–28; 227–8.

35 A. Koyré, *From the Closed World to the Infinite Universe*, Baltimore, Johns Hopkins Press, 2nd ed., 1968, 278, n. 7.
36 EN, 4, 103.
37 Ibid., 4, 732. Galileo's theory of fluids came from *Timaeus* 61A in which the melting of ice and metals was explained by the intromission of air or fire between the particles. The Archimedean Galileo understood that such a corpuscular view of ice as expanded water was consistent with its flotation.
38 EN, 4, 88.
39 See Lodovico delle Colombe, *Discorso Apologetico*, ibid., 331. See also Castelli replying to Coresio, Colombe, Di Grazia, ibid., 273; 340; 586; 594; 736 and Galileo's letter to Nozzolini, ibid., 295–310; 299. See also S. Drake, *Cause, Experiment and Science*, Chicago, Chicago University Press, 1981, 97–8; M. Biagioli, *Galileo Courtier*, 191–202; Michele Camerota, "Virtù calamitica: analogia magnetica e ruolo dell'aria nella teoria galileiana degli arginetti," in Antonio Cadeddu, a cura di, *Filosofia, scienza, storia*, Milano, F. Angeli, 1995, 273–93; 274–88.
40 EN, 4, 103, 301–2.
41 EN, 8, 115; transl. Drake, *New Sciences*, 74.
42 *De Revolutionibus*, 1:1, transl. Edward Rosen, ed., *Copernicus, On the Revolutions*, London, Macmillan Press, 1978, 8.
43 EN, 4, 133.
44 Ibid., 416.
45 Ibid., 211. For Aristotle's refusal of an instant-view of time and motion cf. *Physica*, IV, 2:220a.
46 EN, 4, 67.
47 EN, 7, 127; transl. Drake, *Dialogue Concerning the Two Chief World Systems*, Berkeley, University of California Press, 2nd ed., 1967, 101.
48 Ibid.
49 Ibid., 260; transl. ibid., 234.
50 EN 3, 60; 80; 56; transl. adapted from Drake, *Discoveries and Opinions of Galileo*, New York, Doubleday, 1957, 52; 28; 24. See Albert Van Helden, *Sidereus Nuncius or Sidereal Message*, Chicago, Chicago University Press, 1989, 31; Isabelle Pantin, ed., *Le Messager céleste*, Paris, Les Belles Lettres, 1992, 53.
51 See *Dissertatio cum Nuncio Sidereo*, in Max Caspar, Franz Hammer, eds., *Johannes Kepler Gesammelte Werke*, Munich, Beck, vol. 4, 1941, 282–311; transl. by E. Rosen, *Kepler's Conversation with Galileo's Sidereal Messenger*, New York, Johnson Reprint, 1965 and I. Pantin, ed., Kepler, *Discussion avec le Messager céleste*, Paris, Les Belles Lettres, 1993, 45. Odo van Maelcote, *Sidereus Nuncius collegii Romani*, EN, 3, 293–8.

On Galileo's "concettismo" about *nuntius/nuncius* see S. Drake, "The Starry Messenger," *Isis*, 49, 1958, 346–7; Pantin, *Le Messager céleste*, xxxiii–xxxvi.

52 Thomas Seggett, *Epigrammata*, *Kepler Gesammelte Werke*, vol. 4, 323, lines 19–24. Campanella to Galileo, January 13, 1611, E. N., 10, 21–6; 21. Libert Froidmont, *Saturnalitiae coenae, variatae somnio, sive peregrinatione caelesti*, Lovanii, P. Dormalius, 1616, 78, on which see Pietro Redondi, "Libert Froidmont, opposant et allié de Galilée," in Anne-Catherine Bernès, ed., *Libert Froidmont et les résistances aux révolutions scientifiques*, Haccourt, Ass. Vieilles familles d'Haccourt, 1988, 83–104; 86.

53 Galileo to Dini, March 23, 1615, EN, 5, 297–305, 300; transl. of this letter in Richard J. Blackwell, *Galileo, Bellarmin and the Church*, Notre Dame, Notre Dame University Press, 1991, 212, and also in Maurice Finocchiaro, *The Galileo Affair*, Berkeley, University of California Press, 1989, 60–7. On the censorship of *Letters on Sunspots*, see EN, 5, 138–9; 11, 439, letter no. 804; 446–7, no. 812; 450–1, no. 815. Cf. Giorgio Stabile, "Linguaggio dela natura e linguaggio della Scrittura in Galilei," *Nuncius*, 9, 1994, 37–64, especially 43–6; Bruno Basile, "Galileo e il teologo Foscarini," in *L'invenzione del vero*, Roma, Salerno, 1987, 9–48.

54 Cf. Augustine, *De Ordine*, 2:18:47. On Galileo's Augustinian quotations also through Benedictus Pereira's *Commentariorum et Disputationum in Genesi* see R. J. Blackwell, *Galileo*, 20–22. On Cusanus's influence on the Benedictine Order and Sarpi see M. Bucciantini, "Un trattatello cusaniano della prima metà del secolo XVII," *Rinascimento*, 23, 1983, 329–44; Luisa Cozzi, Libero Sosio, eds., Paolo Sarpi, *Pensieri naturali, metafisici e matematici*, Milan and Naples, Ricciardi, 1996, 351, note. Cusanus appears with Cesalpino in a letter that Favaro attributed to Foscarini, cf. EN,12, 214–20; 216. Given that Cusanus's *De Concordantia Catholica* was on the Index and his influence in Giordano Bruno's works, Galileo's lack of direct reference to Cusanus is not surprising.

55 EN, 5, 95; transl. Drake, *Discoveries*, 90. Emphasis added.

56 Ibid., 187; transl. Drake, *Discoveries*, 124.

57 Ibid., 186; transl. ibid., 123.

58 EN, 130; transl. Drake, *Dialogue*, 104.

59 *Quaestiones Conviviales*, VIII, q. 2:718B–C; transl. Paul A. Clement, Herbert B. Hoffleit, eds., Plutarch, *Moralia*, London, Loeb, Heinemann, 1964, vol. 9, 119.

60 EN, 5, 187; transl. Drake, *Discoveries*, 124. Galileo's words followed closely Augustine's *Enarrationes in Psalmos*, 1, 7 on Psalm *Caeli enarrant gloriam Dei*.

61 *Letter to Castelli,* December 21, 1613, EN, 5, 281–8; 288; transl. R. J. Blackwell, *Galileo,* 201. On the eternal combustion of the Sun cf. Cozzi, Sosio, eds., Sarpi, *Pensieri,* 238, and Castelli to Galileo, 8 May 1612, EN, 11, 294–5.

62 *De Revolutionibus,* 1:10; transl. Rosen, *On Revolutions,* 22. For the Copernicus misquotation of Aristotle's *De Generatione,* IV:10:777b, on the kinship between the Earth and the Sun, ibid., 360.

63 Galileo to Dini, March 23, 1615, EN, 5, 288; transl. Blackwell, 212.

64 On the astrological identification of the Sun with the heart see C. A. Staudenbaum, "Galileo, Ficino and Henry Moore's *Psychatanasia,*" *Journal of the History of Ideas,* 29, 1968, 657–78; Eugenio Garin, *Lo Zodiaco della vita,* Bari, Laterza, 1976, 12–13, and the critical remarks by Paolo Rossi in "Galileo Galilei e il Libro dei Salmi," in *La scienza e la filosofia dei moderni,* Torino, Bollati Boringhieri, 1989, 67–89. Galileo's concept of solar fluid was very different from Ficino's and Fernel's *spiritus mundi.* He distinguished the Sun from its creator according to Augustine in *Enarrationes in Psalmos,* 85, 12 and to Cusanus who stated that "God is not in the sun as a sun." See Ernest Hoffmann, Raymond Klibansky, eds., Nicolai de Cusa, *De Docta Ignorantia,* II, 4:20, *Opera Omnia,* Lipsiae, F. Meiner, 1932, vol. 1, 74. Secondly, Galileo's aethereal fluid was caused by an *anima nutritiva* draining and replenishing the Sun's *aetherea facula.* For Cesalpino's Galenic theory of cardiac–pulmonary nutritional function, see his *Peripateticarum Quaestionum Libri Quinque,* Florentiae, 1569, 2nd ed., Venetiis, apud Iuntas, 1571, book v, q. iii, 102E; and q. iv: *De Respiratione,* 111B;117E. Cesalpino's treatise on tides, *Maris fluxum et refluxum ex motu terrae,* was also published in this book. For Sarpi's view of the circulation to and from the heart, cf. Cozzi, Sosio, eds., Sarpi, *Pensieri,* 25–7.

65 EN, 5, 304; 302; transl. Blackwell, 215; 214.

66 EN, 5, 347; transl. Drake, *Discoveries,* 214–15.

67 Ibid., 317; transl. ibid., 183.

68 Ibid., 348; transl. ibid., 215.

69 On the metaphor of the "book of the heavens," see the *Letter to Christina,* ibid., 329; transl. ibid., 196.

70 Augustine, *De Genesi, ad litteram,* 4:32:49. Transl. mine.

71 EN, 5, 329; transl. Drake, *Discoveries,* 196.

72 EN, 7, 489; transl. Drake, *Dialogue,* 464. Cf. *Eccl.* 3:11: "Cuncta fecit bona tempore suo, et mundum tradidit disputationi eorum, ut non inveniat homo opus quod operatus est Deus ab initio usque ad finem," *Biblia Sacra iuxtam vulgatam Clementinam,* Matriti, Biblioteca de Autores Cristianos, 1982, 65.

73 EN, 7, 448; transl. Drake, *Dialogue*, 422.

74 Ibid., 128; transl. ibid., 102.

75 Ibid., 44; transl. ibid., 20.

76 EN, 8, 284; transl. Drake, *New Sciences*, 233–4.

77 EN, 7, 44; transl. Drake, *Dialogue*, 20.

78 Ibid., 45; transl. ibid., 21.

79 *De Civitate Dei*, 12:19; transl. Levine, *The City of God*, vol. 4, 92–3.

80 EN, 7, 397; transl. Drake, *Dialogue*, 370.

81 Ibid., 45; transl. ibid., 21. See *Summa theol.*, q. 7:2; *De Docta ignorantia*, 2:2, Hoffman, Klibanski, eds., N. de Cusa, *Opera omnia*, vol. 1, 67.

82 Cf. *Confessions*, 13:21:29; transl. Watts, vol. 2, 427:

> ... The earth brings [a living soul] forth, because the earth is the cause that they work this in the soul: like as the sea was the cause that they wrought upon the moving things that have life in them, and the flows that fly under the firmament of heaven, of whom the earth hath not need.

Augustine repeated this allegory in *De Genesi ad litteram*, 3:7:9.

83 EN, 7, 566. For Aquinas's principle that "natura nihil facit frustra" see *In De anima*, 3:14:17. See William J. Courtenay, "The Dialectics of Divine Omnipotence in the High and Late Middle Ages," in Tamar Rudavsky, ed., *Divine Omniscience and Omnipotence in Medieval Philosophy*, Dordrecht, Reidel, 1985, 243–70; Luca Bianchi, "Uccelli d'oro e pesci di piombo; Galileo Galilei e la *potentia dei absoluta*," in Mariateresa Beonio-Brocchieri, ed., *Sopra la volta del mondo*, Bergamo, Lubrina, 1986, 139–46.

84 EN, 8, 200–1; transl. Drake, *New Sciences*, 157. Cf. T. Bruce Birch, "The Theory of Continuity of William of Ockham," *Philosophy of Science*, 3, 1963, 494–505.

85 EN, 8, 284; transl. Drake, *New Sciences*, 233–4. For Galileo's reapprisal of the method of Oresme's *De Latitudinis formarum* see EN, 7, 255–6; transl. Drake, *Dialogue*, 228–9. On Oresme's metaphor of the clock-maker God cf. A. D. Menut, A. J. Denomy, eds., Nicolas Oresme, *Livre du ciel et du monde*, Madison, University of Wisconsin Press, 1968, 298.

86 *Timaeus*, 36D; 38C–E; transl. Cornford, 105; 112. On Galileo's sources in *Timaeus* 38C–39A see Stephan Sambursky, "Galileo's Attempt to a Cosmogony," *Isis*, 53, 1962, 460–3; Bernard I. Cohen, "Galileo, Newton and the Divine Order of the Solar System," in Ernan Mc-Mullin, ed., *Galileo Man of Science*, New York, Basic Books, 1967, 207–31:210; Bruno Basile, "Galileo, Platone e il Demiurgo," *Romanistische Zeitschrift für Literaturgeschichte*, 9, 1985, 455–67. Kepler had also relied on the *Timaeus* in reaching the conclusion that the world

was first created through linear motions: cf. F. Hammer, ed., *Mysterium Cosmographicum, Kepler Gesammelte Werke*, vol. 8, 1963, 44–6. For Newton's objections about Galileo's cosmogony cf. Alexandre Koyré, "Newton, Galileo and Plato," in *Newtonian Studies*, Cambridge, MA, Harvard University Press, 1965, 201–20.

87 See EN, 7, 474–9; transl. Drake, *Dialogue*, 452–7.

88 EN, 8, 224; transl. Drake, *New Sciences*, 182.

89 Ibid., 225; transl. ibid., 183.

90 Ibid., 226; transl. ibid.

91 Trans. John A. Symond, ed., *Michelangelo, The Sonnets*, London, Vision Press, 1957, 46–7, also quoted in EN, 7, 130; transl. Drake, *Dialogue*, 104. For the Aristotelian origin of such a metaphor see *Metaphysica*, 1032a–1033b.

92 Galileo to Cioli, May 3, 1631, EN, 14, 259.

93 EN, 7, 27; transl. Drake, *Dialogue*, vii.

94 Antonio Rocco, *Esercitazioni Filosofiche*, Venetia, F. Baba, 1633, EN, 7, 573–4.

95 Ibid., 576. Rocco maintained the Aristotelian eternity of nature "being God ab eterno" against Galileo's cosmo-theological conception of acceleration, cf. ibid., 601. On Rocco see G. Spini, *Ricerca dei libertini*, Firenze, La Nuova Italia, 1983, 149–76.

96 Micanzio to Galileo, November 8, 1634, EN, 16, 161. For Sarpi's insight of condensation, rarefaction, and melting point in terms of vacuities and continuum cf. Cozzi, Sosio, eds., Sarpi, *Pensieri*, 116; 130–6; 205; 273–4; 111–16; 334; 419.

97 EN, 8, 66; transl. Drake, *New Sciences*, 27.

98 EN, 6, 352; transl. Drake, *Discoveries*, 278. For Dionysius's and Augustine's infinitive theory of light also adopted in Cusanus's *De Docta ignorantia* see Klaus Hedwig, *Sphaera Lucis*, Munster, Aschendorff, 1980, 235–6; 265 ff. For a physical version of such a metaphysics of light cf. Cozzi, Sosio, eds., Sarpi, *Pensieri*, 236; 348; 433; Castelli's letter to Galileo on thermal absorption, August 15, 1637, EN, 17, 156–69, 163–5. In the latter, Castelli repudiated his former atomism for religious scruples. See also Castelli's mystical letter to Galileo, August 12, 1634, EN, 16, 121–2.

99 Ibid., 6, 75.

100 Galileo to Micanzio, November 19, 1634, EN, 16, 163.

101 See *Exigit Ordo executionis* in J. R. O'Donnel, "Nicholas of Autrecourt," *Medieval Studies*, 1, 1939, 179–280; Pierre Duhem, *Le Système du monde*, Paris, Hermann, vol. 7, 1956, 50–3; Edith Sylla, "Autonomous and Handmaiden Science: St. Thomas Aquinas and William of Ockham on the Physics of the Eucharist," in John E. Murdoch, E. D.

Sylla, eds., *The Cultural Context of Medieval Learning*, Dordrecht, Reidel, 1975, 361–72.

102 See Cusanus, *De Mathematica Perfectione*, in Nicolai De Cusa, *Opera*, Basileae, Ex Officina Henricpetrina, 1565, 1110–57, especially 1110.

103 EN, 8, 96; transl. Drake, *New Sciences*, 58; Ockham, *Centuriae Theologicae*, 17c; *Quodlibet* I, q. 9.

104 EN, 8, 79; transl. Drake, *New Sciences*, 41. Cf. Augustine, *De Genesi ad litteram*, 8:19:38.

105 *De Civitate Dei*, 12:19; transl. Levine, 91, and also Aquinas, *Comm. Phys.*, 1, Lect. 9, n. 7.

106 EN, 8, 83; transl. Drake, *New Sciences*, 45–6.

107 Ibid., 83; transl. ibid., 45–6. *De Docta ignorantia*, I, 22:8; 24:19–21, Hoffmann, Klibansky, eds., N. de Cusa, *Opera omnia*, vol. 1, 45; 49.

108 Galileo to Liceti, September 24, 1639, EN, 18, 106.

109 *Ecclus.*, 1:2.

110 EN, 8, 72; transl. adapted from Drake, *New Sciences*, 34: "santo" is translated as "devout." In the previous English translation, Henry Crew and Alfonso de Salvio, eds., *Dialogues Concerning Two New Sciences*, New York, Macmillan, 1914, 26, "santo" was translated as "God-fearing." On the meaning of this adjective in Galileo's times, see *Vocabolario degli Accademici della Crusca*, Venezia, G. Alberti, 1612, 748–9.

6   Galileo's Copernicanism: The science and the rhetoric

When Galileo left the University of Pisa without taking a degree in the spring of 1585, he was a promising young mathematician with an experimental bent, but there was nothing to foretell his later interest in astronomy. He earned his living by giving private lessons in Florence and Siena, and it is probably at this time that he wrote a short *Treatise on the Sphere* or *Cosmography* for the use of his pupils.

This elementary textbook of spherical astronomy is based on the thirteenth-century *Sphere* of John Holywood, better known under his Latinized name of Sacrobosco. It is conventional in its geocentrism and makes no mention of Copernicus. Galileo may have used it when he became a Professor of Mathematics at Pisa (1589–92) and during the first years of his professorship at Padua (1592–1610).

In Pisa, Galileo made the acquaintance of Jacopo Mazzoni, a philosopher who sought to combine the insights of Plato and Aristotle, and with whom he stayed in touch after he had left Tuscany for the Venetian Republic. It was this friend who, in 1597, provided Galileo with his first opportunity of stating his opinion that the heliocentric theory of Copernicus was more probable than the geocentric system of Aristotle and Ptolemy.

Mazzoni had just published a book in which he claimed to have found a new and decisive argument against the motion of the Earth. Taking for granted Aristotle's assertion that Mount Caucasus is so high that its summit is illuminated by the Sun for a third of the night, Mazzoni inferred that from the top of the mountain one could see two thirds of the celestial vault. Mazzoni then boldly concluded that if the Earth moved around the Sun, and hence shifted its position with respect to the stellar sphere, at least two thirds of the heavens would be visible in the course of a year.

Galileo immediately saw the flaw in his friend's reasoning and sent him a letter in which he used simple trigonometry to show that the revolution of the Earth around the Sun would not entail any difference in the number of visible stars.

Galileo's argument did not have an immediate impact on his contemporaries but it played a vital role in his personal development. Mathematics had been called upon to refute the latest argument against Copernicus and had emerged victorious. This was a considerable psychological boost for a junior professor who had yet to muster the courage to express his Copernican leanings.

A month later, Galileo proudly informed the German astronomer Johann Kepler that he had managed to account, on the Copernican hypothesis, for a number of natural events that could not be explained on the received geocentric doctrine. He added, however, that he refrained from publishing for fear of ridicule, which shows that he was not utterly sure of being right.

In this essay, we shall examine in the first part how Galileo's celestial discoveries confirmed him in the opinion that the Earth moves around the Sun; in the second part, we shall discuss the arguments that he presents in his literary masterpiece, the *Dialogue on the Two Chief World Systems*; and in a concluding section, we shall contrast his method with that of his predecessors.

GALILEO'S CELESTIAL DISCOVERIES

The appearance of a nova in the autumn of 1604 caused a considerable stir among the students in Padua, and Galileo gave three public lectures to large audiences in which he explained that the absence of any apparent displacement of the new star against the background of fixed stars (what is technically called parallax) indicated that the new star had been produced beyond the lunar region, namely in that part of the world that the Aristotelians held to be immune from change. Copernicanism was not the issue; the debate revolved entirely on the Aristotelian doctrine of the immutability of the heavens.

Matters might have rested at this level of general conjecture had not something new occurred. The novelty did not descend from the ethereal regions of speculation. It was the mundane outcome of playing around with concave and convex lenses, in Italy around 1590, in the Netherlands in 1604, and in the whole of Europe by the summer of 1609. Out of a toy to make objects appear larger, Galileo made, first, a naval, and then a scientific instrument. In the *Starry Messenger*, which appeared in April 1610, he tells us how he heard of the telescope:

About 10 months ago a report reached my ears that a certain Fleming had constructed a spyglass by means of which visible objects, though very distant from the eye of the observer, were distinctly seen as if nearby. Of this truly remarkable effect several experiences were related, to which some persons gave credence while others denied them. A few days later the report was confirmed to me in a letter from a noble Frenchman at Paris, Jacques Badovere, which caused me to apply myself wholeheartedly to investigate means by which I might arrive at the invention of a similar instrument. This I did soon afterwards, my basis being the doctrine of refraction.[1]

The phrase "my basis being the doctrine of refraction" has sometimes been interpreted as though Galileo claimed to have worked out the properties of lenses the way Kepler was to do a year later in his *Dioptrics*. Actually Galileo's theory was more modest and, significantly, more empirical, as he himself makes clear:

My reasoning was this. The device needs ... more than one glass ... The shape would have to be convex ... concave ... or bounded by parallel surfaces. But the last-named does not visible objects in any way ... the concave diminishes them, and the convex, though it enlarges them, shows them indistinct and confused ... I was confined to considering what would be done by a combination of the convex and the concave. You see how this gave me what I sought.[2]

Rumors of the invention of the telescope probably reached Galileo in July 1609 when he visited friends in Venice to explore ways of increasing a salary that had become inadequate for an elder brother expected to provide dowries for two sisters. He received little encouragement from the Venetian patricians who controlled the University of Padua, but he had a flash of insight when he heard that someone had presented Count Maurice of Nassau with a spyglass by means of which distant objects could be brought closer. The Venetians might not see how they could increase his salary, but what if he succeeded in enhancing their vision?

When Galileo returned to Padua on August 3, his fertile mind was teeming with possibilities. By August 21, he was back in Venice with a telescope capable of magnifying eight times. He convinced worthy senators to climb to the top of a tower from whence they were able to see boats coming to port a good two hours before they could be spotted by the naked eye. The strategic advantages of the new instrument were not lost on a maritime power, and it suddenly became clear to all that Galileo's salary should be increased from 520 to 1,000 florins per year.

Unfortunately, after the first flush of enthusiasm, the senators heard the sobering news that the telescope was already widespread throughout Europe, and when the official document was drawn up it stipulated that Galileo would only get his raise at the expiration of his existing contract a year later, and that he would be barred, for life, from the possibility of subsequent increases.

This incident understandably made Galileo sour. He had not claimed to be the inventor of the telescope, and if the Senators had compared his instrument with those made by others they would have found that his own was far superior. Let the Venetian Republic keep the eight-power telescope! He would make a better one and offer it to a more enlightened patron. Better still, he would show that much more could be revealed not only on land and sea, but beyond the reaches of human navigation.

The Moon's new face

The telescope was pointed to the heavens; and for the first time the human eye had a close-up view of the Moon.

Galileo's reason for examining the Moon was probably to confirm a conjecture that he had made in a satirical book published under the pseudonym of Alimberto Mauri in 1606. The changes in the features of the lunar surface that can be seen with the naked eye had been adduced as evidence that there are mountains on the Moon. His eight-power telescope was sufficient to strengthen this hypothesis and by November 1609 he had a fifteen-power telescope that enabled him to set all doubt aside. By March 1610, he had devised an instrument that magnified thirty times.

Galileo's construction of the telescope was the result of ingenuity and inventiveness rather than theoretical know-how. To his dying day, he remained in the dark about the laws of optics that lay behind his success. But although he could not determine the magnifying

power from the focal lengths of the concave and convex lenses as
we do today, he found a practical and reliable method that bypassed
geometrical considerations:

Now, to determine without great trouble the magnifying power of an instrument, trace on paper the outlines of two circles (or two squares) of which one
is 400 times as large as the other, as will be the case when the diameter of
one is 20 times that at of the other. Then, with two such figures attached to
the same wall, observe them both simultaneously from a distance, looking
at the smaller one through the telescope and at the larger one with the other,
unaided eye. This may be done without difficulty, holding both eyes open at
the same time, and the two figures will appear to be of the same size if the
instrument magnifies objects in the said ratio.[3]

This simple technique gives us a good idea of Galileo's resourceful-
ness and his practical cast of mind.

A didactic problem

As we have seen, the first celestial object that Galileo observed was
the Moon. The drawings that he published in the *Starry Messenger*
were to transform existing knowledge about our satellite. They also
give us a glimpse into the didactic problems that he faced.

The illustrations of the Moon first and last quarter show a libra-
tion (apparent oscillation by which parts near the edge of the lunar disk are alternately visible and invisible) of 9° vertically measured from a crater (later called Albategnius) that Galileo chose to
illustrate the shadow cast by mountains on the Moon. This feature
enabled Guglielmo Righini to determine the date of the observations
as December 3 and 18, 1609.[4] A comparison of the Moon at last quarter as seen through a modern telescope and as sketched by Galileo
reveals that the size of the crater is greatly enlarged in Galileo's drawing (see Figure 6.1).

Galileo noticed the difference between the illumination of the
crater at first and last quarter, and he realized that this indicated
that there were mountains on the Moon. He was anxious that this
should not be overlooked by his readers, and like many good teachers, before and after him, he exaggerated the size of what he had
observed in order to bring out the salient features. This was all the
more necessary since, in a small woodcut, Galileo could not highlight

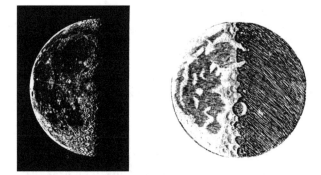

Figure 6.1.   Moon at last quater, (*left*) as seen through a high-power tele-scope (Lick Observatory Photographs) and (*right*) as drawn by Galileo (from his *Starry Messenger*). (From Stillman Drake, *Galileo at Work*. Chicago University Press, 1978, p. 145).

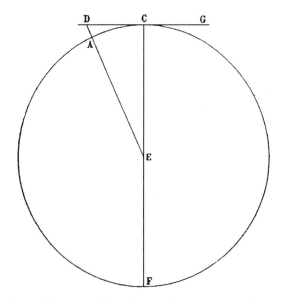

Figure 6.2.   Diagram of the Moon with mountain of height AD.

the shifting pattern of shadows without giving the crater consider-able width. There is no telescopic enigma here, just good pedagogy.

The problem of communication comes to the fore again in the dia-gram that Galileo used to illustrate his trigonometric determination of the height of mountains on the Moon (see Figure 6.2). This shows a mountain AD whose peak is just touched by a ray of sunlight GCD. The rest of the mountain still lies in the dark region beyond the boundary of light CF. From his knowledge of the radius of the Moon (CE or AE) and his observational determination of the distance DC, Galileo arrived at the figure of four terrestrial miles for the height of the mountain AD.[5]

In October 1610, Galileo received a note from the German scientist Johann Georg Brengger pointing out that the phenomenon that Galileo recorded could not have been observed on the rim of the Moon for reasons that Galileo himself had clearly stated. Namely, the rim of the Moon appears perfectly circular, not toothed or dented, because the space between the mountains is concealed by other ranges of mountains. The illuminated spots in the dark region could only have been observed near the center. The unevenness of the boundary line between light and darkness made precise measurement impossible, but it seemed incontrovertible to Brengger that no more than three hours could have elapsed between the time of the first illumination of a peak in the darkened area and its joining the illuminated boundary. Because the Moon goes around the Earth (i.e., describes a circle of 360°) in roughly 29 days, in 3 hours it covers about 1°. This means that the distance CD (see Figure 6.2) is much shorter than Galileo claimed and, hence, that the mountain AD need only be one third of a mile high. A mountain four miles high would imply a rotation of 5° and a time of 8 hours, much more than Galileo had intimated.

In a lengthy reply, which is one of the first detailed discussions of the application of geometry to the new celestial data, Galileo granted that Brengger's reasoning was valid but claimed that some peaks are indeed illuminated more than eight hours before reaching the boundary of light. All that could be concluded was that mountains on the Moon are of varying heights! More interesting, perhaps, is Galileo's avowal that his data were taken from the central part of the Moon. He had to draw the mountain as though it were on the very rim of the Moon in order to make his geometrical point clear. Galileo did not distort his data; he merely bowed to the requirements of sound teaching.

Sharpening the image

The spherical and chromatic aberrations of Galileo's first telescope were such that they probably blurred the difference in appearance between stars and planets. Galileo also suffered from a problem with his eyes which caused him to see bright lights as irradiated with colored rings. He could improve his vision by peering through clenched fists, and it is almost certainly personal experience and not theoretical consideration that led him to stop down the objective lens of his telescope, as he explains in the *Starry Messenger*:

> If we now fit to the lens CD thin plates, some pierced with larger and some with smaller apertures, and put now one plate and now another over the lens, as required, we may form at will different angles, subtending more or fewer minutes of arc, and by this means we may easily measure intervals between two stars separated by but a few minutes, with no error greater than one or two minutes.[6]

Galileo began placing a cardboard stop on the objective lens of his telescope early in January 1610. This greatly reduced the haziness of the image and the rainbow discoloration, but it did not drastically narrow the field of view as Galileo believed. Perforated plates could only reduce the field of vision if they were fitted not to the lens but well beyond.

Kepler discovered this when he used the telescope that Galileo had sent the Archbishop of Cologne. This was equipped with a "window" that Kepler removed only to find that the field of vision was barely enlarged. The device might not have narrowed the field as Galileo had surmised; it did something more important: It reduced the fuzziness around small bodies and made it possible to detect satellites.

The satellites of Jupiter

By January 1610, Galileo had considerably improved his telescope and his means of observation. His device now magnified twenty times, and the lenses were fixed at the ends of tubes in such a way that the one with the eyepiece slid up and down the one containing the objective to allow for proper focusing. The instrument was about a meter long and was mounted on a stable base to free his hands for drawing. Finally, the objective lens was partly covered with an oblong piece of cardboard.

On the evening of January 7, Galileo saw three small but very bright stars in the immediate vicinity of Jupiter. The idea that they might be satellites did not occur to him. What struck him was the fact that they were in the unusual configuration of a short straight line along the ecliptic.

Looking at Jupiter on the next night, he noticed that whereas two had been to the east and one to the west of Jupiter on the previous evening, they were now all to the west of the planet. Again, he did not suspect that they might be in motion but wondered whether Jupiter might not be moving eastwards contrary to what the standard astronomical tables asserted.

On the 9th, the sky was overcast. On the 10th, he observed two stars to the east of Jupiter. This seemed to dispose of the conjecture that Jupiter might be moving in the wrong direction. On the 11th, he again saw two stars to the east of Jupiter but the furthest from the planet was now much brighter. On the 12th, the third star reappeared to the west of Jupiter. On the 13th, a fourth star became visible; three stars were now to the west and one the east of Jupiter. On the 14th, the sky was again overcast, and on the 15th, only three remained to the west (see Figure 6.3).

By the 11th, Galileo had concluded that the three stars he had observed were moving but he probably did not think that they were circling Jupiter, but oscillating back and forth along a straight line. Under these circumstances, it is impossible to point to an instant in time and say, "At this hour, he saw the satellites for what they really were!"

Galileo himself probably found it difficult to remember the genesis of his discovery from the first observation of three stars in the neighborhood of Jupiter to the full realization that they were satellites. But why was this discovery so exciting? Galileo tells us himself:

Here we have a powerful and elegant argument to quiet the doubts of those who, while accepting without difficulty that the planets revolve around the sun in the Copernican system, are so disturbed to have the moon alone revolve around the earth while accompanying it in an annual revolution about the sun, that they believe that this structure of the universe should be rejected as impossible. But now we have not just one planet revolving around another; our eyes show us four stars that wander around Jupiter as does the moon around the earth, and that all together they trace out a grand revolution about the sun in the space of 12 years.[7]

To those who objected that the Earth could not orbit around the Sun without losing its moon, Galileo could now point to the skies and show Jupiter circling around a central body (be it the Earth, as they believed, or the Sun, as Copernicus argued) without losing not one but four satellites. If Galileo could not explain why the Earth did

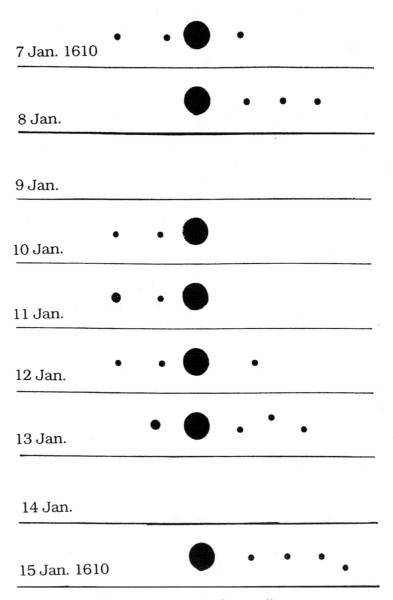

Figure 6.3. Jupiter and its satellites.

not shed its moon, the Aristotelians were equally at a loss to say why Jupiter held on to its satellites. From challengers, the geocentrists were rapidly becoming the challenged!

From time immemorial, no new planets had been sighted, and Galileo saw that the satellites of Jupiter could be made to serve not only a terrestrial but a mundane cause. Anxious to ingratiate himself with the Grand Duke of Tuscany, he named the new "stars" *Medicean* after the family of the reigning Prince, Cosimo II. He was suitably rewarded by being recalled to Florence in the summer of 1610.

The Mother of Love and Cynthia

The satellites of Jupiter were the last of Galileo's discoveries in Padua. Shortly after his return to Florence, Venus, Saturn, and the Sun provided more celestial news.

Among the difficulties raised against Copernicus's theory was the fact that Mercury and Venus, like the Moon, should display phases since they lie between the Sun and the Earth. Copernicus had replied that the phases were invisible to the naked eye, and Galileo was anxious to see whether his telescope would enable him to see them. Venus was usually too close to the Sun to be observed and it was only in the autumn of 1610 that he was able to confirm that Copernicus had been right.

At the time, anagrams were frequently used to guarantee the priority of a discovery without having to rush into print. On December 11, Galileo wrote to the Ambassador of Tuscany in Prague and enclosed the following mock sentence for Kepler: "*Haec immatura a me iam frustra leguntur o y.*" Kepler made a number of attempts to find the hidden message but he had to give up and wait for Galileo's letter of January 1 to learn that the letters, once transposed, read: "*Cynthiae figuras aemulatur mater amorum,*" namely, "The mother of love (Venus) imitates the appearances of Cynthia (the Moon)."[8]

The point is the following: If Venus revolves around the Sun, it will not only go through a complete series of phases, but it will vary considerably in size. At its greatest distance from the Earth, it will be seen as a perfectly round disk, fully illuminated. As it moves toward the Earth it will grow in size until at quadrature (corresponding to the first and third quarter of the moon) it will be half-illumined. At

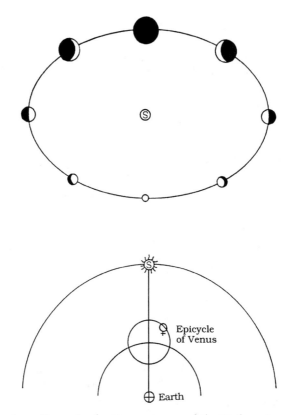

Figure 6.4.   Venus in the Copernican and the Ptolemaic systems.

its closest to the Earth, it will have become invisible (like the Moon when it is new).

This is exactly what Galileo observed. Such a phenomenon would be impossible in the Ptolemaic system where Venus is said to move on an epicycle attached to a larger deferent circle whose center always lies on the line that joins the Earth to the Sun. Because Venus never goes behind the Sun, the complete sequence of phases is ruled out in this system (see Figure 6.4).

The discovery of the phases of Venus was a powerful argument against the ancient astronomy but it did not supplant the rival hypothesis of the Danish astronomer Tycho Brahe, who agreed that Venus and Mercury and all the other planets went around the Sun but maintained that the Sun itself revolved around the Earth.

The ears of Saturn and the sun's spots

Since Jupiter had four "assistants," it was natural that Galileo should examine the other planets to see whether they also had satellites. He searched for many months in vain.

The result was a disappointment but it was also a source of complacency, for it was becoming clear that he was the only one whom God had predestined to discover new celestial bodies. Nonetheless, he was sorry not to be able to meet the request of the French Court which *begged* him to find a new planet and name it after their King Henry IV.

In the summer of 1610, however, Saturn presented an unsuspected aspect and showed itself as a conglomerate of three stars. Galileo, fearing that someone else might publish the news before him, immediately sent an anagram to the Tuscan ambassador in Prague, but he waited until November 13, 1610, before disclosing its meaning and offering the following information:

I have observed that Saturn is not a single star but three together, which always touch each other. They do not move in the least among themselves and have the following shape oOo, the middle being much larger than the lateral ones.

Galileo went on to say,

If we look at them with a telescope of weak magnification, the three stars do not appear very distinctly and Saturn seems elongated like an olive, thus ◯. But with a telescope that multiplies the surface over a thousand times (i.e., magnifies a little over 30 times) the three globes will be seen very distinctly and almost touching, with only a thread of dark space between them. A court has been found for Jupiter, and now for this old man two attendants who help him walk and never leave his side.[9]

Galileo had barely send off his letter when the two attendants began to dwindle to the point of vanishing entirely by the end of 1612. With a fine sense of melodrama, Galileo commented upon their disappearance to his friend Mark Welser:

What can be said of so strange a metamorphosis? Were the two smaller stars consumed like spots on the sun? Have they suddenly vanished and fled? Or has Saturn devoured his own children? ... I cannot resolve what to say in a change so strange, so new, so unexpected.[10]

But Galileo soon plucked up his courage and, in the same letter, conjectured that the two attendants would reappear after revolving around Saturn, and that by the summer solstice of 1615, they would not only be again visible, but more luminous and larger. When they reappeared they had the shape of "ears" on each side of Saturn, but soon they vanished again!

As was later discovered, Galileo had been observing Saturn's rings, which are sometimes at right angle to the line of sight and virtually invisible while at other times they are more or less slanted and can be detected. The so-called ears were the most visible parts of these rings, and they remained a mystery until Christiaan Huygens was able to identify them with a better telescope in 1656.

It was natural for Galileo to wish to explore the Sun as well as the planets, but he could not observe the flaming ball of the Sun for more than a fleeting instant without being blinded. A neutral blue or green lens could be placed over the objective of the telescope, or the glass could be covered with soot. But the best method was found by one of Galileo's former students, Benedetto Castelli, who had the idea of projecting the image of the Sun on a screen just behind the telescope. Galileo was therefore able to see clearly the black spots on the surface of the Sun.

A Jesuit professor, Christoph Scheiner, who observed the sunspots at the same time, believed they were hitherto unknown satellites revolving close to the Sun. With geometrical rigor and devastating wit, Galileo was able to show that the spots lie on the surface or very near the Sun.

This was a momentous discovery at the time since, as we have seen, the Aristotelians maintained that nothing could change in the heavens, and surely not the eternal and immutable Sun! Galileo's discovery that devastating change occurred on the very face of the Sun was yet another blow to the traditional world view.

The decisive proof that the Earth moves

Galileo's celestial discoveries strengthened the case for Copernicanism but they fell short of being compelling. What Galileo wanted was a physical proof that the Earth moved. This proof eluded him for years but came to him in a flash on one of his frequent trips from Padua to Venice in a large barge whose bottom contained a certain amount of water that splashed up and down when the boat went faster or slower.

Galileo noticed that the water tended to pile up at the back of the boat when it accelerated and at the front when it slowed down. This struck Galileo as a kind of tidal motion, and he wondered whether the to and fro oscillation of the tides could not be explained by a combination of acceleration and deceleration. But where would the increase and decrease of speed come from?

Galileo thought he had the answer. What if the speeding up and slowing down resulted from a combination of the diurnal and annual revolutions of the Earth! As befitted an astronomer used to describing the motion of bodies on epicycles and deferents, Galileo visualized the daily rotation of the Earth as occurring along the circumference of a small circle BCDL whose center A is attached to a larger circle ACGL that represents the annual revolution around the Sun (see Figure 6.5). The small circle revolves once every twenty-four hours. The axial and orbital speeds of the Earth are so combined that a point on the surface of the Earth moves very fast once a day when both revolutions are in the same direction (point B in the diagram) and very slowly once a day when they are going in opposite directions (at point D).

The land masses are not displaced by these combined motions, but the water in the oceans are tugged to and fro. If the Earth did not spin on its axis while it goes around the Sun, Galileo was convinced that "the ebb and flow of the oceans could not occur."[11]

Galileo was so proud of his argument and so convinced of its power that he resolved to change the title of his book on Copernicanism from *The System of the World*, as he had provisionally called it, to *A Dialogue on the Tides*. He tried his argument out in Rome in 1616.

It was considered clever but unconvincing, and the fuss generated over the issue led the Roman censors to examine Copernicus's *De Revolutionibus Orbium Caelestium*, which had been published almost three quarters of a century earlier. The work was banned for claiming, without scientific proof, that the Sun was at rest in opposition to the commonsensical language of the Bible, which plainly speaks of the Sun (and not the Earth) as rising and setting. Galileo's writings were not mentioned and he even returned to Florence with a flattering testimonial from Cardinal Bellarmine, the Head of the

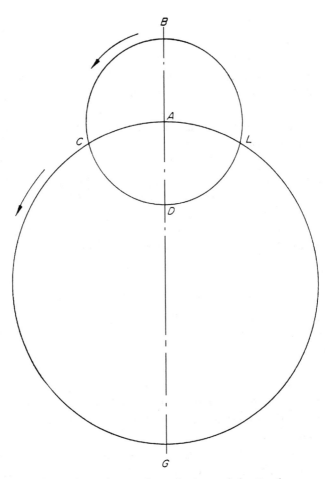

Figure 6.5. The daily and annual revolutions of the Earth represented by an epicycle on a deferent.

Tribunal of the Inquisition, but he was bitterly disappointed and realized that it would be unwise to push the theologians too hard.

THE DIALOGUE ON THE TWO CHIEF
WORLD SYSTEMS

Galileo had practically resigned himself to silence when, in 1623, Cardinal Maffeo Barberini, a patron of the arts, a poet, and a Florentine to boot, was elected Pope and took the name Urban VIII. At the suggestion of his friends in the Vatican, Galileo journeyed to Rome in the spring of 1624, and he was received six times by the Pope in the course of six weeks.

He failed in his attempt to have the ban on Copernicanism lifted, but he nevertheless derived the impression that he was free to write in support of the heliocentric theory as long as he "kept out of the sacristy" as a Roman prelate had advised him. Thus encouraged, he embarked, at the age of sixty, on his epoch-making *Dialogue on the Two World Systems*, which he completed in 1630 and saw through the press two years later.

Galileo chose to cast his argument for Copernicianism in the form of a discussion between three interlocutors. The two first, the Florentine Filippo Salviati (1583–1614) and the Venetian patrician Giovanfrancesco Sagredo (1571–1620), had been his friends; the third, the Aristotelian Simplicio, was an imaginary character.

They are presented as having gathered in Sagredo's palace at Venice for four days to discuss the arguments for and against the heliocentric system. Salviati is a militant Copernican, Simplicio an avowed defender of geocentrism, and Sagredo an intelligent amateur already half-converted to the new astronomy.

Never before Galileo had any critic of traditional astronomy been so apt at convincing an opponent by the sheer brilliance of his presentation, or so masterful at laughing him off the stage when he refused to be persuaded. Galileo drew from the literary resources of his native Italian to convey insights and to stimulate reflection, but his style does not possess the bare factualness of the modern laboratory report or the unflinching rigor of a mathematical deduction.

Words are more than vehicles of pure thought. They are sensible entities, and they possess associations with images, memories, and feelings. Galileo knew how to use these associations to attract, hold, and absorb attention. He did not present his ideas in the nakedness of abstract thought but clothed them in the colors of feeling, intending not only to inform and to teach, but to move and to entice to action. He wished to bring about nothing less than a reversal of the 1616 decision against Copernicanism, and the dialogue form seemed to him most conducive to this end.

Although the written dialogue may be deprived of the eloquence of facial expression and the emphasis of gestures and of the support of modulated tone and changing volume, it retains the effectiveness of pauses, the suggestiveness of questions, and the significance of omissions. Galileo made most of these techniques, and it is important to keep this in mind when assessing his arguments, for too often passages of the *Dialogue* have been paraded without sufficient regard for their highly rhetorical content. During the first three days the interlocutors debate astronomical issues; the fourth is devoted to a brief but powerful presentation of the physical proof from the tides that we have already considered.

The old world dismantled

The First Day of the *Dialogue* is devoted to a refutation of Aristotle's assumption that the sphere of the Moon divided the universe into two sharply distinct regions, the terrestrial and the celestial. Bodies in the celestial were said to be composed of a special kind of matter, the quintessence, which was incorruptible and underwent only one kind of change, uniform motion in a circle. Bodies below the Moon were subject to all kinds of change, and if they moved the motion natural to them was a straight line toward their proper place. Evidence for this view could be seen in fire which always moves straight up or in a clod of earth which always falls straight down.

To replace this *double-tiered cosmos* by the Copernican *universe*, Galileo had to show that the heavens are also subject to change. When the Aristotelian expert, Simplicio, states that the heavens are immutable because no change has ever been observed there, Salviati asks him how he can affirm that China and America are subject to change when he has only seen Europe. If the Mediterranean Sea was created, as many maintain, by water rushing in from the Atlantic through the straits of Gibraltar, the flood could have been noticed from the Moon.

But the Earth was obviously subject to generation and corruption before this happened. Hence why should the Moon not be equally corruptible even though humanity has failed to record any appreciable change? Indeed the novae of 1572 and 1604, and the sunspots, provide clear evidence that change does occur in the heavens.

Simplicio shifts his ground and denies that change makes sense on heavenly bodies,

which are ordained to no other use than the service of the earth, and need nothing more than motion and light to achieve their purpose, [for] we plainly see and feel that all generations, changes, etc. that occur on earth are either

directly or indirectly designed for the use, comfort and benefit of man ...
Of what use to the human race could generations that might happen on the
Moon or on other planets ever be?

This argument can be met either by denying that man is the center
of all things or by postulating the existence of human beings on the
Moon. Sagredo prefers to disclaim the anthropocentric assumption
altogether. Although it is true that we can only imagine what we
have already seen or what we can piece together from our past experience, we should not allow ourselves to be fettered by our limited
knowledge when thinking on a cosmic scale.

Thus on the Moon, separated from us by such a great distance and perhaps
made of a very different material from the earth's, it might be the case that
substances exist and actions occur, not merely remote from, but completely
beyond our imaginings.[12]

Galileo compares our speculations about the Moon to guesses that
someone, who has never seen a lake or a stream, might make if he
were told that animals move without wings or legs in a world made
of water. Unless he were taken to a lake or shown an aquarium, he
might indulge in the wildest fantasies without fear of disproof.

But if this is the case, and nothing can be proved, how can anything
be disproved? What about the hard and impenetrable celestial matter
of the Aristotelians? Galileo recognizes that it can only be ridiculed,
as in the following witty exchange between Sagredo and Salviati.

Sagr. What excellent stuff, the sky, for anyone who could get hold of it for
building a palace! So hard, yet so transparent!
Salv. Rather, what terrible stuff, being completely invisible because of its
extreme transparency. One could not move about the rooms without grave
danger of running into the doorposts and breaking one's head.
Sagr. There would be no such danger if, as some Peripatetics say, it is
intangible; it cannot even be touched, let alone be bumped into.
Salv. That would be no comfort, for celestial matter, although it cannot
be touched because it lacks tangible properties, can nevertheless touch elemental bodies, and it would injure us as much, and more, by running into
us as it would if we had run into it.[13]

More interesting than Sagredo's and Salviati's devastating satire,
is Simplicio's comment: "The question you have incidentally raised

is one of the difficult problems in philosophy." The question is, of course, perfectly sensible and legitimate in the Aristotelian framework, but it appears ludicrous in the new conceptual scheme. The world must not only be seen through the telescope, it must be looked at through a new set of intellectual categories.

The new world unveiled

Once the assumption that there is a radical difference between the terrestrial and the supra-lunar world is abandoned, what we know about objects on Earth can be used to know something about the Moon and the planets if they display phenomena similar to those with which we are familiar. Analogies can be brought into play to know what the lunar surface is like.

For instance, as Galileo points out, the suggestion that the Moon's surface is polished like a mirror must be discarded because the phenomena observed on the Moon cannot be reproduced with either flat or spherical mirrors. This can be achieved, however, by rotating a dark ball with prominences and cavities proportional in size to those on the Moon.

Out of the countless different appearances that are revealed night after night during one lunation, you could not imitate a single one by fashioning as you please a smooth ball out of more or less opaque and transparent pieces. On the other hand, balls may be made of any solid and opaque material which, merely by having prominences and cavities and by being variously illuminated, will display precisely the scenes and changes that are seen on the Moon from one hour to the next.[14]

Models are instruments, and if it is necessary to establish their relevance, it is no less important to determine when they break down. Simplicio brings the issue to the fore by asking Salviati how far he is prepared to extend the parallel between the Earth and the Moon. Would he be willing to say, for instance, that the large spots on the Moon are seas? Salviati replies with a brief lecture on models and analogies:

If the only way two surfaces could be illuminated by the sun so that one appeared brighter than the other was by having one made of land and the other of water, it would be necessary to say that the moon's surface is partly land and partly water. But because several other ways of producing the same effect are known, and there are perhaps others we are not aware of, I shall not make bold to affirm one rather than another to exist on the moon.[15]

Salviati is certain, however, that the darker parts are plains and the brighter ones mountain ranges because "the boundary which separates the light and the dark part makes an even cut in traversing the spots, whereas in the bright part it looks broken and jagged."[16]

He is also willing to say that life on the Moon would be unlike anything known to us because of different climatic conditions. First, a lunar day is equal to a terrestrial month, and no earthly plant and animal could survive fifteen days of relentless and scorching heat. Secondly, the seasonal changes, which are considerable on the Earth because of a variation of 47° in the rising and setting of the Sun, are much less on the Moon where the variation is only 10°.

Finally, although oceans cover a large part of the terrestrial globe, the Moon must be waterless since it has no clouds. Sagredo suggests that this last difficulty might be overcome by postulating storms or great dews during the night. Salviati's reply is again instructive:

If from other appearances we had any indication that there were species similar to ours there, and that only occurrence of rain was lacking, we should be able to find something or other to replace it, as the inundations of the Nile do in Egypt. But finding no property whatever that agrees with ours of the many that would be required to produce similar effects, there is no point in troubling ourselves to introduce one only, and even that one, not from sure observation but because of a mere possibility.[17]

In Aristotelian physics, terrestrial models were deemed irrelevant because celestial bodies were made of an entirely different material. In Galileo's unified cosmos, analogies from familiar objects can be used to explain features of the Moon and the planets, but the limitations of this method are made clear. Galileo's caution is dictated by the prudence of the experimentalist for whom the world always hold surprises.

Every kind of change, for Galileo, is merely a reorganization of matter in motion. On this view, it becomes easier to know the course of the planets in the sky than the nature of generation and corruption on the Earth. The underlying assumption is that all bodies move in mathematically describable paths and arrange themselves in geometrical patterns. Although Aristotle was right in asserting that bodies are three dimensional, he should have proved his point instead of appealing to the consensus of the Pythagoreans and the fitting character of the number three:

I do not believe that the number three is more perfect for legs than four or two, nor that the number four is imperfect for the elements, and that they would be more perfect if they were three. It would have been better for Aristotle to leave these tropes to rhetoricians and to prove his point with rigorous demonstrations as is required in the demonstrative sciences.[18]

Simplicio expresses surprise and dismay. How can Salviati, a mathematician himself, ridicule the opinion of the Pythagoreans? Simplicio's astonishment serves a dual purpose.

First, it discloses the authoritarian frame of mind of the Aristotelian scholar, an intellectual stance Galileo is always eager to expose. Simplicio views disagreements as incidents between warring schools of thought. He thinks, and he assumes others do, as the member of a school, as the disciple of some ancient master. Secondly, Simplicio's reaction provides Galileo with the opportunity of distinguishing the Pythagoreanism of the mathematicians from that of the astrologers and the alchemists.

I know very well that the Pythagoreans held the science of numbers in high esteem, and that Plato himself admired the human intellect and considered it to partake of divinity simply because it understood the nature of numbers. I would not be far from making the same judgment myself. But I do not believe that the mysteries which caused Pythagoras and his school to have such veneration for the science of numbers are the follies that abound in the sayings and the writings of the common man.[19]

Salviati proves that bodies have only three dimensions by showing that no more than three lines can be drawn at right angles to each other. Simplicio initially fails to see the cogency of the argument because he lacks the elementary training that would enable him to think rapidly and consistently (a quality that can only be acquired by studying mathematics). "The art of demonstration is learnt by reading works which contain demonstrations," says Salviati, who adds, "these are mathematical treatises, not books on logic."[20]

This statement, which comes at the beginning of the First Day, sets the tone of the *Dialogue*. Galileo rejects the mystical number-juggling of pseudoscience, but he firmly believes that the human intellect partakes of divinity because it understands mathematics, the language of nature.

At the end of the First Day, when the use of mathematics has been vindicated in a variety of ways, Salviati returns to the theme of "divine" mathematical knowledge. The human mind is restricted in many respects, but it can attain certainty

in the pure mathematical sciences, that is, geometry and arithmetic, of which the divine intellect indeed knows infinitely more propositions, since it knows them all. But with regard to the few that the human intellect understands, I believe that its knowledge equals the divine in objective certainty, for it succeeds in grasping their necessity.[21]

The unity of all things in the mind of God "*is not entirely unknown to the human intellect, but it is clouded in deep and thick mists.*"[22] The haze is dispersed when a mathematical proposition is so firmly mastered that it can be run over rapidly and with ease. What the divine intellect perceives in a flash, the mortal mind fits together bit by bit.

Galileo's concept of nature implies a revolution in the way we think about the world. Against the Aristotelians who dismiss mathematics as irrelevant and futile, he affirms that it is the divine feature of the human intellect. The implication is clear: For centuries, Aristotelians have ignored the divine principle in man. God is a geometrician in his creative labors. This is why Galileo declares in a letter to the Grand Duchess Christina that doubtful passages in Scripture should be interpreted in the light of science rather than the reverse:

It seems to me that in discussing natural problems we should not begin from the authority of scriptural passages, but from sensory experiences and necessary demonstrations. Holy Scripture and nature proceed alike from the divine World. . . . Everything that is said in the Bible is not bound by rules as strict as those which govern natural events, and God is no less excellently revealed in these than in the sacred pronouncements of Scripture.[23]

Galileo uses all the rhetorical gifts at his command to persuade his readers that science is not mere rhetoric. A few years earlier, he had

written in the same vein against the Jesuit professor, Orazio Grassi
(whose pseudonym was Sarsi):

I believe Sarsi is firmly convinced that it is essential in philosophy to support
oneself by the opinion of some famous author, as if when our minds are
not wedded to the reasoning of some other person they ought to remain
completely barren and sterile. Perhaps he thinks that philosophy is a book of
fiction created by one man, like the *Iliad* or *Orlando Furioso* (books in which
the least important thing is whether what is written in them is true). Sig.
Sarsi, this is not the way matters stand. Philosophy is written in that great
book which ever lies before our eyes (I mean the universe) but we cannot
understand it if we do not first learn the language and grasp the symbols
in which it is written. This book is written in the mathematical language,
and the symbols are triangles, circles and other geometrical figures, without
whose help it is humanly impossible to comprehend a single word of it, and
without which one wanders in vain through a dark labyrinth.[24]

The Second Day of the *Dialogue* will show that in the real world
the Earth rotates on its axis; the Third Day will establish that it
revolves around the Sun.

The diurnal rotation of the Earth

Galileo could not devise an experiment to prove that the Earth rotates
on its axis but he could show that the traditional objections were no
longer valid. For instance, it had been objected that if the Earth turned
from west to east (instead of the Sun rising in the east and setting in
the west), arrows shot to the west would carry further.

Sagredo suggests testing this by mounting a crossbow on an open
carriage. What if an arrow that travels 300 yards when it is shot from
a stationary crossbow were shot from a carriage that covers 100 yards
in the same time? Simplicio, anxious to display his computational
skills, immediately declares that it will travel 200 yards in the direction of motion and 400 yards in the opposite direction.

Salviati then leads him to the correct solution by pointing out that
the speed could be equalized if the strength of the crossbow were
increased in the first case and reduced in the second. This is, in fact,
what happens since the crossbow shares the motion of the carriage.
In the direction of motion, the arrow is given an impetus of 400 yards,
and in the opposite direction it receives one of only 200 yards.

Since the carriage moves 100 yards during the time of the arrow's
flight, the distances are equalized! The same holds for shots fired

from a moving Earth: Regardless of the direction in which they are aimed, they will fall at the same distance from the mouth of the cannon.[25]

Galileo realized that vertical shots could be interpreted in the same way. Assuming that the Earth moves, a cannon ball shot straight upward will climb vertically while continuing to move horizontally at the same velocity as the rotating Earth whose motion it shares. Galileo's recognition that the vertical and horizontal motions are independent components represents a major conceptual advance. It was failure to grasp this principle that hampered his opponents and led them to believe that the impulse from the gunpowder would have to be added to that of the Earth's rotation.

If the Earth moves, its inhabitants share its uniform motion which therefore remains imperceptible to them. Ballistic experiments on Earth are of no avail.

The correct strategy is to call upon the heavens, to seek a motion common to all celestial bodies, and then to ask (in the light of the principle of simplicity) whether the phenomena could not be explained more profitably by postulating that the Earth also moves. Now clearly all the bodies that we observe in the heavens naturally move in a circle! It is legitimate therefore to consider the rotation of the Earth as something that is natural. Galileo's argument then takes the form of an appeal to simplicity:

Who is going to believe that nature (which by general agreement does not perform by means of many things what it can do by a few) has chosen to make an immense number of very huge bodies (i.e, the planets and the stars) move with incalculable speed, to achieve what could have been done by a moderate movement of one single body around its own center?[26]

The diurnal motion of the Earth would do away with a host of complexities in the geocentric system. First, it would remove the anomaly of a heavenly sphere of stars moving westward when all the planets move eastward. Secondly, it would explain the apparent variations in the orbits and periods of the stars, and, finally, it would dispense with the solid crystalline spheres that carry the stars around in the Ptolemaic system.

The motion of a stationary Earth is so firmly embedded in the imagination of the Aristotelians that when they hear that it moves they "foolishly assume that it started moving when Pythagoras (or whoever it was) first said that it moved."[27]

The correct and indispensable procedure is to replace the Ptolemaic frame of reference by the Copernican one. If this is done, Galileo assumes, somewhat too easily, that all becomes clear, and he goes on to argue in the Third Day that the same can be said for the Earth's annual revolution around the Sun.

The annual motion of the Earth

The telescope made it possible to see that Venus has phases like the Moon, that the apparent diameters of Mars and Venus vary considerably, and that Jupiter orbits with not only one but four moons. Furthermore, because the telescope does not magnify the distant stars but reduces them to tiny dots, Tycho Brahe's fear that the stars would have to be gigantic in size becomes groundless.

With the removal of these difficulties, Salviati claims that there is no longer any bar to admitting the Copernican hypothesis. Among other advantages, this nongeocentric view accounts for apparent irregularities in the motions of the planets without cluttering the heavens with deferents and epicycles as in the Ptolemaic system. In Figure 6.6(a), the sighting lines from the Earth, E, show why a planet farther from the Sun than the Earth such as Mars, M, seems to reverse its direction against the background of distant stars.

The retrograde motion is merely apparent and results from Mars traveling around the Sun more slowly than the Earth does. The motion of Venus, whose orbit lies between the Earth and Sun is explained on the same principle in Figure 6.6(b). This time the planet travels faster than the Earth. In the Ptolemaic model, these stations and retrogressions could only be explained by postulating an intricate series of deferents and epicycles. Such a complicated celestial machinery violated nature's basic laws, as Sagredo points out:

If the universe were ordered according to such a multiplicity, one would have to remove from philosophy many axioms commonly adopted by all philosophers, such that nature does not multiply things unnecessarily, that she makes use of the easiest and simplest means for producing her effects, that she does nothing in vain and the like.[28]

It is only with the heliocentric system, he adds, that the principle of uniform motion in a circle can be retained without filling the heavens with an intricate series of gears and wheels. Ideal physical

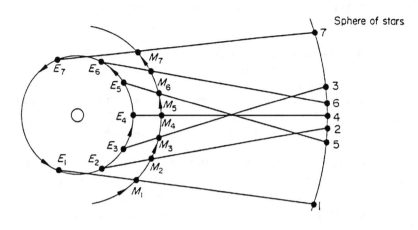

(a)

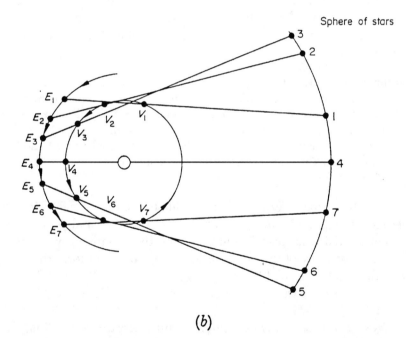

(b)

Figure 6.6.   The motion of an outer planet (a) and an inner planet (b) against the background of the stars.

proofs for Galileo should approximate geometrical demonstrations in rigor and simplicity. He praises Gilbert for his experimental work on the lodestone, but he cannot help wishing

that he had been somewhat better at mathematics, and especially well grounded in geometry, the practice of which would have made him more cautious in accepting as rigorous proofs the reasons he puts forward as the real causes of the conclusions which he himself observed. These reasons, candidly speaking, do not compel with the strength which those adduced for natural, necessary and eternal conclusions should undoubtedly possess.[29]

For want of mathematical training, otherwise intelligent people raise ridiculous objections against the motion of the Earth, asking, for instance, why they do not feel themselves transported to Persia or to Japan. Mathematics would sharpen their intellect and enable them to penetrate beyond the veil of the senses.

When Salviati lists the astronomical evidence in favor of the heliocentric theory, Sagredo is astonished that everyone has not embraced it yet. Salviati marvels rather that anyone should have upheld it prior to the invention of the telescope. Such a feat of intellectual daring is the hallmark of genius:

I cannot sufficiently admire the intellectual eminence of those who received it and held it to be true. They have by sheer force of intellect done such violence to their own senses as to prefer what reason told them over that which sense experience plainly showed them to be the case ... I repeat, I cannot find any bounds for my admiration when I consider that reason in Aristarchus and Copernicus was so able to conquer sense that, in spite of it, it became the mistress of their belief.[30]

Aristarchus and Copernicus were unable to see the phases of Venus and the variations in the apparent diameters of Mars and Venus. Yet, "they trusted what reason told them and they confidently asserted that the structure of the universe could have no other form than the one they had outlined."[31]

"What pleasure the telescope would have given Copernicus," says Sagredo.

"Yes," comments Salviati, "but how much less the fame of his sublime intellect among the learned. For we see, as I have already mentioned, that he persistently continued to affirm, assisted by rational arguments, what sense experience showed to be just the opposite."[32]

CONCLUSION: REASON AND EXPERIMENT
IN GALILEO'S PROCEDURE

For Galileo, the scientific revolution, the passage from the old to the
new world-view, is not primarily the result of more and better observations. It is the inspired mathematical reduction of a complex geometrical labyrinth into a beautifully simple and harmonious system.
The crucial distinction no longer lies between mental and factual but
between mathematical and crudely empirical. Experiments (be they
mental or real) are equally valid if they are set up in accordance with
the requirements of mathematics.

Galileo replaces the qualitative approach of the Scholastics by a
more rigorous method where measurement, at least in principle, becomes fundamental. When objects are not open to direct inspection,
real or imagined models are invoked to determine the spatial and
temporal relationships that are basic to scientific understanding.

Whether a stone dropped from the mast of a moving ship falls at the
foot of the mast is a question that is settled by a thought experiment.
We are asked to "observe, if not with our physical eyes, at least with
those of our mind, what would happen if an eagle, carried by the
force of the wind, were to drop a rock from its talons." Salviati adds:

You will see the same thing happen by making the experiment on a ship
with a ball thrown perpendicularly upward from a catapult. It returns to the
same place whether the ship is moving or standing still.[33]

This is surely not an experiment that the captain of a ship would have
welcomed! But even if Galileo had performed the experiment and had
dropped balls from the mast of a ship, the issue would not have been
settled. Aristotelians knew of the alleged result and remained not
only impenitent but unperturbed. The margin of experimental error
was too great, they said, for how could the mast remain straight as
the ship rolled or pitched when pushed by the wind.

Galileo was conscious, however, that the results of mathematical
reasoning must be open, at least in principle, to empirical verification. This was less important for his Aristotelian opponents, who
viewed science in a different light. They accepted an instrumentalist interpretation of astronomy, and they considered explanations
in terms of human purposes more real than explanations in terms
of efficient causality which pointed the way to the regulative use of
experiments.

The world, as they saw it, existed for man's enjoyment, instruction, and use; it was subordinate to him and made sense in relation to him. The realm of nature was not only Earth-centered but man-centered. It is largely a result of the Galilean revolution that many have come to view this attitude as a piece of intellectual arrogance.

The World and its purpose

The Middle Ages rediscovered and handed down to their successors a world vision inherited from the Greeks, whose main concern was not to seek out new facts but to provide an all-encompassing justification of world order. They were not interested in detailed explanation and prediction but in seeing how things formed part of a connected, rational, and aesthetically satisfying whole. Under the influence of Judeo–Christian theology, this led to the belief that the entire realm of nature was subordinate to man and to his eternal destiny.

There is a neatness and tidiness about this conception that is not only gratifying to the mind but pleasing to the eye. The imagination was left with an orderly picture of the world where each thing had its proper place. In time, this world-view acquired a deceptive obviousness which went unchallenged for want of a better alternative.

Man could, and did, marvel at the size of the universe, but he never doubted that it had been created for his use and benefit. Astrology was both popular and respectable because it was commonly assumed that human affairs would prosper when undertaken under the right conjunction of stars. Simplicio takes it for granted that the celestial bodies "are ordained to no other use than that of service to the earth." He is boggled by the empty space the Copernicans wish to introduce between Saturn and the stellar sphere:

Now when we see the beautiful order of the planets, arranged around the earth at distances commensurate with their producing upon it their effects for our benefit, why go on to place between the highest orb, namely that of Saturn, and the stellar sphere an enormous, superfluous and vain space without any star whatsoever? To what end? For the use and convenience of whom?[34]

Under these rhetorical questions lies a method of philosophizing, indeed a philosophy of life. From this view, before one gets down to the details of building and testing the Copernican hypothesis, one must know whether it "stands to reason." It is pointless to construct a new intellectual edifice, or even to examine its design, until its possibility has been ascertained.

It would be wrong to say that Galileo shirks the problem of man's privileged status in the cosmos or that it fails to impinge on his intellectual consciousness. Galileo claims that man's unique position does not derive from the fact that he occupies the spatial center of the universe but from his ability to encompass the entire world by grasping its mathematical structure. If we are to think in spatial images, it would be more appropriate to say that man's intellect goes around the universe than to describe him as sitting at the center of things.

Since what qualifies as a scientific explanation for Galileo is no longer an analysis in Aristotelian terms of act and potency, matter and form, but a mathematical theory verifiable in nature, he rejects the very concept of substantial change. In the new perspective, only "a simple transposition of parts" is amenable to mathematical treatment and, consequently, intelligible. The Aristotelians abuse themselves with words.

When Salviati is asked whether the motive force of the planets is inherent or external, he professes ignorance, but it is the ignorance of a Socrates who exposes the sham knowledge of those who claim to know. If his adversaries can tell him what moves the planets and the stars, Salviati will have found the force that moves the Earth. Simplicio replies that everyone knows that this is gravity.

"You are wrong, Simplicio," says Salviati, "you should have said that everyone knows that it is called gravity. But I am not asking you for the name, I am asking you for the essence of the thing, and you do not know a bit more about that essence than you do about the essence of whatever moves the stars around."[35] All the Aristotelians offer are mere names for observed regularities.

Galileo, however, continues to think of natural motion as a tendency, an inclination, a natural instinct. The main objection to the diurnal motion of the Earth is solved by granting the Earth a natural tendency to revolve around the center of its mass once every twenty-four hours. In other words, the answer to the Aristotelians who suppose that the Earth is naturally at rest is to postulate that it moves naturally in a circle.

Galileo never formulated Newton's first law of motion, not because he was unwilling to postulate an infinite universe about which he remained uncommitted, but because he had to make circular inertia a cornerstone of his heliocentric system in order to answer the objections of his opponents. We see this in the way he conceives circular motion as a balance between force and resistance:

Acceleration occurs in a moving body when it is approaching the goal toward which it has an inclination, and retardation occurs because of its reluctance to leave and go away from that point; and since in circular motion the moving body is always receding from its natural terminus and at the same time moving toward it, therefore the reluctance and the inclination are always of equal strength in it. The consequence of this equality is a speed that is neither retarded nor accelerated, that is, uniform motion.[36]

This brings Galileo close to modern physics, but he never formulated the correct principle of inertia because he was thinking in terms of an eternally *ordered* motion. Because circular motion is natural, Galileo does not need a force acting on the planets to keep them orbiting. His great achievement remains his brilliant demonstration that the Aristotelian dichotomy between heavenly and terrestrial motion was not only wrong but stultifying and that the metaphysical barrier that precluded the presence of two *natural* motions in one body was no more than a mental block. Science and rhetoric won the day. Astronomy and physics could now forge ahead.

NOTES

1 Galileo Galilei, *Starry Messenger*, translated by Stillman Drake in his *Telescopes, Tides and Tactics*, Chicago: University of Chicago Press, 1983, p. 19 (*Nuncius Sidereus, Opere di Galileo*, Vol. III, p. 60). On the telescopes that Galileo used, see Stillman Drake, "Galileo's First Telescopic Observations," *Journal for the History of Astronomy*, VII (1976), 158–9, and his commentary in the form of a dialogue in *Starry Messenger*, pp. 19–21.

2 Galileo, *Il Saggiatore*, 1623, *Opere di Galileo*, Vol. VI, p. 259. I quote Drake's translation in his *Galileo at Work*, Chicago: University of Chicago Press, 1978, pp. 139–40.

3 *Starry Messenger*, pp. 21–2 (*Opere di Galileo*, Vol. III, p. 61).

4 Guglielmo Righini, "New Light on Galileo's Lunar Observations," in M. L. Righini-Bonelli and W. R. Shea, eds., *Reason, Experiment and Mysticism in the Scientific Revolution*, New York: Science History Publications, 1975, p. 75.

5 *Starry Messenger*, pp. 36–7 (*Opere di Galileo*, Vol. III, pp. 71–2).

6 *Starry Messenger*, pp. 22–3 (*Opere di Galileo*, Vol. III, p. 62).

7 *Starry Messenger*, pp. 88–9 (*Opere di Galileo*, Vol. III, p. 95).

8 *Opere di Galileo*, Vol. XI, p. 12.

9 *Opere di Galileo*, Vol. X, p. 474.

10 *Opere di Galileo*, Vol. V, p. 237.

11 Galileo, *Dialogue Concerning the Two Chief World Systems* (*Ptolemaic Copernican*) translated by Stillman Drake, Berkeley and Los Angeles: University of California Press, 1962, p. 417 (*Opere di Galileo*, Vol. VII, p. 443). In this and in following quotations, I have sometimes amended the translation.

12 *Dialogue*, pp. 59–62 (*Opere di Galileo*, Vol. VII, pp. 84–6). The reader interested in a general account of Galileo's life and works can turn to Annibale Fantoli, *Galileo: For Copernicanism and for the Church*, second edition, Vatican City: Vatican Observatory Publications, 1996.

13 *Dialogue*, p. 69 (*Opere di Galileo*, Vol. VII, p. 94).

14 *Dialogue*, p. 86 (*Opere di Galileo*, Vol. VII, pp. 111–12).

15 *Dialogue*, p. 99 (*Opere di Galileo*, Vol. VII, p. 124).

16 *Dialogue*, p. 99 (*Opere di Galileo*, Vol. VII, p. 125).

17 *Dialogue*, p. 101 (*Opere di Galileo*, Vol. VII, p. 126).

18 *Dialogue*, p. 11 (*Opere di Galileo*, Vol. VII, p. 35). On science and rhetoric in the Copernican Controversy, see Jean Dietz Moss, *Novelties in the Heavens*, Chicago: Chicago University Press, 1993.

19 *Ibid.*

20 *Dialogue*, p. 35 (*Opere di Galileo*, Vol. VII, p. 60). See Maurice A. Finocchiaro, *Galileo and the Art of Reasoning*, Dordrecht and Boston: Reidel, 1980.

21 *Dialogue*, p. 103 (*Opere di Galileo*, Vol. VII, pp. 128–9).

22 *Dialogue*, p. 104 (*Opere di Galileo*, Vol. VII, p. 129).

23 Galileo, *Letter to Christina of Lorraine*, *Opere di Galileo*, Vol. V, pp. 316–17.

24 Galileo, *The Assayer*, translated by Stillman Drake in *Galileo Galilei et alii, The Controversy of the Comets of 1618*, Philadelphia: University of Pennsylvania Press, 1960, pp. 183–4 (*Il Saggiatore, Opere di Galileo*, Vol. VI, p. 232).

25 *Dialogue*, pp. 169–70 (*Opere di Galileo*, Vol. VII, p. 195).

26 *Dialogue*, p. 117 (*Opere di Galileo*, Vol. VII, p. 143).

27 *Dialogue*, p. 188 (*Opere di Galileo*, Vol. VII, p. 215).

28 *Dialogue*, p. 397 (*Opere di Galileo*, Vol. VII, p. 423).

29 *Dialogue*, p. 406 (*Opere di Galileo*, Vol. VII, p. 432).

30 *Dialogue*, p. 328 (*Opere di Galileo*, Vol. VII, p. 355).

31 *Dialogue*, p. 335 (*Opere di Galileo*, Vol. VII, pp. 362–3).

32 *Dialogue*, p. 339 (*Opere di Galileo*, Vol. VII, p. 367).

33 *Dialogue*, pp. 143, 174 (*Opere di Galileo*, Vol. VII, pp. 169, 200).

34 *Dialogue*, p. 367 (*Opere di Galileo*, Vol. VII, p. 394).

35 *Dialogue*, p. 234 (*Opere di Galileo*, Vol. VII, p. 260).

36 *Dialogue*, pp. 31–2 (*Opere di Galileo*, Vol. VII, p. 56).

7 Galileo's discoveries with the telescope and their evidence for the Copernican theory

Galileo's researches in astronomy were more than original, they were unprecedented. He was not an astronomer in the sense of Copernicus, Tycho, and Kepler, making observations, devising models, and deriving parameters in order to compute tables and ephemerides for finding the positions of the Sun, Moon, and planets. Nor did he search for the physical principles governing the motions of the heavens as Kepler and later Newton did. Most of his work was concerned with two issues, the refutation of the Aristotelian and the defense of the Copernican "System of the World," and his originality lies not so much in what he found as in how he interpreted his discoveries. Even his discoveries with the telescope, as interesting as they are in themselves – and it is hard to think of more surprising discoveries in the entire history of science – are of still greater interest for the conclusions that he drew from them, for nearly all of them could be turned to the criticism of Aristotle and the defense of Copernicus, and in his *Dialogue on the Two Great Systems of the World* that is just what Galileo did. Our concern here, however, is with his initial discoveries and his initial interpretations, which, although not as far-reaching as the conclusions he reached in the *Dialogue*, were upsetting enough to anyone who was not already a friend of Copernicus.

In late 1608 Galileo's friend Paolo Sarpi heard a rumor of an optical device, recently invented in the Netherlands, that made distant objects appear close, and by May of 1609 he must have alerted Galileo. It was not hard to make one of these things using spectacle lenses, a plano-convex lens as an objective and a plano-concave lens as an eyepiece. When placed in a tube, the result is a 'spyglass' giving an upright image of 3× or 4× magnification. Galileo did this much, and since he wanted something better, he learned to grind and polish

244

lenses, and by August made an instrument of 8× or 9×. He called it a *perspicillum*, and he arranged through Sarpi a demonstration for the Venetian Senate, on whom its naval application for spotting distant ships was not lost. Galileo therefore donated sole rights to the manufacture of the instrument to the Republic of Venice – which is curious since he was not the inventor and Venice could hardly prevent manufacture elsewhere – asking in return only an improvement in his position at the university. This he received. His salary was nearly doubled to 1,000 florins, although not until the following year, after which it would be frozen. So Galileo promptly renewed overtures to his former pupil Cosimo de' Medici for a court appointment in Florence, sending him a very fine telescope. He soon had a more splendid gift for Cosimo.

By the beginning of 1610 he had made a telescope of 20×, but even before that he began making observations of the heavens, in which it was not so much the magnification as the light gathering and resolving power of the telescope that allowed him to see what had never been seen before. In about two months, December and January, he made more discoveries that changed the world than anyone has ever made before or since. He began with the irregular surface of the Moon, went on to the uncountable number of the stars, and then in early January found the satellites of Jupiter, which made him resolve to publish quickly, before someone else had the bright idea of turning a telescope on Jupiter. In fact Simon Mayr later claimed to have observed the satellites in December of 1609, but he did not publish until 1614 and his claim to prior discovery is generally discounted. Galileo's latest observation is dated 2 March, and by 13 March the *Sidereus Nuncius*, the "Sidereal Messenger" (or Message) appeared in Venice, dedicated to Cosimo II de' Medici, Fourth Grand Duke of Tuscany, after whom he named the four satellites of Jupiter the "Medicean Stars." This is particularly appropriate, he points out in the dedication, since at the time of Cosimo's birth Jupiter occupied the midheaven, the royal planet in the tenth house of royal authority, and there are yet other pleasing astrological conceits to flatter the young Grand Duke's vanity. Within a few weeks Galileo's discoveries were known throughout Europe, and by June he had resigned his position at Padua to become Chief Mathematician of the University of Pisa, with no teaching responsibilities, and Philosopher and Mathematician to the Grand Duke of Tuscany. He continued his observations, and in the course of the year discovered the peculiar shape of Saturn, the phases of Venus, and irregular moving spots on the Sun, all of which he mentioned, along with the periods of Jupiter's satellites, in the preface to the *Discourse on Bodies in Water* in 1612 and then discussed in greater detail in his *History and Demonstrations Concerning Sunspots*, usually called the *Letters on Sunspots*, in 1613.

Within a year of publishing the *Sidereal Messenger*, Galileo was the most celebrated natural philosopher in Europe. In the spring of 1611 he visited Rome in what appeared to be a triumph. Cardinal Robert Bellarmine (1542–1621), statesman, theologian, member of the Congregation of the Holy Office, and head of the Collegio Romano, asked his mathematicians for their opinion of Galileo's discoveries, and they confirmed every one, with the proviso that Father Clavius believed that the surface of the Moon is not rough, but has denser and rarer parts. Christopher Clavius (1537–1612), with whom Galileo had earlier corresponded, then the most distinguished astronomer in Italy, had taken some time to be convinced of the discoveries and wished more time to interpret them properly, as he wrote in the last, posthumous, edition of his *Commentary on the Sphere of Sacrobosco*. Galileo met with Clavius and Bellarmine, and was feted by the Collegio with a dinner and speech in honor of his discoveries. He was also elected the sixth member of Federigo Cesi's (1585–1630) Accademia dei Lincei (lynxes), which published his *Letters on Sunspots* in 1613 and ten years later *The Assayer*. Galileo was very proud of this honor, and from this time he regularly signed his name Galileo Galilei Linceo.

Galileo's discoveries changed the world, but first they changed Galileo. Before, he was favorable to Copernicus and critical of Aristotle, but had published nothing on these subjects, at least under his own name. After, he became the strongest proponent of Copernican theory in Italy and the most hostile critic of Aristotelian physics anywhere, and for the latter distinction there was no lack of competition. And the transformation was immediate. In the *Sidereal Messenger* he states unequivocally that the planets move around the Sun and that in his *System of the World* he will show that the Earth is a planet. In the *Letters on Sunspots*, following the discovery of the phases of Venus, the heliocentric theory is treated as a fact, especially in the third letter. While it is true that Galileo's discoveries with the telescope do not *by themselves prove* the heliocentric theory – and he never quite claimed that they do, although he certainly believed they came very close – they did provide a great deal of evidence in its favor and remove a number of objections. Just as important as their evidence for Copernican theory was the evidence his discoveries provided against the Aristotelian theory of the heavens as perfect and unchanging – because they have only circular motions – and utterly unlike the Earth. And although the evidence for Copernicus now has the greater fame, it appears that to Galileo's contemporaries the evidence against Aristotle had the more disturbing effect. Here the *Sidereal Messenger* is not explicitly anti-Aristotelian, although Galileo had no doubts about the implications of his demonstrations of the similarities between the Earth and the Moon, while the devastatingly polemical *Letters on Sunspots* are in part a pointed attack on the Aristotelian perfection of the heavens. Truly, Galileo's discoveries changed the world, and it is not surprising that each one was received with everything from the greatest acclaim to the greatest hostility. On the one side was Kepler, who responded by May of 1610 with his enthusiastic and fanciful *Conversation with the Sidereal Messenger*, and Galileo's students and friends, who were soon to be known as *Galileisti*. On the other, the philosophers and, yes, the astronomers, including at first the learned and refined Jesuits of the Collegio Romano, who either refused to believe the observations or sought ways of explaining away their troubling consequences.

We have touched upon Galileo's discoveries and their implications in general. Now let us consider them specifically, noting that Galileo did not discuss their full implications until the *Dialogue* of 1632.

THE MOON

Galileo first turned his telescope on the Moon. He found that it had a rough surface with mountains and plains, which was especially evident by examining the terminator between the illuminated and dark portions. For bright points of light were seen in the dark that gradually extended toward the terminator, just as the light of the rising Sun first strikes the tops of mountains and then gradually extends down to the surrounding plain. He drew and had engraved five illustrations of crescent and quarter phases, two of which are shown in Figure 7.1 – seven of his hand drawings also survive – of remarkable

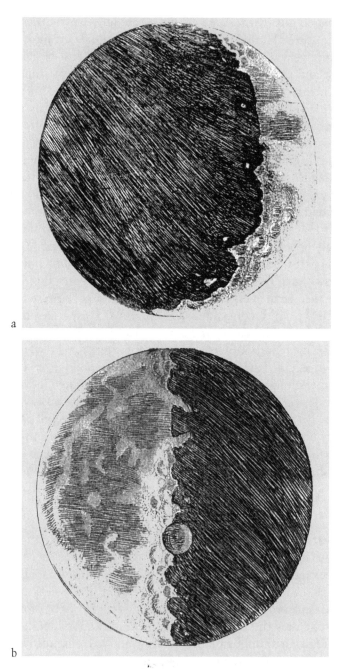

a

b

Figure 7.1.

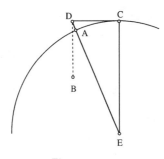

Figure 7.2.

realism if not altogether accurate, showing the points of light in the dark part, clear distinctions between the lunar seas and highlands, as they are now known, and a number of circular features that we know to be craters. The one of exaggerated size in Figure 7.1b is Albategnius, and others are also identifiable: the large dark region to the left is Oceanus Procellarum, and the roughly circular feature in the upper part Mare Imbrium with part of the illuminated rim of Mare Serenitatis extending into the dark half. Of course these large features are also visible without a telescope, but not in such detail. Estimating the distance of a lighted point from the terminator as 1/20 the diameter of the Moon, he determined that the height of a mountain exceeded four miles. Thus, in Figure 7.2, with the Moon at quadrature, suppose a point of light at B in the dark part projected to the limb at D. Let the radius of the moon $CE = 1,000$ miles and the distance $DC = (1/10)CE = 100$ miles. Then $DE = (CE^2 + CD^2)^{1/2} \approx 1,005$ miles, and the height of the mountain $DA = 5$ miles, although Galileo gives $DA > 4$ miles. To explain why such mountains do not give the Moon an irregular edge, like a toothed wheel, he suggests that the ranges of mountains overlap to form a smooth curve, and further, that the Moon, like the Earth, is surrounded by a vaporous orb.

Galileo also used the opportunity to discuss a problem he had solved several years earlier, the secondary light of the Moon. When the Moon is in its crescent phase, the dark part of its body is also faintly lighted, sufficiently to detect the large spots with a good telescope, an effect that disappears around quadrature. The nonuniformities of shading in the dark part of Figure 7.1a may be intended to show the effect of the secondary light. After refuting a number

of incorrect causes, as the intrinsic light of the Moon, or light imparted by Venus or the stars, or sunlight passing through the body
of the Moon, he explains the secondary light as reflected light from
the Earth. Just as the Moon when nearly full illuminates the Earth
at night, so the nearly full Earth illuminates the Moon. He adds that
he will explain this in more detail in his *System of the World*, where
he will show with many reasons and experiments that there is a very
strong reflection of sunlight by the Earth; and against those who exclude the Earth from the choric dance (*corea*) of the stars because
it is without motion and light, he will confirm by demonstrations
and countless reasons drawn from nature that the Earth is a planet
(*vagam*, wandering) and surpasses the Moon in light. This is the
most direct statement concerning the motion of the Earth in the
Sidereal Messenger, and it is significant that it is in connection with
the secondary light of the Moon, which Galileo thus takes as very
important evidence that the Earth may be regarded as a heavenly
body.

What is to be inferred from all this is that the Earth is like the
Moon, a body shining by reflected light from the Sun, and the Moon
is like the Earth, a solid body with a rough surface made, not of
some fifth element of the heavens, but of the same solid stuff as the
Earth. This in itself was not new. There had been speculation since
antiquity that the Moon was like the Earth and also inhabited. In
the *Considerations of Alimberto Mauri*, a controversial work on the
new star of 1604 published pseudonymously in 1606, Galileo had
noted the irregularity of the terminator at quadrature as evidence
that the Moon has large mountains and flat planes. Kepler believed
the curious circular features were built by the inhabitants to shelter
themselves from the scorching Sun – they lived in caves along the
rims – and some years before the telescope Michael Maestlin thought
he saw rain clouds on the Moon. But these were just fancies. Galileo
would have none of them, but he knew that the Aristotelian theory
of the heavens was finished, or at least in serious trouble, and that if
the solid and earthlike Moon could move about the Earth, the bright
and moonlike Earth could move about the Sun. None of Galileo's
discoveries provoked more hostility and more preposterous attempts
at refutation than the rough surface of the Moon and the explanation
of the secondary light, and with good reason because for none were

the stakes as high. The controversy even extended to the depiction of the Moon in the iconography of the Immaculate Conception, drawn from Revelation 12.1-2, showing a pregnant woman with a crown of twelve stars standing on a crescent Moon with its horns downward that may be either smooth, immaculate, even translucent, according to traditional opinion, or rough, maculate, and opaque, according to Galileo's description.

THE STARS

In observing stars Galileo found that their enlargement was much less than that of the Moon and planets, which appear as globes, like little moons. The telescope, he concluded, removes the stars' extraneous rays and shows them to be much smaller than previously thought, although so much brighter that a star of the fifth or sixth magnitude appears equal to Sirius. The removal of the stars' "irradiation," as he later called it, which he found to apply also to planets, was one of Galileo's most important discoveries, to which he returned in his later works, refining its explanation and extending its implications. Still more strikingly, countless fainter stars were seen, amounting to more than six additional magnitudes of brightness. Within a space of one or two degrees in Orion, he found more than five hundred new stars, and to illustrate this he showed eighty new stars around the nine original stars in the belt and sword and thirty-six within half a degree of the six Pleiades. The head of Orion and Praesepe in Cancer, listed in Ptolemy's star catalogue as "nebulous," were found to consist of many small stars very close together, and the most spectacular of all, the Milky Way, whose nature had provoked endless discussion, turned out to consist of vast numbers of stars beyond all counting grouped into clusters.

The small apparent size, large range of brightness, and immense number of the stars were Galileo's most ambiguous, and potentially most important, discoveries. Were stars now to be very small objects at a single small distance, say, just beyond Saturn, or objects of indeterminate size distributed over many large but indeterminate distances? The latter interpretation makes the diurnal rotation of the celestial sphere implausible to the point of impossibility, and removes the one purely astronomical objection to the motion of the

Earth about the Sun: the absence of any detectable effect on the positions of stars. However, after the speculations about an infinite universe filled with innumerable inhabited worlds by the unfortunate Giordano Bruno, the subject was, let us say, rather sensitive, and Galileo approached it cautiously even in the *Dialogue*. Nevertheless, there can be no doubt that Galileo's observation of the stars was the first step toward the universe of vast numbers of stars and systems of stars at vast distances of modern cosmology.

THE SATELLITES OF JUPITER

On 7 January 1610 Galileo observed Jupiter and found two small bright stars to the east of the planet and one to the west in a straight line parallel to the ecliptic. On the 8th all three stars were equally spaced in a line to the west. He wondered if perhaps Jupiter could be moving to the east, although by computation, from tables or an ephemeris, it was moving retrograde to the west. The 9th was cloudy, but on the 10th two stars were to the east and the third, he guessed, was hidden behind Jupiter. At this point he realized, with astonishment, that the motion must belong, not to Jupiter, but to the stars. By the next night, 11 January, he says that he reached his conclusion: the three stars were moving about Jupiter just as Venus and Mercury move about the Sun (although Stillman Drake has presented evidence that this conclusion was not reached until the 15th). On 13 January he observed a fourth star and noted that none of them twinkle like stars. That all four were moving around Jupiter was confirmed by nightly observations, continuing until 2 March, with measurements of their distances from Jupiter and each other in apparent diameters of Jupiter, taken as one arc minute, along with estimates of their size or brightness, and from 26 February their passing of a nearby star (see Figure 6.3 in previous chapter). Since Galileo wished to demonstrate beyond doubt that these four stars were indeed moving around Jupiter, he published sixty-five illustrations of the configuration at each observation showing stars aligned about an open circle to indicate their distances, with the sizes of the stars distinguishing their apparent size, and in the last five showing the nearby fixed star. Their variation in size or brightness he assumed was due to Jupiter's being surrounded by a vaporous orb, like the

Earth and Moon, which dimmed the light of the stars when they were seen through it.

The satellites of Jupiter were a total surprise, first to Galileo, then to everyone else (except Kepler who immediately concluded that they must exist for the inhabitants of Jupiter as our Moon exists for us). Because the reliability of the telescope itself was suspect, and the satellites could only be seen with a fairly good telescope, there was some skepticism about whether they were really there even after the evidence of Galileo's observational reports and sixty-five diagrams. Galileo says he did an excellent job of convincing the entire University of Padua of their existence at public lectures – although the noted Aristotelian Cesare Cremonini refused even to look through a telescope – but when he tried to show them to Giovanni Antonio Magini in Bologna, he did not do as well, for Magini failed to see them even with Galileo's telescope. By the end of 1610, however, there had been a number of independent confirmations, including those of Magini and the astronomers of the Collegio Romano, and the existence of the satellites was well established. The term "satellites" (from *satelles*, an attendant upon an important person), incidentally, was introduced by Kepler in 1611; Galileo called them "planets," "stars," and "little stars" (*stellulae*). The significance of the satellites, aside from their own interest as the very first additions to the planetary system since the most remote antiquity, was that they showed that a planet could move and have satellites, since Jupiter was obviously moving, answering a perfectly reasonable objection to Copernican theory that it seemed odd that the Earth could have the Moon moving around it while it moved about the Sun.

After the publication of the *Sidereal Messenger*, Galileo continued to observe the satellites and set about determining their synodic periods. He did so in an "Atlantic labor," as he called it, that remains his most important contribution to mathematical astronomy. Kepler thought the task to be nearly impossible because of the difficulty of distinguishing the three inner satellites. In fact the order of brightness is III, I, II, IV, but all are variable, especially when close to the planet, and the whole problem nontrivial. The most obvious way of distinguishing the satellites is by their characteristic greatest elongations from the planet, identifying first the outermost IV, then III, then II, and last the innermost I. But the moment of greatest elongation is not well defined since the satellite is sensibly unmoving for some time, so these are useless for finding the periods, without which it is impossible to keep track of any one of them and continue to distinguish it from the others. A precarious way of estimating the periods without necessarily distinguishing the inner satellites is to look for identical or nearly identical configurations. Galileo found something like this on 3 and 10 December of 1610, seven days less one hour apart, in which IV had moved nearly from one greatest elongation to the other, completing about half a revolution, and the inner satellites occupied the same positions, presumably completing integral numbers of revolutions. Hence, one might guess that the period of IV was two weeks – in the *Sidereal Messenger* it was "semimonthly" – III one week, II one-half week, and I one-quarter week, which is nearly correct for all but IV. On 11 December Galileo wrote to Giuliano de' Medici, the Tuscan ambassador in Prague, that he had found a way of determining the periods of the Medicean planets, and that he should give his regards to Signor Kepler!

However, this was only a rough indication, by itself not very helpful without identifying the inner satellites. Galileo next turned to observations in which a satellite was hidden by conjunction with Jupiter, either at apogee above or perigee below the planet – now called occultation and transit – which could be distinguished by the direction of the satellite's motion, west to east with respect to Jupiter near apogee, east to west near perigee, as a means of establishing an epoch, a location at a known time. This too was precarious for a number of reasons, the first being that the brightness of Jupiter could well conceal a satellite separated from the planet by more than one diameter, a problem made all the worse by spherical and chromatic aberration in Galileo's telescope, enlarging Jupiter's image with a colored halo. His observational records show that on 29 December satellite I was at perigee, on 24 January 1611 III at apogee, on 13 February II at perigee, and on 7 March IV at perigee. Then on 15 March, after two observations showing three satellites very close to the planet, no satellite could be seen from three hours after sunset until the setting of Jupiter four hours later. He took this "great conjunction," as he called it, as his fundamental epoch and, estimating times that II, III, and IV were at apogee and I at perigee, used earlier observations to derive provisional periods and mean motions. On 23

March he left Florence for Rome, continuing his observations each night, and after he arrived in Rome on 29 March for his great visit began the "Atlantic labor" of correcting the periods by calculating backwards to compare with earlier observations. In the preface of the *Discourse on Bodies in Water* (1612), he gives periods for the satellites that he says he worked out in Rome in April of 1611. It is, however, certain that these were not reached so early, for there were still problems in the method of determining periods. Also, it would not be characteristic of Galileo to wait a full year to publish, or at least report in correspondence, periods in which he had confidence, since he was not the only one trying to find them and he wished to be the first.

When he returned to Florence in June, he made two extended series of calculations to examine and refine the periods, probably worked out in Rome, forward from 15 March to 15 June and backwards from 10 March to the preceding 15 November, each containing drawings of the configurations to compare with the observations. The satellites were located in the drawings by means of a graphical analogue computer, called a *giovilabi* on the analogy of *astrolabi*, by which motion in a circle around the planet in degrees from apogee could be converted to an elongation in radii of Jupiter by means of a perpendicular to the diameter of the circle. But the results were inconsistent, particularly when the satellites were close to the planet, and for this there were two sources of error. The first is that *he forgot to take into account that the Earth was moving around the Sun*, which changes the direction of the apogee and perigee of Jupiter's satellite system by as much as $\pm 11\frac{1}{2}°$, the angle subtended by the radius of the Earth's orbit at Jupiter. Of course this does not mean that Galileo had any reservations about the Earth's motion, and the same effect would occur if the Earth were fixed and Jupiter moving on an epicycle, it is just that the problem of the satellites was so new and complex that he only gradually comprehended all that had to be done to solve it correctly. But in the worst case, in which two observations or calculations were made at the maximum positive and negative parallactic corrections, the difference in direction could amount to $23°$, producing errors in the epochs and any subsequently calculated positions. Thus in Figure 7.3 in which the Sun is at S and Jupiter at P, when the Earth is at O_1 or O_2 the apogee and perigee will be A_1 and B_1 or

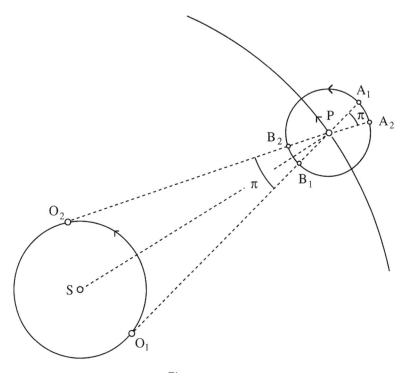

Figure 7.3.

A_2 and B_2 respectively, differing by $\pi \approx 23°$, which can produce a difference of three hours in the time of apogee or perigee for I and of more than one day for IV. By late 1611 or early 1612 Galileo had introduced a correction into his calculations, angle SPO, under the name *prosthaphaeresis* (addition–subtraction), the term for the same correction in computing a planet's position, used by Ptolemy for the correction due to the motion of the planet on its epicycle and by Copernicus for the parallactic correction due to the motion of the Earth. He later carried out a series of calculations for 17 March to 16 July of 1612 using this correction, but the periods in the *Discourse on Bodies in Water* were already found with it not long before the manuscript was delivered to the printer in late March, for tables of mean motions implying periods from which these were rounded were either derived or confirmed by Galileo in notes using the correction. The published periods, the periods implied by the tables in Galileo's notes, and the modern values from Sampson's tables (1910) are as follows:

	Published		Notes		Modern	
I	1^d	$18\frac{1}{2}^h$	1^d	$18;28,26^h$	1^d	$18;28,36^h$
II	3	$13\frac{1}{3}$	3	$13;20,51$	3	$13;17,54$
III	7	4	7	$3;55,14$	7	$3;59,36$
IV	16	18	16	$17;56,14$	16	$18; 5, 7$

Hence by March of 1612 Galileo had reached periods accurate to a few minutes. However, a second problem remained, which he had earlier noted, that at times a satellite remained invisible at apogee for an excessively long time. A note on the calculation for 18 March shows that he had found the solution: "It is clearly certain that IV was in the shadow of Jupiter, for it had not yet appeared at the sixth hour." He had discovered that a satellite could be invisible some-what before or after it was behind the planet because it was eclipsed. In Figure 7.4 the satellite is in occultation from *Oc.D* to *Oc.R* and in eclipse from *Ec.D* to *Ec.R*, the excess time of invisibility being from *Oc.R* to *Ec.R*, and in the same way the eclipse may also occur before

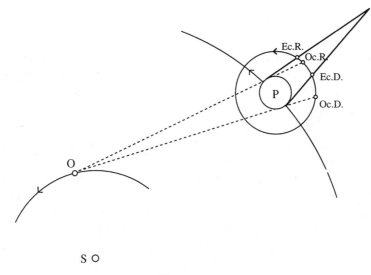

Figure 7.4.

occultation. This was the last piece of the puzzle to be discovered by Galileo – recognition of the latitudes and inequalities of the satellites, transits of the satellites' shadows across the disc of Jupiter, and the equation of light came only in the second half of the century – and he again set to work refining his periods and epochs. He now had another device to aid his observations: a micrometer of sorts consisting of a grid ruled in radii of Jupiter attached to the side of his telescope. When an observation was made with one eye looking through the telescope and the other eye looking at the grid, the image of Jupiter and the satellites was superimposed on the grid and elongations could be found very precisely by simply counting lines of the grid. This device also allowed him to improve his measurements of the greatest elongations of the satellites and of the apparent diameter of Jupiter s by taking the diameter of the image i on the grid divided by the focal length f and magnification m of the telescope, $s = \sin^{-1}(i/fm)$. In this way an estimate of 0;0,50° for the diameter of Jupiter as a fraction of the elongation of IV was reduced using observations in January and June to 0;0,41,37° and 0;0,39,24°. The modern mean value is about 0;0,38°; Galileo's slightly larger results are due to the enlargement of Jupiter's image by spherical and chromatic aberration. On the night of 27–28 December of 1612 and on 28 January 1613 he made measurements of the distance of Jupiter from a star that it passed twice in direct and retrograde motion. These have turned out to be the first sightings of Neptune. Still more remarkably, on 28 January he noted the location, in a straight line with Jupiter and a fixed star, of the same star, "which was also observed the preceding night, but they (the stars) appeared more distant from each other" (*sed videbantur remotiores inter se*)!

By early 1613 Galileo had worked out the theory of the satellites to his own satisfaction, and as a demonstration he prepared diagrams showing their elongations from Jupiter from 1 March to 8 May, the first of which is shown in Figure 7.5, published as an appendix to the third of the *Letters on Sunspots*, which appeared by late March. In a postscript he discussed the difficulties of observing the satellites when close to Jupiter because of its "irradiation," and he explained and gave the dates of four eclipses, remarking that whether eclipses occur and their durations depend upon the annual motion of the Earth, the latitude of Jupiter, and the distance of the satellite from Jupiter. Evidently he now took the distinction of eclipses

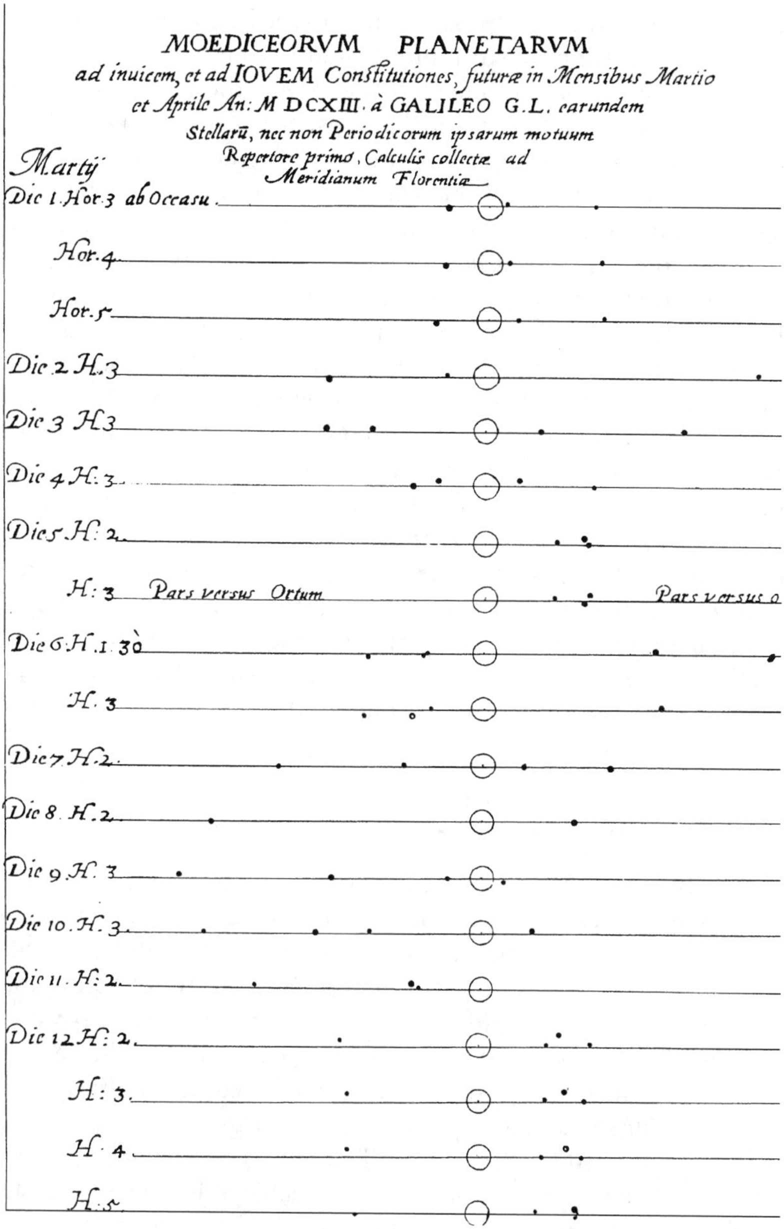
MOEDICEORVM PLANETARVM
ad inuicem, et ad IOVEM Constitutiones, futuræ in Mensibus Martio
et Aprile An: M DCXIII. à GALILEO G.L. earundem
Stellarū, nec non Periodicorum ipsarum motuum
Repertore primo, Calculis collectæ ad
Meridianum Florentiæ
Martij
Die 1. Hor. 3 ab Occasu
Hor. 4
Hor. 5
Die 2 H. 3
Die 3 H. 3
Die 4 H: 3
Die 5 H: 2
H: 3
Pars versus Ortum
Pars versus O
Die 6 H. 1 30
H. 3
Die 7 H. 2
Die 8 H. 2
Die 9 H. 3
Die 10 H. 3
Die 11 H: 2
Die 12 H: 2
H: 3
H. 4
H. 5

Figure 7.5.

and occultations as evidence of the Earth's annual motion – as well he should – for, although possible, it is exceedingly cumbersome to attribute the distinction to Jupiter's motion on its epicycle in the Ptolemaic theory or the Sun's motion about the Earth in the Tychonic. There was also a practical purpose to Galileo's Atlantic labor on the theory of the satellites, namely, the determination of longitude, a proposal for which he sent to the government of Spain in September of 1612. The principle is that if identical phenomena of Jupiter's satellites, as occultations or eclipses, are observed from different locations, the difference in local time will correspond to the difference in geographical longitude. Thus tables and diagrams of the phenomena computed for the meridian of, say, Florence, would allow the difference in longitude from Florence to be determined from wherever the phenomena were observed. Negotiations with Spain and work on this project were to occupy Galileo for years – about 2,000 observations and calculations survive among his papers from 1613 to 1619 – and in 1636 he made the same proposal to the Netherlands. Again nothing came of it, but the idea was to occupy the attention of astronomers into the eighteenth century and was responsible for much of the study given to the great system of Jupiter and the four Galilean satellites, to this day, it should be noted, along with the Moon the most interesting satellites in the planetary system.

SATURN

On 25 July 1610 Galileo observed Saturn and found that it looked like a large star with two smaller stars on each side that nearly touched it and never moved. He announced his discovery to Kepler in an anagram, which Kepler assumed to refer to two satellites of Mars (since the Earth had one and Jupiter four). The first published report was in the preface to the *Bodies in Water* in 1612, but by late in the year the smaller stars had disappeared; Galileo predicted in the third of the *Letters on Sunspots* that they would reappear in 1613, and they did. In 1616 he noticed that their form had changed to what later came to be called "handles" (*ansae*). He now realized that whatever they were, they were not spherical, and he predicted another disappearance for 1626, which also happened. He suspected their changing appearance had something to do with the alignment of Saturn and the Earth – in this sense he regarded the changes as evidence for the Copernican theory – and possibly with a slow rotational period of Saturn and its two companions, but it was not until 1659 that Huygens gave the correct explanation, that Saturn was surrounded by a thin, flat ring, not touching the planet and inclined to the plane of the ecliptic.

VENUS

There was another discovery in 1610 that Galileo could explain completely: the appearance of Venus. If Venus were below the Sun, as in Ptolemy's theory, when observed from the Earth it would always appear as a crescent of greater or lesser size and width. If it were above, which is now seldom mentioned but was still a possibility, it would always appear as a disc. But if it moved around the Sun, as in the Copernican or Tychonic theories, it would change from a small round disc near superior conjunction to a large crescent near inferior. That is exactly what Galileo found between October and December, when he received a letter on the phases of Venus from his former student Benedetto Castelli (1578–1643), to whom he reported his observations. It has been suggested that Galileo did not understand the significance of the phases of Venus until he received the letter from Castelli, but that is to misunderstand the period required to see the succession of phases and eliminate two of the three possible arrangements. The significance was now apparent and conclusive, for it meant that Venus, and presumably Mercury, must move about the Sun. Even before he reached his final conclusion, on 11 December he sent Kepler an anagram, explained on 1 January as "The mother of loves emulates the figures of Cynthia" (the moon). Kepler later wrote Galileo that this came as a surprise to him for, as Venus is so bright, he had believed it to be self-luminous. To Father Clavius on 30 December Galileo wrote that Venus and all the planets shine only by the light of the Sun and that the Sun is "without any doubt the center of the great revolutions of all the planets." The phases of Venus were also first mentioned in the preface to the *Bodies in Water*, and in the third *Letter on Sunspots* he reported the apparent diameter to vary from less than 1/200 the diameter of the Sun at greatest distance to more than six times as great at least distance, that is, from less than $0;0,10°$ to more than $0;1°$, both quite accurate and far smaller than the traditional value of $1/10$ the diameter of the Sun or $0;3°$. He probably measured them using the grid micrometer just as he did for Jupiter.

SUNSPOTS

Galileo was not the first to see sunspots with a telescope, nor was he the first to conclude that they were on the Sun and showed that the Sun rotated. Johann Fabricius had published a book on this in 1611. Galileo began observing them in 1610, showed them in Rome the following year, and made a careful study of their motions and changing appearance, later with help from Castelli, but kept his own counsel on a subject of such complexity. He mentioned them briefly in the preface to *Bodies in Water* as a strong argument either that the Sun revolves, or that there are other planets moving about the Sun with elongations smaller than that of Mercury, which only become visible when seen against the Sun, or both. In a paragraph added to the second printing, he reported that continued observation had convinced him that the spots are contiguous to the Sun's body and carried about by its rotation in about a lunar month, "a great event, and even greater for its consequences."

What provoked him into serious publication was a pamphlet called *Three Letters on Sunspots* by one "Apelles hiding behind the painting" published by Marcus Welser in Augsburg early in 1612. The letters were sent to Welser in November and December 1611 by the Jesuit Father Christopher Scheiner (1573–1650), professor in Ingolstadt, who wrote under a pseudonym on instructions from his order lest he be wrong and prove a source of embarrassment; hence he used the name "Apelles hiding behind the painting" (the story is in Pliny 35.85), showing that he was willing to take correction. Scheiner thought it impossible that the Sun have on it spots darker than the dark parts of the Moon, and that the spots do not return regularly to the same positions shows that they are not carried around by a rotation of the solar body. Rather, he believed that the spots were many small planets moving about the Sun like Mercury and Venus, although much closer, the possibility that Galileo considered and rejected. One of his arguments for this was that the spots are broad near the center of the Sun but grow thin as they approach the limb where, similar to the crescent phase of Venus, part of the body of the small planet is lighted and not visible against the Sun. Thus, he was aware of the phases of Venus, but he also believed he had independent, and superior, evidence that Venus moved around the Sun. Magini's *Ephemerides* predicted that on 11 December 1611 Venus would reach superior conjunction with a latitude less than the semidiameter of the Sun; hence if Venus moved on an epicycle below the Sun a transit lasting no less than 40 hours should be visible, and this should be easily observable since Venus would be moving in the direction opposite to sunspots and Scheiner assumed the traditional apparent diameter of 0;3°. Venus was not seen beneath the Sun. As he delicately put it: "She blushed, rushed forward, but we did not gaze upon her nuptials. What follows from this I do not say – it is clear in itself – even if we were deprived of all other arguments, from this one it would be proved that the sun is encircled by Venus."

Galileo received Apelles's letters from Welser in late March with a request for his opinion, which Welser seems to have supposed would be favorable. Little did he know. Galileo answered in two letters in May and October and, following a reply to the first letter by Apelles, called *A More Accurate Inquiry Concerning Sunspots and the Wandering Stars about Jupiter*, a third in December. The *History and Demonstrations Concerning Sunspots*, published by the Accademia dei Lincei in March of 1613, is a masterpiece, of science and of invective. What aroused Galileo's ire was not so much Scheiner's incorrect explanation of sunspots, which was bad enough, as his smug insinuation that the absence of the transit was by itself the best evidence that Venus moved around the Sun. It is for this reason that he devotes so much attention to the phases of Venus, with a patronizing explanation as though Scheiner had never so much as heard of them, and to refuting the gross exaggeration of Venus's apparent diameter and with it the use of the absence of a transit as evidence. Venus could still, he points out, be entirely above the Sun or self-luminous, both of which possibilities are only refuted by its phases.

Sunspots, he says, cannot be dark bodies like planets or, as Scheiner believed, darker than the dark parts of the Moon, because they are not even dark, are in fact at least as bright as the brightest parts of the Moon and only look dark in contrast to the Sun. Galileo argued that, whatever they were, perhaps something like clouds, sunspots

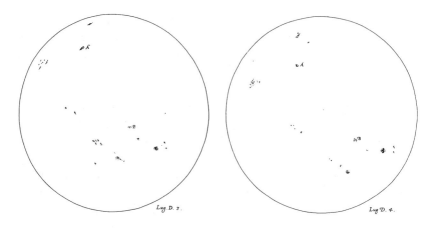

Figure 7.6.

were on the surface of the Sun, as shown by their changing speed and separation as they move across the solar body and their fore-shortening near the edge, all characteristic of motion on a sphere, as he then demonstrates. He noted that they all appeared within about 30° of the Sun's equator, moved with the same angular speed much too slowly for planets – he estimated the period of the Sun's rotation as about a month – and had irregular shapes that changed, appeared, and disappeared with considerable irregularity, and they could be of enormous size, much too large for planets. These were illustrated by thirty-eight plates in the second letter from drawings made in June through August 1612, using a method invented by Castelli of projecting the image of the Sun on to a piece of paper in a darkened room. Those for 3–4 July are shown in Figure 7.6, in which the motion, foreshortening, and change in appearance of the spots are evident. The implications of these discoveries for the Aristotelian perfection and immutability of the heavens need hardly be mentioned, but Galileo does so with scathing invective against philosophers who never raise their eyes from the pages of Aristotle. The letters are not confined to sunspots, for they consider his other discoveries with the telescope, including the predicted positions of Jupiter's satellites, are solidly Copernican, and contain discussions of scientific method that have become deservedly well known. They are scientifically unanswerable, brilliantly, and caustically, witty, and made Apelles look foolish. Galileo won hands down, which may have been a miscalculation because it made an implacable enemy for life of Scheiner, who was really quite a competent scientist, later writing the definitive work of the century on sunspots, the gigantic *Rosa Ursina* (1630), in which he decided that the spots were on the surface of the Sun after all.

CONCLUSION

Even more so than 1604 when he discovered the law of the acceleration of falling bodies, 1610 was Galileo's *annus mirabilis*, and his discoveries with the telescope were to affect, perhaps even determine, most of his subsequent work. Although this point is certainly debatable, I believe that Galileo was an absolutely convinced Copernican years before he made use of a telescope. His reasons were: first, the sense of the heliocentric theory itself, how it determines the order and distances of the planets in a unified system and explains the behavior of geocentric planetary theory, but not *vice versa*, which has something close to an inevitability about it, at least for those who truly understood it, who were few; second, Galileo's explanation of the tides through the variable velocities of the seas caused by the Earth's annual and diurnal motions – never mind that it is incorrect by Newtonian mechanics and perhaps even by Galilean mechanics – which he reported to Paolo Sarpi by 1595, two years before he wrote to Kepler that he had arrived at the Copernican opinion "many years ago"; and, third, the explanation of the secondary light of the Moon, showing that the Earth and Moon are similar bodies – and the Moon most certainly does move – supported by the speculation that the Earth and Moon have similar rough surfaces, both conclusions reached by 1605. It is in connection with the explanation of the secondary light in the *Sidereal Messenger* that Galileo promised his *System of the World*, which he described in May of 1610 as "two books on the system and constitution of the universe, an immense conception full of philosophy, astronomy, and geometry". This "immense conception" had surely been in the works for some time, certainly in Galileo's head and possibly also on paper; it was surely Copernican, and Galileo surely believed that the telescope had given him what he needed to bring it to completion, that is, to prove the Copernican theory, which, as evident from his correspondence prior to 1616, he believed he could do.

But it was not to be, at least not for another twenty years and not as Galileo had originally planned. The work was stopped dead by the prohibition against writing on Copernicus in 1616, lifted only conditionally in 1624. However, even before the prohibition something restrained Galileo's hand, which could have been no more than his work on sunspots and the satellites of Jupiter, to both of which he devoted a great amount of time, but it also could have been that he was still not ready to set out his full evidence and argument. It is difficult to know how much of the *Dialogue* of 1632 actually goes back to work, whether in his head or on paper, done by Galileo twenty years earlier in the way that much of the *Two New Sciences* of 1638 goes back to work done thirty years earlier. Most of Galileo's evidence, although not necessarily most of his argument, was in place by 1613, when he learned of the seasonal change in the motion of sunspots, but it appears that the argument from sunspots, which Galileo considered, along with the tidal theory, his best proof of the motions of the Earth, was not formulated until 1629, and it is possible, although in no way certain, that many of the arguments of the Second Day in refutation of Aristotelian criticisms of the diurnal rotation of the Earth were also formulated years after Galileo had reached the conclusions in mechanics that underlay them.

Nevertheless, it is the discoveries with the telescope and their interpretation that made the *Dialogue* possible, and whatever Galileo had previously written or thought about the *System of the World* must have been radically transformed by what he found in 1610–1613. Except for the sense of the Copernican theory itself and the theory of the tides, a physical theory that Galileo believed to prove the two motions of the Earth, all of the *positive* arguments for the heliocentric theory and all but one of the refutations of astronomical, not physical, arguments against it depend directly or indirectly upon what was shown by the telescope. (The exception is the refutation of Scipione Chiaramonti's large parallaxes of the new stars by a prescient application of probability, the first theory of errors.) Among these arguments are obviously the phases of Venus, showing that it must move around the Sun, extended by induction to all the planets since, aside from the superior planets reaching opposition, their motions do not differ from that of Venus; the removal of the "irradiation" of Venus and Mars, showing that their apparent sizes varied in proportion to their change of distance, which Kepler correctly pointed out was no argument since the change of distance is the same in the geocentric system, although Galileo seemed to think differently; the variation in the motion of sunspots, reasonably explained by the annual motion of the Earth and the rotation of the Sun, which is also evidence by analogy for the rotation of the Earth, and not reasonably explained in any other way; the similarity of the surfaces of the Earth and Moon, showing that if one can move, so can the other; the satellites of Jupiter, dark bodies that suffer eclipse just as our moon, showing that a planet can move and carry with it satellites; and the removal of the "irradiation" of stars, showing that they are much smaller than had been supposed and so can be sufficiently distant for parallactic effects to be negligible without their bodies being any larger than the Sun.

This is not a small list, and although philosophers may quibble over whether each point *proves* anything or not, as philosophers did and apparently still do, Galileo himself believed that together, by a preponderance of evidence, their force was overwhelming, and so apparently did anyone who read the *Dialogue* with an open mind, that is, without Aristotelian or theological prejudice that precluded appeal to empirical evidence and logical argument. If one wonders why the Copernican theory, with almost no adherents at the beginning of the seventeenth century, had pretty much swept the field by the middle, the answer, with no disrespect to Kepler, is above all the *Dialogue* – whether people actually read it themselves or not, it changed everything – and the *Dialogue* itself was grounded in a few months of telescopic observations that first established Galileo as the most celebrated scientist of his age and, with good reason, have kept him there ever since.

NOTE ON SOURCES AND FURTHER READING

Virtually all of Galileo's works, many writings of contemporaries concerned with Galileo, correspondence, and documents are published in *Le Opere di Galileo Galilei*, Edizione Nazionale, edited by Antonio Favaro, 20 vols., G. Barbèra, Florence, 1890–1909; reprinted with additions in 1929–39 and 1964–66. The earlier *Le Opere di Galileo Galilei, prima edizione completa*, edited by Eugenio Albèri et al., 15 vols., Società Editrice Fiorentina, Florence, 1842–56, is still valuable and contains some materials not included in the Edizione Nazionale.

The *Sidereal Messenger* (1610) has been translated by Edward S. Carlos, London, 1880; nearly completely by Stillman Drake in *Discoveries and Opinions of Galileo*, Doubleday, Garden City, NY, 1957; completely by Drake in *Telescopes, Tides and Tactics. A Galilean Dialogue about the Starry Messenger and Systems of the World*, University of Chicago Press, Chicago, 1983; and by Albert Van Helden in *Sidereus Nuncius or The Sidereal Messenger*, University of Chicago Press, Chicago, 1989. The two last are recommended. The *Discourse on Bodies in Water* is translated by Drake in *Cause, Experiment and Science*, University of Chicago Press, Chicago, 1981. Excerpts from the *History and Demonstrations Concerning Sunspots* (1613) can be found in Drake's *Discoveries and Opinions of Galileo*; a complete translation, including Scheiner's letters and contemporary correspondence, by Mario Biagioli and Van Helden is in progress and will be of great interest.

The *Dialogue on the Two Great Systems of the World, Ptolemaic and Copernican* (1632) was translated by Thomas Salusbury in *Mathematical Translations and Collections*, London, 1661, and has been revised by Giorgio de Santillana in *Dialogue on the Great World Systems*, University of Chicago Press, Chicago, 1953. Salusbury's translation is faithful but literal and archaic in language, and the freer modern translation by Drake, *Dialogue Concerning the Two Chief World Systems – Ptolemaic and Copernican*, rev. ed., University of California Press, Berkeley, 1967, has become the standard version. An abridged translation with an extensive commentary, mostly on philosophical issues, by Maurice A. Finocchiaro, has recently been published by the University of California Press, 1997.

There are many studies of various aspects of Galileo's astronomy. Of more comprehensive treatments, one must first note the works of Stillman Drake: the delightful presentation in dialogue in *Telescopes, Tides and Tactics, Discoveries and Opinions of Galileo*, and *Galileo at Work, His Scientific Biography*, University of Chicago Press, Chicago, 1978 (reprint Dover, New York, 1995), the finest book ever written on Galileo. The subjects of sunspots, comets, and the *Dialogue* are treated by William R. Shea, *Galileo's Intellectual Revolution, Middle Period, 1610–1632*, 2nd ed., Science History Publications, New York, 1977. A critical but nevertheless insightful survey is Willy Hartner, "Galileo's Contribution to Astronomy" in *Galileo, Man of Science*, ed. by Ernan McMullin, Basic Books, New York, 1967 (reprint The Scholar's Bookshelf, Princeton Junction, 1988), pp. 178–94.

Studies of the discoveries with the telescope include Van Helden, *Measuring the Universe, Cosmic Dimensions from Aristarchus to Halley*, University of Chicago Press, Chicago, 1985, Chap. 7, and "Galileo, Telescopic Astronomy, and the Copernican System" in *Planetary Astronomy from the Renaissance to the Rise of Astrophysics*, ed. René Taton and Curtis Wilson, *The General History of Astronomy*, vol. 2, Cambridge University Press, Cambridge, 1989, pp. 81–105; Drake, "Galileo's First Telescopic Observations," *Journal for the History of Astronomy (JHA)*, 7 (1976), pp. 153–68; and Shea, "Galileo Galilei: An Astronomer at Work," in *Nature, Experiment, and the Sciences*, ed. T. H. Levere and W. R. Shea, Kluwer, Dordrecht, 1990, pp. 51–76, a fine study with particular reference to the work of Stillman Drake.

The lunar observations are considered by Ewan A. Whitaker, "Galileo's Lunar Observations and the Dating of the Composition of 'Sidereus Nuncius'," *JHA*, 9 (1978), 155–69, with discussion of papers by Guglielmo Righini and Owen Gingerich in *Reason, Experiment and Mysticism in the Scientific Revolution*, ed. by M. L. Bonelli and W. R. Shea, Science History Publications, New York, 1975, 59–88, and the paper of Drake just mentioned. Whitaker's excellent paper contains all of Galileo's drawings and engravings of the Moon compared with modern photographs, and his analysis of the dating of the observations appears definitive. See also Whitaker's "Selenography in the Seventeenth Century" in *Planetary Astronomy from the Renaissance...*, 119–43. The secondary light and the controversies following Galileo's lunar discoveries are treated by Eileen Reeves, *Painting the Heavens, Art and Science in the Age of Galileo*, Princeton University Press, Princeton, 1997, a highly original study of Galileo's knowledge of art and his influence on contemporary painting.

The manuscripts containing Galileo's observations and calculations for determining the periods of Jupiter's satellites, a sensational discovery in the Biblioteca del Palazzo Pitti by Eugenio Albèri, were first published by Albèri in 1846 in Vol. 5 of *Le Opere di Galileo Galilei.*; a more complete publication by Favaro with many facsimiles followed in 1907 in Vol. 3, Pt. 2 of the Edizione Nazionale with additions in the reprint of 1931. The principal studies are by Albèri in the volume just mentioned, by Pietro Pagnini in the introduction to the additions in the 1931 reprint, and by Drake, "Galileo and Satellite Prediction," *JHA*, 10 (1979), 75–95.

The phases of Venus are treated in a series of papers by Drake, "Galileo, Kepler, and Phases of Venus," Gingerich, "Phases of Venus in 1610," and William T. Peters, "The Appearances of Venus and Mars in 1610," *JHA*, 15 (1984), 198–214. Observations of Saturn and explanations of its curious appearance from Galileo to Huygens are treated by Van Helden, "Saturn and His Anses" and "'Annulo Cingitur': The Solution of the Problem of Saturn," *JHA*, 5 (1974), 105–21, 155–74. The observations and controversy concerning sunspots are discussed by Bernard Dame, "Galilée et les taches solaires (1610–1613)" in *Galilée. Aspects de sa vie et de son oeuvre*, Presses Universitaires de France, Paris, 1968, 186–251, in Shea's *Galileo's*

Intellectual Revolution, and most recently by Van Helden in "Galileo and Scheiner on Sunspots: A Case Study in the Visual Language of Astronomy," *Proceedings of the American Philosophical Society,* 140 (1996), 358–96.

It is only fair to mention that this paper is based in part upon a book in progress on Galileo's astronomy, treated in some detail, and his conflicts with the Church.

8   Galileo on science and Scripture

AT THE ROOT OF THE GALILEO AFFAIR[1]

In Bertolt Brecht's play, *Galileo*, an aged cardinal denounces the upstart astronomer from Florence:

> I am informed that Signor Galilei transfers mankind from the center of the universe to somewhere on the outskirts. Signor Galilei is therefore an enemy of mankind and must be dealt with as such. Is it conceivable that God would trust this most precious fruit of his labor to a minor frolicking star? Would He have sent His Son to such a place? ... (To Galileo) You have degraded the earth despite the fact that you live by her and receive everything from her. I won't have it! I won't have it! I won't be a nobody on an inconsequential star briefly twirling hither and thither.... The earth is the center of all things, and I am the center of the earth, and the eye of the Creator is upon me. About me revolve, affixed to their crystal shells, the lesser lights of the stars and the great light of the sun, created to give light on me that God might see me – Man, God's greatest effort, the center of creation: "In the image of God He created him."[2]

Brecht puts in the mouth of the old cardinal what he himself may well have believed the primary motive to be on the church's side of the "Galileo affair." Certainly, this reading of history has been a common one from the time of the Enlightenment onwards. Why were Galileo's Copernican views met with such hostility on the part of his Church? What could have explained the violent opposition of the Roman authorities to the views of someone who was after all recognized by these same authorities as the leading astronomer in the Italy of his day? Why would they have risked such a clash where the stakes were obviously so high?

271

Brecht's cardinal echoes the many whose Galileo is the principal mover in the "Copernican revolution" that displaced human beings from the center of the cosmos. Had not Christian theology from the beginning portrayed human beings as the focal point of God's creation, the only creatures capable of affirmation or denial, creatures whose history showed the Creator's special concern? And did not the common-sense Aristotelian Earth-centered cosmos give philosophical body to this theological framework of belief? No wonder, then, that the Roman theologians would have been so concerned, so intent to crush the Copernican challenge at all costs, just as later theologians would oppose those other great diminishers of human uniqueness, Darwin and Freud.

In this essay, I want to argue by way of prologue that this reading of Galileo's conflict with the Catholic Church is wrong. Not *entirely* wrong, of course, since cosmological issues were obviously involved in the opposition to Galileo on the part of the Roman Curia, but substantially wrong nonetheless. Brecht located the conflict at just the point where *he* would have seen the threat had *he* been a Roman theologian of that time. And historians of science who take the cosmological thesis propounded in the *Dialogue on Two Chief World Systems* to be the key not surprisingly tend to suppose that the strongly negative reaction of the Church authorities to that book was prompted by their adherence to the "Chief World System" so effectively undermined there, that of Aristotle.[3]

The theologian–consultors who were asked in 1616 to evaluate the Copernican assertion that the Sun is at rest at the center of the world saw the matter differently, however. The Copernican claim was, they said, "foolish and absurd in philosophy" (or, as we would say, in science), but, far more seriously in their eyes, it was

formally heretical, since it explicitly contradicts in many places the sense of Holy Scripture according to the literal meaning of the words and according to the common interpretation and understanding of the Holy Fathers and the doctors of theology.[4]

What these consultors showed themselves committed to defend was not primarily a cosmology. In their own eyes, they were vindicating the authority of Scripture in regard to the truth of its literal content. The Copernican theses about the Earth's motion and the Sun's stability were, in their view, clearly at odds with specific passages in the

Bible. To affirm such theses, therefore, was equivalent to calling the authority of Scripture into question. It was that, and not a presumed link between Aristotelian cosmology and the *content* of Christian doctrine, that led them to condemn the Copernican claim about the Sun as "formally heretical."[5]

Looming just as large in Roman eyes was the challenge that the Copernicans offered to Church authority. At the fourth session of the Council of Trent in 1546, in order to "control petulant spirits," it had been decreed that:

> in matters of faith and morals pertaining to the edification of Christian doctrine, no one relying on his own judgment and distorting the Sacred Scriptures according to his own conception shall dare to interpret them contrary to that sense which Holy Mother Church, to whom it belongs to judge of their true sense and meaning, has held or does hold, or even [to interpret them] contrary to the unanimous agreement of the Fathers....[6]

Yet here were the Copernicans, petulant spirits surely as far as the theologians were concerned, disputing on their own authority as individuals the traditional interpretation of various biblical passages. To the consultors, this would have seemed a direct violation of the mandate of Trent. The challengers were setting themselves dangerously close to the camp of the Reformers for whom the individual's right to interpret Scripture according to his or her own lights was paramount.

The issue that had most bitterly divided the two sides in the century-old dispute that had sundered Christendom was this very one: With whom does authority lie in the interpretation of disputed passages in Scripture? Cosmology offered the occasion for the complaint that had been laid before the consultors, to be sure. And they were convinced that the Copernican cosmology was false even on purely philosophical (in our terms, scientific) grounds, an important link in their overall argument. But, as theologians, their primary motive for rejecting the new cosmology lay deeper: It contradicted the literal sense of the words of Scripture where the literal sense was clearly the proper one, as far as they were concerned. Furthermore, its proponents undoubtedly seemed to the consultors to have arrogated to themselves an authority in interpreting Scripture that belonged properly only to the Church, speaking through its bishops and theologians.

Ponder for a moment a simple counter-factual conjecture. Suppose the biblical writers had not found occasion to refer in passing to the motion of the Sun or the stability of the Earth; this could, so far as one can see, have happened very easily. Would the Church still have condemned the Copernican doctrine? Would the comfortable coherence between the common-sense geocentrism of Aristotle and the anthropocentrism of the Christian tradition have been sufficient of itself to warrant the charge of heresy against the Copernican challenge to the Aristotelian world system? It would surely seem not. At the very least, a completely different argument would have had to be advanced for such a charge, an argument of which there is hardly a hint, to the best of my knowledge, in the theological writings of the day.

Had Galileo made his case for Copernicanism a century earlier or a century later, it seems unlikely that it would have evoked the strong response it did on the part of the Roman theologians. After all, Nicole d'Oresme, a prominent ecclesiastic, had given cautious credence to the arguments for a rotating earth long before Copernicus, without exciting any notable reaction among theologians. When, however, a respectable theologian, like Paolo Foscarini, signified his support for the Copernican arguments in 1615, his book was summarily banned. What had changed in the meantime? It would be risky to rely too much on the comparison between two such diverse and such complex historical contexts. But it seems fair to say that the most significant changes were those associated with the Protestant Reformation, notably the deep division regarding the role of authority in the interpretation of Scripture.

The Council of Trent repeated the traditional view that God is the "author" of the Bible but did little to clarify the nature of the influence by which God was said to move the human writers, other than to describe it in passing by the metaphor of dictation. It is clear in the context that this was not intended in the sense of a direct revelation or of a literal dictation of text, since the "dictation" is said to extend to the later "unwritten traditions" of the Church, whose authority the Council was concerned at all costs to safeguard against the attacks of the Reformers.

Nevertheless, the notion that even the very word choice of the biblical text was God's, and thus inerrant, gained ground among Catholic and Protestant theologians alike, engaged as they were in doctrinal duels where the main weapons were proof-texts drawn from Scripture, deployed quite often independently of biblical context. The Dominican theologian, Melchior Cano, to recall one well-known example of this hardening of exegetical approach, claimed in his *De Theologicis Locis* of 1585 that "not only the words but even every comma has been supplied by the Holy Spirit."[7] A similar view can be found on the Reformation side also, in the *Formula Consensus Helvetica* of 1675, for example, which maintained that even the very letters of the Bible must be regarded as inspired by God. In the defensive climate that prevailed in Roman theological circles by the early seventeenth century, Galileo's attempt to appeal to more tolerant exegetical principles, like that of accommodation, for instance, was not likely to be greeted with any sympathy, even though these principles could find a warrant all the way back to Augustine. Galileo had the misfortune to bring the Copernican claims to public notice at just the wrong time, a time when sensitivities in regard to questions involving scriptural interpretation and Church authority were at their most intense.

The Galileo affair ought not then be construed, as it so often has been, as primarily a clash between rival cosmologies, with the resistance of the Church authorities to the new cosmology to be explained by their stubborn adherence to an outmoded Earth-centered cosmos. The embattled Aristotelian natural philosophers who, when the astronomical evidence went strongly against them, called in their support what Galileo called the "terrible weapon"[8] of Scripture *did*, of course, view their battle with the Copernicans in primarily cosmological terms. But the same was not true of those theologians who came later to the fray. What called them into action was a perceived threat to the authority of Scripture as well as to their own authority as its licensed interpreters. Once *they* entered the lists, the ground of battle shifted, as Galileo very quickly saw. He realized that if he were ever to get a hearing for the new cosmology on its philosophic (scientific) merits, he would have to defend himself on an entirely different front first. And it was on *this* front that the battle was lost before it was ever really joined on the side of cosmology.

Does the authority of Scripture attach to the literal reading of phrases that describe the Sun as being in motion or the Earth as being fixed on its foundations? That was the issue, as far as Rome was concerned. Galileo was convinced that the appeal to Scripture in a case like this was a last-ditch diversionary attempt on the part of the

Aristotelian philosophers to save their position. And he evidently thought that the theologians could be persuaded of this by a mixture of common-sense arguments and appeals to the Church's own exegetical tradition. He must also have believed that the theologians would listen to such a case even if it were being made by someone from outside their own ranks, a layman without theological training. Not for the first time, nor indeed the last, did he overestimate his own powers of persuasion, as well as underestimating the antagonism that his entrance into theological territory would unleash among its professional occupants.

What has come to be called the "Galileo affair" went through two more or less distinct phases, each terminating in a decisive action on the part of the Roman authorities.[9] The first comprises the events leading up to the condemnation of Copernican doctrine in 1616; the second covers the events leading up to Galileo's trial in 1633 as well as the trial itself. Though the second is the more colorful and always has attracted far more attention, the first is, to my mind, much the more important. By that, I mean that without the first, the second would hardly have happened.

Without the decree of 1616 and the events surrounding the condemnation of Copernican doctrine, the writing of a book in support of that doctrine would not have encountered the sort of obstacles that Galileo faced in composing the *Dialogue*. Nor is it likely that its publication would have led its author to be sent to trial before the Holy Office, any more than did the publication of Foscarini's much more daring work prior to 1616. Though matters of personality, political circumstance, and the rest played a major part in the second phase, it seems fair to say that the root of the Galileo affair must be sought in the events that culminated in the banning of Copernicus's work in 1616. The promulgation of this decree set the Church on a collision course with the new astronomy. If Galileo had not offered the occasion, someone else (Descartes perhaps?) would very likely have done so. Given time and wiser counsel, a collision might perhaps have been avoided. But an extended defense of the Copernican claims coming less than twenty years after they had been officially declared to be contrary to Scripture was all too easy to construe as an open challenge.

The focus of this essay will be upon the first, and decisive, phase of the Galileo affair. It will be divided into two main parts. In the first,

I will trace in summary fashion the series of events leading from the first serious theological challenge to the Copernican cosmology in late 1613 to the completion of Galileo's *Letter to the Grand Duchess Christina* in mid-1615.[10] The period covered is only a year and a half, but during those short months the lines were drawn in the debate that would lead to the momentous decision on the part of the Congregation of the Index in March 1616 to "suspend, until corrected" the work of Copernicus and to declare the "Pythagorean doctrine" of the Earth's motion and the Sun's rest to be "altogether contrary to the Holy Scripture."[11] In the second part of the essay, the focus will be on the set of exegetical principles proposed by Galileo as a means of dealing with tensions between science and Scripture. One of their major sources was the *De Genesi ad litteram* of St. Augustine, so we will begin there, pause briefly on Kepler, and then go on to Galileo's formulation of the principles, examining in particular their plausibility and their internal coherence, and asking what moral might have been drawn from them in regard to the Copernican theses.

COPERNICANISM CHALLENGED, 1613–1615

In December 1613, at a breakfast at the Medici palace in Florence attended by the young Grand Duke, Cosimo II, and his formidable mother, the Dowager Grand Duchess, Christina of Lorraine, Galileo's former student, the Benedictine monk Benedetto Castelli, was asked to explain the significance of the new astronomical discoveries. Prompted by an Aristotelian philosopher, Cosimo Boscaglia, who happened to be present, the Grand Duchess pressed Castelli about the apparent contradiction between the Copernican claims and such biblical passages as the one in *Joshua* where the Lord commanded the Sun and Moon to stand still over the valley of Ajalon to allow the Israelites to wreak vengeance on their foes.[12] Castelli, in his own words, "behaved like a champion," and felt that he had deflected this line of attack on the new cosmology.[13]

When he heard of the affair, Galileo was not so sure, and in a long letter to Castelli took the occasion "to examine some general questions about the use of Holy Scripture in disputes involving physical conclusions."[14] His approach was a common-sense one. It seemed to him obvious that the biblical writers would have adapted their mode of expression to the understanding of their readers, and equally obvious that the aim of Scripture was limited to "persuading men of those articles and propositions which are necessary to salvation."[15] Since there could be no real conflict between the two sources of truth, Scripture and what "sense experience or necessary demonstration" establishes concerning nature, one must suppose that when an apparent conflict arises, Scripture has to be interpreted in an alternative, less literal, way. We already know, after all, that passages like those attributing hands and eyes as well as human emotions to God cannot be taken literally. Galileo ended with a telling *ad hominem* argument, directed against his Aristotelian opponents.[16] To stop the apparent motion of the Sun across the sky would require those who defend the Aristotelian world system to suppose that what God *really* did was to stop the *Primum Mobile*, the outermost sphere on which the diurnal motions of all the other celestial bodies depend. To stop the Sun alone in this scheme would actually have shortened the day, not lengthened it. Thus the passage in *Joshua* not only does not support the Aristotelian position but would have to be understood non-literally to be made compatible with it.

His opponents in Florence saw to it that a copy of the letter would find its way to Rome where it eventually reached the Congregation of the Holy Office, the Church's arbiter in matters of faith and morals. But when the letter was submitted to a theologian–consultor of the Congregation for his judgment as to its orthodoxy, he found little to object to.[17] Aware that the letter was under scrutiny in Rome, Galileo took care to send what he describes as the "correct" version to one of his Florentine friends there, Monsignor Piero Dini, suggesting that he might pass on a copy to the most influential member of the Holy Office, Cardinal Robert Bellarmine. This, as Galileo must have realized, was to court risk. Another Roman friend, Prince Federico Cesi, had already reported to him, "As to Copernicus's opinion, Bellarmine himself who is one of the heads of the Congregation dealing with these matters has told me that he holds it to be heretical and that the motion of the earth is without any doubt against Scripture."[18]

Dini did, it seems, pass on a copy of the *Letter to Castelli* to Bellarmine and reported back to Galileo that Bellarmine discounted the likelihood that Copernicus's book would be condemned but indicated that it might be necessary to insert a note in the book reminding readers that the work was to be understood as no more than "a way to save the appearances, in the manner of those who have put forth epicycles but do not really believe in them."[19] There would obviously be no reason to ban the *De Revolutionibus* if it were clearly understood to make no claims about the real motions of Sun and Earth.

This view of the inherent limitations of mathematical astronomy, that its "hypotheses" were no more than calculational devices making no claim on truth, was of course not original with Bellarmine. It went back to medieval natural philosophy and perhaps further, being prompted by the Aristotelian separation between physics and mathematics as well as by the evident inconsistency with one another of the "two chief world systems" of that earlier day, the mathematical astronomy of Ptolemy and the physical astronomy of Aristotle.[20] The favored way among natural philosophers of dealing with this inconsistency was to attribute truth to the causal account given by Aristotle on the grounds that causal argument was required for demonstration, while maintaining that the mathematical formalism of Ptolemy, supported as it was only by its claim to "save the appearances," should be treated as no more then a practical aid to determining planetary positions and periods.

Bellarmine's reasons for adopting this fictionalist account of the constructs of the mathematical astronomer were, however, rather different. As a young man he lectured on astronomy at the University of Louvain. He departed quite radically from Aristotle (and hence from Aquinas) in his account of the heavens.[21] He rejected the Greek method of composition of planetary motions, that is, breaking the irregular observed planetary motion down into a combination of circular motions, thus making a mathematically tractable analysis possible. (Aristotle had physical reasons also for adopting a compositional approach since it allowed him to offer a quasi-mechanical explanation of the planet's motion.) Bellarmine argued that the Sun's *real* motion is the complex variable one: the circles are invention, of practical use, perhaps, but of no ontological significance. Guided much more by the Bible than by Aristotle, he accepted geocentrism but rejected other Aristotelian tenets regarding, for example, the composition of the heavenly bodies (he claimed that they were composed of fire) and their incorruptibility. He would thus have been even less disposed than an Aristotelian would to accepting the Copernican composition of motions as testimony to the "real" motions of Earth or Sun. His evident conviction in this regard undoubtedly played a crucial role in the early stages of the Roman debate regarding the Copernican challenge.

Bellarmine relied for additional support in this regard (as casual readers of the *De Revolutionibus* had from the beginning done) on the fact that the preface to the work had portrayed it in instrumentalist terms as making no claims about real motions. In his response to Dini, Galileo objected strongly to this construal; only those who had not read the text, he responded, could say such a thing. (He was apparently unaware of the true authorship of the preface; Kepler had already noted that it was the work of a Lutheran theologian, Andreas Osiander.)

In the text, Copernicus had "put on philosophical garments" and set out to declare the "true structure" of the world; all six books of the work are in consequence "full of the doctrine of the earth's motion and of explanations and confirmations of it."[22] In reply to Bellarmine's allegation that those who make use of epicycles "do not really believe in them," Galileo drew an interesting distinction, claiming that they believe in the reality of the motions as they describe them but not in:

the solid, material, and distinct orbs, introduced by the builders of models to facilitate understanding by beginners and computations by calculators; this is the only fictitious and unreal part, as God does not lack the means to make the stars move in the immense celestial spaces within well-defined and definite paths, but without having them chained and forced.[23]

According to Dini, Bellarmine had mentioned a passage in *Psalms*, where the Sun is described as "running its course" (18, 6), finding it particularly telling against the claim that the Sun is really at rest. In his letter to Dini, Galileo ventured a cautious suggestion that this passage might also be interpreted in a way that would *support* Copernicus or more exactly support the view that a "penetrating spirit" spreads outward from the Sun and is responsible for warmth, life, and the motions of the planets. He goes on: "It seems to me that from Holy Writ we can acquire *evident certainty* that the solar body is, as I have said, a receptacle and, so to speak, a reservoir of this spirit and this light which it receives from elsewhere."[24]

This was a dangerous ploy. Galileo was, effectively, challenging the leading theologian of the Holy Office on the proper exegesis of a biblical text. And, of course, he was also violating his own prohibition against using Scripture to support a philosophical thesis about the natural world. Perhaps he meant it as an *ad hominem* argument, intended only to counter Bellarmine's own use of this passage. In closing, Galileo suggested to Dini that he might, at his discretion, pass the letter on to Bellarmine. Needless to say, Dini decided against this.

In the meantime, another Roman friend, Giovanni Ciampoli, had written to reassure Galileo that the Dominicans in Rome were not, as he feared, in league against him. But in another quarter, the news was not so good:

Cardinal Barberini, who as you know from experience, has always admired your talents, told me only yesterday evening that with respect to these opinions he would like greater caution in not going beyond the arguments used by Ptolemy and Copernicus, and finally in not exceeding the bounds of physics and mathematics. For to explain the Scriptures is claimed by theologians as their field, and if new things are brought in, even though to be admired for their ingenuity, not everyone has the dispassionate faculty of taking them just as they are said.[25]

Later, as Pope Urban VIII, Barberini permitted Galileo to procced with the writing of the *Dialogo* with the proviso that he treat Copernicanism as a "hypothesis" only. Were the limitations traditionally set on mathematical astronomy and echoed in the preface to Copernicus's work what he had in mind? In part, they must have been. But his unwillingness to allow that the Copernican theses might possibly come to be *demonstrated* almost certainly rested on other grounds also.[26] In any event, in the conversation relayed to Galileo in 1615, he may only have been warning the astronomer to stay out of biblical exegesis.

At this point, Galileo received a copy of a letter Bellarmine had written to Paolo Antonio Foscarini, a Carmelite theologian, author of a treatise, "in which it is shown that [the Copernican] opinion agrees with, and is reconciled with the passages of Sacred Scripture which are commonly addressed against it," to quote the subtitle of the treatise.[27] Foscarini proposed a set of exegetical principles resembling those Galileo had already defended in his *Letter to Castelli*. For example: "The Sacred Scripture speaks in accordance with the common language of popular reason and of ordinary people, and thus according to the appearances and not according to actual reality"; and again: "The Scriptures have no other purpose than the attainment of salvation."[28] Foscarini laid out a natural philosophy that differed significantly from Aristotle's (whose philosophy, he claimed, had "fallen into ruin.")[29] But then he went much further than Galileo had done by setting out to "accommodate many passages of Holy Scripture" to this philosophy and more specifically to the Copernican doctrine, described by him as "clearly probable."[30]

Bellarmine's response to Foscarini is an odd document and has been interpreted very differently by different scholars. It is moderate in tone, given that Foscarini is defending a doctrine that Bellarmine has, according to Cesi at least, characterized as heretical. He begins by giving Foscarini and Galileo the benefit of the doubt: He assumes (or pretends to assume) that they are speaking *ex suppositione* (which he paraphrases as saying that they are claiming only that the Copernican formalism saves the appearances better than the Ptolemaic one does), "as I have always believed that Copernicus spoke."[31] The firm conviction that mathematical astronomy could not *in principle* provide a demonstration of the Earth's motion, and that without such a demonstration the literal sense of Scripture ('literal' in our usage) could not be challenged, seems to have been Bellarmine's guiding light throughout. But of course he knew that both Foscarini and Galileo made the stronger realist claim for the Copernican theses and so he goes on to warn them: To make such a claim "is a very dangerous thing, likely not only to irritate all scholastic philosophers and theologians, but also to harm the Holy Faith by rendering Holy Scripture false."[32] Why would it do that?

Here Bellarmine lays down his own exegetical principle, one that went significantly beyond the declaration of the Council of Trent and the theological tradition that preceded Trent:[33]

Nor can one answer that this is not a matter of faith [as Foscarini had claimed], since if it is not a matter of faith *ex parte objecti* [because of the subject matter], it is a matter of faith *ex parte dicentis* [because of the speaker]. And so it would be as heretical to say that Abraham did not have two children and Jacob twelve, as it would be to say that Christ was not born of a virgin, because both are said by the Holy Spirit through the mouth of the prophets and the apostles.[34]

One can see here the effect on Bellarmine of years of controversy with the leading Reformation theologians. Note his use of the term, "heretical."[35] If the Holy Spirit is, indeed, the principal author of the Bible, Bellarmine presumes that the literal sense must be accorded full authority, down to the last detail of the text. At this point, the gulf between him and the Copernicans seems almost unbridgeable.

The last paragraph of Bellarmine's letter has often been taken to show that Bellarmine was, in fact, open to persuasion in regard to the Copernican issue; all that was required was a proper *demonstration* of the Earth's motion, something that Galileo could not produce.[36] Bellarmine does say that *if* there were a "true demonstration" of the Copernican theses, "one would have to proceed with great caution in explaining the Scriptures that appear contrary and say rather than we do not understand them than that what is demonstrated is false." But in context, one can see that he was not conceding this allusion to the traditional Augustinian principle to be a real possibility. It is his innate courtesy to his correspondent, a respected theologian, that leads him to add the qualifier "until it is shown me" to the assertion: "I will not believe that there is such a demonstration." He has already indicated that he thinks such a demonstration to be permanently out of reach; indeed, he lists three separate reasons for this.

One reason is, once again, that merely "saving the appearances" in astronomy cannot provide a true demonstration of real motion. A second is the "common consensus" of the Fathers and scriptural commentators, here recalling the criterion specified by the Council of Trent. And the third, directed against Foscarini's suggestion that the biblical writers are speaking "in accordance with the appearances," is that we clearly *experience* that the Earth stands still and so this cannot be treated simply as "appearance." None of these arguments leave room for a concession on his part that a demonstration of the Earth's motion might at a later time be discovered. Bellarmine is *not* merely pointing to the fact that the Copernicans have not yet come up with a proper demonstration of the Earth's motion. He is, in his own mind, at least, giving reasons to believe that they never *could*. Thus, he is implicitly setting aside the prudential principle well stated by Foscarini:

Since something new is always being added to the human sciences, and since many things are seen with the passage of time to be false which previously were thought to be true, it could happen that, when the falsity of a philosophical opinion [to which the authority of Scripture has been attached] has been detected, the authority of the Scriptures would be destroyed....[37]

Galileo obtained a copy of Bellarmine's letter and made a series of notes that may have been intended to aid Foscarini in preparing a response to the letter.[38] The notes contain a variety of briefly stated arguments, some good, some surprisingly bad. Among the former: The Council of Trent did not affirm Bellarmine's exegetical principle, which would attach authority to phrases in the Bible that have no bearing whatever on faith and morals. Moreover, even if one were to admit the validity of this principle for such claims as that Tobit had a dog, this would still not validate its application to phrases bearing on the motions of Sun and Earth. The literal sense of the former sort of phrase is not in question, so there would be no reason for the Holy Spirit to use this phrase "if it did not state the truth." However, this is just what *is* in question for the other sort of phrase, where one can argue that the Holy Spirit would "accommodate the words of Scripture to the capacities of the common man."[39]

Galileo's objection points to a serious difficulty for Bellarmine's "*ex parte dicentis*" principle. Bellarmine admits, on the one hand, that the Bible uses metaphorical language when speaking about God. In such a case, the language is clearly being accommodated to our capacities. It has thus to be *established* regarding any given passage whether the language of that passage is to be understood literally or not; it cannot simply be taken for granted, as Bellarmine is evidently doing when discussing the texts that refer to the Sun and Earth. What Foscarini and Galileo are asking is why it is acceptable to allow a principle of accommodation in one case and not in the other. Part of the problem lies in the ambiguity in the notion of the "literal," which Bellarmine understands to refer both to the sense intended by the author and to the "plain" sense that the average reader would take from the words used.

In an earlier discussion of this issue in one of his exegetical works, Bellarmine had urged that arguments regarding the sense of Scripture "ought to be sought in the literal meaning alone. For it is certain that that meaning, which is taken immediately from the words, is the meaning of the Holy Spirit."[40] In his letter to Foscarini, Bellarmine asserts that since the "literal" interpretation of the disputed passages is evidently that the Sun "rotates around the Earth with great speed," and the Earth "stands immobile in the center of the world,"[41] this must be the sense intended *ex parte dicentis* and is therefore "a matter of faith." The argument plainly begs the question.

But the confusion was not all on Bellarmine's side. He had failed, as a theologian, to grasp as fully as he should have, the consequences of the exegetical principle he was employing. However, Galileo likewise failed, as a scientist, to grasp what was called for in the way of proof in the context of cosmology or to appreciate the epistemic value of probable reasoning.

In his notes on Bellarmine's letter to Foscarini, he says that if the Copernicans "were to have no more than 90 percent of the arguments on their side, they would be rebutted."[42] (The implication seems to be that *all* arguments have to be on the Copernican side, otherwise they fail. On theological grounds?) "It is clear that those who are on the false side cannot have any arguments or evidence of value; while on the side of truth, there is the advantage that everything agrees and is consistent." He had already remarked in his *Letter to Castelli*: "The one who supports the true side will be able to provide a thousand experiments and a thousand necessary demonstrations for his side, whereas the other person can have nothing but sophisms, paralogisms, and fallacies."[43] He goes on: "When everything offered by the philosophers and astronomers on the other side is proven to be for the most part false ... then the position of the [Copernican] proponents should not be scorned ... because of the fact that it cannot be demonstrated conclusively."

If the only arguments of value must lie on the side of truth, then it is easy to slip from "well supported" to "demonstrated". The possibility that more than one explanatory hypothesis might have evidence in its support is being set aside. Then, most strangely, he adds:

It is true that to show that the appearances are saved by the mobility of the earth and the stability of the Sun is not the same thing as to demonstrate that this hypothesis is really true in nature. But it is equally or even more true that the other commonly accepted system is not able to give reasons for these appearances. The latter is undoubtedly false, just as it is clear that the former, which corresponds to the appearances perfectly, could be true. No greater truth can be, or ought to be, sought for in a position than that it corresponds to all the particular appearances.[44]

Granted that these notes are no more than jottings, it is still disturbing to find Galileo so uncertain regarding the principal philosophical issue separating Bellarmine and himself. He says first that saving the appearances is not enough to demonstrate the truth of a hypothesis and ends by remarking that saving the appearances is the *most* that can be demanded of an hypothesis. This seems to go a long way toward conceding Bellarmine's contention that a hypothesis in mathematical astronomy cannot, in principle, reveal the true motions of the heavenly bodies. The most that can be said of a hypothesis (like that of Copernicus) that "fits the appearances perfectly" is, apparently, that it *could* be true. But this is far too weak to carry any weight in the face of Bellarmine's objection.

In his *Apologia pro Tychone contra Ursum* (1600), Kepler had earlier faced a very similar objection from Ursus (Nicolaus Baer). Kepler admits that saving the appearances is not sufficient to establish truth. But he goes on to argue that there are other criteria of astronomical theory that, if satisfied, can go far toward achieving that goal. And he sees these as favoring Copernicus over Ptolemy, even though the two systems have roughly equal merit as far as saving the appearances is concerned. The Copernican model can *explain* many features of the planetary motions that had to be arbitrarily postulated in the earlier scheme ("Copernicus did not have to ask why it is that the planets at their evening risings are [at their brightest and therefore] at their nearest to the earth."[45])

In the *Astronomia Nova* (1609), Kepler carried this theme further, as the full title of the work reminds us: *The New Astronomy Causally Explained; or Celestial Physics Based on the Motions of the Planet Mars.* He is reiterating the Aristotelian emphasis on "physical" (causal) explanation as the testimony of truth in natural philosophy. Merely to *save* the planetary motions is not enough, since many other mathematical constructions may save them equally well. One must in addition *explain* them causally.[46] Having successfully saved the motions of Mars by a simple ellipse, he searches therefore for physical reasons why a planet should follow such an orbit. If he can find these and they hold up over time, he is assured that the theory must be true.

Galileo almost surely had not read the *Astronomia Nova* (except perhaps for the preface). And there is little sign in his writings from this period that he had thought through the epistemological puzzles surrounding proof in astronomy in the systematic way that Kepler had. He could not seem to find an appropriate category at this point to describe the epistemic status of the Copernican hypothesis.[47] He wanted to say that it did more than save the appearances (though in the final sentence in the passage from his notes above, he seems to concede that it cannot do this). But he also had to admit that it fell short of demonstration. What lies in between? Perhaps it was because he was so heavily influenced by the traditional Aristotelian emphasis on demonstration that he did not develop in response to Bellarmine the notions of likelihood or probability that he so badly needed. It was all or nothing – and in the intellectual climate of Rome in 1615, the latter was the more likely verdict on Copernicanism.[48]

Nor did he have a *theory* of the planetary motions to offer, even of the most tentative sort. Given that he was still working with the circles and epicycles bequeathed by Copernicus, this was hardly surprising. Kepler had recognized the epistemological significance of such a theory for anyone who would make a claim for the reality of the Earth's motion. Nonetheless, Galileo had high hopes at this stage for his tidal theory which, if it were successful, *would* give him a "physical" argument of the needed sort.[49] But he would have to be able to claim not just that postulating the double motion of the Earth explained, in causal terms, the general phenomena of the tides but that it gave the only *possible* explanation, if his argument were to have the demonstrative form that his Aristotelian critics regarded as canonical.[50]

We are almost to the end of our story. During these months, despite bouts of severe ill health, Galileo had been working on a systematic response to the challenge posed by those who would call on Scripture to refute Copernican cosmology. It was all very well for Barberini to advise leaving theology to the theologians. But the theologians were not leaving science to the scientists! Galileo must have known that his foray into theology would be resented. However, he evidently felt impelled to do everything he could to prevent an outcome that was now beginning to seem imminent, one that would be a tragedy (he was convinced) for the Church itself.

His *Letter to Castelli* had been lacking in one crucial respect: support from the Fathers and major theologians of the Church. Galileo resolved to make that lack good in the new work. He had no expertise whatever in that area, so he evidently asked his Benedictine friend, Castelli, to seek out references that would support the exegetical principles he had outlined in his earlier letter to him. Castelli apparently enlisted the aid of others. He writes from Rome in January 1615 to say that an unnamed Barnabite priest has promised to send citations from St. Augustine and other Fathers in confirmation of Galileo's views on the *Joshua* passage.[51] The list of authorities that Galileo goes on to present in his support was surely not the product of extensive reading on his part; it was needed to persuade his opponents that his exegetical views found support in the tradition, notably in St. Augustine, the most revered of the Church's early theologians.

His main resource would obviously be Augustine's *De Genesi ad Litteram* which was already well known among exegetes for its treatment of the relations between "natural knowledge" and Scripture. Galileo quotes no less than fourteen passages, some of them quite lengthy, from the first two books of that work. These texts could have been passed on to him by Castelli, but it is also possible that he might have been induced to read these two short books for himself. The choice of texts certainly testifies to a close reading of the books in question, as we shall see when we come to examine them for ourselves below.[52]

Galileo also draws on the most authoritative commentary on *Genesis* of the day, by a leading Scripture scholar, Benito Pereira, S. J.[53] Pereira prefaces his massive work with a page where *he* lays out four "rules" intended to guide the exegesis of passages where conflict arises between the literal reading of Scripture and other sources of knowledge.[54] This page was an obvious choice for Galileo's purposes. He quotes the fourth of the rules, one that enjoins the exegete never to interpret Scripture in a way that runs contrary to "manifest evidence and the arguments of philosophy or other disciplines." From the same page, Galileo also almost certainly draws the reference he immediately goes on to make to Augustine's *Seventh Epistle to Marcellinus*, hardly common coin, as well as a passage from Augustine's *De Genesi ad Litteram*, which he quotes in the paraphrase version found in Pereira.[55] There is no evidence, so far as I can tell, of Galileo's drawing any other of his references to Augustine from Pereira's text.[56] Thus it is possible that what he was working with was a copy simply of that single highly relevant page from Pereira listing the four exegetical "rules."

One other likely source was Foscarini's *Defensio*, the brief defense of his position that Foscarini composed when he heard that his *Letter* was under attack in Rome. Foscarini quotes the same passage from Pereira that Galileo uses; it could have been this reference that drew

Pereira's text to Galileo's attention.[57] Further evidence that Galileo had seen the *Defensio* is his use of two quotations from Jerome (commenting on *Jeremiah* and on *Matthew*), which are also featured in the *Defensio*.[58]

The work was finished around June 1615. It took the form of a letter, freeing it from the need to pass through a censorship procedure but enabling it to be circulated privately. Galileo eventually decided[59] to address it to the Dowager Grand Duchess, mother of his patron, the person whose interrogation of Castelli had first led Galileo to realize that a full-scale defense of Copernicanism from theological attack might be necessary. How widely the letter was circulated at that time remains unclear.[60] It was first published in 1636 in Strasbourg, translated by Elio Diodati, with Italian and Latin in parallel columns and later appended to the Latin version of the *Dialogo* that became the standard text of that work for Northern European readers. It thus eventually did reach a wide readership.

One feature of the work that might have commended it to many of those readers was the contemptuous and dismissive tone in which Galileo addressed those with whom he was disagreeing. But in the context of the readership for which the *Letter* was originally intended, this constitutes something of a puzzle. Galileo was not unaware of the maxims of rhetoric, a much studied art in his day.[61] How could he have violated in so obvious a manner the elementary advice for any work of persuasion that one should gain the goodwill of the reader or hearer first (*captatio benevolentiae*)? As one example of such a failure, the *Letter* is addressed to an elderly woman interested in Scripture, yet he quotes a passage from St. Jerome that is hardly calculated to win her favor, to say the least:

The garrulous old woman, the doting old man, and the wordy sophist, one and all take in hand the Scriptures, read them in pieces and teach them before they have learned them. Some with brows knit and bombastic words, balanced one against the other, philosophize concerning the sacred writings among weak women. Others – I blush to say it – learn from women what they are to teach to men...[62]

One may excuse, perhaps, the violence of the language in which he attacks his Aristotelian critics ("superficial and vulgar writers") throughout the letter for their "simulated religious zeal" and their "insincerity"; he was certainly not aiming to win *their* assent.[63] But the people he really needed to persuade were the Roman theologians. It was all very well to appeal to the educated general audience, but if he antagonized those who at that very moment were debating the issues in Rome, he would surely compromise the goal he had clearly set himself in composing the *Letter*: to persuade the Church authorities not to proceed against the work of Copernicus.

Yet when he addresses "some theologians whom I regard as men of profound learning and of the holiest life-style," men whom he holds "in high esteem and reverence" (Bellarmine would be an obvious referent), he confesses himself to be troubled by the fact that these men seem "in disputes about natural phenomena to claim the right to force others by means of the authority of Scripture to follow the opinion they think most in accordance with its statements, and at the same time they think they are not obliged to answer observations and reasons to the contrary."[64] Later, even more devastatingly: "Officials and experts in theology should not arrogate to themselves the authority to issue decrees in professions they neither exercise nor study."[65] In other words, theologians have no business assessing the merits of astronomical arguments (as Bellarmine and his colleagues have, of course, been doing).

The first reaction of theologian readers to passages such as these would surely have been an angry one.[66] And their second one might have been one of incredulity that Galileo could chastise them for trespassing in science, to all appearances in exactly the way he was himself in the process of doing in theology. Had he given up hope of persuading the theologians and was he, effectively, going over their heads to the educated lay people among whom the *Letter* would circulate? It seems unlikely. Or had he simply allowed himself to be carried away by his anger at those who simply would not see the light? Whatever be the answer, one would seem forced to conclude that in strictly rhetorical terms, the *Letter* showed strikingly poor judgment.

However, this is not my main interest. What about the *logic* of Galileo's exegetic analyses? There is no more effective rhetorical device than a good argument. I intend to examine the exegetical principles he proposes, ask how appropriate they were in the context of the time, and reflect on their mutual coherence. Pope John Paul II summed up Galileo's contribution to exegesis: "Paradoxically,

Galileo, a sincere believer, showed himself to be more perceptive [in regard to the criteria of scriptural interpretation] than the theologians who opposed him."[67] How good a theologian was the Galileo of the *Letter to the Grand Duchess*? To answer this question, it will be necessary first to return to Augustine on whom Galileo could rely at (almost) every turn.

BACK TO AUGUSTINE

It was not surprising that Galileo would look back to Augustine for support when he was challenged for his handling of the biblical texts that were being used by his opponents to condemn the Copernican system. For Augustine had had to contend with a very similar challenge when trying to meet the criticisms launched by the Manichaeans, his former co-religionists, against the *Genesis* account of cosmic origins. They claimed to find a variety of inconsistencies between *Genesis* and what we may call the "natural knowledge" (accepted views about the physical world) of the day. How, they asked, could there be "days" before the Sun itself was formed, as the *Genesis* narrative seemed to require? How could there be "waters above the firmament," when the proper place of water is below? Augustine struggled with objections such as these over much of his scholarly lifetime. Two early commentaries on *Genesis*, the second unfinished, left him dissatisfied. Finally, in A.D. 401 he began the composition of what would be one of his major works, the *De Genesi ad Litteram*, a "literal"[68] commentary on *Genesis*, which would eventually run to twelve books and occupy him on and off for fourteen years.[69]

In this work, Augustine goes through the creation narrative systematically, treating problems as they come up. He makes no attempt to give a general account of the principles that guide his exegetical practice. It is, however, possible to reconstruct what this account might look like by examining his frequent asides on how to deal with specific instances of apparent conflict between Scripture and natural knowledge.[70] He presupposes, of course, as a first principle that no *real* conflict can arise between the two, our twin sources of truth. How does he proceed after that? The maxims he offers, drawn from common sense as well as being rooted in the philosophy and theology of the day, were to guide later Christian thought and would be echoed in Galileo's *Letter to the Grand Duchess* more than a thousand years later.

Early in the *De Genesi ad Litteram*, Augustine remarks:

> In matters that are obscure and far beyond our vision, even in such as we may find treated in Holy Scripture, different interpretations are sometimes possible without prejudice to the faith we have received. In such a case we should not rush in headlong and so firmly take our stand on one side that, if further progress in the search for truth (*diligentius discussa veritas*) justly undermines this position, we too fall with it. That would be to battle not for the teaching of Holy Scripture but for our own, wishing its teaching to conform to ours, whereas we ought to wish ours to conform to that of Holy Scripture.[71]

His advice might be summed up in the following principle:

Principle of Prudence (*PP*): When trying to discern the meaning of a difficult Scriptural passage, one should keep in mind that different interpretations of the text may be possible, and that, in consequence one should not rush into premature commitment to one of these, especially since further progress in the search for truth may later undermine this interpretation.[72]

Augustine relies here on two different prudential considerations. First, the Scriptures themselves, dealing as they do with "matters far beyond our vision," do not yield their proper (for him their "literal") sense readily. Furthermore, a deeper consideration of the question involved may well show a too-hastily adopted reading of Scripture to be in error, thus weakening the credibility of the Scriptures gene-rally. This last theme is one to which he often returns; his constant concern is to protect the Scriptures from challenge. He asks whether the heavenly bodies are guided by intelligences, as the philosophers suppose, and is cautious in reply. On matters such as these:

> we should always observe that restraint that is proper to a devout and serious person and on an obscure question entertain no rash belief. Otherwise, if the truth later appear (*quod postea veritas patefecerit*), we are likely to despise it because of our attachment to our error, even though this explanation may not be in any way opposed to the sacred writings...[73]

Notice that Augustine is stressing that progress in knowledge (he does not mention natural knowledge specifically) might force a reevaluation of the interpretation to be given to the scriptural text. In both passages quoted above, the presupposition is that the scriptural text is an obscure one, lending itself to different interpretations. Hence there is need for caution, lest "the truth later appear." But it might be that the fault lies, to begin with, in an overly hasty or overly dogmatic interpretation of Scripture:

Usually, even a non-Christian knows something about the earth, the heavens, and the other elements of this world, about the motion and orbit of the stars and even their sizes and relative positions, about the predictable eclipses of the sun and moon, the cycles of the years and the seasons, about the kinds of animals, shrubs, stones, and so forth, and this knowledge he holds to as being certain from reason and experience. Now it is a disgraceful and dangerous thing for an infidel to hear a Christian, presumably giving the meaning of Holy Scripture, talking nonsense on these topics, and we should take all means to prevent such an embarrassing situation, in which people show up vast ignorance in a Christian and laugh it to scorn. The shame is not so much that an ignorant individual is derided, but that people outside the household of the faith think our sacred writers held such opinions, and, to the great loss of those for whose salvation we toil, the writers of our Scripture are criticized and rejected as unlearned men. If they find a Christian mistaken in a field which they themselves know well and hear him maintaining foolish opinions about our books, how are they going to believe those books in matters concerning the resurrection of the dead, the hope of eternal life, and the kingdom of heaven, when they think their pages are full of falsehoods on facts which they themselves have learnt from experience and the light of reason?[74]

It is worth quoting this long passage in full (as does Galileo) in order to bring out how strongly Augustine felt about the dangers that apparent conflicts between Scripture and natural knowledge pose to the Christian community. For such conflicts to constitute a threat, however, it is clear that the claim to natural knowledge must qualify as "certain from reason and experience." This emphasis recurs over and over in his pages:

But someone may ask: "Is not Scripture opposed to those who hold that the heavens are spherical, when it says [of God] 'who stretches out the heavens like a skin'?" Let it be opposed indeed, if what they say is false. The truth is rather in what God reveals than in what groping men surmise (*humana infirmitas conicit*). But if they are able to establish their doctrine with proofs that cannot be denied (*si forte illud talibus illi documentis probare potuerint, ut dubitari inde non debeat*), we must show that this statement of Scripture is not opposed to the truth of their conclusions.[75]

And again:

Whatever they [the Manichaean critics of Scripture] could demonstrate about the nature of things by means of reliable evidence (*quidquid ipsi de natura rerum veracibus documentis demonstare potuerint*), we shall show not to be contrary to our Scripture. But when they produce from any of their books something contrary to Scripture, that is (*id est*), contrary to the Catholic faith, we shall either by some means or other show, or else without any shadow of doubt believe, that it is absolutely false.[76]

Two complementary principles seem to flow from passages such as these. The first is straightforward:

Principle of Priority of Demonstration (PPD): When there is a conflict between a proven truth about nature and a particular reading of Scripture, an alternative reading of Scripture must be sought.

I am using the term "demonstration" here in a broad sense to include any form of convincing proof and not just deductive proof from principles grasped as true in their own right (the technical Aristotelian sense of the term, to which Augustine does not confine himself). Augustine's emphasis is on the certainty that is needed for the claim to natural knowledge to count as a challenge to a Scripture reading. He uses phrases in this context such like "the facts of experience,"[77] "knowledge acquired by unassailable arguments or proved by the evidence of experience,"[78] and "proofs that cannot be denied" (above).

Augustine accepts the ability of our God-given powers of sense and reason to arrive at truth in our accounts of the natural world. Such truths cannot be in real conflict with Scripture, our other major source of truth. If there is an appearance of conflict, it can only be that an incorrect interpretation has been given of the scriptural passage in question. One would, therefore, be justified in such a case in departing from what appears at first sight to be the obvious sense of the passage and in adopting a metaphorical or other alternative sense instead, assuming that the sense that gives rise to the conflict cannot possibly have been what the original writer intended.

But now suppose that the claim to natural knowledge is something less than certain. What then? Augustine's constant emphasis on the certainty that is required of such a claim for it to constitute a warrant to search for an alternative reading of a scriptural text would seem to imply that in the absence of such certainty, the supposed challenge from natural knowledge no longer materializes. When interpreting the scriptural text that speaks of the heavens as being "suspended like a vault," for example, we would not (he says) want our inter-pretation to contradict the theory that the heavens are spherical, "provided only that this is proved (*si tamen probatur*)."[79] If it is *not* proved, it would, it seems, no longer carry decisive weight in the exe-getical discussion. There are overtones here of the traditional Greek distinction between knowledge (*epistêmê*) and opinion (*doxa*). But there is a more distinctively Augustinian flavor also.

When, for example, he is dealing with the objections raised by those who argue "from the relative weights of the elements" against the placement of waters above the firmament in *Genesis* I, his res-ponse is to give a highly speculative account of how such waters might well exist in the distant planetary regions in the form of ice. He concludes: "Whatever the nature of that water and whatever the manner of its being there, we must not doubt that it does exist in that place. The authority of Scripture in this matter is greater than all human ingenuity.[80] Or, again, when discussing the shape of the heavens in the passage quoted earlier, he asserts: "The truth is rather in what God reveals than in what groping men surmise."[81] When the claim to natural knowledge is a matter, then, only of "surmise," or "human ingenuity" (in other words, it lacks demonstration), the normal meaning of the scriptural text is to be given priority because of its greater dignity.

In Augustine's theory of knowledge, Divine illumination is the source of the intelligibility that enables the human reason to ren-der true judgment. In this perspective, the illumination that comes directly from God through the words of Scripture far outshines the mere products of human ingenuity. Surmise about the world of sense cannot be allowed any weight in a matter as grave as discerning the meaning of God's word. This points to a principle that is comple-mentary to PPD:

Principle of Priority of Scripture (PPS): Where there is an apparent conflict between a Scripture passage and an assertion about the nat-ural world grounded on sense or reason, the literal reading of the Scripture passage should prevail as long as the latter assertion lacks demonstration.[82]

When Augustine says things like "the truth is rather in what God reveals," he is laying aside a difficulty that he himself constantly stresses elsewhere, namely, that deciding just what God *has* revealed in a particular passage may be no easy matter. He is, effectively, assuming that the passage does have a straightforward literal meaning. Attributing priority to Scripture in the context of conflict with natural knowledge, therefore, is still open-ended. If the Scriptural passage lends itself to different interpretations, might not a well-supported (though not demonstrated) knowledge-claim make a difference in deciding on the proper interpretation? This will, of course, be the crucial issue when we come to the Copernican conflict. Note that PPS leaves open the possibility that the claim to natural knowledge might at a *later* time be demonstrated. It merely states that as long as this claim is *not* demonstrated, the literal reading of the scriptural text is to be maintained.

Two other exegetical principles can be found in Augustine's pages. Christian theologians long before his day were aware that in certain scriptural contexts, the normal sense of the terms used might have to be set aside. In speaking of God, the scriptural writers were forced to use human language of a Being for whom such language is clearly inadequate. God does not have a right hand, nor should God be understood to have literally walked in the Garden of Eden.[83] And the manner in which God brought about the creation of the world likewise transcends the capacities of literal language. Augustine does not hesitate, as we have already noted, to attribute to the "days" of Creation a purely metaphorical sense. In contexts such as these, he remarks: "Sacred Scripture in its customary style is speaking with the limitations of human language in addressing men of limited understanding."[84] Obviously, then, we must take into account a further principle:

Principle of Accomodation (PA): The choice of language in the scriptural writings is accommodated to the capacities of the intended audience.

There were two main reasons for admitting such a principle: 1) the inadequacies of human language in the face of realities that lie beyond normal human reach and 2) the inherent limitations of human powers of acquiring knowledge. Augustine mentions a context of particular interest to us where accommodation might be called for.

"We must hold," he says, "to the pronouncement of St. Paul that ... 'star differs from star in glory (brightness).' But, of course, one may reply, without attacking St. Paul, 'they differ in glory to the eyes of men on earth.'"[85] Though he prefers the literal alternative that the heavenly bodies differ from one another in *intrinsic* brightness (the Sun in the Creation narrative is described as the "greater" of the two lights), he admits that it would be acceptable to suppose that Paul is speaking according to the appearances only.

The accommodation here is to the limitations of the human visual perspective. The celestial phenomena are described *as they appear to us;* this form of accommodation is built into the very structure of our language. It would, thus, be unreasonable to insist on a literal reading in such a case: When we speak of the brightness of the heavenly bodies in an everyday context, it is their brightness as it appears to us that is meant. The relevance of this form of PA to the later Copernican conflict hardly needs emphasis. As it happens, Galileo misses this text.[86]

Augustine ends his discussion of this issue with a caution: "For us it is neither necessary nor fitting to engage in subtle speculation about the distances and magnitudes of the stars or to give to such an inquiry the time needed for matters weightier and more sublime." Elsewhere, he is even more explicit:

The sacred writers have omitted [discussing the shape of the heavens]. Such subjects are of no profit to those who seek beatitude, and what is worse, they take up precious time that ought to be given to what is spiritually beneficial. What concern is it of mine whether heaven is like a sphere and the earth is enclosed by it and suspended in the middle of the universe, or whether heaven, like a disk above the earth, covers it on one side? . . . I must say briefly that in the matter of the shape of the heaven, the sacred writers knew the truth but the Spirit of God, who spoke through them, did not wish to teach men such things as would be of no avail for their salvation.[87]

And again, in response to a question about whether the heavens move, given the scriptural use of the term, "firmament," Augustine replies that this usage "does not compel us to imagine a stationary heaven." Furthermore:

There is a great deal of subtle and learned inquiry into these questions for the purpose of arriving at a true view of the matter; but I have no further time to go into these questions and discuss them, nor should they have time whom I wish to see instructed for their salvation.[88]

What he seems to be saying here is that one should not expect to find in Scripture a technical treatment of the details of such sciences as astronomy. The concerns of Scripture and of the sciences are in the end quite different and must be held separate. The Scriptures are written for man's salvation, and astronomy simply does not bear on this.

It must be admitted that these texts are not addressed directly to the issue of how a particular Scriptural passage is to be interpreted, but to why a particular sort of topic has not been treated more explicitly in Scripture. Nonetheless, this way of handling the differences in aim between Scripture and natural science would lead one naturally to a more radical way of defusing tensions between them when they arise:

Principle of Limitation (PL): Since the primary concern of Scripture is with human salvation, texts of Scripture should not be taken to have a bearing on technical issues of natural science.

Augustine might have been reluctant to subscribe explicitly to so limiting a principle, were it to be directed to knowledge of nature in general and not just to technical issues of natural science. Over and over in his commentary on *Genesis* he takes the word of Scripture to carry weight on a wide diversity of issues involving natural knowledge, such as the placement of waters above the firmament. Still, he is obviously impatient with those who would look to Scripture for technical detail on astronomical matters "of no avail for salvation." It is not unreasonable, then, to discern a principle like PL not far from the surface as he struggles with the Manichaean challenge to the credibility of Scripture in the light of the natural knowledge of the day.

This was the first large-scale struggle of this sort, opposing the literal interpretation of specific scriptural texts to accepted natural knowledge. There would not be another until the Copernican controversy erupted more than a millennium later.[89] My use here of the term, "principle," might be challenged, since it could suggest a greater degree of deliberation on Augustine's part then was perhaps the case. The *Literal Meaning of Genesis* was not written as a treatise on the principles of exegesis. Nevertheless, the work does enable us to see what sorts of considerations Augustine relied on in dealing with the conflicts that propelled him to the writing of the commentary in the first place.

Though he does not argue in any detail for these "principles," it is not hard to imagine how he would have defended them, if pressed. PP and PA are no more than common sense, whereas PL follows from a general understanding of the role of Scripture in the life of the Christian. PPD and PPS, taken together, reflect a theory of knowledge that presupposes a sharp distinction between demonstration and anything short of demonstration, as well as a theory of scriptural interpretation that tends to give priority, in matters of dispute, to the literal sense of Scripture. PPS and PL are not explicit in Augustine's text but are suggested by comments he made while discussing the exegetical problems encountered in the texts under study.

Why devote so much space to Augustine in an essay on Galileo? Because later I will make two points: First, the exegetical positions laid out in the *Letter to the Grand Duchess* are already contained in germ in Augustine's work. Despite the claims made for it in recent Galileo scholarship, Galileo's contribution to exegesis was not especially novel. What distinguishes it is the forceful and effective way in which it is argued. That it should have appeared daring says more about the state of theological discourse in his time than about the novelty of its contents. My second point will be that a strain already latent in the Augustinian principles of exegesis reappears, but now with a troublesome consequence beginning to show, one that had far-reaching implications for the Copernican debate.

ON TO KEPLER

It will be instructive to take a brief look at Kepler's foray into biblical exegesis before going on to Galileo, in order to note some significant differences between the ways in which the two faced the problem of reconciling the Copernican system with the authority of Scripture. Kepler was the first major supporter of Copernicus after Copernicus's own day; at a time when his senior, Galileo, was still hesitant to commit to the Copernican cause,[90] Kepler was already building an elaborate theoretical astronomy around the Copernican system. But he had to face the objections from Scripture to this thesis that had already been widely voiced.

In his first work, the *Mysterium Cosmographicum* (1596), a reference to the exegetical issues raised by the Copernican doctrine had to be deleted from the manuscript sent for publication because of objections on the part of the authorities at the University of Tübingen. However, he prefaced his next work, the ground-breaking *Astronomia Nova* (1609), with a forthright treatment of the troublesome scriptural passages, arguing that they pose no real challenge to Copernicanism. These few pages were to attain a wider readership in the seventeenth century than anything else he wrote; they were usually bracketed with the *Letter to the Grand Duchess* from their first publication together in 1636.

His exegetical advice is a sensible combination of PA and PL, as he asks what the original writers would be likely to have intended by the texts under scrutiny. For example, they would surely have accommodated their language in the context of judgments of perception. And it was not their business to teach physics.

The Holy Scriptures, when treating common things, concerning which it is not their purpose to instruct humanity, speak with humans in the human manner in order to be understood by them.... No wonder, then, if Scripture also speaks in accordance with human perception when the truth of things is at odds with the senses....[91]

The psalmist "considered the Sun to move for the precise reason that it appears so to the eyes." When Joshua prayed for the Sun to stop, what he wanted was that it should "appear so to him, whatever the reality might meanwhile be." It would have been "quite inappropriate to think, at that moment, of astronomy and of visual errors."[92] Those who call upon Scripture to settle matters like this ought to "refrain from dragging the Holy Spirit into physics class." The supposed challenges to Copernicanism can be met if we but "turn our eyes from physics to the aims of Scripture." "You do not hear any physical dogma" when Ecclesiastes says that generations come and go, but "the earth stands forever." Rather, "the message is a moral one." Likewise, in Psalm 104, when the Earth is described as "founded on its stability," "nothing could be farther from the psalmist's intention than speculation about physical causes." Regarding other texts, the writer "does not wish to teach things of which men are ignorant"; he "is not writing as an astronomer"; he "tells us nothing that is not generally acknowledged, because his purpose was to praise things that are known, not to seek out the unknown."

Kepler does not cite any authorities, whether contemporary theologians or the early Fathers. Indeed, in a much-quoted passage, he even gently mocks those who do turn to "the opinions of the holy ones in matters of nature":

While in theology it is authority that carries the most weight, in philosophy it is reason. Therefore, Lactantius is holy who denied that the earth is round, Augustine is holy who, though admitting the roundness, denied the Antipodes, and the Holy Office nowadays is holy which, though allowing the earth's smallness, denies its motion. To me, however, the truth is more holy still, and (with all due respect to the Doctors of the Church) I prove philosophically not only that the earth is round, not only that it is inhabited all the way round at the Antipodes, not only that it is contemptibly small, but also that it is carried among the stars.[93]

Galileo could never have dared venture a passage like this. The authority of the Fathers, as we shall see, was one of the weapons most often turned against him.

Had Kepler wanted to quote a theologian, he might have turned to John Calvin who, though he never discussed the Copernican issue, was quite comfortable with both PA and a moderate version of PL:

The Holy Spirit had no intention to teach astronomy; and in proposing instruction meant to be common to the simplest and most uneducated persons, He made use by Moses and the other prophets of popular language, that none might shelter himself under the pretext of obscurity.... The Holy Spirit would rather speak childishly than unintelligibly to the humble and unlearned.[94]

Would he have agreed with Kepler's use of these principles to defuse the Copernican issue? That is impossible to say.[95]

What is most striking from our perspective about Kepler's way of resolving the scriptural objections is that there is no mention of PPD/PPS, no emphasis on the need for demonstration of the Copernican position, and no suggestion that the literal interpretation of the texts regarding Sun and Earth ought to have priority in the absence of demonstration on the side of the astronomers. Though he had early become convinced of the truth of the claims of the Copernican cosmology, he had (as we have seen above) a clear grasp of the hypothetical status of the individual arguments from effect to cause that the astronomer had to accumulate in order to arrive at such an assurance. As a mathematical astronomer, besides, he did not share the preoccupation with demostration that Galileo had absorbed from his early exposure to Aristotelian logic and natural philosophy. In his view, the astronomical texts in Scripture *obviously* ought not be taken literally, both because the writers would have accommodated their references to Sun and Earth to the understanding of their hearers (PA), and because teaching truths about nature was foreign to their aim (PL). His convictions in that regard would have made it seem irrelevant whether the Copernican view could be demonstrated or not. The Scriptures simply had nothing to say about the true states of motion of Sun and Earth.

GALILEO AS THEOLOGIAN

This brings us, finally, to Galileo's treatise on exegesis, the *Letter to the Grand Duchess*. The principles that make up the framework of the *Letter* will by now be familiar since they echo those already announced by Augustine in the *De Genesi ad Litteram*. However, Galileo works them out much more explicitly than Augustine had done and provides arguments, often very persuasive arguments, in their support. The same five principles reappear here. From the rhetorical standpoint, as we have already seen, the *Letter* is an exceedingly complex document. I shall lay aside much of the detail of the text to focus on the principles that propel the main argument. The aim of the *Letter* is simply to reassure his readers that there is no real conflict between the new Copernican doctrine and the Scriptures, properly understood.

In his *Letter to Castelli*, Galileo had, as we have seen, already given a response to the exegetical challenge he was facing because of the recourse of the beleaguered Aristotelians to the weapon of Scripture. The principles he enunciated there were those I have identified in Augustine's work as PP, PA, PL, and PPD. This was all before Galileo had turned for explicit support to Augustine. It is unlikely, to my mind, that he already knew at this time about the texts in the *De Genesi ad Litteram*; had he known, he would almost surely have called explicitly on Augustine in his support. It is not hard to see how he would have hit on PP, PA, and PL; they were pretty much what a thoughtful layman would have been likely to propose in disputes of the kind. And he could well have encountered PA and PL in the preface to Kepler's *Astronomia Nova*. It seems likely also that he would have already discussed these matters with Castelli and others better versed in theology than he, in the aftermath of the astronomical discoveries he had been making. PPD would have been the natural reaction of someone who took the Aristotelian emphasis on demonstration as seriously as Galileo did. Missing in the *Letter to Castelli* is any indication of the problematic Augustinian principle, PPS. More of that later.

Galileo opens the argument of the *Letter to the Grand Duchess* with a forceful statement and lengthy justification of the principle of accommodation (PA). The meaning of Scripture is frequently recondite; the authors are often forced to depart from the literal meaning of the words they use in order to convey a deeper truth. They attribute to God feet, eyes, and hands, human feelings like anger, and human conditions like forgetfulness, in order to accommodate themselves to the capacities of the unlearned, the "common people." This being so:

Who will categorically maintain that in speaking incidentally of the earth, water, sun, or other created thing, the Scripture has... chosen to limit itself rigorously to the literal and narrow meanings of the words. This would be especially implausible when mentioning features of these created things that are very remote from popular understanding and not at all pertinent to the primary purpose of the Holy Writ, that is, to the worship of God and the salvation of souls.[96]

The notion of accommodation presupposes a deliberate action on the part of authors who themselves know better. Galileo quotes the opinion of "the holiest and most learned Fathers," in a somewhat noncommittal way to the effect "that the writers of Holy Scripture not only did not pretend to teach us about the structure and motions of the heavens and the stars, and their shape, size, and distance, but that they deliberately refrained from doing so, even though they knew all these things very well."[97] In this case they *would* have been accommodating their writing to the capacities of their readers.[98] But, of course, for the theologians of Galileo's day, as we have seen, God is the principal author of the Bible, and thus the "accommodating" would ultimately be referred back to God's action in inspiring the human writer.

However, if it be allowed that the language of the Bible is accommodated in this way, a second, more far-reaching, principle suggests itself. In the text above, Galileo asserts that deep truths about the natural world are simply not "pertinent to the purposes of Holy Writ." What he is proposing here is, in essence, a *limitation* of the scope of scriptural authority; the Bible is simply not relevant to discussions about the nature of the physical world. For reasons that are rooted both in a proper understanding of the aims of Scripture and in a reflection on the human ability to arrive at demonstrative knowledge of the world revealed by the senses, he can conclude that the Bible ought not be assigned any special authority in regard to the nature of the physical phenomena alluded to in its pages:

In disputes about natural phenomena one must begin not with the authority of Scriptural passages but with sensory experience and necessary demonstrations. For the Holy Scripture and nature derive equally from the Godhead, the former as the dictation of the Holy Spirit and the latter as the most obedient executrix of God's orders. Moreover, to accommodate the understanding of the common people, it is appropriate for Scripture to say many things that are different (in appearance and in regard to the literal meaning of the words) from the absolute truth. On the other hand, nature is inexorable and immutable, never violates the terms of the laws imposed on her, and does not care whether or not her recondite reasons and ways of operating are disclosed to human capacities. But not every Scriptural assertion is bound to obligations as severe....[99]

Interpreting nature is thus, he suggests, more attuned to our knowing capacities than is interpreting Scripture. Consequently, claims to natural knowledge, provided they can be demonstrated, ought to be given precedence when the issue is one of understanding a scriptural text dealing with natural phenomena (PPD):

So it seems that a natural phenomenon which is placed before our eyes by sensory experience or proved by necessary demonstration should not be called into question, let alone condemned, on account of Scriptural passages whose words appear to have a different meaning.[100]

Or, more emphatically:

In questions about natural phenomena that do not involve articles of faith, one must first consider whether they are demonstrated with certainty or known by sensory experience, or whether it is possible to have such knowledge and demonstration. When one is in possession of this [demonstration], since it too is a gift from God, one must apply it to the investigation of the true meaning of Holy Writ at those places which apparently seem to read differently.[101]

Thus natural science can serve as an "appropriate aid to the correct interpretation of Scripture."[102]

However, the reverse is not the case. The Scriptures are not concerned with, or in the end relevant to, matters of natural science (PL):

The authority of Scripture aims chiefly at persuading men about those articles and propositions which, surpassing all human reason, could not be discovered by scientific research (*per altra scienza*) or by any other means than through the mouth of the Holy Spirit himself.[103]

The authority of Scripture is limited to those truths that are inaccessible to natural knowledge:

I do not think that one has to believe that the same God who has given us senses, language, and intellect would want to set aside the use of these and give us by other means the information we can acquire with them, so that we would deny our senses and reason even in the case of those physical conclusions which are placed before our eyes and intellect by our sensory experiences or necessary demonstrations.[104]

And he adds a second consideration in support of this version of PL:

This is especially implausible for those sciences discussed in Scripture to a very minor extent and in a disconnected way. Such is the case for astronomy, so little of which is contained therein that one does not find there even the names of the planets, except for the Sun, the moon, and only once or twice Venus....[105]

If the authors of Scripture had wanted to teach their readers some astronomy, they would surely have done something more systematic and more explicit.

Later he sums up his discussion of the passages we have already examined in Augustine:

We have seen that the Holy Spirit did not want to teach us whether heaven moves or stands still, nor whether its shape is spherical..., nor whether the earth is at its center or on one side. So it follows... that the Holy Spirit also did not intend to teach us about other questions of the same kind and connected to those just mentioned in such a way that without knowing the truth of the former one cannot decide about the latter, such as the question of the motion or rest of the earth or Sun. But if the Holy Spirit deliberately avoided teaching us such propositions, inasmuch as they are of no relevance to His intention (that is, to our salvation), how can one now say that to hold this rather than that proposition on this topic is so important that one is an article of faith and the other erroneous?[106]

Though Galileo is relying on Augustine here, he goes beyond his predecessor by presenting well-considered arguments in support of PL, some of which would almost surely have given Augustine pause. The reader is meant to be persuaded that mentions of natural phenomena in Scripture are accommodated to the capacity of the reader and, in any event, carry no particular authority as natural knowledge; the aims of those who composed the books of the Bible did not extend to natural science. PL, as we have defined it, applies only to issues bearing on natural science. A much broader principle of limitation would restrict the authority of the Bible to matters that bear specifically on human salvation and *only* to them.

Such a principle is, in fact, suggested by the quip that Galileo attributes to Cardinal Baronio: "The intention of the Holy Spirit is to teach us how to go to heaven, and not how the heavens go."[107] But this is obviously far more debatable.[108] It would, for example, have called into question Bellarmine's assertion that every historical detail in the Bible (that Abraham had two sons, for instance) is a matter of faith. Galileo was skeptical about this latter claim, as we have seen when discussing the notes he made for a response to Bellarmine's letter to Foscarini. He does hint several times at the more sweeping version of a limitation principle in the *Letter to the Grand Duchess*. However, he did not need it for his purposes; the arguments he gave work primarily for PL in the narrower sense, restricting its application to contexts where natural science is involved.

Interspersed in this discussion is a frequent reminder that the sort of natural knowledge Galileo has in mind has to be "demonstrated with certainty or known by sensory experience" (PPD). This leads to a recognition of the other major emphasis of the *Letter*: "Let us go back and examine the importance of necessary demonstrations in conclusions about natural phenomena."[109] In Galileo's eyes, only demonstration or direct sensory evidence carries weight in natural philosophy:

I should like to ask these very prudent [theologians] to agree to examine very diligently the difference between debatable and demonstrative doctrines. Keeping firmly in mind the compelling power of necessary deductions, they should come to see more clearly that it is not within the power of practitioners of demonstrative sciences to change opinion at will, choosing now this, now that one; that there is a great difference between giving orders to a mathematician or a philosopher and giving them to a merchant or a lawyer; and that demonstrated conclusions about natural and celestial phenomena cannot be changed with the same ease as opinions about what is or is not legitimate in a contract....[110]

It is the demonstrated character of natural knowledge that gives it weight, therefore, in scriptural exegesis (PPD). If the proper knowledge-claim is "debatable," this is no longer the case. Galileo's Aristotelian conviction that what distinguishes natural philosophy is its ability to *demonstrate* truths about nature suffuses the language of the *Letter*.[111] He shared this conviction with those for whom he was writing, the Roman theologians who had been schooled in the Aristotelian categories of the Thomist tradition. He quotes Pereira whose commentary on *Genesis* was well regarded in Rome:

One must take diligent care to completely avoid holding... anything which contradicts the decisive observations and reasons of philosophy; since all truths always agree with one another, the truth of Holy Scripture cannot be contrary to the true reasons and observations of human doctrines.[112]

And he adds a comment from Augustine's *Seventh Letter to Marcellinus* (taken almost certainly from Pereira):

If, against the most manifest and reliable testimony of reason, anything be set up claiming to have the authority of Holy Scripture, he who does this does it through a misapprehension of what he has read [in Scripture].

He concludes with a strong affirmation of the principle of priority of demonstration:

The true meaning of the sacred texts... will undoubtedly agree with those physical conclusions of which we are already certain and sure through clear observation and necessary demonstration.

But what if the claim to natural knowledge falls short of demonstration? Historians disagree as to how Galileo answers this vital question. A number of passages suggest that in such a case the literal sense of the scriptural passage should be given priority, thus acknowledging what we have earlier called the principle of priority of Scripture (PPS):

> Even in regard to those propositions which are not articles of faith, the authority of the same Holy Writ should have priority over the authority of any human writings containing pure narration or even probable reasons but no demonstrative proofs (*tutte le scritture umane, scritte non con metodo dimostrativo, ma o con pura narratione o anco con probabile ragione*). This principle should be considered appropriate and necessary inasmuch as divine wisdom surpasses all human judgment and speculation.[113]

This last sentence echoes Augustine's own reasoning in favor of PPS, and it seems a clear endorsement of the principle itself. Since, as we shall see more fully in a moment, there is an obvious tension between PPS and several of the other exegetical principles proposed by Galileo (notably PL and PP), those scholars who argue for the consistency of Galileo's exegetical approach to the disputed texts in Scripture are at some pains to deny that a version of PPS can be found anywhere in the *Letter*.

Commenting on the passage above, Fantoli argues that the "fundamental thesis" of the *Letter* is what he calls "the principle of the autonomy of scientific research."[114] Thus, Galileo cannot be supposed to "give the last word" to Scripture because this would imply that further scientific research on the disputed topic would have to be abandoned, thus belying his fundamental thesis. However, since this response *assumes* consistency, it runs the risk of begging the question. But more to the point, it draws attention to an ambiguity in the claim that priority is being given to Scripture. A *strong* version of PPS would assign priority to the literal sense of the disputed text once for all. But a weaker sense, the one I would take to be more plausible, would give priority to this sense only in the absence of a demonstration of the conflicting claim to natural knowledge. It does not rule out the possibility that such a demonstration might later be discovered.

Fantoli concedes that the text does appear to convey PPS in this weaker sense. But he argues that the emphasis ought not be put (as I am putting it here) on the distinction between demonstration and something short of demonstration but rather upon a contrast between "two altogether different sorts of 'human writings'," one written (as the text, literally translated, puts it[115]) "by a demonstrative method" (thus properly scientific in form), and the other not written in this way (and hence not properly scientific). The priority given to Scripture would therefore, only be in regard to rival *unscientific* claims, leaving the principle of (properly) scientific autonomy untouched.

This reading plays, however, on the ambiguity of the term "scientific." If it be construed in Aristotelian fashion to mean: yielding demonstration, then the principle of "scientific" autonomy would reduce to PPD; autonomy would *not* be conceded to probable argument (which can be "scientific" in the modern sense) where Scripture would still be given priority (PPS). If, in contrast, the term be construed in the modern sense, the principle of "scientific" autonomy cannot be unambiguously identified in the text.

Perhaps, however, "written with a demonstrative method" might be construed as meaning: yielding (or capable in principle of yielding) demonstration. This would not reduce to PPD; it would exempt claims to natural knowledge that might at a *later* time be demonstrated, from subjection to the priority of Scripture. Because such claims would until that time be no more than "probable" or "speculative," they would seem to be denied such exemption in the interim, according to the wording of the original passage.

In favor of such an exemption, however, a distinction of this general sort *is* drawn elsewhere:

Some physical propositions are of the type such that by any human speculation and reasoning one can attain only a probable opinion and a verisimilar [likely] conjecture about them, rather than a certain and demonstrated science; an example is whether the stars are animate. Others are of a type that either one has, or one may firmly believe that it is possible to have, complete certainty on the basis of experiments, long observations, and necessary demonstrations; examples are whether or not the earth and sun move and whether or not the earth is spherical. As for the first type, I have no doubt at all that, where human reason cannot reach, and where consequently one cannot have a science but only opinion and faith, it is appropriate to conform absolutely to the literal meaning of Scripture. In regard to the others, however, I should think as stated above, that it would be proper to ascertain the facts first, so that they could guide us in finding the true meaning of Scripture; this would be found to agree absolutely with demonstrated facts, even though *prima facie* the words would sound otherwise, since two truths can never contradict one another.[116]

This is a distinction that Aristotle would hardly have recognized; he had, after all, like most of his successors up to Galileo's day, believed that discussion of whether or not the motions of the planets were due to the action of immanent intelligences was a proper part of natural philosophy. One wonders whether Galileo was not creating this special category of reasoning about natural phenomena, one that could not in principle arrive at full certainty, as a device for allowing suitably limited scope to Augustine's PPS.

How would one know in a given case whether demonstration of the proposed thesis *could* be reached if this had not yet been achieved? Or, again, might it not turn out that the thesis is, in fact, false? Galileo's sanguine treatment of the category of the demonstrable-though-not-yet-demonstrated appears to assume that demonstration is just a matter of time in such a case. However, this interpretation is obviously open to question. And one would have to ask, in particular, why PPS should *not* apply in the interim to these possibly demonstrable, though not demonstrated, claims.[117] After all, their status could only be probable; they are still for the moment no more than "likely conjecture," the epistemic category that he allows must yield priority to Scripture.

There is one further passage that seems to give unequivocal support to a particularly strong version of PPS. Galileo quotes Pereira's paraphrase of one of the passages in Augustine that lends itself to a PPS interpretation:

In the learned books of worldly authors are contained some propositions about nature that are truly demonstrated and others that are simply taught. In regard to the former, the task of wise theologians is to show that they are not contrary to Holy Scripture; as for the latter (which are taught but not demonstrated with necessity), if they contain anything contrary to Holy Writ, then they must be considered indubitably false and must be demonstrated such by every possible means.[118]

This runs so clearly contrary to some of the other principles Galileo is advocating (notably PP) that commentators have tried to find ways to interpret the passage other than the literal one. Fantoli maintains that Galileo is "certainly aware" that the kinds of assertions that should be shown to be false are *only* those that are, in fact, contrary to the Catholic faith and not those, more generally, that merely seem to conflict with some passage in Scripture.[119] This would make the passage innocuous, though it would also shift the point it makes away from the interpretation of Scripture. But the qualifier "that is, contrary to the Catholic faith" is not in Augustine's text as Galileo reproduces it.[120]

Finocchiaro tries a different tack: the injunction to treat anything taught but not demonstrated as "indubitably false" if it contains anything contrary to Holy Scripture is addressed, he suggests, to "wise theologians," so it could have been intended simply as "a rule of interdisciplinary communication." A methodological directive of this sort is desirable because "the inadequacies of an idea can be discovered more easily by those who reject it."[121] This "ingenious but plausible rule" Finocchiaro takes to be the main conclusion of this part of the *Letter*. But, of course, in this form it does run directly counter to PP. And it appears in Galileo's text as a flat assertion ("must be considered false") rather than in the qualified mode appropriate to an "as if" directive.

In the end, it is difficult to know how best to interpret this enigmatic passage. Fantoli remarks that if Galileo had noticed a contradiction between the passage from Augustine and the principles he is defending elsewhere in the *Letter*, he would presumably not have quoted it.[122] Perhaps so. But these principles all find a precedent in Augustine's commentary, and Galileo might have simply decided to stay as close to his authoritative predecessor as possible. He may well have believed at this point that the Copernican theses were something more than propositions "taught but not demonstrated with necessity."

In the opening paragraphs of the *Letter*, he makes his own conviction of the truth of these theses abundantly clear. His critics are aware, he says that:

on the question of the constitution of the world's parts, I hold that the Sun is located at the center of the revolutions of the heavenly orbs and does not change place, and that the earth rotates on itself and moves around it. Moreover, they hear how I confirm this view not only by refuting Ptolemy's and Aristotle's arguments, but also by producing many for the other side, especially some pertaining to physical effects whose causes perhaps cannot be determined in any other way, and other astronomical ones dependent on many features of the new celestial discoveries; these discoveries clearly confute the Ptolemaic system, and they agree admirably with this other position and confirm it.[123]

Given this degree of confidence in the case he could make for the Copernican claim, it is understandable that he might have been inclined to let pass the dangerously strong wording of the passage from Augustine which, for other reasons, he wanted to draw on.[124] PPD should be enough of itself to carry the day in the debate over the interpretation of the troublesome Scripture passages. In the circumstances, he could afford to concede (or at least appear to concede) PPS, since it could not, if he were right, be invoked against him. If this *was* indeed his reasoning, it would turn out to be a serious miscalculation, prompted by overconfidence in the demonstrative force of the case he could present for the Copernican theses.

Despite a distinct lack of prudence on Galileo's part in this latter regard, he urges a principle of prudence (PP) on interpreters of Scripture and offers several considerations in its support.[125] He quotes a passage from Augustine that we have already seen[126] to the effect that scriptural texts are often ambiguous, so that one ought not rush to judgment in their regard. A second motive is more specific to the issue that was so crucial to the Copernican debate: What about propositions that are possibly demonstrable but not yet demonstrated?

It would be very prudent not to allow anyone to commit and in a way oblige Scriptural passages to have to maintain the truth of any physical conclusions whose contrary could ever be proved to us by the senses and demonstrative and necessary reasons. . . . Who is going to claim that everything in the world that is observable and knowable has already been seen and discovered? . . . One must not. . . block the freedom of philosophizing about things of the world and of nature as if they had all already been discovered and disclosed with certainty.[127]

The reference to the possibility of future discovery in the realm of natural knowledge is more explicit here than it had been in Augustine, reflecting Galileo's own confidence in that regard. Elsewhere, he remarks how particularly unwise it would be, in the context of the Copernican debate, to give premature assent on scriptural grounds to a geostatic doctrine when:

because of many new observations and because of many scholars' contributions to its study, one is discovering daily that Copernicus's position is truer
and truer and his doctrine firmer and firmer. So to prohibit Copernicus now,
after being permitted for so many years when he was less widely followed and
less well confirmed, would seem to me an encroachment on the truth and
an attempt to step up its concealment and suppression in proportion to how
much more it appears obvious and clear.[128]

Though he is recommending prudence here, his choice of language
("concealment," "suppression") is itself not entirely prudent in the
circumstances! But he had already given up on those who were using
Scripture against him, people who were "deficient in the intelligence
necessary first to understand and then to criticize the demonstrations" that the sciences make use of. Regarding the efforts of such
"superficial and vulgar writers," he urges: "It would perhaps be wise
and useful advice not to add without necessity to the articles pertaining to salvation and to the definition of the faith."[129]

Critics of the Copernican doctrine, such as Bellarmine, were making heavy use of an exegetical principle that, in the nature of things,
Augustine would have been unlikely to call on. This was the "consensus of the Fathers" in regard to the interpretation of particular
scriptural passages. Relying on the weight given such a consensus
by the Council of Trent, they urged an independent reason for maintaining the assertion that the Sun is in motion and the Earth at rest:
This was how these texts were understood by the Fathers of the
Church.[130]

Ought this, then, be recognized as an additional principle? Galileo
was insistent that limits had to be set upon it. The consensus of the
Fathers ought to carry weight only in regard to "those conclusions
which the Fathers discussed and inspected with great diligence and
debated both sides of the issue, and for which they all agree to reject
one side and accept the other."[131] This was quite obviously not the
case regarding the astronomical texts in dispute. Nothing can be
inferred from their silence in this matter. It was necessary, after all,
for the writers of Scripture to "accommodate popular understanding"
in such matters. Indeed, even if the motion of the Earth were now
to be demonstrated, popular ways of speech that have the Sun move
across the sky would be unlikely to change.[132]

A consensus on such ways of speech does not testify to truth. And the "consensus" of the Fathers that critics of Copernicanism are calling on is no more than a testimony to the popular usage of their own day. Somewhat daringly, Galileo takes on Bellarmine directly. The authority of the Fathers that was emphasized by the Council of Trent ought to be attributed only to "propositions that are articles of faith or involve morals."[133] And this is clearly not the case regarding the astronomical texts in question. The "holiest Fathers" knew better. Realizing how harmful it would be "to use Scriptural passages to establish conclusions about nature, when by means of observation and necessary demonstrations one could at some point demonstrate the contrary of what the words literally say," they, and among them most notably Augustine, counseled circumspection.[134]

REFLECTIONS ON CONSISTENCY

How are we to sum up Galileo's contributions to biblical exegesis? And to what extent did the principles he formulated influence the course of the Copernican debate that culminated in his own trial for suspicion of heresy in 1633? His exegetical principles were not in any sense novel, as he himself went out of his way to stress. They were all to be found in varying degrees of explicitness in Augustine's *De Genesi ad Litteram*, and, separately, they could call on the support of other earlier theologians.[135]

This is not to say that Galileo originally discovered these principles in Augustine or in other theological sources. The *Letter to Castelli* represents, as we saw earlier, his own first reaction to the way in which his Aristotelian opponents were calling on Scripture to defeat the Copernican challenge; there is no reference in that document to Augustine. Yet we find there four of the principles we first located in Augustine's work, as clearly enunciated as one could wish: PA ("in order to adapt itself to the understanding of all people..."), a strong version of PL ("the authority of Holy Writ has merely the aim of persuading men of those articles and propositions which are necessary for their salvation and surpass all human reason..."),[136] PP ("it would be prudent not to allow anyone to oblige scriptural passages to have to maintain the truth of any physical conclusions whose contrary could ever be proved to us by the senses and demonstrative and necessary reasons"), and finally PPD ("the task of wise interpreters is to strive to find the true meanings of Scriptural passages agreeing with those physical conclusions of which we are already certain and sure from clear sensory experience or from necessary demonstrations").[137]

Significantly there is no suggestion of PPS in that earlier document. Indeed, if anything, the opposite is true ("you see how disorderly is the procedure of those who in disputes about natural phenomena that do not directly involve the Faith give first place to Scriptural passages..."; "it seems to me that in disputes about natural phenomena, [Scripture] should be reserved to last place").[138] The clear implication is that the traces of *PPS* in the *Letter to the Grand Duchess* derive from Augustine, whom Galileo had in the meantime discovered to be an invaluable support, in every other way, of his own position.

Reference has already been made to tensions within the set of principles that Galileo introduces in the course of the *Letter*.[139] It should be clear by now that these tensions did not originate with him; they were implicit long before in Augustine's treatment of the same issues. Of course, Galileo might have avoided them, as Kepler did. But the intellectual backgrounds and rhetorical situations of the two men were altogether different. Given Galileo's early exposure to Aristotelian concepts and methodology and the theological and philosophical standpoints of those he had to persuade, it was, if not inevitable, at least very likely that the exegetical proposals he would lay out would reflect a latent inconsistency that had deep roots in the ancient exegetical tradition, at once Christian and Greek, an inconsistency that had had little practical effect up to this time but that would have significant implications for the Copernican debate.

I use terms like "tension" and "inconsistency" here rather than the more formal logical term "contradiction." The principles themselves are not expressed in formal fashion in the *Letter*. Galileo almost certainly did not think of them as a set of independent rules of interpretation whose mutual consistency would have to be carefully safeguarded.[140]

One of the Augustinian principles, PPS, assigning priority to Scripture where demonstration is lacking on the side of natural knowledge, appears to be implied in the *Letter* but there are, as we have seen, some reasons for hesitation in that regard. Readers, like Bellarmine, for whom PPS was already an exegetical guide, would hardly, however, be persuaded by anything in the *Letter* to relinquish this principle; they would more likely be led to believe that Galileo was allowing epistemic authority to the literal meaning of the biblical text in cases where an apparently conflicting assertion about nature could not summon in its support "sensory observation or necessary demonstration."

The source of the tension within the principles advocated in the *Letter* is easily stated.[141] On the one hand, several of the principles, notably PL and in context PA, imply that Scripture is simply not relevant to matters of natural science, since the biblical writers had something quite different in mind. And their choice of language in describing natural phenomena testifies only to the prevailing usage of the day and not to the underlying reality of the physical situation, particularly when this latter would involve technical issues that would baffle readers and distract them from the real function of the biblical discourse.

On the other hand, PPD emphasizes the importance of demonstration in regard to the relevant claim to natural knowledge. This is the source from which its claim to priority over the normal reading of the scriptural passage is taken to derive. It is not because Scripture is *irrelevant* to the scientific understanding of the natural phenomena involved but because scientist/philosophers can produce an irrefutable opposing claim on their own account. If PL (or, less obviously, PA) were to be the guide, however, it would not matter whether the claim to natural knowledge could be demonstrated or not. Even something well short of demonstration could carry a measure of conviction. Over and over again in the *Letter*, Galileo keeps insisting, effectively, on the *"si tamen probatur"* condition ("as long as it be proved") in regard to scientific claims; this is put forward as the reason why, in this case, the authority of the normal reading of Scripture should be set aside. But if PL is to be heeded, this cannot be the reason.

Might not PL and PPD be regarded as *independent* reasons for giving priority to natural knowledge in the appropriate cases?[142] No, because the practical consequences of the two are significantly different. If PPD be emphasized, the effort will be to find a way to *demonstrate* the claim to natural knowledge. If PL be the guide, this will not be of importance. One might say that if one were to be guided by PL, PPD would be redundant. But this could be misleading, as it might suggest that PPD is a simple consequence of PL.

And this is not the case. PPD conveys the impression that there is a need to achieve the level of demonstration in regard to "physical" propositions, whereas according to PL this is not the case.

The contrast between the two approaches, through PL and PPD, becomes sharper if one asks: What if demonstration is *not* achieved? From the PL standpoint, it does not matter: The Scriptures are not going to be relevant anyway to the scientific understanding of the phenomena in question. So whatever level of probability the natural philosopher can offer in that regard is the best that can be done for the moment in determining the truth of the claim being advanced. However, from the PPD side, the matter is quite different. It depends, of course, on whether a principle of the PPS type be adjoined as corollary, and what precise form it takes. Accepting such a principle inevitably makes it inconsistent with PL. That is, if priority is given to Scripture in the event of the claim to natural knowledge falling short epistemically, this would contravene the assertion made by PL that Scripture is simply not relevant to natural knowledge in the first place.

Drawing on our previous discussion of PPS, suppose we assign a special category to propositions that are "demonstrable though not yet demonstrated." The principle of prudence (PP) could then be applied to these; if there is a chance that they might at some later time be demonstrated, then the theologian should be wary of adopting a Scriptural interpretation that would conflict with them.[143] (Of course, PP would be redundant in such cases, if PL were to be our guide.) But this still leaves a large and mixed category of propositions that Galileo describes as "debatable," relying on "probable reasons," mounting only to "likely conjecture " or "opinion," and so on. Where *these*, at least, are concerned, Galileo most emphatically urges the priority of Scripture.[144] This, of course, would also contravene PL which would forbid assigning priority to Scripture in regard to natural phenomena generally.

What Galileo was trying to combine here, under the inspiration of Augustine's texts, were three themes that do not readily fit together: the irrelevance of problems about nature to the concerns of Scripture, the epistemically problematic character of propositions that are not known with certainty through "sense-observation or strict demonstration," and the claim that "divine wisdom surpasses all human judgment and speculation."[145] The combination of the second and third of these is almost bound to challenge the first one. One could attain consistency by relying on PL alone (with a judicious assist perhaps from PA), as did Kepler. But literalistically inclined theologians might have balked at this. After all, had not Bellarmine asserted that it would be heretical to deny anything that was "said by the Holy Spirit through the mouth of the prophets"? And the stilling of the Sun's motion was surely crucial, was it not, to the miracle in *Joshua*? The literal meaning of the text appeared obvious in this case. It would have seemed safer for the author of the *Letter* to rely on PPD, which no one would question. But then that brought with it a train of questions about how to treat propositions that had some degree of likelihood but lacked the cachet of demonstration.

One might, of course, also achieve consistency by relying on PPD and PP alone, leaving aside PL altogether. One would then assign priority to demonstrated propositions about nature and simply counsel prudent caution in regard to all others, withholding priority claims for Scripture but leaving open the possibility that Scripture might, in individual cases, carry a special warrant for its descriptions of natural phenomena. This would be consonant with the second and third of the themes above but not with the first (PL). Yet PL obviously appealed to Galileo because of its forthright simplicity and common-sense plausibility.

Part of the problem with the exegetical advice offered by the *Letter* is due to what in our eyes might seem a rather cavalier treatment on Galileo's part of the category of the probable.[146] The association of science with demonstration and the consequent characterization of anything short of science in that restricted sense as "opinion," "conjecture," "speculation," or "a matter of faith" conveys the unmistakable impression that he took less seriously than did many others of his contemporaries and immediate successors (Kepler, Boyle, Huygens) the merits of a well-supported hypothesis.[147]

Yet this impression could also be misleading where his actual practice was concerned, for he made extensive and skillful use of hypothetical reasoning in some parts of his own scientific work, notably in his discussions of such astrophysical issues as the natures of the lunar surface, of comets, of sunspots, and the like. In these contexts, it was clear that strict (*propter quid*) demonstration was unavailable, since the natures involved are not directly accessible. Galileo sought causal hypotheses that would best explain the phenomena under study, sometimes citing the optimistic principle that only one cause can properly account for a given effect.[148]

However, the dominant conception of science in his work in mechanics is always the demonstrative one.[149] His early success in formulating a purely kinematic law of falling bodies clearly encouraged him to suppose that demonstration of a broadly geometric sort was achievable in that domain at least, although he had, in fact, set aside entirely the causal issue as to the nature of gravity. And so his language remained that of the "sense observation and necessary demonstration" tradition that we have seen to be characteristic of the *Letter*. This in turn may have prompted him to draw the rather dubious distinction we have seen between physical propositions that are demonstrable and those that can only attain a degree of likelihood short of demonstration, treating the latter of these categories dismissively as no more than conjecture.[150]

He was, consequently, disposed to concede (or, at least, to appear to concede) the priority of Scripture, following Augustine's precedent, where full-scale demonstration was not available. The premium set on the criterion of certainty in assertions about the natural world was unmistakable. Had Galileo been less an Aristotelian in his manner of treating the requirements of natural knowledge, the exegetical advice offered by the *Letter* might perhaps have taken a simpler, and ultimately a more coherent, form.[151]

SIGNIFICANCE OF THE LETTER

Would this have made any difference to the events of 1616 and 1633? Might it have made less likely the condemnation of the *De Revolutionibus*? Would it have influenced the outcome of Galileo's trial? The answer in both cases is almost surely: no. The contents of the *Letter* were quite probably not known to the consultors (the "qualifiers") who took part in the deliberations of the Congregation of the Index in 1616. And once the decree of the Congregation was promulgated, the exegetical issues discussed in the *Letter* were, effectively, shunted aside; they were scarcely noticed, so far as the remaining record goes, in the negotiations between Galileo and his accusers in 1633. The die by then was cast; as far as the *Letter* was concerned, the worst had happened.

The historical significance of the *Letter* has to be sought elsewhere. The *Letter* conveys, better than any other document remaining to us, perhaps, the strains that existed within the principles of exegesis available in Galileo's day for the resolution of conflicts like the one occasioned by Copernican astronomy. Not everyone agrees, however, that the *Letter* exhibits any such strains. Widely different assessments have been offered by different writers.

The strongest challenge, perhaps, comes from Maurice Finocchiaro. He sets out to refute what he terms the "conventional interpretation" of the *Letter*, the one that claims to find some inconsistency between the exegetical principles the *Letter* professes.[152] Instead, he argues that the *Letter* "provides the philosophical theory of which the *Dialogue* is the scientific practice."[153] To show this, he proposes, first, to relate the principles I have called PPD, PL, and PP, in a single logical structure. Galileo, he says, takes PPD for granted ("conclusive proof of a physical truth is *sufficient* to force a non-literal interpretation of the Bible") as a principle with which no one would disagree. But then Galileo "goes on to argue that the reason why *this* principle holds is such as to justify also another more controversial but more relevant principle," that is, PL: "the Bible is not an authority in physical investigation but in matters of faith and morals." Then, Finocchiaro continues, "from this we get the novel principle that biblical statements should not be used to condemn physical conclusions which, though not yet conclusively proved, are capable of being conclusively proved," a prudential principle. Finally: "this novel principle justifies what Galileo does in the *Dialogue*, for all he needs is that the geokinetic thesis should be a proposition capable of being proved."[154]

However, Galileo at no time argues that the reason why PPD holds is such as to justify PL also. In a recent paper, Finocchiaro makes his point even more explicit:

The crucial step in the argument [of the *Letter*] is to ask for the rationale for... Augustine's traditional principle [PPD]: what is the reason why conclusively proved physical truths are (traditionally and uncontroversially) given precedence over conflicting biblical assertions? Baronio's principle [i.e., PL, in its strongest version] gives the answer, and provides the rationale. That is, Baronio's principle explains why Augustine's principle is correct, and this explanation in turn justifies the former's plausibility.[155]

However, PL is not, and could not be, offered either as justification or as explanation for PPD. The latter, according to both Augustine and Galileo, stands in its own right. It is something, as Finocchiaro himself remarks, that is taken for granted. The appropriate testimony of truth in natural philosophy is quite obviously in their eyes "sense experience or necessary demonstration." And two truths cannot contradict. Besides, PL would be far less persuasive in the eyes of the intended readership of the *Letter* than would PPD. (Using Finocchiaro's labels, Augustine would carry much more weight than Baronio!) Most important of all, PL would offer no reason why demonstration *should* be demanded or why demonstration should be thought significant in this context in the first place. The intellectual sources of PPD and PL are ultimately quite different; one of them lies in a philosophical analysis of how truths about nature are to be properly certified and the other in a theological analysis of the aims of Scripture.

Furthermore, PP is not, as we have seen, a novel principle, nor is it derived (either by Augustine or by Galileo) from PL. Indeed, were PL to be insisted on, PP would strictly speaking become redundant. It is hardly correct to describe PP as the "central conclusion" of the *Letter*;[156] this might perhaps be true for a modern reader who is looking at the logical structure of the *Letter* from the perspective of the Copernican debate, but in the rhetoric of the *Letter* as Galileo wrote it, PPD (which Finocchiaro elsewhere describes in fact as the "key premise" of the *Letter*[157]) gets greater emphasis.

Finally, PP does not "justify" what Galileo does in the *Dialogue*. The promulgation of the decree of 1616 superseded PP in the most emphatic way. PP is a principle of *prudence*, not an epistemic principle. Once the Copernican doctrine had been declared to be "contrary to Scripture," it would have been the opposite of prudent to claim it to be demonstrable, though not yet demonstrated.

This leads to Finocchiaro's second major claim, which is that the *Letter* could serve as a defense of Galileo against the charge for which he was condemned in 1633, namely, of holding and defending "as probable an opinion... contrary to Holy Scripture." The *Letter* would (Finocchiaro argues) justify the course Galileo followed in the *Dialogue* on the grounds that "such probable reasoning is a necessary prerequisite for arriving at conclusively demonstrated physical conclusions."[158] Since he had, then, a valid defense against the charge laid against him, the implication is clear: He should not have been found guilty on the grounds cited in the trial sentence.[159]

This is a very far-reaching resolution of a question that has been debated over many years regarding the outcome of the Galileo trial. I do not propose to enter into the details of this convoluted issue here, except insofar as they bear on the principles enunciated in the *Letter*. These principles simply cannot be used in this way to defend the propriety, from the standpoint of those who accepted the authority of the decree of 1616, of defending a doctrine that had been *declared* to be contrary to Scripture.

The principle defended by Galileo (PP) was not (as Finocchiaro defines it) that "physical propositions capable of conclusive demonstration should not be condemned even if they conflict with the Bible."[160] It was, rather, that they should not be condemned if they *appear* to conflict with the Bible, that is, with the literal meaning of the scriptural text. Nothing in Galileo's argument for what is, after all, presented as a prudential principle, would suggest that it would be legitimate to defend a proposition that *actually* conflicted with the Bible.[161] It is because *apparent* conflict may not be real that PP can be allowed as a principle counseling caution. The formal notification that Bellarmine gave to Galileo in 1616 was that he should not "defend or hold" the Copernican theses.[162] There could be no doubt that the *Dialogue* did defend them,[163] and thus that, technically, Galileo had violated Bellarmine's admonition, which was no more than was already implied by the decree itself. None of the arguments of the *Letter* could have prevailed against this clear consideration.[164]

Though the implications of the *Letter* for the 1616 decree and for the decision as to how the argument of the *Dialogue* should be presented are not perhaps as dramatic as those we have just been examining, they are nonetheless significant. The consultors who were asked to adjudicate on the theological orthodoxy of the Copernican claims in 1616 were in no doubt about their answer, which took them only a few days to formulate. Their first finding, significantly, was: "all said that the [heliostatic] proposition is foolish and absurd in philosophy."[165] Thus, before going on to find this proposition to be contrary to Holy Scripture (and therefore in their eyes "formally heretical"), they first declared it to be false from the perspective of natural science. There could thus be no question of invoking PPD in its favor, a principle that they (like Bellarmine) would certainly have accepted. PL they very probably would have questioned.

The consultors would have been open to the idea that the writers of Scripture accommodated their texts to their readers in some contexts (PA), but they would very likely have denied that assertions about the Earth's motion or the Sun's rest would qualify under this heading. The prudence counseled by PP they clearly deemed unnecessary. If the heliostatic claim *could* never be demonstrated (and we have seen that this was almost certainly Bellarmine's view), there was no need to be cautious about condemning this claim on the grounds of its conflict with Scripture, literally understood. They were thus, effectively, guided by PPS and by a second principle that Galileo had argued ought not be applied to the Copernican issue, namely, the invocation of the consensus of the Fathers.

What made all the difference here, I suspect, was the conviction on the part of these theologian–consultors, most of them Dominicans schooled in Aristotelian natural philosophy, that there was no shadow of a case for interpreting Copernican astronomy in a realistic manner. The successes of that astronomy would have been seen only as a testimony to its value as an effective way to save the phenomena, just as Ptolemy's astronomy had done for so many centuries. It gave no reason to suppose that the Earth *really* went around the Sun. The consultors almost certainly were not familiar with the detail of the Copernican arguments, the arguments based on the phases of Venus, for example. But it would have availed little to bring these up, if the best that could be achieved by means of such arguments was to show that the Copernican astronomy was superior to that of Ptolemy in the practical order. The entire weight of Aristotle's physics could be thrown against any attempt to take heliocentric astronomy in any other way.

The principle on which Galileo leant so heavily in the *Letter*, PPD, never had a chance in the eyes of his Roman critics of vindicating the Copernican theses. They would indeed have been happy to cite Galileo's own insistence on the testimony of "sense experience or necessary demonstration" as warrant for their verdict against these same theses. Lacking such testimony (and, once again, Bellarmine's *Letter to Foscarini* gives a strong indication of how their deliberations would have been likely to proceed in that regard), they would have felt entirely justified in proceeding as they did. Even if Galileo had followed Kepler's example and relied on PL and PA alone, leaving aside all mention of the need for demonstration, and even if his *Letter* had been laid before the consultors as a formal brief for the Copernican side, it is unlikely that the outcome would have been any different. PPD was too ingrained as a guide to situations where conflict loomed between Scripture and natural knowledge, and PL would assuredly have seemed too radical, given the literalist climate of Roman theological opinion at the time.[166] And the references in the Bible to the Sun's motion and the Earth's stability could have seemed too closely tied to theological points the biblical texts were making for PA to come into play.

The effect of the decree of 1616 was, therefore, to repudiate much of the exegetical argument of Galileo's *Letter*. And Bellarmine was deputed to make it clear to Galileo that the decision of the Holy Office was such as to exclude further defense of the Copernican position on his part. When, seven years later, Galileo was sufficiently encouraged by the accession of Maffeo Barberini to the papal throne as Pope Urban VIII to renew his efforts in support of the Copernican cause, the work he planned would leave exegesis entirely aside to focus exclusively on the scientific merits of the case. But there would still be one echo of the *Letter to the Grand Duchess*. What sort of epistemic status should he seek for the Copernican argument?

The decree of 1616 and Bellarmine's warning made any sort of public defense of the proscribed view risky. Urban had licensed some sort of "hypothetical" treatment of the arguments, so long as Galileo kept in mind that demonstration was excluded, on both philosophical and theological grounds. But if demonstration was thus formally excluded, how was the case for Copernicus to be made against those who would bring Scripture once more against the Copernican assertion of the Earth's motion? Galileo would not have forgotten PPD; he had made that Augustinian principle his own. Furthermore, if demonstration were to be barred and if "probable reasons" were the best that could be found, would this not automatically sanction the application of PPS to enforce the priority of Scripture?

As Galileo labored to find an acceptable way to present the Copernican case, he found himself therefore in what seems, in retrospect at least, an almost hopeless rhetorical predicament. No wonder, then, that this should be reflected in the argument of the *Dialogue* itself. Was he or was he not claiming to demonstrate the Earth's motions?

Commentators have long disagreed as to how to respond. There is, indeed, ample evidence on both sides. He would clearly have *liked* to claim the status of demonstration for the Copernican theses, but he equally clearly hesitated to do so, as his choice of the dialogue format for the argument would have implicitly conveyed. On one side, he was surely aware at this point that his arguments did not amount to demonstration of the Copernican world system. And he just as surely must have been continually conscious of the warnings given him by Bellarmine and Urban against claiming demonstration. On the other side, readers of the *Letter to the Grand Duchess* would hardly miss the exegetical moral: Nothing *less* then the certainty afforded by "sense experience or necessary demonstration" would serve to validate a claim to natural knowledge that conflicted with the plain literal meaning of a biblical text. Galileo could not claim demonstration, but in its absence his defense of the Copernican doctrine would not persuade his critics who would appeal to PPD and question PL. To modern eyes, at least, it would seem that the author of the *Letter* had left himself no way out when he came to compose the *Dialogue on Two Chief World Systems*.

Could he have done otherwise? He was writing for an audience schooled in the intellectual traditions of Aristotle and Augustine. He could hardly, in the circumstances, have avoided including PPD in his list of proposed exegetical principles. But once this principle be admitted, the task of defending the Copernican theses, the task he set out to accomplish in the *Dialogue*, becomes difficult, if not impossible, of accomplishment. The onus would now be on him, as Bellarmine had long ago said, to produce a demonstration. And this he did not have. Nor in the aftermath of 1616, would he have been permitted to make public such a demonstration were he to have one. The *Letter* reflected all too well an intellectual predicament Galileo had neither created nor, in the end, had the means to resolve.

NOTES

1 An earlier version of this essay was delivered under the title "Galileo as a theologian" as the annual Fremantle Lecture at Balliol College, Oxford, in 1983. I am indebted to a good many Galileo scholars for our

discussions of the topics treated here, notably the late Stillman Drake who communicated some of his own enthusiasm for Galileo studies to me in the early 1960s, Richard Blackwell whose compilation of source material in his *Galileo, Bellarmine and the Bible* (Notre Dame, University of Notre Dame Press, 1991) I have found invaluable, and the late Olaf Pedersen, whose judicious assessment of the historical details of this complex story I long ago came to rely on. I am particularly grateful to Annibale Fantoli for his helpful comments on an earlier draft of this essay.

2 Bertolt Brecht, *Galileo*, adaptation by Charles Laughton, New York: Grove Weidenfeld, 1966, pp. 72–3.

3 Alexandre Koyré suggests a different link between cosmology and the Church's reaction at this time. Giordano Bruno is "the occult but real cause of the condemnation of both Copernicus and Galileo" because he connected the doctrine of the plurality of worlds with Copernicanism in people's minds (*Galileo Studies*, transl. J. Mepham, Atlantic Highlands, NJ: Humanities, 1978, p. 136). Lacking, as we do, the records of the Bruno trial, it is difficult to determine how significant a role Copernican doctrine played in his condemnation by the Roman Inquisition. Dorothy Yates claimed that the role was, at most, a minor one since graver charges regarding the theology of the Eucharist, for example, clearly took precedence (*Giordano Bruno and the Hermetic Tradition*, Chicago: University of Chicago Press, 1964). But Luigi Firpo, on the basis of a broader documentation, has recently emphasized that Bruno's (broadly) Copernican views regarding the motion of the earth and the immobility of the sun did draw criticism from his judges on the grounds that they clashed with specific passages in Scripture (*Il Processo di Giordano Bruno*, Rome: Salerno, 1993). Though the principal charges against Bruno clearly had nothing to do with natural science, there can be no doubt that his trial had already drawn the hostile attention of Roman theologians to Copernican cosmology more than a decade before Galileo first turned his telescope to the skies.

4 Maurice A. Finocchiaro, ed. and transl., *The Galileo Affair* (hereafter *GA*), Berkeley: University of California Press, 1989, p. 146; Sergio Pagano, *I Documenti del Processo di Galileo Galilei*, Vatican City: Pontifical Academy of Sciences, 1984, p. 99.

5 This phrase was not repeated in the official decree of the Congregation of the Index issued two weeks later which said only that the suspect doctrine was "altogether contrary to Holy Scripture"; Finocchiaro, *GA*, p. 149; Pagano, *Processo*, p. 103.

6 Appendix I to Blackwell, *Galileo, Bellarmine, and the Bible* (hereafter *GBB*), p. 183. For a discussion of the link between the Tridentine decree

and the sequence of events leading to the condemnation of Copernicus's book in 1616, see Olaf Pedersen, *Galileo and the Council of Trent*, vol. I, no. 1, in *Studi Galileiani*, Vatican City: Vatican Observatory Publications, 1991.

7 *De theologicis locis*, 2.17. Quoted in Bruce Vawter, *Biblical Inspiration*, Philadelphia: Westminster, 1972, p. 59. A similar view may be found in another Dominican work of the same decade, Domingo Bañez's commentary on the *Summa Theologica* of Thomas Aquinas (Rome, 1584; Venice, 1591): "The Holy Spirit not only inspired all that is contained in the Scripture, he also dictated and suggested every word with which it was written." And to make his meaning doubly clear, he adds: "To dictate means to determine the very words" (I, q. 1, a. 8, *dub.* 3 and conclusion; Vawter, p. 60). Historians of exegesis are divided whether to take assertions such as these at face value, given the complexities of the Thomist doctrine of God's customary action on the human will. But Bañez seems to go out of his way in the remainder of the passage cited to make his commitment to a literal notion of dictation quite explicit. See Richard F. Smith, "Inspiration and inerrancy," in *The Jerome Biblical Commentary*, ed. Raymond E. Brown *et al.*, Englewood Cliffs: Prentice-Hall, NJ, 1968, 2, 499–514; p. 505.

8 Letter to Castelli, *Le Opere di Galileo Galilei*, Edizione nationale (hereafter EN), ed. Antonio Favaro, Firenze: Barbera, V, 285; *GA*, p. 52.

9 These are sometimes called the two "trials" of Galileo, though the first was not a trial in the strict sentence, nor was Galileo mentioned in the resulting Index decree of 1616. He was, however, to be privately enjoined by Bellarmine to abandon the "Copernican opinions."

10 For a more detailed chronicle, see Annibale Fantoli, *Galileo: For Copernicanism and for the Church*, Rome: Vatican Observatory, and Notre Dame: University of Notre Dame Press, second revised edition, 1996, Chapter 3. I have found Fantoli's work a treasurehouse. See also Blackwell, *GBB*, chapter 3.

11 EN XIX, 323; *GA*, p. 149. The decree was issued by the Congregation of the Index but promulgated under the authority of the Congregation of the Holy Office, the supreme doctrinal body of the Church under the Pope, of which the Congregation of the Index was, effectively, a subcommittee.

12 *Joshua*, 10, 12–13.

13 Castelli to Galileo, December 14, 1613, EN XI, 605–6; *GA*, p. 47.

14 Galileo to Castelli, December 21, 1613, EN V, 282; *GA*, p. 49.

15 Letter to Castelli, EN V, 284; *GA*, p. 51.

16 He repeats, and enlarges on, this argument in the *Letter to the Grand Duchess*; he was obviously proud of it. Some commentators have

claimed that it was inconsistent on his part to make use of Scripture here to support the Copernican claim, given his criticism of his Aristotelian opponents for calling on Scripture in support of *their* world-view. But this is to misunderstand Galileo's rhetorical point. He is merely arguing that *if* one wishes to interpret the scriptural texts literally (as his Aristotelian opponents claim they want to do), then this would favor the Copernican world-view, not the Aristotelian one. This was a perfectly fair argument. It does *not* mean that he would himself favor this use of Scripture in support of a scientific theory.

17 He objected only to some turns of phrase in the copy of the *Letter* originally submitted to the Holy Office which do not appear in the version that Galileo later forwarded to Dini. The usual explanation of this discrepancy, one strongly hinted at in Galileo's covering letter to Dini (*EN*, V, 291–2; *GA*, p. 55), is that someone, probably Niccolò Lorini, Galileo's Dominican critic who was responsible for sending the *Letter* to Rome in the first place, had tampered with the text out of ill will towards Galileo (see, for example, Blackwell, *GBB*, pp. 196–7). Against this, however, Mauro Pesce has recently argued that Lorini's copy was, in fact, a fair copy of the original and that Galileo, knowing that the *Letter* was under scrutiny in Rome, prudently deleted some of the expressions most likely to give offence before sending the "correct version" to Dini ("Le redazione originali della Lettera Copernicana di G. Galilei a B. Castelli," *Filologia e Critica*, 17, 1992, 394–417). Fantoli leans to this latter view; see *Galileo*, pp. 177, 240–1.

18 Cesi to Galileo, January 12 1615, EN XII, 129–31; Fantoli, *Galileo*, pp. 175–6. R. S. Westfall thinks this note especially significant in indicating that the original moving force in the process that led to the banning of Copernicus's book was Bellarmine (*Essays on the Trial of Galileo*, Vatican City: Vatican Observatory Publications/Notre Dame: University of Notre Dame Press, 1989, Chapter 1). Fantoli, however, discounts the significance of Cesi's note in this regard, arguing that if Bellarmine had really believed that the Copernican doctrine was heretical, he would hardly have consented to the more moderate wording of the Index decree of 1616. (*Galileo*, pp. 241–2). I am not convinced by this latter argument, for reasons that will become clear later. Bellarmine undoubtedly had a hand in shaping the course of events, particularly the form taken by the 1616 decree, which banned the work of Foscarini outright, never mentioned Galileo, and permitted the work of Copernicus to remain in circulation as long as it was made clear that it was only aimed at saving the appearances. This was just what, as we shall see, one would have expected Bellarmine to advise. But I think it unlikely that Bellarmine wanted the matter to come to a head

as it did in so public a way in 1616; the indications are that although he would have preferred negotiation, overt action was forced on him. Fantoli himself sums up the evidence as indicating that "Bellarmine was one of the principal personages, though certainly not the only one, responsible for the decision of 1616" (p. 233).

19 Dini to Galileo, March 7, 1615, EN XII, 151-2; *GA*, p. 58.

20 Karl Popper was thus wrong to describe Bellarmine as a "founding father" of the instrumentalism Popper criticizes in "Three views concerning human knowledge" (*Conjectures and Refutations*, New York: Basic Books, 1962, p. 68). Pierre Duhem long ago drew attention to the tension between "mathematical" and "physical" astronomy during this early period (*To Save the Phenomena*, transl. E. Dolan and C. Maschler, Chicago: University of Chicago Press, 1969). His account has been challenged by some for imposing a modern brand of instrumentalism on many of the authors in the "mathematical" tradition; see G. E. R. Lloyd, "Saving the appearances," *Classical Quarterly*, 28, 1978, 202-22. It should be emphasized that the "instrumentalist" interpretation of mathematical astronomy found in the works of such medieval philosophers as Thomas Aquinas was confined to astronomy only; the arguments in its support would not have applied to other parts of natural philosophy, notably not to physics, where Aquinas and after him the entire Thomist tradition were resolutely realist (Thomas Litt, *Les Corps Célestes dans l'Univers de St. Thomas d'Aquin*, Louvain: Publications Universitaires, 1963; E. McMullin, "The goals of natural science," *Proceedings of the American Philosophical Association*, 58, 1984, 27-58). Though Bellarmine's views on mathematical astronomy were undoubtedly instrumentalist, he could hardly be described as an instrumentalist in the modern sense since his approach to natural science generally was unquestioningly realist (E. McMullin, "Robert Bellarmine," *Dictionary of Scientific Biography*, ed. Charles Gillispie, New York: Scribner, 1970, vol. 1, 587-90).

21 See Ugo Baldini and George Coyne, *The Louvain Lectures of Bellarmine*, Vatican City: Vatican Observatory Publications, 1984. I am indebted to Dr. Baldini for our discussion of Bellarmine's key role in the events of 1614-1616. See also Bellarmine's own *De Ascensione Mentis in Deum* written in 1614, just as the Copernican controversy was about to spread from Florence to Rome (English translation: *The Mind's Ascent to God by the Ladder of Created Things to God*, in *Robert Bellarmine: Spiritual Writings*, transl. J. P. Donnelly and R. J. Teske, New York: Paulist Press, 1989). Step 7 ("The consideration of the Heavens, the Sun, the Moon, and the Stars," pp. 119-30) is especially revealing. The cosmology it describes draws heavily from the Old

Testament, notably the Psalms. The motion of the Sun is particularly emphasized: the Sun runs "tirelessly and extremely fast," and "covers an immense space in a short time" (pp. 120–1). Regarding the nature of the stars: "we are not seeking opinions," as he describes the views of the philosophers, "but certain knowledge or the teaching of the faith" (p. 125).

22 Galileo to Dini, March 23, 1615, EN V, 299–300; *GA*, p. 60.

23 *GA*, pp. 61–2.

24 Galileo to Dini, *GA*, p. 63; emphasis added.

25 Ciampoli to Galileo, February 28, 1615, EN XII, 145–7; Fantoli, *Galileo*, pp. 179–80.

26 There is evidence from the text of the *Dialogo* itself that the main source of Urban's restriction was the principle that had animated the nominalist challenge to the Aristotelian ideal of demonstration in the fourteenth century: that claims to necessity in demonstration in natural philosophy would unduly constrain the power of God. The fateful argument that Galileo put in the mouth of Simplicio in the closing lines of the *Dialogo* is implicitly attributed to Urban, and it suggests that the reason that the tidal argument cannot *demonstrate* the Copernican thesis is that since one is inferring from observed effect (the tidal motions) to an unobserved cause (the earth's double motion), it has to be admitted that God could, in principle, bring about this effect equally well by some other (unobserved) cause. (The argument has an interesting affinity with the "underdetermination" argument in recent philosophy of science. Theories are said to be "underdetermined" by the data brought in their support, since there will ordinarily be more than one theoretical explanation for a given set of observed effects.) Urban's argument would thus exclude strict demonstration in natural philosophy on purely theological grounds. It should be noted that calling the Copernican proposal a "hypothesis" on these grounds could still allow it some degree of likelihood as a truth-claim, unlike the "hypotheses" of mathematical astronomy in Bellarmine's instrumentalist interpretation.

Cardinal Agostino Oregio mentions in his *De Deo Uno* (Rome, 1629) that Urban had argued around 1615 with a "very learned man" (quite probably Galileo) that since God, being omnipotent, might have arranged earth, sun, planets, and their motions differently, there can be no question of asserting the *necessity* of the present configuration. Copernicans cannot, then, claim to demonstrate their theory; they can at best only claim to save the phenomena (A. Favaro, *Oppositore di Galileo: Maffeo Barberini*, Venice, 1921, p. 27; quoted by Rivka Feldhay, *Galileo and the Church: Political Inquisition or Critical Dialogue*, Cambridge: Cambridge University Press, 1995, p. 209). This is not the same argument as the one that appears in the *Dialogo*, though its conclusion is the same.

It is conceivable, therefore, that Urban had several different objections in mind to the claim that the Copernican proposal could be demonstrated. Niccoló Riccardi, the Dominican Master of the Sacred Palace, whose task as censor was to decide whether or not to allow the printing of the *Dialogo*, may have conflated the several sorts of reservation when reporting on the Pope's intentions in regard to the work, in a letter of May 24, 1631, to the Inquisitor of Florence, Clemente Egidi, to whom he was entrusting the responsibility for giving the *Dialogo* a final *Imprimatur*. He reminds Egidi that the Pope desires the focus of the work not to be on the tidal argument (which Galileo regarded as the best hope for demonstration of the Copernican theses):

> but absolutely on the mathematical examination of the Copernican position on the earth's motion, with the aim of proving that, if we remove divine revelation and sacred doctrine, the appearances could be saved with this supposition; one would thus be answering all the contrary indications which may be put forth by experience and by Peripatetic philosophy, so that one would never be admitting the absolute truth of this opinion, but only its hypothetical truth without the benefit of Scripture. (*EN XIX*, 327; *GA*, p. 212).

The first part of this reminder suggests that Urban wishes Galileo to treat the Copernican hypothesis in instrumentalist terms, merely as a means of saving the phenomena; the second part appears to allow that this could also serve to answer the Aristotelian physical objections, thus granting the Copernican claim a measure of physical likelihood. Riccardi describes without demur the *Dialogo* as discussing the Copernican system "in probable fashion." It makes a considerable difference what sort of "hypothesis" Urban had in mind when it comes to assessing whether the *Dialogo* violated the mandate laid by him on its author. This long parenthetical note carries the story well beyond the cut-off date of 1616 at which our formal narrative ends. It is needed, however, in order to bring out the significance of the discussions of "hypothesis" at the earlier stage of the affair.

27 It was written in the form of a lengthy letter to the General of the Carmelite order. For a translation, see Blackwell, *GBB*, pp. 217–51.

28 *Ibid.*, pp. 228, 233.

29 *Ibid.*, p. 241.

30 *Ibid.*, p. 223.

31 Bellarmine to Foscarini, April 12, 1615, EN XII, 171–2; *GA*, pp. 67–9.

32 *GA*, p. 67.

33 The Council specified that the books of the Bible "in all their parts" are to be regarded as "sacred and canonical" (Blackwell, *GBB*, p. 182).

No further specification of this last provision was given; later theologians would fill it out in very different ways. As late as the nineteenth century, a passionate controversy followed Cardinal Newman's suggestion that *obiter dicta*, such as a reference to Abraham's two sons, ought not be supposed to carry with them the authority (and hence the inerrancy) of Scripture. For a review, see Raymond F. Collins, "Inspiration," *The New Jerome Biblical Commentary*, ed. Raymond Brown *et al.*, Englewood Cliffs, NJ: Prentice-Hall, 1990, 1023–33.

34 *Ibid.*, p. 68.

35 Fantoli, *Galileo*, pp. 185–8. Fantoli thinks that characterizing as "heretical" any departure from the literal sense of such claims as that Abraham had two sons would foreclose any discussion of taking texts about the Sun's motion or Earth's rest nonliterally. But as Galileo himself would point out in response to Bellarmine (see below), a principle of accommodation could well apply to texts of the astronomical kind where it would not to texts of the former simpler sort. For the use of the term, 'literal' in this context, see Note 68 below.

36 See, for example, Pope John Paul II's speech to the Pontifical Academy of Sciences terminating the work of the Galileo Commission, which he had instituted in 1981 to restudy the details of the Galileo affair:

> Robert Bellarmine, who had seen what was truly at stake in that debate, personally felt that in the face of possible scientific proofs that the Earth orbited around the Sun, one "should interpret with great circumspection" every biblical passage that seems to affirm that the Earth is immobile and "say that we do not understand, rather that what had been demonstrated is false." Before Bellarmine, this same wisdom and same respect for the divine word guided St. Augustine .... ("Lessons of the Galileo case," *Origins: Catholic News Service*, November 12, 1992, 22, 370–6; p. 372).

> Rivka Feldhay gives a similarly sympathetic reading of Bellarmine's letter (*Galileo and the Church*: pp. 35–6).

37 Blackwell, *GBB*, p. 261.

38 Foscarini had already composed a spirited *Defensio* in response to a critical assessment of his original letter by an unnamed theologian in Rome. (For the criticism and the *Defensio* see Blackwell, *GBB*, Appendices VIIA and VIIB.) Foscarini argued in his defense that the testimony of the Fathers ought be given weight only in matters of faith and morals, and not at all on issues bearing on natural philosophy. He asserts further that this is not a novel principle, citing in particular the testimony of the leading Dominican theologian, Melchior Cano, to that effect. In the original *Letter*, Foscarini quotes extensively from Scripture but not at all from theological authorities. He rectifies this omission in the *Defensio*, which is mainly concerned with showing that his views find

support in Augustine, as well as in such contemporary authorities as
Cano and Pereira.

39 These notes constitute Appendix IX in Blackwell, *GBB*; see p. 270.

40 *De Controversiis*, I, 3, 3; this chapter is translated as Appendix III in
Blackwell, *GBB*, see p. 190.

41 Blackwell, *GBB*, p. 266.

42 Blackwell, *GBB*, p. 271.

43 EN V, 285; *GA*, p. 52. This rather simplistic mode of assessing rival
hypotheses appears again in his later work: "It is not possible within
the bounds of human learning that the reasons adopted by the right side
should be anything but clearly conclusive, and those opposed to them
vain and ineffective." *Dialogue Concerning the Two Chief World Systems*, translated by Stillman Drake, Berkeley: University of California
Press, 1953, p. 356; EN VII, 383.

44 Blackwell, *GBB*, p. 271.

45 Text and translation of the *Apologia* in Nicholas Jardine, *The Birth of
History and Philosophy of Science*, Cambridge: Cambridge University
Press, 1984; see p. 145. See also E. McMullin, "Rationality and paradigm
change in science," in *World Changes: Thomas Kuhn and the Nature
of Science*, ed. Paul Horwich, Cambridge, MA: MIT Press, 1993, 55–78;
see pp. 71–5.

46 The assumption is that this requirement sets much tighter constraints
on candidate theories than does merely "saving the appearances" by
means of a mathematical formalism. The issue of how to limit the
number of acceptable causal hypotheses in effect-to-cause (retroduc-
tive) reasonings had already been much debated in later Aristotelian
natural philosophy and had attracted ever increasing notice as the seventeenth century wore on. See E. McMullin, "Conceptions of science
in the Scientific Revolution," in *Reappraisals of the Scientific Revolution*, ed. D. Lindberg and R. Westman, Cambridge: Cambridge University Press, 1990, 27–92.

47 Blackwell, *GBB*, p. 85.

48 Later on, in the *Dialogo* of 1632, Galileo did rather better in this regard,
though still groping for the proper way to say that the Copernican hypothesis was much the best one available and thus had a higher degree
of credibility. In the Third Day, he writes:

The principal activity of pure astronomers is to give reasons [the
same phrase he had used in the notes above] just for the appearances
of celestial bodies, and to fit to these and to the motions of the stars
such a structure and arrangement of circles that the resulting calculated motions correspond with those same appearances. (Drake,
Dialogue Concerning the Chief World Systems, p. 341; EN, VII, 369).

But this, he goes on, is not enough. "However well the astronomer might be satisfied merely as a calculator, there was no satisfaction or peace for the astronomer as a philosopher." And then he shows what the "philosopher" can find to recommend Copernicus over Ptolemy: the "wonderful simplicity" that explains planetary retrogression, substitutes the single annual motion of Earth for a plethora of epicycles, and so on. The argument is not nearly as convincing as Kepler had made it; it is never quite clear just why simplicity should carry the epistemic weight that Galileo gives it. With the tidal argument of the Fourth Day, he hoped to provide the causal argument needed to close the gap further, though he did not attempt a causal explanation of the planetary motions themselves and dismissed Kepler's appeal to attraction in that connection as a "puerility" (*Dialogue*, p. 462; EN VII, 486).

49 On January 8, 1616, Galileo presented to Cardinal Orsini in Rome a treatise on the tides, similar in its thrust to the tidal argument for the Copernican motions in the Fourth Day of the *Dialogo* of 1632 (EN V, 377–95). He chose an inauspicious time. By the time Orsini spoke to Pope Paul V on Galileo's behalf on February 23, 1616, the Pope had already set in motion the procedures of the Holy Office that led to the condemnation of the Copernican theses a few days later (March 5, 1616).

50 Matters would get worse for Galileo's hopes of demonstration when he set down to construct the argument of the *Dialogo*. To respond to the crucial Aristotelian objection to the motion of the Earth (why don't winds whistle, towers fall, and birds fall from the air?), he argued that the effects of the shared circular motions of bodies on or near the surface of the Earth are imperceptible (Second Day of the *Dialogo*). But if this is so, how can there be tidal effects of the Earth's motions? Galileo never acknowledged this inconsistency; it was due to the ambiguity in his notion of inertia (is inertial motion rectilinear or circular?) and to the lack on his part of a theory of gravity. If the Earth were to rotate fast enough, gravity would no longer prevent the effects that the Aristotelians asserted should accompany the Earth's motion. See my introduction to *Galileo Man of Science*, New York: Basic Books, 1967, p. 41.

51 Castelli to Galileo, January 6, 1615; EN XII, 126. Fantoli argues plausibly that the Barnabite priest was Pomponio Tartaglia, Superior of the College of San Frediano in Pisa. A number of his Barnabite colleagues are known to have been sympathetic to the Copernican cause. See Fantoli, *Galileo*, pp. 247–8.

52 Galileo misses, as we shall see, just one passage (in II, 16) which could have strengthened his case. Quoted at Note 85.

53 Benedictus Pererius (Benito Pereira), *Commentariorum et Disputationum in Genesim Tomi Quatuor*, Rome: Ferrari, 1591–5; second edition, Cologne: Hierat, 1601.

54 I, 1, p. 8. See Rinaldo Fabris, *Galileo Galilei e gli Orientamenti Esegetici del Suo Tempo*, Vatican City: Pontifical Academy of Sciences, Scripta Varia 62, 1986, pp. 29–31; Blackwell, *GBB*, pp. 20–2. Ironically, however, Pereira devotes a lengthy section of his work to showing that the Biblical texts referring to the Sun's motion and the Earth's immobility must be taken literally, despite his support elsewhere for a principle of accommodation. See Irving A. Kelter, "The refusal to accommodate: Jesuit exegetes and the Copernican system," *Sixteenth Century Journal*, 26, 1995, 273–83; p. 280.

55 Pereira was in the habit of paraphrasing or abbreviating the passages he presents as direct quotations from Augustine. All three of the passages he quotes on this opening page are fairly extensively reworded in one way or another.

56 There is, in fact, counter-evidence. When Galileo quotes another of the three passages from Augustine that Pereira lists on this opening page (*De Genesi ad Litteram*, I, 18), he quotes it exactly as it appears in Augustine's original text, rather than in the Pereira reworded version (see Pierre-Noel Mayaud, "Deux textes au coeur du conflit: Entre l'Astronomie Nouvelle et l'Ecriture Sainte: La lettre de Bellarmin à Foscariin et la lettre de Galilée à Christine de Lorraine," in *Après Galilée*, ed. Paul Poupard, Paris: Desclée, 1994, 19–91; p. 86). Furthermore, in all of the remaining twelve passages from the *De Genesi* quoted by Galileo (seven of these represent Book I, Chapters 18 and 19 quoted almost in their entirety), the text is the authentic original, allowing for small variations in the different editions of Augustine's work.

57 Galileo, however, must have seen this relevant page in Pereira for himself, since he quotes from it in a slightly fuller form than that given by Foscarini. See Mayaud, "Deux textes," p. 27. Pereira had already come to Galileo's attention much earlier in another context. In his notebooks on various physical questions compiled at the beginning of his teaching career, probably while he was still at Pisa, Galileo draws on Pereira's influential textbook on Aristotelian natural philosophy, *De Communibus Omnium Rerum Naturalium Principiis et Affectionibus* (Rome, 1581). See William Wallace, *Galileo's Early Notebooks: The Physical Questions*, Notre Dame: University of Notre Dame Press, 1977, especially pp. 14–15, 257, 294.

58 Galileo received a copy of Foscarini's original *Letter* from Cesi in early March 1615 (EN *XII*, 150). The *Defensio* was composed in late March

or early April; Foscarini sent a copy of the *Letter* and the *Defensio* to Bellarmine, whose response, already discussed above, was sent on April 12. It seems likely that Foscarini would have passed on a copy of the *Defensio* to Galileo whose work he praises in his *Letter*.

59 Galileo evidently had someone else in mind originally as official recipient of the *Letter*; an early draft uses "Paternità" as the form of address instead of the "Altezza Serenissima" of the final version, leading Favaro to guess that the original intended recipient was probably Castelli. Drake thought it more likely to have been one of Galileo's ecclesiastical patrons in Rome. There is much about the *Letter* that seems to me to make Drake's suggestion the more likely one.

60 Favaro lists thirty-six manuscript copies he had consulted in preparing his critical edition (EN V, pp. 272–4). Most are in Italian collections. Many, however, could have been made at a later time since the printed version of 1636 was not readily available in Italy. Fantoli believes that the *Letter* originally circulated only among Galileo's most trusted friends, so that it had "practically no influence on the scriptural debate from 1615 until Galileo's trial in 1633." (He notes in passing that Gianfrancesco Buonamici, in his diary for May 2, 1633, remarks that Pope Paul V was prevented from issuing a stronger condemnation of Copernicanism in 1616 in part by the "learned writing" of Galileo to the Lady Christina of Tuscany. Fantoli, rightly to my mind, finds this account unlikely, p. 262.) Westfall argues that Bellarmine, at least, is likely to have received a copy. There is no reference to the *Letter* in the Roman documents bearing on the decree of 1616. It is mentioned by Melchior Inchofer, a Jesuit philosopher, who was one of those commissioned by the Holy Office to write an evaluation of the *Dialogo* in 1632; in his strongly negative report, he concludes that Galileo does, indeed, defend the Copernican view in the *Dialogo* just as he had done years before in the *Letter to the Grand Duchess*, which, he adds, "if I am not deceived, here in Rome [has] passed through the hands of quite a few" (*GA*, p. 263; EN XIX, 349).

61 For a detailed treatment, see Jean Dietz Moss, "Galileo's *Letter to Christina*: Some rhetorical considerations," *Renaissance Quarterly*, 36, 1983, 547–76. Rhetoric is concerned with the techniques involved in *persuasion*. Where demonstration is available, these techniques are not needed. But when the argument is a probabilistic one (a dialectical argument, in the Aristotelian terminology familiar to Galileo), rhetoric can be an important aid in effecting persuasion.

62 St. Jerome, Letter 53 to Paulinus, EN V, 323; *GA*, p. 99, translation slightly modified.

63 Moss, who regards Galileo as an "astute rhetorician," is puzzled by "his castigation of his adversaries for their stupidity and hypocrisy";

he clearly "departs from advice offered by classical rhetoricians ... not to antagonize the audience or readers through arrogance." The answer, she suggests, "seems not to lie in innate maliciousness: rather it appears that Galileo was very sensitive to criticism" ("Galileo's *Letter to Christina*," p. 555).

64 EN V 323–4; *GA*, p. 99.

65 EN V 325; *GA*, p. 100.

66 Inchofer in his report on the *Dialogo* in 1632 recalls that in the *Letter to the Grand Duchess*, Galileo "ridiculed those who are strongly committed to the common scriptural interpretation of the sun's motion as if they were small-minded, unable to penetrate the depth of the issue, half-witted, and almost idiotic" (*GA*, p. 263).

67 "Lessons of the Galileo case," p. 372.

68 The term "literal" meant something other for Augustine than its usual modern sense. He took it to signify the sense intended by the author (which could well be metaphorical), contrasting it only with "allegorical" usage where the sense attributed is something over and above what the original author intended. His work on *Genesis* features speculative interpretations of all sorts that in his sense of the term count as "literal," though for us they would be metaphorical. See Taylor's introduction to *LMG*, vol. 1, pp. 9–11. I use the term in its more restrictive modern sense in this essay.

69 The Latin text can be found in vol. 34 of the Migne *Patrologia Latina* (1841) as well as in vol. 28 of the Zycha *Corpus Scriptorum Ecclesiasticorum Latinorum* (1894). The full text is now available in English translation for the first time: John H. Taylor, *The Literal Meaning of Genesis*, New York: Newman, 1982, in two volumes (*LMG*).

70 An earlier attempt at a reconstruction of the principles guiding the exegesis of the "conflict" passages in *LMG* will be found in my "How should cosmology relate to theology?" in *The Sciences and Theology in the Twentieth Century*, ed. A. R. Peacocke, Notre Dame: University of Notre Dame Press, 1981, pp. 19–22.

71 *LMG*, I, 18; vol. 1, p. 41. Quoted by Galileo.

72 Blackwell calls this the "Pragmatic Rule," *GBB*, p. 76.

73 *LMG*, II, 18; vol. 1, p. 73. (I have amended Taylor's translation of the Latin phrase above.) Galileo evidently thought this to be a key passage, since he quotes it at the beginning of the *Letter to the Grand Duchess*.

74 *LMG*, I, 19; vol. 1, pp. 42–3. Quoted by Galileo.

75 *LMG*, II, 9; vol. 1, p. 59. Quoted by Galileo.

76 *LMG*, I, 21. Quoted by Galileo. The translation is my own. The passage is a puzzling one. An implicit term needs to be made explicit: "Whatever they demonstrate about the natures of things by means of reliable evidence, we shall show not to be *really* contrary to Scripture

[though it may appear to be]. But when they produce from any of their books something *really* contrary to Scripture [and hence] contrary to the Catholic faith, we shall ... show ... that it is absolutely false." Fantoli argues that the intended contrast must be between "questions in natural philosophy which are open to discussion because not connected with the Christian faith, and those which are not, precisely because they are related to the faith" (*Galileo*, p. 197). But this seems questionable. The first term in the contrast refers rather to propositions about nature known to be true because they are demonstrated. The contrast is thus an imperfect one since it leaves hanging the all-important issue of propositions about nature that *appear* to conflict with the literal sense of Scripture but are neither demonstrated nor clearly contrary to the Catholic faith. The important point, as far as I am concerned, however, is Augustine's continued emphasis on the need for demonstration, if a new meaning for the scriptural text is to be sought.

77 *LMG*, III, 8; vol. 1, p. 81.

78 "quod vel certis rationibus perceperunt vel experimentis manifestissimis probaverunt" (*LMG*, II; 1; vol. 1, p. 48).

79 *LMG*, II, 9; vol. 1, p. 59.

80 *LMG*, II, 5; vol. 1, p. 52.

81 *LMG*, II, 9; vol. 1, p. 59.

82 This principle can take a number of slightly different forms, depending on which of the Augustinian themes one stresses: the epistemic weakness of human surmise or the epistemic strength of scriptural revelation. The crucial implication is that a natural knowledge claim has to qualify as certain for it to carry weight in the matter of scriptural exegesis.

83 *LMG*, *XI*, 33; vol. 2, p. 166. See also *VI*, 12; vol. 1, p. 192.

84 *LMG*, V, 6; vol. 1, p. 157.

85 St. Paul is using this as an analogy for the way in which the bodies of the resurrected differ from one another in glory. (*I Corinthians*, 15, 41) *LMG*, *II*, 16; vol. 1, p. 70.

86 This might lead one to wonder, as we have seen, whether he *had* read these pages of Augustine's commentary for himself or whether the citations he uses had been supplied to him.

87 *LMG*, *II*, 9 , vol. 1, p. 59. Quoted by Galileo.

88 *LMG*, *II*, 10; vol. 1, pp. 60–1. Quoted by Galileo.

89 The protracted struggle between the devotees of Aristotle's "natural" works and more tradition-bound theologians in the thirteenth and fourteenth centuries did indeed concern the relations between natural science and the Scriptures. But the focus was rarely on the interpretation of specific texts; rather, it had to do with more general issues, like

the eternity of the world and the freedom of God in creating. Furthermore, the new Aristotelian "natural knowledge" stayed close to the appearances; its empiricist emphasis ensured that a clash between it and the common sense cosmology of the ancient Hebrew writers would be unlikely to arise.

90 There is some disagreement as to when, finally, Galileo *did* become convinced of the superiority of the Copernican system. See, for example, Willy Hartner, "Galileo's contribution to astronomy," in *Galileo Man of Science*, ed. E. McMullin, 178–94, and Fantoli, *Galileo*, pp. 74–81.

91 Johannes Kepler, *New Astronomy*, transl. William H. Donahue, Cambridge: Cambridge University Press, 1992, p. 60.

92 *New Astronomy*, p. 61. All the texts cited below will be found on pp. 61–5.

93 *New Astronomy*, p. 66. I have translated "sanctus" as "holy" here, instead of "pious" as Donahue has it. At the time Kepler wrote these words (1609), the Holy Office had not, in fact, yet denied the motion of the Earth. Galileo's telescopic discoveries still lay ahead.

94 John Calvin, *Commentary on Psalms*, Grand Rapids: Eerdmans, 1963, vol. 5, p. 184. Quoted in Edward Rosen, "Calvin's attitude toward Copernicus," *Journal of the History of Ideas*, 21, 1960, 431–41; pp. 440–1. Rosen shows, to my mind conclusively, that Calvin's supposed rejection of Copernicus in his *Commentary on Genesis* ("Who will venture to place the authority of Copernicus above that of the Holy Spirit?") repeated by a whole series of authors, including Bertrand Russell, Dean Inge, and Dorothy Stimson, was fictive. It derived originally from A. D. White who enlarged on what he found in Frederic Farrar, who misquoted it to begin with. See also Christopher Kaiser, "Calvin, Copernicus, and Castellio," in *Calvin and Science*, ed. Richard C. Gamble, New York: Garland, 1992, 45–71. Calvin's belief that the message of the Bible should be accessible to everybody may have disposed him to favor the notion of accommodation in this way. For his theory of accommodation, see Reijer Hooykaas, "Calvin and Copernicus," *Organon*, 10, 1974, 139–48.

95 Hooykaas points out that a number of early seventeenth-century defenders of Copernicus, such as John Wilkins and Jacob van Lansbergen, call on Calvin's doctrine of accommodation to deflect biblically inspired attacks on the Copernican theses ("Calvin and Copernicus," p. 143). Still, it should also be noted that Calvin frequently described the Divine authorship of the Bible in terms of dictation to "scribes" or "amanuenses." This would, of course, still be compatible with the notion of accommodation on the part of *God* as author.

96 *Letter to the Grand Duchess Christina*, transl. M. Finocchiaro, EN V, 316; *GA*, p. 93.

97 EN V, 318; *GA*, p. 94.

98 See Carlo M. Martini, "Galileo e la teologia," in *Saggi su Galileo Galilei*, ed. Carlo Maccagni, Firenze: Barbèra, 1972, vol. 3(2), 441–51.

99 EN V, 316–7; *GA*, p. 93.

100 EN V, 317; *GA*, p. 93.

101 EN V, 332; *GA*, p. 105.

102 EN V, 317; *GA*, p. 93.

103 EN V, 317; *GA*, pp. 93–4.

104 EN V, 317; *GA*, p. 94.

105 Ibid.; translation slightly modified.

106 EN V, 319; *GA*, p. 95.

107 EN V, 319; *GA*, p. 96.

108 Nonetheless, Pope John Paul II quotes Baronio's *bon mot* from Galileo approvingly in his 1992 allocution, already alluded to (Note 36). But he evidently interprets it in the narrower sense expressed in the formulation of PL above: "The Bible does not concern itself with the details of the physical world, the understanding of which is the competence of human experience and reasoning" (p. 373).

109 EN V, 319; *GA*, p. 96. Moss writes that Galileo mentions "the importance of demonstration some 25 times [in the *Letter*], speaking as if such proofs exist" ("Galileo's *Letter to Christina*," p. 567). And she goes on to quote each occurrence of the phrase: "sense experience and necessary demonstration" or its equivalent, noting wryly that "the expressions form almost a litany to mesmerize his readers." See also her "The rhetoric of proof in Galileo's writings on the Copernican system," in *The Galileo Affair: A Meeting of Faith and Science*, ed. G. V. Coyne S. J., *et al.*, Vatican City: Specola Vaticana, 1985, 41–65.

110 EN V, 326; *GA*, p. 101. The opening distinction here is between the "demonstrative" sciences, the sciences where demonstration can be reached, and those fields where demonstration is not possible and whose claims thus always remain debatable. But the distinction that matters in the context of Scriptural debate is clearly between "demonstrated conclusions" which "cannot be changed" and assertions that fall short of that. It is the *demonstrated* nature of these conclusions that makes them privileged; *possibly* demonstrable ones, i.e. ones that may or may not achieve demonstration at a later time, *might* be changed and hence lack the all-important privilege. Speculative claims in natural philosophy would, in this view, carry no weight against the literal word of Scripture merely because they pertain to the "demonstrative sciences."

111 Galileo's youthful notes on Aristotle's *Posterior Analytics* have undergone intensive study in recent years. William Wallace makes a strong case for the claim that much of the content of these notes derives from lectures of Paolo Valla S. J. at the Collegio Romano in 1587–8, and he argues that this Aristotelian formation in the terminology of proof was to influence Galileo throughout his career. See his edition of the notes, *Galileo's Logical Treatises*, Dordrecht: Kluwer, 1992, and his accompanying commentary, *Galileo's Logic of Discovery and Proof*, Dordrecht: Kluwer, 1992.

112 EN V, 320; *GA*, p. 96.

113 EN V, 317; *GA*, p. 94.

114 Fantoli, *Galileo*, pp. 198, 200, 249. It turns out, however, that this principle is "applicable only in the case of questions which are open to discussion," p. 200. (It excludes matters bearing on Christian faith.) In the context of the Copernican debate, this could prove a significant limitation, as Bellarmine's response to Foscarini (see Note 41 above) illustrates.

115 In his translation of the *Letter*, Stillman Drake puts it: "written in a demonstrative way," *Discoveries and Opinions of Galileo*, New York: Doubleday, 1957, p. 183.

116 EN V, 330; *GA*, p. 104. The version of PPS in the sentence beginning: "As for the first type" is clearly incompatible with PL.

117 Finocchiaros claim that the "main epistemological distinction" propounded in the *Letter* lies between physical propositions that are *capable* of demonstration (whether or not they are yet demonstrated) and those that are not, rather than between propositions that "have and those that have not been conclusively proved" This seems, questionable ("The methodological background to Galileo's trial," in *Reinterpreting Galileo*, ed. William Wallace, Washington: Catholic University of America Press, 1986, 241–72; p. 268). The issue that is central to the *Letter*, after all, is the proper interpretation of scriptural texts dealing with the physical world. Yet until the conflicting physical proposition is *demonstrated* (according to PPD), the literal meaning of the scriptural passage cannot, on that account at least, be challenged. To say that it is demonstrable (as we have already seen) carries no weight in that regard; it may, after all, turn out eventually to be false.

118 EN V, 327; *GA*, p. 102. Why did Galileo make use of Pereira's version of this passage? After all, he did not use Pereira's paraphrases elsewhere (see Note 56). Was it because it is conveniently abbreviated? Was it because it substitutes "worldly authors" for the "they" of the original, suggesting that Augustine's text was intended for the philosophers of

his day? But Pereira's paraphrase omits a key qualifier that could have softened the extraordinarily strong version of PPS conveyed by the latter part of the quoted passage. Pereira drops the qualification "that is, contrary to the Catholic faith" after "anything contrary to Holy Writ" when speaking of the second sort of assertion, those that are not demonstrated. But it is this qualifier that makes sense of Augustine's original injunction (see Note 76). Omitting it makes Galileo appear to support an even stronger version of the controversial PPS principle than did Augustine. Perhaps Galileo simply did not notice the troublesome omission in the Pereira version.

119 Fantoli, *Galileo*, p. 198.

120 It is in the original text of Augustine, as we saw earlier (Note 76), but not in the version that Galileo found in Pereira.

121 Finocchiaro, "The methodological background to Galileo's trial," p. 266.

122 Fantoli, *Galileo*, p. 199.

123 EN V, p. 311; *GA*, pp. 88–9.

124 Michael Sharratt, *Galileo: Decisive Innovator*, Oxford: Blackwell, 1994, pp. 125–6.

125 Unlike the four preceding principles, the prudential principle he advocates does not instruct us how to arrive at the proper reading of a disputed scriptural text. It is, instead, purely pragmatic in nature, urging the withholding of judgment in the absence of a secure exegesis.

126 EN V, 339; *GA*, p. 111; quoting *LMG*, I, 18 (see Note 71).

127 EN V, 320; *GA*, pp. 96–7. Drake inserts a phrase here that makes the reference to scientific progress more explicit: "when *at some future time* the senses and demonstrative or necessary reasons may show the contrary," *Discoveries and Opinions of Galileo*, p. 187. Emphasis added.

128 EN V, 329; *GA*, p. 103.

129 EN V, 321; *GA*, p. 97.

130 See Pedersen, *Galileo and the Council of Trent*, pp. 26–9.

131 EN V, 335; *GA*, p. 108.

132 EN V, 333; *GA*, p. 106.

133 Finocchiaro, EN V, 337; *GA*, p. 109.

134 EN V, 338–9; *GA*, p. 110.

135 Many commentators have implied that Galileo's hermeneutic principles were novel, particularly his version of PL. See, most recently, Giorgio Stabile, "Linguaggio della natura e linguaggio della scrittura in Galilei," *Nuncius*, 9(1), 1994, 37–64; Mauro Pesce, "L' interpretazione della Bibbia nella Lettera di Galileo a Cristina di Lorena e la sua ricezione," *Annali di Storia dell' Esegesi*, 4, 1987, 239–84. Quoted in

William E. Carroll, "Galileo, science, and the Bible," *Acta Philosophica*, 6, 1997, 5–37; pp. 7–8.

136 Carroll notes that when Galileo repeats this passage in the *Letter to the Grand Duchess*, he softens it by altering *"solamente"* ("has merely the aim") to *"principalmente"* ("has principally the aim"). Galileo does not need the more sweeping (and more vulnerable) claim for the purposes of his argument in the later *Letter*. But Galileo is not, it seems to me, in this way implicitly conceding that the Bible may serve as a source of truths about the physical world, though it may contain truths about other matters, historical events, for example. ("The authority of the same holy Writ should have priority over the authority of any human writings containing pure narration," EN V, 317; *GA*, p. 94.) When he says that a knowledge of natural science would help theologians interpret more correctly ambiguous scriptural passages bearing on the physical world (EN V, 332; *GA*, p. 105), he clearly does not mean to imply that these passages, correctly interpreted with the aid of the scientist, ought be said to "contain" scientific truth.

137 EN V, 282–4; *GA*, pp. 50–1.

138 EN V, 285, 282; *GA*, pp. 52, 50.

139 A number of writers have pointed to such tensions: Jerome J. Langford, *Galileo, Science and the Church*, New York: Desclée, 1966, pp. 72–4; McMullin, introduction to *Galileo Man of Science*, pp. 33–5, and more fully in "How should cosmology relate to theology?," pp. 19–22; Blackwell, *GBB*, pp. 78–82; Sharratt, *Galileo: Decisive Innovator*, pp. 123–6; Edith Sylla, "Galileo and probable reasons," in *Nature and Scientific Method*, ed. Daniel Dahlstrom, Washington: Catholic University of America Press, 1991, 211–34. Two historians have recently argued that this claim is based on a misreading of the *Letter*: Fantoli, *Galileo*, Chap. 3; Finocchiaro, "The methodological background to Galileo's trial." Their arguments will be discussed below. Earlier writers most often assumed that the *Letter* constituted "solid argumentation" (as does, for example, Mario Vigano S. J., "Galileo e l'esegesi biblica," *La Civilta Cattolica*, 116(1), 1965, 228–39; p. 236).

140 PL and PA, for example, are clearly not independent of one another. If God "did not want to teach men such things as would be of no avail for their salvation" (*LMG*, II, 9) (i.e., PL), some sort of accommodation of the language of Scripture would automatically follow. Strictly speaking, PL makes PA redundant. But because the arguments in favor of the two principles are so different, there were sound rhetorical reasons for retaining both.

141 It is noteworthy that something of the same tension reappears in the encyclical, *Providentissimus Deus*, issued by Pope Leo XIII in 1893, a

THE CAMBRIDGE COMPANION TO GALILEO

document that has often been described as a vindication of the exegetical principles of Galileo's *Letter* (*The Papal Encyclicals* 1878–1903, ed. Claudia Carlen IHM, Raleigh: McGrath, 1981, 325–39). On the one hand, the encyclical takes a version of PL from Augustine and quotes Aquinas in support of PA (the writers of Scripture "went by what sensibly appeared," *Summa Theologica*, I, q. 70, a. 1, *ad* 3). On the other hand, it also calls on Augustine to the effect that interpreters of Scripture must not "depart from the literal and obvious sense, except only where reason makes it untenable or necessity requires" (p. 332). Further, they "should show that those facts of natural science which investigators show to be now quite certain are not contrary to the Scripture, rightly explained," adding as a cautionary note that "much which has been held as proved certain has afterwards been called into question and rejected," a cautious affirmation of PPD (p. 335). And in a familiar passage Augustine says: "Whatever they can really demonstrate to be true of physical nature, we must show to be capable of reconciliation with our Scriptures" (p. 334). But if the Holy Spirit "did not intend to teach men these things, i.e. the essential nature of the visible universe, things in no way profitable unto salvation" (Augustine again, PL), why should it matter whether the scientists can "really demonstrate" their claims, show them to be "quite certain," for them to be taken seriously in the context of potential conflict with Scripture? Might not this once more require Galileo to *demonstrate* the Copernican theses in order to make his case? This troubling implication will appear once again in more recent Roman documents; see Note 151.

142 Among the defenders of the consistency of the Galilean exegetical principles, Fantoli takes the "principle of the autonomy of scientific research" to be "the fundamental thesis of the *Letter*" (*Galileo*, p. 198). Finocchiaro, in contrast, takes PPD to be "the key premise of Galileo's argument" in the *Letter* ("Methodological judgment and critical reasoning in Galileo's *Dialogue*," *PSA* 1994, ed. D. Hull *et al.*, E. Lansing, MI: Philosophy of Science Association, 1995, vol. 2, 248–57; p. 253). Pesce takes PL and PPD to be two "convergent" means of limiting the authority of Scripture ("L'interpretazione della Bibbia," p. 251; quoted in Carroll, "Galileo, science, and the Bible" p. 22).

143 As a regulative principle, not an epistemic one like the other four, PP only tells theologians not to commit themselves publicly, but it is strictly speaking, consistent with PPS, that is, with the claim that the normal reading of the Scripture passage is more likely to be correct, as things stand, in cases where the conflicting physical proposition is not demonstrated, though potentially demonstrable.

144 Fantoli believes that it is "perfectly self-consistent" for Galileo to urge "absolute conformity to the literal meaning of Scripture" in cases where the best the natural philosopher can aspire to is (in Galileo's words) "probable opinion or verisimilar conjecture." He adopts Galileo's alternative description of such cases as ones "where human reason cannot reach," or as Fantoli himself puts it, that are "beyond the capacity of human comprehension" (*Galileo*, p. 251). However, where probable reasons can be given or likely conjecture supported by argument, the issues are not entirely beyond human comprehension. If one were to be guided by PL, Scripture would *not* be assigned priority in such cases. On the face of it, PL and Fantoli's "principle of autonomy of scientific research" might seem to be equivalent. But if "scientific" be defined restrictively to refer only to propositions that are demonstrated or strictly demonstrable, then well-supported hypotheses that are not, in Aristotelian terms, demonstrable would not enjoy autonomy and Scripture could thus be given priority over them. This would violate PL but not Fantoli's principle of autonomy.

145 EN V, 317; *GA*, p. 94.

146 Many commentators have pointed also to the ambiguity in the notion of *hypothesis* current in Galileo's day; see Note 26 above. Was it a saving of the phenomena for practical ends, or an explanatory account with some degree of likelihood? The later course of the Galileo story hinged to a significant extent on this ambiguity. See, for example, Guido Morpurgo-Tagliabue, *I Processi di Galileo e l'Epistemologia*, Milan: Edizione di Comunità, 1963; Feldhay, *Galileo and the Church*; Sharratt, *Galileo: Decisive Innovator*, especially 118–19.

147 E. McMullin, "Conceptions of science in the Scientific Revolution," passim. In his *Galileo's Logic of Discovery and Proof* and elsewhere, Wallace presents a much more positive account of Galileo's handling of probable reasoning, emphasizing the sophisticated treatment of the varieties of *suppositio* in the Jesuit source from which Galileo derived his early notes on Aristotelian demonstration and Galileo's own description of the demonstrative *regressus* in those notes. Edith Sylla notes that Galileo's shift from the context of the formal Aristotelian treatise to that of the dialogue would occasion a shift of expectation on the part of the reader. In the former case, probability would count for little, whereas in the latter it would be what the reader would look for and would carry corresponding weight. She concludes that "this is why, I think, the judges at Galileo's trial could condemn him," i.e., for assigning *real* likelihood to a doctrine that had been condemned ("Galileo and probable arguments," p. 230).

148 *Dialogue*, EN VII, 444, 471.

149 E. McMullin, "The conception of science in Galileo's work," in *New Perspectives on Galileo*, ed. R. Butts and J. Pitt, Dordrecht: Reidel, 1978, 209–57.

150 We saw above that Galileo sometimes asserted that only a true explanation can have valid arguments in its favor: "Those who are on the false side cannot have any arguments of value" (Note 42). If one were to rely on this principle, the gap between what is potentially demonstrable and what is actually demonstrated might come to seem very small.

151 The exegetes of today are not likely to demand demonstration from natural scientists when an apparent conflict looms. Yet one catches an occasional echo of PPD even still. In the report he presented to the Pope on the occasion of the official termination of the work of the Galileo Commission in 1992, Cardinal Paul Poupard argued that the key to the Galileo affair was that Galileo "had not succeeded in proving irrefutably the double motion of the earth," as Bellarmine had challenged him to do. When, however, an "optical proof" of the Earth's motion around the Sun became available in the following century, Pope Benedict XIV had the Holy Office grant an *Imprimatur* to Galileo's works in 1741 ("Galileo: Report on Papal Commission findings," *Origins: Catholic News Service*, November 12, 1992, 22, 375–6). The implication seems to be that Galileo ought to have had a proper demonstration of the Earth's motion before he challenged the literalist reading of the disputed biblical passages; it was the "transitional situation" in astronomy, apparently, that was at fault. This was, of course, precisely Bellarmine's response. But it is hardly the exegetical lesson that one would expect today. The cardinal frankly acknowledges the "exegetical confusions" of the theologians of that distant day (and he could have included in this admission Bellarmine and the Congregation of the Holy Office, as well as the consequent error in the 1616 decree of the Congregation of the Index). But, of course, from our perspective the principal exegetical confusion was precisely to require demonstration of the Copernican thesis in the first place, a confusion compounded by the delay in clearing Galileo's works until an "optical proof" of that thesis had been found.

152 Whether this *is*, in fact, the conventional interpretation might be challenged. Finocchiaro takes this interpretation of the *Letter* to be part of a larger "anti-Galilean myth"; it is based, he asserts, on an "untenable misreading" of the *Letter* and is "the result of insufficient analysis" ("The methodological background to Galileo's trial," pp. 259, 246–7, 261).

153 Ibid., p. 260.

154 Ibid., pp. 260–1.
155 Finocchiaro, "Methodological judgment and critical reasoning in Galileo's *Dialogue*," *PSA* 1994, ed. D. Hull *et al.*, E. Lansing MI: Philosophy of Science Association, 1995, vol. 2, 248–57; p. 253. See my comment in the same volume, "Scientific classics and their fates," 266–74; p. 270.
156 Ibid., p. 271.
157 Finocchiaro, "Methodological judgment," p. 253.
158 Finocchiaro, "Methodological background," p. 270.
159 Finocchiaro strengthens this last claim in "Methodological judgment."
160 Ibid., pp. 271–2.
161 In the texts quoted by Galileo, Augustine makes it clear how he intends PP to be taken: Prudence is to be exercised in asserting the priority of scripture where the scriptural texts in question are in one way or other "obscure."
162 This is according to the certificate Bellarmine subsequently gave Galileo, and which the latter produced at the trial (*GA*, p. 153).
163 Over and over again, the arguments he advances in the *Dialogue* are said to favor the Copernican side, to "strengthen the Copernican hypothesis until it might seem that this must triumph absolutely," as the Preface puts it. This surely constitutes "defending." See McMullin, "Scientific classics," p. 271.
164 Finocchiaro leaps to the conclusion that to claim this is equivalent to saying that "the Church was right to condemn Galileo" ("Methodological background," p. 247). But there were many other factors involved besides the technical one of Galileo's defense of a doctrine proscribed by a decree issued with the authority of the Holy Office. The major error on the part of the Church authorities was made in 1616. The verdict in 1633 could claim the 1616 Decree as warrant, though a warrant that we would say, with the benefit of hindsight, should not have been invoked, considering all the circumstances.
165 EN XIX, 321; *GA*, p. 146.
166 Pope Leo XIII in *Providentissimus Deus* (1893) strongly disapproved of the attempt to limit inspiration to "matters of faith and morals" on the part of various Catholic theologians of the centuries after Trent. But the less constraining notion that the aim of Scripture is to communicate "salvific truth," "that truth which God wanted to put into the sacred writings for the sake of our salvation" (from the declaration of the Second Vatican Council, "On Revelation," 3:11) now seems widely accepted in Catholic theology. See R. F. Smith, "Inspiration and inerrancy," p. 514.

9 Could there be another Galileo case?

Galileo's conflict with the Roman Catholic Church has long held a very special fascination. The prime reason for this, of course, is that the Galileo affair has come to be seen as the paradigm case of the troubled interaction between science and religion.

Another reason is the sheer dramatic power of the events involved, which continue to attract the attention of the scholar, the novelist, and the playwright. Images easily multiply of the flawed tragic hero, of the struggle for intellectual freedom, of the unprotected individual pitted against a powerful institution committed to its self-preservation, and of plots and subplots and counterplots worthy of the best mystery writer.

At yet another level, the Galileo case has, unfortunately, long provided many with an ideal arena for ideological posturing for and against both the scientific and the religious world views.

Still another reason for our fascination with the Galileo case is that it irresistibly invites comparisons with the unstable interactions between science and religion in other ages as well as in our own. What can we learn from it, and what have we learned from it, for our understanding of the relations between contemporary scientific culture and our inherited religious beliefs and traditions? Are we now confident that we have reached a stage of peaceful coexistence between science and religion? And, if so, why? Or are we still uneasy about the possibility of future conflicts arising between the two? In short, could there be another Galileo case?

At first sight, there seems to be no grounds for concern here at all. No one today would seriously wonder whether the Earth revolves around the Sun, or vice versa, no matter what the literal sense of the Bible might be. This is a completely settled issue. Even the Catholic

Church, in its most recent formal reassessment of the Galileo case, which was announced on the last day of October of 1992, has frankly admitted that the Church was wrong in its decisions and that its errors were based in large part on its use of erroneous principles of biblical exegesis. With these admissions, the Galileo case has supposedly come to an end.

We might mention in passing that Pope John Paul II's address[1] on the occasion just mentioned is peculiar in several respects. First, in some ways it develops its own line of thought about the Galileo case, one not based on the findings of the four study groups of the Commission which the Pope himself had established a dozen years earlier, specifically to reexamine the case for him.

Second, although it is admitted that errors were committed, these errors are not specifically identified. Moreover, they are attributed repeatedly to the theological advisers at the time of the Galileo case, and not to the members of the hierarchy who made the decisions, nor to the two popes who approved them.

Third, it is not clear from the documents whether the errors admitted relate to the doctrinal decision that Copernicanism is false, or to the later judicial decision that Galileo was personally guilty of heresy, or to both. We will see later how important that distinction is.

These ambiguities in the latest Vatican statements will no doubt keep the issue alive among Galileo scholars for years to come. Nevertheless, there is no present concern that the Galileo case itself will reoccur, if by that we mean a rekindling of the same specific debates.

But this leaves the more general question unanswered. Could something reasonably similar to what happened in the Galileo case happen again in the future over some other scientific theory, for example, evolution or a comprehensive neurophysiological account of the human mind, if such were to be discovered some day? This is the fallout issue in the contemporary scene to which the Galileo case invites attention.

Even on this more general level, Pope John Paul II is quite optimistic. At the same meeting of the Pontifical Academy of Sciences referred to above, at which the Galileo case was to be closed, the Pope said:

From the Galileo affair, we can learn a lesson that remains valid in relation to similar situations that occur today and that may occur in the future ...

There exist two realms of knowledge, one that has its source in revelation and one that reason can discover by its own power. To the latter belong especially the experimental sciences and philosophy. The distinction between the two realms of knowledge ought not to be understood as opposition. The two realms are not altogether foreign to each other; they have points of contact. The methodologies proper to each make it possible to bring out different aspects of reality.[2]

The Pope's views here are quite in keeping with the tradition and break no new ground. He is saying that in regard to their subject matters, science and religion usually encompass different realms, and thus they do not come into confrontation in such cases. But they do overlap on some topics. It is in this relatively small but often quite significant area of common subject matter that conflicts can arise. But such conflicts can be avoided, we are told, if we are sufficiently attentive to the different sources from which the two bodies of knowledge are derived, namely, revelation for religion and the power of human reason based on empirical facts for science. As a result, we are presented in science and religion with two quite distinct realms of knowledge. And, most importantly, these two bodies of knowledge are declared not to be in opposition but to be complementary to each other.

This latter point is, of course, the key claim. Why is there – or, at least, why should there be – no conflict? The answer given is that the methodologies of science and religion are different, a point that was not at all adequately understood by the contestants on both sides in the Galileo case, as the pope correctly indicates elsewhere in his address. If this be granted, then these different methodologies reveal different aspects of reality, thus making science and religion not merely consistent but even complementary.

As an ideal, one can hardly quarrel with this analysis. But does it hold up when embedded in the concrete daily life of science and religion? The focus is on the methodologies. But does a more fine-grained analysis and comparison of the method of appealing to revelation in religion and of the method of appealing to reasoned empirical facts in science support the optimistic view of a peaceful coexistence between science and religion?

We are skeptical as to whether this is so. We wish to argue, rather, that such a fine-grained analysis uncovers what we will call a "logic of centralized authority," which is essentially required by the scripturally based revelation that serves as the source of religion, at least as this has been understood in the Catholic tradition.

Furthermore, this "logic of centralized authority" is in certain respects antithetical to the scientific method, which is based on an authority, indeed, but on an authority of a quite different type. If so, then no matter how much agreement there may be between science and religion at the level of their respective world-views, there still remains a potential locus of conflict between the two at the level of competing authorities. Their methodologies can and do lead to conflict. That is the root of the problem.

The above remarks constitute the main thesis that we wish to defend in this paper. The historical and philosophical analyses that follow are an attempt to defend this thesis.

GALILEO'S TWO TRIALS

So we ask again, "Could there be another Galileo case?" The first step toward answering that question is to take a close look at precisely what happened to Galileo in the seventeenth century. This will reveal quite explicitly that what we have called the "logic of centralized authority" was at the heart of the matter in the Galileo case.

The central point to be noted at the outset is that the Galileo affair consisted of two trials, not one. The first occurred in February 1616, and the second seventeen years later in the spring of 1633. Both trials were conducted by the Congregation of the Holy Office in Rome, and in each case, the final judgment of the Congregation was submitted to and approved by the reigning pope.

The similarities end there. In the two trials, there were very substantial differences in the defendants being judged, in the complaints brought against them, in the character of the relevant evidence and theological argumentation, and even in the judicial processes and technical legal grounds used to justify the proceedings.

In the trial of 1616, the defendant was actually a scientific idea, namely, the Copernican hypothesis about the structure and motion of the solar system. To submit an idea to a trial may sound odd to us now, but this was not so in Galileo's day of high sensitivity to heretical views. The charge brought against Copernicanism was that it seemed to contradict numerous passages in Scripture that speak of a stationary Earth and of the motion of the Sun. To be more specific, the issue was whether the following two propositions were unorthodox:

1. That the Sun is the center of the world and, thus, is immobile of local motion.
2. That the Earth is not the center of the world, nor is it immobile, but it moves as a whole and also with a diurnal motion.[3]

Both of these claims were judged to be false because they contradict the Bible. The promulgation of this decision and its consequences took the form of a decree issued by the Congregation of the Index on March 5, 1616. This decree publicly announced that the Copernican hypothesis was "false and completely contrary to the divine Scriptures" and then proceeded to condemn several books that taught heliocentrism, including the writings of Copernicus himself.

However, none of Galileo's own writings were mentioned. As far as the Church was concerned thereafter, the substantive topic of the assessment of Copernicanism was a closed issue. This disastrous decision at the first trial was so erroneous from our present day perspective that a few words are in order to throw some light on how it came about.

First, on the scientific side, everyone involved realized that no strict proof had yet been found for Copernicanism. Galileo's observations with the telescope, and in particular his discovery of the phases of Venus, made the new theory more probable, but not conclusive. He fully realized this, and for the remainder of his life he searched without success for definitive proof.

However, Cardinal Bellarmine, who at the time served as the chief theological adviser to the pope, admitted frankly that the traditional interpretation of Scripture would have to be changed if a conclusive proof of Copernicanism were forthcoming. But as no such proof was either at hand or on the horizon, he concluded that no scriptural reinterpretations were in order.

Second, on the theological side, two developments heavily influenced the theologians of Galileo's day. The first was the decree concerning the interpretation of the Bible, which had been adopted as official church teaching at the Fourth Session (April 8, 1546) of the Council of Trent in response to Luther's doctrine of private interpretation of the Bible. The relevant passage, which was used as part of the legal grounding of the first trial, reads as follows:

Furthermore, to control petulant spirits, the Council decrees that, in matters of faith and morals pertaining to the edification of Christian doctrine, no one, relying on his own judgment and distorting the Sacred Scriptures according to his own conceptions, shall dare to interpret them contrary to that sense which Holy Mother Church, to whom it belongs to judge of their true sense and meaning, has held and does hold, or even contrary to the unanimous agreement of the Fathers, even though such interpretations should never at any time be published. Those who do otherwise shall be identified by the ordinaries and punished in accordance with the penalties prescribed by the law.[4]

It is important to note that this statement is not about the principles to be used for biblical interpretation. Rather, it is about who has the authority to undertake an interpretation or reinterpretation of the Bible. It is unequivocally clear that on matters of faith and morals, this authority is claimed to belong to the Church (i.e., to the hierarchy). Any individual, for example, Galileo, who would suggest a new interpretation, thus faced a double jeopardy: 1. Is the content of the new interpretation a correct or incorrect reading of the Scripture?, and 2. even if it is correct, is the person presuming to make that interpretation authorized to do so?

As a result, if Galileo's work took him into this terrain, he had to lose on the second question, even if he had won on the first. This simply was not his business, but a matter for church authority. And after the recent struggles of the Reformation, the Church was especially concerned about defending and maintaining that authority.

Moreover, in the half century that had passed since the Council of Trent ended, Catholic biblical exegesis had become increasingly more literalistic. This, again, was part of the highly defensive posture assumed by the Church during the Counter-Reformation. The result was a great hesitation to introduce any novelties or to depart in any way from the common opinions of the church fathers, who, of course, spoke of the world in terms of the common-sense viewpoint of geocentrism. Perhaps the cause of the church's overreaction of condemning Copernicanism was the fear of facing a second Reformation, growing this time out of science. It seems so obvious to us now that a mere suspension of judgment on the matter would have been much wiser and quite adequate for the church's interests.

It should be noted that Galileo personally was not involved at all in the first trial. We know that, at that time, he had long been personally convinced of Copernicanism, and three years earlier he stated so publicly in one of his books. However, he did become involved indirectly in a curious way. The pope at the time, Paul V, directed Bellarmine to meet with Galileo to explain to him the Holy Office's decision at the first trial and to ask Galileo to accept that decision under the threat of an injunction. Discussion of the merits of the substantive question of the truth of Copernicanism was not the purpose of this meeting. Rather, the issue was Galileo's acceptance of the decision as a matter of personal obedience to the Church.

This famous meeting took place on February 26, 1616. Precisely what happened is not known, since there are two inconsistent and ambiguous accounts of the interview, which no one has yet been able to reconcile. One version is contained in the relevant record in the files of the Holy Office; the other is in a later letter requested by Galileo from Bellarmine to summarize the gist of the meeting.

The key issue is whether, and in what sense, Galileo had understood and accepted the wording of the injunction which said that he should not "hold, teach or defend (Copernicanism) in any way whatsoever, verbally or in writing." The inconsistency arises from the fact that Bellarmine's letter to Galileo contains the much weaker language that Copernicanism "cannot be defended or held" (period). That seems to rule out only definite claims that Copernicanism is true but to allow hypothetical discussion, orally and in writing, of the merits of both theories, as Galileo himself seems to have understood the matter. It is one of the terrible ironies of history that such a basic confusion rules the day in a proceeding that was to poison the relations between science and religion ever since.

Be that as it may, in the proceedings of 1616, one could hardly have a stronger distinction between two quite different levels of concern. First, there is the intellectual content issue of Copernicanism, which was the explicit focus of the first trial. The second is the authority issue of implementing that decision, which was partially carried out through the injunction imposed on Galileo. To put this in another way, there are two aspects of the religious revelation operating here: the meaning content of the message (which Copernicanism was judged to offend) and the centralized authority of the Church itself, which gives credence to the revelation (and which Galileo was asked to accept in the injunction.) It was essential, and perhaps even more essential for the church authorities, that the latter be asserted and defended as well as the former.

This key distinction becomes even clearer when we look at what happened at the second trial in 1633. This time, Galileo was directly involved as the defendant. In the previous year, he had published what was to become his most famous book, the *Dialogue Concerning the Two Chief World Systems*. Using the model of a Platonic dialogue, he presented all the evidence and arguments for and against the theories of both Ptolemy and Copernicus, with the latter clearly having the advantage. The charge against Galileo was that the publication of this book had violated the conditions of the injunction of 1616.

It is essential to notice that the charge against Galileo in 1633 was the purely technical issue of his obedience to the terms of the earlier injunction, and had nothing whatever to do with the original substantive question of whether or not Copernicanism contradicts the Bible. As far as the Holy Office was concerned, that issue had been settled for good in 1616, and was not up for reconsideration. When one reads through the testimony at the second trial, one finds no mention of scientific discoveries or theories, nor any discussion of reinterpreting the Bible, nor of the principles of scriptural exegesis, nor of the views of the earlier theologians of Church Fathers. Rather all the testimony relates to the injunction and its proscriptions, and to the securing of Church permissions for the publication of the *Dialogue*.

This time no scientific theory was on trial. Rather it was Galileo's acceptance of, and obedience to, the 1616 decision that came under question. It was a matter of authority now, not truth. And this authority was making new and quite different demands on Galileo. He was found guilty, of course, for indeed his new book did seem to violate the conditions of the injunction. And the famous formula of adjuration, which he was forced to read, was intended to bend – or break – his will rather than his reason.

In summary what this examination of the Galileo affair rather clearly shows is that the appeal to revelation as the source of religion is a two-fold appeal. In one sense it is an appeal to the meaning content, the religious message, the world view, which the revelation communicates. In this sense the revelation is either true or false – which was the concern of the first trial. In a second sense the appeal to revelation is an appeal to the authority which stands behind the message, which "authorizes" the message, as it were, in the sense of empowering it as credible and reliable. In this sense of appealing to revelation the issue is not its specific truth or falsity, but rather whether the authority behind the message is freely accepted or rejected as legitimate – which was the concern of the second trial.

Seen in this light the heart of the matter in Galileo's personal trial in 1633 was not whether a scientific theory was consistent with the Bible, but rather was whether Galileo had attacked the centralized authority of the Church by his apparent violation of the injunction of 1616.

If we now return to our original distinction of revelation as the source of religion and reasoned empirical facts as the source of science, the picture has become more complex. Science and religion can and do interact at the first level of their respective messages or world-views. At this level, science may or may not be in agreement with religion. Hopefully, disagreements are in principle avoidable here, if both science and religion stay within their proper and complementary realms. That was also Pope John Paul II's point.

But science and religion also intersect at the meta-level in regard to the character of the authorities giving each its legitimacy. Each is indeed based on an authority at this second level. However, the authorities are quite different, and we cannot claim that these authorities will not conflict with each other without closer examination.

THE LOGIC OF CENTRALIZED AUTHORITY

Our central theme then boils down to these questions: What is the nature of the foundational authorities that give legitimacy to science and to religion, and how are these authorities related to each other? Although the nature of each of these authorities is well known and has been studied in detail, surprisingly little effort has been made to compare them.

On the scientific side, the foundational authority of the entire enterprise is the appeal to empirical facts. If this appeal is rejected as illusory, then science as a whole collapses. From this factual base science proceeds by induction to form generalized empirical laws and ultimately to the genesis of explanatory theories. The second phase of the scientific enterprise consists in testing these laws and theories by use of the methods of verification and falsification. Here, again, empirical facts serve as the authority of last appeal for the acceptance or rejection of scientific laws and theories.

It has long been recognized, of course, that both the methods of induction and of verification are logically invalid. As a result, since at least the time of Galileo, the brief sketch of scientific method outlined above has undergone an elaborate evolution to soften the impact of these logical objections to the authority of science. For example, complex models of probability logic have been developed to supplement, or to supplant, the straightforward use of induction and verification in science.

To make matters more complex, it has gradually come to be realized, especially in recent years after the influential work of Thomas Kuhn, that the appeal to empirical facts in science is not itself theory-neutral. To put this in another way, it is now widely granted that interpretive perspectives on facts are unavoidable in the scientist's observations of the world and that these interpretations can and do change over time.

In contrast, unlike verification, the logical process of falsification is formally valid. In effect, no finite number of positive cases can prove that a scientific law is conclusively true, but one negative case does prove that it is false. In the latter case, the negative instance prompts a reexamination of the previously accepted body of truths to see where a correction is needed. As a result, authority in science is self-corrective and the scientific attitude is characteristically one of fallibilism, to use the term standardized by C. S. Peirce. This means that the mind of the scientist should always be open to the possibility that whatever is accepted as true to date in science may, in time, turn out to be false or only partially true. Epistemological humility is, thus, a virtue built into the mindset of scientific authority, precisely because the logic of scientific method requires it.

But, despite all these complications, the appeal to empirical facts has always remained the foundational authority of science, serving as both its starting point and final guarantor of truth. Furthermore, the very nature of scientific method requires that this authority be exercised in a pluralistic and democratic way. The work of one individual scientist, or a small group of scientists, can never embody the full authority of science. Rather, that work must be submitted publicly for others to repeat it and to verify or falsify it independently.

Witness the recent much publicized dispute in science over the alleged discovery of cold fusion. Such open and public assessment is essential to science, as the means it uses to move beyond the subjective convictions of the original worker to the public status of the truth it claims to seek. The authority that grounds science is thus pluralistic, democratic, public, fallibilistic, and self-corrective.

In regard to religion, the parallel situation is equally well understood. The foundational authority of the entire religious enterprise is God as the author of the religious revelation. If this appeal to God is rejected as illusory, then religion as a whole collapses. However, a truthful God would give us only an absolutely reliable and truthful message. This notion is so basic and so ancient that it is even preserved in the etymology of the terms we have been using. An "authority" was originally understood to be an "author" – namely, God as the author of the revelation.

A favorite metaphor used in Galileo's day was to speak of God both as the author of the book of nature, which is the object of science, and as the author of the book of Scripture, which grounds religion. If the one, truthful God is seen as the author of both "books," then we are guaranteed a unity of truth between the two. This is the oldest and still the most common argument for the conclusion that, in the last analysis, science and religion cannot come into conflict, no matter how we may at the moment understand either.

Like the authority that stands behind science, the authority behind religion has also undergone a considerable evolution over time. The original oral revelation and the later Apostolic tradition were gradually – and perhaps only partially – committed to writing. This in turn generated an immense body of devotional and explanatory literature at a secondary level of authority.

Meanwhile, in the early centuries after the death of Christ, the Catholic Church, which saw itself as the custodian of the revelation, slowly became institutionalized, and thus so did the original authority behind the revelation. For complex historical reasons over many centuries, which are too involved to examine here, that institution became progressively more centralized through such developments as the conciliar movement, the Reformation debates over the individual versus the church as the ultimate interpreter of the Scriptures, and the declaration of papal infallibility in the late nineteenth century. As an outgrowth of these issues, the protection of the inherited religious authority has become all important to the hierarchy of the Church. This concern may be the reason for the ambiguities pointed out earlier in the present pope's address on the Galileo case.

The situation is considerably complicated by another factor. Unlike science, religious belief is not purely, or even primarily, an intellectual matter. It is also based, in part, on an act of the will. This, in turn, influences the ways in which religious authority is exercised.

This role of the will in religious belief is twofold. First, such belief is not simply a matter of understanding the meaning of the religious message. It requires, in addition, a willingness to accept the authority that guarantees its truth, an authority that, as we have seen, has evolved in the Church in complex ways through history. Second, the religious believer is also expected to choose a practical life-style that embodies the religious message and its values. As a result, authority in religion is as much, if not more, concerned with the pursuit of goodness in the world as with the pursuit of truth.

The result is that the contemporary sense of religious authority, at least in the Catholic tradition, is monolithic, centralized, esoteric, resistant to change, and self-protective. By contrast, authority in science, as we have seen earlier, is pluralistic, democratic, public, fallibilistic, and self-corrective. It is obvious that these two modes of authority are quite different, and understandably so.

Despite these differences, it does not follow that the exercise of authority in science and in religion must result in conflict. That conclusion would be too strong. These authorities can function harmoniously; and they often do. The important thing to see is that the mindset of each is quite different from the other. Those who have become habituated to think in only one of these modes, unfortunately, often find it difficult to understand and to communicate with those who think otherwise.

To make matters worse, the way we train scientific and religious professionals in our universities seems almost designed to exaggerate and to perpetuate the gulf between these two mindsets. The theologian who really understands science from the inside and the scientist who really understands religion from the inside are indeed rarities. Such a situation almost invites conflict.

Applying all this to the Galileo case, we saw that what happened in the seventeenth century was due, in significant part, to a clash of these two types of authority. In the nearly four centuries since, the characteristics of these two types of authority have not lessened but have become even more accentuated.

So the conclusion must be that the same forces that produced the Galileo affair are still in play now. As a result, it is quite possible that another Galileo affair could occur today. How *likely* it is that this will happen again is, however, quite another matter. All we are arguing for is that the possibility remains. But, of course, there are some major differences as well.

In the seventeenth century, the power of the Church was dominant in Western society, while science was a weakling just entering the picture. Today, these roles are almost completely reversed. Science and technology are the overwhelmingly dominant cultural forces of our day, while religion continues to have less and less vitality and influence in modern life. This perennially puts the Church in a reactionary and defensive posture as innovation in the sciences continues to shape the debate. This role reversal, plus today's candid admission of how great the damage to religion was from the Galileo affair, may make a recurrence rather unlikely. However, should a new and sufficiently great threat to religion arise from science, the conditions for the possibility of a recurrence may come into play.

THREE FANCIFUL SCENARIOS

In conclusion, we will break one of the basic rules of philosophical discourse by talking about some concrete cases. Three very brief scenarios suggest themselves.

First, what would have happened if Darwin had been a Catholic? Evolution is even more apparently in conflict with the Bible than was Copernicanism. Moreover, the origin of the human species is of much greater concern to religion than is the topic of how the heavens move. Furthermore, in the late nineteenth century, the Catholic Church was again in a very defensive posture, this time in reaction to the Italian Resorgimento. Papal infallibility was defined at the First Vatican Council.

Under all these circumstances, could there have been another Galileo case? Was the Church simply lucky that Darwin was not a Catholic? It is, of course, impossible to answer these counterfactual questions, but if our suggestion has caught your imagination, then perhaps the thesis of this paper may be worth a second thought.

Second, has another Galileo case actually happened in our own day? We are thinking of Teilhard de Chardin, who was not only a Catholic but a Jesuit priest. As a scientist, he was convinced of the truth of evolution. He then proceeded to construct a new evolutionary philosophy and theology, for which he has since become famous. These writings were so upsetting to the authorities in Rome that he was forbidden to publish them during the last twenty years of his life. Only after his death in 1955 did copies of these writings, left with friends, find a public audience.

Third, let us assume that in the near future science succeeds in developing an as-yet-unknown theory that successfully accounts for all the operations of the human mind, purely in terms of neurophysiological functions. This may seem impossible to us now, especially if we are thinking of reducing consciousness to matter in the Newtonian sense of inert, passive matter. But twentieth-century science after Einstein has long since replaced this with a new conception of matter as dynamic energy.

Some of my well-informed professional friends are of the opinion that this sort of reduction of mind to matter as energy is actually taking place at present. As a minimum, we can say beyond doubt that many investigators are today hard at work on this project. If they are successful, what will be the reaction of the Church to the prospect of seeing human consciousness accounted for naturalistically and without appeal to any transcendent factors? If this fanciful scenario were to actually occur, the impact on the Church's interests would be truly monumental. Would there then occur again something very much like what happened in the Galileo case?

EPILOGUE: THE ADULTERATION OF PIO
PASCHINI'S *Vita e Opere di Galileo Galilei*

In many ways, the Galileo affair centered around issues of intellectual honesty and the freedom of human thought. This was recognized explicitly, even in Galileo's own day, as can clearly be seen in Tommaso Campanella's eloquent defense of these values in his defense of Galileo.[5]

However, present-day concern for intellectual freedom is certainly much stronger than it was then. Consequently, one might argue that for this reason alone, anything resembling a repetition of the Galileo affair is exceedingly unlikely – if not impossible – in our day.

Our response to this objection is to call attention to a series of developments in the Vatican in recent years, which indicate that concern for intellectual honesty and freedom of thought may still not be strong enough within the Church to prevent a reoccurrence. Ironically, these events, which themselves constitute another scandal, dealt directly with the Galileo affair and how it should be assessed by the contemporary Church. These developments were first uncovered by Italian scholars in 1979, but because they are still relatively unknown in the English-speaking world, a brief summary of them is in order here.[6]

The year 1942 was the 300th anniversary of Galileo's death. That prompted a decision by the Pontifical Academy of Sciences, whose president at the time was Agostino Gemelli, to sponsor the writing and publication of a new book on Galileo. In an article in the Vatican newspaper *L'Osservatore Romano* for Dec. 1–2, 1941, Gemelli announced that Msgr. Pio Paschini, the rector of the Pontificio Ateneo Lateranense, had been selected to undertake this new project, which was described as being not merely a biography of Galileo but also a study of his work in the intellectual context of his own times, so as to place "the great astronomer in his true light."

Gemelli went on to characterize the book as follows

The projected volume will be an effective proof that the Church did not persecute Galileo, but helped him considerably in his studies. It will not be an apologetic book, for that is not the task of scholars, but will be a historical and scholarly study of the documents.

Announcing the expected results before the research on the project had even begun was not an encouraging sign.

Pio Paschini (1878–1962), a native of Friuli, had lived in Rome since 1913, where he was a seminary professor who had become a widely experienced, highly respected, and scrupulously honest scholar working on the textual resources of the Vatican libraries. His field of expertise was church history, but he had no background in the history of science, and he had undertaken no previous studies of the Galileo case. After some initial but futile objections expressed to Gemelli that this was outside his area of expertise, Paschini began his research into the Galileo documents. His work occupied the next three years, the darkest days of World War II in Italy, and was completed in 1944.

Following regular procedures, Paschini next submitted his manuscript for the book to the Vatican authorities for prepublication review. To make a long story short, the book was then rejected as "non opportuna" (unsuitable) for publication. Because the Holy Office (today called the Congregation for the Doctrine of the Faith) has, to date, still not made public the relevant documents relating to this judgment of the book (e.g., the assessments and the identities of the reviewers), we do not know the specific points of objection that were raised.

However, other indirect sources, including especially Paschini's extensive correspondence with his close friend Guiseppe Vale, indicate that the objections did not relate primarily to factual errors or to misstatements of scientific ideas, both of which could, in due course, have been easily corrected by Paschini before publication. Rather, it appears that the book was withheld from publication because of its interpretive judgments, namely, it was too pro-Galileo, too critical of the role of the Jesuits (especially Christopher Scheiner, S. J.) in the Galileo affair, and too forceful in assigning responsibility to the Church for the condemnation of Galileo. Thus, it seems quite clear that ideological, not factual, issues were the central concern.

Paschini objected vigorously, but fruitlessly, to this decision and refused to modify the book, although even he did not receive a full account of the rationale behind the rejection. From then on up to his death in 1962, he simply dropped the matter and remained silent about what had happened, as was requested of him "for the good of the Church." But in his will, he left the manuscript of the book to his literary heir M. Maccarrone, who, a few years later, gave it to a public library in Udine, where it is still held today.

Oddly enough, the book that was originally intended to be published on the 300th anniversary of Galileo's death was destined to be published on the 400th anniversary of his birth. In 1964, a considerably revised version of Paschini's book was published, for reasons to be explained below, by the Pontifical Academy of Sciences, whose president now was the eminent scientist Msgr. George Lamaître. The changes in the book were made by the noted textual scholar,

Edmond Lamalle, S. J., the archivist of the Archum Romanum Societatis Iesu in Rome.

Lamalle's changes are not identified in the textual apparatus of "Paschini's book," and in an introductory note, Lamalle says merely that his changes in the texts and in the footnotes are "deliberately very moderate, being limited to some corrections which seem to us to be required and to a minor updating of the bibliography."[7] The impression given is that this is essentially Paschini's book with minor editorial changes.

This impression could have been verified by comparing the published book with Paschini's original draft, but no one did this until 1979. It was then found that the changes were extensive, not "moderate." There are several hundred modifications in both the body of the text and in the footnotes. They range from relatively trivial one-word substitutions to complete reversals of the sense of the text. Some whole passages are dropped, others added, and others replaced; the overall interpretive thrust of the book has been reversed to a view less favorable to Galileo and more favorable to the Church and to the Jesuits.

To present this book as if it were essentially Paschini's own work was intellectually dishonest, to say the least. There is little room to doubt that Paschini would have disowned "his own" book if he had lived to see it in print. This was a large-scale adulteration of his work (earlier judged to be "unsuitable" for publication) if not simply a forgery.

To complicate matters further, we should add that the occasion to publish the adulterated version of Paschini's book was the need to deal with the Galileo affair at the Second Vatican Council, which was then nearing its conclusion. The theme of that Council was "the church in the modern world," and its central closing document, *Gaudium et spes*, could not avoid the question of the relationship between science and religion. Early drafts of that Council document show that some of the bishops wished to mention Galileo by name in the body of the text as having been unjustly treated by the Church, in the hope of putting an end to the matter. Other speakers strongly disagreed.

A compromise was introduced into the Council's debates by Msgr. Pietro Parente, ironically a former student of Paschini, who apparently was one of the few participants in the Council who knew about

Lamalle's changes in Paschini's book. The compromise was that the body of the text would include only a general statement affirming the autonomy of scientific research and the compatibility of science and religion, while any explicit mention of Galileo would be moved to a footnote. As a result, the key sentence in paragraph 36 of *Gaudium et spes*, approved on December 7, 1965, at the Council, reads as follows:

One can, therefore, legitimately regret attitudes to be found sometimes even among Christians, through an insufficient appreciation of the rightful autonomy of science, which have led many people to conclude from the disagreements and controversies which such attitudes have aroused, that there is opposition between faith and science.

At the end of this sentence there is attached the following footnote #7: "See P. Paschini, *Vita e Opere di Galileo Galilei*, 2 vols. Pont. accademia delle scienze, Vatican City, 1964."

The ironic impact of this situation is forceful. Here we have a religiously authoritative statement asserting the "rightful autonomy of science" that is itself partially justified by a reference to an intellectually dishonest source. Here we have an attempt to put an end to the Galileo affair that has become yet another intellectual scandal. Here we find that an attempt to remove opposition between science and religion may actually have increased that opposition.

In the years that have passed since the end of the Second Vatican Council, paragraph 36 of *Gaudium et spes* has often been quoted in Church circles in discussions of the relationship between science and religion, thus reemphasizing its official status. For example, the key sentence quoted above, along with its footnote, is restated verbatim in Pope John Paul II's speech to the Pontifical Academy of Sciences at the November 10, 1979, Einstein centennial celebration when he asked scholars to reexamine the Galileo case to "dispel the mistrust that this affair still raises in many minds."[8] Although at that time, the adulteration of Paschini's book was not publicly known, this same paragraph 36 was also quoted by the pope in his October 31, 1992 address.

There may be more to this unfortunate story that could throw a more favorable light on what happened in 1945, when Paschini's original text was rejected as "unsuitable" for publication, and in 1964, when the adulterated version was prepared and published. But we will not know the full saga until the full documentation of what happened, still held in secret, is made public. In the meantime, it is difficult to avoid the conclusion that intellectual honesty and freedom of thought may still not be strong enough in the Church to prevent the recurrence of another clash between science and religion, one similar to the Galileo affair.

NOTES

1 For the Pope's statement and the report of the Pontifical Commission presented at the same time by Cardinal Paul Poupard, see *Origins* 22:(22) (November 12, 1992), 370–5.
2 *Ibid.*, 373.
3 For the origin and an analysis of these two statements, see R. J. Blackwell, *Galileo, Bellarmine and the Bible*, Notre Dame, IN: University of Notre Dame Press, 1991, pp. 112–25.
4 Quoted from Blackwell, *op. cit.*, p. 183.
5 Campanella, Thomas, O. P., *A Defense of Galileo, the Mathematician from Florence*. Translation by R. J. Blackwell, Notre Dame, IN: University of Notre Dame Press, 1994.
6 For more detailed scholarly and documentary accounts of the origin and the fate of Pio Paschini's *Vita e Opere di Galileo Galilei*, see the following sources: P. Bertolla, "Le vicende del 'Galileo' di Paschini," in *Atti del convegno di studio su Pio Paschini nel centenario della nascita: 1878–1978*, Udine: Poliglotta Vaticana, 1980, pp. 172–208; P. Nonis, "L'ultima opera di Paschini, Galilei," *Ibid.*, pp. 158–72; M. Maccarrone, "Mons. Paschini e la Roma ecclesiastica," *Ibid.*, pp. 49–93; S. Tramontin, "Galileo Galilei nella recente storiografia," in *Galileo Galilei e Padova* (Padua: Studia Patavina, 1982), pp. 159–67; P. Scandaletti, *Galileo privato* (Milan: Camunia Editrice, 1989); Annibale Fantoli, *Galileo per il Copernicanesimo e per la Chiesa* (Vatican City: Specola Vaticana, 1993), pp. 406–9; and especially Paolo Simoncelli, *Storia di una censura: "Vita di Galileo" e Concilio Vaticano II* (Milan: Franco Angeli, 1992).
7 Lamalle, Edmond, S. J., "Nota introduttiva all'opera," in *Miscellanea Galileiana*, Vatican City: Pontifical Academy of Sciences, 1964, vol. I, xiii.
8 See *Science*, 207 (March 14, 1980):1166.

10 The god of theologians and the god of astronomers: An apology of Bellarmine

In his theological writings, Galileo maintained what might be called the "independence principle" – science and religion belong to, and are competent on, two distinct and different domains: the factual domain of natural phenomena and the domain of faith of supernatural phenomena. As he put it, a distinction is to be drawn between "purely physical propositions which are matters of faith [and] supernatural propositions which are articles of faith." Accordingly, Galileo held the view that all factual statements about natural phenomena contained in the Scriptures have no value for salvation and, therefore, can be revised or dismissed on scientific grounds.

Bellarmine adopted a different principle, which can be called the "limitation principle." According to it, certain factual statements contained in the Scriptures are necessary for their salvation value and, therefore, cannot be revised in the light of any contrary scientific theories. This has the consequence that, if such theories are advanced, they cannot be held to be true and, at the most, have to be treated as "hypotheses," in the technical sense of devices for calculating or systematizing phenomena, deprived of truth and epistemic value.

Accepted by many theologians and most scientists as well, Galileo's principle has apparently become the official hermeneutic criterion of the Catholic Church. It is alluded to in the Encyclic Providentissimus Deus by Pope Leo XIII (1893), referred to in the Pastoral Constitution Gaudium et Spes of the Vatican Council II (1965), and often invoked by the present Pope John Paul II as a means for avoiding conflicts between science and religion. Bellarmine's principle was instead advocated by the Pope Pius XII in his Encyclic Humani Generis (1950).

368 THE CAMBRIDGE COMPANION TO GALILEO

The aim of this essay is to maintain that the independence principle cannot be accepted by a Catholic believer, because although it
favors science it may damage faith. In particular, I examine Galileo's
allegiance to the independence principle and Bellarmine's opposition to it, the recent, ambiguous acceptance of this principle by the
Church, and the reasons why, in spite of the official homage it pays
to it, the Church is actually suspect of it. As a consequence, it will
be shown that the fire of new Galileo affairs is still smoldering under
the ashes that were thought to be cold.

Such cases do not depend on historical circumstances, the imprudence of men, the transition from one tradition to another, or the
power and prerogatives of institutions; they are constitutive. The
clash between science and religion is linked to two overlapping, although irreducible, forms of experience and the "logics" of their conceptual organization.

"TWO EXTREMES: TO EXCLUDE REASON, TO ADMIT REASON ONLY."[1]

At the end of a new series of lectures on psychoanalysis in 1932, Freud
contrasted scientific Weltanschauung and religious Weltanschauung
and raised the question why the latter does not accept putting an end
to the controversy with the former by explicitly admitting:

> It is a fact that I cannot give you what is commonly called "truth"; if you
> want that, you must keep to science. But what I have to offer you is some-
> thing incomparably more beautiful, more consoling and more uplifting than
> anything you could get from science. And because of that, I say to you that
> it is true in another, higher sense.[2]

The words Freud puts into the believer's mouth here express what
may be called the independence principle between science and religion, according to which religious statements (or beliefs or truths)
cannot interfere or conflict with scientific statements (or beliefs or
truths) because they refer to different domains and have different
purposes.

Freud was of the opinion that such a principle is neither accepted
by religion nor acceptable to science. The reason why he claims
the principle is not accepted by religion shows how a genius sometimes lets himself be attracted by mere banalities. Freud writes that

"religion cannot make this admission because it would involve its forfeiting all its influence on the mass of mankind."[3]

The reason why he maintains the principle is not acceptable to science shows how a genius may sometimes indulge in a mediocre scientism. Freud maintains that the growth of science has gradually eroded the foundations of religions and finally showed, thanks to psychoanalysis, that it is a transient illness, a "neurosis which individual civilized men have to go through in their passage from childhood to maturity."[4]

If science has not yet solved "the problems of the universe" (no less!), this depends, according to Freud, on the fact that "it has truly not had time enough yet for these great achievements."[5] Ironically, enough, Freud's archaic nineteenth-century view that in science, "there is even today a solid groundwork which is only modified and improved but no longer demolished,"[6] is at odds with his aim at confuting religion. The groundwork of science (however solid it may be) is quite different from that of religion, because although the former is based upon empirical experience and aims at explanation, religion is based upon revelation and aims at salvation.

If, as Freud himself maintains, religion, in one of its functions "issues precepts and lays down prohibition and restrictions,"[7] how can one maintain that science interferes with religion? Precepts, prohibitions, and restrictions are (and should be kept) outside the domain of science.

But if we reject Freud's arguments, should we accept the independence principle? This is the subject of this paper. I shall focus on the relationship between the idea of God that believers, specifically Christian Catholic believers, trust in and the idea of God that scientists, in particular modern cosmologists, sometimes refer to. I shall uphold two main points. First, by provisionally accepting the independence principle, I shall try to show that on the basis of such a principle, scientists and theologians (or believers) have nothing to fear from each other but nothing to say to each other either, at least nothing more than, say, Van Gogh depicting sunflowers has to say to a seed oil producer. Secondly, I shall question the independence principle and suggest why believers should reject it. My view is that, contrary to what is nowadays held by the Catholic Church, that principle, although favoring science, damages faith. My apology of Bellarmine stems from this. I believe that religion may clash with science and there is no guaranteed way to avoid such a clash. If I am right, Bellarmine was also right and, what is more and worse, we continue to have the source of new Galileo affairs on our hands.

The current formulation of the independence principle is mainly the work of Galileo, who introduced it in his famous letters on the Copernican question. By basing the principle on such authors as Augustine and Thomas, Galileo's move was rhetorically clever.

If many authoritative Fathers of the Church maintain that science is to be given freedom of inquiry and cannot conflict with religion, how should we refute extending this principle to the Copernican theory and allowing it to be examined as any other empirical theory? Yet, as has been acutely noted,[8] Galileo's principle is much stronger and more demanding than Augustine's and less favorable to faith. As will be seen in a while, it is the last of a series of theses that are increasingly sympathetic with the reasons of science.

To make this point clear, let us suppose a scientific statement or a statement purporting to be cognitive T conflicts with a factual statement S contained in, or drawn from, the Holy Scriptures, in the sense that T and S cannot be both true. As different situations are possible, different attitudes can be adopted. The first situation is when T is not scientifically demonstrable. In this case, Galileo holds the following thesis:

Thesis 1: If T is not demonstrable, then accept S and reject T.

As Galileo himself says, this is the case with such statements as "the stars are animate"[9] and in general with those "articles and propositions which, surpassing all human reason, could not be discovered by scientific research or by any other means than through the mouth of the Holy Spirit himself."[10]

The second situation is when T is demonstrable and already demonstrated. In this case, Galileo holds a different thesis, namely:

Thesis 2: If T is demonstrable and demonstrated, then accept T and reject S.

Galileo puts forward this thesis when he writes that

a natural phenomenon which is placed before our eyes by sensory experience or proved by necessary demonstrations should not be called into question, let alone condemned, on account of scriptural passages whose words appear to have a different meaning.[11]

Like the previous one, this thesis, too, stems from Augustine and Thomas, and it is apparently harmless. There is no problem about rejecting or reinterpreting S when, to use Augustine's example quoted by Galileo, it is a statement such as "The heavens are stretched out like a hide," or, to make use of Thomas's example also quoted by Galileo, such as "The earth hangeth upon nothing," which are both demonstrably false.

But there is a third, more complicated situation. It is when T is demonstrable but not yet demonstrated. This is the case with Copernican theory. Here, Galileo's view is that, in case of doubt, one has to follow the holy Scriptures but to allow science to pursue T as a hypothesis until either T is proved to be true and, then, on the basis of Thesis 2, S is rejected or revised or T is proved to be false and then, on the basis of the same Thesis, S is accepted. Then Galileo's third thesis is:

Thesis 3: If T is demonstrable but not demonstrated, then keep S and pursue T as a hypothesis.

This thesis seems to be reasonable and tolerant but, as we shall see, it is a source of controversy. First, it is important to note that, according to Theses 2 and 3, S and T may conflict and the conflict is settled in favor of S or T according to the proofs that support T. If T is proved, then S is to be rejected or reinterpreted, for example, with the argument that the Scriptures in which S is included do not aim at proving the truth of S or with the argument that S has been introduced in the Scriptures with the aim of making them understandable to primitive, uneducated people.

More generally, Theses 2 and 3 come to say that factual questions belong to science, which has the right to treat them according to its own methods. Thus the consequence of Theses 2 and 3, at least the consequences Galileo draws from them, is another, more demanding thesis. It can be formulated in the following terms:

Thesis 4: All factual statements S are revisable in light of T.

Galileo professes this thesis when he writes that the factual statements contained in the Scriptures have no explanatory purpose but aim at salvation. In particular, when he writes that

the Holy Scripture did not want to teach us whether heaven moves or stands still, not whether the earth is spherical or like a discus or extended along a plane, not whether the earth is located at its center or in one side.[12] And this the Holy Spirit did not want "deliberately," because "they are of no relevance to His intention (that is, to our salvation)." In other words, to use Cardinal Baronio's formula, "the intention of the Holy Spirit is to teach us how one goes to heaven and not how heaven goes."[13]

Let us now consider Copernican theory. Although it is at odds with the Scriptures, Galileo, consistently with his own Theses 3 and 4, calls for freedom of inquiry and demands one be allowed to pursue it at least as a probable, promising hypothesis. As he explicitly writes:

One is not asking that in case of doubts, the interpretation of the Fathers should be abandoned, but only that an attempt be made to gain certainty regarding what is in doubt, and that therefore no one disparage what attracts and has attracted very great philosophers and astronomers. Then, after all necessary care has been taken, the decision may be made.[14]

The reaction of the Church to this demand was twofold and ambiguous. On the one hand, Bellarmine gave the impression of being willing to put Copernican theory under the protection of Thesis 3, for by writing to Father Foscarini that it could be considered as a hypothesis ("Your Paternity and Mr. Galileo are proceeding prudently by limiting yourselves to speaking suppositionally and not absolutely"), he seemed to admit that it can be pursued until, one might argue, it was proved to be true or false, although he personally appeared to be skeptical ("but I will not believe that there is such a demonstration until it is shown to me.")

On the other hand, Bellarmine, set a limit to inquiry, because in the same letter to Foscarini, he maintained that the rest of the Earth is upheld by the Scriptures and if it is not a matter of faith "as regards the topic" (ex parte objecti), it is a matter of faith "as regards the speaker" (ex parte subjecti).[15]

As one can see, the point here does not concern the treatment to be granted to Copernican theory alone. The crucial point, the one that gave rise to the conflict, is whether all factual knowledge included in the Scriptures is in principle revisable and is actually to be revised should it conflict with scientific knowledge. Bellarmine's view is that not all is. In particular, Bellarmine's view is that factual knowledge included in the Scriptures that is essential to the salvation message of faith cannot be revised. Thus, Bellarmine contrasted Galileo's Thesis 4 with the following:

Thesis 5: Certain factual statements S are not revisable in the light of T.

In support of Thesis 5, Bellarmine mentioned some examples of factual claims that are not revisable. He writes that

> it would be heretical to say that Abraham did not have two children and Jacob 12, as well as to say that Christ was not born of a virgin, because both are said by the Holy Spirit through the mouth of the prophets and the apostles.[16]

Clearly, to declare that these are factual statements that are "of faith" is tantamount to negating Thesis 4, suspending the validity of Thesis 3, and preserving such statements from (the possible revision due to) scientific inquiry.

In his reply, Galileo insisted that the cosmological question is a purely empirical question not belonging to the domain of those factual questions that have a salvation value. But such a reply was patently ineffective because Bellarmine did not deny this. He denied that the solution of the cosmological question, *because it has a salvation value*, could be different from one asserted by the scriptures.

Thus, Bellarmine took Galileo's own argument and turned it against him. His counterargument came down to this: If, as Galileo maintains, "two truths cannot contradict one another,"[17] then if one of them is essential for the salvation of man, the other is to be rejected or reinterpreted.

Here, for Bellarmine, the tolerance of Thesis 3 could not be invoked. According to him, the burden of proof is not on the person who condemns T but on anyone who wants to reject or revise S. Patently this is not the astronomers' concern, because when S is "of faith," the Church has legitimate authority over it, not astronomers. In order not to beg the question, Galileo had only one way out. He had to deny that factual assertions of the Scriptures are relevant to faith, that is, to maintain that the purpose of the Scriptures is for salvation alone and not to be used for empirical description or scientific explanation.

This is precisely what he did when, as we have seen, he wrote that the cosmological assertions of the Scriptures are not essential to its message. He tried to avoid a conflict between science and religion by arguing that if salvation assertions are not revisable while factual assertions are, then the assertions of the Scriptures are not factual. Thus, he puts forward the following thesis:

Thesis 6: Factual statements S have no salvation value.

Theses 5 and 6 go in opposite directions. Whereas Galileo's Thesis 6 supports the independence principle, Bellarmine's Thesis 5 is the expression of a different principle, which we may call the "limitation principle," according to which science and religion overlap and there are limits to the revision of statements concerning their overlapping area.

At least at first sight, the independence principle has advantages over the limitation principle. It is tolerant and mutually satisfactory, because it gives science and religion authority in different domains. According to this principle, if a conflict arises and science ascertains a truth that is contrary to a religious statement, this statement is to be rejected or revised. Yet this would not be harmful to religion because the rejected or revised statement would be irrelevant to salvation.

GALILEO AND THE INDEPENDENCE PRINCIPLE

As the subject is important and usually neglected, before continuing, I would like to go further into the question of Galileo and Thesis 6. Did he really maintain that all factual statements of the Scriptures are not essential to salvation?

In certain passages, Galileo seems to refer to cosmological statements alone, in particular to those statements of the Scriptures from which the rest of the Earth can be drawn. He claims that such a view cannot be said to be of faith for two reasons: First, because "it is not enough to say that all the Fathers accept the earth's rest, etc., and so it is an article of faith to hold it, rather one would have to prove that they condemned the contrary opinions."[18] Second, because on this matter, the Fathers do not share the same opinion, "given that one can read in the Fathers different interpretations of the same passages."[19] But if the Earth's rest is not of faith for these reasons alone, then one might think it is of faith for other reasons or that certain other factual statements may be considered to be so. Such a conclusion might be drawn from the following passage:

Next consider the principle that the collective consensus of the Fathers, when they all accept in the same sense a physical proposition from Scripture, should authenticate it in such a way that it becomes an article of faith to hold it. I should think that at most this ought to apply only to those conclusions which the Fathers discussed and inspected with great diligence and debated on both sides of the issue and for which they then all agreed to reject one side and hold the other.[20]

However, the view Galileo advocates here is more general. He takes Thesis 2 literally. On the basis of Thesis 3, he asks for freedom of inquiry into natural phenomena. As a consequence, he invokes Thesis 4 as regards the factual statements of the Scriptures. And in order not to stop the progress of science with contrary scriptural statements, he advocates Thesis 5, although for obvious reasons of prudence, he does not profess it explicitly. Several steps lead Galileo to this conclusion.

He starts by raising

doubts about the truth of this prescription, namely whether it is true that the Church obliges one to hold as articles of faith such conclusions about natural phenomena, which are characterized only by the unanimous interpretation of all the Fathers.[21]

Then he goes on to say that, as regards natural conclusions, certain Fathers "consider it useless to spend time trying to ascertain those conclusions."[22]

But Galileo does not stop here, for he adds that natural questions are not only useless for the salvation message of the Scriptures, but that they are not even its subject matter. He distinguishes two kinds of questions: natural questions that belong to science and supernatural questions that pertain to theology.

Thus, not only does Galileo write that theology is worthy of the title of "queen," insofar as its topic "surpasses in dignity all the other topics which are the subject of the other sciences and also insofar as its teaching proceeds in more sublime ways,"[23] he also maintains that theology "does not come down to the lower and humbler speculations of the inferior sciences, but rather . . . it does not bother with them, inasmuch as they are irrelevant to salvation."[24]

Galileo's next step therefore consists in saying that theology concerns only transcendent and not mundane questions, or that its topic is the salvation of man and not the explanation of nature. In the letter to Castelli he writes:

I should believe that the autonomy of the Holy Writ has merely [solamente] the aim of persuading men of those articles and propositions which are necessary for their salvation and surpass all human reason, and so could not become credible through some other science or any other means except the mouth of the Holy Spirit itself.[25]

In the corresponding passage of the letter to the Grand Duchess Christina, "merely" is replaced by "chiefly" (principalmente), but this change is dictated by caution, as is clear from the fact that he writes it would be prudent not to allow anyone to commit the Scriptures on natural questions.

Finally, and this is his last step, Galileo distinguishes between "purely physical propositions which are not matters of faith [and] supernatural propositions which are articles of faith."[26] If, as it seems, this classification is exhaustive, then according to Galileo, there are no natural questions that are of faith. But this is precisely what Thesis 6 says: Natural questions in the Scriptures have no salvation value. And this supports the independence principle: There can be no conflict between science and religion.

THE INDEPENDENCE PRINCIPLE VERSUS THE MUTUAL SUPPORT PRINCIPLE

It is not my intention to question the practical effects of the independence principle. As a matter of historical fact, it has favored both science and religion. By protecting them both from possible mutual conflict, it has smoothed the way for the growth of the former and allowed the latter freedom of prediction. But I have doubts about the theoretical status of the principle and the legitimacy of the consequences sometimes drawn from it. First of all, let us note that the independence principle seems nowadays to be accepted by both scientists and Christian Catholic theologians or believers.

In 1893, with his *Encyclic Providentissimus Deus*, Pope Leo XIII declared that the Scriptures are not concerned with scientific matters; they make use of the language of the people they were addressed to. In a speech dating from December 20, 1931, Pope Pius XI said that "when one speaks of alleged contrasts between faith and science, either one makes science say what it does not say or makes faith say what it does not teach."[27]

Eventually, in 1965, using almost the same words Galileo had used 350 years before, the Vatican Council II, with the Pastoral Constitution *Gaudium et Spes*, established that

the methodic inquiry of each discipline, if it really proceeds scientifically and according to moral norms, will never be in real contrast with faith, because profane reality and reality of faith stem from the same God.[28]

More recently, in 1980, Pope John Paul II has declared:

Between reason, which, according to its own nature stemming from God aims at truth and is qualified for knowledge and faith, which stems from the same divine source of every truth, there can be no substantial conflict. We do not fear, but rather exclude, that science, which is based itself on rational motives and proceeds with methodological seriousness, may produce knowledge that conflicts with truths of faith. This can only happen when the distinction between the domains of knowledge is neglected or denied.[29]

As I have said, I doubt this is really the case. But before examining this problem, I shall provisionally accept the independence principle. It is my opinion that, if we stick to this principle, then science and religion cannot conflict but neither can they support each other.

And it is also my opinion that many of those who have professed the independence principle have, in actual practice, resorted to a different principle, that I shall call the "mutual support principle," between science and religion. In my view, this latter principle commits a "category fallacy." Such a fallacy is often involved in the use of the concept of creation by both cosmologists and theologists.

Let us take a closer look at this concept. Both the main cosmological theories of this century have made use of it, either to affirm that science has solved the problem of creation or to deny it. Thus, Bondi wrote that, thanks to the steady state theory,

the problem of the origin of the universe, that is, the problem of creation, is brought within the scope of physical inquiry and is examined in detail instead of, as in other theories, being handed over to metaphysics.[30]

For their part, certain cosmologists, either supporters of the Big Bang theory or interpreters of it, have maintained either that "we may perhaps not improperly refer [to the initial singularity] as to the creations"[31] or that the initial singularity is the effect of an act of creation, so that "we can 'witness' the Creator's existence."[32]

On this point, I agree with Grunbaum's view[33] that the concept of creation as it appears in modern cosmology is different from the concept of matter formation *ex nihilo* as it appears in theology and that the latter concept gives rise to a pseudo-scientific problem, both in the steady state theory, because in this theory, such a problem cannot be raised any more than, in classical physics, the problem of uniform motion can be raised, and in the Big Bang theory, because, according to this theory, there is no time before the singularity and therefore no problem about its cause. I also adhere to Hume's and Kant's indictments concerning the use of the concept of a cause beyond empirical domains. But rather than stress these points, I prefer a different line of argumentation.

Let us suppose, for the sake of argument, that we can refer "not improperly" to the initial singularity as an act of creation. What conclusion can we draw from it? That a Creator exists? Suppose, still for the sake of argument, that this, too, is conceded. The problem now is twofold: Is this creator theologically relevant? Can this creator serve the purpose of faith?

My answer to the first question is decidedly negative. A creator proved by cosmology is a cosmological agent that has none of the properties a believer attributes to God. Even supposing one can consistently say the cosmological creator is beyond space and time, this creator cannot be understood as a person or as the Word made flesh or as the Son of God come down to the world in order to save mankind.

Pascal rightly referred to this latter Creator as the "God of Abraham, Isaac and Jacob, not of philosophers and scientists."[34] To believe that cosmology proves the existence of a creator and then to attribute to this creator the properties of the Creator as a person is to make an illegitimate inference, to commit a category fallacy.

My answer to the second question is also negative. Suppose we can grant what my answer to the first question intends to deny. That is, suppose we can understand the God of cosmologists as the God of theologians and believers. Such a God cannot (and should not) serve the purpose of faith, because, being a God proved by cosmology, he would be at the mercy of cosmology. Like any other scientific discipline that, to use Pope John Paul II's words, proceeds with "methodological seriousness," cosmology is always revisable. It might then happen that a creator proved on the basis of a theory will be refuted when that theory is refuted. Can the God of believers be exposed to the risk of such an inconsistent enterprise as science?

My conclusion on this point is that if cosmology is really taken as independent from theology and faith as regards its domain and purposes, then cosmology neither proves nor confutes (or neither should prove nor confute) the traditional proofs of the existence of God.[35] Thus Pope Pius XII's view, according to which "the idea of the creation of the universe [is] perfectly compatible with the scientific view,"[36] may be accepted but not in the sense the Pope intended it. That is, modern cosmology supports theology, although it does not provide an "absolute proof" of the existence of God.

The God of cosmologists and the God of believers are compatible because they are two quite different entities. But if they are two distinct entities, they cannot support each other. Thus when Pope Pius XII, after examining the results of modern cosmology, concluded, "Therefore creation in time; thus a Creator; so, God!"[37] his "therefore" is not scientifically proved, his "thus" is logically invalid, and his "so" is risky and in any case insufficient for the believer. Pope John Paul II seems to have rightly corrected his predecessor when he admitted that scientific rationality "is not enough to lead [one] to know a personal and transcendent God."[38]

The same conclusion holds in the opposite direction, that is, if one uses theology to support cosmology. My first negative reason is the same: By so doing, we make a category fallacy. My second negative reason is also the same but inverted. If, by using cosmology as support for theology we endanger the God of believers, by using theology as support for cosmology, we endanger scientific theories. This is what happened when Pope Pius XII considered the steady state theory as a "solely gratuitous hypothesis."[39] If the independence principle holds good, then what is or is not gratuitous is to be decided by science, independently of any theological assertion that may sound to the contrary.

But does the independence principle hold good? This is my last point.

I shall examine this question from the standpoint of a Catholic believer. For him or her, God is a source of knowledge. Thus, a Catholic believer has two sources, experience and revelation.

According to the independence principle, these two sources can never clash because the former concerns factual questions whereas the latter concerns salvation questions. The problem is: Are there factual questions that a Catholic believer takes (or has to take) as essential for his or her salvation?

It can be readily admitted that many factual questions are not essential to the believer's faith. For example, it does not matter for him or her whether the Earth moves or stands still or whether life originated on Earth or elsewhere, in our galaxy or in other galaxies. However, not all factual questions are of this sort. Certain factual questions are essential to faith and cannot be removed or revised. This is the case with such dogmas as the virginity of Mary or Jesus Christ's resurrection, which, in spite of the fact that they patently clash with science, the believer cannot reject.

This is also the case with those questions concerning miracles that the believer accepts, although they are obviously contrary to scientific knowledge. But there are further factual questions that, though they are not dogmas, are essential to faith in the sense that the latter would make no sense without the former. Consider the following claims:

1. The universe is infinite in time.
2. Life in the universe stems from inorganic matter.
3. Life originated in more than one place.
4. Psychical life is reducible to biological and social conditions.

Granted, none of these claims is nowadays a scientific truth. But what matters is that all of them are open to scientific inquiry. Although they are not empirically testable in a strict, direct sense and can be better understood as metaphysical cores of research programs, they belong to those questions on which scientists claim to have a right of investigation and to which they consider positive solutions possible. Suppose one day, these solutions are put forward and eventually, after discussion and critical examination, transformed into *truths of science*. Might a believer accept them?

A Christian Catholic has two orders of commitments. He is committed to God from whom revelation comes and he is committed to Church, by which the right interpretation of the content of such a revelation is established and authenticated. The first commitment concerns faith, as a personal experience of revelation. The second concerns religion, as a set of concepts, beliefs, and practices required by faith according to the interpretation of the Church. If a conflict arises between a truth of science and a factual statement the believer attributes to revelation, the Church may revise such a statement and even drop it from the content of revelation the believer has to respect, that is, religion.

Such a move, however, has a limit. The believer and the Church may revise or reinterpret many statements, but they cannot give up those theses without which faith loses its meaning. Let us call these theses *truths of faith*. Here are a few of them for a Catholic believer:

1. God created the universe.
2. God gave the gift of life.
3. God gave the gift of life only to one original couple.
4. God gave man a body and a soul independent of that body.

All these truths of faith interfere with the previous claims of science. If God created the universe, then the universe has not always existed, for in such a case there would be no need to create it. If God gave the gift of life, then life cannot be taken as deriving from inorganic matter, for in that case, it would be a natural phenomenon. If God gave the gift of life to a single, original couple, then life cannot have originated in more than one place. And if man has a soul that is independent of the body, then man's consciousness and physical life cannot be reduced to (an organization or function of) biological and physical properties. For if this were the case, the term "soul" would become devoid of meaning.

Thus if the four truths of faith hold, the four truths of science cannot be maintained. It follows that a Catholic is committed to certain truths of faith that clash with certain truths of science. If he does not want to give up the former, he has to reject the latter. That is, he has to declare that there are questions that, although factual, cannot be corrected by science. But this is Bellarmine's Thesis 5, which is contrary to Galileo's Thesis 6. Consequently, the independence principle cannot be accepted by a believer.

Here is, in my view, the real source of the conflict between Bellarmine (and the Church) and Galileo (and modern science). One can say that Galileo was doubly imprudent, because he tried to credit Copernican theory with an epistemtic value higher than his "sensory experiences and necessary demonstrations" allowed him and because he also tried to show that Copernican theory was more compatible with the Scriptures than the Ptolemaic theory.[40]

However, one can also say that the Church insisted beyond any reasonable limit, because it tried to commit the Scriptures on a question such as the rest of the Earth that (as the Church itself eventually admitted) is not essential to salvation. But neither Galileo's imprudence nor the Church's obstinacy (its "errors and deficiencies," as Pope John Paul II called them[41]) is the real source of the conflict.

The conflict was much deeper and transcended the *dramatis personae* of the time. It was a conflict between two principles, that is, the principle that science can investigate any factual question (Galileo's independence principle, supported by his Thesis 6) and any principle that certain factual questions cannot be investigated by science because they are articles of faith (Bellarmine's limitation principle, stemming from his Thesis 5). Or, if one wants, it was a conflict between two traditions: the new tradition of science, according to which science and science alone is competent on questions of truth, and the old religious tradition, according to which human experience cannot be dissected into different domains and the Scriptures, too, have something to say about it.[42]

If this is the real nature of the conflict that arose at that time, then it can arise at any time. And, indeed, it arose again at the middle of this century with Pope Pius XII's *Encyclic Humani Generis*.

Pius XII rejected Theses 1–4 as contrary to articles of faith. I have already mentioned point 1, which the Pope considered as "gratuitous hypothesis," because it is in conflict with the idea of creation in time by a Creator. As for Thesis 2, the Pope did not express himself, but his view can be seen from what he said about Thesis 3.

Speaking about evolutionism, the Pope wrote that an examination of this theory

has to be carried on in such a way that the reasons for the two opinions, that is, that for and that against evolutionism, are considered and evaluated with the necessary seriousness, moderations and control, and provided everyone is willing to submit to the judgment of the Church, which Christ entrusted with authentically interpreting the Holy Scriptures and with defending the Dogmas of Faith.[43]

But as regards polygenism, that is, Thesis 3, the Pope wrote:

As far as the other hypothesis is concerned, that is polygenism, the sons of the Church are not allowed the same freedom. Believers cannot adopt that opinion whose supporters teach that after Adam there have existed here on earth true men which did not come, by natural generation, from him, or that Adam represents the whole of many parents.[44]

Thus, Thesis 3 cannot be accepted by believers and even less so Thesis 2. As for Thesis 4, the Pope was equally clear, for he wrote that "Catholic faith obliges us to believe that souls have been created by God immediately."[45]

Rather than following the independence principle, which he never accepted as a hermeneutic principle for the Scriptures, Pope Pius XII adhered to the mutual support principle and accepted Bellarmine's Thesis 5. For those questions that have not yet been proved by science but that might be, Galileo had called for tolerance and put the burden of proof on the shoulders of those who intended to damn them. Pope Pius XII (like Bellarmine before him) not only shifted the burden of proof but declared there can be no proof and not even any search for it, because no truth of the Scriptures with salvation value, however different it may be from a truth of science, can ever be rejected or revised. The following passage leaves no room for doubt:

Finally, we must speak about those questions which, though belonging to positive sciences, are more or less linked with the truth of Christian faith. Not a few insist that Catholic religion has to take great care of those sciences. This is undoubtedly commendable as regards those facts that are really demonstrated; but one has to be prudent if they are hypotheses, however in some way or another scientifically based, which touch upon the doctrine contained in the Holy Scriptures or in Tradition. If such hypotheses are directly or indirectly against the revealed doctrine, then they cannot be maintained in any way.[46]

The relevant points of this passage are the following: according to the Pope:

1. There are questions that, "though belonging to positive sciences, are more or less linked with the truths of Christian faith."
2. Such questions are "in some way or another scientifically based."
3. As a consequence, scientists advocate their own right to examine them and, if proved, they ask that the Catholic religion should take "great care of the results, that is, it should correct or reinterpret the Scriptures accordingly," and yet
4. "if such hypotheses are directly or indirectly against the revealed doctrine, then they cannot be maintained in any way."

This means that

5. There are factual questions essential to the salvation message of the Scriptures that cannot be revised.

This was Pius XII's view and this was Bellarmine's opinion (his Thesis 5). The conclusion is that, at least on some important points, science and Catholic religion are in conflict.

One might object that this conflict concerns the relationship between truths of faith and scientific hypotheses, not scientific truths. But the objection is untenable. Firstly because, according to a more adequate epistemology than Pius XII's, all scientific truths are hypothetical. Secondly, because the Pope denied that hypotheses contrary to articles of faith can be maintained even *qua* hypotheses. One might also object that Pius XII's *Encyclic* did not give rise to a new Galileo affair.

A new Galileo affair did not arise in 1950 (at the time of Pius XII's *Encyclic*) as it arose in 1633 (at the time of Galileo's trial) because of the contingent, historical circumstances. However, the real source of the affair, that is, the conflict between the independence principle and the limitation principle, has not been removed.

In summary, in a period in which scientific culture is so pervasive and its impact so impressive, it may be prudent and wise, as John Paul II has recently done, to invoke "a dialogue in which the integrity of both religion and science is supported and the advance of each is fostered" and to stress that "both religion and science must preserve their autonomy and their distinctiveness."[47] But it would also be dangerous to forget that the risk of a conflict, like a fire smoldering under the ashes, is still there.

NOTES

1 Blaise Pascal, *Pensees*, translated by W. F. Trotter, *Great Books of the Western World*, vol. 33 (Encyclopedia Brittanica Inc.), the University of Chicago, Chicago, 1952, n. 253, p. 220.
2 Sigmund Freud, *New Introductory Lectures on Psycho-Analysis* (1933), the *Standard Edition of the Complete Psychological Works of Sigmund Freud*, edited by J. Strachey, Hogarth Press, London, 1953–1974, 24 vols., vol. XXII, p. 172.
3 Ibid.
4 Freud, p. 168.
5 Ibid.
6 Freud, p. 174.
7 Freud, p. 162.
8 See E. McMullin, "How Should Cosmology Relate to Theology?, in A. R. Peacocke, ed., *The Sciences and Theology in the 20th Century*, London, Oriel, 1981, pp. 17–57.
9 Galileo Galilei, *Letter to the Grand Duchess Christina* (1615), English translation in *The Galileo Affair, a Documentary History*, edited by M. Finocchiaro, University of California Press, Berkeley, 1989. See p. 104.
10 Finocchiaro, see pp. 93–4, see also p. 104.
11 Finocchiaro, p. 93.
12 Finocchiaro, p. 95.
13 Finocchiaro, pp. 95–6.
14 Galilei, "Considerations on the Copernican Opinion," 1615, in *The Galileo Affair*, p. 85.
15 *Letter of Bellarmine to Foscarini* (April 12, 1615), in Finocchiaro, *The Galileo Affair*, pp. 67–8.
16 Finocchiaro, p. 68.
17 *Letter to the Grand Duchess Christina*, p. 96, also p. 93.
18 Finocchiaro, p. 108.
19 Finocchiaro, p. 109.
20 Finocchiaro, p. 108.
21 Ibid.

22 Finocchiaro, p. 109.
23 Finocchiaro, p. 100.
24 Ibid.
25 Galilei, *Letter to Castelli* (December 21, 1613) in Finocchiaro, *The Galileo Affair*, p. 51.
26 Finocchiaro, p. 101.
27 Quoted in *I Papi e la Scienza*, edited by M. Gargantini, Milan, Jaca Books, 1985, p. 137.
28 Ivi, p. 63.
29 Karol Wojtyla (Pope John Paul II), Speech of December 15, 1980 to scientists and students in the Cathedral of Cologne, reprinted in K. Wojtyla, *L'Uomo nel Mondo*, edited by A. Rigobello, Rome, Armando, 1981, pp. 115–16.
30 H. Bondi, *Cosmology*, 2nd ed., Cambridge, Cambridge University Press, 1961, p. 140.
31 This was Sir E. Whittaker's view as referred in Pope Pius XII's speech of November 22, 1951. See *Discorsi Indirizzati dai Sommi Pontefici Pio XI, Pio XII, Giovanni XXIII, Paolo Vi, Giovanni Paolo II ala Ponfitica Accademia delle Scienze dal 1936 al 1986*, Pontificiae Academiae Scientiarum Scripta varia in Civitate Vaticana, 1986, p. 812.
32 C. I. Borghi, "Mentalita scientifica e religiousa. Considerazioni di un fisico," *Serie Cristiani e Societa Italiana*, no. 12, Milano, 1980, p. 20.
33 See A. Grunbaum, "The Pseudo-Problem of Creation in Physical Cosmology," *Philosophy of Science*, 56, 1989, pp. 373–94.
34 Pascal, "Memorial," in *Oeuvres Completes*, edited by J. Chevalier, Biblioteque de la Pleiade, Paris, Líbrairíe Gallimard, 1954, p. 554.
35 I completely agree with McMullin when he writes that "what one cannot say is first, that the Christian doctrine of creation 'supports' the Big Bang model or, second, that the big Bang Model 'supports' the Christian doctrine of creation." See E. McMullin, "How Should Cosmology Relate to Theology," p. 39. In my view, this holds good for any other scientific theory, cosmological or not.
36 Pope Pius XII, Speech of November 22, 1954, p. 80.
37 Pope Pius XII, p. 81.
38 Pope John Paul II, Speech of April 2, 1981, to the Secretariat for Non-believers in *I Papi e la Scienza*, p. 49. Later, John Paul II corrected Pius XII's view more dramatically when he warned theologians about "making uncritical and overhasty use for apologetic purposes of such recent theories as that of the Big Bang in cosmology." See his Message of June 1, 1988, as reprinted in *John Paul II on Science and Religion*, edited by R. J. Russell, W. R. Stoeger S. J., G. V. Coyne S. J., Vatican Observatory Publications, Notre Dame, the University of Notre Dame Press, 1990

(the quotation is from pages M 11–12).

39 See Pope Pius XII's Speech of November 22, 1951, p. 77.

40 For this latter imprudence of Galileo's, see C. M. Martini, "Galileo e la teologia," in *Saggi su Galileo Galilei*, edited by C. Maccagni, Florence, Barbera, 1972, vol. III, tome 2, pp. 441–51.

41 Speech of December 15, 1980, p. 116.

42 On this point, I agree with Feyerabend, who also describes "the conflict between Galileo and the Church as a conflict between traditions." See P. K. Feyerabend, *Farewell to Reason*, London, Verso, 1987, p. 248.

43 Pope Pius XII, *Encyclic Humani Genersis* (August 12, 1950), Gregoriana Editrice, Padova, 1952, p. 24. I examined the content of this encyclic in the light of the relationship between science and religion in my "Scienza e trascendenza," *Studium*, 77, 1981, pp. 517–43.

44 Ivi, p. 25.

45 Ivi, p. 24.

46 Ivi, p. 23.

47 John Paul II, Message of June 1, 1988, pp. M 7 and M 8.

11 The never-ending Galileo story

This essay is concerned with the myth of Galileo and, thus, with his image as a hero and martyr. It does not endeavor to state who Galileo was or what he did, but deals rather with people's expectations of who he was; in other words how his image and the image of his science have evolved from his time to the present day.

Galileo's great qualities and skills as a scientist are well known, but he was also an accomplished writer, wielding his sharp pen as a major protagonist in an age of upheaval, and he was the most famous martyr of science. His fate is, therefore, an endless source of material for an epic, enough to satisfy every age's demand for hero worship. This is why Bertolt Brecht chose to write his famous play *Galileo*.[1]

It is nothing new that Galileo has been a subject of worship since his own day.[2] It is agreed among Galilean scholars that the Galileo story is often distorted by popular as well as scholarly literature.[3] Moreover, Galileo is naturally idolized.[4] If we cannot, or do not wish to, safeguard historical description from circumstantial influences or fashions, let us at least try to explore the twilight zone between "true" history and myth.

At times this myth, as we shall see, has even been useful in fostering scholarship. In describing various metamorphoses of Galileo's image, however, I would call for caution or – to borrow the expression of a leading Galilean scholar, Maurice Finocchiaro – judiciousness, and I would suggest that even today we occasionally fail to notice, whether unconsciously or consciously, when quasi-hagiography disguises itself as scholarship.

GALILEO IN THE EYES OF HIS CONTEMPORARIES

In his own day, Galileo was a celebrity and a hero, receiving endless praise during his lifetime from admirers, friends, and opponents alike throughout Europe.[5] Even Maffeo Barberini, before becoming Pope Urban VIII and having him condemned by the Inquisition, composed an ode in 1620, *Adulatio Perniciosa*, in Galileo's honor, praising his astronomical discoveries.[6] And the most famous contemporary Italian poet, Giambattista Marino, devoted the following lines to Galileo in his *Adone* (1623):[7]

> Through thee, O Galileo, the telescope,
> to present age unknown, shall be composed,
> the work which brings remotest object close
> and makes it show much larger to one's sense.
> Thou only, the observer of her motion
> and of what in her parts has concealed,
> thou shalt, without a veil to shroud her form,
> behold her nude, O new Endymion.[8]

> In this same glass thou'lt spy not only each
> of her minute details from near at hand,
> but also, by my aid, thou shalt observe
> Jupiter girt round with other lights,
> whence in the sky the Arno's demigods
> will leave their names inscribed forevermore.
> Then Julius[9] shall yield to Cosimo,
> Augustus vanquished by thy Medici.

Despite the condemnation of Galileo in 1633 under the Pontificate of Urban VIII, the latter's *Adulatio* was published in Antwerp in 1636 and again in Paris in 1642, the very year of Galileo's death.[10]

No doubt, however, Galileo's misfortune meant that there would be little open enthusiasm for him in the Catholic world for well over a century. His death was given little public attention, in sharp contrast to the tide of feeling that accompanied the death of other giants such as Michelangelo and Newton.[11] In the years following his death, he was mentioned and praised in contemporary literature but not worshipped; or rather, worship was not allowed.[12]

Louis Moreri's successful *Grand Diction[n]aire Historique* (1674) devoted a flattering, though balanced, article to Galileo saying that never had there been a greater spirit for the sciences of the heavens.[13]

Pierre Bayle's erudite and historically oriented *Diction[n]aire Historique et Critique* (first edition in 1695–97) did not even in its fourth edition of 1730 devote an entry to Galileo and mentioned him only in the entry devoted to his pupil Vincenzio Viviani (1622–1703).[14]

Every age creates its own heroes, and Galileo is a perennial candidate for that position; his extraordinary life adventure has all the necessary elements for a promising career as a superstar. In post-Renaissance Italy, the Renaissance genius was heroized, and the prototype of the contemporary genius was the "divine" Michelangelo Buonarroti.

Many illustrious writers shared the shaping of the latter's image as a hero, above all Michelangelo's famous pupil, the pioneer art historian and biographer Giorgio Vasari, and the contemporary writer and historian Benedetto Varchi. So did the Church representative, the Apostolic Nuncius to Florence, Giorgio Bolognetti.[15] This image was also the ideal of Galileo's worshipers, who, while the Inquisition was on watch to ensure Galileo's memory remained low-profile, were secretly preparing to celebrate his comeback as a second Michelangelo.[16]

GALILEO AS A RENAISSANCE GENIUS

On January 12, 1642, four days after Galileo's death, Bolognetti wrote, evidently in great distress, to the Pope's nephew Cardinal Francesco Barberini in Rome: "They say that the Grand Duke wants to erect to him [Galileo] a sumptuous mausoleum comparable with and opposite that of Michelangelo Buonarroti."[17] The aim of Galileo's followers and admirers was thus clear from the very beginning, and, despite difficulties, they persisted. Galileo's canonization as a hero was carried out above all by his young disciple, Vincenzio Viviani, who, indeed, devoted most of his creative career to the memory of his teacher. The first important step was his biography of Galileo.[18]

Viviani began writing *Life of Galileo* in 1654 at the request of another admirer of Galileo, Prince Leopold de Medici, the brother of the Grand Duke of Tuscany. Since Viviani was a perfectionist, he went on writing it and improving it for the rest of his life, and the short, eloquent essay appeared only posthumously in 1717.[19]

In Viviani's eyes, Galileo was the Renaissance ideal of a genius, and his *Life of Galileo* followed the typical pattern of contemporary literary "hagiography," which ascribed to its heroes supernatural qualities from the moment of birth (often a birth accompanied by some cosmic event), the childhood qualities of a prodigy, a knowledge more profound than that possessed by normal mortals, and extraordinary talents (preferably practical ones).[20]

Viviani introduces Galileo thus: "Nature chose Galileo as one who should reveal part of those secrets."[21] His main inspirer, as his papers in Florence's National Library clearly reveal, was none other than Vasari: One sentence in Viviani's *Life* is closely copied from Vasari's *Life of Giotto*.[22] Viviani's particular ideal was, naturally, Michelangelo, and, as a fortunate coincidence, Galileo was born three days before Michelangelo died (February 15 and 18, 1564). Viviani's papers include all sorts of calculations related to Michelangelo's death; perhaps he was trying to find some additional, transcendental, links. Although nobody mentioned reincarnation – after all, all parties involved were good Christians – it must have been, subconsciously at least, a most welcome event.[23]

Admittedly, Viviani made an effort to seek out sources and was certainly more conscientious a historian than many of his contemporaries. Yet, in order to achieve his ideal, he had to embellish historical facts – a common practice at the time – and his biography is of course not very reliable for the purposes of modern historians of science. Above all he related – or invented – anecdotes indicating the deep, magical, practical insights of Galileo. Thus Viviani reports, and today we question, that Galileo discovered the principle of the pendulum as the result of his having observed the swinging of a lamp in the cathedral of Pisa. The same kind of embellishment holds, even more emphatically, for the legendary experiment of dropping weights from the Leaning Tower of Pisa.[24]

Viviani's *Life of Galileo* was one of the most authoritative texts on Galileo's life until the twentieth century, if not to date. The reason is obvious: Despite its shortcomings, this kind of embellishment in Viviani's essay is altogether both a good piece of contemporary "hagiographical" literature, and (considering his time) a relatively accurate history of science. It is the excellence of Viviani's essay that makes it so difficult to interpret; even today, historians have difficulties in distinguishing between reality and myth in its pages. The details related by Viviani and his embellishments were considered by later historians to be the unvarnished truth.

Above all, by presenting Galileo as a practical man, Viviani was the originator of the historiographical tradition, in popular as well as scholarly history of science, which considered and considers Galileo the founder of experimental sciences, based on sheer common sense. This view has been seriously questioned in the present century by some modern historians of science, especially Emil Wohlwill, Lane Cooper, and, most significantly, Alexandre Koyré.[25] I will return to this later in this essay.

Nor was writing Galileo's *Life* in the style of Renaissance hagiographies the only undertaking of Viviani to turn his teacher into a hero.[26] In 1674 he reminded the Tuscan Grand Duke, Cosimo III, of the old plan of Cosimo's father to erect a monument in honor of Galileo similar to that erected in the same church, Santa Croce, in honor of Michelangelo. In a letter to another follower of Galileo, Ottavio Falconieri, he suggested how the monument should look: with three statues, representing geometry, astronomy, and philosophy, just like the statues representing architecture, sculpture and painting in Michelangelo's monument.[27]

Unfortunately, Viviani did not live to see such a monument. For the time being, all he could do was to place, in 1693, a bust of Galileo above the entrance of his own house and an inscription in Galileo's memory fixed to its wall.[28] Five years later, the widespread small guide of Florence, *Ristretto delle Cose Più Notabili della Città di Firenze*, praised Viviani's initiative and expressed the long endeavor for an adequate memorial for Galileo in Florence.[29] Such a monument, just as Viviani would have wished, was erected only in 1737, in the Church of Santa Croce, in front of Michelangelo's.

In the century that followed Viviani's death, the age of Newton, the details of Galileo's life and work remained relatively unknown. His works and the scientific controversies associated with them had by then receded in importance and all that remained was his fame as a genius and as a martyr of science. Yet he remained (and in many senses is still today) an icon. Newton mentioned him in his *Principia* on occasions in which he agreed with him, namely when stating the laws of motion.[30] Newton's system of the world, based on his theory of gravitation, nevertheless surpassed and contradicted

Galileo's system, in which planets had circular orbits. In this case, Newton concealed the discrepancy by not mentioning Galileo's name (he said "others" instead) though he was referring precisely to the latter's law. In his *The System of the World* he said:

> But it has been long ago observed by others, that (allowance being made for the small resistance of the air) all bodies descend through equal spaces in equal times. And, by the help of pendulums, that equality of times may be distinguished to great exactness.[31]

This, however, was no more than contemporary scientific reverence. Galileo came to be much more than a Renaissance genius and a scientific sacred cow.

GALILEO, THE MARTYR OF SCIENCE

In April 1633, in the midst of Galileo's trial, the eclectic scholar Gabriel Naudé wrote to the philosopher Pierre Gassendi, making "the machinations of Father Scheiner, and other Jesuits, who wish to get rid of him" responsible for Galileo's fate.[32] Today we know that the Galileo affair was much more complex. Naudé's letter is one of the earliest attempts to turn Galileo into a martyr of science, an attempt that, thanks to the ideas of the Enlightenment, had full success.

Naudé's letter is a private document. The earliest public presentation of Galileo as a martyr of science came from the Protestant world, out of the pen of none other than John Milton. Milton was an admirer of Galileo and in his *Areopagitica – Speech for the Liberty of Unlicenc'd Printing* (1644), he mentions his meeting with "the famous *Galileo* grown old, a prisoner to the Inquisition, for thinking in Astronomy otherwise then the Franciscan and Dominican licenser thought."[33]

Galileo's martyrdom as a legend, however, prospered in the eighteenth century. In 1703, a work under the title *Naudaeana et Patiniana* appeared in Amsterdam. It said under the entry "Galileo:"

> Everybody knows that the fame of Galileo has increased the list of unlucky intellectuals. After having languished in the prisons of the Inquisition, having been obliged, in order to come out, to revoke publicly his belief that probably had no fault other than that of not being liked by the Inquisitors.[34]

This vague description, in a book dedicated to Naudé, repeats and adds invented details to the latter's pronouncement and well illustrates the neglect of the vast documentation concerning Galileo's life. Even Viviani's relatively well-documented and detailed description of Galileo's life was still unpublished. Its publication, in 1717, came just as the ideas of the Enlightenment, with their anticlerical bias, were gaining popularity in Europe.[35] In the eyes of that age, like Newton, Galileo was an exemplary hero.

Thus Viviani's *Life of Galileo* suited the eighteenth century's spirit, despite Viviani's caution in describing the controversy between his teacher and the Church. He had merely said of Galileo's discussion of the two world systems:

> Galileo showed himself to be more adherent to the Copernican hypothesis which had been condemned by the Holy Church as repugnant to the Divine Scripture. Thus, after the publication of his *Dialogues*, Galileo was summoned to Rome by the Congregation of the Holy Office, where he arrived around 10 February 1632 ab incarnatione.[36] By the supreme clemency of that Court and by the sovereign Pontiff Urban VIII who also knew him very well from the republic of men of letters, he was placed under arrest in the residence of the Tuscan ambassador in that exquisite Palace of the Trinità de' Monti, and, for a short time (having been shown his error), he withdrew as a true Catholic this opinion of his.[37]

Viviani's biography may have been at the birth of the Galileo myth but does not touch on those traits that transformed Galileo into a martyr of science. As historian Rupert Hall points out, despite the evident naivete of Viviani's statement, "most eighteenth-century writers cast 'Peripatetics' in the role of villains."[38] Yet in 1754, Voltaire, the Enlightenment's most celebrated caricaturist-mouthpiece, wrote, in his *Dictionnaire Philosophique*:

> The persecutors were the party that happened to be mistaken. Those who enjoined penance upon Galileo were more mistaken still. Every inquisitor ought to be overwhelmed by a feeling of shame in the deepest recesses of his soul at the very sight of one of the spheres of Copernicus. Yet if Newton had been born in Portugal, and any Dominican had discovered a heresy in his inverse ratio of the squares of the distances, he would without hesitation have been clothed in a 'san-benito,' and burned as a sacrifice acceptable to God at an 'auto-da-fé.'[39]

(A footnote added to the above quotation by the English translator in 1835 says: "This is as true in fact, as piquant in description; and although san-benitos and autos-da-fé are out of fashion, the disposition to persecute and run down abstract truths is nearly as strong as ever.")

In the same year in which Voltaire was writing about Galileo (1754), the fourth volume of Diderot and D'Alembert's *Encyclopédie* appeared. Although it did not contain an entry on Galileo, the entry on Copernicus clearly presented Galileo as a martyr of science and appealed to the pope to put an end to the restrictions imposed on scientific research in Italy. It said:

It would be very desirable that a country as full of spirit and knowledge as Italy, should finally admit an error so damaging to the progress of science ... Such a change would well suit the enlightened pontiff governing the Church today.[40]

The pressure of the Church was lessening, but the Enlightenment's hostility toward it persisted.[41] Its ideas influenced dedicated Italian historians; they had at their disposal sources for Galileo's life which they scarcely used. In 1793, the Florentine historian Giovanni Bat[t]ista Clemente de' Nelli published the most detailed biography of Galileo til then.[42] It was particularly important and authoritative because Nelli had discovered Galileo's papers and had at his disposal an impressive collection of sources, now forming a substantial portion of the Galilean Collection of manuscripts in the Florence National Library.[43]

Yet – as other of Nelli's own manuscripts and drafts kept in the same library testify – what he did was mainly to amplify Viviani's biography.[44] This is why his attitude to the Church is particularly relevant to the theme of this essay, namely Galileo's image. His critique of the Church reflects a fashion rather than documentary evidence. He says, inter alia:

It is amazing to see the extent of the friars' hatred and the attitude of the Pontiff to his divine author ... The Pope, the Inquisition, the friars, the ignorant peripatetics, with the utmost extravagance, found unheard ways to torment the spirit of that unfortunate philosopher.[45]

Galileo's image as the martyr of science as presented by the anti-clerical spokesmen of the Enlightenment is well summarized by the authoritative contemporary Florentine naturalist and historian Giovanni Targioni Tozzetti in his balanced assessment (1780):

Galileo's ill-fortune, though partly brought upon himself, caused much noise in the world, and if it brought little honor to the Tuscan Government of those days, it also brought no small dishonor to the Roman Court; since it has given and will give to the heterodox, and even slightly recalcitrant orthodox, an opportunity not to support its [the Church's] course.[46]

Targioni Tozzetti was right in his judgment: Galileo remained a martyr of science long after the Enlightenment. In 1821, for instance, the British writer, Walter Savage Landor, began writing in Florence his monumental work, *Imaginary Conversations*, wherein he imagines the meeting between Milton and Galileo.[47] Landor's "conversation," like Milton's *Areopagitica* and Brecht's *Galileo*, is historically inexact, but it was extremely important in the diffusion of a certain image of Galileo's martyrdom in the English-speaking world.

Anticlericalism was one feature of the Enlightenment response to the case of Galileo. Another feature is the conviction that correct reasoning leads to demonstrated truth, namely knowledge – although there was no consensus on what correct reasoning or knowledge was. The leaders of the Enlightenment movement included philosophers of contradicting views, notably the inductivist Francis Bacon and the intellectualist René Descartes.

Galileo was recognized as one of the pioneers of the modern method of investigation, but since the details of his work and methodology were little known and less understood, contemporary thinkers adopted and adapted him and his work to their own philosophy. Thus, the eighteenth century also saw the rebirth of a different Galileo, at times inconsistent, and his heroization began to take different paths.

GALILEO, SCIENTIFIC METHOD,
AND THE ENLIGHTENMENT

Colin Maclaurin, the mathematician and follower of Newton, described Galileo in 1748 as one who

did no less service by treating, in a clear and geometrical manner, the doctrine of motion, which has been justly called the key of nature. The rational part of mechanics had been so much neglected, that there was hardly any improvement made in it, from the time of the incomparable Archimedes to that of Galileo; but this last named author has given us fully the theory of equable motions, and of such as are uniformly accelerated or retarded, and of these two components together.[48]

Maclaurin stressed the importance of geometry in Galileo's contribution, including in the concept the view of acceleration and velocity (i.e., the view that velocity is the time differential of position and that acceleration is the time differential of velocity). He praised Galileo's mathematics, as here he was on safe ground (although not quite, since Newtonian time differential is not a Galilean concept and, moreover, this is not quite geometry).

Other philosophers preferred to stress the empirical aspects of Galileo's work. In his *Saggio sopra il Cartesio*, written in 1754, Francesco Algarotti, the popularizer of Newton, friend of Voltaire, and admirer of British empiricism, regarded Galileo and Newton as empiricists in contrast to the rationalist Descartes. For Algarotti, Galileo had been an "enemy of Hypotheses, modest and patient discoverer, at the mercy of the experimental and geometrical help of the doctrine of motion."[49] Similarly, Nelli described Galilean methodology in the following words:

Galileo in Tuscany, in Italy, and I would nearly say in Europe, was the one that introduced the right manner of philosophizing, and the first that not with litigious arguments, but with founded, firm experiments proved true his opinions.[50]

There were, of course, more balanced presentations of Galileo, such as that of David Hume, who in *The History of England* (1759) wrote:

Bacon pointed out at a distance the road to true philosophy: Galileo both pointed it out to others, and made himself considerable advances in it. The Englishman was ignorant of geometry: the Florentine revived that science, excelled in it, and was the first that applied it, together with experiment, to natural philosophy. The former rejected, with the most positive disdain, the system of Copernicus: the latter fortified it with new proofs, derived both from reason and the senses.[51]

Similarly, Paolo Frisi, Barnabite, mathematician, physicist, and astronomer, and author of *Saggio sul Galileo* (1765), presented Galileo as "a philosopher, a geometer, a mechanician and an astronomer, not less theoretical than practical."[52]

Yet the view that modern science is essentially empirical and detached from prejudices prevailed, and with it the belief that Galileo, as one of the earliest modern scientists, grounded – and perhaps even founded – experimental science. Galileo became (and still is) the model for the empiricist scientist who, unlike the natural philosophers of his day, sought to answer questions not by reading philosophical works, but rather through direct contact with nature. As support for this view of science, Viviani's anecdotes were particularly important.

Thus, by the end of the eighteenth century, the picture that emerged of Galileo was that of Galileo as freethinker, martyr of science, and founder of experimental science. The Enlightenment, no doubt, erected statues to honor great scientists, and it was during this period that Galileo's myth grew. However, as the philosopher of science Joseph Agassi points out, Enlightenment writers did not expect a scientist to be a genius.[53]

"The intellectual leaders of the Age of Reason, Bacon and Descartes, agreed," says Agassi, "that common intelligence suffices for the pursuit of knowledge. The last great philosopher of the Age of Reason, Immanuel Kant, also endorsed this view."[54] The age that followed, Romanticism, was different in essence. It was reactionary and irrationally condemned all rebels. How did the Galileo tale survive this period?

Romanticism was a revolt against authority and tradition, as well as against reason and science. It had, according to Joseph Agassi, "acceptance or popular success as the criterion of correctness."[55] Science, to be "good," had to be useful.

A typical example is John Herschel's A Preliminary Discourse on the Study of Natural Philosophy (1830).[56] For Herschel, Galileo was more than the pioneer of science: He was also the pioneer of applied science. "Among the Greeks," he says, "this point was attained by Archimedes, but attained too late, on the eve of that great eclipse of science which was destined to continue for nearly 18 centuries, till Galileo in Italy, and Bacon in England, at once dispelled the darkness:

the one, by his inventions and discoveries; the other, by the irresistible force of arguments and eloquence."[57]

Because for Herschel experience, which includes both observation and experiment, was the "only ultimate source of our knowledge of nature and its laws,"[58] Galileo must have reached his discoveries by means of experience:

A fair induction from a great number of facts led Galileo to conclude that the accelerating power of gravity is the same on all sorts of bodies, and on great and small masses indifferently; and this he exemplified by letting bodies of very different natures and weights fall at the same instant from a high tower, when it was observed that they struck the ground at the same moment, abating a certain trifling difference, due, as he justly believed it to be, to the greater proportional resistance of the air to light than to heavy bodies.[59]

Moreover, Galileo was a kind of prophet and already knew what was discovered after him, and Herschel remarks: "the gravity of every material body is in the direct proportion of its mass, which is only another mode of expressing Galileo's law."[60] The Galileo tale had to become utilitarian, and Alexander von Humboldt related in his *Cosmos* (1846) that Galileo used a pendulum to measure the height of the cathedral in Pisa. This invented story is nothing but a Romantic addition to the Renaissance embellishment in Viviani's story.[61]

In summary, the only way to cope with a prominent rebel such as Galileo in the age of Romanticism was to let him escape forward, namely to turn him into a modern genius. It would be hard to describe the innumerable representations produced by the eighteenth century of Galileo as a genius. The outstanding editor of Galileo, Antonio Favaro, has devoted two essays to Galilean iconography, amply documenting the contemporary blooming of paintings depicting Galileo's genius.[62] It would be enough to glance at the "Tribuna di Galileo," erected in 1841 by Grand Duke Leopold II on the first floor of the Palazzo Torregiani in Florence.[63] Pietro Redondi has recently written a long study of nineteenth-century literature and painting concerning Galileo, showing how "the martyr has been sanctified."[64]

Romanticism influenced the political changes in Europe during the nineteenth century, including the Risorgimento, the movement for Italian unification.[65] It was in the wake of the Risorgimento that, in 1887, a royal decree issued by Umberto I, second King of Unified Italy, ordered the collection of Galileo's writing in the National Edition. The decree announced

a consideration of supreme national pride to satisfy in this manner the long-lasting desire of the scholars, the raising of a new and permanent monument of glory to the marvelous Genius who created experimental philosophy.[66]

Pathos aside, as the decree itself said, the National Edition, published between 1890 and 1909, is not only a monument, but also a masterpiece of scholarly work, and of course a most reliable source for Galilean studies. Indeed, this was also the period in which modern history of science was emerging, whose critical approach would sooner or later come to question the heroic model of Galileo.

MODERN HERESY BEGINS

In the middle of the nineteenth century, modern history and philosophy of science were emerging. From 1837 onward, the philosopher and historian William Whewell produced a series of original and powerful studies combining history of science, philosophy of science, and theory of knowledge.[67] Although Whewell did not contribute directly to dispelling the mythical image of Galileo, his modern approach certainly challenged it.

Whewell stressed the importance of intuition and imagination against the worthlessness of induction in the development of science, and he noticed that small modifications to theories are important to the growth of science.[68] Whewell noticed, for instance, incompatibilities between theories in science, such as Kepler's laws and Newton's Theory of Gravitation: They are, in fact, equivalent only for a two-body system.[69] Whewell's views implicitly questioned the traditional image of Galileo by suggesting that all great scientific discoveries, including Galileo's, are sooner or later surpassed. Whewell's work, however, had little impact: Because he went against current opinion his work was set aside and forgotten.[70]

Yet scholarship was making progress. In 1876–1877, Karl von Gebler published a masterly edition of the documents of Galileo's Trial.[71] In 1893, the historian of art Igino Benvenuto Supino found that the so-called Galilean Lamp in the cathedral of Pisa was hung there in 1587, contradicting Viviani's report that Galileo had observed it swinging four years earlier.[72] The more legendary aspects of the Galileo myth began to crumble.

The most radical step in the demythologization of Galileo came toward the end of the century. Between 1891 and 1900, Raffaello Caverni, a Florentine priest, wrote a monumental work (six volumes), relying on many previously unpublished documents, attempting to study the position and importance of Galileo's work in relation to his predecessors, his followers, and other seventeenth-century European scientists.[73]

The result was a totally new presentation of Galileo's work, claiming that too much credit had been given to him at the expense of other Renaissance scientists and of his contemporaries. Despite his great admiration for Galileo, Caverni boldly questioned what the latter pretended to have discovered, going as far as to denounce him for having claimed priority for the discoveries of many natural philosophers who were his predecessors, such as Tartaglia or Stevin, or even his own followers such as Castelli or Cavalieri. Galileo's false claims, says Caverni, were reported and, in a few cases, amplified by his biographers.

Caverni's work has many merits. Most important of all, he drew attention to the work of many scientists whom Galileo had overshadowed. He also pinpointed one of Galileo's most important contributions to science – the recognition of the basic importance of geometry.[74] Admittedly, Caverni let his "anti-Galileanism" carry him too far, and his claims are at times exaggerated and no less mythical than the views he criticized.

Caverni's presentation of Galileo as an antihero naturally encountered much opposition, and this was not just restricted to philosophical polemic.[75] Caverni was isolated outright: He was excluded from the board of editors of the National Edition, and his claims were to a great extent ignored. The printing of his work was even interrupted in the middle of the sixth volume when he died in 1900, although he left a complete manuscript. Incredibly, Volume 6 abruptly ends in the middle of a sentence. It took three quarters of a century to rediscover and reprint his work.[76]

Yet even in his own day, Caverni's work had an impact, though initially outside Italy, marking a turning point in Galilean studies and encouraging critical study of Galileo's work. In 1903, Emil Wohlwill, a German chemist and historian, pointed out that there is no evidence that several additional details in Viviani's story ever occurred.[77] Wohlwill doubted, among other things, the truthfulness of stories such as that of the lamp in the cathedral of Pisa and the Leaning Tower experiment.

Moreover, before Caverni, to the best of my knowledge, no one had investigated Galileo's intellectual predecessors – indeed, it was taken for granted that Galileo had none. A few years after Caverni had published his work, the French physicist, philosopher, and historian of science Pierre Duhem, in the wake of Whewell and Caverni, studied the development of science as constant modification to theories, known as the "conventionalist" approach to the history of science. Duhem published a monumental study of Galileo's predecessors, emphasizing the former's debt to their work.[78] All these studies, of course, reshaped Galileo's image.

Official history of science could not abide these heresies. Favaro, in a series of articles, attempted to refute Wohlwill's claims.[79] Favaro's arguments were plausible, but the tone in which they were written displayed an irritation that went beyond scholarly argument. For instance, Wohlwill had claimed that there was no evidence that King Gustav Adolf of Sweden had been a student of Galileo in Padua as Viviani had related.

Favaro replied with an article with the angry title: "Ancora, e per l'ultima volta, intorno all'episodio di Gustavo Adolfo di Svezia nei racconti della vita di Galileo" ("Again, once and for all, concerning the episode of Gustav Adolf of Sweden in the stories of Galileo's Life"). The article accuses Wohlwill of being no less than anti-Italian and anti-Latin.[80] On another occasion he wrote: "Nobody had ever doubted, until, regrettably, in the past few months, one of the most authoritative and profound Galilean scholars argued against him [Viviani]."[81] Wohlwill had violated the sanctum.

But heresy went on. In 1935, Lane Cooper, an American professor of English, published a small humorous book, *Aristotle, Galileo and the Tower of Pisa*.[82] Cooper's aim was to assemble the literature relevant to the Leaning Tower story for the use of English-speaking readers, and he repeated Wohlwill's doubts, pointing out that there was no evidence that the episode ever took place. The book was not so much directed against Viviani's story as against that mythological literature that presented the Leaning Tower demonstration as a dramatic turning point in the history of science.

The reaction was excessive.[83] Shortly after its appearance, Cooper's book was reviewed and criticized by two leading scholars, the historian of science Aldo Mieli and the classicist Harold Cherniss.[84] Both reviewers focused their criticism on a secondary feature of Cooper's book – his presentation (or misrepresentation) of Aristotle's law of fall – and practically disregarded the rather more important point raised by him and, earlier, by Wohlwill, namely that no documentation exists to prove Viviani's story.

Mieli was particularly scornful, and in his four-page review he ridiculed Cooper by referring to him no less than six times as "the Professor of English" who tried to meddle in matters that did not concern him. Mieli's irrational arguments were soon picked up by Giuseppe Boffito, who in 1940 updated the Galilean bibliography. He commented on the entry for Cooper's book: "The author is a philologist, not a physicist: this deficiency is evident throughout the book."[85]

Neither Mieli nor Boffito say, however, how a better knowledge of physics or history of science can produce evidence in favor of Viviani. The disproportionate and irrational reaction to Cooper's book confirms that progress not only failed to dispel the mythological aspects of the Galilean story but probably emphasized them.

KOYRÉ

Shortly after the publication of Cooper's book, Alexandre Koyré began a series of Galilean studies that became fundamental for the history of science in general.[86] Koyré conjectured that neither experience nor experiment played any essential role in Galileo's work and even suggested that some experiments Galileo described in detail had never been performed, basing his claim both on evidence and even more on his view of Galileo's apriorist view of method.

Koyré's claim was frankly presented as an outcome not so much of his remarkable study of the Galilean heritage as of his own views concerning the role of experiment in science. An experiment, he maintains, is a question put before nature and the "facts" resulting from asking this question have to be ordered, interpreted, and explained within the language in which it is formulated; thus the results are necessarily formulated a priori.[87] This interpretation, claims Koyré, is particularly appropriate when applied to the birth of modern science, when mathematical language had evolved further than experimental ability.

It is Galileo's work on method rather than on the physical world that fits this interpretation, having much in common with the Platonic and, more specifically, Archimedean view of scientific method. According to Koyré, Galileo's great contribution to science was in going one step beyond Plato and Archimedes, by successfully granting movement to the abstract and immovable Archimedean bodies. The laws of his physics are thus deduced abstractly, without recourse to experiment on real bodies. Therefore, says Koyré, the experiments Galileo claims to have performed, even the ones he really carried out, cannot be anything but thought experiments.[88]

Koyré ridiculed, for instance, the description of Galileo's inclined-plane experiment in the *Two New Sciences* as "An accumulation of sources of error and inexactitude,"[89] adding: "It is obvious that the Galilean experiments are completely worthless: the very perfection of their results is a rigorous proof of their lack of correction."[90] These words, if taken out of the context of Koyré's general apriorism, do indeed sound blasphemous. Yet this still does not mean that, according to Koyré, Galileo did not perform empirical work, but only that his empiricism was conceived a priori.[91]

Koyré's fascinating view is difficult to criticize because, as one of his critics, Maurice Finocchiaro, has pointed out to me, it concerns what Galileo should have done rather than what he actually did. Indeed, Koyré's view may be considered part of the Galilean myth, more precisely of the anti-Galilean myth, and it suffers from the main weaknesses of the Galilean myth in that it attempts to use Galileo as a mouthpiece through which to expound Koyré's own view of science.

Koyré's challenge raised different types of criticism. One attempt to invalidate Koyré's arguments by checking his precision came from a number of prominent scholars, such as Eugenio Garin and Maurice Finocchiaro, who indeed showed that Koyré had been imprecise. The latter, in particular, found in Koyré's treatment "superficiality in logical analysis, oversimplification, injudicious exaggerations, and questionable manipulation of the text by means of excessive quotations, of taking passages out of context, and of not infrequent scholarly carelessness."[92] Finocchiaro's criticism is strong because it is rational but does not prevent Finocchiaro from praising Koyré:

Nevertheless, Koyré does deserve the credit for having called attention to the logical structure and validity of Galileo's arguments and to his rationalism, even though he misunderstands the former as circular and misinterprets the latter as apriorism. Finally, it would be unhistorical to deny that the study of the history of science made great progress with Koyré; to turn the clock backwards is simply unthinkable.[93]

Yet there were those who tried to turn the clock back, to invalidate Koyré's arguments, by irrational criticism. It all started in 1961, when Thomas Settle repeated Galileo's inclined-plane experiment ridiculed by Koyré.[94]

Settle's description of the repetition of Galileo's experiment in a nice short article is among the most quoted in Galilean studies. It concluded, in contradiction to Koyré, that the experiment could be performed with the means Galileo described. Settle's experiment, however, neither refuted nor claimed to refute Koyré's general methodological argument that since all experiments are premeditated, whether or not Galileo performed some experiments is not important for understanding his intentions.[95]

Settle's interesting result, however, was twisted by several later empirically oriented works. Typical of these is Stillman Drake's complaint, in his classic and outstanding article on Galileo's experimental confirmation of horizontal inertia: "Koyré's paper was reprinted years later in book form without so much as a note by the editors concerning Settle's refutation of its thesis."[96]

In his article, Drake attempted to reconstruct Galileo's inclined-plane experiment on the basis of unpublished manuscripts. Drake's work initiated a new rich trend of Galilean studies, in attempts to interpret Galileo's working notes. It would be beyond the boundaries of this article, and frankly monotonous, to outline the ramifications of this research (which include, among other things, many modern ball-rolling experiments). Let me here only quote Jürgen Teichmann, a scholar who had the perseverance to follow it throughout and study its results.[97] His conclusion was that these studies as a whole strengthen the Galileo myth.

The myth of Galileo's empiricism is only part of the Galileo myth. In recent times no less emphasis has been placed on the myth of Galileo the martyr of science.

GALILEO'S MODERN MARTYRDOM

Gebler and Favaro's edition of the manuscripts of Galileo's trial was followed by many studies of the "Galileo Case." Two exciting books are particularly relevant to the present article: Giorgio De Santillana's *The Crime of Galileo* and Arthur Koestler's *The Sleepwalkers*.[98] The first relies on Gebler, argues in favor of Galileo, and adds one more link to the long literary chain of Galileo's martyrdom. The second blames, in the wake of Caverni, Galileo's arrogance as the source of his misfortunes, rather than the "obscurantism" of his opponents, and adds one more link to the chain of the Galileo antimyth.

There is a basic difference between these works. Santillana's was written as a more scholarly work, its intention apparently to provide "an objective" account of the case.[99] Koestler's main purpose seems to have been to present a more popular history of cosmology from the Greeks to Newton (I. Bernard Cohen even suggested that "One almost has the feeling that what began as a biography of Kepler ended up as a history of cosmology"[100]). Indeed, the book, with over 600 pages and subtitled "A History of Man's Changing Vision of the Universe," is divided into five parts and does not deal with Galileo until the middle of Part Four (p. 352).[101]

Koestler was a novelist; he did not make an effort to get his facts right, and history of science would have done better to treat his book as a work of divulgation, in the same way as Brecht's *Galileo* was treated as fiction. But Brecht's Galileo is "good" and Koestler's Galileo is "bad."

A violently hostile review article by Santillana and Stillman Drake branded Koestler as a heretic and elevated his book to the rank of a scholarly work. Of the seven points discussed at length in that article, six deal with Galileo.[102] It is hard to blame the two prominent Galilean scholars of having been irrational in their criticism.

There is no doubt, however, that the reaction that provoked the review was emotional: Joseph Agassi, after a meticulous analysis of the controversy, points out,

Generally, every time Galileo's defenders are apologetic, Koestler stresses the point which causes them discomfort; and every time the Catholic apologists show a weak point in Galileo's scientific view, Koestler follows them. And he regularly attributes some unpleasant motives to Galileo.[103]

Koestler, the iconoclast, did not escape the fate of his predecessors.

ON GOES THE GALILEO TALE

"So well have we defended the pantheon of science from any suggestion of stain," says the late Richard Westfall in a classic article on Galileo's science and patronage, "that only after I had pursued this question nearly to its conclusion did I discover it had been raised once before, nearly a century ago, by an Italian scholar, Raffaello Caverni. Caverni, who wrote during the springtime of Italian unity, was summarily drummed right out of the Italian learned community for casting a shadow on the name of the national hero. Since I have no desire to suffer a similar fate, I trust that I am far enough removed from the seat of such emotions. I do wish to emphasize that it is not my purpose in any way to call Galileo's position in the history of science into question."[104]

If a scholar of the stature of Westfall found it appropriate to make a declaration such as the one above, I feel all the more impelled to repeat it at the end of this article dealing with heroes and heretics. For a historian who repeated Galilean experiments did me the honor of placing me in the company of Caverni & Co.[105] I had dared, in my book *In the Wake of Galileo*, on the successors of Galileo, to devote about two pages to the discussion of Galileo's empiricism, saying that although there is no doubt that Galileo experimented a great deal, one cannot say exactly what role he assigned to experiment.[106]

The myth-ridden image of Galileo's work as perfect remains, and his (little-studied) critics and disciples are still considered better ignored. Criticism in science and its history can endure as long as it is rational, respects intellectual propriety and fair play. Only under these conditions may history be distinguished from legend.

NOTES

I am indebted to Joseph Agassi for having read an early version of this article and suggesting many improvements. Just before the completion of this article, Neil Harris gave me invaluable criticism and suggestions: Not all could be incorporated in the manuscript but they contributed greatly to its improvement. I am also indebted to Alison Moffat for her editing work as well as her improvements to the contents.

1 Bertolt Brecht, *Leben des Galilei*, Berlin: Hen schelverlag, 1956, English adaptation, *Galileo*, by Charles Laughton, edited and introduction by Eric Bentley (New York: Grove Press, 1966).

2 For Galileo's changing image in Italian culture during the seventeenth and eighteenth centuries, see Gianni Micheli's informative "L'idea di Galileo nella cultura Italiana dal XVI al XIX secolo," in *Galileo: La Sensata Esperienza*, Cinisello Balsamo: Amilcare Pizzi, 1988, pp. 163–237.

3 One should of course distinguish between scholarship and more divulgative forms of writing or between the use of the figure of Galileo and the story (or myth) of his life in creative writers. Some of these episodes seem high art, such as Brecht's, but the interpretation is linked with the preoccupations of these writers. In many cases, they also have only a partial and imperfect knowledge of Galileo's writings and thus accept the myth. Most of this article concerns the figure of Galileo in the work of specialists, yet history itself is often a myth, and one finds the Galileo myth in different nuances but basically the same traits in all types of literature.

4 A delicious presentation of the Galileo myth in relation to the story of the Leaning Tower Experiment is Lane Cooper's, *Aristotle, Galileo, and the Tower of Pisa* Ithaca: Cornell University Press, 1935, which was ignored for decades before it achieved its present status as a classic. Both his philosophy and his history of science were heretical, and at that time heresy was less tolerated than today. For the rejection of Cooper see my "Galileo, Viviani and the Tower of Pisa," *Studies in History and Philosophy of Science* (1989), pp. 435–51.

5 It would be enough to look at Galileo's wide correspondence, collected in volumes 10–18 of *Le Opere di Galileo Galilei*, Edizione Nazionale, 20 vols., ed. Antonio Favaro (henceforth abbreviated as EN), Florence Barbèra, 1890–1909; reprint: 1929–1939, 1964–1966, 1968. For a compilation of the poetic references to Galileo in contemporary works see Nunzio Vaccaluzzo, *Galileo Galilei nella Poesia del Suo Secolo. Raccolta di Poesie Edite e Inedite, Scritte da Contemporanei in Lode di Galileo*, Milan: Remo Sandron, 1910. This useful work, with a long introduction, clearly shows how the Galileo myth existed already in his own day. For some other examples see also Micheli, "L'idea di Galileo," pp. 166–8.

6 *Pernicious Adulation*. The poem was sent to Galileo by Barberini accompanied by a letter dated August 28, 1620. Galileo thanked him with a letter written on September 7; EN 13:48–50. As Giorgio de Santillana points out in his exciting though biased *The Crime of Galileo* (London: Mercury Books, 1961, first published 1955), p. 156, in the *Adulatio* Galileo's discoveries "are brought in as an example of how greatness and glory deemed to be above the changes of fortune will eventually show their weakness and come to grief."

7 *Adone*, x, 43. Quotation from *Adonis. Selections from L'Adone of Giambattista Marino*, Harold Martin Priest, trans., Ithaca: Cornell Univ. Press, 1967, p. 190. Marino's and others' attitude to Galileo's discoveries is discussed by Giovanni Aquileia, "Da Bruno a Marino," *Studi Secenteschi* 20, 1979; pp. 89–95. Not everybody agreed with Galileo's Copernicanism but his telescopic discoveries were highly acclaimed.

8 A handsome youth, loved by Cynthia.

9 Julius Caesar.

10 The first publication is quoted by Favaro, EN, 13:48, note 2; the second one in Maphaei S. R. E. Card. Barberini nunc Urbani Papae VIII poemata, Parisiis, e Typographia Regia, anno 1642.

11 For public indifference to Galileo's death and burial see Paolo Galluzzi, "I sepolcri di Galileo: le spoglie 'vive' di un eroe della scienza," in Luciano Berti, *Il Pantheon di Santa Croce Firenze*, Florence: Cassa di Risparmio di Firenze, 1993 (this bank publication is not available commercially), pp. 145–82. Galileo's funeral was attended by only a small number of relatives, friends, and followers (see p. 145). Galluzzi relates the efforts made by Galileo's followers to grant Galileo a mausoleum appropriate to his standing and the difficulties they encountered, and he adds another interesting piece to the mosaic of the growth of the Galileo myth.

12 Three sonnets composed in his honor in 1642 by one Paganino Gaudenzio, "In morte del famosissimo Galileo," disappeared without trace from Florence's Magliabechi library; see Antonio Favaro and Alarico Carli, *Bibliografia Galileiana* (1568–1895), Rome, 1896, p. 40. This was not necessarily censorship, but when Galileo's pupil Vincenzio Viviani wanted to describe Galileo's "supernatural talent" ("talento sopranaturale"), he was dissuaded by a churchman; see Luigi Tenca, "Relazione fra Vincenzio Viviani e Michel Angelo Ricci," *Rendiconti dell'Istituto Lombardo di Scienze e Lettere, Classe di Scienze*, 87 (1954):212–28, p. 219. Things were however significantly different in Catholic France: Pierre Gassendi, an admirer of Galileo, in his *Institutio Astronomica* (London, 1653), praised Galileo's astronomical discoveries (I was not able to find this early edition of Gassendi's work and I rely on Favaro and Carli, *Bibliografia Galileiana*, p. 52).

13 Louis Moreri, *Le Grand Dictionaire Historique*, 2 vols., Lyon, 1681, 2:11. I quote this edition since it is the earliest available to me.

14 Pierre Bayle, *Diction[n]aire Historique et Critique*, 4 vols., Leiden, 1730, 4:463. This edition, too, was the only one I had available.

15 For Bolognetti see next section on "Galileo as a Renaissance Genius."

16 Galileo was already compared to Michelangelo during his own lifetime: In 1612, reacting to criticism of Galileo's highly controversial

Bodies in Water, Galileo's friend, the painter Ludovico Cardi da Cigoli, wrote him an encouraging letter saying that Michelangelo too had been criticized and was alleged to have ruined architecture. See EN 12:361.

17 EN 18:378.

18 See my "Viviani's Life of Galileo," *Isis*, 80 (1989):207–31. See also my *In the Wake of Galileo* New Brunswick: Rutgers University Press, 1991, where his life's work is outlined in some detail.

19 Ibid. Viviani's *Life* [of Galileo] was published for the first time in *Fasti consolari dell'Accademia Fiorentina*, ed. Salvino Salvini, Florence, 1717, pp. 397–431, and included in EN 19:597–646.

20 This pattern has been vividly described by Ernst Kris and Otto Kurz, *Legend, Myth, and Magic in the Image of the Artist: A Historical Experiment*, transl. Alastair Laing, transl. rev. by Lottie M. Newman New Haven, CT: Yale University Press, 1979; based on Kris and Kurz, *Die Legende vom Künstler: Ein historischer Versuch*, Vienna: Krystall Verlag, 1934, with additions to the original text by Otto Kurz.

21 EN 19:602.

22 Vasari says of the young Giotto: "mostrando in tutti gli atti ancora fanciulleschi una vivacità e prontezza d'ingegno," and Viviani says of Galileo: "ne' prim'anni della sua fanciullezza a dar saggio della vivacità del suo ingegno." The first quotation is from Giorgio Vasari, *Le Vite de' Più Eccellenti Pittori, Scultori e Architettori nelle Redazioni del 1550 e 1568*, ed. Rosanna Bettarini, annotated by Paola Barocchi, vol. 2 Florence: Sansoni, 1966, pp. 96 and 139 for the 1550 and 1568 editions respectively. The second is from EN 19:601.

23 Viviani's papers related to his *Life* [of Galileo] have been collected in vol. 11 of the Galilean Collections of MSS in the National Library in Florence. For full details see my "Viviani's Life of Galileo," pp. 221–5, and *In the Wake of Galileo*, pp. 116–22. In his article "I sepolcri di Galileo" (1993) Galluzzi, too, deals with the myth of Michelangelo as Viviani's source and with the providential coincidence between Michelangelo's death and Galileo's birth. Galluzzi flatters me by devoting a footnote to my book, *In the Wake of Galileo*, referring to my account of Viviani's efforts to scrutinize this coincidence (pp. 169–70 in Galluzzi's article, pp. 116–22 in my book). Galluzzi also criticizes my having allegedly said that Viviani had falsified dates. I neither ascribed to Viviani any such misconduct nor have I dated any falsification, observing instead that it is not known when Viviani wrote the different drafts of his *Life*. Galluzzi also reproaches me for having spoken of Viviani's juxtaposition of dates only in relation to a biographical *cliché*, without exploring the intellectural drives behind such a juxtaposition. Such an exploration would be, indeed, too ambitious for

me: I am eager to hear more from him about his own work in this direction.

24 EN 19, pp. 603 and 606 respectively.

25 For the creation of the myth of Galileo as the common-sense founder of experimental science, see my *In the Wake of Galileo*.

26 See Galluzzi, "I sepolcri di Galileo."

27 Ibid., p. 169.

28 The building, known as "Palazzo dei Cartelloni," and the bust and inscription still exist in Via dell'Amore (near S. Maria Novella, now called Via S. Antonino).

29 Raffaello Del Bruno, *Ristretto delle Cose Più Notabili della Città di Firenze* (2nd ed., Florence, 1698). This guide appeared in many editions, especially in the eighteenth century; I was not able to find this particular edition. It is missing today in the Florence National Library, though not in its Magliabechi catalog. I rely on Galluzzi "I sepolcri di Galileo," p. 145.

30 For instance at the beginning of the *Principia* or when speaking of parabolic motion or of free fall. Newton does not mention Galileo anywhere in Book III of the *Principia*.

31 Isaac Newton, *A Treatise of the System of the World*, translated from Latin into English by I. Bernard Cohen, London: Dawson of Pall Mall, 1969, p. 36 (italics mine). Newton's difficulty is discussed by Joseph Agassi in "Newtonianism Before and After the Einsteinian Revolution," in Frank Durham and Robert D. Purrington, eds., *Some Truer Method: Reflections on the Heritage of Newton*, New York: Columbia University Press, 1990, pp. 145–74. What disturbed Newton, according to Agassi (p. 166), "was his realization that a theory which is an approximation to the truth, no matter how good, is false, and that no falsehood is provable, so that he was pressed by the theory of rationality as proof to declare Galileo's or Kepler's theory absolutely true, or not rational!" Agassi's solution is to devise a new theory of rationality.

32 EN 15:87–8.

33 *The Works of John Milton*, ed. Frank Allen Patterson, vol. 4, New York: Columbia Univ. Press, 1931, p. 330. For a study of Milton's references to Galileo and their historical context see Neil Harris, "Galileo as a Symbol: The "Tuscan Artist" in Paradise Lost," *Annali dell'Istituto e Museo di Storia della Scienza di Firenze* 10 (1985) 2:3–29; "The Vallombrosa Simile and the Image of the Poet in Paradise Lost," in *Milton in Italy: Contexts, Images, Contradictions*, ed. Mario A. Di Cesare, New York: Binghamton, 1991, pp. 71–94.

34 No author or editor is mentioned on the title page: *Naudaeana et patiniana ou singularitez remarquables, prises des conversations de Mess. Naudé & Patin*, Amsterdam, 2nd ed., 1703, pp. 153–4.

35 For an outline of Galileo's image in the eighteenth century, see A. Rupert Hall, "Galileo in the Eighteenth Century," in Haydn Mason (general ed.), *Transactions of the Fifth International Congress on the Enlightenment*, vol. 1, Oxford: The Voltaire Foundation at the Taylor Institution, 1980, pp. 81–99. For a detailed presentation of the scientific controversies in the Age of Enlightenment in Italy see Vincenzo Ferrone, *Scienza Natura Religione: Mondo Newtoniano e Cultura Italiana*, Naples: Jovene, 1982.

36 In Florence in Viviani's day, the years were counted *ab incarnatione*, so that they began with the feast of the Annunciation (March 25). Thus February 10, 1632 in Viviani's biography refers to February 10, 1633 in today's dating.

37 EN 19:617 (my translation).

38 Hall, "Galileo in the Eighteenth Century," p. 89.

39 Translation from *A Philosophical Dictionary, from the French of M. De Voltaire With Additional Notes*, Abner Kneeland, Boston, 1835, p. 172.

40 *Encyclopédie ou Dictionnaire Raisonné des Sciences, des Arts et des Métiers*, vol. 4, reprint of the first edition 1751–1780, Stuttgart-Bad Cannstatt: Friedrich Frommann, 1966, p. 174 (my translation).

41 See Bernard Jacqueline, "La Chiesa e Galileo nel secolo dell'Illuminismo," in *Galileo Galilei: 350 Anni di Storia (1633–1983). Studi e ricerche*, Rome: Edizioni Piemme, 1984. This article relies on Hall's "Galileo in the Eighteenth Century".

42 Giovanni Batista Clemente De' Nelli, *Vita e Commercio Letterario di Galileo Galilei*, Lausanne, 1793.

43 The story of Nelli's discovery of Galileo's manuscript is related in Giovanni Targioni Tozzetti, *Notizie degli Aggrandimenti delle Scienze Fisiche Accaduti in Toscana nel Corso di Anni LX del Secolo XVII*, 3 vols., Florence, 1780; reprint, Bologna: Forni, 1967, 1:124–5. Targioni Tozzetti was a Florentine naturalist and historian and his *Notizie* are an impressive description of the development of science in Tuscany in the seventeenth century, focusing on Medici patronage.

44 The documentation used by Nelli and the drafts of his work are collected in MSS 318–22 of the Galilean Collection.

45 Nelli, *Vita*, pp. 557 and 558 (my translation).

46 Targioni Tozzetti, *Notizie*, 1:120 (my translation).

47 Walter Savage Landor, "Galileo, Milton, and a Dominican, in Imaginary Conversation," *Imaginary Conversations*, vol. 4, London: Aldine House, 1916, pp. 384–93.

48 *An account of Sir Isaac Newton's Philosophical Discoveries, in Four Books by Colin Maclaurin*, reprint. New York, 1968, p. 55.

49 "Saggio sopra il Cartesio," in Francesco Algarotti, *Saggi*, edited by Giovanni Da Pozzo, Bari: Laterza, 1963, pp. 405–31. Quotation from p. 427.

50 Giovanni Batista Clemente Nelli, *Saggio di Storia Letteraria Fiorentina del Secolo XVII*, Lucca 1759, p. 84.

51 David Hume, *The History of England*, vol. IV, London, 1830, p. 391.

52 Frisi's *Saggio* has been republished and commented on in Micheli, *Galileo, la Sensata Esperienza*, pp. 207–12 (my translation from p. 211).

53 Joseph Agassi, "Genius in Science," in Joseph Agassi, *Science and Society*, Dordrecht: Reidel, 1981, pp. 192–222.

54 Ibid., p. 193.

55 Ibid., p. 202.

56 John F. W. Herschel, *A Preliminary Discourse on the Study of Natural Philosophy*, London, 1830; reprint, The University of Chicago Press, 1987. John Herschel (1792–1871), son of William Herschel, was an important astronomer in his own right, as well as a philosopher of science. Joseph Agassi has stressed the importance of Herschel in "Sir John Herschel's Philosophy of Success," *Science and Society*, pp. 388–420.

57 Herschel, *A Preliminary Discourse*, p. 72.

58 Ibid., p. 76.

59 Ibid., pp. 167–8.

60 Ibid., p. 169.

61 Alexandre De Humboldt, *Cosmos: Essai d'une Description Physique du Monde*, transl. H. Faye, 4 vols., Paris 1846, 1:189.

62 Favaro, *Studi e Ricerche per una Iconografia Galileiana*, Venice: Carlo Ferrari, 1913, and *Nuove Ricerche per una Iconografia Galileiana*, Venice: Carlo Ferrari, 1914.

63 Reference from Micheli, *La Sensata Esperienza*, reproducing these paintings, pp. 166–72.

64 Pietro Redondi, "Dietro l'Immagine. Rappresentazioni di Galileo nella Cultura Positivistica," *Nuncius*, 9, (1994) 1:65–116, p. 73.

65 The Risorgimento was essentially anticlerical and its leaders searched for a list of martyrs of the Church, such as Giordano Bruno, Tommaso Campanella, and, of course, Galileo, to designate as Italian heroes.

66 Antonio Favaro, *Per la edizione nazionale delle opere di Galileo Galilei sotto gli auspici di S. M. il Re d'Italia. Esposizione e disegno* (Florence, 1888), p. 3: "Considerando di supremo decoro nazionale l'appagare per tal guisa il lungo desiderio degli studiosi, elevando ad un tempo nuovo e durevole monumento di gloria al Genio meraviglioso che creava la filosofia sperimentale."

67 In particular, William Whewell, *History of the Inductive Sciences*, 3 vols., London, 1837, and *The Philosophy of the Inductive Sciences Founded upon Their History*, 2 vols., London, 1840.

68 I am indebted to John Wettersten for summarizing to me Whewell's contribution to the history of science (I did not find anywhere in the literature a concise presentation of Whewell's contribution to the history of science.) Wettersten's book on Whewell, *Whewell's Critics: Have they Prevented Him from Doing Good?* is forthcoming, Amsterdam, Atlanta: Rodopi.

69 See "On Hegel's Criticism of Newton's Principia," in William Whewell, *On the Philosophy of Discovery*, London, 1860, Appendix H.

70 As claimed and described by John Wettersten and Joseph Agassi in "Whewell's Problematic Heritage," in Menachem Fisch and Simon Schaffer, *William Whewell: A Composite Portrait*, Oxford: Clarendon Press, 1991, pp. 345–69.

71 Karl Von Gebler, "Galileo Galilei und die Römische Kurie," 2 vols., Stuttgart, 1876–1877. Translated into English by Jane Sturge under the title *Galileo Galilei and the Roman Curia*, London, 1879; reprint, Merrick, NY: Richwood Publishing Company, 1977. For the history of the documents and of their publication see Sergio M. Pagano, ed., *I Documenti del Processo di Galileo Galilei*, Vatican City: Pontificia Academia Scientiarum, 1984, pp. 26–35 concerning Gebler.

72 Igino Benvenuto Supino, "La lampada di Galileo," *Archivio Storico dell'Arte*, 6 (1893), 3:215–18.

73 Raffaello Caverni, *Storia del Metodo Sperimentale in Italia*, 6 vols., Florence, 1891–1900; reprint. Bologna: Forni, 1970.

74 Ibid., 1:143.

75 As post-Risorgimental Italy was anticlerical and Caverni was a priest he was at a disadvantage.

76 The story of Caverni's work is related by Giorgio Tabaronni at the beginning of the reprinted work and by Cesare S. Maffioli in "Sulla genesi e sugli inediti della Storia del metodo sperimentale in Italia di Raffaello Caverni," *Annali dell'Istituto e Museo di Storia della Scienza di Firenze*, 10 (1985), 1 : 23–85.

77 Wohlwill's doubts were expressed at first in a meeting reported by the *Münchener Medizinische Wochenschrift* 50 (1903):1849–50, and later, in detail, in his series of articles "Galilei-Studien: Die Pisaner Fallversuche," *Mitteilungen zur Geschichte der Medizin und der Naturwissenschaften*, 4 (1905):229–48; "Der Abschied von Pisa," *Mitteilungen zur Geschichte der Medizin und der Naturwissenschaften*, 5 (1906): 230–49, 439–64, 6 (1907):231–42.

78 Pierre Duhem, *Études sur Léonard de Vinci*, published in three se-
ries, Paris: Hermann, 1906–1913, and *Le systéme du Monde:
Histoire des Doctrines Cosmologiques de Platon a Copernic*, 10 vols.,
Paris: Hermann, 1913–1959.

79 Favaro, "Ancora, e per l'ultima volta, intorno all'episodio di Gustavo
Adolfo di Svezia nei racconti della vita di Galileo," *Atti e Memorie della
R. Accademia di Scienze Lettere ed Arti in Padova*, 365 (1906–1907),
nuova serie – vol. 23, pp. 6–12. "Sulla veridicità del 'Racconto istorico
della vita di Galileo' dettato da Vincenzio Viviani," *Archivio Storico
Italiano*, disp. 2a, 1915, Florence: Tipografia Galileiana, 1916; and "Di
alcune inesattezze nel 'Racconto istorico della vita di Galileo' dettato
da Vincenzio Viviani," *Archivio Storico Italiano*, disp. 3a, 4a, 1916,
Florence: Tipografia Galileiana, 1917.

80 Favaro, "Ancora, e per...," p. 8.

81 Favaro, "Sulla veridicità," p. 6.

82 *Op. cit.*

83 For a full account, see my "Galileo, Viviani and the Tower of Pisa."

84 Aldo Mieli, *Archeion, Archivio di Storia della Scienza*, 17 (1935):303–7.
Harold Cherniss, *Modern Language Notes*, 51 (1936):184–5.

85 Giuseppe Boffitto, *Bibliografia Galileiana* (1896–1940), primo supplemento, Rome: Libreria dello Stato, 1943, p. 198.

86 *Alexandre Koyré, Études Galiléennes* (Paris; Hermann, 1939; reprint,
1966). English translation by John Mepham as *Galileo Studies*, Has-
socks, Sussex: The Harvester Press, 1978. The work is dated 1939, but
it appeared only in 1940. It collected studies published from 1935. For
details see Redondi's useful study of Koyré's work: *Alexandre Koyré, De
la Mystique à la Science. Cours, conférences et documents, 1922–1962*,
edited by Pietro Redondi, Paris: École des Hautes Études en Sciences
Sociales, 1986, pp. 36–7 and 217.

87 See Alexandre Koyré's outstanding, "An Experiment in Measurement"
(1953), republished in *Metaphysics and Measurement* London: Chapman & Hall, 1968; reprint, Yverdon: Gordon and Breach, 1992, pp. 89–
117. Koyré also believed that the Leaning Tower experiment did not
take place, see "Galilée et l'Expérience de Pise: a propos d'une légende,"
Annales de l'Université de Paris, 12 (1936):441–53. See p. 443.

88 See Koyré, *Galileo Studies*, pp. 36–8.

89 Koyré *Metaphysics and Measurement*, p. 94.

90 EN 8:212–13. Koyré, *Metaphysics and Measurement*, p. 94.

91 See, in particular, *Galileo Studies*, p. 37. Cf. William Shea's outstanding
Galileo's Intellectual Revolution, New York: Science History Publications, 1972, pp. 150–63.

92 Note of Eugenio Garin, in *Giornale critico della Filosofia Italiana*, 36, terza serie, vol. 11 (1957):406–9. Maurice A. Finocchiaro, *Galileo and the Art of Reasoning: Rhetorical Foundations of Logic and Scientific Method*, Dordrecht: Reidel, 1980, Chapter 9. Quotation from p. 221.

93 Ibid., p. 222.

94 Thomas Settle, "An Experiment in the History of Science," *Science*, 133 (1961):19–23.

95 Settle says: "Thus far I can only reproduce the end product of a process of evolution (in Galileo's own mind)." Ibid., p. 20.

96 Stillman Drake, "Galileo's Experimental Confirmation of Horizontal Inertia: Unpublished Manuscripts," *Isis*, 64 (1973):291–305. Quotation from p. 291.

97 Jürgen Teichmann, "Der freie Fall bei Galilei: Experimente und Mythos," paper given at the Berlin Galileo Conference (November 10–13, 1994), to be published in the forthcoming proceedings.

98 Giorgio De Santillana, *The Crime of Galileo*; Arthur Koestler, *The Sleepwalkers: A History of Man's Changing Vision of the Universe*, London: Hutchinson, 1959.

99 See Santillana's Preface, p. xiii.

100 I. Bernard Cohen, Review of Koestler's *The Sleepwalkers*, *Scientific American*, 200 (June 1959):187–92. Quotation from p. 188.

101 Agassi, *Science and Society*, p. 322.

102 Giorgio de Santillana, and Stillman Drake, "Arthur Koestler and his Sleepwalkers," *Isis*, 50 (1959):255–60.

103 Joseph Agassi, "On Explaining the Trial of Galileo," in Agassi, *Science and Society*, pp. 312–51. Quotation from p. 324. Agassi says that Galileo was a sincere and brave Catholic reformer (pp. 337–41).

104 Richard S. Westfall, "Science and Patronage: Galileo and the Telescope," *Isis*, 76 (1985):11–30. Quotation from p. 28.

105 Ron Naylor, "Old Myths and New," *Nature*, 355 (February 1992):597–8; *Annals of Science*, 50 (1993):496–7.

106 pp. 40–41.

12 The sepulchers of Galileo: The "living" remains of a hero of science[1]*

Galileo died on January 8, 1642, in the unpleasant predicament of a man who had been condemned and then forced to abjure, as "vehemently suspected of heresy." His will[2] indicated that his remains should be placed beside those of his father Vincenzo and of his ancestors, in the Basilica of Santa Croce, where the family tomb can still be seen.

The death of such a remarkable person was not marked by solemn ceremonies or orations attesting either to his virtues as a man or to his sensational discoveries as a scientist and astronomer. On the day after his death, Galileo's body was removed to the Basilica of Santa Croce without the slightest hint of pomp or ceremony,[3] accompanied by his son Vincenzo, by the Curate of S. Matteo in Arcetri, by Vincenzo Viviani, by Evangelista Torricelli, and by a few members of his family. The Grand Duke remained in Pisa, and no other important figures of Florentine public life made an appearance.

The furtive nature of the removal was a consequence of the fear that the ecclesiastical authorities might issue a formal interdict on the burial of Galileo's remains in the church of Santa Croce. This fear was not without grounds, as is demonstrated by a theological argument, almost certainly written at the request of the Grand Duke, in support of the legitimacy of the Christian burial of one vehemently suspected of heresy.[4] It is extremely probable that the author was Giovanni Paolo Bimbacci, personal theologian of the Grand Duke and author of another contemporary argument, sustaining the absolute validity of Galileo's will.[5]

* Translated by Michael John Gorman.

417

Given the circumstances, it was impossible to guarantee that all of the requests made by Galileo in his will would, in fact, be carried out. His mortal remains were not in fact placed in the family tomb. Fear of provoking the church authorities caused the family and disciples of Galileo to "conceal" the corpse in the tiny chamber under the bell tower of the church, access to which is, even to this day, by means of a small door on the left-hand side of the Cappella del Noviziato (Chapel of the Noviciate) dedicated to Saints Cosma and Damian (Figure 12.1).

Despite the fact that the burial process was carried out with extreme circumspection and discretion, the tender actions of the relatives and the disciples of the scientist were attentively observed and immediately reported to the Roman authorities. On January 12, 1642, the Florentine Nuncio, Giorgio Bolognetti, hastened to inform Cardinal Francesco Barberini, nephew of the pope, of the events following the death of Galileo and of the rumors in the city concerning the worrying proposals of the Grand Duke:

> Galileo died on Thursday at 9 o' clock: the following day his corpse was deposited privately in Santa Croce. It is said that the Grand Duke wishes to construct a sumptuous tomb, opposite that of Michelangelo Buonaroti in order to establish a *paragone* with him, and that he intends to entrust the Accademia della Crusca with the design of the model and the monument itself. With all due respect, I judged that it would be better for your Eminence to know this.[6]

The alarm bells had been sounded and Cardinal Barberini hurried to inform Urban VIII. A few days later, Francesco Niccolini, the Medici representative in the Papal See who had been an eyewitness to the trial and condemnation of Galileo, was called up before Urban VIII. As Niccolini reported to the Secretary of State of the Grand Duchy,

> [the Pontiff] came to ask me to discuss a matter in confidence and only for his own business, not that I had anything much to write about; and it was that the Holy See had heard that the Grand Duke might have thought to have a tomb erected in Santa Croce. He wanted to tell me that it would not be a good example to the world for you to do so, as that man had been here before the Holy Office for a very false and erroneous opinion, which he had also impressed upon many others, there giving rise to a universal scandal against Christianity by means of a damned doctrine...[7]

Figure 12.1

The same day, Cardinal Francesco Barberini gave instructions to the Florentine Inquisitor. He was told that he should let it come to the

ears of the Grand Duke that it is not good to build mausoleums to the corpse of those who had repented before the Tribunal of the Holy Inquisition and who had died while in penance, because the good people might be scandalized and prejudiced with regard to Holy Authority.[8]

The combined dissuasive actions of the pope and his cardinal nephew produced the desired effects. On January 29th, Gondi, the Tuscan Secretary of State, reassured Niccolini:

There was much talk here too, of the tomb to the late mathematician Galileo, but without resolution, even in the mind of the Grand Duke. But, in any case, the considerations brought forward by Your Eminence about that which the Pope discussed with such delicacy will lead us to draw appropriate conclusions ...[9]

The dream of the monumental tomb thus lasted only a few days: the remains of Galileo were destined to stay a long while in the narrow room attached to the Chapel of the Noviciate.

After this first rebuff, many years were to pass before the opportunity of erecting a monumental tomb to Galileo arose. The driving force behind this attempt to resuscitate the project was Vincenzo Viviani. He understood that the goal of bestowing sepulchral honor on Galileo was an essential part of the fight to promote the legitimacy and importance of Galileo's work and guarantee the liberty of Galileo's disciples to carry on his research and extend it to new fields. The image of Galileo as a heretic resulting from the 1633 trial obstructed the fulfillment of these objectives.

The rehabilitation of Galileo's reputation represented, for Viviani, not so much a defense of the Pisan from the insanity of his detractors and from many true or supposed usurpers of his discoveries, but, above all, an attempt at establishing the belief in the profound and unfailing Christian *pietas* of the Master. In the *Life of Galileo* of 1654, when dealing with the "incident" of the trial and the condemnation of the *Dialogo*, Viviani affirms that Galileo erred in not maintaining the presentation of the Copernican idea on a purely hypothetical level. For this error, the Church had rightly admonished

him, and he had recognized his error and purged himself by a public
and formal abjuration, in a fully sincere act of submission:

But, given that the fame of Sig.r Galileo had traveled even to the heavens
through admirable speculations on other issues, and with many novelties
which made him appear almost a divine being, Eternal Providence permitted
him to demonstrate his humanity through error. Thus, in his discussion
of the two systems he demonstrated himself to be more in favor of the
Copernican System, already condemned by the Church as repugnant to Holy
Scripture. For this reason Sig.r Galileo, after the publication of his *Dialogues*,
was called to Rome by the Congregation of the Holy Office: where . . . by the
highest clemency of that Tribunal and the Sovereign Pontiff Urban VIII . . .
he was arrested and in brief (having publicly recognized his error) retracted,
as a true Catholic, this opinion of his.[10]

This conciliatory thesis has been widely used by Catholic apologists up to this day to demonstrate Galileo's responsibility in the
"affair" surrounding the trial. Viviani, however, adopted this position for purely instrumental reasons. To be convinced of this, one
has only to consider Viviani's violent reaction in June 1678 when
informed that the Jesuit Athanasius Kircher intended to include a
eulogy of Galileo in his *Etruria Illustrata*,[11] in which the scientist
was accused of not having proceeded with the necessary caution in
the *Dialogo* and in his Copernican writings.

The analogy between such an interpretation and the presentation of the condemnation of Galileo in Viviani's *Vita* appears evident. Notwithstanding this, Viviani took immediate action, plead-
ing with the Jesuit Father Baldigiani to exert every possible pressure
on Kircher to persuade him to remove the statement about Galileo's
imprudence from the eulogy, suggesting that this would also greatly
please the Grand Duke, to whom the work was dedicated.[12] Despite
Baldigiani's reservations, Viviani continued to insist, until the Jesuit replied angrily that if he considered the circumstances with a
modicum of objectivity Viviani would see that the tone of Kircher's
eulogy for Galileo was anything but hostile:

He was summoned, interrogated and condemned: what could one say? That
it was carried out in a state of complete innocence, that an entire Congregation was mistaken, that the most holy tribunal was unjust: who would
ever speak in such a way, even if he believed it to be true? And even if he
had spoken in such a way, how many would have been persuaded? Is it not

better to say that he was mortified, that on those occasions he should have comported himself with more prudence, that he had caused injury to Urban VIII and the Barberini, and that they were justifiably irate.[13]

The line of conciliation assumed by Viviani aimed at removing force from the image of Galileo as a heretic, an image that clearly obstructed the propagation of the new science.

While conceding the fundamental point of the purely hypothetical value of the new science, Viviani was confident that he would be able to reopen a free space for research, which had been closed off since the condemnation of 1633. He never missed an opportunity to emphasize the moral dignity of Galileo and his exemplary conduct as a Catholic, ready to submit to the decrees of the Church. He reacted with heated indignation to the image, widespread outside Italy and especially in the Protestant countries, of Galileo as a "libertine," unfettered by the dogmas of faith and thus both protagonist and martyr of the battle against the degeneration of the Roman Church.

This is shown by an extremely worried letter that Viviani wrote to Lorenzo Magalotti, then in Flanders, on July 24, 1673, asking him to intervene in order to prevent the forthcoming Amsterdam publication of the letters between Galileo and Paolo Sarpi.

... suddenly it came into my mind that if that were to happen, much material would be given to the perpetual detractors of Galileo, of which you know that there are whole regiments, to cause them to suspect that he was that which he certainly never was, not even in thought ... I know that if I was in those parts, I would go straight to Amsterdam to see the letters for myself..., and, having seen them, whichever they turned out to be ... I would not merely employ every skill and every possible means to impede their publication, but would also attempt to remove the originals and any existing copies, however great the cost... [14]

This strategy of conciliation was shared and encouraged by Grand Duke Ferdinand II and Prince Leopold. In order to continue to exploit the extraordinary celebratory potential of the protection given by Cosimo I and Ferdinand II to Galileo, and of the dedication of the satellites of Jupiter to the Medici dynasty, it was necessary to blur the conflict with the ecclesiastical hierarchy.

It seemed opportune to stimulate, on the one hand, the exaltation of the Galilean research tradition as an instrument particularly well suited to display the extraordinarily ordered structure of nature, an evident demonstration of the omnipotence of its Author. On the other hand, every care was taken to erase the intellectual trauma of the trial and condemnation of the Pisan scientist from the general memory.

When it was impossible to avoid mentioning the episode, it was stressed that although Galileo had erred, he had asked sincerely for forgiveness, expiring his last breath in the fold of the Holy Mother Church. In clear contrast with the image of Galileo the hero and martyr of *libertas philosophandi*, so widespread in Europe, and especially in France, the "Medicean" myth elaborated by Viviani presented Galileo as the promoter of a radical, but not traumatic, renewal of knowledge and as a man who respected the values and traditional disciplinary hierarchies, fully conscious of the relativity and transience of human knowledge.

Through a reduction of their cognitive significance, the results of the new science were "tranquilized." The same purpose was served by the reductive experimentalism imposed on the Accademia del Cimento by the Medici princes.[15] This emphasized the impossibility of man ever attaining full knowledge of the principles that determine the workings of nature. During the same period, it appeared crucial to repropose the major works of Galileo, especially the *Dialogo*, applying this new and reassuring interpretative key. Galileo's works were to be read not as sound evidence of the truth of the Copernican hypothesis, but as a demonstration of the unsurpassable limits of human understanding.

Finally, it became fundamentally important to give tangible form and full visibility to the image of Galileo as a Christian hero of science, whose faith had been reinforced by means of error, purified by sincere repentance and by a genuinely sincere act of submission to the Church. It appears evident that the erection of the tomb in the Basilica of Santa Croce represented a decisive step in this strategy. Thus, it is not surprising that the efforts carried out by Viviani to achieve the revocation of the prohibition of the *Dialogo* were inextricably bound up with his attempts to reopen the opportunity to erect a monumental sepulcher in the Basilica of Santa Croce.

The results obtained from his attempts to validate and promote the literary heritage of his master were relatively modest. In Florence, Viviani was responsible for the first complete edition of the works of Galileo. This was produced not in Florence, but by the Bolognese publisher Manolessi, undoubtedly to conceal Medicean support of the edition.[16] Despite Viviani's labors, the edition, finally published in 1656, was full of errors and, necessarily, incomplete. Ecclesiastical permission for the insertion of the *Dialogo* and other Copernican writings was refused.

During the same period, Viviani did not miss an opportunity to affirm the importance of providing a decorous resting place for the mortal remains of Galileo. While waiting for this desired event, he devoted his attention to the preparations for the enterprise at hand. He had a clay model made from Galileo's death mask by the sculptor Antonio Novelli.[17] He ordered Ludovico Salvetti to cast a bronze bust of Galileo with the aid of the model of Galileo's head that had been made by Giovanni Caccini around 1612, which has unfortunately been lost to us.[18] Later, he commissioned Giovanni Battista Foggini, a friend of the scientist and the most enthusiastic "Galilean" artist, to sculpt a marble bust of Galileo.[19] Viviani also asked Foggini to provide a rough sketch of the sepulcher for which the bust was destined.[20] He carried out a successful petition to collect the necessary funds for the construction of the funeral monument,[21] the symbolic and conceptual scheme of which he was busily working out in great detail. But the results of his efforts were disappointing. The project of the tomb was met with active opposition by the ecclesiastical authorities and the defenders of traditional intellectual culture.

When, in June of 1674, Paolo Falconieri, on behalf of Cosimo III, asked Viviani to provide him with a portrait of Galileo to serve as a model for a marble bust that the Grand Duke wished to place in the Gallery,[22] Viviani seized the occasion to exhort Falconieri to remind Cosimo III of the far more ambitious wishes of his father Ferdinand II and of his uncle Leopold to give an honorable burial to Galileo.[23] The noble and heartfelt peroration, however, went unheeded. Viviani's disappointment and discouragement are evident in his decision, taken some weeks later, to ornament Galileo's resting place with a bust and an epitaph exalting the merits of the deceased.

Evidence for Viviani's melancholy awareness of the futility of his efforts appears in many other events of the time. In December 1688, at the age of sixty-six, he wrote his will. This obliged his beneficiaries to carry out the project of realizing Galileo's funeral monument, which was to serve also as a resting place for his own mortal remains.[24]

With lucid and desperate determination Viviani went on to dedicate the last years of his life to the elaboration of every detail of the sepulchral monument. He reiterated that the monument had to be built in the Basilica, in symmetrical juxtaposition to that of Michelangelo. Like in the tomb of the great artist from Caprese, which was ornamented by three statues representing Architecture, Painting, and Drawing, three statues (Astronomy, Geometry, and Philosophy) were intended to stand guard over the relics of Galileo.[25]

Among Viviani's papers, numerous autograph versions of the inscription, which he intended for the sepulcher, have survived. These presented Galileo as a symbol of knowledge itself,[26] emphasizing the admiration his works had elicited from literati the world over, who had frequently lamented the lack of a suitable funereal monument to the great scientist.[27] Aware of the necessity of acting with extreme prudence if his project were to be approved, Viviani avoided any reference to the trial and condemnation of Galileo. The composition of the text of the epitaph for Galileo's tomb can be placed between the years 1691 and 1692.

In the same period, Viviani completed his final documented attempt to obtain a mitigation of the condemnation of Galileo, a fundamental prerequisite for the realization of the sepulcher. In an exquisite letter to the Jesuit Antonio Baldigiani of August 1690, Viviani made an able attempt to win the respectable father over to the noble cause of the rehabilitation of Galileo. The explicitly stated objective of the letter was to stimulate a priest well-versed in mathematics and the Consultor of the Holy Office, who had, on numerous occasions, expressed his deep admiration for Galileo, to use his position to obtain authorization to put the *Dialogo* back in circulation, with the corrections deemed necessary to restore to the work its character as an impartial illustration of two opposing conceptions of astronomy, both of which were defendable on a purely hypothetical level.[28]

Yet again, Viviani had been painfully overoptimistic. His request to treat Galileo's *Dialogo* on a par with Copernicus's *De Revolutionibus* was not accepted. Consequently, he decided to concentrate his efforts on a solemn "private" homage to his master, conceived, however, with remarkable originality, in such a way that it could be visible to the public.

Viviani had acquired a house in need of structural work on the Via dell'Amore (today Via S. Antonio) in Florence. He gave to his friend, the fervently Galilean architect Giovanni Battista Nelli, the task of transforming the facade of the palace into a structure documenting and celebrating the extraordinary intellectual achievements of Galileo. Giovanni Battista Foggini, to whom the bronze bust of Galileo which is still there to this day is attributed, also collaborated in the enterprise.[29]

Foggini designed the template for the tablets and was probably also responsible for the scrolls placed alongside the bust.[30] The illustrations present in the two scrolls, based on the graphical model of medals, allude to Galileo's principal achievements in astronomy and mechanics. The two tablets of enormous dimensions placed on the sides of the main entrance, from which the name Palazzo dei Cartelloni (Palace of the tablets) is derived, bear texts of exceptional length for a commemorative epitaph.[31]

Thus conceived, the house was transformed into an extraordinary piece of propaganda, a memorial that was accessible to those passing, to whom Viviani made no casual appeal in the opening phrase: "passerby of upright and generous mind."

The facade constituted the first memorial to Galileo visible in a public place in the city of Florence. It represented a sort of "lay" sepulcher to Galileo, pointing with implicit recrimination to the absence of a religious memorial. At the same time the tablets offered a conspicuous compendium of his works and life, conceived in accordance with the motivations of Viviani's strategy of reconciliation.

The tablet on the left gave abundant information about the details of Galileo's multiple conquests in the fields of astronomy, mechanics, and natural philosophy, emphasizing that the keystone of the extraordinary success of the Pisan scientist was to be found in the profitable union between geometrical analysis and experimental investigation which he had been the first to establish. Viviani listed the many celestial novelties discovered by Galileo with the aid of the telescope, but avoided every reference to the polemic *de systemate mundi* and to the dramatic conclusion of that controversy in the condemnation of 1633. In the final passage of the tablet, Viviani emphasized the moderation, and above all the piety of Galileo, "who had the greatest respect for God and Truth. The penetration by the depth of his mind of the stars, the sea and the earth is comparable only to that of God."[32]

The tone of the tablet on the right-hand side was no different. This gave details of the fundamental events of Galileo's life. Regarding Galileo's birth in Pisa, to Vincenzo Galilei and Giulia Ammannati, Viviani insisted on the legitimacy of Galileo's conception and birth. He was concerned to refute the belief, propounded by Ianus Nicius Erythraeus (alias Giovanni Vittorio de' Rossi[33]) and exploited by other authors, that Galileo was illegitimate. This bears witness to the importance, in the eyes of Viviani, of emphasizing the moral dignity and piety of the Master and is confirmed by the insistence, again in the right-hand tablet, of the Christian end to the life of Galileo.

The final years of Galileo are portrayed as the actualization of a design of Providence which, in order to allow the Pisan scientist better to perceive the magnitude of the Creator, deprived him of material vision. In preparing to abandon his earthly shackles, Galileo's conduct displayed the same exemplary degree of piety:

This great mathematician who had among his distinguished qualities a remarkable constancy, philosophical no less than Christian, strengthened by the repeatedly invoked spiritual help of the Church, rendered, in a most serene manner, his immortal soul to God.[34]

The addressee of the message inscribed on the second tablet was no longer merely the passerby, but the city of Florence itself, "cara Deo prae aliis urbibus." Which other city could boast the privilege of having received from Providence, on the same day and at the same hour as the death of its celebrated son Michelangelo Buonarroti, reviver of the arts of Painting, Sculpture, and Architecture, the generous reparation of a new extraordinary hero, namely Galileo, perpetrator of the renewal of the whole of natural philosophy?

In acknowledgment of the privileged destiny bestowed upon her by Providence, Florence should express, by means of appropriate action, full recognition of the divine gift of these prodigious sons. The rhetorical device was, thus, a cautious, but nonetheless quite clear, means of publicly lamenting the lack of a sepulchral monument to Galileo.

Viviani's insistence on the coincidence of the death of Michelangelo and the birth of Galileo is striking. We must remember the news that circulated, just after Galileo's death, of Ferdinand II's intention to build a monument to him in Santa Croce "opposite that of Michelangelo Buonarroti, in order to establish a *paragone* with him."[35]

The coincidence between the dates of the death of Michelangelo and the birth of Galileo which both occurred, according to Viviani, on February 18, was first put forward between 1691 and 1692, on the drafts of the epitaphs produced by Viviani, for the supposedly imminent construction of the sepulcher.[36] In fact in the *Vita* of 1654, Viviani had established a chronological continuity and a comparison not between Galileo and Michelangelo, but between Galileo and Vespucci.[37] Additionally, the *Vita* gave Galileo's date of birth as the 19th of February.[38]

During the course of 1692, while attending to the last changes to the texts for the tablets for the house of via dell'Amore, Viviani took great pains to establish the precise dates of Galileo's birth and of Michelangelo's death. From Pisa he obtained a copy of Galileo's original baptismal certificate, which bore the date of February 19. At the same time, he had confirmed with Baldinucci[39] and Filippo Buonarotti[40] that Michelangelo had died on February 18 at around 6 p.m. At this point, by assuming that Galileo was born the day before his baptism, the two dates were made to coincide perfectly.

The issue of continuity between the lives of Buonarroti and Galileo, represented, in Viviani's imagination, a guiding principle of the greatest importance.[41] Viviani toyed with the idea of suggesting that a providential design had bestowed upon Florence the privilege of nurturing two great heroes, protagonists of radical renovation of the arts, in the one case, and of science, in the other.

His exaltation of the privileged role of the city recalled the magnificent patronage of the Medici dynasty, whose most important members had offered protection and amplification of the talents of these extraordinary celebrities. The subtle celebratory strategy which gave life to the Michelangelo–Galileo *paragone* was founded on the revival and extension of the well-tested *cliché* of the "Medicean" myth of Buonarroti.[42] This myth had been constructed, mainly by Varchi and Vasari, immediately after the death of the great artist. It found eloquent expression, for the first time, in the somber trappings of the funeral rites conducted initially in 1564 in the Basilica of San Lorenzo and, subsequently, in the monumental sepulcher erected in Santa Croce.[43]

The Medicean Michelangelo displayed the combined countenance of a hero and a saint. In a remarkable distortion of his actual position and role as a defender of the Florentine Republic from the Imperial army, which brought the Medici back to power in Florence, he became the crowning glory of the propagandistic exercise, so dear to the heart of Cosimo I, to publicize the patronage and good government of the Medici.

Additionally, he was praised as a man perfectly in conformity with the Counter-Reformation canons of art as an effective instrument for the propagation and defense of orthodoxy.[44] His whole intense existence, which also included a series of not entirely edifying episodes, was presented as a model of exemplary moral conduct and Christian piety.

To give plausibility to this complex and arduous operation, the authorities did not hesitate to cleanse the *Canzoniere* of the artist, of the more vulgar and earthly images it contained to render it more consonant with Christian ideals.[45] Similar "corrections" were made to the provocative naked figures of the *Giudizio Universale*.[46]

Upon the death of Galileo, the idea of following, with the necessary adaptations, the model of the magnificent and advantageous Medicean celebration of Michelangelo must surely have occurred to Ferdinand II, and this was promptly seconded by Viviani.

In Galileo's case, celebratory emphasis on his harmonious synthesis of cultural and civil merit, on the one hand, and religious belief, on the other, was made increasingly difficult after the 1633 condemnation. For this reason, it was necessary to attempt to redefine the global significance of the Galilean program, according to the model that Viviani had outlined in his *Vita* of 1654. Galileo's piety had to be stressed above all other qualities, and his Copernican excesses in the *Dialogo* had to be seen to be redeemed by his subsequent repentance and abjuration. The abjuration itself represented, in Viviani's scheme, the highest and most emotionally charged testimony to Galileo's religious faith.

Thus, the heroic Galilean lesson was reshaped in consonance with Counter-Reformation ideals, in accordance with the model elaborated by Vasari and Varchi to construct the Medicean myth of Michelangelo.

It thus becomes clear why the construction of a Galileian sepulcher acquired such a deep significance. The veneration of Galileo's disciples for their master, the princes' need to give public amplification to their role as protectors of an extraordinary genius, and the need to underline the continuation of Florentine cultural primacy under Medici direction, from the golden period of the Renaissance up to the present,[47] all combined to reinforce the importance of a triumphal memorial. The falsification of Galileo's date of birth and the direct continuity so happily established between the lives of Galileo and Michelangelo gave new life to the image of a dynasty which, after having favored the rebirth of the arts by protecting Michelangelo, baptized the discoveries of new worlds and the birth of new methods and new sciences by supporting Galileo.

The image of the handing of the torch from Michelangelo to Galileo, established by Viviani, met with remarkable fortune. Among the many to reiterate the continuity was none other than Giovanni Battista Clemente Nelli, in his monumental *Life of Galileo*.

Nelli did have the courage to contest the additional happy coincidence established between the death of Galileo and the birth of Newton, the fruit of a much more brazen fabrication, which was, nevertheless, attested by numerous authors.[48] Even Kant was moved by this distortion of the historical record, claiming that Michelangelo had been reincarnated in Newton, through the intermediary of Galileo.[49]

The construction of the Medicean myth of Galileo and the function that this had in the articulation of the project to erect a sepulcher in Santa Croce should not blind us to the other important factors and motivations at work in those who maintained a powerful bond between Michelangelo and Galileo. Despite the fact that Medicean mythcraft and clumsy Counter-Reformation amendments had substantially altered the original and tormented character of Michelangelo's religious spirit, the artist from Caprese remained the author of the *Giudizio*, a work that had perturbed many pious spirits by the overflowing and sensual nudity of its figures.

It was Michelangelo who had rebelled against Counter-Reformation canons, refusing to reduce painting, sculpture, and architecture to mere instruments of propaganda and defense of an orthodoxy rigidly determined by the ecclesiastical authorities. For his obstinate choice of freedom and for his unfettered articulation of his conscience he was not only discussed and criticized, but actually denounced and, especially after his death, heavily censored.

Michelangelo's true character, as a rebel against convention and the traditional models of knowledge, must have served to reinforce the comparison between the two celebrities among the disciples of Galileo. Both had been radical innovators in their cultural production and in the ways in which they interpreted the function and nature of religious feeling. Both suffered persecution and censorship for recklessly pursuing the truth.

From this point of view, the *Last Judgment* and the Copernican *Letters* offered multiple points of symmetry and analogy. Both works expressed, in their different genres and styles, intellectual experiences interwoven with a profound religious spirit. Both also met with the immediate and severe opposition of the ecclesiastical authorities.

It is, thus, difficult to remove the impression that what was at work in the persistent emphasis placed on the comparison by Viviani and the other Galileans was not only the calculated recasting of the Medicean myth of Michelangelo but also an awareness of a profound and objective symmetry between the two great and dramatic intellectual experiences.

Even in 1612, Ludovico Cardi, called Cigoli, had sown the seeds of this relationship by establishing a precise and suggestive comparison between Galileo and Michelangelo, based on emphasizing the common innovative character of their work, condemned precisely for this reason, faced with the incomprehension and opposition of the representatives of traditional culture. To comfort Galileo, who was worried about the discouraging reactions to his treatise *Delle Cose che Stanno in su l'Acqua*, Cigoli reminded him of the similar reception of the work of the great artist from Caprese:

As for the book you have printed, I heard from a man of letters that it was little to the liking of those philosophers; and, I believe, the same happened as when Michelagniolo began to design buildings outside the orders of the others up to his time, when all united to claim that Michelagniolo had ruined architecture by taking so many liberties outside of Vitruvius; I replied to them that Michelagniolo had ruined not architecture but the architects, because if they lacked designs such as his and continued to work as before, they appeared to be worthless things.[50]

The suggestion embodied in this comparison was continued even after the death of Viviani in 1703. Although he was not successful in his plan to build a monumental sepulcher to Galileo, by means of his will, he put into motion a mechanism that would be started as soon as the circumstances were favorable.

The auspicious moment was soon offered by a conspicuous series of attempts to promote the Galilean legacy, the key actors in which were a group of authoritative Catholic intellectuals, in the first third of the eighteenth century.[51] At the forefront of a heated battle to modernize the Catholic Church, these people supported the abandonment of the traditional hostility that emerged in confrontations with new scientific and philosophical ideas.

These initiatives led to, among other things, the Florentine republication of the works of Galileo in 1718,[52] which, however, still lacked the *Dialogo* and Copernican *Letters*, pending ecclesiastical authorization. The same desire to stress the importance of convergence between faith and the new Galilean science led to the publication of Torricelli's *Lezioni Accademiche*[53] in 1715, and, more significantly, to the 1727 Florentine reprint of the complete works of Gassendi,[54] a figure who assumed emblematic value, as a Galilean whose religious comportment was entirely beyond reprehension.

In the presentation and introductions of these editions the image of Galilean science as an intrinsically Christian doctrine was constantly reiterated.

After the death of Cosimo III, in 1721, the ferment of renewal and the attempts to revive the Galilean heritage underwent an acceleration and a slight shift in significance. The new Grand Duke, Gian Gastone, with the help of a group of powerful intellectuals, became involved in a courageous battle to circumscribe the enormous power of the Church and to restore full power to the State. His brief reign witnessed a number of extremely heated encounters between the ecclesiastical authorities and the Grand-Ducal functionaries. Many intellectuals trained by the Galilean professors at the Pisan Studio[55] supported Gian Gastone's cause. Additionally, the proposals for reform of the Pisan studio made by the Proveditore Monsignor Gaspare Cerati drew support from similar considerations and conferred dignity upon the demand for full cultural and didactic recovery of the Galilean heritage.[56]

The Masonic phenomenon, the origins of which in Tuscany went back to 1735, presented itself as a movement animated by strong demands for cultural, scientific, and civil renovation and also adopted a clear and forceful anticlerical position.[57] The influence of the new intellectual circles, which aimed to renovate not only the Studio of Pisa but also the academies and cultural institutions of Florence, and the determination with which Gian Gastone fought to secularize the State finally combined to elicit the appropriate moment for the erection of a sepulchral monument to Galileo. In those years, and in that intellectual climate, the realization of the old project acquired extreme political significance.

From a letter of June 8, 1734 from the Florentine Inquisitor, Paolo Antonio Ambrogi, to the Holy Office, we learn that he inquired to know if "there remained any order of the Supreme and Sovereign Congregation prohibiting the erection in this our Church of Santa Croce of a sumptuous tomb in marble and bronze in memory of the late Galileo Galilei."[58] The Consulters of the Congregation examined the case with extraordinary speed and decided, after deliberation, that the project would not be obstructed. It was recommended to the Inquisitor that he should ensure that the ceremony was not used to recriminate the ecclesiastical authorities. Moreover, he was required to approve the text of the epitaphs and of the official orations.[59]

Documents giving further details of the realization of the project were missing until March 12, 1737, when the remains of Galileo were exhumed and transferred to the base of the new tomb, already nearing completion. The monument was finished on June 6 of the same year (Figure 12.2).[60]

It is clear that the operation represented a significant moment in the jurisdictional battle between the State and the Church. To bury the "heretic" Galileo with honors in Santa Croce, almost a century after his death, was an affirmation of the autonomy of the Prince from ecclesiastical power. The very way in which the ceremony was carried out and, above all, the people who played prominent roles confirmed that this was no mere act of pious homage, but an event of visible political significance.

The ceremony that took place on that memorable day in March 1737 is illustrated in detail in an *Istrumento notarile* (the Notary's official report), a public act that gives emblematic evidence for the official character bestowed upon the event.[61] The *Istrumento* indicates with precision the composition of the official delegations charged with the solemn mission. The overriding criterion for

Figure 12.2

inclusion seems to have been that of ensuring the most authoritative representation of the cultural institutions of Florence and of the entire Grand Duchy. Glancing down the list of delegates in the *Instrumento*, one is immediately struck by the lack of representatives of the ecclesiastical authorities.

Nonetheless, the cultural identity of the members of the official delegations is homogeneous and clearly characterized. Many of them, such as Antonio Cocchi[62] and the abbot Antonio Niccolini,[63] were known for their positions in the defense of the prerogative of the State, for the sympathies they displayed when dealing with progressive and materialist ideals, and, in particular, for the function they fulfilled in the Masonic circles of the city.

In the spring of 1737, there was already a violent conflict in progress between the Florentine Masons and the Inquisitor. This was to lead, a few months later, to the inquisition of the Mason Tomasso Crudeli,[64] in the proceedings of which the names of many of the respected members of the delegation presiding over the exhumation and transfer of Galileo's corpse featured frequently, with explicit reservations about the solidity of their Christian faith.

Neither does it seem insignificant that in the proceedings of the trial the Florentine Masons were suspected not only of atheism and immorality, but also of being convinced Copernicans, that is to say, followers of the heretical Galileo.[65] The identity of the notary Cammillo Piombanti is in tune with the general features of this group of intellectuals, and indeed he was himself very close to Masonic circles.[66]

From these remarks, it is evident that the fulfillment of the objective to which Viviani devoted much of his life occurred in an intellectual climate very different from that which saw its conception. Its significance, too, was modified profoundly in the new circumstances. Although Viviani had dreamed of a mutual embrace between the Church and a repentant Galileo, the 1737 ceremony became a challenge to the abuse of power by the ecclesiastical authorities who had long obstructed public homage being paid to the Pisan scientist.

Despite these changes, the new protagonists revived the central importance of the Michelangelo–Galileo comparison. The removal of the remains of Galileo to the new sepulcher actually took place on March 12, 1737 at 6 p.m. That is, on the same day and at the same time as the mortal remains of Michelangelo, in 1564, clandestinely brought to Florence from Rome, were solemnly deposited in the Basilica of Santa Croce, to await the erection of a tomb.[67] This episode indicates the continued fascination that this comparison exerted, even in the new situation. It also reasserts that behind the juxtaposition of the two tombs in Santa Croce lay the desire to point out the symmetry and continuity between the two great men.

The precise limitations issued by the Holy Congregation with respect to the authorization of the construction of the Galilean tomb forced the promoters of the project to make certain compromises. It was, above all, decided to decorate the tomb with only two statues, of astronomy and geometry, and to abandon the original project of adding a third statue representing philosophy, which would have brought the tomb into full symmetry with that of Michelangelo. Caution suggested abandoning philosophy, which might have been considered an implicit reference to the realistic dimension of Galileo's Copernicanism. To avoid conflict with the Inquisitor and the Holy Congregation it was also decided to avoid making a solemn funeral oration.

On the evening of March 12, 1737, only the prudent epitaphs written by Simone di Bindo Peruzzi, Member of the Accademia Columbaria and Reader in the Tuscan language at the Florentine Studio, were permitted to be read out. In Peruzzi's first epitaph, later placed in the small chamber adjacent to the Cappella del Noviziato, it is at least possible to discern a reference to the dissatisfaction of citizens and foreigners for having had to wait nearly 100 years before seeing Galileo buried with due honor.[68]

The second epitaph, placed on the tomb in a very prominent position, displayed even greater prudence. It ended up more as a general homage to the Pisan, evasive about the details of his philosophical and scientific achievements, and entirely silent about the reasons why a recognition of these achievements in the form of a monumental tomb had not been given closer to the time of Galileo's death.[69] The reticence of Peruzzi's inscriptions display that the Inquisitor, by whom the texts had to be approved, was closely guided by the mandate issued by the Congregation.

In the modest, yet intense arrangements for the March 12 ceremony, every detail was studied with meticulous attention. The *Instrumento* of the notary Piombanti indicates that a rigorous protocol was followed. To complete the monument required exhuming the bodies of Galileo and Viviani to enable their transfer to a position beneath the base of the sepulcher, already in an advanced phase of construction.

The Cappella del Noviziato was rigged out for the display of the bodies, to permit their public recognition, an operation that would have been impossible in the restricted space of the small chamber in which the original tomb was located. A great number of candles and torches, suitably positioned, allowed the crowd of bystanders to follow closely the different stages of the operation.

The *Instrumento notarile* describes how the operation began with the demolition of the brick tomb containing the remains of Viviani.[70] A wooden coffin was removed from the tomb and taken to the Cappella del Noviziato. When the cover was removed, it was possible to see the remains of the last direct disciple of Galileo, as was attested by the inscription on the lead plate underneath the cover of the coffin. When the corpse had been identified, the coffin was placed inside a cask, draped in black, and carried to the new sepulcher in a solemn procession.

The ceremony was then repeated for the second tomb, on the left-hand side of the chamber, which was presumed to contain the mortal remains of Galileo. Following the same procedure, the brick tomb was taken apart. A wooden coffin with a broken lid emerged and "in removing [the cask], it was observed that immediately underneath it lay another wooden coffin of the same shape and size as the first, that is to say, capable of containing a human body."

The detached account of the notary does not register the gasp of surprise the discovery must have elicited from the bystanders. None of those present was prepared for this find. The *Instrumento notarile* records only the series of actions carried out by the members of the delegation, after they had recovered from the initial shock, in order to deal with this embarrassing situation.

First, the upper coffin was removed to the Cappella del Noviziato, and its contents were examined. The corpse of an old man, "which had once been cut and opened, as was demonstrated by the anatomy professors present" was observed. The skeleton had fallen apart in many places, and the jawbone, which was detached from the rest of the skull, contained only four teeth. Next, the group proceeded to make accurate measurements of the skeleton.

At this point, the *Instrumento* registered a sense of panic that spread among those present:

In the view of all, a diligent search was made of the cask, amongst the remains of the clothing of the corpse, on the interior and exterior parts of the cask and among the bones removed thence, but no trace was found of any letters or characters or any other record of any kind.

The examination of the contents of the third and unexpected coffin assumed a crucial importance at this moment. Once again, the *Instrumento*, in detailed and clinical prose, describes the accurate examination of the corpse by the anatomy professors who also availed themselves of the knowledge of anatomical proportions of the professors of sculpture present that evening. The unanimous verdict that they came to was, fortunately, reassuring. The coffin contained the remains of a young woman who had died long ago. It was not possible to establish her identity, but her gender was enough to guarantee that the other corpse was that of Galileo.

Everybody breathed a sigh of relief. If the result of the examination of the remains of the third cask had been more equivocal, the ceremony which had been planned with such care would have turned into an atrocious farce. Once the identity of the remains of Galileo had been verified, the procedure that had been carried out with Viviani's remains was repeated. This time, however, the cask was borne to the new sepulcher only "after it had been displayed for long enough to allow the spectators to satisfy themselves with the sight of the revered bones of such a great man."

For the organizers of the ceremony, the initial surprise on discovering the third mysterious cask must have been quickly followed by dismay on finding that the coffin supposed to contain the remains of Galileo lacked any sign to confirm the identity of the corpse. The intensity of this emotion can be seen in the decision of those present to remain silent about the event, fearing that any comments could lead to substantial doubts about the full success of the operation.

Even the slightest shadow of a doubt about the identity of the corpse transferred to the new tomb could have produced embarrassing consequences. Thus, all of those present agreed to forget the traumatic experience and to avoid inquiring as to the identity of the woman who had died at a young age and ended up under the coffin containing the remains of Galileo.

Many of the witnesses subsequently described the solemn ceremony of that evening while systematically avoiding mention of the unfortunate surprise, to avoid nourishing the doubt, malicious or otherwise, that the man who was being celebrated had not, in fact, been present.

That evening, the witnesses saw what was convenient to see, erasing from their memories any details that could have jeopardized the plan that had inspired the solemn display. As for the unobjective notary, Piombanti, it must be added that he did not even record the macabre rite of loving appropriation of fragments of Galileo's remains, carried out by the same authoritative members of the official delegation.

As can be deduced from indubitable and convergent testimonies, Antonio Cocchi, Anton Francesco Gori, and Vincenzio Capponi removed no less than three fingers, a vertebra, and a tooth from the decrepit remains of the Pisan, with the aid of a knife provided by Targioni Tozzetti.[71] One of the fingers, placed immediately after the event in an urn inscribed with a solemn epitaph by Tomasso Perelli, is still preserved in the collection of the Institute and Museum of the History of Science of Florence,[72] while the vertebra removed by Cocchi constitutes one of the most precious Galilean "relics" at Padua University.[73]

No doubt the notary, Piombanti, felt that this excessive expression of devotion to Galileo, considered as a saint whose relics were endowed with extraordinary evocative powers, could damage the image of the solemnity and decorum of the ceremony that the *Instrumento* was intended to portray.

However, Piombanti was not the only person to transform the events of that magical night for his own purposes. In the embellished account of the exhumation and the examination of Galileo's body, written many years later, Giovanni Targioni Tozzetti stated that

the face of the corpse had been preserved extremely well and in very close resemblance to the bust made by Gio. Caccini in the year 1610 from life ... and to the portrait painted around 1636 by Monsieur Giusto Substerman, with that fine big sweeping head.[74]

The need to remove the memory of the anxious uncertainty of the identity of the corpse, by means of the highly improbable alleged resemblance to the iconographic records, induced Targioni Tozzetti to transfigure the bare and unrecognizable skull described accurately in Piombanti's *Instrumento* into a florid face with a penetrating gaze.

Even the accounts of the ceremony of March 12, 1737, written many decades later, maintained the character of the early reports. In his *Vita* of Galileo of 1793, Giovanni Battista Clemente Nelli gave substantial coverage of the solemn ceremony of 1737. He too considered it ill-advised to mention the little surprise that had animated the evening's proceedings. He published the entire text of Piombanti's *Instrumento*, taking care to omit the part describing the discovery and examination of the third corpse.[75]

The systematic cover-up operation surrounding this episode was so successful that it went completely forgotten. Nobody has felt the need to go back to the original *Instrumento* still preserved in the Archivio di Stato. Thus its "censored" version contained in Nelli's *Vita* of Galileo has been the only one consulted. No one has, therefore, taken the trouble to enquire further as to the identity of the woman in question, nor to wonder about the reasons for her singular and mysterious place of rest.

Let us pause to reflect on the facts. The cask containing Galileo's remains was found in the small chamber adjoining the Cappella del Noviziato. It had a damaged lid and was full of plaster fragments, which seemed to have been there for a very long time.

This suggests that, at a certain point, the brick tomb that had been built on Galileo's death in 1642 had been demolished to insert the second coffin. In the process of dismantling the tomb, pieces of plaster presumably broke the lid and penetrated the coffin. A number of clues suggest that the original tomb was opened in the summer of 1674, at the very time when the original tomb was decorated and adorned with the bust of Galileo and Viviani's laudatory inscription.

When the present arrangement of the small chamber adjoining the Cappella del Noviziato is examined with care, it can be seen that in 1737, after the tomb was demolished, its imprint remained on the wall, acting as a frame for Peruzzi's inscription. The frame is two braccia [a little less than four feet] in height, corresponding exactly to the height indicated in Piombanti's *Instrumento*. Above the frame, the epitaph placed there by Father Pierozzi in September 1674 stands with perfect graphical symmetry.

These observations suggest that the original tomb was transformed into a container with two levels at the same time as the decorations to the tomb were performed in 1674. If this were indeed the case, it comes almost naturally to the imagination to suppose that Viviani, wishing to carry out an act of profound devotion and sincere love towards his Master, had devised the touching idea of reuniting him with the remains of his favorite daughter, Sister Maria Celeste, whose burial place has never been identified.

Virginia, as she was known before taking the veil, had been very comforting to Galileo during the traumatic months of his trial, and her unexpected death in April 1634 was the cause of extreme and profound grief to the Pisan scientist. It was probably in this way that a desire expressed by Galileo on his deathbed was finally carried out in secret. The decision to bury the body of the unidentified woman in the monumental tomb indicates that it must have occurred also to those attending the ceremony on March 12, 1737, that they were in the presence of a person who had been very dear to Galileo.[76]

In the absence of direct documentary evidence, this must remain as a hypothesis. However, it is tempting to believe that in the long and complex story of the attempts to erect a tomb to Galileo, constantly marked by cynical political stances, by vested interests in celebrating Galileo's career, by compromises inspired by opportunism, and, finally, by continuous and significant distortion of his thought, the desire to carry out an act of pure love and compassionate solidarity, at least on one occasion, played its part.

NOTES

1 This essay is a shortened and revised version of "I sepolcri di Galileo. Le spoglie 'vive' di un eroe della scienza," published in *Il Pantheon di Santa Croce a Firenze*, ed. L. Berti, Florence: Giunti, 1993, pp. 145–82.

2 Galileo Galilei, *Le Opere*, Edizione nazionale, ed. A. Favaro, 20 vols., Florence: G. Barbèra, 1890–1909 (henceforth EN), XIX, pp. 522–34 (second will, drawn up on the 19th November, 1638).

3 Ibid., p. 558, n. 6.

4 Ibid., p. 559–62.

5 Ibid., pp. 535–7.

6 EN XVIII, p. 378.

7 Ibid., pp. 378–9 (letter of January 25, 1642). On January 23, the Congregation of the Holy Office too, had discussed this delicate problem (see "I documenti del processo di Galileo," ed. Sergio M. Pagano, *Pontificiae Academiae Scientiarum, Scripta Varia*, 53, Rome, 1984, pp. 239–40).

8 Ibid., pp. 379–80.

9 Ibid., p. 380.

10 EN XIX, p. 617.

11 Unfortunately this work is lost.

12 "If you delete these few words (that [Galileo] should have been more cautious etc.) the Great Duke will be very pleased" (A. Favaro, *Miscellanea Galileiana imedita, Memorie del Reale Istituto Veneto di Scienze Lettere ed Arti*, xxii, 1882, p. 829).

13 Letter from A. Baldigiani to Vincenzo Viviani, 12th July, 1678 (ibid., pp. 837–8).

14 Ibid., pp. 809–10.

15 For an analysis of the motives that persuaded the Medici Princes to promote the Accademia del Cimento, see my "L'Accademia del Cimento: 'gusti' del Principe, filosofia e ideologia dell'esperimento," in *Quaderni Storici*, 48 (1981), pp. 788–844.

16 On the Bologna edition of the works of Galileo (*Opere di Galileo Galilei ... in questa nuova edizione insieme raccolte e di vari trattati dell'istesso autore non più stampati accresciute*, 2 vols., Bologna, for the heirs of Dozza, 1656), see A. Favaro, *Amici e Corrispondenti di Galileo*, XXIX. *Vincenzio Viviani*. The whole series of *Amici e Corrispondenti* has been reprinted by P. Galluzzi, 3 vols., Florence, 1983, III, pp. 1106–8. See, also by Favaro, "Documenti inediti per la storia dei manoscritti galileiani nella Biblioteca Nazionale di Firenze," *Bullettino di Bibliografia e di Storia delle Scienze Matematiche*, XVIII (1885), pp. 1–230. Cf. also *Le Opere dei Discepoli di Galileo*, Natl. Ed. edited by P. Galluzzi and M. Torrini, *Carteggio*, 2 vols., Florence: Giunti, 1975, II, pp. VIII–XII and the vast number of letters relating to the Bologna edition.

17 On the busts of Galileo, see A. Favaro, "Studi e ricerche per una iconografia galileiana," *Atti del Reale Istituto Veneto di Scienze, Lettere ed Arti*, A. A. 1912–1913, vol. LXXII, second part, pp. 1035–47; cf. also Giovanni Battista Clemente Nelli, *Vita e Commercio Letterario di Galileo Galilei ...* 2 vols., Florence: Moücke, 1793, I, pp. 867–74. Amongst recent contributions, one should consult the excellent work of Frank Büttner, "Die ältesten Monumente für Galileo Galilei in Florenz," in *Kunst der Barock in der Toskana*, Munich, 1976, pp. 1013–27. See, lastly, also M. Gregori, "Le tombe di Galileo e il palazzo di Vincenzo Viviani," in *La città degli Uffizi*, Exhibition catalogue (Florence, 9th October 1982–6th January 1983) Florence: Sansoni, pp. 113–18.

18 Büttner, *op. cit.*, pp. 105–7.

19 Ibid., p. 107.

20 Ibid., p. 110.

21 In MS Galileiano 13 of the Biblioteca Nazionale Centrale in Florence, at ff. 55r–56r, one reads the "Note of those Signori Florentine Academicians who, as true connoisseurs and grateful admirers of the teaching and incomparable reputation of the famous Signor Galileo Galilei willingly bind themselves to the expense of the sum of 3,000 Scudi, which they intend to use for a noble deposit of marble with statues and following the drawing of . . . ."

22 The June 30 letter is found in MS Galileiano 164, f. 334r.

23 See the minute autograph of the letter from Viviani to Paolo Falconieri, dated July 10, 1674 (MS Galileiano 159, ff. 34r–36v).

24 Favaro, *Amici e Corrispondenti XXIX cit.*, pp. 1127–9.

25 Such a design was clearly expressed in the letter to Falconieri of July 10, 1674 cited above.

26 The drafts of the epigraphs are titled "Galilaeo ac Sophiae." Cf. MS Galileiano 318, ff. 328r and 811r.

27 Ibid., f. 811v.

28 The letter was sent only after having received from Baldigiani, who had been previously informed of the confidential nature of the communication, the indication of a "safe" address to which it should be sent.

29 Büttner, *op. cit.*, p. 113.

30 We deduce this from a letter from Lorenzo Bellini to Viviani, dated 8th February, 1693 (probably from Pisa), in MS Galileiano 257, f. 120r: "I am told Signor Foggini is working on, and wants to do the designs of the scrolls, but he needs the inscriptions. I send them to You Sir that you may correct them all, and that you may let me know if you are pleased that they are arranged as indicated."

31 V. Viviani, *De locis solidis secunda divinatio geometrica in quinque libros iniuria temporum amissos Aristaei Senioris Geometrae*, Florentiae, Typis Regiae Celsitudinis Apud Petrum Antonium Brigonci, 1701. The inscriptions are published on pp. 120–8 together with engravings of the view of the facade and principal architectural details, the work of Fra Antonio Lorenzini Minore Conventuale. Clemente Nelli (*op. cit.*, I, p. 855) accused Lorenzini of having depicted the facade in an imprecise manner. A. Favaro ("Inedita Galilaeiana. Frammenti tratti dalla Biblioteca Nazionale di Firenze," in *Atti e Memorie dell'Istituto Veneto di Scienze, Lettere ed Arti*, XXI, 1880, pp. 35–43) shows the edition of the engraving of the Palazzo dei Cartelloni opposite the text of *De locis solidis*. They do not differ in important respects.

32 EN, V, p. 39.

33 Pinacotheca imaginum illustrium virorum qui auctore superstite diem suum obierunt. Coloniae Agrippinae, 1643.

34 Favaro, *Inedita Galilaeiana cit.*, p. 42.

35 See note 6 above.

36 MS Galileiano 318, ff. 328r and 811r.

37 Cf. EN, XIX, p. 624: "and thus, no less than in life, honoring after death the immortal fame of the second Florentine Amerigo, not just discoverer of a little land, but of innumerable worlds and new heavenly lights."

38 Ibid., p. 599. It is worth remembering that Galileo's correct date of birth is February 15.

39 MS Galileiano 11, f. 168v (requests for information from Viviani to Baldinucci, and his reply).

40 Ibid., f. 171r (letter from Filippo Buonarroti of June 7, 1692 to Baldinucci, who had forwarded Viviani's request to him). At f. 168r one reads, moreover, the autograph extract of Viviani of the passage from the expanded edition of Vasari's *Vita of Buonarroti* where the date and time of the artist's death are specified.

41 Recent attention has been drawn to the falsification of Galileo's date of birth to make it coincide with that of Michelangelo's death, by M. Segre (*In the Wake of Galileo*, New Brunswick, NJ: Rutgers Univ. Press, 1991, pp. 106–26). According to Segre, Viviani developed the *paragone* because he intended to propose Galileo as a hero in his *Vita*, following the model adopted by Vasari for the *Vita of Buonarroti*. The coincidence between one's date of death and the other's birth would have made more obvious the heroic character of the Pisan's life. Nevertheless, it seems to have escaped Segre that the operation of falsification does not arise with the drafting of the *Vita of Galileo* (1654) but is verified a good forty years later, at the start of the 1690s. Furthermore, Segre attributes the emphasis of the *paragone* on the part of Viviani simply to his wish to adhere to a Renaissance biographic cliché, and he avoids questioning himself on the intellectual suggestions of the *paragone* between the Pisan and the Caprese artist established since Galileo's death.

42 On the myth of Michelangelo, see Romeo De Maio, *Michelangelo e la Controriforma*, Rome–Bari: Laterza, 1978, especially pp. 447 ff. (but the entire volume is well worth consulting for the many interesting transfigurations of the image of Buonarroti after his death). For the comparison of the two editions of the *Vita of Michelangelo* by Vasari, with the development, in the second, of the Medicean myth of Buonarroti, see G. Vasari, *La Vita di Michelangelo nelle Redazioni del 1550 e del 1568*, edited with notes by Paola Barocchi, Milan–Naples: R. Ricciardi, 1962. On the political and celebratory meaning of Michelangelo's funeral, see R. and M. Wittkower, *The Divine Michelangelo. The Florentine Academy's homage on his death in 1564*, London: Phaidon Publishers 1954.

43 Cf. A. Cecchi, "L'estremo omaggio al 'Padre e Maestro di tutte le arti.'
    Il monumento funebre di Michelangelo," in *Il Pantheon di Santa Croce
    a Firenze*, ed. L. Berti, Florence: Giunti, 1993, pp. 57–82.
44 Cf. De Maio, *op. cit.*, especially pp. 17–107.
45 Ibid., p. 456; cf. also E. N. Girardi, "La poesia di Michelangelo e
    l'edizione delle Rime del 1623," in *Studi su Michelangelo Scrittore*, Flo-
    rence, 1974, pp. 79–95.
46 De Maio, *op. cit.*, pp. 17–107.
47 I fully endorse the observations of Eugenio Garin on the fascination
    wrought on Viviani by the "thesis of the continuity of the Renaissance
    and of the resurrection from Antiquity of the fields of art and scientific
    enquiry": "Galileo e la cultura del suo tempo," in *Scienza e Vita Civile
    nel Rinascimento Italiano*, Rome–Bari: Laterza, 1965, pp. 109–10 and
    notes 1–2, p. 134.
48 Cf. Nelli, *op. cit.*, p. 840.
49 Cf. De Maio, *op. cit.*, p. 3 and note 2 (p. 11).
50 EN XI, p. 361 (letter from Rome, July 14, 1612).
51 See Vincenzo Ferrone, *Scienza, Natura, Religione. Mondo Newtoniano e
    Cultura Italiana nel Primo Settecento*, Naples: Jovene, 1982, especially
    pp. 109–68.
52 *Opere di Galileo Galilei*, Nuova Edizione coll'aggiunta di vari trattati
    dell'istesso autore non più dati alle stampe, 3 vols., Florence: G. Gaetano
    Tartini and Santi Franchi, 1718. On the significance of the edition and
    its promoters, see Ferrone, *op. cit.*, pp. 131–5.
53 *Lezioni Accademiche*, Florence: G. Gaetano Tartini and Santi Franchi,
    1716. Cf. Ferrone, *op. cit.*, pp. 135–8.
54 *Petri Gassendi, Opera Omnia in Sex Tomos Divisa Curante Nicolao
    Averanio*. Florentiae, apud J. Tartini and S. Franchi, 1727. For the famous
    and impassioned promoters of this enterprise, cf. Ferrone, *op. cit.*, pp.
    155–62.
55 The thesis of the close relationship, under Gian Gastone, between civil
    rebirth and valorization of the Galilean tradition was already marked
    out by Riguccio Galluzzi in *Istoria del Granducato di Toscana sotto
    il Governo della Casa Medici*, 8 vols., Florence, 1781. Such a thesis
    was proposed again by Niccolò Rodolico (*Stato e Chiesa in Toscana
    durante la Reggenza Lorenese*, reprint from the first edition of 1910
    with Introduction by Giovanni Spadolini, Florence, 1972). One still lacks
    exhaustive investigations that would allow the reconstruction of whe-
    ther, and to what extent, this welding between the exigency of civil re-
    newal and the fertile rebirth of the Galilean lesson was the consequence
    of an intentional strategy firmly adopted by the Prince.

56 Cf. Nicola Carranza, *Monsignor Gaspare Cerati Provveditore dell'Università di Pisa nel Settecento delle Riforme*, Pisa: Pacini, 1974.

57 On the diffusion and characterization of Freemasonry in Tuscany, see Carlo Francovich, *Storia della Massoneria in Italia. Dalle Origini alla Rivoluzione Francese*, Florence: La Nuova Italia 1989, especially pp. 49–85. See also the excellent essay by Fabia Borroni Salvadori, "Tra la fine del Granducato e la Reggenza: Filippo Stosch a Firenze," *Annali della Scuola Normale Superiore di Pisa*, serie III, vol. VIII (2) (1978), pp. 565–614.

58 Cf. *I documenti del processo di Galileo Galilei*, pp. 214–15.

59 Ibid., p. 216.

60 Cf. Umberto Dorini, *La Società Colombaria, Accademia di Studi Storici, Letterari, Scientifici e di Belle Arti. Cronistoria dal 1735 al 1935*, Florence: Chiari 1935, p. 230.

61 The original Act is at the State Archive of Florence, Notarile Moderno, notary G. Camillo Piombanti, Prot. 25,439, March 12, 1737. Thanks to Dr. Orsola Gori of the State Archive of Florence, who, at my request, swiftly traced this, providing me also with additional extremely interesting information about other personalities involved in this event.

62 On Cocchi, see the excellent entry of U. Baldini, in the *Dizionario Biografico degli Italiani*, Rome, 1960, Istituto della Enciclopedia Italiana, XXVI (1982), pp. 451–61.

63 On the masonic inclinations of Abbot Niccolini, see Francovich, *op. cit.*, pp. 54 ff. Cf. also Carranza, *op. cit.*, *passim*.

64 Cf. the classic work of Ferdinando Sbigoli, *Tommaso Crudeli e i primi Framassoni in Firenze. Narrazione storica corredata di documenti inediti*, Milan, 1884.

65 Ibid., p. 148. For a presumed adoption of the Copernican thesis on the part of the notorious Baron Stosch, see Borroni Salvadori, *op. cit.*, p. 592.

66 Information on Giovanni Camillo di Pasquale di Piero Piombanti and on his functions as a frequently used notary of many Florentine public magistracies and cultural institutions, as well as a number of major families (Ginori, Nelli, Neri, Niccolini, Rucellai, etc.) that played an important civic role in the passage from Medicean dynasty to the Regency, has generously been given to me by Dr. Orsola Gori, to whom I express many thanks. For the familial relationship of Piombanti with Antonio Cocchi, see the entry *A. Cocchi* by U. Baldini, in the *Dizionario Biografico degli Italiani*, p. 437. Some letters of C. Piombanti are to be found amongst the Cocchi papers (cf. A. M. Megal Valenti, *Le Carte di Antonio Cocchi*, Milan: Bibliografica 1990). See also M. A. Timpanaro Morelli, *Per una Storia di Andrea Bonducci*, (Firenze 1715–1766), Rome 1996, pp. 249–254.

67 See the description by Vasari in the second and expanded edition of the *Vita di Michelangelo* (Giorgio Vasari, *Le Vite ... nelle redazioni del 1550*

e 1558, text edited by R. Bettarini, historical commentary by P. Barocchi, vol. VI, Florence: Spes, 1987, pp. 126–7).

68 The epigraph can be read in G. B. Clemente Nelli, *Vita cit.*, p. 880. On the personality of Peruzzi and the official role he played on the occasion of the solemn funeral rites of Gian Gastone, see Marcello Verga, *Da Cittadini a Nobili. Lotta Politica e Riforma delle Istituzioni nella Toscana di Francesco Stefano*, Milan: Angeli, 1990, pp. 53–5.

69 Ibid., pp. 876–7.

70 See above, note 61.

71 Cf. A. Favaro, "A proposito del dito indice di Galileo," *Scampoli Galileiani*, CXLI, reprint with introduction and indices by Lucia Rossetti and Maria Laura Soppelsa, 2 vols., Padua: Antinore, 1992, II, pp. 679–88. The reconstruction of the exact number and nature of the fragments (or should one say, relics) taken from Galileo's remains, as well as their fates, gave origin to an erudite, colorful, and bitter historiographical–documentary dispute, in which there competed, among others, Giuseppe Palagi (*Del Dito Indice della Mano Destra di Galileo. Memoria*, Florence: Le Monnier's heirs, 1874) and, later, his severest critic Pietro Gori *Le Preziossime Reliquie di Galileo Galilei. Reintegrazione Storica*, Florence: Tipografia Galletti e Cocci, 1990.

72 Cf. *Museo di Storia della Scienza, Catalogo*, ed. M. Miniati, Florence: Giunti, 1991, p. 62. Before being displayed in its current location, the famous finger suffered noteworthy vicissitudes, to the point of being considered lost. It was finally rediscovered in the Biblioteca Medicea Laurenziana, whence, in March 1804, it was moved to the Museo di Fisica. The delivery was marked by a solemn and long speech, which is today conserved in the Archive of the Istituto e Museo di Storia della Scienza di Firenze (MS 189).

73 See the *Processo verbale pel collocamento di una vertebra di Galileo Galilei nella Sala di Fisica dell'I. R. Università di Padova*, Padua: Tipografia Crescini, 1823.

74 G. Targioni Tozzetti, *Notizie degli Aggrandimenti delle Scienze Fisiche Accaduti in Toscana nel Corso di Anni LX del Secolo XVII*, 3. vols., Florence: Giuseppe Bouchard, 1780, I, p. 142.

75 Nelli, *op. cit*, pp. 878–80.

76 Cirri, in the *Sepoltuario* (Biblioteca Nazionale Centrale, Florence, Manuscripts Room), immediately after having reported the hypothesis that the woman in the coffin was Alessandra Bandini, puts forward this suggestive hypothesis: "Oh, why could it not be the remains of Sister Maria Celeste, daughter of Galileo, whose tomb at Arcetri in the Church of S. Matteo has been sought in vain?" (f. 992). But then he adds in parentheses "(it cannot be)" without, nevertheless, indicating the motives that led him to this conclusion.

(Also see more complete references in footnotes to individual chapters.)

Agassi, Joseph. 1981. *Science and Society*, Dordrecht: Reidel.

Baldo Ceolin, M., ed. 1995. *Galileo e la Scienza Sperimentale*, Padua: Dipartimento di Fisica "Galileo Galilei."

Benvenuto Supino, Igino. 1893. "La lampada di Galileo," *Archivio Storico dell'Arte*, Anno 6, Fasc. 3, 215–18.

Berti, Enrico, 1991. "La Theoria Aristotelica della Dimostrazione nella 'Tractatio' Omonima di Galilei," in M. Ciliberto and C. Vasoli, eds., 1991, 327–50.

Biagioli, Mario. 1993. *Galileo Courtier*. Chicago, IL: University of Chicago Press.

Blackwell, R. J. 1991. *Galileo, Bellarmine, and the Bible*, Notre Dame, IN: The University of Notre Dame Press.

Brecht, Bertolt. 1956. *Leben des Galilei*, Berlin: Henschelvelverlag; English version: *Galileo*, 1966, edited with introduction by Eric Bentley, New York: Grove Press.

Burtt, E. A. 1949. *Metaphysical Foundations of Modern Physical Science*, revised edition, London: Humanities Press.

Butts, R. E. and J. C. Pitt, eds. 1978. *New Perspectives on Galileo*, Dordrecht and Boston: D. Reidel Publishing Co.

Camerota, Michele. 1991. "Movimento circolare e *motus neuter* negli scritti *de motu* di Galileo Galilei," *Annali della Facoltà di Magistro dell' Università di Cagliari*, NS 15:1–37.

  1992. *Gli scritti de motu antiquiora di Galileo Galilei: Il MS Gal. 71, Un analisi storico-critica*, Cagliari: CUEC Editore.

Campanella, Thomas. 1994. *A Defence of Galileo, the Mathematician from Florence*, translated by R. J. Blackwell, Notre Dame, IN: The University of Notre Dame Press.

Carugo, Adriano. and A. C. Crombie. 1983. "The Jesuits and Galileo's Ideas of Science and of Nature," *Annali dell' Istituto e Museo di Storia della Scienza di Firenze*, 8.2:3–36.

Cassirier, Ernst. 1927. *The Individual and the Cosmos in Renaissance Philosophy*, translated by Mario Domandi, 1972, Philadelphia, PA: University of Pennsylvania Press.

Caverni, Rafaello. 1891–1900. *Storia del Metodo Sperimentale in Italia*, 6 vols., Florence; reprint, 1970, Bologna: Forni.

Chalmers, Alan. 1993. "Galilean Relativity and Galileo's Relativity," in S. French and H. Kamminga, eds., *Correspondence, Invariance and Heuristics*, Amsterdam: Kluwer, 189–205.

Ciliberto, M. and C. Vasoli, eds. 1991. *Filosofia e Cultura, per Eugenio Garin*, Rome: Editori Riuniti.

Clagett, Marshall. 1959. *The Science of Mechanics in the Middle Ages*. Madison, WI: University of Wisconsin Press.

Clavelin, Maurice. 1974. *The Natural Philosophy of Galileo*. transl. A. J. Pomerans. Cambridge, MA: M.I.T. Press.

Cohen, Bernard I. 1959. Review of Koestler's *The Sleepwalkers*, *Scientific American* 200 (June 1959):187–92.

1960. *Birth of a New Physics*, Garden City, NY: Anchor Books.

1980. *The Newtonian Revolution*, New York: Cambridge University Press.

Cooper, Lane. 1935. *Aristotle, Galileo and the Tower of Pisa*, Ithaca, NY: Cornell University Press.

Crombie, Alistair C. 1975. "Sources of Galileo's Early Natural Philosophy," in M. L. Rignini-Bonelli and W. R. Shea, eds., 1975, 157–75, 304–5.

1977. "Mathematics and Platonism in the Sixteenth-Century Italian Universities and in Jesuit Educational Policy," in Y. Maeyama and W. G. Salzer, eds., 1977. 63–94.

Damerow, P., G. Freudenthal, P. MacLaughlin and J. Renn. 1992. *Exploring the Limits of Preclassical Mechanics*, New York: Springer.

Dear, Peter. 1988. *Mersenne and the Learning of the Schools*. Ithaca, NY: Cornell University Press.

1995. *Discipline and Experience: The Mathematical Way in the Scientific Revolution*. Chicago, IL: University of Chicago.

De Caro, M. 1993. "Galileo's Mathematical Platonism," in J. Czermak, ed. *Philosophie der Mathematik*. Wien: Holder-Picher-Tempsky.

De Pace, Anna. 1990. "Galileo Lettore di Girolamo Borri nel de Motu," in De Motu: *Studi di Storia del Pensiero su Galileo, Hegel, Huygens, e Gilbert*, Università degli Studi di Milano, Facoltà di Lettere e Filosofia, Quaderni di Acme 12, 3–69.

1992. "Archimede nella Discussione su Aristotelismo e Platonismo di Jacopo Mazzoni," in Corrado Dollo, ed., 1992, 165–97.

1993. *Le Matematiche e il Mondo: Ricerche su un Dibattito in Italia Nella Seconda Metà del Cinquecento*. Filosofia e Scienza nel Cinquecento e nel Seicento, 38. Milan: Franco Angeli.

Di Cesare, Mario A. 1991. *Milton in Italy: Contexts, Images, Contradictions*, New York: Binghamton.

Dollo, Corrado. 1990. *Galileo a la Fisica del Collegio Romano*, Catania: Università di Catania, Dipartimento di Scienze Storiche, Anthropologiche, Geografiche. Quaderno 17.

— 1992. *Archimede: Mito, Tradizione, Scienza*, Florence: Olchki.

Drabkin, I. E. and Stillman Drake. 1960. *Galileo Galilei, On Motion and On Mechanics*, Madison, WI: The University of Wisconsin Press.

Drake, Stillman, translated and with Introduction and Notes. 1957. *Discoveries and Opinions of Galileo*, New York, NY: Anchor.

— 1960: *Galileo Galilei et al., The Controversy of the Comets of 1618*, Philadelphia, PA: The University of Pennsylvania Press.

— 1969. *Mechanics in Sixteenth Century Italy*, Madison, WI: University of Wisconsin Press.

— 1970. *Galileo Studies: Personality, Tradition and Revolution*, Ann Arbor, MI: The University of Michigan Press.

— 1973. "Galileo's Experimental Confirmation of Horizontal Inertia: Unpublished Manuscripts," *Isis*, 64:209–305.

— 1978. *Galileo at Work: His Scientific Biography*, Chicago, IL: The University of Chicago Press.

— 1981. *Cause, Experiment and Science*, Chicago, IL: University of Chicago Press.

— 1983. *Telescopes, Tides and Tactics*, Chicago, IL: The University of Chicago Press.

— 1986. "Galileo's Pre-Paduan Writings: Years, Sources, Motivations," *Studies in History and Philosophy of Science*, 17:429–48.

Duhem, Pierre. 1906–1913. *Etudes sur Leonard de Vinci*, published in three series, Paris: Hermann.

— 1913–1959. *Le Systeme du monde: Histoire des Doctrines Cosmologiques de Platon a Copernic*, 10 vols., Paris: Hermann.

Durham, Frank and Robert D. Purrington, eds. 1990. *Some Truer Method: Reflections on the Heritage of Newton*, New York: Columbia University Press.

Fantoli, Annibale. 1986. *Galileo: Per il Copernicanesimo e per la Chiesa*. 1994. *Transl. George Coyne, Galileo: For Copernicanism and for the Church*. Vatican City: Vatican Observatory Publications.

Favaro, Antonio. 1888. *Per la Edizione Nazionale delle Opere di Galileo Galilei sotto gli Auspici di S. M. il Re d'Italia. Esposizione e Disegno*, Florence.

— 1913. *Studi e Ricerche per una Iconografia Galileiana*, Venice: Carlo Ferrari.

— 1914. *Nuove Ricerche per una Iconografia Galileiana*, Venice: Carlo Ferrari.

1915. "Sulla Veridicità del 'Raccondo Istorico della Vita di Galileo' dettato da Vincenzio Viviani," *Archivio Storico Italiano*, Disp. 2 a, Florence: Tipografia Galileiana, 1916.

1916. "Di Alcune Inesattezze nel 'Racconto Istorico della Vita di Galileo' dettato da Vincenzio Viviani," *Archivio Storico Italiano*, Disp. 3a, 4a, Florence: Tipografia Galileiana, 1917.

Ferrone, Vincenzo. 1982. *Scienza Natura Religione: Mondo Newtoniano e Cultura Italiana*, Naples: Jovene.

Finocchiaro, Maurice A. 1980. *Galileo and the Art of Reasoning. Rhetorical Foundations of Logic and Scientific Method*, Dordrecht and Boston: Reidel.

ed. 1989. *The Galileo Affair. A Documentary History*, Berkeley, CA: The University of California Press.

Transl. and ed. 1997. *Galileo on the World Systems: A New Abridged Translation and Guide*. Berkeley, CA: University of California Press.

Feldhay, Rivka. 1995. *Galileo and the Church: Political Inquisition or Critical Dialogue*. New York, NY: Cambridge University Press.

Fredette, Raymond, 1972. "Galileo's *De Motu Antiquiora*," *Physis*, 14:321–48.

1975. "Bringing to Light the Order of Composition of Galileo Galilei's *De Motu Antiquiora*." Unpublished paper delivered at the Workshop on Galileo, Virginia Polytechnic Institute and State University.

Frisi, Paolo. 1765. *Saggio sul Galileo*, republished and commented in Michelli, 1988, 207–12.

Galilei, Galileo. 1890–1909. *Le Opere di Galileo Galilei*, Antonio Favaro, ed., 20 vols., Florence: G. Barbèra Editrice. Reprint: 1929–1939, 1964–1966, 1968.

1590. *On Motion, and On Mechanics, Opere di Galileo*, Vol. I; transl. 1969. by I. Drabkin and S. Drake, Madison, WI: University of Wisconsin Press.

1610. Drake transl. 1983. *Nuncius Sidereus, Opere di Galileo*, Vol. III; *Starry Messenger* in Drake, 1983, and Van Helden, ed. 1989.

1623. Drake transl. 1960. *Il Saggiatore, Opere di Galileo*, Vol. VI; *The Assayer* in Drake, 1960.

1632. *Dialogo Sopra i Due Massimi Sistemi del Mondo. Opere di Galileo*, Vol. VII; S. Drake transl. 1962. *Dialogue Concerning the Two Chief World Systems – Ptolemaic & Copernican*, transl. by S. Drake. Berkeley, CA: The University of California Press.

1638. *Discorsi e Dimostrazioni Mathematiche intorno a Due Nuove Scienze Attinenti alla Mechanica i Movimenti Locali. Opere di Galileo*, Vol. VIII; 1974. S. Drake transl., *Two New Sciences*, Madison, WI: University of Wisconsin Press. Also 1914. transl. Henry Crew and Alfonso de Salvio, *Dialogues concerning the Two New Sciences*, New York, NY: Dover.

Galluzzi, Paolo. 1973. "Il Platonismo del tardo cinquencento e la filosofia di Galileo," in P. Zambelli, ed. *Richerche sulla Cultura dell'Italia Moderna*, Bari: Laterza.

1979. *Momento: Studi Galileiani*, Rome: Ateno and Bizzarri.

ed. 1984. *Novità Celesti e Crisi del Sapere*, Florence: Giunti Barbera.

1993. "I Sepolcri di Galileo: Le spoglie 'vive' di un eroe della scienza," in Luciano Berti, 1993, 145–82.

Gargantini, M., ed. 1985. *I Papi e la Scienza*, Milan: Jaca Book.

Garin, Eugenio. 1957. *Giornale Critico della Filosofia Italiana*, anno 36, erza serie, vol. 11:406–9.

1965. *Scienza e Vita Civile nel Rinascimento Italiano*, Bari: Laterza.

1969. Transl. by Peter Munz, as *Science and Civic Life in the Italian Renaissance*, Garden City, NY: Anchor.

Geymonat, Ludovico. 1965. *Galileo: A Biography and Inquiry into his Philosophy of Science*. Transl. S. Drake. New York, NY: McGraw-Hill.

Hall, A. Rupert. 1963. *From Galileo to Newton*: 1630–1720. New York, NY: Harper and Row.

Harris, Neil. 1985. "Galileo as a Symbol: The 'Tuscan Artist' in *Paradise Lost*," in *Annali dell' Istituto e Museo di Storia della Scienza di Firenze*, Anno X, Fasc. 2, 3–29.

Helbing, Mario. 1989. *La Filosofia di Francesco Buonamici, Professor di Galileo a Pisa*. Pisa: Nistri-Lischi Editore.

Hill, D. K. 1986. "Galileo's Work on 116v.: A New Analysis" *Isis* 77:283–91.

1988. "Dissecting Trajectories: Galileo's Early Experiments on Projectile Motion and the Law of Fall," *Isis*, 79:646–68.

Holton, Gerald. 1972. *Thematic Origins of Scientific Thought: Kepler to Einstein*, Cambridge, MA: Harvard University Press.

Jacqueline, Bernard. 1984. "La Chiesa e Galileo nel secolo dell'Illuminismo," in *Galileo Galilei: 350 anni di storia 1633–1983) Studi e Ricerche*, Paul Poupard et al., eds., Rome: Edizioni Piemme.

Koestler, Arthur. 1959. *The Sleepwalkers: A History of Man's Changing Vision of the Universe*, London: Hutchinson.

Koyré, Alexandre. 1936. "Galilee et l' Experience de Pise: A Propos d'une Legende," in *Annales de l'Universite de Paris*, 12:441–153.

1939. *Etudes Galiléennes*, Paris: Hermann; reprint, 1966; translated into English by John Mepham, 1978, as *Galileo Studies*, Atlantic Highlands, NJ: Humanities Press.

1953. "An Experiment in Measurement," republished in Koyré, 1968.

1957. *From the Closed World to the Infinite Universe*, Baltimore, MD: The Johns Hopkins University Press.

1957. "Galileo and Plato," reprinted in P. P. Wiener and A. Noland, eds., *Roots of Scientific Thought*, New York: Basic Books.

1965. *Newtonian Studies*, Chicago, IL: University of Chicago Press.

1968. *Metaphysics and Measurement*, London: Chapman & Hall; reprint, 1992, Yverton: Gordon & Breach.

Koyré, Alexandre and Bernard Cohen, eds. 1972. *Isaac Newton's Philosophiae Naturalis Principia Mathematicae*, 2 vols., Cambridge: Cambridge University Press.

Kretzmann, N., ed. 1982. *Infinity and Continuity in Ancient and Medieval Thought*, Ithaca, NY: Cornell University Press.

Landor, Walter Savage. 1916. "Galileo, Milton, and a Dominican, in Imaginary Conversation," Vol. 4, London: Aldine House, 384–93.

Lennox, James G. 1986. "Aristotle, Galileo and 'Mixed Sciences'," in W. A. Wallace, ed., 1986c, 29–51.

Levere, Trevor and W. R. Shea, eds. 1990. *Nature, Experiment and the Sciences. Essays on Galileo and the History of Science in Honour of Stillman Drake*, Boston Studies in the Philosophy of Science, 120. Dordrecht and Boston: Kluwer Academic Publishers.

Ludwig, Bernd. 1992. "What is Newton's Law About?, Philosophical Reasoning and Explanation in Newton's *Principia*," *Science in Context*, 5, 139–62.

Machamer, Peter. 1973. "Feyerabend and Galileo," *Studies in History and Philosophy of science*. 4:1–46.

1978. "Galileo and the Causes," in R. E. Butts and J. C. Pitt, eds., 1978, 161–80;

1991. "The Person Centered Rhetoric of Seventeenth Century Sciences," in M. Pera and W. R. Shea, eds., *Persuading Science: The Art of Scientific Rhetoric*, Canton, MA: Science History Publications.

Machamer, Peter and Andrea Woody. 1994. "A Model of Intelligibility: Using the Balance as a Model for Understanding the Motion of Bodies," in *Science and Education*, 3, 215–44.

McMullin, Ernan ed. 1967. *Galileo: Man of Science*, New York, NY: Basic Books.

1981. "How Should Cosmology Relate to Theology?" in A. R. Peacocke, ed., 1981.

Mancuso, P. 1996. *Philosophy of Mathematics and Mathematical Practice in the Seventeenth Century*, New York, NY: Oxford University Press.

Manno, Antonio, ed. 1987. *Cultura, Scienze e Tecniche nella Venezia del Cinquecento*, atti del Convegno Internazionale de Studio "Giovan Battista Benedetti e il suo Tempo," Venezia: Istituto Veneto de Scienze, Lettere ed Arti.

Maeyama, Y. and W. G. Salzer, eds. 1977. *Prismata: Naturwissenschafts-geschichtliche Studien*, Wiesbaden: Franz Steiner.

Maffioli, Cesare, S. 1985. "Zulla geneso e sugli inediti della Storia del metodo sperimentale in Italia di Raffaello Caverni," *Annali dell' Istituto e Museo di Storia della Scienza di Firenze*, Anno 10, Fasc. 1:23–85.

Masotti, Arnoldo. 1975. "Ricci, Ostilio," *Dictionary of Scientific Biography*, New York: Charles Scribner's Sons, 11:405–6.

1976. "Tartaglia, Niccolò," *Dictionary of Scientific Biography*, New York: Charles Scribner's Sons, 13:258–62.

Mayr, Otto. 1986. *Authority, Liberty and Automatic Machinery in Early Modern Europe*, Baltimore, MD: The Johns Hopkins University Press.

Michelli, Gianni. 1988. "L'idea di Galileo nella Cultura Italiana dal XVI al XIX Secolo," in *Galileo: La Sensata Esperienza*, Cinicello Balsamo: Amilcare Pizzi.

Moody, Ernest. 1951. "Galileo and Avempace: The Mechanics of the Leaning Tower Experiment," *Journal of the History of Ideas*, 12, 163–93, 375–422.

Moss, Jean Dietz. 1993. *Novelties in the Heavens*, Chicago, IL: The University of Chicago Press.

Murdoch, John E. and Edith D. Scylla. 1978. Chapter 7 in *Science in the Middle Ages*. David C. Lindberg, ed., Chicago, IL: Chicago University Press, 206–64.

Naylor, Ron H. 1974. "Galileo and the Problem of Free Fall," *British Journal for the History of Science*, 7:105–34.

1977. "Galileo's Theory of Motion: Processes of Conceptual Change in the Period 1604," *Annals of Science*, 34:365–92.

1980. "Galileo's Theory of Projectile motion," *Isis*, 71:550–70.

1992. "Old Myths and New," *Nature*, 355, (February 1992), 597–8.

1993. Review of Segre, *Annals of Science*, 50:496–7.

Olschki, Leonardo. 1927. *Galileo und seine Zeit*, Paris: Halle.

1943. "Galileo's Philosophy of Science," *Philosophical Review*, 349–65.

Pagano, Sergio M., ed. 1984. *I Documenti del Processo di Galileo Galilei*, Vatican City: Pontificia Academia Scientiarum.

Paschini, Pio. 1941–1944. *Vita e opere di Galileo Galilei*, 2 vols., Vatican City: Pontifica Accademia delle Scienze, 1964.

Peacocke, A. R., ed. 1981. *The Sciences and Theology in the Twentieth Century*, London: Oriel.

Pedersen, Olaf. 1992. *The Book of Nature*, Vatican City: Vatican Observatory Publications.

Pepper, Stephen. 1948. *World Hypotheses*, Berkeley, CA: University of California Press.

Pitt, Joseph. 1992. *Galileo, Human Knowledge, and the Book of Nature: Method Replaces Metaphysics*, Dordrecht: Kluwer.

Purnell, Frederick. 1972. "Jacopo Mazzoni and Galileo," *Physis*, 3:273–94.

Redondi, Pietro. 1983. *Galileo Eretico*. Torino: Einaudi. 1987. Translated by Raymond Rosenthal, *Galileo Heretic*, Princeton, NJ: Princeton University Press.

   1986. Alexandre Koyré, *de la Mystique a la Science. Cours, Conferences et Documents, 1922–1962*, Paris: Ecole des Hautes Etudes en Sciences Sociales.

   1994. "Dietro l'Immagine. Rapresentazioni di Galileo nella Cultura Positivistica," *Nuncius*, Anno 9, Fasc. 1:65–116.

Reston, James, Jr. 1994. *Galileo: A Life*, New York, NY: Harper Collins.

Righini, Guglielmo. 1975. "New Light on Galileo's Lunar Observations," in M. L. Righini-Bonelli and W. R. Shea, eds., 1975.

Rignini-Bonelli, M. L., and W. R. Shea, eds. 1975. *Reason, Experiment and Mysticism in the Scientific Revolution*, New York: Science History Publications.

Rose, P. L. 1976. *The Italian Renaissance of Mathematics. Studies on Humanists and Mathematicians from Petrach to Galileo*, Geneve: Droz.

Rosen, Edward. 1947. *The Naming of the Telescope*, New York, NY: Henry Schuman.

Santillana, Giorgio de. 1953. *The Crime of Galileo*, revised edition of T. Salusbury's translation, Chicago, IL: University of Chicago Press.

Santillana, Giorgio de and Stillman Drake. 1959. "Arthur Koestler and his Sleepwalkers," *Isis*, 50:255–60.

Schmitt, Charles B. 1981. *Studies in Renaissance Philosophy and Science*, London: Variorum Reprints.

Scylla, E. 1986. "Galileo and the Oxford *Caculatores*," in W. A. Wallace, ed. *Reinterpreting Galileo*, 1986.

Segre, Michael. 1989a. "Galileo, Viviani and the Tower of Pisa," *Studies in History and Philosophy of Science*, 20:435–51.

   1989b. "Viviani's Life of Galileo," *Isis*, 80:207–31.

   1991. *In the Wake of Galileo*, New Brunswick, NJ: Rutgers University Press.

Settle, Thomas B. 1961. "An Experiment in the History of Science," *Science* 133:19–23.

   1971. "Ostilio Ricci, a Bridge between Alberti and Galileo," *XIIe Congres Internationale d'Histoire des Sciences*, Paris: Tome IIIB:121–6.

Shapere, Dudley. 1974. *Galileo: A Philosophical Study*, Chicago, IL: University of Chicago Press.

Shea, William R. 1972. *Galileo's Intellectual Revolution: Middle Period, 1610–1632*, New York: Science History Publications.

Simoncelli, Paolo. 1992. *Storia di una Censura: 'Vita di Galileo' e Concilio Vaticano II*, Milan: Franco Angeli.

Strong, W. 1936. *Procedures and Metaphysics. A Study in the Philosophy and Mathematical-Physical Sciences in the Sixteenth and Seventeenth Centuries*, Berkeley, CA: University of California Press.

Supino, Igino Benvenuto. 1893. "La Lampada di Galileo," *Archivio Storico dell'Arte*, 6, 3:215–18.

Tyson, G. B. and Sylvia Wagonheim, eds. 1986. *Print and Culture in Renaissance: Essays on the Advent of Printing in Europe*, Newark, DE: University of Delaware Press.

Van Helden, Albert. 1989. ed. and transl. *Sidereus Nuncius, or the Sidereal Messenger*, Chicago, IL: University of Chicago.

Viviani, Vincenzio. 1717. *Life of Galileo*, first published in Salvino Salvini, ed., *Fasti Consolari dell' Accademia Fiorentina*, Florence, 397–431; included in Galileo's *Opere* XIX:597–646.

Von Gebler, Karl. 1876–1877. *Galileo Galilei und die Romische Kurie*, 2 vols., Stuttgard. Translated into English by Jane Sturge under the title *Galileo Galilei and the Roman Curia*, London, 1879; reprint, Merrick, New York: Richwood Publishing Co., 1977.

Wallace, William A. 1977. *Galileo's Early Notebooks: The Physical Questions. A Translation from the Latin, with Historical and Paleographical Commentary*, Notre Dame, IN: The University of Notre Dame Press.

    1978. "Galileo Galilei and the *Doctores Parisienses*," in R. E. Butts and J. C. Pitt, eds., 1978, 87–183; reprinted and enlarged in 1981, 192–252.

    1981. *Prelude to Galileo: Essays on Medieval and Sixteenth-Century Sources of Galileo's Thought*, Boston Studies in the Philosophy of Science, 62, Dordrecht and Boston: D. Reidel Publishing Co.

    1983. "Galileo's Early Arguments for Geocentrism and His Later Rejection of Them," in Paolo Galluzzi, ed., 1983, 31–40.

    1984a. *Galileo and His Sources: The Heritage of the Collegio Romano in Galileo's Science*, Princeton, NJ: Princeton University Press.

    1984b. "Galileo and the Continuity Thesis," *Philosophy of Science*, 51: 504–10.

    1986a. "Galileo's Sources: Manuscripts or Printed Works ?" in G. B. Tyson and Sylvia Wagonheim, eds., 1986, 45–54.

    1986b. "Galileo and His Sources," (Reply to A. C. Crombie), *The Times Literary Supplement*, January 3 (No. 4318):13, 23.

    ed. 1986c. *Reinterpreting Galileo*, Studies in Philosophy and the History of Philosophy 15, Washington, DC: The Catholic University of America Press.

    1990. "The Dating and Significance of Galileo's Pisan Manuscripts," in Trevor Levere and W. R. Shea, eds., 1990, 3–50.

1991. *Galileo, the Jesuits and the Medieval Aristotle*, Collected Studies Series, CS346, Hampshire, UK: Variorum Publishing.

1992a. *Galileo's Logic of Discovery and Proof. The Background, Content and Use of his Appropriated Treatises on Aristotle's* Posterior Analytics. Boston Studies in the Philosophy of Science, 137, Dordrecht, Boston, London: Kluwer Academic Publishers.

1992b. *Galileo's Logical Treatises. A Translation, With Notes and C Commentary, of his Appropriated Latin Questions on Aristotle's* Posterior Analytics. Boston Studies in the Philosophy of Science, 138, Dordrecht, Boston, London: Kluwer Academic Publishers.

1993. "Dialectics, Experiments and Mathematics in Galileo," in Peter Machamer, Marcello Pera and Aristides Baltas, eds., *Controversies in Science*, New York: Oxford University Press, 1999.

1995. "Circularity and the Demonstrative *Regressus*: From Pietro d' Abano to Galileo Galilei," *Vivarium*, 3.1:76–97.

Weisheipel, James A. 1967. "Galileo and His Precursors," in *Galileo: Man of Science*, Ernan McMullin, ed., New York: Basic Books, 85–97.

Westman, Robert. 1984. "The Reception of Galileo's *Dialogue*," in Galluzzi, 1984.

Westfall, Richard S. 1971. *Force in Newton's Physics*, New York: American Elsevier.

1985. "Science and Patronage: Galileo and the Telescope," *Isis*, 76:11–30.

1989. *Essays on the Trial of Galileo*, Vatican City and Notre Dame, IN: University of Notre Dame Press.

Wisan, Winifrid L. 1974. "The New Science of Motion: A Study of Galileo's De Motu Locale," *Archive for the History of the Exact Sciences*, 13:103–306.

1978. "Galileo's Scientific method: A reexamination," in R. E. Butts and J. C. Pitt, 1978.

1984. "Galileo and the Process of Scientific Creation" *Isis*, 75:269–86.

Wohlwill, Emil. 1905. "Galilei-Studien: Die Pisaner Fallversuche," *Mittenlungen zur Geschichte der Medizin und der Naturwissenschaften*, 4:229–48.

1906–1907. "Der Abschied von Pisa," *Mitteilungen zur Geschichte der Medizin und der Naturwissenschaften*, 5:230–49, 439–64, 6:231–42.

INDEX